GREAT CHRISTIAN JURISTS AND LEGAL COLLECTIONS IN THE FIRST MILLENNIUM

Great Christian Jurists and Legal Collections in the First Millennium is a systematic collection of essays describing how Christian leaders and scholars of the first millennium in the West contributed to law and jurisprudence and used written norms and corrective practices to maintain social order and to guide people from this life into the next. With chapters on topics such as Roman and post-Roman law, church councils, the papacy, and the relationship between royal and ecclesiastical authority, as well as on individual authors such as Lactantius, Ambrosiaster, Augustine, Leo I, Gelasius I, and Gregory the Great, this book invites a more holistic and realistic appreciation of early-medieval contributions to the history of law and jurisprudence, suitable for entry-level students and scholars alike. *Great Christian Jurists and Legal Collections in the First Millennium* provides a fresh look, from a new perspective, enabling readers to see these familiar authors in a new light.

Philip L. Reynolds is Charles Howard Candler Professor of Medieval Christianity and Aquinas Professor of Historical Theology at Emory University. A senior fellow of Emory's Center for the Study of Law and Religion, Reynolds directed the Center's project on the Pursuit of Happiness (2006–11). Reynolds was a Henry Luce III Fellow in Theology (2013–14) for his work on contemplative and apophatic theology and on the medieval reception of the pseudo-Dionysius. His books include *Food and the Body* (1999) and *How Marriage Became One of the Sacraments* (2016).

LAW AND CHRISTIANITY

The Law and Christianity series publishes cutting-edge work on Catholic, Protestant, and Orthodox Christian contributions to public, private, penal, and procedural law and legal theory. The series aims to promote deep Christian reflection by leading scholars on the fundamentals of law and politics, to build further ecumenical legal understanding across Christian denominations, and to link and amplify the diverse and sometimes isolated Christian legal voices and visions at work in the academy. Works collected by the series include groundbreaking monographs, historical and thematic anthologies, and translations by leading scholars around the globe.

Books in the Series

Great Christian Jurists and Legal Collections in the First Millennium Philip L. Reynolds

English Ecclesiastical Lawyers: A History of Their Life and Work R. H. Helmholz

Law, Love, and Freedom: From the Sacred to the Secular Joshua Neoh

Abbreviations

ACO	*Acta conciliorum oecumenicorum*. vols. 1–3 & 4.2, ed. E. Schwartz (Strasbourg, Berlin, Leipzig, 1914–40); vol. 4.1, ed. J. Straub (Berlin, 1971)
ACW	*Ancient Christian Writers: The Works of the Fathers in Translation* (New York, Newman Press)
AHC	*Annuarium historiae conciliorum*
ANF	*The Ante-Nicene Fathers: Translations of the Writings of the Fathers Down to A.D. 325*. Ed. Alexander Roberts and James Donaldson. 10 vols., 1885–1887
BMCL	*Bulletin of Medieval Canon Law*
c.	*circa* [date]
CCL	*Corpus Christianorum Series Latina* (Turnhout, Brepols)
CCM	*Corpus Christianorum Continuatio Medievalis* (Turnhout, Brepols)
CIC	*Corpus Iuris Civilis*
CICan.	*Corpus Iuris Canonici*. Ed. Aemilius Friedburg. 2 vols. Leipzig, 1879–81
COD	*Conciliorum oecumenicorum decreta*
Cod. Iust.	*Codex Iustinianus*
Cod. Theod.	*Codex Theodosianus*
CSEL	*Corpus Scriptorum Ecclesiasticorum Latinorum* (Vienna, 1865)
d.	died [date]
DB	*Decretum Burchardi*
Dig.	The *Digest* of Justinian
ed.	editor; edited by
EME	*Early Medieval Europe* [journal]
Ep.; *Epp.*	*Epistula; Epistulae*

Since the initial consultation, I have benefited from correspondence with Professor Abigail Firey and (recently) with Professor Michael Heil, as well as with several of the authors of the chapters. These colleagues have helped me to grapple with the special problems that the first millennium in the West presents from the perspective of legal history.

I am grateful to Sarah Bogue, Brian Gronewoller, Gary Hauk, and Micah Miller for editorial and other assistance in the planning and preparation of this volume.

I am grateful, as always, to the CSLR and to its director, John Witte. The Center is a blessing, enhancing humanistic inquiry and collegial conversation at our university in extraordinary ways.

Finally, I am grateful to the McDonald Agape Foundation and to its founder, Ambassador Alonzo L. McDonald, for the Foundation's generous funding in support of this volume.

As a first step, we convened a consultative meeting at Emory with several experts in early Christianity and in legal history: Professors Patout Burns, Judith Evans Grubbs, David Hunter, Abigail Firey, Willemien Otten, Kenneth Pennington, and Robert Somerville. The purpose of the meeting was to decide which topics, chapters, and "great Christian jurists" ought to be included, and to gather suggestions as to who might be invited to write about them.

This initial meeting confirmed two convictions that I had already reached regarding the design of the volume. One was that we needed to cover not only laws but also such lawlike norms as monastic rules and penitential prescriptions, with the institutional settings that gave rise to all these norms. Another was that whereas the typical method of the series is to devote each chapter to a particular author, proceeding in chronological order, that approach was not wholly suited to the first millennium in the West. Fundamental developments in ecclesiastical regulation during this era occurred collectively, and some important work in the field was written anonymously or pseudonymously. Thus, the book is divided into two parts. Part I is thematic, with each chapter addressing a broad, collective development. Part II is devoted to individual authors, following the model of the series.

There are two deliberate anomalies in Part II. One is a chapter on a nonexistent but influential author, Isidore the Merchant – a pseudonym attached to a forgery. The other is a chapter on the *Rule of Benedict*. The Benedict of tradition is inseparable from his *Rule*.

There are diverse criteria for selecting which authors are "great" enough to be the subject of a chapter in a book such as this, and some of these criteria are retrospective and might run the risk of anachronism: a grave sin in historical studies. My solution was to separate each author from his reception and historical significance. (I say "his" because sadly, as far as we know, all the first-millennial authors in this context were male.) Thus, each chapter in Part II focuses on an author of the period writing in response to a current historical situation, as heir to a tradition of thought and practice, but it concludes with a section on the subject's subsequent reception and significance.

With one exception, the chapters were written specially for this volume. The exception is Professor Mayke de Jong's chapter in Part I, of which a French version had previously appeared in *Annales*.[1] An English version of this article is included here by kind permission of the editors of *Annales*. Our version is based on the original, unpublished English text, provided to us by the author, which had been expertly translated into French for *Annales* by Pauline Baggio-Huerre. I compared the original text carefully with the French translation, which represented a more advanced stage of editing, and I incorporated some minor amendments proposed by the author, but we did not attempt to update the contents.

[1] Mayke de Jong, "*Sacrum palatium et ecclesia*. L'autorité religieuse royale sous les Carolingiens (790–840)," *Annales HSS*, 58.6 (2003): 1243–1269. © Éd. de l'Ehess, Paris.

Preface and Acknowledgments

This book belongs to a series on notable Christian jurists over the ages. Volumes that have already appeared include *Great Christian Jurists in English History* (2017) and *Great Christian Jurists in Spanish History* (2018). The "great Christian jurists" formula follows the precedent of Erik Wolf, *Grosse Rechtsdenker der deutschen Geistesgeschichte*, first published in 1951 (4th edition, 1963). The project as a whole is proceeding under the aegis of Emory's Center for the Study of Law and Religion (CSLR). Professor John Witte, Jr., director of the Center, is general editor of the series.

Departing from the nation-centered pretext, John Witte invited me to edit an anthology for the series on the first Christian millennium in the West. I was and am very grateful to John for this opportunity. The focus posed some special challenges. On the one hand, legal historians usually regard the early Middle Ages teleologically, in light of categories and institutions that emerged later. The boundary of AD 1000 precludes that perspective. Moreover, this is considered to have been an era of "law without jurists," in view of the absence of juristic writing after the sixth century as well as of an academic culture of law. The *interpretationes* (comments) that were added to the *Lex Romana Visigothorum* were arguably the last examples of explicitly juristic writing in the West before the late eleventh century. On the other hand, the focus provided me with a welcome opportunity to consider law not in isolation but as one mode of normativity among others. And this is a better way for the historian to spread the net widely, in my view, than using the term "law" vaguely, equivocally, or in an unexamined way. Although there were no jurists in the classical sense after the sixth century, there were scholars and clerics who thought deeply and inquiringly about law and about other lawlike norms, such as penitential prescriptions and monastic rules, in relation to their Christian faith and to their understanding of the Scriptures. Moreover, a conspicuous feature of the era is the compiling of canonical collections, which sometimes involved judicious editing and even forgery. This work, too, presupposed juristic thinking, and the collections are generally regarded today as constituting a body of canon law.

David G. Hunter is Cottrill-Rolfes Professor of Catholic Studies at the University of Kentucky.

Luca Loschiavo is Full Professor for Medieval and Modern Legal History at the University of Teramo and Roma Tre.

Rob Meens is Lecturer in Medieval History at the Department of History and Art History at the University of Utrecht, The Netherlands.

Alexander Callander Murray is Professor of History, Emeritus, Department of History and Centre for Medieval Studies, University of Toronto.

Bronwen Neil is Professor of Ancient History and Director of the Ancient Cultures Research Centre at Macquarie University, Australia.

Philip L. Reynolds is Charles Howard Candler Professor of Medieval Christianity, Aquinas Professor of Historical Theology, and a senior fellow of the Center for the Study of Law and Religion at Emory University in Atlanta.

Stefan Schima is Associate Professor for the Study of Law and Religion in the faculty of law at the University of Vienna.

Robert Somerville is Tremaine Professor of Religion and Professor of History at Columbia University in New York City.

Carole Straw is Emeritus Professor of History at Mount Holyoke College in Massachusetts.

Francesco Veronese is a post-doctoral fellow at the Istituto Storico Italiano per il Medioevo, Rome, and he teaches in the Department of Historical, Geographical, and Ancient Sciences (DiSSGeA) at the University of Padova.

Susan Wessel is Professor of Theology and Religious Studies at the Catholic University of America in Washington, DC.

Contributors

Greta Austin is the Dolliver / National Endowment for the Humanities Professor of the Humanities, Professor of Religious Studies, and Director of the Gender & Queer Studies program at the University of Puget Sound.

Mayke de Jong is Emeritus Professor of Medieval History, University of Utrecht.

Elizabeth De Palma Digeser is Professor of History at the University of California, Santa Barbara, and the founding editor of *Studies in Late Antiquity*

Albrecht Diem is Associate Professor of History at Syracuse University.

Hugh Feiss, OSB, is a monk of the Monastery of the Ascension in Jerome, Idaho.

Roy Flechner is Lecturer in Early Medieval History at University College Dublin.

Clemens Gantner is Researcher on Early Medieval History at the Institute for Medieval Research of the Austrian Academy of Sciences.

Brian Gronewoller is Adjunct Professor of Early Christianity at Emory University in Atlanta.

Gregory Halfond is Associate Professor of History at Framingham State University in Massachusetts.

Clara Harder is a postdoctoral scholar at the University of Cologne, Germany, where she teaches Medieval History.

Jill Harries is Emeritus Professor of Ancient History in the School of Classics, University of St Andrews, Scotland, UK.

David Heith-Stade holds a doctorate in theology from Lund University, as well as a master's degree in theology and bachelor's degree in religious studies from Uppsala University. An independent scholar, he is the Vice Secretary of the Society for the Law of the Eastern Churches (Vienna).

Contents

CAMBRIDGE
UNIVERSITY PRESS

University Printing House, Cambridge CB2 8BS, United Kingdom

One Liberty Plaza, 20th Floor, New York, NY 10006, USA

477 Williamstown Road, Port Melbourne, VIC 3207, Australia

314–321, 3rd Floor, Plot 3, Splendor Forum, Jasola District Centre, New Delhi – 110025, India

79 Anson Road, #06–04/06, Singapore 079906

Cambridge University Press is part of the University of Cambridge.

It furthers the University's mission by disseminating knowledge in the pursuit of education, learning, and research at the highest international levels of excellence.

www.cambridge.org
Information on this title: www.cambridge.org/9781108471718
DOI: 10.1017/9781108559133

First published 2019

Printed in and bound in Great Britain by Clays Ltd, Elcograf S.p.A.

A catalogue record for this publication is available from the British Library.

Library of Congress Cataloging-in-Publication Data
NAMES: Reynolds, Philip Lyndon, 1950– editor.
TITLE: Great Christian jurists and legal collections in the first millennium / edited by Philip L. Reynolds.
DESCRIPTION: Cambridge, United Kingdom ; New York, NY, USA : Cambridge University Press, 2019. | Series: Law and Christianity
IDENTIFIERS: LCCN 2019001101 | ISBN 9781108471718 (hardback)
SUBJECTS: LCSH: Canonists – Europe, Western – Biography. | Europe – History – 392-814 – Biography. | Canon law – History – To 1500. | Roman law – History – To 1500. | BISAC: LAW / Jurisprudence.
CLASSIFICATION: LCC KBR122 .G74 2019 | DDC 340.092/874–dc23
LC record available at https://lccn.loc.gov/2019001101

ISBN 978-1-108-47171-8 Hardback

Great Christian Jurists and Legal Collections in the First Millennium

Edited by

PHILIP L. REYNOLDS

Emory University

CAMBRIDGE
UNIVERSITY PRESS

Great Christian Jurists in French History Olivier Descamps and Rafael Domingo

Church Law in Modernity: Toward a Theory of Canon Law Between Nature and Culture Judith Hahn

Common Law and Natural Law in America: From the Puritans to the Legal Realists Andrew Forsyth

Care for the World: Laudato Si' and Catholic Social Thought in an Era of Climate Crisis edited by Frank Pasquale

Church, State, and Family: Reconciling Traditional Teachings and Modern Liberties John Witte, Jr.

Great Christian Jurists in Spanish History Rafael Domingo and Javier Martinez-Torron

Under Caesar's Sword: How Christians Respond to Persecution edited by Daniel Philpott and Timothy Samuel Shah

God and the Illegal Alien Robert W. Heimburger

Christianity and Family Law John Witte, Jr. and Gary S. Hauk

Christianity and Natural Law Norman Doe

Great Christian Jurists in English History edited by Mark Hill, QC and R. H. Helmholz

Agape, Justice, and Law edited by Robert F. Cochran, Jr and Zachary R. Calo

Calvin's Political Theology and the Public Engagement of the Church Matthew J. Tuininga

God and the Secular Legal System Rafael Domingo

How Marriage Became One of the Sacraments Philip L. Reynolds

Christianity and Freedom (Volume I: Historical Perspectives, Volume II: Contemporary Perspectives) edited by Timothy Samuel Shah and Allen D. Hertzke

The Western Case for Monogamy Over Polygamy John Witte, Jr.

The Distinctiveness of Religion in American Law Kathleen A. Brady

Pope Benedict XVI's Legal Thought Marta Cartabia and Andrea Simoncini

FC	*Fontes Christiani* (Fontes Christiani Institut, Bochum. Published by Brepols or Herder)
Inst.	Justinian's *Institutes* (*Institutiones Iustiniani*)
J^1, J^2, J^3	*Regesta pontificum Romanorum*, 3rd edition, ed. Marcus Schütz et al., 3 vols. (Göttingen: Vandenhoeck & Ruprecht, 2016–2017)
JE, JK, JL	*Regesta pontificum romanorum*, ed. Philipp Jaffé, 2nd edition, with F. Kaltenbrunner (JK: 64–599), P. Ewald (JE: 590–882), and S. Loewenfeld (JL: 882–1198) (Leipzig, 1885)
JECS	*Journal of Early Christian Studies*
JEH	*Journal of Ecclesiastical History*
JTS	*Journal of Theological Studies*
Kéry, *Collections*	Lotte Kéry, *Canonical Collections of the Early Middle Ages (ca. 400–1140): A Bibliographical Guide to the Manuscripts and Literature*. Washington, DC: Catholic University of America Press, 1999
MGH	*Monumenta Germaniae Historica*
MGH AA	MGH Scriptores: *Auctores antiquissimi*
MGH Capit.	MGH *Capitularia regum Francorum* (Leges, Sectio II)
MGH Capit. Episc.	MGH Concilia, *Capitula Episcoporum*
MGH Conc.	MGH Concilia (Leges, Sectio III)
MGH Const.	MGH *Constitutiones et acta publica imperatorum et regum* (Leges, Sectio IV)
MGH Epist.	MGH, *Epistolae* (in Quart)
MGH Fontes	MGH, *Fontes iuris Germanici antiqui in usum scholarum separatim editi*
MGH LL	MGH, Leges (in Folio)
MGH NG	MGH *Leges Nationum Germanicarum* (MGH Leges, Sectio I)
MGH RF	MGH *Capitularia regum Francorum* (MGH Leges, Sectio II)
MGH SRG	MGH Scriptores: *Scriptores rerum Germanicarum in usum scholarum seperatim editi*
MGH SRM	MGH Scriptores: *Scriptores Rerum Merovingicarum*
MGH SS	MGH Scriptores
MS; MSS	manuscript; manuscripts
NPNF	*A Select Library of Nicene and Post-Nicene Fathers of the Christian Church*. Ed. Philip Schaff and Henry Wace. 28 vols. in 2 series, 1886–1889
NRSV	The Bible, New Revised Standard Version
PG	J.-P. Migne (general editor), *Patrologia Cursus Completus, Series Graeca* (Paris, 1857–)

PIMS	Pontifical Institute of Mediaeval Studies (Toronto)
PL	J.-P. Migne (general editor), *Patrologia Cursus Completus, Series Latina* (Paris, 1844–)
Prefaces	Robert Somerville and Bruce C. Brasington. *Prefaces to Canon Law Books in Latin Christianity: Selected Translations, 500–1245*. New Haven: Yale University Press, 1998
r.	reigned [dates]
RB	*Regula Benedicti* (The Rule of St. Benedict)
RHE	*Revue d'Histoire Ecclésiastique*
RM	*Regula Magistri* (The Rule of the Master)
SC	Sources Chrétiennes (Paris, Cerf)
Serm.	*Sermon*
trans.	translator; translated by
ZRG	*Zeitschrift der Savigny-Stiftung für Rechtsgeschichte*
ZRG Kan. Abt.	*Zeitschrift der Savigny-Stiftung für Rechtsgeschichte*, kanonistische Abteilung

Abbreviations for books of the Bible follow *The SBL Handbook of Style*, 2nd ed. (Atlanta: SBL Press, 2014).

PART I

1

Normative Texts and Practices of the First Millennium

Philip L. Reynolds

This book explores how Christian leaders, scholars, and clerics of the first millennium in the West[1] understood, interpreted, and contributed to law and to lawlike normative texts and practices. The book covers four categories of normative texts, each with the corresponding practices: laws (*leges*), monastic rules (*regulae*), penitential prescriptions (*iudicia poenitentiae*), and canons (*canones*). These categories were not necessarily mutually exclusive. For example, the earliest surviving penitential prescriptions are canons decreed by church councils. Again, although the distinction between penance and judicial punishment is clear in principle, penitential regimes could be used to maintain social order, with penances functioning as quasi-judicial punishments. There were other Christian norms that might be considered in this normative setting, such as creeds and the canon of sacred Scripture, but the aforesaid fields were the most lawlike and the most relevant to the long history of Christian law and jurisprudence.

Scholars who study any of these normative fields during the first millennium are necessarily preoccupied with collections of texts. These include compilations of laws, ranging from private collections to promulgated codes (see Chapters 2–3); penitential books, or penitentials, which reflect early-medieval penitential practice (Chapter 8); and canonical collections (Chapter 7). The collecting and comparison of monastic rules by the Carolingian monk Benedict of Aniane (d. 821, see Chapter 9) was a crucial stage both in the West's conception of the regular life and in the establishment of the *Rule of Benedict* (see Chapter 16) as the monastic rule *par excellence*.

Although the texts and collections can be studied in themselves as literary artefacts, normative texts are essentially practical and performative. They cannot be understood in abstraction from their use and intended results, just as one cannot understand the tools of ancient artisans without knowing how they were meant to be used and to what end. Each class of texts was designed to achieve a certain practical good, or desirable result.

[1] In what follows, for convenience, the term "first millennium" refers by default only to the West, and not to Byzantium or to Eastern Orthodox Christianity.

Moreover, in most cases the texts achieved their ends by means of corresponding normative practices. A penitential prescription, for example, was designed to achieve reconciliation with God and with the Christian community by means of the prescribed penitential performance. Each set of texts and practices, considered in relation to the desired result, constitutes what I have called a normative field. But whereas many normative texts and collections from the first millennium have survived intact, independent evidence of how the texts were applied and of the corresponding practices is scarce, uneven, and sometimes difficult to interpret.

The four normative fields shared a common purpose, which was to guide and correct human action or right living by means of explicit rules or measures.[2] The terms "norm," "canon," and "rule" (*regula*), which are conspicuous in Christian writing of the period, referred to externally imposed standards and correctives. For example, the Latin word *norma* denoted literally a square used in carpentry and masonry to check right angles, and by extension any standard or measure. In the Latin versions of Jeremiah 31:39, the term denotes a long measuring cord. Christian writers used the term "norm" metaphorically to denote anything proposed externally to regulate or correct human action, such as a teaching, an exemplar, an Idea (in the Platonic sense), or sacred Scripture. For example, Augustine spoke of the need to discipline children by teaching them a "norm of living" (*norma vivendi*).[3] The phrase "norm of justice" (*norma iustitiae*) was common and could describe any external measure of equity. Benedict of Nursia, advising advanced monks who had outgrown his own "little rule" as to what they should read, recommends Scripture above all, for "what page or what word [of Scripture] is not the straightest norm [*rectissima norma*] of human life?" (RB 73.3)

Each normative field involved something preconceived and imposed from without by persons of authority and power. As external means to right living, these were quite different from such means as virtue, prayerful intimacy with God, and divine grace, which were understood to work from within, often in unpredictable ways. Again, inasmuch as the texts stated explicit rules of conduct, they needed to be univocal and unambiguous. In this respect, they were unlike beatitudes, aspirational maxims, and moral counsels, which invited personal reflection, new interpretations, and diverse appropriations – although some monastic rules, including Benedict's, *included* aspirational maxims and moral counsels.

The history of creeds, such as the so-called Nicene and Apostle's creeds (which are Trinitarian in structure), illustrates the points that I have made in the foregoing remarks.[4] Although their early history is murky and contested, they probably began

[2] I am echoing Thomas Aquinas, *Summa theologiae* I–II.90.1, resp., who characterizes law as a species of "rule [*regula*] and measure [*mensura*] of actions by which someone is induced to act or restrained from acting."

[3] Augustine, *Enarratio in Ps* 37, §34, CCL 38, 398, line 21.

[4] J. N. D. Kelly, *Early Christian Creeds*, 3rd ed. (London: Longman Group, 1972) is still valuable for details, but for a more up-to-date appraisal, see W. Kinzig and M. Vinzent, "Recent Research on the Origin of the Creed," JTS 50.2 (1999): 535–59.

as interrogatory confessions of faith that were performed when converts were baptized by triple immersion in the name of the Father, the Son, and the Holy Spirit (cf. Matt 28:19). From there, they soon acquired a second application: in catechesis (the instruction of converts). A third application first appears in formulations of a creed-like "canon of truth" (*kanōn tēs alētheias*) or "rule of faith" (*regula fidei*) as a defense against heterodoxy, which we find in Irenaeus (d. c. 200) and Tertullian (d. 225). These authors used rules of faith not only to articulate core beliefs but also to proscribe "heresies" – i.e., Gnostic sects – by setting limits on what could be taught and on how the Scriptures might be interpreted. The use of declaratory creeds as rules of faith became prominent in the fourth century, when church councils used them to exclude heterodox teachings about the Godhead and Christ. The earliest known examples of this dogmatic use come from two councils held at Nicaea in 325, which proposed creeds to proscribe Arius's theology. The second of these two councils was convened by Constantine and came to be regarded as the first Ecumenical Council. Finally, the liturgical recitation of creeds probably began during the fifth century. Thus, although the creeds can be studied as theological and literary texts – the so-called Nicene Creed, for example, while Trinitarian in structure, also outlines a cosmic narrative of going forth and returning – the history of creeds is a story of normative *use* and of *performance*: baptismal, catechetical, dogmatic, and liturgical.

Again, from around 350, the term *kanōn*, which literally denoted a measuring reed or rod, was used to denote the sacred Scriptures as constituting a rule or norm of life. This usage coincided with an effort to determine what was and was not included in the Word of God. Scholars and bishops asked which books were canonical and which non-canonical.[5] The designation of certain texts as canonical meant that special uses and performances were exclusively appropriate to them, for example, as regards liturgical reading and accompanying rituals, preaching, the application of "spiritual" (i.e., nonliteral) methods of interpretation, and monastic meditation. Countless texts were worthy of reading and study, but only canonical texts were the subject of these special practices.

LAWS (*LEGES*)

To introduce his treatise on laws in the *Etymologies* (*De legibus*, V.1–27), Isidore of Seville (d. 636) reviews the lawgivers and legal systems known to him (V.1). He begins with ancient Jewish law, explaining that "Moses, of the Hebrew race, was the first of all to explicate, in the Holy Scriptures, the divine laws." King Phoroneus was the first to make laws for the Greeks, Isidore continues, Hermes Trismegistus for the Egyptians, Solon for the Athenians, and Numa Pompilius for the Romans. Isidore

[5] Carl Holladay, *Introduction to the New Testament: Reference Edition* (Waco: Baylor University Press, 2012), 398.

then outlines the history of Roman law before coming at last to Constantine's constitutions and the *Theodosian Code*: the most advanced form of law known to him.

After his initial survey of legislators and legal systems, Isidore distinguishes between divine law (*lex divina*) and human law (*lex humana*). Whereas human law is different for each people (*gens*), since it is a form of custom (*mos*), divine law is universal (and presumably unchanging as well, although Isidore does not say so). Isidore equates divine law (*lex divina*) with *fas*, and human law (*lex humana*) with *ius*. In classical, polytheistic tradition, *fas* regulated interactions among the gods and between human beings and the gods, whereas *ius* regulated the interactions among human beings.[6] Isidore takes a more philosophical view, equating *fas* with the natural law (*ius naturale*), the notion of which he owed to Roman jurisprudence (V.2, V.4).[7]

The Mosaic Law as Christians Understood It

Christ said that he had come to fulfill the law, not to abolish it (Matt 5:17). On one occasion, however, pressed to condemn a sinner according to the law, Christ remained silent while writing in the dust (John 8:1–11). Christians inherited from St. Paul a complex argument about the relationship of their religion to Jewish law (*nomos* in Greek, *lex* in Latin), which was a species of written law. In their view, the Old Testament recorded a phase in which the people of God had tried to attain righteousness through laws alone, which operated from the outside inward; and this effort had proved inadequate and counterproductive, albeit in a salutary, divinely disposed way: "Wherefore the law was our pedagogue in Christ, that we might be justified by faith. But after the faith is come, we are no longer under a pedagogue" (Gal 3:24–25).

From the Christian point of view, then, Christ had bestowed instead an interior transformation – a gracious change of heart – which worked from the inside outward. In his treatise *On the Spirit and the Letter*, Augustine elaborated metaphors of writing to expound this claim. Augustine combined in particular two ideas from Paul: that there is a law "written in their hearts" (Rom 2:15); and that Christ wrote the Gospel "not with ink, but with the Spirit of the living God; not on tablets of stone, but on the fleshy tablets of the heart" (2 Cor 3:3).[8] Christian authors sometimes construed this inward transformation as something that had superseded law, and

6 On the classical *fas / ius* distinction, see Matthew M. McGowan, *Ovid in Exile: Power and Poetic Redress in the Tristia and Epistulae ex Ponto* (Brill: Leiden, 2009), 121–33.

7 Isidore based his exposition of natural law creatively on opinions by the jurists Ulpian (*Dig.* 1.1.2–4, *Inst.* 1.2 pr.) and Gaius (*Dig.* 1.1.9, 1.2.1–2). See P. L. Reynolds, "Isidore of Seville," in R. Domingo and J. Martínez-Torrón (eds.), *Great Jurists in Spanish History* (Cambridge: Cambridge University Press, 2018), 31–48, at 36–40.

8 Augustine, *De spiritu et littera*, esp. cc. 21–22, 29–30, 46 (CSEL 60:175–76, 183–84, 200–201). As well as Rom 2:15 and 2 Cor 3:3, Augustine cites Rom 5:5 ("the charity of God is poured forth in our hearts by

sometimes as law of a new and radically different kind: Paul's "law of Christ" (*lex Christi*, Gal 6:2), or Augustine's "law of faith" (*lex fidei*), which is "not letter but spirit."[9] The four gospels spoke *about* the New Law, but they did not state it, for it was essentially unwritten.

The usual view of the Mosaic law among Christian writers and clerics of the first millennium was that it had been futile as the exclusive means to righteousness and excessive in its details. But they did not infer that Christian communities should not use laws and other norms as means to achieve right living. Indeed, a conspicuous feature of the Christian view of life during the early Middle Ages was an anxious determination to guide human action through extraneous regulations and practices. There was perhaps no period in European history when people were less confident that their "fleshy hearts" alone would guide them adequately. This preoccupation may have owed something to the relative weakness and instability of centralized secular governance, in contrast to the relative strength, coherence, and authority of ecclesiastical organization. Among pious persons, it seems, the question, "Good Master, what good thing shall I do, that I may have eternal life?" (Matt 19:16) was urgent and terrifying and called for explicit and detailed answers.

Unlike the Decalogue, which was revealed in writing only as a last resort, much of the Mosaic law was strictly positive, which is to say that the "force" (*virtus*) of the law, and thus one's reason for obeying it, was due solely to the acknowledged power of the lawgiver. Consider the following law from Leviticus, the first in a series on clean and unclean foods:

> And the Lord said to Moses and Aaron: Say to the people of Israel: These are the living things which you may eat among all the beasts that are on the earth. Whatever parts the hoof and is cloven-footed and chews the cud among the animals, you may eat. Nevertheless, among those that chew the cud or part the hoof, you shall not eat these: The camel, because it chews the cud but does not part the hoof, is unclean to you. And the rock badger, because it chews the cud but does not part the hoof, is unclean to you. And the hare, because it chews the cud but does not part the hoof, is unclean to you. And the swine, because it parts the hoof and is cloven-footed but does not chew the cud, is unclean to you. Of their flesh you shall not eat, and their carcasses you shall not touch; they are unclean to you. (Lev 11:1–8)

Here, deductions are drawn from a premise: that the flesh of four-footed beasts is clean if and only if the beast is both cloven-hooved and ruminant. Nevertheless, regardless of whatever historical or anthropological reasons one might invoke to explain how this premise emerged, it demanded obedience only because it expressed a divine command. Christians assumed, on the contrary, not only that

the Holy Spirit, who is given to us") and Jer 31:33 ("I will give my laws* in their hearts, and I will write it in their heart"). *Sic: The word was *leges* (plural) in Augustine's Old Latin version.

9 Ibid., c. 22 (CSEL 60:176). On Paul, see T. R. Schreiner, "Law of Christ," in G. F. Hawthorne and R. P. Martin (eds.), *Dictionary of Paul and His Letters* (Downers Grove, Ill: InterVarsity Press, 1993), 542–44.

canonical norms ought to be reasonable, but also that the reasons were sufficiently accessible to guide interpretation and application. For example, a church council at Orléans in 538 rejected the belief that Christians ought not to travel on horseback or use vehicles on Sundays, explaining that these were matters of Jewish, and not of Christian observance. (Anxiety about Jewish influence on Christians was a recurrent issue throughout the Middle Ages.) But the canon adds that the church prohibits routine work in the fields and vineyards on Sundays – not because of Sabbath observance, but because it prevents the faithful from coming to church.[10]

The Mosaic law was what first came to mind when Christians considered law from a theological point of view. Precepts were paramount in this conception: commandments determining what must or must not be done. The Mosaic law reminded Christians of the limitations of written law as a means to righteousness, but it was also a form of divine law, expressing at some level norms that were unchanging and universal. Moreover, it had prefigured Jesus Christ, who had come to fulfill the law, not to abolish it (Matt 5:17).

Biblical, theological, and pastoral reflection gave rise to ways of talking about law that roamed far from the mundane regulation of mortal human life in community. Christian writers used the term *lex* to denote Scripture as the truest written norm of human life, and even to describe God as the ultimate norm. When Christians thought about law on a grand scale, reflecting theologically on the Christian life and its underlying reasons and structures, their models came chiefly from Scripture, even if they borrowed some of their terms and distinctions from Roman law and jurisprudence and from pagan philosophy. Laws were typically enacted by a legislator, written down, applied through judgment, and enforced with penalties. But when God was the lawgiver, the notions of enactment, writing, judgment, and punishment could be greatly extended by analogy. For example, the New Law is "written" on the heart. Although the term *lex* in Latin was not as expansive in its meanings and connotations as *nomos* was in Greek, its semantic range in Christian discourse was still very broad.

Roman Law

Early Christians were familiar in their daily lives with Roman private law (Chapter 2), which typically ensured fairness by fine-tuning and limiting civil interactions that were basically instinctive and customary. In this context, written law was used as the last resort, when custom and instinctive fairness failed to function or were insufficient. Consider this example:

> If any man should contract for the marriage of a girl to himself and should fail to effect such marriage within two years, and if after this time has elapsed the girl should proceed to marry another, no fraud should be imputed to her for hastening

[10] Conc. Aurelianense A. 538, can. 31, CCL 148A, p. 125.

> her marriage and not allowing her marriage vows to be mocked any longer. (*Cod. Theod.* 3.5.4)[11]

This law pertained to an established custom whereby a man would give a substantial gift to his bride-to-be to confirm their betrothal. What if the betrothal failed, and the two never came together in marriage? Then a law determined that if the breakdown was the suitor's fault, he forfeited the gift, whereas if it was the fault of the girl or her parents, they had to return to the gift (*Cod. Theod.* 3.5.2.1–2). The point of the law quoted above was that a girl and her family were not liable if the suitor had failed to fulfill his promise and they had accepted another offer of marriage rather than waiting any longer, for then the failure of the betrothal was the suitor's fault. To make this principle work, it was necessary to define how long betrothed girls or their parents should be expected to wait, and this limit was set at two years.

Educated Christians of the Western Roman Empire, especially those of Rome, Milan, and North Africa, were steeped in Roman law. Legal advocacy was a popular way to earn a living, and it required skills in rhetoric. Augustine of Hippo, for example, would have offered instruction in legal argument as a professor of rhetoric (see Chapter 12). Conversely, the study of rhetoric, which was fundamentally necessary for any educated person, included at least basic information on law. Although expertise in jurisprudence was a secondary consideration for run-of-the-mill advocates, therefore, rhetorical manuals included some law and jurisprudence. Isidore of Seville's most extended discussion of law in his *Etymologies* (V.1–27) was dependent on juristic sources, but his treatment of rhetoric, too, included paragraphs on law in general (II.10) and on legal argument (II.5), which he must have collected from rhetorical sources.

Roman law was the obvious example of merely human law during the patristic period. Although it did not have much theological significance, it provided Christian writers with categories and techniques of argument. Among Latin patristic authors, the presence of legal language and concepts is especially evident in Tertullian and Ambrosiaster.

The North African theologian Tertullian, active during the first quarter of the third century, freely adapted legal concepts in denouncing the Gnostic heresies and defending Christianity against its pagan Roman opponents. He also demonstrated skills in legal argument. Indeed, according to what used to be the standard account of his life – until T. D. Barnes demolished it in 1971 – Tertullian had been a professional lawyer who practiced in Rome.[12] This claim was based on Eusebius's remark that Tertullian was knowledgeable in the laws of the Romans and had belonged to a circle of distinguished men in Rome (*Ecclesiastical History* II.2.4). The fact that there had been a Roman jurist of the same name bolstered the

[11] Trans. Pharr, 67.

[12] T. D. Barnes, *Tertullian: A Historical and Literary Study* (Oxford: Clarendon Press, 1971; revised edition, 1985).

notion. But the claim that Tertullian dwelled in Rome is otherwise unsupported, and the identification of the two Tertullians is implausible – although Jill Harries has reflected playfully on the possibility that the jurist and the Christian Apologist were father and son.[13] While it is possible that the latter practiced as an advocate, he could have acquired his familiarity with Roman law from rhetoric or even from the ambient culture of North African cities.

Ambrosiaster is perhaps a more interesting example. As David Hunter explains in Chapter 11, Ambrosiaster's thought was permeated with language and concepts from Roman law and administration. He saw parallels between traditional Roman models of authority and the new Christian ones, and he spoke about church offices in Roman terms, which had legal implications. For example, bishops were "legates" (*legati*) and "vicars" (*vicarii*) of Christ, and they acted as judges (*iudices*) and as agents of God (*actores Dei*). Likewise, the emperor was the "vicar of God," and both emperor and bishop derived their authority (*auctoritas*) from God.

Several chapters in this anthology explore how Christian thinkers regarded law from a perspective that was informed by Scripture, theology, and an understanding of God's gradually unfolding plan. (See especially Chapter 10, on Lactantius; Chapter 11, on Ambrosiaster; Chapter 12, on Augustine; Chapter 13, on Leo the Great; Chapter 14, on Gelasius I; Chapter 17, on Gregory the Great; and Chapter 21, on Hincmar.) Thus, Ambrosiaster reflected theologically on the nature, purpose, and divisions of law in relation to sacred history and to the fall from original righteousness, applying insights from Roman jurisprudence to an essentially biblical account of law. So, too, did Augustine of Hippo and Hincmar of Reims. Ambrosiaster distinguished among the natural law, the Mosaic law, and the laws of the secular "nations," such as the Roman Empire (Chapter 11). Augustine distinguished among eternal, temporal, natural, and divine law (Chapter 12). Hincmar's legal categories included natural law, written law, Mosaic law, and human law. Hincmar also attributed the force of law to the four gospels and to at least some of the church's canons, especially those of the first four Ecumenical Councils (see Chapter 21). Of all such divisions, Augustine's would prove to be the most enduring and fruitful after the first millennium. It is striking that canonical regulations were either not included in these divisions and schemata or at best had only a tenuous or implicit presence. (The same is still true of Thomas Aquinas, although he lived in an era replete with canon law and its processes, professions, and jurisprudence.)

The term "divine law," as used in writing of the first millennium, is tricky and often difficult to interpret. It implies a distinction between *lex divina* and human law (*lex humana*).[14] Although Isidore equated divine law with the natural law, the term

13 D. I. Rankin, "Was Tertullian a Jurist?" *Studia Patristica* 31 (1997): 335–42. David E. Wilhite, *Tertullian the African: An Anthropological Reading of Tertullian's Context and Identities* (Berlin: De Gruyter, 2007), 20–22. Jill Harries, "Tertullianus & Son," in Zuleika Rogers (ed.), *A Wandering Galilean: Essays in Honour of Seán Freyne* (Leiden: Brill, 2009), 385–98.

14 Compare Philip L. Reynolds, *Marriage in the Western Church* (Leiden: Brill, 1994), 121–72, where I discuss the *lex divina / lux humana* distinction as regards marriage, especially in Gregory I and Leo

"divine law" usually denoted revealed law, and it often referred nonspecifically to sacred Scripture. Remarkably, medieval theologians rarely explained or remarked on the relationship between divine law and the church's canons, even after the emergence of the *ius canonicum* as a branch or body of law in the twelfth century.

Post-Roman Law

After the collapse of the Western Roman Empire, the laws of the successor kingdoms superseded Roman law, but these were more or less Romanized and incorporated legislation from the *Theodosian Code*. As Alexander Callander Murray explains in Chapter 3, these diverse legal systems used to be regarded as variant manifestations of a single ethnic substratum of "Germanic" law, construed in binary fashion as the alternative to Roman law. This interpretation still lingers in historical writing, but it is arguably untenable.[15] With the demise of "Germanic" law as a plausible category of historical scholarship, it has become difficult to generalize about the influence of post-Roman law on Christian thought and practice. Scholars today who refer to "Germanic" law do not necessarily have any ethnic, nationalist, or essentialist conception in mind, but specialists in the field prefer less descriptive terms, such as "post-Roman" law.

The Nature and Concept of Laws

The following provisional account is not intended to capture every norm that might be considered as law but focuses instead on enacted laws, for this was chiefly what the plural term *leges* denoted in medieval usage. In the absence of any widely accepted general theory about the essence of law from the period, one must depend chiefly on a descriptive account of the salient features of what they and we call "laws." But Isidore of Seville's observations are also helpful. Situated at the historical boundary between late-Roman culture and a new Gothic Spain, Isidore considered Justinian's Byzantium to be corrupt and in decline. He was culturally Roman, but he vested his hopes for the future of Christian civilization in the Visigothic regime and worked to foster its order and stability. Meanwhile, Isidore took it upon himself to preserve for this new world what was most useful from patristic and classical learning.

Isidore claims that the term *lex* (plural: *leges*) comes from the verb *legere*, "to read," for law in the proper sense is a "written statute" (*constitutio scripta*) (*Etym.*

I. I now think that I failed to appreciate how often the term *lex divina* referred to Scripture, and that I exaggerated the extent to which it denoted church law.

15 The idea that a static "folklaw" prevailed throughout the early Middle Ages, as expounded by Harold J. Berman, *Law and Revolution: The Formation of the Western Legal Tradition* (Cambridge, MA: Harvard University Press, 1983), 47–84, is still more remote from reality. On this point, see P. Landau's review of Berman's book in *University of Chicago Law Review* 51.3 (1984): 937–43, at 938–39.

V.3.2). Being written may seem unlikely as a distinguishing feature of anything, for writing was used for many different purposes. (To the modern reader, Thomas Aquinas's etymology, whereby *lex* comes from *ligare* – "to bind" – may seem more convincing.)[16] One reason for Isidore's emphasis on written law was that he wanted to distinguish laws in the proper sense from enduring, stable customs. Although these could be construed as unwritten law (*lex non scripta*) – an insight that Isidore owed to Roman jurisprudence – he thought that custom functioned as law only in the absence of written law (V.3.2–3). Moreover, whereas unwritten laws were usually customary, enacted laws were usually written. Written law, therefore, was law par excellence.

Isidore may have had another reason for emphasizing that laws were typically written, for the written word manifested the fixity of laws, even though written law is presumably easier to change than customary law.[17] Writing showed not only that laws were authoritative (for authority was closely associated with writing in the first millennium) but also that they were external, inflexible constraints. Not only were laws usually stated absolutely, as if they would endure forever, but they also enjoyed a certain objectivity, so that experts could inquire how to interpret and apply them and how to extend them to unforeseen situations. By the same token, laws were blunt instruments, even a necessary evil. They were good if and only if they were useful and beneficial, but to meet that criterion they needed only to improve matters in the majority of cases, not in all. Written law makes up for the inconsistency and unreliability of practical wisdom, but its consistent application generates inconsistencies of fairness and benefit.

Laws are typically written texts, then, but they cannot be understood simply as texts. One cannot choose to make a law as one might choose to write a sonnet. Laws are functional, performative texts.[18] They express the imperative will of whoever holds supreme political power over the community that the law binds. During the first millennium, supreme power was usually vested in an individual sovereign (the supreme *princeps*), such as a king or an emperor. Laws can be applied only by designated authorities, acting as agents of the sovereign's authority.

The purpose of law is to regulate human action at the level of a political community. Thus, laws are designed to regulate the life of the community as a whole, and they regulate the lives of individuals, families, classes (*statūs*), and voluntary associations only in relation to the larger community. Isidore says that good laws are made "not for private advantage, but for the common benefit of the citizens" (V.21), and that a law is a "statute of a people" (*constitutio populi*), imposed by the senior members of the community upon the juniors, but with the consent of the latter

[16] Thomas Aquinas, *Summa theol.* I–II.90.1, resp.: "dicitur enim lex a ligando, quia obligat ad agendum."

[17] On the presumed "static character" of customary laws, see H. L. A. Hart, *The Concept of Law*, 3rd ed. (Oxford: Oxford University Press, 2012), 92–93.

[18] For an accessible introduction to this consideration, see Lorenzo Fiorito, "On Performatives in Legal Discourse," *Metalogicon* 19.2 (2006): 101–12.

(V.10). Classical theories of law were inherently political and based on an account of the *polis* or the commonwealth (*res publica*), which was construed as a complete community: the "body politic."[19] The purpose of law was to preserve and foster the "common good." Aristotle regarded the *polis* as a visible, palpable entity.[20] The notion became complicated and fraught when applied to larger, more complex political communities, such as kingdoms and empires, but it was no less necessary for understanding the nature of law. The word of a *pater familias* within his household was sometimes said to be law, but only metaphorically. The notion that laws might be made for particular private individuals or voluntary associations was at best highly problematic.

Law is closely related to punishment (*poena*), which is meted out through judgment. Because laws are binding by definition, it is hard to make sense of laws that are not enforceable, and one rationale for judicial punishment is as an aid to enforcement – although another rationale is retributive, and retribution (a measured form of revenge) may be understood as an intrinsic restoration of due order: a communal or even cosmic rebalancing.

Whether the threat of punishment is an essential feature of laws or legal systems is disputable. Isidore claims that laws have three purposes: to permit, to prohibit, and to punish, as if these were three distinct goals. But Isidore also observes that laws in general are made "to restrain human audacity through fear," since "human life is moderated by reward and punishment" (V.20, II.10.4–5). The analytical legal positivist Joseph Raz, arguing that "sanctions" are not essential to the existence of a legal system, considers the objection that without sanctions there would be no courts, and without courts no legal system. In reply, Raz argues that even a community of perfect people ("angels") might settle disputes in courts but without any need for the threat of punishment.[21] In the real world, however, legislation is coextensive with the possibility of punitive justice.

It is interesting that Raz does not question the premise that without courts (i.e., a judicial process) there would be no legal system – which is perhaps not the same as there being no laws. Laws are judicable, arguably by definition.[22] Laws exist to be applied, and they are applied through judgment. The judicial process is the chief normative practice corresponding to this class of normative texts. As Luca Loschiavo explains in Chapter 18, Isidore's most valuable and lasting contribution to central-

19 Joseph Raz, *Practical Reason and Norms* (Oxford: Oxford University Press, 1999), 150–54, achieves a similar result in a positivist, analytical context (where goods are incidental) by claiming that legal systems, in relation and in contrast to other normative systems, are "comprehensive" and "supreme."

20 N. Aroney, "Subsidiarity in the Writings of Aristotle and Aquinas," in M. Evans and A. Zimmermann (eds.), *Global Perspectives on Subsidiarity* (Dordrecht: Springer, 2014), 9–27, at 14–15.

21 Raz, *Practical Reason*, 159–60.

22 Hermann Kantorowicz, *The Definition of Law* (Cambridge: Cambridge University Press, 1958), 21, defines law (i.e., any legal system) as "a body of rules prescribing external conduct and considered judiciable [*sic*]." On the uncertainty as to what Kantorowicz meant by the last requirement, see Goodhart's introduction, xxiii–xxiv.

medieval canon law was his account of the procedure of a court of law (*De foro*: *Etym*. XVIII.15). It is because laws are meant to be judicable and applied by judges that a good law, according to Isidore, must be "clearly stated [*manifesta*], lest through obscurity it contains something deceitful" (V.21).

Finally, a conspicuous characteristic of legal systems is the positing and proliferation of *de iure*, supra-physical qualities and entities, such as rights and privileges, culpability, obligations, and the validity of contracts, vows, and marriage. We might refer to this field as the descriptive (rather than analytical) "ontology" of law.

The Meanings of *Ius*

"*Ius* is said in many ways," according to the jurist Paul (*Dig*. 1.1.11). In other words, it is equivocal. The term *ius* (plural *iura*) entered Christian Latin from classical usage and Roman law. Although the term was important in the canon law of the central Middle Ages, however, it occurred only infrequently in Christian writing of the early Middle Ages, where its meaning is often unclear or debatable.

In the context of Roman law and jurisprudence, *ius*, like *lex*, is usually translated into modern English as "law" (e.g., *ius civile*, "civil law"), although the nouns "right" and "justice" are sometimes more appropriate. The use of the word "law" today to translate *ius* is a consequence of a narrowing of the semantic range of the noun "right" in English, where it now refers almost exclusively to subjective rights, such as a person's right to do or to use something. The term formerly enjoyed a broader range of senses, encompassing whatever was "considered proper, correct, or consonant with justice" (OED). In contrast, several other modern European languages have a pair of terms, such as *loi* / *droit* in French, that functions in a similar way to *lex* / *ius* in classical Latin. That is not to say that terms such as *droit* in French, *recht* in German, and so forth, are univocal or straightforward. In French, for example, *loi* and *droit* are systematically distinguished only in legal discourse (*discours juridique*), whereas they are often interchangeable in ordinary discourse. Even in legal discourse, the term *droit* may refer either to subjective or to objective rights, and both *loi* and *droit* in the singular number may denote a legal system considered as a whole: as a body of law. Thus, where an English speaker might refer to the redress available "under French law," a French speaker might use either *droit* or *loi*, although a purist might insist on *droit*.

Although *ius* was equivocal or nonspecific in Roman law, it often referred to something more fundamental than *lex*. The close relationship between *ius* and justice (*iusticia*) was fundamental. "It is called *ius*," said Isidore, "because it is just [*iustum*]" (*Etym*. V.3.1). Laws and the judicial process existed so that a member of the political community who had been treated unfairly or inequitably could seek and obtain redress. This basic sensibility presupposed subjective rights, whether explicit or implicit – albeit arguably not of *natural* rights in the modern sense, for slaves were effectively nonpersons. In its most general sense, therefore, *ius* was "that which is always equitable and good," as the jurist Paul put it.[23] In medieval Latin, *aequitas* (fairness) and *iusticia* are often synonyms.

More fundamental to Roman law and jurisprudence, however, was the use of the term *ius* to denote a person's subjective right in relation to others in the community, such as a right in the strong sense (presupposing a correlative duty in others), or a mere privilege (presupposing from others only noninterference), or a power (i.e., what the scholastics called a *facultas*: a legal capacity).[24] Thus, Ulpian defines the virtue of justice as "a steady and enduring will to give to each his *ius*" (*Dig.* 1.1.10 pr., *Inst.* 1.1.1). In the language of classical Roman law, subjective rights are indicated when someone is said "to have a right" (*ius habere*), and possession of a right may be signified by a possessive pronoun (e.g., *ius meum*), by use of the genitive (*ius alicuius*), or by the dative of possession (*ius est alicui*).[25]

The term *ius* was also used collectively to denote everything legal or juridical as a whole made up of numerous parts, or as a genus containing several species. Thus, the jurist Gaius identified as the *iura* (plural) of the Roman people their statutes (*leges*), plebiscites, resolutions of the Senate, imperial constitutions, edicts of those with the power (*ius*) to issue them, and the responses of juristic experts.[26] Likewise, Isidore says that "*ius* is the general term, and law [*lex*] is a species of *ius*." Again, the term *ius* sometimes denoted the justice available to a specific community or under a specific jurisdiction, as in the terms *ius civile* ("civil law," i.e., the justice available to citizens qua citizens) and *ius militare* ("military justice").

From these generic and inclusive senses came the central-medieval use of *ius* to denote a body of laws or a legal system, especially inasmuch as this was the object of academic study and jurisprudence. By the fourteenth century, both the *ius canonicum* ("canon law") and the *ius civile* (Roman civil law, construed as secular) were recognized as universal bodies of learned law. Together, they constituted the *ius commune*, in contradistinction to the statuary laws of particular political communities or jurisdictions (the *iura propria*). It would be a mistake to attribute the notion of *ius canonicum* in this sense to clerics and scholars of the first millennium.

The equivocity of *ius* in Roman law was arguably a measure of its grandeur and of the respect due to justice. As Kenneth Pennington puts it:

> the jurists never attributed the rich penumbras of meanings to *lex* that they did to *ius*. *Lex* was a plebian hod carrier of the law; *ius* was a term rich in resonances. *Ius* reminded the jurists constantly of the transcendental significance of a legal system.

23 *Dig.* 1.1.11. Paul identifies *ius* here with natural law (the *ius naturale*).

24 For example, someone who owns a house (a strong subjective right) has the privilege of living in it and the power to transfer ownership to another.

25 Charles Donahue, Jr., "*Ius* in Roman Law," in J. Witte, Jr., and F. S. Alexander (eds.), *Christianity and Human Rights: An Introduction* (Cambridge: Cambridge University Press, 2011), 64–80, at 66–67.

26 Gaius, *Institutes* 1.2.

It existed not just to establish right and wrong and to punish the wicked. It was the source of justice, equity, and rights.[27]

For Christians of the first millennium, however, *lex* was hallowed by its biblical use and embedded in a complex and sometimes theological discourse, whereas *ius* was a merely legal term, not a theological one, and it had been appropriated from a pagan culture. Despite its aura of justice and fairness, *ius* was not embedded in the sacred discourse.

In Christian writings of the first millennium, therefore, although *ius* suggested a certain grandeur, it was a term of convenience, used reflexively without any clear intention when *lex* was too specific. It encompassed whatever, according to context, was considered right or required. Less often, it hinted at some form of justice: some process of inquiry and judgment. The reflexive modern use of the term "law" or "laws" to translate *ius* or *iura* in writings of the first millennium, while inevitable (unless one resorts to obsolete uses of "right"), is often problematic and misleading, for *ius* was less specific than *lex*, being either equivocal (as Gaius claimed) or generic (as Isidore claimed). All *lex* was *ius*, but not all *ius* was *lex*.

MONASTIC RULES

From the earliest days of coenobitic (communal) monasticism, Eastern and Western monastic leaders wrote guides to the religious life for their followers. Typically, a leader would address his (or perhaps her) own community while keeping in mind the possibility that the document might be copied and disseminated, and that others might find it helpful. These early guides followed no fixed pattern and varied widely in content, scope, and composition. Nor was there any general descriptive title for them. Only later did they become known in the West generically as *regulae*, or rules.

The *Rule of Benedict*, written around the middle of the sixth century, bequeathed to Western monasticism a definitive notion of the monastic rule and its function, which Benedict had appropriated from the anonymous *Rule of the Master*, written perhaps two or three decades earlier. Hitherto, as Adalbert de Vogüé has pointed out, coenobitic monks lived in immediate obedience not to a written rule but solely to their abbot. Communities followed a largely oral tradition of monastic lore that John Cassian referred to as the discipline (*disciplina*).[28] The abbot directed his followers on behalf of Christ, and all religious recognized Scripture as their ultimate law (*lex*).

The term *regula* was used of the monastic life during this early period in several senses. It could denote obedience to the abbot, or the religious way of life, or the common discipline of monastic communities, or Scripture.[29] The Master and

27 Kenneth Pennington, "*Lex naturalis* and *ius naturale*," *Jurist* 68 (2008): 569–91, at 573.

28 A. de Vogüé, "Sub regula vel abbate: A Study of the Theological Significance of the Ancient Monastic Rules," in B. Pennington (ed.), *Rule and Life: An Interdisciplinary Symposium*, Cistercian Studies Series 12 (Spencer, Mass.: Cistercian Publications, 1971), 21–64.

29 Ibid., 51–52.

Benedict, without entirely excluding earlier and broader connotations, used the term chiefly to denote a written norm, conceived as including detailed prescriptions covering every aspect of the community's life, as if the rule was a codification or reduction to writing of the community's version of the discipline. Moreover, both the Master and Benedict regarded the written rule as something to which obedience was due. The written rule was the norm by which the abbot governed and led his community.

The Carolingian abbot and monastic reformer Benedict of Aniane was responsible for a further development (see Chapter 9). This "second Benedict" gathered and collated all the monastic guides known to him, construing them all as monastic rules, and comparing them with the *Rule of Benedict* to show that this was the monastic rule par excellence. Henceforth, to be a monk or a nun would for centuries require obedience to the *Rule of Benedict* – although what that entailed in practice was complicated and varied widely.

A monastic rule was a document that functioned as the norm defining right living for a community of religious. The term *regula* had connotations of governance and royalty (compare the verb *regere*, "to rule"), but this sense was secondary. The term denoted literally a straightedge: a tool enabling someone to draw a straight line between two points. The Latin *regula* (or sometimes *rigula* in late Latin) passed through the cognate Old- and Middle-English words *rhegel* and *reule*, both commonly used also to denote monastic rules, to our modern words "rule" and "ruler," denoting a straightedge or measuring tape.[30]

Monastic rules, as envisaged by the Master and Benedict, differed from laws in the literal sense (i.e., written laws regulating political communities) in several salient respects. First, whereas laws were designed primarily to control external actions (since grudging obedience sufficed), monastic rules were designed to inculcate virtues and to foster spiritual transformation. Second, whereas the scope of laws was minimal – as Augustine noted, they left the judgment of most transgressions to divine providence[31] – the scope of monastic rules was maximal, extending to minute details of daily life. Third, whereas accidents of location or birth were sufficient to make someone subject to the laws of a particular community, subjection to a monastic rule, albeit lifelong, was voluntary: a result of personal commitment expressed in a vow. Monastic communities were usually cautious about accepting new members, and reception required determination and perseverance on the part of the newcomer, after which there was a period of opportunity for second thoughts. Fourth, whereas laws by definition regulated life at the level of the political community as a whole, monastic rules regulated a small community within the larger community from which the monks or nuns, while spiritually "dead to the world," could not be isolated in fact. From a political point of view, monastic communities

30 I am grateful to Albrecht Diem and to James Morey for clarifying this etymology for me.

31 Augustine, *De libero arbitrio* I.5(13), CSEL 74, 13–14.

were and are voluntary associations. Fifth, although monks could be held to account and even corporeally chastised for infractions, the normative practice corresponding to a monastic rule was not a judicial process but a way of living (*modus vivendi*): a way that was centered on constant vigilance. Sixth, whereas the desired result of law was mundane equity and orderliness, that of the monastic life was a spiritual well-being that began now but would be fully realized only in the life to come.

Subjection to a particular monastic rule, while defining a community's way of life, did not preclude the use of other regulatory documents and traditions. From the ninth century, monastic communities supplemented the *Rule of Benedict* with their own statutes (additional regulations) and customaries (written records of the community's particular traditions). Later, as new orders and new modes of the religious life emerged, beginning with the Canons Regular in the eleventh century, each order was defined by its subjection to an approved written rule – or at least to something that served as a rule, for a wide range of documentary resources met that requirement. Some rules for new orders and movements, such as the Canons Regular and the mendicants, were much less detailed than the *Rule of Benedict*, the general outlines of which could be presupposed. Again, the Cistercians, whose order emerged in the twelfth century as a reformist movement within the Benedictine family, continued to follow the *Rule of Benedict* but supplemented it with their own charter (the *Carta caritatis*) and *Constitutiones*. Notwithstanding such complications, religious orders were defined and attained status in canon law through the approved written rules to which they professed obedience. The seeds of this institutional and legal dependence on written rules in the central Middle Ages, which was extended to non-monastic orders such as the mendicants (friars), lay in the idea of a monastic rule proposed long ago by the Master and Benedict, who were innocent of any notion that a community's rule implied situating the community's way of life in a larger legal framework.

PENITENTIAL PRESCRIPTIONS

The administration of penance was a quintessentially ecclesiastical performance. Although penance presupposed moral crime and guilt, its essential purpose was not to punish but to forgive and to reconcile. In practice, however, this distinction could become blurred. For example, when the alternative to penance was excommunication, penance could function as a disciplinary measure, and so as something akin to judicial punishment.

Until the new historical approaches to early and medieval penance that have emerged during the last two decades, historians writing on the topic understood their task as explaining the transition from the public, once-only penance of the early church, administered by a bishop, to private, repeatable penance, administered by any priest, and still familiar today as one of the seven sacraments of the church – a status that it acquired during the first half of the twelfth century. Both were modes of formal penance, in which an ordained minister of the church, by virtue of his office and using prescribed rites and formulas, assigned an appropriate penitential practice to a repentant sinner.

Penance as Reconciliation with the Christian Community

The early practice of formal penance emerged during the second century and flourished in the fourth. It was still the only form of penance recognized by Merovingian church councils during the sixth century. Often referred to today as canonical penance, this ancient practice offered a second chance to someone who had committed a grievous sin after baptism, such as murder, adultery, or apostasy: a transgression that threatened the peace and unity of the Christian community and merited irrevocable excommunication and eternal damnation. Reconciliation was administered either by an individual bishop or by the bishops who had assembled for a council. Although the details of the sin might be kept confidential, to become a penitent was to adopt a marginal but transitional social status. The sinner was morally exiled from the community, lived austerely, wore penitential garb, and was prohibited from receiving eucharist. He or she would be ceremonially reconciled only after living as a penitent for a lengthy period. Normally, there was only one such opportunity in a person's lifetime. The practice was considered inappropriate both for children (who should not use up their second chance too soon) and for clergy in holy orders. The latter might instead be demoted, after which penance was possible. Even after reconciliation, the penitent remained in some respects a second-class member of the Christian community. For example, reconciled penitents were usually prohibited from clerical ordination.

Formal penance during the early Christian centuries, therefore, was applicable only to extreme transgressions, and because Christianity was a deeply penitential faith, it is likely that the practice of penance at that time was mostly informal. Faithful persons troubled by guilt and not confident that their prayers were being heard would presumably have undertaken some purgative practice either on their own initiative or with the counsel of a priest or a monk. As Richard Price remarks, "The system of canonical penance was never as important as the traditional histories of the sacrament have tried to make out, distorted as they have been by having as the prime objective not the description of early Christian practice, but finding a respectable ancestry for the discipline of a later period."[32]

Although the chief theological function of formal penance in the early church was to reconcile the sinner with God and to enable him or her to escape eternal damnation, the means to achieve this end was reconciliation with the *people* of God. Regarded from a sociological point of view, public penance was a way to limit the

[32] Richard Price, "Informal Penance in Early Medieval Christendom," in K. Cooper and J. Gregory (eds.), *Retribution, Repentance, and Reconciliation* (Suffolk, UK: Boydell Press, 2004), 29–38, at 30.

cost to a community that would have been incurred by the permanent exile of transgressors and by the fracture of marriages and families.

Among the earliest surviving penitential prescriptions are several canons from the Council of Ancyra (modern-day Ankara) in 314. This is among the earliest councils from which reliable records of the decisions have survived, and it was the first such Eastern council.[33] Roughly one-third of the twenty-five canons concern men in clerical orders, and all but one of the others concern the laity. (The exception concerns consecrated virgins.) Among the canons that pertain to lay persons, roughly half are penitential prescriptions; and half of those pertain to persons who had lapsed in a time of persecution.

The council was preoccupied with the fallen (*lapsi*) because of the recent anti-Christian persecution by emperor Maximin Daia. Some had denied their faith by sacrificing: specifically, by burning incense in front of a temple and then eating some of the meat that had been ritually offered to the deity. Apostasy was a heinous crime, but measurement of the sin's gravity depended on the circumstances. Complicating or mitigating factors included the degree or manner of coercion, the willingness or unwillingness of the transgressor, and the use of subterfuge to obtain a certificate of sacrifice without sacrificing. Among the roughly one-third of the canons from Ancyra that address the issue of the lapsed, three determine the consequences regarding clerical orders: the appropriate course of action for an ordained cleric who had lapsed, and whether a layman who had lapsed was capable of being ordained. But most concern the reconciliation of lay persons through penance.

The penitential canons from this council presuppose three intermediate stages along the path to full communion. These should be interpreted in light both of the spatial disposition of the liturgy and of the limited participation of catechumens, who were permitted to hear the readings and any homily but had to leave before the celebration of the mysteries of eucharist. At the first and most remote stage are those called hearers, who must have followed the liturgy from the rear of the church or from the narthex. Next are the prostrators, who could not remain for the mystery of eucharist. They presumably mingled with the congregation during the "word" phase of the service but left with the catechumens. Then there are the penitents described as those who pray – the supplicators, we might say. They remained with the community during the celebration of eucharist but could not yet receive it.

The last of the canons of Ancyra records a particular case that had come before the council (canon 25). Perhaps the details were too complicated or peculiar for any general rule to be extrapolated from them. A certain man who was already betrothed

[33] See Hefele-Leclercq, *Histoire des conciles*, vol. 1 (Paris, 1907), 298–326; Ulrich Huttner, *Early Christianity in the Lycus Valley* (Boston: Brill, 2013), 279–84; R. B. Rackham, *The Text of the Canons of Ancyra: The Greek, Latin, Syriac and Armenian Versions*, =Analecta Gorgiana, 15 (Piscataway, NJ: Gorgias Press, 2006), first published in *Studia Biblica et Ecclesiastica*, ed. S. R. Driver et al. (Oxford: Clarendon Press, 1981), 3:139–216.

to a woman had had sexual intercourse with her sister and made her pregnant. When he married his betrothed, her sister committed suicide. The council ruled that he must do ten years of penance, appropriately divided into stages, in order to become a supplicator. The canon does not determine how long the penitent was to remain in this penultimate stage, perhaps leaving this for a subsequent council to determine.

The other penitential canons from this council are general rules, although they, too, may have originated in particular cases. Lapsed Christians who sacrificed not because they were physically coerced but because they were threatened with confiscation of property, and who are only now, some years later, seeking reconciliation, must do penance as hearers until the next Easter council (these councils apparently took place annually in the fourth week after Easter), then as prostrators for three years, and finally as supplicators for two years (canon 6). Persons who have practiced magic or divination must do penance as hearers for five years, as prostrators for three years, and as supplicators for two years (canon 24). Persons who have committed sodomy with irrational animals must do penance for many years, but the specifics depend on age and marital status. If the transgressor was married and at least twenty years of age when the sodomy occurred, he must be a prostrator for twenty-five years and then a supplicator for five years (canon 16). A person guilty of deliberate, premeditated murder must do lifelong penance as a prostrator (canon 22). Reconciliation was possible, presumably, when the person was dying.

These penitential canons presupposed a crime for which the just punishment would have been permanent exile from a people of God. Exile from the Christian community was a spiritual death, just as exile beyond the borders of the Roman Empire was a civic death, classified as capital punishment. In some cases, a tribunal of some sort must have been necessary to establish the precise circumstances of the transgression for which the penance was prescribed. And the prescriptions imply, among other things, an assessment of the gravity of the offence. Nevertheless, the canons presuppose that the guilt (*reatus*) of the penitent has already been established, and in this respect, among others, they are unlike laws. Rather than imposing a just punishment (*poena*) on an unwilling subject as the sentence of a judicial process, they offer a merciful and reparative penance (*poenitentia*) to someone who opts to undertake it.

Penance and the Cure of Souls

The Fourth Lateran Council of 1215 mandated that all persons had to confess their sins at least once a year to their own priest (i.e., to their parish priest in most cases), as well as to attend eucharist at Easter. The interview with a priest is likened to a consultation with a skilled physician, who puts questions to the patient so that he can prescribe the appropriate remedy, just as the Good Samaritan applied wine and oil to the wounds of the injured one. The priest must not reveal the penitent's guilt to others. He may seek counsel from another priest as to what prescription is appropriate, but then he must not reveal the identity of the sinner (canon 21).[34] Penance in this form, which had been counted as one of the seven sacraments of the church since the 1140s, was repeatable, administered by a priest (not necessarily a bishop), and applicable to sins of any degree, minor or major.

Church historians have understood since the nineteenth century that this practice could be traced to sixth- or early-seventh-century Celtic monastic practices. Although there are records of oral prescriptions in the Lives of Celtic saints, prescriptions in this tradition were mainly transmitted in penitential books, or penitentials, which flourished in insular communities and were transmitted to the Continent with missionary movements, especially those associated with the monk Columbanus. (One should keep in mind, however, that reception presupposes receptivity, which may take the form either of perceived need or of comparable precedents.) By providing examples of prescriptions regarding a wide range of sins, the penitentials helped confessors to administer a measured, tariffed system of penance. The method was capable of handling not only grave, socially disruptive sins, such as murder and illicit sex (for which the penance might be a lengthy period of geographical exile), but also minor infractions. Tariffed penance was directed more to cure of souls than to the common good. It was readily repeatable, and it fostered a culture of self-examination. Texts such as penitentials, questionnaires, and canonical collections helped the clergy to administer it.

In secret, or private penance, the focus was not on reconciliation with the community but on the individual penitent's reconciliation with God. Considered in itself, such penance was even less lawlike than public penance. The obvious model was not judicial but medical. Secret penance was a means of *cura animarum*: the cure and care of souls.

Alcuin (d. 804), formerly advisor to Charlemagne, used the themes of remedy and judgment in an epistolary treatise on penance that he wrote for the "boys" of St. Martin's abbey, of which he was abbot.[35] He encourages the boys to bring their guilty secrets out into the open from the dark recesses of their consciences through "sincere" (*pura*) and "salutary" confession, which is the proper remedy for guilt (§2). God's justice is terrifying, but God is a merciful physician as well as terrible judge. "If the physician does not intervene," Alcuin explains, "the sick person will not be cured. Confession is the remedy to your wounds, the most certain assistance for your health [*salus*] ... No one restores you better than he who made you. No one else heals you but the one who scourges and cures" (§3). It is good to exchange a painful moment of shame and embarrassment now, Alcuin points out, for eternal damnation in the life to come (§§4, 6, 8). Although the twin themes of cure and judgment recur throughout the treatise, that of cure is developed more fully, and the judgment

34 Tanner, 245.

35 Michael S. Driscoll, "*Ad Pueros Sancti Martini*: A Critical Edition, English Translation, and Study of the Manuscript Transmission," *Traditio* 53 (1998): 37–61. For Driscoll's edition and facing-page translation, see pp. 48–61. The likely date of the treatise is 796–98.

to which Alcuin refers, with one exception, is post-mortem. Alcuin posits cure now as the alternative to future condemnation. In the exceptional passage, Alcuin interprets confession itself as a judicial process, but one that occurs in the private forum of confession, where the accuser is the penitent himself. As a "most benign judge," God permits penitents "to accuse ourselves of our sins before a priest of God, lest the devil accuses us of them later before Christ as judge" (§4). At no point in the treatise does Alcuin construe penance itself as judicial punishment.

The Historiography of Penance

The work of Bernard Poschmann, beginning in the 1920s, provided generations of church historians and historical theologians with a framework for understanding and analyzing the two kinds of formal penance and the historical passage from one to the other. This was a teleological approach, designed to explain the ancestry of penance as one of the sacraments of the church, and tending to impose schematic divisions and categories on complicated historical data.[36]

The work of Cyrille Vogel in the 1960s supplemented Poschmann's schema.[37] Vogel recognized the importance of public penance during the Carolingian era, when normative sources advocated the retention of the ancient form, which was appropriate especially for high-profile, scandalous cases (see Chapter 6). The Carolingians introduced the distinction between public penance and penance done secretly (e.g., *occulte, absconse*: the adverbial idiom was more common than the adjectival in canons on penance during this period, and the term "private penance" did not become current until the eleventh century). Vogel brought to light the Carolingian principle that hidden sins required secret penance, whereas public sins required public penance.[38] He also confirmed, as Anciaux had argued, that there was a shift of emphasis during the twelfth century from the tariffed evaluation of actions to the evaluation of the agent's intentions, and thus from penance to confession.[39] The presumed shift is consistent with the moral reflection on intention found in the early-scholastic sentences and treatises of the twelfth century, with their focus on the "adultery of the heart" (Matt 5:27–28) and a new interest in the propassions of Stoic ethics (immediate responses of the carnal appetites that are reflexive and pre-voluntary).

36 Bernhard Poschmann, *Die abendländische Kirchenbusse im Ausgang des christlichen Altertums* (Munich: Kösel & Pustet, 1928); Bernard Poschmann, *Die abendländische Kirchenbusse im frühen Mittelalter*, Breslauer Studien zur historischen Theologie 16 (Breslau, 1930); Bernard Poschmann, *Penance and the Anointing of the Sick*, trans. F. Courtney (New York: Herder and Herder, 1964).

37 Cyrille Vogel, *Le pécheur et la pénitence au moyen âge* (Paris: Cerf, 1969); Cyrille Vogel, *Les 'Libri paenitentiales,'* with supplement by A. J. Frantzen, *Typologie des sources du moyen âge occidental* 27 (Turnhout: Brepols, 1985).

38 Vogel, *Le pécheur*, 24–27.

39 P. Anciaux, *La théologie du sacrament de pénitence au XIIe siècle* (Louvain; Nauwelaerts; and Gembloux: Duculot, 1949), 7–55. Vogel, *Le pécheur*, 27–36.

Whereas the leading historians of penance around the middle of the twentieth century, such as Poschmann and Vogel, were historical theologians, the new approaches that have flourished since the 1990s originated in social history. Resistance to the schematizing theories of historical theologians has been a conspicuous trait of this work. The end result has not been a demolition of the schemata of Poschmann and Vogel, which have held up fairly well, but rather a broadening of scope and a shift from normative sources to sources arguably more closely related to practice. Mary Mansfield's *The Humiliation of Sinners* – which was the text of her doctoral dissertation, completed in 1989, although the book was not published until 1995 because of her untimely death – documented the continuing importance of public humiliation during the central Middle Ages.[40] Sarah Hamilton acknowledged a debt to Mansfield in *The Practice of Penance* (2001),[41] and Hamilton's book in turn inspired a workshop in Utrecht (2002), the proceedings of which were published in a special edition of *Early Medieval Europe*, edited by Rob Meens (2006).[42] Meens's own extensive writings on the history of penance include what is currently the standard book on the topic.[43] Professor Meens is also the author of the chapter on penance in this volume (Chapter 8).

These historians take a more inclusive view of the subject matter as regards the practices involved, the function of penance, and the sources. For example, Hamilton and Meens, as well as Mayke de Jong (see Chapter 6), have emphasized the use of public penance among the Carolingians as a way to quell scandals that were dividing rulers from their subjects, and Meens has drawn attention to the use of penance in conflict resolution. Moreover, rather than focusing exclusively on normative sources, such as conciliar canons and episcopal capitularies, these scholars prefer sources that were arguably closer to actual practice. For example, the Carolingian distinction between public and secret penance is found in a few normative texts but very rarely in liturgical *ordines* (scripts). Nor is it easy to see how the distinction would apply to the Carolingian practice whereby several members of a parish or a monastic community would be enrolled collectively as penitents on Ash Wednesday and then reconciled on Maundy Thursday. Nor is it easy to define which element of the process was public in public penance, or secret in secret penance.[44] The crux, it seems, pertained neither to the act of confession (which was usually secret in either process) nor to the penance itself (which was often visible in

40 Mary Mansfield, *The Humiliation of Sinners: Public Penance in Thirteenth-Century France* (Ithaca, NY: Cornell University Press, 1995).

41 Sarah Hamilton, *The Practice of Penance 900–1050* (Royal Historical Society and Boydell Press: Woodbridge, UK, 2001), esp. 16–20.

42 EME 14.1 (2006). Meens observes in his introduction, 1–6, at 6: "From the ensuing papers it will be clear that all speakers were inspired by Sarah Hamilton's wonderful study of the practice of penance in the tenth and eleventh centuries."

43 Rob Meens, *Penance in Medieval Europe 600–1200* (Cambridge: Cambridge University Press, 2014).

44 See M. de Jong, "What Was Public about Public Penance? Paenitentia publica and Justice in the Carolingian World," in *La giustizia nell'alto medioevo (secolo 9.-11), Settimane 44* (Spoleto: Centro italiano di studi sull'alto Medioevo, 1997), 863–904; and Tom Tentler, review of Hamilton, *Practice of*

both forms of penance) but to accusation and to reconciliation. In public penance of this period, other members of the community accused someone of transgressions, and the aim was public, even political reconciliation. In secret penance, the penitents accused themselves (as Alcuin observed), and reconciliation was usually quiet and unobserved.

CANONS

In the narrow and original sense of the term, canons were the decrees of church councils (Chapter 4). More precisely, they were the disciplinary decrees, as distinct from doctrinal definitions, creeds, and so forth, for councils also settled matters of doctrine and defined the faith. But this distinction is not always clear. For example, the anathematizing of those who taught a certain error or who worshipped in a certain way was in itself a disciplinary ruling, but it implied a doctrinal one. Again, rules regarding the performance of the sacraments and the validity of marriage refused to belong unambiguously on one or the other side of the division.

Conciliar Canons

So that this discussion is not too abstract, I begin with two disciplinary canons from the great Council of Nicaea in 325, chosen almost at random:

> CANON 3: This great synod absolutely forbids a bishop, presbyter, deacon or any of the clergy to keep a woman who has been brought in to live with him, with the exception of course of his mother or sister or aunt, or any person who is above suspicion.
>
> CANON 10: Concerning catechumens who have lapsed, this holy and great synod decrees that, after they have spent three years as hearers only, they shall then be allowed to pray with the catechumens.[45]

Whereas as the first example pertains to the discipline of the clergy, the second pertains to the laity: specifically, catechumens (i.e., those still under instruction and not yet baptized) who have sacrificed under threat, thereby denying the faith that they have not yet formally professed.

Most disciplinary conciliar canons were either administrative regulations, directed toward the clergy on holy orders, their status, and their ministry, or regulations for the laity, sometimes including clerics in minor orders (e.g., regarding marriage). Regulations of the former sort defined the structure and organization of the ecclesiastical institutions and the clergy's role in relation to the community at large. Penitential

Penance, The Medieval Review 02.07.19 [on-line resource], III.3: "Public and Private: What Was Private About Private Penance?"

45 Trans. Tanner, pp. 3, 11.

canons belonged to the second class. Another, much smaller class of canons consisted of regulations affecting religious, such as consecrated virgins and monks and nuns.

Councils were, in essence, formally convened, decision-making assemblies of bishops. The bishops (Greek, *episkopoi*; Latin, *episcopi*) might be assisted by advisors and secretaries, and sometimes abbots participated as prelates. Councils presupposed colleges of bishops, and this collegiality in its fully developed form entailed at least two levels of organization, respectively diocesan and provincial. On the first level was the institution known as "monoepiscopacy" (also spelled "monepiscopacy"), whereby one bishop was assigned to each urban center (*polis*) and presided over the presbyters and deacons who ministered to the churches of the corresponding diocese. The higher, provincial level of organization, in its fully developed form, depended on the assignment of a senior bishop to the metropolis (the "mother city"). The metropolitan bishop presided over the suffragan (subordinate) bishops of the corresponding province.[46] This two-tiered structure of episcopal governance, which mirrored administrative divisions of the Roman Empire, was in place by the end of the third century, although neither the organization nor the nomenclature was as clear or consistent as it would have become within a couple of centuries. The institution of the church council, therefore, in its fully developed form, presupposed the existence of provinces, each encompassing a college of bishops.

How did this hierarchical structure come about? The idea of assembly (*ecclesia*) had been fundamental to Christianity from the beginning. The *ecclesia* was manifest on several levels, from the local congregation to the universal church. Moreover, the *ecclesia* was considered to be not only a domestic, political, and administrative association, but also a sacred, supernaturally receptive one. It was chiefly as a community that Christians received guidance from the Holy Spirit. Mainstream Christians assumed from a very early stage that they constituted in some sense a single, universal community.

The earliest Christian writings refer both to *presbyteroi* ("elders") and to *episkopoi* ("overseers"), as well as to the deacons and deaconesses who served the congregation. The term "presbyter" was Semitic in origin, whereas the term *episkopos* was Greek and borrowed from secular administration. The two terms seem to have been used coextensively during the New Testament era, but they were obviously not synonyms. Rather, these were two descriptions of the same leaders of the early communities, who are sometimes referred to in the modern literature as presbyter-bishops. In a recent study of the emergence of monoepiscopacy, Alistair Stewart proposes that in the beginning each church was headed and administered by a single leader called the *episkopos*, but that the several leaders of the churches in an urban center or a region were known as elders (*presbyteroi*) when they met collegially, either to manage their own affairs or to confer with neighboring colleges.[47] At this

46 Metropolitans are also known as archbishops, but this title is less precise because it was sometimes bestowed on prelates who were not metropolitans.

47 Alistair C. Stewart, *The Original Bishops: Office and Order in the First Christian Communities* (Grand Rapids: Baker Academic, 2014).

early stage, when Christians assembled in house-churches, the bishop was comparable to a householder or a *paterfamilias*. Monoepiscopacy had emerged by the end of the second century as a result of centralization, institutionalization, and hierarchy. One can perhaps understand why the term *episkopos*, with its connotations of singular leadership and authority, came to denote the *monoepiskopos*, whereas the term *presbyteroi*, with its connotation of teamwork and collegiality, came to denote the many ministers or priests of a diocese.

As the *ecclesia* became more organized, there was sometimes tension between hierarchical, episcopal structures, on the one hand, and enthusiastic movements emphasizing special prophetic gifts, on the other, such as the New Prophecy movements of the second and third centuries (also known as Montanism). Moreover, the fourth century saw the rapid development of monasticism: the way of life of hermits and communities of religious who had turned away from the world and yet, as holy men or (on a smaller scale) holy women, were powerfully influential and authoritative. These two great collective institutions, episcopacy and monasticism, would always be somewhat at odds with each other. In principle, a community of religious was subordinate to the bishop of the diocese in which the community was situated. In practice, monks and nuns belonged to a different and unrelated mode of communal organization, headed by abbots and pursuing a different mode of community.

Although Christians looked back to the Jerusalem council of the mid-first century (Acts 15:2–35) as the precedent for holding councils, the earliest reliable records of regional assemblies of bishops involve Cyprian (d. 258), who as bishop of Carthage convened meetings with his North African bishops. The earliest councils from which the decisions have survived are the Council of Elvira in Spain (c. 305), near modern Granada, and the Council of Ancyra (314), mentioned earlier. The great council of Nicaea (325), in an effort to solve the problems and uncertainties arising when persons who had been excommunicated in one diocese moved to another, ruled that the bishops of each province should assemble at least twice a year.[48]

By the fourth century, therefore, a church council was typically a formally convened and constituted decision-making gathering of the bishops from one or more provinces – "typically," because episcopal assemblies during the patristic period and the early Middle Ages were pragmatic events driven by need and beset by contingencies.

As already noted, councils were sacred as well as administrative events, whose purpose was to receive the guidance from the Holy Spirit. It is remarkable that surviving conciliar canons are nearly always expressed absolutely, in quasi-legal fashion, rather than as expressions of consensus regarding what should be done in the particular provinces that were represented. This owes something to the influence of secular legislative procedures in the early days, such as those of the Roman senate,

48 Canon 5 (Tanner, 9).

but more to the sacred pretext of the event. The bishops were trying to express the will of God. The practice of holding church councils to discern God's will is known in modern scholarship as "conciliarism."[49]

In the East, an episcopal assembly was known as a *synodos* (a "coming-together"). The Latins sometimes appropriated the Greek term, which was exclusively ecclesiastical in their understanding, but they generally preferred the Latin term *concilium*, denoting a meeting or consultative body. Sometimes in the early Middle Ages a church council was called a "synodal council" (*concilium synodale*) or a "synodal assembly" (*conventus synodalis*). Here, the term "synodal" was little more than an embellishment, but it indicated that this was an ecclesiastical or episcopal meeting. By the Carolingian period, the terms "synod" and "synodal" were being used for episcopal meetings and interventions that operated at a lower level than provincial councils, such as episcopal and archiepiscopal visitations.

Modern scholars sometimes reserve the term "council" for formally constituted meetings of bishops in one or more provinces, while referring to more irregular or ad hoc assemblies with less-than-provincial representation as "synods," even when these are called *concilia* in the medieval records. But because it is not always obvious or certain how an early-medieval council was convened or which bishops attended, there is less risk of confusion if we refer to all such assemblies as "councils" by default, using the term "synod" only when it occurs in the Latin record.

Two further developments in organization shaped the role of councils and the authority of conciliar canons. One was the theological recognition that some councils were not provincial but rather "ecumenical," or worldwide. Such councils were especially qualified to determine matters of doctrine and creed. The notion of worldwide councils emerged gradually and retrospectively. The great Council of Nicaea in 325 was on an unprecedented scale, and for the first time a Roman emperor, Constantine, presided over it and attended some of the sessions. Some of the bishops who attended had lived through the Great Persecution initiated by the emperor Diocletian in 303, which was the most concerted imperial effort to eradicate Christianity. Within a few years after 325, churchmen were describing Nicaea as having been an ecumenical synod, but at first only to indicate its scale, for the designation initially had no particular theological significance.[50]

It is hard to assign a precise date to the emergence of the theological concept, but Chalcedon, in 451, was crucial. In their preamble to Chalcedon's declaration of faith regarding Christology, Marcian and Valentinian (the Eastern and Western emperors respectively) described the assembly as a "great and ecumenical synod," affirmed

49 This broad use of the term should be distinguished from its special use to denote a late-medieval theory, originating in canon law, that supreme authority in the church belonged not to the pope but to major church councils, which had the power to depose and appoint popes.

50 H. Chadwick, "The Origin of the Title 'Oecumenical Council'," *JTS* 23.1 (1972), 132–35.

the orthodoxy of the preceding councils of Nicaea (325), Constantinople (381), and Ephesus (431) as regards Trinity and Christology, and underscored the role of Constantine at Nicaea.[51] This declaration helped to establish both the status of these four councils as truly ecumenical (in a theological sense) and the role of emperors in convening such councils. The doctrine that these councils had been ecumenical was a measure not of the level of representation at them but of their orthodoxy and their perceived authority. None of them was "worldwide" in a merely representative sense, least of all Ephesus in 431. They were ecumenical because they were doctrinally authoritative, and not vice versa. Their partisans claimed that they spoke for the entire church (i.e., all who were orthodox), but in no sense did the entire church or even a majority of its bishops assemble and deliberate at each council.

Three of the first four ecumenical councils segregated different "dialects" of Christian practice, and some of these divergences gave rise to enduring denominational traditions – above all, the so-called Nestorian churches, or Churches of the East, which rejected Ephesus; and the Miaphysite, Oriental Orthodox Churches, such as the Coptic Orthodox, which rejected Chalcedon. What has come to be regarded as the mainstream Byzantine tradition recognized, by definition, that of all four of these early councils had been ecumenical, and it also recognized three more: Constantinople II (553), Constantinople III (680–81), and Nicaea II (787). The West, too, accepted all these councils as ecumenical, attributing special value to the first four and often comparing them to the four Gospels.

The second development was the establishment of the five patriarchates, which constituted a third tier of episcopal governance. Although the title was not new, the formal institution emerged in the sixth century, building on the special status attributed traditionally to the churches of Alexandria, Antioch, and Rome, which the Council of Chalcedon had extended to Constantinople (Constantine's "New Rome") and to Jerusalem. In Byzantine and Eastern Orthodox thought, representation of all five patriarchs would be necessary for an ecumenical assembly – something that would no longer be possible after the schism between East and West. But the formalization of the five patriarchates mattered little in the West because it emerged during a period when the claim of papal supremacy over the worldwide church was emerging (see Chapter 5, on the papacy, and Chapter 17, on Gregory the Great). The popes of this period resisted the title "Ecumenical Patriarch" that the metropolitans of Constantinople were assuming. The West later developed a different notion of what made a council ecumenical – or "general," to use the preferred Western term – which was predicated, in a manner never adequately defined, on the authority of the pope. The series of general, papally convened councils, which claimed to speak for the whole church but were not recognized in

51 Tanner, 83–84.

the East, began with the First Lateran Council of 1123 – but that is a story that lies beyond the scope of this book.

Canonical Collections and Decretals

One can hardly overstate the importance of textual compilation in the intellectual and normative cultures of the Middle Ages – especially during the first millennium, when books were scarce and precious. (There were monastic *scriptoria*, or writing workshops, during this period, but as yet no "mass production" of manuscripts, as there would be in the universities of the central Middle Ages.) By collecting brief, easily digestible texts in a single book or a codex, a scholar or cleric was not only providing a convenient resource but also defining the scope of a discipline or a branch of ministry. The collection tacitly proposed what someone needed to know to be proficient in a certain field, and it seemed to promise a grasp or a view of the field as a whole. Moreover, a collection of normative texts added its own claim of authority to whatever force of obligation the individual texts already possessed. This is most obvious with formally promulgated legal codes, when a sovereign gave a compilation of statutes or constitutions the collective force of law, but any gathering of normative texts into a collection or in a codex implied that the items now had special authority.

The gathering of conciliar canons into collections must have altered their status in several other ways. By further detaching them from the contingencies of particular times and places, it must have enhanced their status as universally valid norms. And by making them more available and accessible, it must have imposed on busy bishops a sense that they ought to be familiar with the ever-expanding canonical tradition. Did bishops consider them to be a valuable resource or a nuisance?

Collections also created a space in which rulings from other sources could be included and thereby given an authority comparable if not equal to that of conciliar canons. In the East, canonical collections included not only canons in the proper sense, issued by councils, but also directives "issued by individual bishops on their own authority ... in response to request for guidance from other bishops."[52] The equivalent of these episcopal rescripts in the Western canonical tradition were papal decretals: letters written by bishops of Rome to settle points regarding ecclesiastical regulation and its application, usually in response to inquiries from other bishops. Decretals presupposed the special authority of the bishops of Rome in the Western church. (See Chapter 5, on the evolution of the papacy; Chapter 13, on Leo I; Chapter 14, on Gelasius I; and Chapter 17, on Gregory I.) Decretals are comparable to imperial rescripts, although it is not clear that the latter served as a model for the

[52] A. Louth, "Conciliar Records and Canons," in F. Young et al. (eds.), *The Cambridge History of Early Christian Literature* (Cambridge: Cambridge University Press, 2004), 391–95, at 394.

former. The similarity may be a case of convergence: the independent development of parallel solutions to similar needs.

Canonical collections included other texts that might serve the same end as conciliar decisions and decretals, including excerpts from Scripture, from patristic writings, and even from Roman law (sometimes misattributed to councils or popes): anything, in fact, that could be used to define the discipline regarding a particular matter. Utility as well as the identity of sources and their presumed authenticity determined what should be included. As Greta Austin points out in her chapters on Regino and Burchard (Chapters 22 and 23), compilers sometimes altered the ascription as well as the wording of canons, deeming the utility of the rule to be more important than its originality.[53] All of this material constituted "the canons" in a broad sense of the term.

A letter that Siricius, bishop of Rome 384–399, sent to Himerius, bishop of Tarragona, in 385 is probably the earliest surviving authentic decretal. Siricius was replying to questions that Himerius had sent to his predecessor, Damasus I (366–384). The letter presupposed that the custom of such rescripts was already established, and it includes some remarks that suggest how decretals were composed and how they were supposed to be used. Siricius says that he has considered Himerius's inquiry carefully with an "assembly of brethren" (*conventu fratrum*: 1132B), and he asks Himerius to circulate his reply among his fellow bishops (*coepiscopi*): not only those in Himerius's own region but also those in the neighboring regions (1146A). Siricius says that all bishops should be familiar with "the statutes of the Apostolic See and the venerable determinations of the canons" (*statuta sedis apostolicae vel canonum venerabilia definita*: 1146B).[54]

A single decretal might address several questions. For example, the issues covered in Siricius's response are as follows: the prohibition of re-baptism for those who have already been baptized in a schismatic sect (in this case, that of the Arians), since the original baptism is valid; the correct practices for baptism, including the preparatory acts (prayer, fasting, exorcism) and the most appropriate seasons of the liturgical year; the treatment of apostates who have participated in pagan rituals (they are to be excommunicated for life, with appropriate penance, and can be reconciled only at the point of death); that a woman who is already betrothed to one man may not be married solemnly, with conjugal veiling, to another man (the precise import of this passage is unclear and was much disputed during the Middle Ages); the treatment of monks and nuns who have lapsed and broken their vows of celibacy; the prerequisites for admission to the ranks of the senior clergy; the requirements for admission to the orders of acolyte, exorcist, and subdeacon, and for subsequent promotion to priest or bishop (the principle that a married man can

53 See also G. Austin, "Authority and the Canons in Burchard's *Decretum* and Ivo's *Decretum*," in M. Brett and K. G. Cushing (eds.), *Readers, Texts and Compilers in the Earlier Middle Ages* (Farnham, UK: Ashgate, 2009), 35–58.

54 *Epist.* 167, PL 13:1131B–1147A. Translated in *Prefaces*, 36–46.

be ordained only if he has been the "husband of one wife" [I Tim 3:2, 12] was crucial here, and the impediment of digamy was extended to a man who had married a widow); the appointment of monks as clerics, which Siricius permits; and the lifelong exclusion from clerical orders of persons who have been reconciled after penance: a prohibition that Siricius extrapolates from the premise that penance is not appropriate for men already in orders.

Among the Western canonical collections of Late Antiquity, the most formative were those that Dionysius Exiguus compiled around 500 (Chapter 15), which initiated a long tradition. Dionysius's work was a "watershed in the Western canonical tradition" (Flechner, Chapter 7). His initial aim was to make Greek canons available in Latin, and to that end he translated material from Eastern councils, including the great councils of Nicaea (325), Constantinople (381), and Chalcedon (451). But Dionysius compiled a second book, consisting of papal decretals. The two books were combined in various ways in what is known as the *Collectio Dionysiana*, which was fundamental to the ensuing canonical tradition. The *Collectio Hispana*, the earliest version of which was contemporaneous with the Third Council of Toledo in 633, over which Isidore presided, was also formative.

Collections were sometimes arranged chronologically and sometimes systematically, by topic. The canons were furnished with inscriptions identifying the material (i.e., original) sources as well as with titles and rubrics.[55] These refinements must have been designed to make the information more accessible and to facilitate cross-references.

The level of authority usually attributed to decretals during the first millennium was somewhat less than that attributed to conciliar canons, although the forged early decretals pseudonymously compiled by Isidore the Merchant during the Carolingian period (Chapter 19) must have enhanced their status. Their status changed radically during the twelfth century. Gratian claimed that decretals had the same kind and level of authority as conciliar canons (D. 3, dictum post c. 2), and during the second half of the twelfth century decretals became the chief resource of learned canon law. During the same period, the popes issued decretals much more frequently as a result of the appointment of prelates (bishops and abbots) as judge-delegates to hear cases appealed to the Holy See in the region of the appellant.

Terminology

The Eastern church at first used several terms to denote conciliar canons but eventually settled on *kanōn*, probably by the sixth century. Hitherto, *horos* had been more common: a term that denoted literally a limit or boundary, and thus by extension a determination, decree, or rule.[56] In its literal senses, the term *kanōn* was

55 On this use of the distinction between formal and material sources (terms that have other uses in modern law), see *Prefaces*, 3–4.

56 Hamilton Hess, *The Early Development of Canon Law and the Council of Serdica* (Oxford: Oxford University Press, 2002), 77–78. See also Louth, "Conciliar records," 393, on the terms used.

used of various instruments for measuring or drawing straight lines, especially a rod or reed marked off for measuring.

Byzantine scholars treated laws (*nomoi*) and canons as distinct classes of regulation, showing little tendency to construe canons *as* laws. But because many matters of ecclesiastical administration, monastic and priestly profession, marriage, and so forth were regulated both by imperial laws and by canons, ecclesiastical jurists studied both kinds of regulation. From the late sixth century, the two resources, laws and canons, were combined in collections that later became known as "nomokanons." This hybrid, canonical-legal resource became the basis of learned Byzantine church jurisprudence.[57] The genre resulted from the more predictable association between secular and ecclesiastical governance in the East. The relationship was more complicated and fraught in the West, with its political fractures and dislocations.

In the West, ecclesiastical writers either appropriated the Greek term "canon"[58] or used instead the Latin term *regula*, which had a similar etymology (noted earlier). The terms "canon" and "rule" in this context were synonyms. Dionysius Exiguus usually referred to his canons as "canons," but he also referred to them as "ecclesiastical rules" (*regulae ecclesiasticae*).[59] He even described them as "the most sacred *iura*, issued by bishops assembled through the grace of God."[60]

The "rule" metaphor is nicely explained in a passage that occurs in two seventh-century Spanish sources: Isidore of Seville's *Etymologies* (in the section on church councils, or synods), and the preface to the *Collectio Hispana*. (Isidore's contribution to the *Hispana*, if any, remains unclear.) A canon was called a rule, according to this account, because it functioned like a straightedge, although there had been other plausible suggestions:

> What is called a canon in Greek is called a rule [*regula*] in Latin. It is called a rule because it leads in a straight line [*recte*], never drawing one astray. Others say that it is called a rule inasmuch as it rules [*regat*], or inasmuch as it presents a norm of living rightly [*norma recte vivendi*], or inasmuch as it straightens [*corrigat*] what is bent or distorted.[61]

Just as the Greeks distinguished between *nomoi* and *kanōnes*, so the Latins distinguished between *leges*, whether secular or biblical, and the ecclesiastical *canones*, or *regulae*. The pairing was relevant, as in the East, because some secular

57 Spyros Troianos, "Byzantine Canon Law to 1100," in W. Hartmann and K. Pennington (eds.), *The History of Byzantine and Easter Canon Law to 1500* (Washington, DC: Catholic University of America Press, 2012), 115–69, at 137–43.

58 On the earliest appearance of *canon* as a loan word in Latin, see Hess, *Early Development*, 79.

59 PL 67:141A.

60 PL 67:140D: "sacratissima iura, pontificalibus per Dei gratiam digesta conventibus."

61 Isidore, *Etym*. VI.16.1. For the same text in the Hispana, see G. Martínez Díez and F. Rodríguez (eds.), *La Colección canónica Hispana III: Concilios Griegos y Africanos*, Monumenta Hispaniae Sacra, Serie Canónica 3 (Madrid: Consejo Superior de Investigaciones Científicas, 1982), 46. The same text occurs in the preface to Pseudo-Isidore, PL 130:7B.

laws, like all ecclesiastical canons, regulated ecclesiastical, spiritual, or religious matters. For example, Hincmar of Reims (Chapter 21), who was more inclined to regard canons as laws than most first-millennial authors, spoke of the "sacred laws [*leges sacrae*] by which, together with the canons, the church is moderated."[62] Likewise, a letter of Charles the Bald, which Hincmar must have written on the king's behalf, refers to "the sacred laws, which the catholic church observes together with the holy canons."[63] Hincmar used the term "sacred laws" to denote legislation by Christian kings and emperors, especially when this regulated ecclesiastical matters. In most cases, he was referring to the constitutions of Christian Roman emperors, but he sometimes referred to statutes and capitularies of Carolingian emperors, too, as sacred laws.[64] Benedictus Levita (see Chapter 16) claimed that the reason why the capitularies of the Carolingian rulers contained excerpts from divine law (*lex divina*) – i.e., from Scripture – was to show how the canonical rules (*regulae canonicae*) were in harmony with the divine laws (*leges divinae*).[65] Abbo of Fleury explains in the preface to his *Canons*, which he wrote around 1000 to defend the rights and privileges of monasteries against secular lords, that he had gathered material from "laws and canons" – i.e., from secular laws and ecclesiastical canons.[66] Even after the establishment of the *ius canonicum* in the twelfth century, the plural form *leges* referred by default to secular laws in contradistinction to ecclesiastical canons and decretals.

The Canons and Canon Law

Writers of the first millennium used the terms *lex*, *ius*, and *iura* with reference to canons occasionally albeit infrequently, and they referred to canons as *leges* (plural) very rarely. For the most part, as already noted, *canones* and *leges* were treated as constituting distinct but complementary categories of norms.

Nevertheless, the collective term today for the canonical collections of the period 500–1100 is "canon law." In regard to this early period, the term is used almost exclusively of a body of literature, and often in a quantitative sense, so that one may speak of how much canon law was being produced or was available in a given period.

One reason for this usage is that the canonical collections of the first millennium belong to the first chapter of a narrative whose second chapter focuses on the *ius*

62 *Libellus ... adversus Hincmarum Laudunensem episcopum*, PL 126:567D: "sacras leges, quibus una cum canonibus moderatur Ecclesia."

63 PL 124:893B.

64 On the meaning of the phrase *leges sacrae* in Hincmar in relation to both Roman constitutions and Frankish capitula, see Karl F. Morrison, *Two Kingdoms: Ecclesiology in Carolingian Political Thought: Ecclesiology in Carolingian Political Thought* (Princeton: Princeton University Press, 1964), 247–50.

65 PL 97:701A.

66 PL 139:473B.

canonicum of the central Middle Ages, which was explicitly a branch or body of law, practiced in ecclesiastical courts. But the latter development presupposed several fundamental innovations, including the Gregorian Reform, with the papal monarchy and centralization of ecclesiastical administration; a well-organized system of episcopal courts, with the routine possibility of appealing cases to the papacy; the rapid development of canonical jurisprudence as a scholastic discipline, beginning with Gratian's *Decretum* in the 1140s; a massive, barely manageable flow of canonical litigation; and the refinement and professionalization of the judicial process in church courts. In the final essay of this book (Chapter 24), Robert Somerville provides readers with a "preview" of some of these new legal horizons.

If one disregards developments after 1000 and concentrates exclusively on canonical regulation and collections of the first millennium, the status of the canons as laws, or of the canonical collections as constituting canon law in bulk, becomes unclear, problematic, and disputable. On the one hand, the role of the papacy during Late Antiquity and the early Middle Ages (Chapter 5) seems to have been judicial and quasi-political, as the chapters on Leo I (Chapter 13) and Gelasius I (Chapter 14) illustrate. More important, early-medieval authors such as Jonas of Orléans (Chapter 20) and Hincmar of Reims (Chapter 21) construed the role of canons as being so lawlike that to question whether in their view canons were truly laws may seem pedantic or otiose. On the other hand, to presume without argument or debate that canons were laws during the first millennium not only pre-empts some reasonable questions and objections but also fails to set in appropriate relief the exceptional instances in which clerics or scholars of the period *did* refer to canons as laws. Such examples should call for commentary and analysis, whereas if we presume a priori that all canons were laws, the examples will fail to attract our attention. The authors of the relevant chapters in this anthology are mindful that positing "canon law" before 1000 is problematic and risks anachronism, and they have handled this issue circumspectly, but in a variety of ways.

To illustrate the difference of perspective in question here, we may compare Isidore of Seville's treatment of laws and canons in his *Etymologies* (c. 625) with the opening distinctions of Gratian's *Harmony of Dissonant Canons*, commonly known as the *Decretum* (1140s). These distinctions are heavily dependent on Isidore, but the authors' respective approaches to canons and laws are quite different.

Isidore's discussion of laws (*De legibus*) in Book V of the *Etymologies* (2–27) is devoted exclusively to secular law, with no reference to anything ecclesiastical. The same is true of his briefer treatment of law and legal argument in the section on rhetoric (II.5–8, 10) and of his treatment of judicial procedure (*De foro*: XVIII.15). The term *forum* ("court") itself had decidedly secular connotations during the first millennium, when "forensic" justice was by definition secular justice, meted out by kings or emperors or by dukes or counts acting on their behalf. Elsewhere in the *Etymologies*, Isidore writes about the canons and the councils of the church (VI.16) – and here he does not even allude to laws, judges, or courts.

In contrast, Gratian begins his book on the canons with a sequence of distinctions that amount to a treatise on law. In the first two distinctions, using material from Isidore's discussion of laws (*De legibus*) in the *Etymologies* (V.9–17), Gratian describes law in general, with its parts and varieties, and Roman law in particular. Then, in distinction 3, Gratian notes that all the foregoing categories are species of secular law, but he adds that as well as secular statutes, which make up the *ius civile*, there are also ecclesiastical statutes, which are known as "canons" (D. 3, dictum ante c. 1). A brief account of the canons follows, taken from Isidore's *Etymologies* (VI.16.1–2). Gratian explains that the term "canons" embraces not only the "statutes of councils" but also the "decrees of pontiffs" (i.e., papal decretals), which have the same legal force (D. 3, dictum post c. 2). Gratian refers to both secular and ecclesiastical statutes as "laws" (*leges*) here, and he claims that the work (*officium*) of both is the same: to command what must be done, to prohibit what is bad, and to permit what is licit (D. 3, dictum post c. 3): a division adapted from Isidore's account of (secular) laws in the *Etymologies*, V.19. Later, when Gratian discusses legal privileges, he notes that his treatment of this topic "pertains to both secular and ecclesiastical laws" (*leges*; D. 5, dictum ante c. 1). Thus, as well as prefacing his textbook on canons with a treatise on law, Gratian combined material from what had been separate discourses in Isidore, respectively on laws and on canons. Rather than positing laws and canons as distinct species of regulations, Gratian posits two species of laws, respectively secular and canonical. This usage was extremely rare before 1100, but it expresses an equivalence that is fundamental to Gratian's project.

It is reasonable to assume not only that Isidore's failure to regard canons as laws was typical of his period but also that Gratian's reworking of Isidore, in which canons were construed as laws, was innovative but not unprecedented. The idea had been hinted at, implied, and occasionally stated outright, albeit sometimes hyperbolically, for centuries. Recent trends, such as the legal reasoning evident in Ivo's letters, had been taking the idea toward the threshold of inevitability.

Efforts in modern scholarship to demonstrate that early-medieval canons functioned as laws are rare. But in two successive chapters of his monograph on Frankish church councils during the sixth through eighth centuries, Gregory Halfond, who contributes the chapter on church councils to this volume (Chapter 4), sets a good example by inquiring whether conciliar canons amounted to a form of law. Halfond's response is cautiously affirmative.[67] In the first of these chapters, Halfond inquires whether conciliar canons were enforceable, whether "canonical pronouncements were common knowledge among clerics and laymen," and whether "their status was equivalent to that of secular law" (*lex*).[68] Halfond answers affirmatively for the most part, focusing on three areas: the dissemination and promulgation of canons; the merging of secular legislation and canonical

67 Gregory Halfond, *Archaeology of Frankish Church Councils, AD 511–789* (Leiden: Brill, 2010), ch. 4 (132–58) and 5 (159–84).

68 Ibid., 134.

regulation, with kings demanding that conciliar canons be obeyed, and bishops concerning themselves with law and order in the community; and the use of penitential regimes as a means to enforce discipline, especially when penance was proposed as the alternative to excommunication. In the next chapter of the monograph, Halfond considers the process by which the canons decreed at councils were gathered into canonical collections: a process that he construes as the transforming of canons into canon law. Halfond points out that although the bishops at councils made their disciplinary decisions to meet particular needs in their dioceses and provinces, they drew on existing collections and must have been well aware that they themselves were in turn contributing to a growing body of canonical literature.[69]

Rather than assuming that canons or canonical collections of the first millennium constituted canon law, therefore, we might usefully inquire to what extent and in what ways the canons were lawlike, both in fact and in the minds of writers and clerics of the period. Several overlapping areas of inquiry would shed light on the question, each of which would present both reasons for and objections to the construing of canons as laws. The following remarks are designed only to illustrate some of these areas, and not to reach any firm conclusions. I recognize that I am tacitly comparing canons of the first millennium to the *ius canonicum* that emerged during the twelfth century. One might also inquire whether, how, and to what extent the secular laws of kings and emperors during the early Middle Ages functioned as laws in some theoretically convincing sense, but I shall not pursue that line of inquiry.

VOCABULARY: How authors and prelates of the period referred to canons provides an obvious point of entry. As already noted, use of the plural form "laws" (*leges*) to refer to canons was very rare in the first millennium. Use of the less specific term *ius / iura* is more common, albeit still infrequent. Occasionally, the singular form *lex* is used, apparently with the same meaning as *ius / iura*.

I offer here a few examples, not to prove a point but to illustrate how such an inquiry might proceed. (I owe most of these examples to Halfond's book.) In some cases, canons were described as the church's *ius* or *lex* to emphasize that the Christian faith demanded different or higher standards than the world at large, with its secular laws and customs. For example, in a plea for greater influence, the bishops at the Council of Clermont (535) urged Theudebert I in a letter that "the institutes of the canons" and "canonical law [*lex*]" should be studied and restored.[70] The contrast between secular and sacred norms is especially marked in relation to nuptial impediments and sexual taboos. For example, Gregory of Tours remarks that Merovech should not have married Brunhilda because marrying the wife of a paternal uncle is "contrary to canonical law [*lex*] and *fas*."[71] Gregory also observes

69 Ibid., 174.

70 CCL 148A, p. 111: "ad replicanda canonum instituta uel studio elucedande legis ecclesiasticae ... "

71 Gregory of Tours, *Historia* V.2, MGH SRM 1.1, p. 195: "contra fas legemque canonicam uxorem patrui accepisset."

that clerics should not fornicate or have sexual relations with women because "canonical law [*lex canonica*] and all the holy Scriptures forbid it."[72] Again, the Council of Orléans in 541 pointed out that the promotion to the diaconate or the priesthood of a man who had been married twice or was married to a woman who had been married previously was "contrary to the *ius* of the canons [*contra ius canonum*]."[73] In a closely related sense, the Council of Soissons in 744 referred to the *ius canonicum* applied by bishops when making parish visitations.[74] But here the term *ius* was appropriate also because bishops were attempting to impose social discipline and order on the citizens in their dioceses, exercising something akin to judicial authority. This *ius canonicum* was a branch of justice, applied in tribunals, with bishops acting in a quasi-judicial capacity.

The term *ius* could also denote the church's rights and privileges, especially when they seemed to be under threat. For example, when Benedictus Levita (see Chapter 16) spoke of the *ius* of churches, monasteries, and priests, he was referring to their inviolable property rights and social privileges.[75] This was probably the sense intended when Carloman, at the Council of Germania (742), commanded that a council should be held every year in his presence in order that "the decrees of the canons and the rights [*iura*] of the church are restored, and the Christian religion repaired."[76] This may be a case of rhetorical hendiadys, but if the phrases "decrees of the canons" and "*iura* of the church" denote different things, as a more cautious reading would suggest, then the term *iura* probably refers to the clergy's rights and privileges, or perhaps to the internal ordering and discipline of the clergy.

Pseudo-Isidore (Chapter 19) goes much further, claiming that "the holy fathers made laws [*leges*], which they called holy canons," to protect priests from false accusations.[77] Pseudo-Isidore claims here, as Gratian will do, that canons *are* laws – at least inasmuch as they define the rights and privileges of the clergy – but that churchmen prefer to call their own laws "canons."

The Political Framework: Another area of inquiry pertains to the perceived relationship between political and ecclesiastical governance, since each domain attempted to impose its own order through regulation: through laws on one side, and through canons on the other. Clerics and scholars of the period regarded the two orders of governance as distinct but complementary. Whether ecclesiastical regulations amount to laws in such circumstances depends partly on whether they apply to an entire political community, and thus on whether one system is subordinate to the other in certain matters, and on whether clergy are isolated from secular jurisdiction.

72 Ibid., VIII.19, p. 386.

73 *Conc. Aurelianense* A. 541, c. 10 (CCL 148A, 134).

74 Soissons 744, c. 4, MGH Conc. 2.1, p. 35.

75 PL 97:937, 744C–D (Book I); and 784D, 796D, 798B (Book II).

76 Germania 742, c 1, MGH Conc. 2.1, p. 3: " … canonum decreta et aecclesiae iura restaurentur, et relegio Christiana emendetur."

77 PL 130:8A–B: "Ideo sancti Patres leges constituerunt quas sanctos canones appellaverunt."

The best-known and most influential attempt to formulate the relationship between the two orders of governance during the first millennium is contained in a letter that Pope Gelasius I sent to emperor Anastasius I in the early 490s, complaining about the emperor's meddling in ecclesiastical and doctrinal matters (Chapter 14).[78] The relevant passage is known by its first two words, *Duo sunt*: "There are two" . . . but two what? The noun is not supplied in the Latin, but the context permits us to supply "domains," "realms," or "orders of governance." Gelasius contrasts the "authority" of bishops and priests with the "power" of emperors and kings. The priestly order has greater dignity, for only the priests care for the eternal welfare of their subjects. But Gelasius's argument is dualistic. Since *we* do not interfere with *your* governance of secular matters, he argues, so *you* should not interfere with *our* governance of spiritual matters.

During the central Middle Ages, *Duo sunt* became the basis of a hierocratic political theology that went much further than anything Gelasius could have envisaged, even maintaining that the political, coercive power of sovereigns and secular princes was delegated to them by the priesthood or the pope, who by rights possessed all power.[79] Gelasius, on the contrary, had in mind a harmonious separation of realms, each with its own area of duty and concern. But while it is clear that it would be anachronistic to attribute medieval hierocratic political theologies or the "two swords" theory expounded by Bernard of Clairvaux to Gelasius, the proper interpretation of what Gelasius said about the two orders of governance remains debatable. According to Alan Cottrell, for example, Gelasius was not proposing a "formulation of the proper roles of ecclesiastical and temporal powers." Instead, Gelasius "merely intended to offer a descriptive statement of the informal relations between the two powers as they then existed in actual practice."[80] But even if the pretext of the argument was descriptive or rhetorical and inconsequential at the time, Gelasius presupposed a distinction between secular power (*potestas*) and ecclesiastical authority (*auctoritas*) that must have been familiar and clearly understood at the time.[81]

Like Leo I and Gregory I, Gelasius lived in an era of political and ecclesiastical dislocation, when the church whose supreme leader (in their view) was the bishop of Rome acknowledged the secular supremacy of a remote emperor in the East. The

78 Epist. 12, in Andreas Thiel (ed.), *Epistolae Romanorum pontificum genuinae et quae ad eos scriptae sunt a S. Hilaro usque ad Pelagium II*, vol. 1 (Brunsberg: Eduard Peter, 1867), 349–58. Translated in Bronwen Neil and Pauline Allen, *The Letters of Gelasius I (492–496)* (Turnhout: Brepols, 2014), 74.

79 J. A. Watt, "Spiritual and Temporal Powers," in J. H. Burns (ed.), *The Cambridge History of Medieval Political Thought c. 350–c. 1450* (Cambridge: Cambridge University Press, 1988), 367–23.

80 A. Cottrell, "*Auctoritas* and *Potestas*: A Reevaluation of the Correspondence of Gelasius I on Papal-Imperial Relations," *Mediaeval Studies* 55 (1993): 95–109.

81 On the meaning and source of the *potestas / auctoritas* distinction, as well as the later reception of Gelasius's *Duo sunt*, see R. L. Benson, "The Gelasian Doctrine: Uses and Interpretations," in George Makdisi et al. (eds.), *La notion d'autorité au Moyen âge: Islam, Byzance, Occident: Colloques internationaux de La Napoule, session des 23–26 octobre 1978* (Paris: Presses Universitaires de France, 1982), 13–54.

typical early-medieval regime, on the contrary, was diarchic, with secular and priestly leaders of the same region or territory working closely together and depending on each other. Such was the polity both of Visigothic Spain and of the Carolingian empire. Churchmen counseled and assisted kings and emperors, while the latter, acting as God's agents (Rom 13:1), fostered the church, made use of clerical literacy, and participated in church councils. Each domain needed the other.

In Book III of his *Sententiae*, Isidore of Seville explains how the leaders of the church and the "princes of this world" (*principes saeculi*) should pursue their respective God-given duties of governance (*regimen*).[82] He regards the two domains as distinct yet interdependent.

On the one hand, Isidore argues, the "leaders of the churches" (*praesules ecclesiarum*), or priests (*sacerdotes*), govern both by preaching "words of instruction" (*sermo doctrinae*) and by setting a good example (36.1). Only those called by Christ should serve as leaders of his church, and they are required to meet very high standards of holiness. A "man of the church" must be "crucified to the world through the mortification of his own flesh" (33.1). Again, priests must fearlessly correct the errors of the princes and defend the poor against them when they act unjustly (45.1–5).

On the other hand, although the princes (*principes*) or kings (*reges*) of this world govern through laws and coercive power (*potestas*), Christ has charged them with the defense of his church. They should not forget that in the final judgment they will be asked how well they have fulfilled this duty (48.9–10, 51.6). Justice requires that the princes should be subject to their own laws (51.2), but they are also subject to the "discipline of religion." They should "preach the faith of Christ through their laws and maintain that preaching of the faith in their good behavior" (51.3). Princes must sometimes even intervene in church matters, exercising their coercive power to "defend ecclesiastical discipline." When priestly "words of instruction" have proved ineffective in governing the church, the princes should take control, exercising their power "through fear of discipline" (51.4). Then "the princely power imposes [discipline] on the necks of the proud," and "the heavenly kingdom . . . makes progress through the earthly kingdom" (51.5).

In 802, at a special "universal synod" at Aachen, Charlemagne not only reminded the churchmen present of canonical norms (including the *Rule of Benedict*) but also summoned the counts, dukes, and other leaders of the people, speaking to them not only as their emperor but also as the sovereign of Christendom, which the Carolingians sometimes called the *ecclesia*.[83] As Mayke de Jong explains in Chapter 6, interpreting such a regime in the dualistic modern terms of church and state is anachronistic and misleading. Whenever sovereigns lent their authority to canonical regulations, the distinction between *canones* and *leges* became indistinct.

[82] Book III, 33–51, CCL 111, 272–304,

[83] Rosamund McKitterick, *Charlemagne: The Formation of a European Identity* (Cambridge: Cambridge University Press, 2008), 275–76. Robert L. Wilken, *The First Thousand Years: A Global History of Christianity* (New Haven: Yale University Press, 2012), 341.

THE JUDICIAL PROCESS: Another area of inquiry pertains to judgment, for a system of laws is by definition judicable. Indeed, if there is a "duck test" for what should be regarded as law, it is the existence of something recognizable as a judicial process. Thus, philosophical questions as to whether military justice is a branch of law today can seem otiose because the procedures, offices, and rituals of military courts look very similar to those of civilian courts.

There are two questions to be considered here: not only whether bishops acted as judges in a legal or quasi-legal capacity, but also, if so, whether they applied the ecclesiastical canons or decretals as statutes in so doing.[84]

To answer the first question, one would need to consider the role of bishops in episcopal hearings, conciliar tribunals, dispute settlements, and episcopal visitations.

i) *Episcopal hearings:* The *episcopalis audientia*, which features in several of the chapters that follow, acquired institutional recognition under Constantine.[85] Such hearings fulfilled Paul's counsel (1 Cor 6:1–8) that Christians should settle their disputes within their own community ("before the saints") rather than in the secular courts ("before the unjust"). But the practice was a special application of the well-established right of disputants under Roman law to appoint any citizen to arbitrate between them. An arbitrator's decision was recognized in law, and it could be fortified by penal stipulations.[86]

The episcopal hearing was intended chiefly for the laity, and in their regard the bishop was less judge then arbitrator, whereas he had absolute power over his clergy. We know from narrative evidence that these hearings were popular and kept bishops busy, but the surviving laws regulating them are difficult to interpret, and there is scant evidence as to the kinds of cases that came before them.[87] It is clear enough,

84 Wilfried Hartmann, "L'éveque comme juge: la pratique du tribunal épiscopal en France du Xe au XIIe siècle," in C. Carozzi and H. Taviani-Carozzi (eds.), *Hiérarchies et Services au Moyen Âge* (Aix-en-Provence: Université de Provence, 2001), 71–92, is a handy summary of this field. For references to Hartmann's extensive writings in German on this general topic, see Additional Readings at the end of this chapter.

85 Peter Brown, "Christianization and Religious Conflict," in A. Cameron and P Garnsey (eds.), *The Cambridge Ancient History*, vol. 13: *The Late Empire, AD 337–425* (Cambridge: Cambridge University Press, 1998), 632–64, at 658–59. Caroline Humfress, "Bishops and Law Courts in Late Antiquity: How (Not) to Make Sense of the Legal Evidence," JECS 19.3 (2011): 375–400, argues that the constitutions on the episcopal hearing included in the *Cod. Theod.* were originally "specific responses to circumstances thrown up by courtroom practice" (375, abstract).

86 A. J. B. Sirks, "The *episcopalis audientia* in Late Antiquity," *Droits et cultures* 65.1 (2013): 79–88. Sirks cites Humfress's *Orthodoxy and the Courts* (Oxford: Oxford University Press, 2007) critically, using it as a foil for his own arguments, but he seems to have been unaware of Humfress's JECS article of 2011.

87 The most relevant laws are *Cod. Theod.* 1.27.1 (318?), 16.11.1 (399), and 1.17.2 (408); and *Cod. Iust.* 1.4.7 (398). Their chief purpose was to establish the authority of the episcopal hearing vis-à-vis the judgment of secular courts. Whereas *Cod. Iust.* 1.4.7 restricted the legal authority of the episcopal hearing to civil matters, *Cod. Theod.* 16.11.1 restricted it to religious matters. *Sirmondian Constitution* 1 (supposedly from 331/3), which includes the strongest affirmation of the bishop's judicial authority, is probably not authentic. Sirks (cited in the previous note, pp. 81–82) proposes that it was a Merovingian forgery.

though, that episcopal hearings were chiefly intended to settle disputes according to Roman civil law. While the institution was arguably a step toward the establishment of bishops as judges, and although the bishops were presumably informed in their decisions by their Christian convictions and their familiarity with Scripture, there is little evidence that the laws applied in these hearings were canons.

ii) *Conciliar tribunals*: At least until the Carolingian period, a common ecclesiastical setting for disciplinary decisions regarding the laity was a church council. The usual result was the assignment of a penance, but decisions affecting the validity of marriage could have legal consequences in the community at large, at least when the partners belonged to the nobility.[88]

Thanks to an epistolary treatise by Hincmar, bishop of Reims, we are unusually well informed about the circumstances of one such case. It came before a council held at Tusey in 860.[89] The assembled bishops received a complaint from Raymund, a count of Toulouse, regarding his son-in-law, an Aquitanian nobleman called Stephen. Stephen had been formally betrothed to Raymund's daughter, but he had refused to complete the marriage by taking her as his wife and had gone into hiding. After some discussion, the council summoned Stephen. He explained that because he had had sexual intercourse with a close relative of his betrothed, sexual intercourse with his spouse would be incestuous. Stephen, by his own account, had sought the advice of his confessor. If he and his partner first did penance secretly, could they then complete their marriage without suffering eternal damnation? The priest consulted a book entitled *The Canons*, in which he found a text establishing that the relationship between the spouses was incestuous. No penance would suffice as long as they remained in their forbidden relationship. Stephen seemed to be both bound to his betrothed and prevented from consummating his marriage with her.

As well as presenting a theologically informed but largely canonical rationale for dissolving the marriage, Hincmar remarks on the proceedings and the points of due process. For example, he explains that bishops are not permitted to conduct a tribunal unless the accuser appears in person, and that in this case the accusation would have to come not from Raymund but from his daughter, since the former had relinquished his power over his daughter by handing her over in marriage.

The bishops were reluctant to adjudicate until the parties had exhausted other means of resolution. Raymund's daughter should seek her father's counsel, and Raymund should try to reconcile daughter and son-in-law. Nevertheless, the bishops

88 See Adhémar Esmein, *Le marriage en droit canonique*, 2nd edition, ed. R. Génestal and J. Dauvillier, 2 vols. (Paris: Sirey, 1929, 1935), esp. vol. 1, 1–66, on the control of marriage (as regards its validity, necessary and sufficient requirements, and so forth) in relation to ecclesiastical regulation and secular law: the classic study, still indispensable, of a topic long overdue for historical reexamination.

89 Hincmar, *Epist.* 136, MGH Epist. 8, 87–107. What follows is based on Philip L. Reynolds, *How Marriage Became One of the Sacraments* (Cambridge: Cambridge University Press, 2016), 222–30.

felt obliged to intervene, for the affair was already notorious. Unless it was resolved quickly, it would surely become the occasion of "very great scandal in the church and damage in the kingdom." It was at this point that the bishops had summoned Stephen, who came willingly but asked for a private audience as distinct from a public hearing. Stephen agreed to accept the council's decision as final, but having heard his explanation in camera, the bishops decided that they could not reach a decision without a public hearing.

The bishops proposed a dual procedure. On the secular side, King Charles the Bald and his nobles should attempt to make peace between Raymund and Stephen. Hincmar remarks he will say "nothing about secular justice, knowledge of which we bishops do not need to have" – which suggests that he envisaged a parallel legal process on the secular side, although he seems to have assumed that the validity of the marriage was an entirely canonical matter. On the ecclesiastical side, the council commissioned two archbishops to conduct an inquiry, and they asked Hincmar to counsel them on the sacred and ecclesiastical dimensions of the case. (The result was Hincmar's epistle.) Hincmar advised that the archbishops should invite Raymund to the tribunal and hear what he had to say, but that they must also interrogate the daughter, who had to appear before them in person.

In Hincmar's judgment, Stephen was right to have shunned sexual intercourse with his spouse. (Hincmar did not question the veracity of Stephen's narrative.) If the impediment of incest had not arisen, Stephen would have been obliged to remain with his wife even if they agreed never to consummate their marriage (as Mary and Joseph had done). But if they consummate their incestuous marriage, not only will it have to be dissolved, but the partners must both remain unmarried. As things stand, both are free to separate and then to remarry, although Stephen will have first to do penance for his transgression, whereas the woman is blameless.[90]

iii) *Dispute settlements*: During the Carolingian period, bishops acted individually as judges in dispute settlements. The tribunals over which they presided were akin to the secular *placita* of the period. A *placitum* (in the relevant sense) was a public tribunal held to settle a dispute, usually over property. The judges at *placita* were dukes or counts, acting on behalf of the king or the emperor, and the hearings took place in the court (*curtis*) of the ducal or comital residence. Similarly, a bishop, or a cleric whom the bishop appointed, with the help of legal advisors, sometimes adjudicated a public settlement in the episcopal residence (*domus*). Whether bishops based their judgments on the canons, however, is unclear. A detailed study by Michael Heil of the public tribunals in Carolingian Lucca suggests that here, at least, bishops handled only disputes between churchmen (clerics or monks),

[90] Ibid., 98, 105–06.

whereas dukes handled disputes in which at least one of the two parties was a lay person.[91]

iv) *Episcopal visitations*: Bishops assumed their most judge-like role in the periodic episcopal visitations of the Merovingian and Carolingian eras.[92] In this setting, the bishop's chief deterrent was excommunication (a frightening prospect), to which the alternative was penance; and penance, therefore, took on the role of punishment. The best evidence for this procedure is the *Libri duo de synodalibus causis et disciplinis ecclesiasticis* (*Two Books concerning Synodal Investigations and Ecclesiastical Judgments*), a canonical collection that Regino of Prüm compiled during the first decade of the tenth century – perhaps 906 or a little later (see Chapter 22). Whereas the first of the two books focuses on discipline among the clergy, with instructions on the interviewing of priests, the second book is concerned with discipline among the laity.

In the first chapter of the second book, Regino describes – or perhaps proposes – a procedure for visitations. An archdeacon or archpresbyter[93] of the diocese arrives in the parish two days before the bishop. He summons the people and announces the bishop's forthcoming visitation. With the help of the local priests, he deals with any minor infractions to lighten the bishop's agenda. When the bishop himself arrives, with due ceremony, he gathers seven trustworthy laymen, who are sworn in. Their task is to inform the bishop of any transgressors in the community. After preliminary inquiry, the suspected transgressors are brought before the bishop for trial. The bishop passes judgment, imposing an appropriate penance when necessary.

Here, it seems, we find a clear instance of the application of canonical and penitential procedures in something akin to criminal justice. Regino must have intended his collection of canons, which includes some Roman law, to be used in such visitations, although we have little idea as to how the canons might have been applied. Nor do we know whether the procedure that Regino outlined was typical, or even whether he was describing an already-established practice or advocating a new one.[94] In his preface, Regino refers to the canons not only as "rules" (*regulae*) but also as "statutes." One of his aims in writing the *Libri duo*, he explains, was to achieve greater consistency by returning to ancient norms. Regino regrets that the various regional churches of his day are pursuing diverse "customs," whereas "Scripture warns that the bounds [*termini*] that our fathers proposed, that is, their laws and decrees [*leges et decreta*], should be observed in every way and never transgressed

91 Michael W. Heil, "Clerical Disputes in the *Gerichtsort* in Carolingian Lucca," *Zeitschrift Quellen und Forschungen aus italienischen Archiven und Bibliotheken* 96 (2016): 66–87.

92 Meens, *Penance in Medieval Europe*, 144–46.

93 A senior priest who oversees several parishes.

94 W. Hartmann, "Zu Effektivität und Aktualität von Reginos Sendhanbuch," in W. P. Müller & M. E. Sommar (eds.), *Medieval Church Law and the Origins of the Western Legal Tradition* (Washington, DC: Catholic University of America Press, 2006), 33–49.

through any rash presumption."[95] How literally one should read the phrase "laws and decrees," however, is unclear, for Regino was speaking rhetorically and echoing Proverbs 22:28: "Pass not beyond the ancient bounds which your fathers have set."

Because the Carolingian episcopal visitation, such as Regino described, was probably the remote ancestor of the *Sendgericht* (synodal tribunal) of German-speaking regions,[96] the latter term is sometimes used today to describe the Carolingian institution. But this is a late-medieval vernacular term for an institution that emerged during the late Middle Ages and continued into the Reformation period.[97] The term *Send-* was apparently a corruption of "synod." Although the term *Sendgericht* has been common in German-language church historiography since the early twentieth century, it has only recently begun to appear in English-language writing. Salient features of the late-medieval and Reformation *Sendgerichte* include the cooperation of clergy and laymen in the prosecution of crimes; the application of criminal punishments, such as fines, whipping, and public humiliation; the use of spaces that were both ecclesiastical and public, such as churches (for the tribunals) and church yards (for punishments); and the focus on "mixed" crimes, involving infractions that were matters of keen interest to clerics and had figured prominently in the penitential tradition, but which also undermined public order. Sex crimes, such as adultery, fornication, and sodomy, were especially prominent in this area of justice. The proceedings of archdiaconal courts during the late Middle Ages exhibited similar traits.[98] Indeed, the distinctions and relations among *Sendgerichte*, episcopal visitations, and archdiaconal courts in recent literature on late-medieval and Reformation canon law are not always clear.

There was arguably a "branching off," therefore, within ecclesiastical jurisdiction during the late Middle Ages from penance (*poenitentia*) to punishment (*poena*).[99] Without losing their traditional focus on sin, penance, and cure, ministers of the church now assumed more competence than hitherto over crime and punishment. Such developments are of particular interest both to social historians who interpret religion as a means of social control and to legal historians who find in late-medieval canon law precedents for the development of criminal law and jurisprudence. Although these developments occurred long after the first millennium, they are

95 Regino, *Libri duo de synodalibus causis et disciplinis ecclesiasticis*, ed. F. G. A. Wasserschleben (Leipzig: Engelmann, 1840), 2.

96 Rudolf Schieffer, "Zur Entstehung des Sendgerichts im 9. Jahrhundert," in Müller and Sommar, *Medieval Church Law*, 50–56.

97 Albert M. Koeniger, *Die Sendgerichte in Deutschland* (Munich: Lentner, 1907). Albert M. Koeniger, *Quellen zur Geschichte der Sendgerichte in Deutschland* (Munich: Lentner, 1910).

98 Joel F. Harrington, *Reordering Marriage and Society in Reformation Germany* (Cambridge: Cambridge University Press, 1995), 112–18.

99 For a preliminary survey of this field of inquiry, see Per Ingesman, "Sin and Crime, Penance and Punishment: Ecclesiastical Discipline in the Middle Ages," in P. Lodberg (ed.), *Religion, Politics, and Law* (Aarhus: Aarhus University Press, 2009), 129–37. For a detailed study, see Lotte Kéry, *Gottesfurcht und irdische Strafe: der Beitrag des mittelalterlichen Kirchenrechts zur Entstehung des öffentlichen Strafrechts* (Köln: Böhlau, 2006); on *Sendgerichte*, see 65–118.

relevant here because one might trace their history to the episcopal visitations, or "synodal cases," of the Carolingian period.

LEGAL REASONING: Another area of inquiry pertains to the presence or absence of legal reasoning and argument. Such discourse is directed not to the pursuit of truth but to the practical application of norms. The reasoning pertains to laws inasmuch as they are judicable. Typically, the aim of legal reasoning is to show which norms apply to a particular issue or case and how they should be applied. This is so regardless of whether the issue is an actual situation (as in the letters of Ivo of Chartres) or a hypothetical one, proposed for the sake of discussion (as in the second part of Gratian's *Decretum*). In legal reasoning, norms function as first principles of argument. These include not only enacted statutes but also underlying principles and presuppositions of the legal system and of its laws, standard modes of reasoning about the application of laws to diverse issues, maxims that are generally accepted in the profession or the culture, and norms that are considered to be self-evident. Did canons often feature as enacted statutes in such reasoning during the first millennium? It is hard to know.

In an important (albeit never formally published) paper, Rachel Stone questions whether there was such a thing as "canon law" prior to and during the Carolingian period, and most of her observations pertain to legal reasoning, although she does not put the matter in those terms.[100] Some of Stone's objections pertain to an absence of system. In the decretals of Innocent I and Leo I and in the letters of Augustine, Stone points out, there is little effort to apply particular canons to particular cases. Instead, these authors rely on custom, precedent, and general principles, notwithstanding their conviction that the canons were vital to church discipline. Stone concedes that "canons as texts matter to Carolingian rulers and reformers far more conspicuously than they do in earlier periods," but she finds little evidence of the care to identify particular canons as authoritative and to apply them to particular cases. Moreover, some of the forged canons and decretals of Pseudo-Isidore seem to have been composed with little regard for how they might be applied to particular cases. Stone notes that whereas some modern scholars have been astonished by the muddled approach of ecclesiastical writers of the first millennium to canon law and by their failure to be consistent and systematic, that may be because what those churchmen were engaged in was not canon law but something else. One might object, following Berman, that what was missing was a "legal system" and not a "legal order," which Berman characterizes as the presence of any "legal constituted authorities that applied law."[101] But that objection is less

[100] R. Stone, "Canon Law before Canon Law: Using Church Canons, 400–900 AD," paper presented to CLANS (Cambridge Late Antiquity Network Seminar), 11 February 2014. The paper is currently posted on Stone's Academia.edu page. Stone touches briefly on the same topic in her *Morality and Masculinity in the Carolingian Empire* (Cambridge: Cambridge University Press, 2012), 61.

[101] *Law and Revolution*, 51.

convincing when the culture in question is profoundly scholarly and devoted to texts and commentary.

From a more constructive point of view, we might take special note of anything akin to legal argument before 1000. Consider, for example, the epistolary treatise on Stephen's improperly constituted marriage (discussed previously), in which Hincmar attempted to illumine the role of the various elements and episodes in the formation of valid marriage, especially sexual union. Among the authorities cited are a forged decretal ascribed to Pope Evaristus, the authentic decretal of Pope Siricius, quotations from Augustine, Ambrosiaster, and Gregory the Great, and, above all, a decretal that Leo I sent the bishop of Narbonne in 458/9. In the relevant passage from the last source, Leo had argued on theological and scriptural grounds (Gal 4:30 and Eph 5:31–32) that a certain man (in the original text, a cleric) who had been living with a servile woman (*ancilla*) and had begotten children by her was free to leave her and marry another woman.[102] Leo's reasoning was that the relationship in question did not adequately conform to Christ's union with the church, since Christianity was a way not of servitude but of freedom. Lacking the "sacrament" of that great union (cf. Eph 5:32), the relationship between the cleric and the *ancilla* was not marriage but only concubinage, as it would have been under Roman law. Hincmar claims that by extrapolating from Leo's response[103] he is able to show that a marriage that cannot be validly consummated is deficient in an analogous way. Whereas Leo's argument was wholly theological (although he noted corroboration in Roman law), Hincmar's attempt to apply Leo's ruling on a different matter to this case, to which no canon or decretal was directly applicable, exhibits legal reasoning. A trait of legal reasoning is perceptible also in Hincmar's effort to gather the few authoritative texts that he could find that seemed to have some bearing on the issue for the benefit of the archbishops commissioned to adjudicate.

There is a clearer example of legal argument in a dossier that Leodoin, bishop of Modena, included in a letter that he sent around 883/87 to Theodoric, abbot of Nonantola. Michael Heil has discussed and analyzed this letter in detail. Leodoin protested that as bishop of the region he had rightful authority over the churches and the clergy within the monastery's estates, and that the monastery was usurping these rights. Only the bishop, for example, had the right to establish parish churches in the territory and to appoint priests to them. Moreover, those monks of the abbey who were also priests were, as priests, subordinate to him as to their bishop. To support his case, Leodoin assembled several decretals from Isidorus Mercator as well as three canons from the councils of Antioch (341) and Chalcedon (451). Heil notes that whereas Leodoin adapted the decretals rather freely, usually without noting to which pope they were ascribed, he used the conciliar canons more carefully, noting the source – presumably because he considered canons to be more authoritative or

[102] Leo I, *Epist.* 167, PL 54:1199–1209. The relevant passage is 1204B–1206B.

[103] P. 93, line 3: "Et nos e regione hinc etiam ostendere possumus . . . "

statute-like than decretals. Heil observes that Leodoin "displayed a keen awareness of his episcopal rights and responsibilities ... [which] he expressed in terms of canonical precedents and procedures."[104]

How were the canonical collections used, or meant to be used? Much of the forgoing discussion of canons in relation to law comes under this broad topic. The fact that the term "canon law" is used to denote a body of literature from this period is itself a sign of how little is known about how the collected canons were applied. The prefaces to canon law collections from the period 500–1000 included in Somerville and Brasington's splendid collection are full of interesting observations, but they provide us with no consistent thesis as to how the compilers expected their collections to be used. I shall cite here the three most informative proposals.

First, in the preface to his *Harmony of Canons* (*Concordia canonum*), probably written in Italy during the second half of the sixth century, Cresconius emphasizes that he intends his collection to provide the details missing from the *Breviary of Canons* by Ferrandus, deacon of Carthage. The *Breviary* frustrates its readers because it provides only summaries. Readers are constantly referred to other sources, which may not even be available. By writing out the "ecclesiastical statutes [*constituta*], as they are called, in their entirety," and by providing such finding tools as titles and ascriptions, Cresconius hopes to contribute to the instruction of the young (*parvuli*). The benefit in the long run will be that a "very fair judge" (*aequissimus iudex*), having established which "canonical decrees" are relevant to a given proceeding, will be able to ascertain "by probing examination" whether he should be severe or lenient.[105] As Somerville and Brasington note in their own preface, Cresconius "did not elucidate principles for reaching that decision, and his advice to rely on proven authorities remains vague."[106] In fact, while Cresconius assumes that the "judge" will have gathered a dossier of all the canons relevant to the case in hand, he does not claim that his own *Harmony* will be used thus, but rather that it should be used to instruct students, so that they will acquire the necessary skills of judgment.

Second, Regino explains to his dedicatee, archbishop Hatto, that his "little" collection is designed for use in synodal visitations and tribunals, and that in preparing it he has been mindful that the esteemed archbishop not only governs his province with the "sanctions of the holy canons" but also labors tirelessly for the well-being of the entire kingdom. Regino acknowledges that the archbishop is a man of great wisdom and erudition, and that his library is well stocked with appropriate books. But perhaps his little handbook (*manuale*) will be useful when the archbishop travels around his province:

104 M. W. Heil, "Bishop Leodoin of Modena and the Legal Culture of Late Ninth-Century Italy," ZRG 134, Kan. Abt. 103 (2017), 1–75 (quotation from p. 7).

105 Klaus Zechiel-Eckes, *Die Concordia canonum des Cresconius* (Frankfurt am Main: Peter Lang, 1992), vol. 2, 420–22. PL 88:831A–832A. *Prefaces*, 52–53.

106 *Prefaces*, 28.

> But because the transcendent loftiness of your wisdom is constantly preoccupied with public matters, perhaps it seems very burdensome that many volumes of councils should be carried around with you far and wide. Therefore, I have arranged this handbook of texts for your lordship, so that you may have it with you as a manual [*enchiridion*] when the plenitude of your books is not available.[107]

This sounds like a mixture of flattery and advocacy. Did Regino really assume that Hatto and his senior clergy pored over books of canons when they were at home, or that they carted many precious books around with them during visitations? Why does Regino say nothing about the already existing collections and handbooks?

Third, Burchard explains that his motive for compiling what he describes as canonical *iura* and prescriptions for penitents (*iudicia poenitentium*) is that the available canons and penitential prescriptions are confusing, inconsistent, poorly studied, and often based on insufficient authority. Burchard focuses on penance. Because penitential texts are confusing and priests are ignorant, those who come to the clergy seeking the remedy of penance do not receive consistent or reliable prescriptions. One might wonder why Burchard singled out penance here, since many of the canons in his collection were not penitential. One reason was that he was borrowing words written around 829 by archbishop Ebbo of Reims, in a letter requesting a penitential book from bishop Haltigar of Cambrai.[108] To these, Burchard adds that rather than defining for each offense the gravity of the sin and a precise penance with its proper duration, the canons rule that such determinations should be left "to the judgment of an understanding priest."

These observations lead the reader to expect that Burchard will provide prescriptions with the desired level of detail and consistency. But Burchard does not claim that his collection will meet this need directly. Instead, he claims that because the consistency that he seeks can only be achieved by clerics who are "wise and learned in divine law [*lex divina*]," he has written his collection for "boys" (*pueri*) to study. What the priests of today are failing to do, these students, having studied his *Decretum*, will be able to achieve when they become the priests of tomorrow.[109] Despite his pretext, therefore, Burchard, too, leaves determinations to the judgment of understanding priests – but he wants them to be properly trained. Like Cresconius, Burchard aims to enhance the understanding and skills of future priests through study and education. As Greta Austin has pointed out, no collection of canons or penitential prescriptions could possibly address every offense and every situation that a cleric or a bishop would be required to adjudicate. What Burchard's *Decretum* could offer was training and formation in canonical thinking. By studying how the canonical tradition would handle certain

107 Ed. Wasserschleben, Praefatio, 1–2 (my translation).

108 *Prefaces*, 76. MGH Epist. 5 (Epist. Kar. Aevi 3), 617.

109 Burchard of Worms, *Decretorum libri XX: ex consiliis et orthodoxorum patrum decretis*, ed. G. Fransen and T. Kölzer (Aalen: Scientia Verlag, 1992), 45–46.

particular cases, a cleric would acquire skills that could be applied to any situation.[110]

It seems, then, that whereas the canons and decretals, in their original settings, were designed for specific contingencies, the genre of canonical collections was detached from any particular utility or application. The compilers of these collections and the prelates who commissioned them had diverse motives and various uses in mind. Bishops were busy administrators who had to make countless judgments (in a broad and not necessarily legal sense of that term), for example, regarding the promotion and discipline of the clergy, the clergy's ministry to the laity, and the laity's adherence to Christian norms. To fulfill that role, what bishops needed above all was practical wisdom. Study of the canons enhanced and informed such wisdom. It must have been useful, too, to other literate clerics in their ministry, for example, in their performance of the sacraments, in confession, in preaching, and in the supervision of marriages. In short, canonical collections were not statute books but practical resources that were useful in diverse ways. Bishops and their advisors must sometimes have looked for specific solutions to particular problems in such collections. Above all, though, study of the canons, like that of Scripture, was one strand in the pastoral formation of bishops and their senior clergy.

SOURCES

Gratian, *Decretum*, *CICan.*, vol. 1.

Isidore of Seville. *Etymologiarum sive originum*. Ed. W. M. Lindsay. 2 vols. Oxford: Clarendon Press, 1911.

Pharr, Clyde (trans.). *The Theodosian Code and Novels and the Sirmondian Constitutions*. Princeton, NJ: Princeton University Press, 1952.

Tanner, Norman (ed. and trans.). *Decrees of the Ecumenical Councils*. In 2 vols. (continuously paginated). London: Sheed and Ward; and Washington, DC: Georgetown University Press, 1990.

ADDITIONAL READINGS

The section headed "Further Reading" that follows each of the chapters that follow is designed chiefly to suggest where a reader pursuing the topic might go next, after reading the chapter. Since this introduction is designed as a prelude to the anthology, the chapters that follow constitute the "further reading." Instead, therefore, I mention here some sources that are pertinent to but not required for documentation of the foregoing discussion.

My elementary remarks on the Mosaic law reflect the Christian view as it had developed in the West by the fourth century. For earlier patterns and developments,

[110] G. Austin, "Jurisprudence in the Service of Pastoral Care: The Decretum of Burchard of Worms," *Speculum* 79 (2004): 929–59, at 955.

see Luke T. Johnson, "Law in Early Christianity," in Luke T. Johnson, *Contested Issues in Christian Origins and the New Testament* (Leiden: Brill, 2014), 643–58.

Paul's ideas about Mosaic law were the subject of prolonged scholarly controversy during the twentieth century. This controversy has no bearing on anything said in the foregoing introduction, but for an overview see F. Thielman, "Law," in G. F. Hawthorne and R. P. Martin (eds.), *Dictionary of Paul and His Letters* (Downers Grove, Ill: InterVarsity Press, 1993), 529–42. On Paul and that debate as seen from a lawyerly perspective, see J. Hall, "Paul, the Lawyer, on Law," *Journal of Law and Religion* 3.2 (1985): 331–79.

On the *episcopalis audientia*, see also Noel E. Lenski, "Evidence for the *Audientia episcopalis* in the New letters of Augustine," in R. W. Mathisen, *Law, Society and Authority in Late Antiquity* (Oxford: Oxford University Press, 2001), 83–97. Lenski argues on the basis of this evidence that the hearings were often concerned with ecclesiastical and clerical matters.

Thomas Tentler's reviews of Mary C. Mansfield, "The Humiliation of Sinners," in *Catholic Historical Review* 83.2 (1997): 309–11, and of Sarah Hamilton, *The Practice of Penance*, in the online *Medieval Review* (TMR), 02.07.19 (2002), are valuable. The author himself had made an important contribution to the history of penance: Thomas Tentler, *Sin and Confession on the Eve of the Reformation* (Princeton, NJ: Princeton University Press, 1977), which includes a general history of penance (3–50). In the reviews, Tentler welcomes the new approaches but is skeptical about some of the bolder claims of innovation. Moreover, while critical of the teleological aspect of Poschmann's work, he resists the notion that the historical outline delineated by Poschmann has been debunked.

Wilfried Hartmann has written extensively on bishops as judges in the Middle Ages (with passing references to *Sendgerichte*) and is the ranking expert in this field. See "Der Bischof als Richter. Zum geistlichen Gericht über kriminelle Vergehen von Laien im früheren Mittelalter (6.-11. Jahrhundert)," *Römische Historische Mitteilungen* 28 (1986): 103–24; idem, "Der Bischof als Richter nach den kirchenrechtlichen Quellen des 4. bis 7. Jahrhunderts," in *La giustizia nell'alto medioevo, secoli V-VIII* (Spoleto: Presso la Sede del Centro, 1995), 805–42; idem, "Probleme des geistlichen Gerichts im 10. und 11. Jahrhundert: Bischöfe und Synoden als Richter im ostfränkisch-deutschen Reich," in *La giustizia nell'alto medioevo, secoli IX-XI* (Spoleto: Presso la Sede del Centro, 1997), 631–74; idem, *Kirche und Kirchenrecht um 900: die Bedeutung der spätkarolingischen Zeit für Tradition und Innovation im kirchlichen Recht* (Hannover: Hahnsche Buchhandlung, 2008).

On sub-episcopal church courts in the late Middle Ages, see Lawrence R. Poots, *Lower Ecclesiastical Courts in Late-Medieval England: The Courts of the Dean and Chapter of Lincoln, 1336–1349, and the Deanery of Wisbech, 1458–1484* (Oxford: Published for the British Academy by Oxford University Press, 2001).

On post-medieval episcopal visitations, see P. Ingesman, "Visitations as an Instrument of Discipline in Early Modern Denmark," in S. H. Berg et al. (eds.),

The Protracted Reformation in Northern Norway: Towards a Protestant North, vol. 2 (Hannover: Wehrhan Verlag, 2016), 205–35.

For essays illustrating a variety of recent approaches to penitential culture in the Carolingian era, see Abigail Firey, *A Contrite Heart: Prosecution and Redemption in the Carolingian Empire* (Leiden: Brill 2009).

On the seeds of criminal law in medieval canon law, see H. Pihlajamäki and M. Korpiola, "Medieval Canon Law: The Origins of Modern Criminal Law," in M. D. Dubber and T. Hörnle (eds.), *The Oxford Handbook of Criminal Law* (Oxford: Oxford University Press, 2014), 201–24.

Finally, some writers on the modern penal system have noted parallels with ecclesiastical penance. Nick Smith, "The Penitent and the Penitentiary: Questions Regarding Apologies in Criminal Law," *Criminal Justice Ethics* 27.2 (2008): 2–85, observes how expressions of remorse (in ecclesiastical terms, of contrition) can offset litigation and shave time off sentences. Andrew Skotnicki, *Criminal Justice and the Catholic Church* (Plymouth, UK: Sheed & Ward, 2008), and Michael Griffin, *The Politics of Penance: Proposing an Ethic for Social Repair* (Eugene, OR: Cascade Books, 2016), discuss, in light of ecclesiastical penance, ways in which judicial punishment may be construed or applied as reparative.

2

The Many Voices of Roman Law

Jill Harries

CONTROLLING LAW

In 534 CE, lawyers of the Byzantine emperor Justinian completed the onerous task of compiling all valid Roman law into three major works, known collectively as the *Corpus Iuris Civilis* (CIC), the Compendium of Civil Law. The three were the *Codex of Justinian* (the second edition, 534, superseding the first of 529), consisting of imperial legislation in concise form from the time of Hadrian (r. 117–138) to the present, and promulgated as a whole by Justinian; the *Institutes*, a basic academic guide to the principles of law in four books; and the *Digest*, a fifty-book collection of selected authoritative interpretations of, mostly, private law, written by classical Roman jurists "wise in the law" (*iuris prudentes*). Although it was compiled in Constantinople, the predominant language of the *Corpus Iuris Civilis* was Latin, the language of law and administration in the Roman Empire.

The *Corpus Iuris Civilis* was the product of a distinctively Roman and Western legal culture. This is especially true of the *Digest*, the material of which dated from the first through the early fourth centuries CE. With the exception of Book 48, on what we should term criminal law and procedure (pertaining to matters such as murder, adultery, violence, penalties, and the regulation of judicial torture), the *Digest* was devoted to private law, that is, to how Romans dealt with each other to define legal relationships and rights, and to provide legal remedies when problems arose concerning such matters as status, property, contracts, obligations, and infringements of legal rights (*iniuriae*: "injuries"). The *Corpus Iuris Civilis* would have been impossible without a thriving culture of legal studies and jurisprudence, to which private law was central.

The enterprise marked both a beginning and an end. Justinian's intention was that the three collections were in the future to be used for citation in lawsuits to the exclusion of all material omitted by the compilers, and the *Digest* would both be used in court and supply the syllabus for law students. In that sense, the *Corpus* was the start of a new and supposedly more coherent legal era. Thus, "ambiguities" would be "cut out" (*Constitutio Tanta* 1 = *Cod. Iust.* 1.17.2.1, of December 533);

everyone would understand clearly what the law was; and the power to change the law would rest with the emperor alone, through the issue of *Novellae constitutiones* (novels, or new laws).[1]

Justinian's project reveals much about the ambitions of the Christian emperors regarding law, but things did not work out as planned, especially in the West. In Italy, which was briefly reconquered by Justinian in the sixth century, local understandings of Roman law, albeit not the full text of the *Corpus*, continued to be relevant. Elsewhere, in the Frankish and other post-Roman successor kingdoms, the *Theodosian Code* (438), a massive official compilation of constitutions issued from the reign of Constantine to that of Theodosius II (without juristic writings), had more impact.[2] By the ninth century, what bishop Hincmar of Reims (archbishop 845–882) called "the law of Justinian" was in fact based on the Latin *Epitome* of Justinian's *Novels*, a law course prepared by Julian, a professor in Constantinople, in the mid-sixth century.[3] Only in the late eleventh and early twelfth centuries did the *Corpus Iuris Civilis* in general and the *Digest* in particular become relevant again in Western law and jurisprudence. Eventually, it would shape secular law in Europe and beyond, becoming, with canon law, a component of the *ius commune*, or "learned law."[4]

Unbeknownst to its authors, Justinian's *Corpus* marked the end of the evolution of Roman law, which had been based on a continuous tradition extending back, by Justinian's reckoning, 1,400 years. In Justinian's mind, as he looked forward, the project demonstrated the divine favor of his Christian God: "*Deo auctore* [by the authority of God]," Justinian declared, he had succeeded in war and peace, placing his trust not in weapons, soldiers, or generals, or even his own abilities, but "solely in the providence of the Highest Trinity" (*Const. Deo Auctore praef.* = *Cod. Iust.* 1.17.1 *praef.*). But there was some tension between two conflicting agendas: that of the emperor and that of his lawyers. Whereas Justinian sought to reorder law to make it "Christian" in ways that his predecessors could not even envisage, still less attempt,

1 The "constitutions," or imperial laws, launching the projects and confirming completion of the stages of the CIC, are known by their opening word or words: C. *Haec* (13 February 528) launches the *Cod. Iust.*; C. *Summa* (7 April 529) confirms the first edition of the *Cod. Iust.*; C. *Deo Auctore* (15 December 530) and C. *Tanta* (16 December 533) launch and confirm completion of the *Digest*; both are included in the second edition of the *Cod. Iust.*, confirmed by the C. *Cordi* (16 November 534). On the *Cod. Iust.*, see S. Corcoran, "The Codex of Justinian: The Life of a Text Through 1,500 years," in Bruce Frier and Fred H. Blume (eds.), *The Codex of Justinian: A New Annotated Translation with parallel Latin and Greek Text* (Cambridge: Cambridge University Press, 2016), xcvii–clxxxi.

2 On the Theodosian project, see Tony Honoré, *Law in the Crisis of the Empire, 379–455 AD: The Theodosian Dynasty and Its Quaestors* (Oxford: Oxford University Press, 1998), ch. 6, "Understanding the Theodosian Code" (pp. 123–53).

3 For a brief account of the *Epitome* with references, see Timothy G. Kearley, "The Creation and Transmission of Justinian's Novels," *Law Library Journal* 102.3 (2010): 377–97, at 383–85.

4 Peter Stein, *Roman Law in European History* (Cambridge: Cambridge University Press, 1999); Paul Vinogradoff, *Roman Law in Mediaeval Europe*, with a new foreword by Peter Stein (Cambridge: Speculum Historiale, 1968).

his lawyers would use their best efforts to preserve intact their unbroken tradition of legal knowledge, which predated the rise of Christianity.

THINKING LAW

By privileging imperial law in the *Codex*, and the learned interpretations of the jurists down to the early fourth century in the *Digest*, Justinian's advisers, who were all the products of a formal and centralizing juristic culture, attempted to impose limits, from an official standpoint, on the forms that "law" could take. Five hundred years earlier, when Rome was a republic governed by the "Senate and People of Rome" (*Senatus populusque Romanus*, or SPQR), the picture had looked very different. Cicero, who was both a lawyer and an advocate, defined the purpose of civil law (the law applying to Roman citizens) in 44 BCE as being the right of citizens to obtain what was due to them (*Topica* 9), and he listed the parts or subdivisions of "law" deployed in the discourse of advocates (*Topica* 28). These parts included statutes (*leges*) passed by the people and plebiscites (*plebiscita*), the resolutions of the Senate (*senatus consulta*), the edicts (*edicta*) of magistrates, the interpretations of jurists, decided cases (used for purposes of argument by analogy rather than as formal precedents), custom (*consuetudo*), and equity or fairness (*aequitas*). The same range, with modifications, still applied in the second century CE: "the laws [*iura*, plural of *ius*, legal right] of the Roman people," wrote the jurist Gaius, "consist of statutes [*leges*], plebiscites, resolutions of the Senate, constitutions of emperors, edicts of those [magistrates] with the right [*ius*] to issue edicts, and the responses of the learned in law [*prudentes*]."[5]

These are often described as the "sources" of Roman law, but they are also indicative of the versatility of Roman legal discourse. Rather than seeing "law" or "legal right" (*ius*) as a single entity, the Romans saw "law" as operative in different ways in different contexts, often entailing a choice of courts (the so-called *praescriptio fori*), of legal actions, or of processes.[6] Alternative forms of dispute resolution, such as informal arbitration hearings before an agreed adjudicator, negotiations between the parties, and mediation through the good offices of a third party, might have legal consequences, but they required no recognition in law except in certain limited situations, when state enforcement of an agreement's provisions was required (see *Dig.* 4.8 on formal arbitration agreements, or *compromissa*).[7] Moreover, the Romans acknowledged the importance of unwritten law, which was based on such social values as fairness (*aequitas*) or on legal custom: the ways things

5 Gaius, *Institutes* 1.2.

6 Caroline Humfress "Thinking Through Legal Pluralism: 'Forum Shopping' in the Later Roman Empire," in J. Duindam, J. Harries, C. Humfress, and N. Hurvitz (eds.), *Law and Empire: Ideas, Practices, Actors* (Leiden: Brill, 2013), 225–50.

7 Jill Harries, *Law and Empire in Late Antiquity* (Cambridge: Cambridge University Press, 1999), 175–84.

had been done in the past. As the Romans acquired an empire, their recognition that law and legal process could take many forms, combined with an aversion on the part of the center to unprofitable interventions in local cultures, allowed for the maintenance of a culture of legal pluralism. This ran counter to the urge, expressed by Justinian and other imperial legislators, to impose uniformity.

Law was a specialist discipline, with its own discourse and distinctive structure as a system of knowledge. It could be imparted by teacher to pupil and thus passed down through the generations (for "dynasties" of jurists, see Pomponius [second century] at *Dig.* 1.2.2). Juristic writing was deceptively simple in merely linguistic terms, but the *concepts* deployed were far from simple, and the jurists' use of a private form of shorthand acted as a deterrent to the nonspecialist and a provocation to the public in general, who, along with many of their emperors, demanded clarity, simplicity, and certainty.

From the publication of the Twelve Tables (the archaic Roman law code) in c. 450 BCE onward, Roman law had revolved around the concept of "legal right" (*ius*): a word that was related, as the opening extract by Ulpian (writing c. 213–217 CE) in the *Digest* declared, to the Latin term for justice (*iustitia*). "Right" was defined in terms of *iniuria*: damage to or offense against "right," and it was thus in a constant process of being tested and redefined on a case-by-case basis. In Twelve-Tables terminology, to "go to law" was to "go to right" (*in ius ire*), and much effort was devoted to explaining how and where legal remedies for injuries were to be sought. In civil cases, this involved a "judge or arbitrator" (*iudex arbiterve*), ideally one agreed on by the parties, although this requirement proved impossible to sustain as Roman citizenship expanded. A plaintiff seeking a remedy had to find the right court, ensure his legal action was valid, and frame it in the correct words. For example, the jurist Gaius (*Institutes* 4.11) noted that a litigant complaining about having had his vines cut down lost his case because he wrote "vines" (*vites*) in his plea, not "trees" (*arbores*), the inclusive term employed in the Twelve Tables. Although the obsession with precise terminology decreased over time, partly because of the wish of Roman emperors that law should be accessible to all their citizens, much of Roman law was "remedial" and, therefore, devoted to identifying what was correct procedure, who was eligible to bring a legal action, and which kind of legal action should be used.

What we think of today as Roman law – *ius* in the collective sense – is a set of written texts with legal force created by elites, but Roman law was also found in action: in the pleas of petitioners, in private legal documents such as wills, and in the projection of power through the legal inscription. Written texts had a material presence, projecting their identity and authority. They ranged from the papyrus will, folded in accordance with the rules and signed by the requisite number of witnesses, to the "Books of Theodosius" in which the *Code* of the emperor Theodosius (issued in 438) was enshrined, and to the bronze tablets or stone inscriptions, giving perpetual form to Roman statutes, municipal charters, or privileges granted to cities by emperors, such as exemptions from taxes.[8] Ironically, the Twelve Tables, which was arguably the most authoritative Roman legal inscription, survives only in fragmentary form, not as an inscription but through later literary citations. Nonlegal texts, such as the tenth book of letters by the Roman senator, Pliny the Younger, governor of Bithynia (c. 110–112), also show both law in action and how new law was created through legal decisions that emperors made in response to questions from their governors and other officials.

By Late Antiquity, the imperial letter or rescript (*epistula* or *rescriptum*) had become, alongside edicts, the principal method by which new laws, drafted and agreed to by the emperor's council or *consistorium*, were communicated to the peoples of the empire. Multiple copies of imperial letters were sent out to provincial officials, who were responsible for making their contents known by public recitation and by the posting of the text, often with the provincial official's decree on implementation attached. Each "law" was accompanied by a rubric stating the date and place where it was issued (*data*), received (*accepta*), and posted in public (*proposita*). The imperial letters were often highly rhetorical and ornate in their language, designed not only to explain the law but also to justify both it and imperial policy in general. They could also be surprisingly vague or unspecific, assuming a wider knowledge of imperial policy on the part of their readers. The anti-Christian emperor Maximin Daza, for example, in his letter to Tyre and other Eastern cities, ordered the expulsion of certain "impious" persons, otherwise undefined (Eusebius, *Church History* 9.7.3–14), but the locals would have also been aware of the separate circulation of the so-called Acts of Pilate, forged to discredit the Christians (Eusebius, *Church History* 9.5.1). On the other side, the Hispellum rescript, issued to an Italian town by Constantine's youngest son, the Caesar Constans, in the early 330s, permitted observance of the imperial cult provided there were no blood sacrifices or concessions to "the deceits of contagious superstition." Here it was left to the recipients to work out, in the light of what was known from other pronouncements on imperial policy, what practices counted as "superstition."[9]

The term *rescriptum* could mean both "reply" in a general sense and, more narrowly, a technical response to an individual query on a detailed point of law. The language of the *rescriptum* in the latter sense, issued not by the emperor himself but by his officials on the emperor's behalf, was brief and to the point. These special rescripts were replies to queries from judges or litigants, addressed to individuals. They made no judgment on the facts, which it was the job of the judge in charge of the case to determine. In the 290s, Gregorius and Hermogenian, two lawyers

8 Elizabeth A. Meyer, *Legitimacy and Law in the Roman World: Tabulae in Roman Belief and Practice* (Cambridge: Cambridge University Press, 2004). For Republican legal inscriptions, see M. H. Crawford et al. (eds.), *Roman Statutes*, vol. 1 (London: Institute of Classical Studies, School of Advanced Study, 1996).

9 Timothy D. Barnes, *Constantine: Dynasty, Religion and Power in the Later Roman Empire* (Chichester: Wiley-Blackwell, 2011), 20–23.

working for the emperor Diocletian, compiled a collection of legal rescripts going back to the time of Hadrian. The original *Codex Gregorianus* (c. 292) was updated by the second lawyer, Hermogenian, in 295, and the combined result is often known under both names. Rescripts were applicable in theory only to the case addressed, but in practice they acquired general application. The contribution of Gregorius and Hermogenian was to provide an authoritative collection for use by lawyers and advocates.[10] Their work does not survive independently, aside from extracts, but much survives through its incorporation into Justinian's CIC.

THE THEODOSIAN CODE

Over a century after Diocletian, and a century before Justinian commissioned the *Corpus Iuris Civilis*, the emperor Theodosius II codified extracts from imperial legislation in his sixteen *Libri Theodosiani*, known collectively as the *Theodosian Code*.[11] The extracts were drawn from imperial edicts and letters, which were classified as "laws of general application" (*leges generales*). "Superfluous verbiage" – the overblown rhetoric in which legal decisions were embedded – was to be excluded. Being the work of a committee, the draft project as envisaged in March 429 (*Cod. Theod.* 1.1.5) compromised over whether to include all laws, some of which documented past thinking that had been superseded, or to restrict itself to laws that were currently valid. Entries under each heading (*titulus*) were arranged chronologically by day, month, and consular year of issue, so that judges faced with contradictions could be guided by the most recent version. The project was completed by autumn 437, to coincide with the marriage of the Western emperor, Valentinian III, to Theodosius's daughter in Constantinople. It was formally promulgated, with instructions for publicity and dissemination, on February 15, 438 (Theodosius, *Novel* 1). Unlike the later *Corpus Iuris Civilis*, the project did not include any compilation of writings by the jurists, or jurisprudence.

Could this exercise in codification be regarded as a specifically Christian enterprise? Theodosius was an emperor celebrated by his contemporaries for his Christian piety; the laws of the *Theodosian Code* began with the first Christian emperor, Constantine; and its last book consisted of laws *about* Christianity, defining the privileges of churches and clergy while outlawing various forms of "pagan" activity and heresy. Despite these indications to the contrary, however, the *Theodosian Code* remained true to the essentially secular traditions of Roman law

10 On the *Codex Gregorianus* and *Codex Hermogenianus*, see Serena Connolly, *Lives Behind the Laws: The World of the Codex Hermogenianus* (Bloomington: Indiana University Press, 2010); and Simon Corcoran, *The Empire of the Tetrarchs: Imperial Pronouncements and Government AD 284–324*, rev. ed. (Oxford: Clarendon Press, 2000). Papal decretal letters had a function analogous in some respects to imperial rescripts, although whether there was any historical connection is unclear. It is possible that decretals were an independent but convergent response to a similar need.

11 On the creation of *Cod. Theod.*, see John Matthews, *Laying Down the Law: A Study of the Theodosian Code* (New Haven: Yale University Press, 2000).

as a structured system of knowledge. It was designed as a continuation (*Cod. Theod.* 1.1.5 *ad similitudinem*) of the Codices of Gregorius and Hermogenian. The structure of the first five books generally follows that of one of Roman law's master texts, the Praetorian Edict, issued annually under the Republic by the Roman magistrate in charge of justice, the text of which was fixed in perpetuity by Hadrian in the 130s.[12] Laws relevant to Christianity are not confined to the last book but rather distributed throughout, again following long-standing traditions.

About one third of the *Theodosian Code* survives only through its reuse or citation in later sources. Its modern, only partial reconstruction owes much to a lesser, non-Roman autocrat: Alaric II, king of the Arian Visigoths in Aquitaine. In 506, Alaric organized a reworking of the *Theodosian Code* for the benefit of those of his subjects who still saw themselves as Roman. The result is properly known as the *Lex Romana Visigothorum*, although it is often referred to as Alaric's *Breviary* (*Breviarium Alaricianum*). Its language was Latin, the administrative language of the former Roman Empire. Alaric's committee consisted of a mix of Romans and Visigoths. Their task was not only to select laws but also to explicate and update the material by providing their own interpretations where necessary. These juristic *interpretationes* (comments, or glosses), as John Matthews states, "expound, summarize, give the meaning of terms, abbreviate or expand, as seems appropriate. In some cases they also update."[13] The background to this initiative is significant. First, the Gothic kingdom of Aquitaine already had a law code, issued by Alaric's father Euric, which was also in Latin. It drew both on the Roman jurists and on Gothic customary law, and it was not modeled on the *Theodosian Code*. Second, Alaric's kingdom was under direct threat from the Franks to the north, who would drive the Goths out of France and into Spain the following year. The *Breviarium*, therefore, can be seen as an attempt to conciliate Alaric's Roman subjects. But its purpose was also to enable the Gothic king to assert his ownership of Roman law – and of its imperial language, Latin – within his kingdom. The process of selection and interpretation broke the link both with the Roman past and with the Roman Empire in the Byzantine East. The result may have looked like an interpretative update of a somewhat abbreviated version of the *Theodosian Code*, but it now bore the name of Alaric, for the Romans of Aquitaine now belonged to him, and not to the Eastern emperor.[14] As later

[12] Jill Harries, "How to Make a Law Code," in M. M. Austin, J. Harries, and C. J. Smith (eds.), *Modus Operandi: Essays in Honour of Geoffrey Rickman*, BICS Suppl. 71 (London: Institute of Classical Studies, 1998): 63–78

[13] John F. Matthews, "Interpreting the *Interpretationes* of the *Breviarium*," in Ralph W. Mathisen (ed.), *Law, Society and Authority in Late Antiquity* (Oxford: Oxford University Press, 2001): 11–32, at 28. See also the essays in M. Rouche and E. Dumézil (eds.), *Le Bréviaire d'Alaric. Aux origines du Code civil* (Paris: Presses de l'Université Paris-Sorbonne, 2008).

[14] Jill Harries, "Legal Culture and Identity in the Fifth-Century West," in G. Greatrex and S. Mitchell (eds.), *Ethnicity and Culture in Late Antiquity* (London: Duckworth, 2000): 45–57, at 54–55. Contrast with Ian Wood, *The Merovingian Kingdoms 450–71* (London: Routledge, 1994), 47. Whether Goths and Romans in the Visigothic kingdom were subject to different laws during this period, and the *Breviary* was intended exclusively for *Romani*, are disputed issues today.

chapters will illustrate, it was the *Libri Theodosiani* (the books comprising *Cod. Theod.*), not the CIC of Justinian, which had the most relevance to the evolution of "Roman" law in the early mediaeval West.

As Fergus Millar has shown, Roman imperial law evolved through responses to external prompts, although emperors were far from passive.[15] The in trays of emperors regularly featured proposals (*suggestiones*), reports (*relationes*), petitions, and referrals (*consultationes*) on matters of law. Their originators could be court officials, provincial administrators, local interest groups, or, from the time of Gallienus (r. 252–268), bishops. Originators of proposals had a powerful voice in the creation of the imperial agenda as they regulated (and could distort) the information that reached the center. Hard-working and politically vulnerable officials, like the pagan senator Symmachus, Prefect of the City of Rome in 384, also needed imperial endorsement for their actions if they had the potential to provoke political or legal controversy. His dossier of state papers (*Relationes*) shows Symmachus referring upward to the emperor for decision in cases that were politically sensitive (*Relatio* 49, the situation of an imperial spy), or so tangled after repeated hearings that only the emperor could sort them out, or, mischievously, implicating a Christian senator in shady property dealings and the unlawful imprisonment of an entire town council (*Relatio* 28).[16]

The responsive nature of much imperial governance affects how imperial constitutions should be read. They were part of a conversation between emperor and subjects of which only fragments remain. For example, a constitution addressed by Constantine to Helpidius, an official at Rome, in 320 agrees that manumissions should be valid on the "day of the Sun" (*Cod. Theod.* 2.8.1). Read in isolation, this appears to be a law validating manumission. In fact, the constitution as a whole was about what kinds of work could take place on holidays, and it was classified as such in both Codes. Legal transactions were, in general, banned on holidays; but Sunday was a holiday; therefore, were such manumissions valid? Constantine's cheerful response was that good things happen on holidays, and that manumissions, being good things, should be allowed as well. In the same law, he also agreed (*Cod. Iust.* 3.12.2) that farmers could work on Sundays to take advantage of good weather.

Eusebius of Caesarea's love of documentation, too, allows us to see the process of report and response at work. He records that the aged empress Eutropia, the mother-in-law of Constantine, visited the sacred shrines at Mamre and reported, luridly, on the pagan abominations she found there. Constantine, knowing nothing directly of the situation, dispatched a letter to the Bishop of Jerusalem, himself a skilled lobbyist, directing him to cooperate with the emperor's enforcer, the count

15 Fergus Millar, *The Emperor in the Roman World (31 BC–AD 337)* (Ithaca, NY: Cornell University Press, 1977).

16 Jean-Pierre Callu (ed.), *Symmaque. Discours – rapports* (Paris: Belles lettreso, 2009). R. H. Barrow, *Prefect and Emperor: The Relationes of Symmachus, AD 384* (Oxford: Clarendon Press, 1973). For a summary, see Harries, *Law and Empire in Late Antiquity*, 114–17.

Acacius, to make the appropriate architectural and other adjustments to ensure that Mamre, hitherto multifaith, became an exclusively Christian holy place (Eusebius, *Life of Constantine*, 3. 51–53). Although, thanks to Eutropia's (mis)representations, his letter castigated the local bishops for excessive tolerance, Constantine seems to have been unaware of the fact that pagans, Jews, and Christians had coexisted peacefully on the site for decades, tolerated by, among others, Eusebius himself.[17]

Christians under Christian emperors were not the only lobbyists to evoke legislation with some foreknowledge of how the emperor would react to their *suggestio*. Eusebius, recalling how the emperor Maximin Daza revived persecution of the Christians after Galerius's Edict of Toleration in 311, alleged that the emperor had prompted embassies from Antioch to "request" the expulsion of Christians from the city (Eusebius, *Church History* 9.2). Those who prompted a law could be relied on to see that the legislation was enforced; but, if a law was a response to representations by a clique, or lacked majority support, enforcement was patchy. For example, the Diocletianic edicts against Christianity issued from 303 onward (Lactantius, *On the Deaths of the Persecutors*, 13–15) were largely ignored in NW Europe, the part of the empire controlled by Constantius I, the father of the future Christian emperor Constantine.

The exact terms of the "persecution edicts" of the emperors Decius and Valerian in the 250s, like those of Diocletian later, were usually strictly observed. Valerian appears to have targeted both wealthier Christians (Cyprian, *Letter* 81.1.2) and unlawful assemblies by Christians in general; the bishop Dionysius of Alexandria wryly observed that the judge, Aemilianus, had tried to avoid the right question (about meetings) in favor of enforcing a ban on being Christian at all (Eusebius, *Church History* 7.11.3). Similarly, under Diocletian, when would-be African martyrs responded to interrogation with the formulaic declaration "We are Christians," the proconsul Anulinus dismissed their answer as irrelevant, insisting that they address the question put them, which had been framed in terms of the edicts: Had they engaged in either of the two activities explicitly outlawed by the edicts, namely, the holding of unlawful assemblies and owning copies of the sacred books?[18] From their perspective, officials like the much-reviled Anulinus were not engaging in "persecution" (an emotive term). Rather, they were enforcing the law in accordance with its exact wording.

HANDBOOKS

To apply the law, lawyers had to know what it was. But few practicing lawyers in the provinces, be they advisers or advocates, could benefit from the specialist libraries in

17 G. S. P. Freeman-Grenville, Rupert L. Chapman, and Joan E. Taylor, *The Onomasticon: Palestine in the Fourth Century A.D.* (Jerusalem: Carta, 2003), under entry for Mamre.

18 Maureen A. Tilley, *Donatist Martyr Stories: The Church in Conflict in Roman North Africa*, TTH 24 (Liverpool: Liverpool University Press, 1996), 38.

Rome or in other capitals. Nor could they match the extensive private collection of Tribonian, for example, Justinian's chief lawyer, which would prove indispensable to the compilation of the *Digest*. Yet the winning of a case could depend on access to the most recent relevant imperial decision. New imperial laws, having been proclaimed and posted publicly, vanished into the archives in due course. The response of lawyers and other interested parties to the problem of access was to put together collections of useful imperial constitutions and extracts from the writings of the jurists. Private collections of this sort may have supplemented the official archives from which the *Theodosian Code* was compiled.

Jurists, aware of the need for access to the basics on the part of imperial officials and others, compiled small guides entitled *Institutes* or *Regulae* (rules), reflecting a more practical and perhaps less sophisticated culture in the outer reaches of imperial governance. But handbooks were useful to anyone interested in or likely to be affected by the operation of Roman law. One such handbook was the *Sententiae* (opinions) ascribed to the jurist Paul but probably the work of a minor lawyer in Africa in the late third century. Another was the so-called *Fragmenta Vaticana*, parts of a legal manual, perhaps compiled at Rome, consisting mainly of extracts from the Severan jurists Papinian, Paulus, and Ulpian, and selected rescripts of third- and early fourth-century emperors. It also drew on the Codices of Gregorius and Hermogenian, updated to include a clutch of decisions of Valentinian I (r. 364–375; see FV 37, FIRA 2nd ed., 471–72). The subject headings under which the extracts were listed reflect the world of the legal hack: the laws of sale, usufruct, dowry, and (extensively) gifts.

Perhaps the most original adaptation of the handbook format was the so-called *Comparison [Collatio] of Mosaic and Roman Law*, thrown together at Rome in the early years of Constantine, and subsequently revised with the addition of a law against homosexuality dating from 390.[19] During a period when rather more sophisticated attempts were being made to integrate the Judeo-Christian past with that of the Greeks and Romans, the Collator's aim was to prove that the laws of Moses (the Ten Commandments) and those of the Romans were in mutual agreement. His use of a structure based mainly on the Ten Commandments was, by implication, a challenge to the traditional arrangement of material employed by Roman lawyers. Within each chapter, the structure was simple: "Moses [with minor variants] said," followed by the Biblical text, and then an appropriate selection from the Roman jurists and the Diocletianic Codes. The identity of the Collator is unknown, but he is assumed to be either Christian or Jewish. His legal knowledge appears to derive from a small collection of books by jurists and from the Diocletianic Codes, which was respectable but not extensive and had a marked bias in favor of criminal law: a branch in general rather despised by the jurists.

[19] Robert M. Frakes, *Compiling the Collatio Legum Mosaicarum et Romanarum in Late Antiquity* (Oxford: Oxford University Press, 2011).

LAW ON THE GROUND

Only limited areas of Roman law, such as the collection of taxes, required active enforcement by the central authorities. The preservation of order was also a government priority, hence legislation to control the activities of guilds and other suspect organizations, including "illicit" religions. Magistrates exercised a discretionary power known as *coercitio*, the right to "coerce" or forcibly prevent bad behavior. One sign of trouble for Paul of Tarsus was his expulsion from various cities on his journey for causing public disorder (Acts 16.19–39). Fearing that he would undermine their livelihoods, the Ephesian manufacturers of silver statuettes of Artemis organized a demonstration against him in the theatre (Acts 19.24–41). For the most part, however, Roman law existed for the citizens to make use of or appeal to it. Criminal prosecutions were triggered by information brought by individuals who claimed to be injured. In Late Antiquity, they were required to lodge a formal "inscription" (*inscriptio*), which made them liable to the penalty threatening the defendant if the charge failed.

Non-imperial agents also affected the operation of the law. The arguments of advocates, who were often advised behind the scenes by legal experts (*iuris prudentes*), reflected the social mores and expectations of the judges. Over time, therefore, they shaped how the law operated.[20] Some judges, such as the Prefect of Egypt, were formally empowered to create precedents through their court decisions, which were preserved in the archives.[21] But judges also created bad precedents by making mistakes. When caught out, their victims claimed they had suffered *iniuria iudicis* through the judge's violation of *ius*, but despite – or perhaps because of – the complex and extensive procedures for appeal, many judicial mistakes must have passed uncorrected.[22] It is likely, for example, that the evolution of "judicial savagery" under the later Roman Empire, including the increased use of judicial torture, was driven more by the courts, by the prejudices of judges (who had some discretion in sentencing), and by vengeful litigants than by imperial pronouncements.[23]

Early accounts of Christian martyrdoms, such as those of Polycarp at Smyrna in 155 and of a Christian group at Lyons in 177, show the Christians as victims of lynch mobs, which acted with the connivance of the governor. But the official policy was to ensure that Christians, like everyone else, had the protection of proper procedure. As Trajan stated to his governor, Pliny (Pliny, *Letters* 10, 97), and as Hadrian reported in a rescript to a later governor, Minucius Fundanus (Justin, *Apology* 1.69; Eusebius,

20 John A. Crook, *Legal Advocacy in the Roman World* (London: Duckworth, 1995).

21 Ranon Katzoff, "Sources of Law in Roman Egypt: The Role of the Prefect," in *Aufstieg und Niedergang der römischen Welt II* 13 (Berlin, 1980), 807–44.

22 Jill Harries, *Law and Crime in the Roman World* (Cambridge: Cambridge University Press, 2007), 38–41.

23 Ramsay MacMullen, "Judicial Savagery in the Roman Empire," *Chiron* 16 (1986): 147–66; repr. in Ramsay MacMullen, *Changes in the Roman Empire: Essays in the Ordinary* (Princeton: Princeton University Press, 1990): 204–17.

Church History 4.9), anonymous denunciations and "angry shouting" were unacceptable, as were attempts at blackmail. According to Hadrian, those shown to be acting "contrary to the laws" were to be punished in line with the severity of the offense. According to Trajan and Pliny, refusal to sacrifice was sufficient proof of guilt, but Christians were not to be "hunted out." This last was a significant limitation on state intervention. Prior to Decius's edict enforcing sacrifice in 250, Christians were safe as long as no one denounced them.

The status of Christianity as an "unlawful" religion was problematic in the Roman Empire and has long been problematic in modern scholarship. The absence of a formal enactment against Christianity caused problems for Pliny (*Letters* 10. 96), who executed Christians but was uncertain of his grounds for doing so. In fact, Christianity existed in the legally grey area inhabited by the *religio illicita* (unlawful religion), which was disapproved of socially and perhaps, but not necessarily, by the law as well. Pliny had investigated accusations of illegal practices among Christians, such as incest and cannibalism, and he had found no evidence of wrongdoing. These accusations are now understood as an expression of social disapproval of an (apparently) deviant cult. Christians were social outsiders, a target group both because of their exclusiveness and because of their refusal to sacrifice to or for the emperor, whether what was to be offered up was an animal, a libation, or a pinch of incense. Precedents for condemnation of Christians on various grounds accumulated and became, without formal statute, a part of judicial practice. Despite this, the extent of "persecution" was limited until the Christians refused to conform to Decius's edict of universal sacrifice in 250.

The converse to the question of "persecution" is when Christianity became a "legal" religion (*religio licita*). In one sense, Christianity was "legal" by default during periods when the bans on meetings and other disabilities imposed from time to time by emperors and then revoked, were inoperative. In another sense, Christianity "became legal" when, in 313, Christians were allowed to own property as a collective.[24] As often happened, we may be in a world where people behaved informally *as if* a certain legal situation existed but did not formally ratify the law until a later date. T. D. Barnes has argued that the emperor responsible for making Christianity "legal" was Gallienus, who, after 260, reversed his father Valerian's policy of persecution. In a rescript to bishop Dionysius of Alexandria (who had recently been restored from exile) and the other bishops in Egypt (Eusebius, *Church History* 7.13.2), Gallienus ordered that opponents of Christianity should vacate the places of worship used by Christians, who could use the rescript to ensure that they were not molested and could do "what you are now lawfully empowered to do." Christians could once again hold meetings. The proscribed bishops' problem under Valerian had been that they had found it hard to find fellow Christians to share their

[24] Charles Saumagne, "*Corpus Christianorum*," *Revue internationale des droits de l'Antiquité*, 3rd series, 7 (1960): 437–78, and 8 (1961): 257–79.

meetings with in their remote places of exile in Libya (7.11.11–12; 17–18). But the rescript does not specify that *ownership* of the places of assembly was an issue. By excluding the opponents of Christianity from the Christians' "places of worship," Gallienus guaranteed the Christians' right to use their places of assembly, but not necessarily to own them. The emphasis in general was on the Christians' need to meet *somewhere*. Bishop Dionysius's concern while in exile had been to find Christians with whom he could meet and places where he could meet them. In the outer reaches of Libya, the question of ownership did not arise.

In 313, however, a decision of Constantine and Licinius, recorded in a letter issued by the latter,[25] formally recognized the right of the Christian communities (*ecclesiae*) to own property as a collective association, or corporation (in Latin, a *corpus*). The emperors ordered that

> since the same Christians are recognized to have had [*habuisse*] not only those places in which they were accustomed to assemble but other places too, pertaining by legal right [*ad ius pertinentia*] to their *corpus* [i.e., corporation], that is of the churches, not of individuals, you will order that all the assets in the law set out above without any dispute or questioning at all be handed back to those same Christians, that is to their *corpus* and to their places of assembly [*conventiculis*]." (Lactantius, *On the Deaths of the Persecutors* 48.9.)

Christians, therefore, "had" places, which "pertained by legal right" to their corporation (*corpus*); but the absence of the formal terminology of ownership (*dominium*, *possession*, etc.) suggests that this was the point at which the Christians' de facto ownership of their *conventicula* were retrospectively recognized as *de iure* as well. Thus, Licinius gave personal instructions that "the *conventicula* be returned to their former state" (48.13).

ALTERNATIVE LAW

Christians and other Romans lived in a world of many courts and many laws. There were special courts for groups, such as the military or, from the fourth century, the clergy; it was in the interest of both to protect the independence of their jurisdiction. In addition, there were informal ad hoc hearings run by local "big men," such as village elders or local military commanders, who had no official role as judges but acted as informal arbitrators, when requested to by disputing parties, both of whom had to agree that his decision would "end" the case. Such men could also be petitioned for redress for wrongs by individuals reluctant to become entangled with formal process. A cavalry officer, Fl. Abinnaeus, for example, based at Dionysias in the Fayyum, Egypt, in the 340s, left an archive of petitions addressed

[25] This letter is widely but incorrectly known as the Edict of Milan. For the history of the scholarship and correction of the terminology, see Timothy D. Barnes, *Constantine: Dynasty, Religion and Power in the Later Roman Empire* (Chichester: Wiley-Blackwell, 2011), 93–97.

to him, rather than to the more distant Prefect of Egypt.[26] One such petition was from Aurelia Atiaris, a female landowner and daughter of a veteran. Claiming that she had been beaten up and wrongfully imprisoned, she petitioned for redress. Abinnaeus would have been required to call witnesses to assess the facts and establish compensation, if appropriate (Documents 51 and 52). Even Christians were not above trying to fix the system. For example, the priest Mios asks Abinnaeus to exempt his brother-in-law, the son of a veteran, from military service (Document 19), regardless of the legal duty imposed on a son to follow his father's profession. Both petitioners had a military connection, which led them to hope for a favorable response. Mios trusted that his mission would succeed "on God's account."

The *episcopalis audientia*, an episcopal hearing or court designed to settle civil disputes, evolved in a context where alternative dispute-settlement, through arbitration, negotiation, and mediation, was commonplace. (On the history of the papal court under Gelasius I, see Bronwen Neil in Chapter 14.) The official state process operating in the provinces of the Empire was the *cognitio*, a trial before the provincial governor, a process that dated from Rome's first acquisition of provinces, when governors found themselves required to exercise judicial powers.[27] This was expensive and, given the many opportunities to appeal, likely to be long drawn-out (and to favor the wealthier or better-connected litigant). Paul's advice to the Corinthians (1 Cor 6:1–8), that they should avoid cheating each other and keep the Gentiles out of it, hints at the perceived advantages of self-help dispute settlement over resort to formal state procedures. The regulations set out in the third-century *Didaskalia Apostolorum* show that leaders of Christian communities were expected to act as healers rather than adjudicators and to reconcile the disputing parties, preferably in time for Sunday worship; only under Constantine were the authorities required to take note of how this process related to the recognized state courts (*Cod. Theod.* 1.27.1, text corrupt).

During the fourth century, the imperial lawyers attempted to interpret episcopal jurisdiction in terms of pre-existing Roman legal practice with regard to arbitration. They declared that the judicial decisions of bishops were valid under Roman law in the same sense as arbitration awards were, which "ended" the dispute and could not be appealed against. On that ground, the state could intervene to enforce the bishops' judgments (*Cod. Theod.* 1.27.2, July 398). Earlier in the same year, the emperor Arcadius had conceded similar rights to Jewish courts in civil matters; again, their judgments could be enforced by the governors.[28] Despite the eagerness

[26] H. I. Bell, V. Martin, E. G. Turner, and D. van Berchem (eds.), *The Abinnaeus Archive: Papers of a Roman Officer in the Reign of Constantius II* (Oxford: Clarendon Press, 1962).

[27] On the *cognitio*, see Harries, *Law and Crime in the Roman World* (Cambridge: Cambridge University Press, 2007), 28–42.

[28] On the two laws of 398, see Jill Harries, "Creating Legal Space: Settling Disputes in the Roman Empire," in Catherine Hezser (ed.) *Rabbinic Law in Its Roman and Near Eastern Context* (Tubingen: Mohr Siebeck, 2003), 63–82.

of Christian emperors to put the state enforcement apparatus at the disposal of the *ecclesiae*, however, the role of the bishops as conciliators remained important; the effective administration of law within small communities still depended on consent.[29] It must have been a relief to humbler bishops that decisions were often about matters of fact rather than of law. When bishop Plousianos, in fifth-century Egypt, heard a case of a nun who had allegedly abstracted books from an estate, he ruled that the nun must either restore them or swear an oath that she had not removed them. Then "all those things left behind in the house" were to be divided among the heirs.[30]

New situations required new laws. When Constantine adopted Christianity as his favored religion after his victory over his rival Maxentius at the Milvian Bridge in 312, he was doing no more than previous emperors had done. Despite Galerius' Edict of Toleration issued in 311 (Lactantius, *On the Deaths of the Persecutors* 34, Greek version at Eusebius, *Church History* 8.17), the status of Christians required clarification, hence the decisions reached jointly with Licinius at Milan in 313. At the same time, Constantine diverted new financial resources to the support of Christian communities and began a program of church building at Rome. But Christians, as Constantine quickly discovered, would make unprecedented demands on their emperor over matters of right belief and church unity. Despite his persistent attempts to devolve such decisions to church councils, Constantine became ever more implicated, first in an unsuccessful attempt to suppress by force the Donatist schism in Africa, and then at the ecumenical Council of Nicaea in 325, which condemned Arianism. (The Arians were accusing of saying that the Son of God was not eternal but created and, consequently, of denying the divinity of Jesus Christ.)[31] By involving himself with matters of doctrine and heresy, Constantine set a precedent for his successors. Emperors henceforward would be required to legislate not only on correct religious observance but also on right belief.

Legislation against heresy, therefore, was a new type of law, but the sanctions against wrong-thinkers were traditional. Emperors after Constantine legislated against heretics, using devices similar to those employed against Christians by Diocletian. Although heretics were neither tortured nor sent to the wild beasts, as the Christian martyrs had been, their meetings were banned, their property (including meeting places) was confiscated, and their leaders were exiled (*Cod. Theod.* 16.5

[29] See Caroline Humfress, "Bishops and Law Courts in Late Antiquity. How (Not) to Make Sense of the Legal Evidence," JECS 19.3 (2011): 375–400. The article provides extensive bibliography and some critique of previous secondary literature on the topic.

[30] James G. Keenan, J. G. Manning and Uri Yiftach-Firanko (eds.), *Law and Legal Practice in Egypt from Alexander to the Arab Conquest* (Cambridge: Cambridge University Press, 2014), 523–25.

[31] What beliefs Arius and the Arians really held, as distinct from what others accused them of holding, is a complicated and fraught matter. On this see David M. Gwynn, *The Eusebians: The Polemic of Athanasius of Alexandria and the Construction of the 'Arian Controversy'* (Oxford: Oxford University Press, 2007). The term "Arianism" serves to capture both what Arius was accused of teaching and how pro-Arian, anti-Nicene strands of thought developed in the century following Nicaea I.

[65 laws]; *Cod. Iust.* 1.5 [22 laws] updates and heavily revises the equivalent *Cod. Theod.* section). One feature of the extreme rhetoric used by bishops against dissidents was the allegation of serious crimes, intended as a form of character assassination. In the 330s, Athanasius of Alexandria refuted one such charge of abduction and murder by producing the alleged victim safe and well (Socrates, *Church History* 1.27–29). In one extreme case in 383, however, a Spanish heretic, Priscillian of Avila, and his followers were found guilty of magic by a non-ecclesiastical court set up by the local emperor in Gaul, Magnus Maximus, and executed, although the consequent uproar among the local bishops ensured that this tactic was not repeated.[32]

JUSTINIAN AND THE CHRISTIANIZING OF ROMAN LAW

Roman law spoke with many voices, reflecting a Roman cultural preference for multi-legalism, which was perpetuated in the diversity of the laws and customs that the empire acquired over many centuries. The aim of Justinian's codification of law between 529 and 534, however, was to restrict the operation of that diversity. Legislative power was to be concentrated in the hands of the emperor; law was to be taught in educational establishments approved by him; and changes to the law could be made only by imperial fiat.

This concentration of power was articulated and justified on Christian grounds. Roman law was itself restructured accordingly. In a clear break with Theodosian precedent, Justinian transposed all the "Christian" titles of Theodosius's Book 16, with a few significant modifications, to the beginning of his Code. This rearrangement was accompanied by other innovations. For example, Theodosius had created a catchall second *titulus* (a subsection with a heading, or title) containing forty-seven enactments on bishops, churches, and clergy. But Justinian separated his twenty-five laws on churches, their property, and their *privilegia* (*Cod. Iust.* 1.2), which related to the law of property, from the fifty-three laws covering bishops, clergy, monks, and ascetics, with their various charitable and personal activities (*Cod. Iust.* 1.3). His most eye-catching innovation was the creation of a separate headed section, or "title" (*titulus*), for *episcopalis audientia*, (*Cod. Iust.* 1.4), containing thirty-four laws on the "law, care and respect due to bishops,": a *titulus* that has no direct parallel in Theodosius.

The re-rendering of Roman law as Christian law reflected the more assertive presence of the emperor as orthodox Christian lawgiver. The *Codex Justinianus* opens with a *titulus* defining and affirming Christian orthodoxy and outlawing the expression of public dissent. In contrast, the corresponding opening title in *Codex Theodosianus* 16 is simply "on the catholic faith" (*de fide catholica*), and the

[32] Edward Iricinschi and Holger M. Zellentin (eds.), *Heresy and Identity in Late Antiquity*, Texts and Studies in Ancient Judaism 19 (Tübingen: Mohr Siebeck, 2008). Henry Chadwick, *Priscillian of Avila: The Occult and the Charismatic in the Early Church* (Oxford: Clarendon Press, 1976).

prohibition of public disputation emerges only later at 16.4. Justinian's elevation of the ban on public disputations of orthodoxy to prime position was a significant structural alteration. Not only was "catholic" orthodoxy affirmed, but its affirmation was conjoined with an upfront ban of public dissent from the official line. Moreover, although Justinian defined orthodoxy with reference to approved authorities, he went several steps further. Out of eight constitutions, the last four – all of which appear unabridged, and at least three of which were in the second but not in the first edition – refer to the orthodoxy sponsored by Justinian himself. The constitutions are combined with denunciations of various heretics. Three are in Greek, but the last (*Cod. Iust.* 1.1.8), "on the catholic faith," is in Latin. It granted to the bishop of Rome, John II (533–35), the unique distinction of authoring an imperial constitution. The text is a letter from John himself, dated 25 March, 534, accompanied by an enclosure detailing Justinian's personal statement of faith (*Cod. Iust.* 1.8.7–24, dated 6 June, 533). John's missive praised the emperor's orthodox understanding of the universal faith (*fides catholica*), since it was based (as the emperor's letter demonstrated) on the teachings of the Apostolic See (*sedes apostolica*) as well as on the doctrines decreed by the church fathers (i.e., by the most respected ancient authorities and by the great councils). This apparent deference to the authority of the Rome as the Apostolic See should not mislead. As Claire Sotinel has observed, while Justinian required the authority of Rome to bolster his position, he did not allow Rome any autonomy in religious policy.[33]

Placed in the last, most authoritative position in the section, Justinian's statement *de fide catholica* was intended to be definitive. By including Rome's endorsement, Justinian protected his own position with the full authority of the Western church; by placing himself last, he superseded anything inconsistent that had gone before; and by providing the full text – departing from the general practice of abridgment featured in the Codes – Justinian rendered this statement of orthodoxy personal and, he would hope, perpetual. Justinian's innovatory arrangement was not, therefore, only about Christianizing the entire contents of the *Codex Justinianus* going back to Hadrian, giving legislation on Christianity pride of place. By reclassifying selected laws from the *tituli* of the first fifteen books of the *Theodosian Code* as "Christian," Justinian also redefined what was now meant by Christian law. His Christian authority, reinforced by the bishop of Rome, no less, reinforced his "rightness" and outlawed dissent. Both legal and religious pluralism were unacceptable. Past legal writing was "corrected," and both the irrelevant and the "wrong" were excluded. The authority to define "right" law would rest with emperors now and in the future.

33 Claire Sotinel, "Emperors and Popes in the Sixth Century: The Western View," in Michael Maas (ed.), *The Cambridge Companion to the Age of Justinian* (Cambridge: Cambridge University Press, 2005), 267–90.

CONCLUSION

Roman law was shaped by the input of many actors and agents, who were engaged in a continuing work of interpretation in multiple contexts. The classical jurists had pride of place as the officially recognized interpreters of statute and custom, but law evolved through interactions among emperors, officials, and interest groups; through judicial decisions and the resolutions of church councils; through alternative methods of dispute settlement; and, more broadly, in response to cultural change. This long and rich legal tradition, with its contending authorities, and the abiding vitality of local cultures, ensured that law and legal decisions were vigorously contested. Christianity itself evolved in the many spaces where Roman law was peripheral or ambiguous. With the formal recognition of Christianity in 313 came assimilation to Roman legal institutions, which enabled Christians to enjoy "corporate" ownership of their assets. But the efforts of Justinian to impose legal uniformity were doomed to fail, not only because they clashed with the diverse cultures of empire, but also because they also denied the variegated legal heritage of Christianity itself.

SOURCES

The entire CIC, consisting of the *Codex, Digest, Institutes,* and *Novels,* was edited by Theodore Mommsen, Paul Krueger, Rudolph Schoell, and Wilhelm Kroll, and eventually published in three volumes (Berlin: Weidmann, 1895). This Latin edition is available, with several other texts, as part of the online *Roman Law Library,* edited by Y. Lassard and A. Koptev.[34] *Cod. Iust.* was edited by Paul Krueger (1877, modified 1914). The Greek and Latin texts with English translation are now available in Bruce W. Frier, *The Codex of Justinian,* 3 vols., based on a translation by F. H. Blume (Cambridge: Cambridge University Press, 2016). An English translation of the *Novels* by David Miller (edited by Peter Sarris) – the first complete translation to be made from the original Greek – is now available from the same publisher (2018). The *Digest* was edited by Theodor Mommsen and Paul Krueger (Berlin: Weidmann, 1868) and translated into English by Alan Watson and others (Philadelphia: University of Pennsylvania Press, 1984).

For an accessible text and translation of Gaius, see William F. Gordon and O. F. Robinson, *The Institutes of Gaius* (Ithaca, NY: Cornell University Press, 1988). For Justinian's *Institutes* (*Inst.*), the edition and commentary in two volumes by J. B. Moyle, 5th edition (Oxford: Clarendon Press, 1913; 1st edition, 1883). See also Justinian's *Institutes,* trans. by Peter Birks and Grant McLeod (Ithaca, NY: Cornell University Press, 1987).

[34] Home page: https://droitromain.univ-grenoble-alpes.fr; CIC: https://droitromain.univ-grenoble-alpes.fr/corpjurciv.htm (both accessed May 16, 2018).

The *Cod. Theod.* was edited by Theodor Mommsen and Paul M. Meyer in 3 vols. (Berlin: Weidmann, 1905); English translation by Clyde Pharr and others (Princeton, NJ: Princeton University Press, 1952). The original sources of *Cod. Theod.* are available in Salvatore Riccobono et al. (eds.), *Fontes Iuris Romani Anteiustiniani* (FIRA), 2nd ed. The second volume (Florence: Barbèra, 1940–1943) has Paulus's *Sententiae* (317–417), the *Fragmenta Vaticana* (463–540), and the *Collatio of Mosaic and Roman Law* (543–89), as well as other fragmentary handbooks. The influential *Lex Romana Visigothorum*, also known as the *Breviarium Alaricanum*, was edited by Gustav F. Haenel (Leipsig, 1848), and reprinted in Aalen (Scientia, 1962).

Text with translation of Eusebius's *Ecclesiastical History* (cited above as *Church History*) is available in the Loeb Classical Library (2 vols.). For translation and commentary of the Life, see Eusebius, *Life of Constantine*, trans. Averil Cameron and Stuart G. Hall (Oxford: Clarendon Press 1999).

FURTHER READING

For a brief guide to Roman law and jurisprudence, see O. F. Robinson, *The Sources of Roman Law: Problems and Methods for Ancient Historians* (London: Routledge, 1997). To understand Roman legal thinking, private law, and litigation, see David Johnston, *Roman Law in Context* (Cambridge: Cambridge University Press, 1999); and Andrew M. Riggsby, *Roman Law and the Legal World of the Romans* (Cambridge: Cambridge University Press, 2010). (The latter, regrettably, lacks footnotes.) W. W. Buckland, *Textbook of Roman Law from Augustus to Justinian*, 3rd edition revised by Peter Stein (Cambridge: Cambridge University Press, 1963), is a weighty guide to Roman law for specialists. On court procedure, see Leanne E. Bablitz, *Actors and Audience in the Roman Courtroom* (London: Routledge, 2007); and for Roman law, the law courts, and Christianity, see Caroline Humfress, *Orthodoxy and the Courts in Late Antiquity* (Oxford: Oxford University Press, 2007). David Johnson (ed.), *The Cambridge Companion to Roman Law* (Cambridge: Cambridge University Press, 2015), contains fairly detailed but accessible guides to many features of Roman law, including legal processes, the cultural and intellectual contexts, and subsequent historical continuities and reception.

On the *Theodosian Code*, see J. Harries and I. Wood (eds.), *The Theodosian Code: Studies in the Imperial Law of Late Antiquity*, 2nd edition (London: Duckworth, 2010); John Matthews, *Laying Down the Law: A Study of the Theodosian Code* (New Haven: Yale University Press, 2000); A. J. B. Sirks, *The Theodosian Code: A Study* (Friedrichsdorf: Éditions Tortuga, 2007); and Tony Honoré, *Law in the Crisis of the Empire, 379–455 AD: The Theodosian Dynasty and Its Quaestors* (Oxford: Oxford University Press, 1998), esp. ch. 6, "Understanding the Theodosian Code" (pp. 123–53).

On the continuation of Roman legal thinking and jurisprudence in the West after the passing of the Western Roman Empire, see Ralph W. Mathisen (ed.), *Law,*

Society and Authority in Late Antiquity (Oxford: Oxford University Press, 2001), especially the chapters by John Matthews and Antti Arjava on the *interpretiones* that were added to the *Lex Romana Visigothorum* (also known misleadingly as the *Breviary*) and appended (according to Arjava) to *Cod. Theod.* itself.

On the *Digest*, in addition to works cited in the notes, see Tony Honoré, *Justinian's Digest: Character and Compilation* (Oxford: Oxford University Press, 2010). On the CIC in general, see Tony Honoré, *Tribonian* (Ithaca, NY: Cornell University Press, 1978). On the jurists in general, see Fritz Schulz, *History of Roman Legal Science* (Oxford: Clarendon Press, 1946), which is dated but still useful. On Ulpian in particular, who was among the most lucid ancient exponents of Roman law, see Tony Honoré, *Ulpian: Pioneer of Human Rights* (Oxford: Oxford University Press, 2002).

For an introduction to Justinian's *Codex* and its reception, see Simon Corcoran, "The Codex of Justinian: The Life of a Text Through 1,500 years," in Blume and Frier (eds.), *The Codex of Justinian* (Cambridge: Cambridge University Press, 2016), xcvii–clxiv.

3

The Law of the Post-Roman Kingdoms

Alexander Callander Murray

This chapter is a profile of law in the Continental post-Roman kingdoms until around 750, with some comments on society, legal administration, and the church. That legal systems existed throughout the period is obvious, but the effort to characterize them in general terms is fraught with difficulty, especially as regards their relation to Roman law. We begin, therefore, with the ways in which legal historians have construed the law of the post-Roman kingdoms.

APPROACHES TO THE FIELD

Broad surveys of European law and institutions usually deal with the post-Roman, successor kingdoms in two ways. If the focus is Roman law and ultimately the legal systems of Modern Europe, the period is seen as a grim interlude of deteriorating civilization before Europe happily regained its direction with the rediscovery of Roman law, especially Justinian's *Digest*, in the era of Irnerius, the famous scholar of Roman law and jurisprudence active during the late eleventh and early twelfth centuries. If the focus is abbreviated to legal and institutional themes in medieval history, the period is presented as an unimportant and primitive prologue to the vigorous, if in fact faltering, work of the Carolingians, followed by the state-building policies of the central Middle Ages – where, again, Irnerius plays a central role. Both approaches move quickly across what is regarded as the bleak terrain of the successor kingdoms to settle in the apparently more verdant pastures of later medieval history. These perversely dramatic narratives obfuscate much, in particular the continuous history of European law from the late Roman Empire, through the kingdoms that succeeded it, and onward to the Medieval and Modern periods.

There have been exceptions to the indifference to the post-Roman period, and they are long-standing. Carl von Savigny (1779–1861), whose name now graces a venerable and prestigious German journal dealing in three *Abteilungen* with Roman, Germanic, and Canon law respectively, devoted two of his six volumes on the history of Roman law in the Middle Ages to the period before Irnerius. These volumes appeared between 1815 and 1831, with the first two in the years 1815 and 1816.[1] They are still rewarding.

Savigny's broad, if still compartmentalized, view of European legal history, however, was not the one that prevailed. The history of German (*deutsch*) law, generally understood to subsume the Germanic (*germanisch*) law of the post-Roman kingdoms, arose as the foundational subject for the history not just of Germany but of the entire West, resting on the rough-hewn legal and political ideas of the barbarians that occupied the Roman provinces. The perceived primitiveness of the period that had discouraged many from treating it seriously was recast here as the vigorous, pregnant beginnings of Western institutions. Such ideas had famous and doughty exponents such as Georg Waitz (1813–1886) and especially Heinrich Brunner (1840–1915) – fine scholars and, again, still worth reading.[2]

This approach produced what can be thought of as the traditional teaching of early-medieval institutions and law, as influential in Romance- and English-language scholarship as in German-language works. The Germanic order was basically seen as having been transferred into the Roman imperial provinces during a distinctive period of migration (*Völkerwanderungszeit*) or invasion – both concepts that, as generalizations, are seriously flawed descriptions of historical processes.[3] Popular institutions and popular sovereignty were supposed to be at the heart of this order. Its original foundation, it was claimed, was visible in the legal sources as the *liberi*, understood as the common freemen, the center point of the political and legal system; and by the time of the settlements in the empire, this order had produced a Germanic form of monarchy, construed as elective but with dynastic elements claiming priority in the selection of kings. The general acceptance of the theory in the English-speaking world is perceptible for instance in the lectures given at Cambridge in the early part of the last century by the noted classicist J. B. Bury (1861–1927) who told his students that while the Germanic state outside the frontiers in late imperial times might have a king or not, in either case "it was virtually a democracy" in which the people were sovereign.[4]

1 Frederick Carl von Savigny, *Geschichte des Römischen Rechts im Mittelalter* (Heidelberg: Mohr/Zimmer, 1815–31). I cite this work by the section numbers of the 2nd edition (1834). I shall also cite the pages for the English translation of vol. 1 (Edinburgh: Black, 1829) where applicable. The journal mentioned is *Zeitschrift der Savigny-Stiftung für Rechtsgeschichte* (ZRG). James Q. Whitman, *The Legacy of Roman Law in the German Romantic Era: Historical Vision and Legal Change* (Princeton: Princeton University Press, 1990), outlines the broad context of Savigny's time. For further information on translations of ancient texts cited in this chapter, see under Sources at the end.

2 Georg Waitz, *Deutsche Verfassungsgeschichte*, 8 vols. (Kiel: Schwers, 1844–78). Heinrich Brunner, *Deutsche Rechtsgeschichte*, 2 vols. (Leipzig: Duncker & Humblot 1887–92); 2nd ed. with Claudius Freiherrn von Schwerin (Leipzig: Duncker & Humblot, 1906–28).

3 Walter A. Goffart, *Barbarian Tides: The Migration Age and the Later Roman Empire* (Philadelphia: University of Pennsylvania Press, 2006).

4 J. B. Bury, *The Invasion of Europe by the Barbarians* (London: Macmillan, 1928; Norton reprint, 1967), 12.

The implications for legal history of this view were fairly straightforward, establishing popular sovereignty not just at the big level of kingship, but also down through a layer of administration to the adjudication of law and justice. The significant number of law codes from the period, sometimes outfitted by modern scholarship with contrived ethnic denominators (see further below), suggested the ready division of the legal components of the successor kingdoms into the binary components of Germanic and Roman law. The latter was thought to have been reduced to an ancillary role, focused mainly on the church and secondary populations, and a sometime, and often delayed, influence on the prevailing forms of essentially Germanic custom.

In the heyday of this approach, dissenters were few and far between.[5] The most famous challenge to the Germanic focus of general history was mounted by the French historian Fustel de Coulanges (1830–1889). Beginning as a classicist, he eventually became an historian of the Merovingian monarchy and an advocate of Roman continuity in the institutions of the incipient French kingdom.[6] But neither he, nor those of like mind, could prevail in their day against the Germanic interpretation of medieval institutions.

Even in fairly recent times, English-language scholars have still felt obliged to decry the traditional interpretation of medieval institutions in its general form and especially its notions about the roots of early-medieval kingship, which today seem more plausibly traceable to Christian and imperial ideas of authority.[7] But before English-language criticisms took hold, politically driven ideas arose in German-language scholarship that effectively inverted how the Germanic order of the successor kingdoms was understood. A new school, or more broadly approach, to European history eventually came to prevail among German scholars from the 1930s through the decades following the Second World War. Though in the post-war period, it often presented itself more cautiously as focused narrowly on German lands, it still, like the view it replaced, argued for a fundamental continuity from the late Roman Iron Age through the Middle Ages into later periods of German history in an attempt to define the eternal verities of German history and its influence on the

5 Hector Munro Chadwick (1870–1947) is a distinctive example worth noting for pre-WWI Britain. Roughly at the time Bury was giving his lectures, Chadwick was developing a much harder view of Germanic (and Celtic) society in a trilogy of works: *Studies on Anglo-Saxon Institutions* (Cambridge: University Press, 1905); *The Origin of the English Nation* (Cambridge: University Press, 1907); and *The Heroic Age* (Cambridge: University Press, 1912). Although he worked along Germanist tracks, he anticipated more recent trends of social and political analysis (see Murray, "Wenskus on Ethnogenesis," 53, 54, 58, 67, as cited in n. 8 below).

6 N. D. Fustel de Coulanges, *Histoire des Institutions Politiques de l'Ancienne France*, 1st ed. (Paris, 1875). More volumes followed until his death in 1889. The standard edition is in 6 vols., edited in part by Camille Jullian (Paris: Hachette, 1900–1914). Later editions followed.

7 P. Grierson, "Election and Inheritance in Early Germanic Kingship, " *The Cambridge Historical Journal* 7.1 (1941): 1–22. Joseph Canning, *A History of Medieval Political Thought 300–1450* (London: Routledge, 1996). P. D. King, "The Barbarian Kingdoms," in J. H. Burns (ed.), *The Cambridge History of Medieval Political Thought c. 350–1450* (Cambridge: Cambridge University Press, 1998), 123–54.

West. This claim of Germanic continuity meant by necessity that the new approach had to drive its interpretation, which was often based on questionable readings of Carolingian and post-Carolingian conditions, at least back to Merovingian Gaul and beyond that to imperial texts describing the peoples to the east of the Rhine and their relations with Rome.

Called at the time the new constitutional history and, once the bloom was off the rose, just the lordship theory, this new approach delighted – sometimes for clearly modern ideological reasons – in turning the old traditional interpretation on its head. The heart of the Germanic order, now transplanted into the Roman provinces, was supposedly not popular or democratic institutions but rather noble lordships of an ancient Germanic aristocracy whose powers derived originally from the domestic authority of the houselord. Lordships ruled their dependents on the basis of autogenous rights that existed independent of the monarchy. The class of common freemen (*liberi*) of the old literature, formerly presumed to be the very foundation of law and political life, was now rechristened the "king's free." Their freedom was thought to have been conditional, linked to the monarchy, and derivative because it supposedly sprang from military service and settlement on royal land. The non-noble element in society was now to be envisioned as a servile appendage of monarchy and nobility. What the old literature had always seen as public law and public administration was reinterpreted as the private law arrangements of the monarchy for its dependents – though it was admitted that notions of a public sphere might still have relevance for southern, apparently Roman, areas of the Frankish kingdom. What had been freedom, with all its political implications in the old teaching for law and political authority, now became a dependent condition restricted to royal service, thereby overturning decades upon decades of the reading of major legal sources of early medieval and, especially, Merovingian history. The old-style history was now deemed, pointedly, to be the result simply of the wishful thinking of the nineteenth-century bourgeoisie.[8] As part of the new history's own wishful thinking, its proponents tossed aside conventional institutions and overlaid their seemingly realistic, if grim, reading of early society with the purportedly defining (though indemonstrable) irrational forces of sacrality and charisma. The former, thought to characterize monarchy, was supposed to be supported by widespread ideas of the divine descent of kings; the latter, a little less potent, was believed to be an attribute of nobility.[9]

What were the implications for law in this new approach to institutional history? The new history did make occasional use of the codifications to document its odd

8 Alexander C. Murray, "Reinhard Wenskus on 'Ethnogenesis,' Ethnicity, and the Origin of the Franks," in A. Gillett (ed.), *On Barbarian Identity: Critical Approaches to Ethnicity in the Early Middle Ages*, Studies in the Early Middle Ages 4 (Turnhout: Brepols, 2002), 39–68, at 53–54.

9 The case, and the sources, for a Merovingian sacral kingship – the only case still argued – is critiqued by Alexander C. Murray, "*Post vocantur Merohingii*: Fredegar, Merovech, and 'Sacral Kingship'," in *After Rome's Fall: Narrators and Sources of Early Medieval History, Essays Presented to Walter Goffart* (Toronto: University of Toronto Press, 1998), 121–52.

idea that the *liberi* were actually the "king's free," a completely modern construct, or to search for the existence of an allegedly ancient Germanic aristocracy that must have imprinted itself, it was believed, on Gallic sources. This history was also more inclined than the traditional teaching to recognize the role of Roman institutions, the parade piece here being the *centena* or hundred as a subdivision of the county in Merovingian Gaul.[10] But here it took hold of an old motif of traditional German history: It relied on the argument that widespread Roman forms were adaptations to what was essentially Germanic content. Despite occasionally employing legal sources for its own ends, the lordship theory was fundamentally incapable of treating law seriously as a subject central to the character and development of society. Law was an accessory to power and privilege and supposedly ancient thinking, which rested on ideas intangible, irrational, even transcendent, divorced from the irrelevant and mundane process of law, legal institutions, and their administration in courts of law.

There is a comment that needs to be made here in passing with regard to the long, patently German struggle to define the nature of early society. The efforts of the old and the new history, quite variable in their manifestations and confident in their expression, were part of a psychological struggle to define German identity, not just in itself but also, given its recurring assertiveness, in its placement at the center of Europe and European history. The struggle was also linked at its various stages with contemporary politics. Why so much of this self-interested self-reflection was taken on so earnestly by other Western scholarly communities is a question that must be postponed to another time.

The "aristocratic turn," prominent in lordship theory, was not limited in twentieth-century historiography to German-speaking lands, but as outlined above this new history was originally a product of a distinctively German right-wing milieu, although some of the ideas that survived the decline of this approach have found a congenial home on the political left. The lordship theory's demotion of law as the key to popular sovereignty and societal forms in particular has contributed to an acceleration of the disparagement of law as an historical source. Normative forms like law codes are presently a subject of suspicion and often blithely sold short in comparison to documentary sources such as charters, though all source types take special handling and skeptical evaluation when used to suggest social reality.[11] There is no reason today, it seems, to think that legal history, since its dislodgment, will quickly regain its former position in the exposition of the general history of the early Middle Ages – and perhaps that is not entirely a bad thing. In any case, historians of

10 The literature with a critique is in Alexander C. Murray, "From Roman to Frankish Gaul: *Centenarii* and *Centenae* in the Administration of the Merovingian Kingdom," *Traditio* 44 (1988): 59–100.

11 Compare Alexander C. Murray's review of W. Davies and P. Fouracre (eds.), *Property and Power in the Early Middle Ages* (Cambridge: Cambridge University Press, 1995), in the *English Historical Review* 112: 1235–36. And see also below n. 47 for a work that shows how efforts to extract social and political reality from certain kinds of judicial charters (*placita*) can go rather off the rails without an understanding of legal form and procedure.

law will continue to explore the legal foundations of the period and to assert the role of law and legal institutions in the development of European history. Master theories marginalize, which after all is their purpose and nature, and in the process they co-opt the legal evidence wherever they can and dismiss it when they have to. But legal scholars, and those with the same interest who recognize another remit, should persevere with their own agendas.

While lordship theory was gripping and reconfiguring German-language scholarship, the German scholar Ernst Levy (1881–1968), was developing a new approach to the law of the late empire and the Western successor kingdoms. He carried out this work far from the centers of Roman and Germanic legal history. As a German Jew, Levy had been caught up in the Nuremberg laws of 1935 and forced to retire from his university at the age of fifty-four, whereupon he moved to the United States and took up a position at the University of Washington in Seattle. There, he wrote in English on the *Sentences* of the classical jurist Paulus and on the Roman law of property, and in German on the law of obligations in Western Roman sources. He also wrote English-language articles about the nature and course of his research.[12] This body of work was organized around the idea of "Roman vulgar law" as a defining concept of Western law between the time of the classical jurists and Justinian's codification and beyond. A recent, patronizing critic of Levy has suggested that the "scientific loneliness of America" freed him to erect his edifice of law to "an astonished public."[13]

The idea of Roman vulgar law was no product of an American sojourn, as indeed his critics, including the last mentioned one in a less polemical mood, recognize. It began elsewhere and in fact has never particularly resonated in English-language scholarship. Where its public was, and where it has had traction, was in Germany. Levy was a thorough product of a German legal education, which included, as it had for Savigny, not just Romanist but Germanist teaching on law – indeed Levy seems often to have a disconcerting sense of just what constitutes Germanic law in our sources. And Levy did not come up with the idea of Roman vulgar law. It arose in 1880 with an (Austrian) Germanist, Heinrich Brunner (already mentioned). He identified it as the Roman law of practice in the Western provinces and successor states that often varied within itself and fell short of classical juristic standards because of local conditions or even because of the influence of geographically

[12] See, e.g., Levy's "Reflections on the First 'Reception' of Roman Law in Germanic States," *American Historical Review* 48 (1942): 20–29; "Vulgarization of Roman Law in the Early Middle Ages," *Mediaevalia et Humanistica* 1 (1943): 14–40; *West Roman Vulgar Law: The Law of Property* (Philadelphia: American Philosophical Society, 1951); *Weströmisches Vulgarrecht: Das Obligationenrecht* (Weimar: Böhlaus, 1956). Various works by Levy are collected in W. Kunkel and M. Kaser (eds.) *Ernst Levy Gesammelte Schriften* (Cologne: Böhlau, 1963).

[13] Detlef Liebs, "Roman Vulgar Law in Late Antiquity," in Boudewijn Sirks (ed.), *Aspects of Law in Late Antiquity: Dedicated to A.M. Honoré* (Oxford: All Souls College, 2008), 35–53, at 44. Despite questionable judgments about some of Levy's contemporaries, Liebs provides valuable criticisms on the problem of determining what is vulgar and what is not. He accepts the term in specific, limited, contexts. His own term "Germanic Roman law" requires a separate critique, only some of which can be found here.

contiguous "tribal" (i.e., Germanic) law. Brunner also felt he had to gloss his general depiction of this "continuation of Roman law" with the phrase "or if one wishes, degeneration of the pure Roman law."[14] This particular perception, slightly awkward but retained by Levy, remains a problem in the exposition of the concept.

There was an analogy intended by use of the term "vulgar." Brunner saw it as a parallel to the concept of "vulgar Latin," the term for everyday Latin speech as opposed to literary Latin. He noted in passing that, alongside the distinctive coloring of legal and documentary language in Western sources (often expressed in what his readers would have thought of as vulgar Latin), there also existed a comparable vulgar law. (Both vulgar Latin and vulgar law, the curious might note, are concepts that have not always been limited to the late Empire and successor kingdoms – by many views, they were always in existence, no matter the prevailing high culture.) The point hardly escaped Brunner that it was vulgar, not classical, Latin that led to Romance.

The concept of vulgar law was not left in hiatus after Brunner. It was acknowledged by other European scholars, and Ludwig Mitteis (1859–1921), another Austrian, accepted it in a famous study (1891) of the eastern Roman provinces, treating it as distinct but complementary to a broader category of peregrine/indigenous law (*Volksrecht*).[15] But, as even his critics acknowledge, it was Levy who established the concept in the basic discourse of West Roman legal studies, and indeed of Constantinian and later imperial law.

What did Levy say? He basically took Brunner's concept of a simplified, and thus divergent, often common-sense Roman law and argued it out in technical detail in West Roman sources. Although varied influences on the development were possible, including non-Roman thought, the principal force driving the process was, in his view, a perpetual quest for simplification and popularization that from the late third century was no longer held in check by, what he understood to be, a creative and orderly jurisprudence. In casting the subject in this way, Levy was not always consistent. He said, for instance, that he used the term "vulgar" to replace the negative term "post-classical," commonly used to characterize the law between the classical period and Justinian, yet at the core of his thinking were his own values as a classicist and jurist. He could be gushing in his praise of classical law, and he repeatedly saw departure from it as a process of the disintegration of superior modes of traditional legal thinking. The departure was vulgar law.

Why is Levy's work important? Apart from the analysis of particular provisions in the sources, there were two observations that are of lasting importance for those studying the laws of the new kingdoms in the Western provinces. The first – and

14 Heinrich Brunner, *Zur Rechtsgeschicht der Römischen und Germanischen Urkunde* (Berlin, 1880; reprint Aalen: Scientia, 1961), 113. Cf. *Deutsche Rechtsgeschichte* 1:255 in the1887 edition, or 1:378 in the 1906 edition.

15 Ludwig Mitteis, *Reichsrecht und Volksrecht in den östlichen Provinzen des römischen Kaiserreichs* (Leipzig: Teubner 1891).

obviously correct at his time and beyond – was that modern handbooks and monographs on Roman law tended to understand it in terms of two distinct periods: the classical law of the Republic and the jurists of the early Empire, on one hand, and the codification efforts of Justinian (especially the *Digest*) on the other. These two perspectives were usually the points in the literature on which a contradistinction was made between Roman law and so-called Germanic law of the new kingdoms. This distinction, Levy rightly said, was based on a fallacy. The law that the legislators, teachers, notaries, and the general population knew in the late empire was pre-Justinianic and thus possibly classical, but also post-classical, or in Levy's terms vulgar, the law of the intervening period. This was the law that constituted what he called, rather affectedly, the "first reception" of Roman law among the Germans, even though it happened in the Roman provinces – and about a millennium before such a reception was commonly deemed to have occurred in Germany.

Levy's second enduring observation is already implied by the first, namely, that supposedly Germanic laws of the successor kingdoms were affected by the legal culture of the provincials, and also, perhaps less obviously, that the Roman vulgar law of the provinces was in turn influenced by the customary practices of the new settlers, a point Brunner had earlier acknowledged. Wolfgang Kunkel, a student of Levy, and a notable scholar in his own right, caught the implication of Levy's work when he claimed, not completely inaccurately but a little precipitously, that the notions that underlay the codifications of the new kingdoms, even the codes designed for their Germanic populations, were Roman in origin; and noted, more modestly and importantly, that as a result of Levy's work the "question of Roman influence on the Germanic law of the early Middle Ages must now be posed anew."[16]

Work on both his points, haltingly under way at the time he wrote and continuing thereafter, has even now hardly reached a point where broad generalizations are likely to garner consensus, though some historians have proceeded to suggest that notions of vulgar law or, a variant conception, provincial law, underlie what moderns regard as the codes of Germanic law in the successor kingdoms.[17] Whether this

16 Wolfgang Kunkel, *An Introduction to Roman Legal and Constitutional History*, trans. J. M. Kelly (Oxford: Clarendon Press, 1966), 140. The importance of Levy's ideas for the West gained early, though anything but universal, recognition. Franz Wieacker used the term "vulgar law" rather broadly and indefinitely at the beginning of his *Privatrechtsgeschiichte der Neuzeit* (1st ed. 1952, 2nd ed. 1967), English translation, *A History of Private Law in Europe: With Particular Reference to Germany*, translated by Tony Weir (New York: Clarendon Press, 1995), 13–25. Better, more specialized, and more focused are J. Gaudemet, "Survivances Romaines dans le droit de la monarchie Franques du Vème au Xème siecle," *Tijdschrift voor Rechtsgeschiedenis* 23 (1955): 149–206; and Hermann Nehlsen, *Skavenrecht zwischen Antike und Mittelalter*, Göttinger Studien zur Rechtsgeschichte 7 (Göttingen: Musterschmidt, 1972) – both still important works. In English, cf. Alexander C. Murray, *Germanic Kinship Structure: Studies in Law and Society in Antiquity and the Early Middle Ages*, Studies and Texts 65 (Toronto: Pontifical Institute of Medieval Studies, 1983), 116–18, 179, recognizing Levy's importance but not employing his method; and see 117 for a broad characterization of the contents of the codes.

17 One assumes the concept of vulgar law is influential in Ian N. Wood, "Disputes in Late Fifth- and Sixth-Century Gaul: Some Problems," *The Settlement of Disputes* (Cambridge: Cambridge University Press, 1986), 7–22, though Levy's name is consigned to a bare mention in the glossary.

is true requires more detailed research than has yet been undertaken and a revision of terminology. The details are in fact in the process of accumulation but will take time. The picture that emerges will surely differ from the old one, but its precise profile is yet to reveal itself.

The effect of post-classical law on so-called barbarian laws is just one aspect of Levy's work. This particular focus has been a subject of little interest to most Romanists who have tended to direct criticisms at those ideas of his more pertinent to historians of Roman jurisprudence itself. He suggested for example that vulgar law from the time of Constantine (the magnet since antiquity for claims of major changes in Roman institutions) entered into imperial legislation as a major force in its configuration. This premise, which has generated significant criticism, is part of a larger issue on the influences, eastern and peregrine, shaping the production of imperial law that are beyond this exposition. So too is the extent to which changing rhetorical conventions in both a low style and an excessively high (and inexact) style have disguised the basic continuity of classical notions of law. Central also to Levy's thinking was the "interpolation problem": the view that the texts that were taken up by Justinian's commission to compose the *Digest* had already been emended by authors of the intervening period, even before the commission did its own smoothing to conform with the juristic thinking of Justinian's time. Again, this problem, important for understanding Levy's method as a whole, is outside the present remit.

For those focused on post-classical and "barbarian law," there still remains the question of the utility of the term "vulgar" to mark out the legal character of the period to which it is applied. Despite the value of Levy's work both in general and in detail, much depends on our conceptualization of both Roman law in a broad sense and its supposed counterpart and rival in the successor kingdoms, namely what is generally called Germanic law. It is not at all that clear how the term "vulgar" provides a key or tells us something generally significant about Roman law, its teaching, and its influence in the West. Perhaps these points will be clearer if we discuss the terminology that is commonly used to discuss the law of the period.

TALKING ABOUT LAW IN THE SUCCESSOR KINGDOMS

The vocabulary of this subject may seem obvious, and so it appears to general histories, especially those of law. But it is not. And the terms that are in use, especially "Roman law" and "Germanic law," contain traps, misdirections, and clichés.

P. S. Barnwell, "Emperors Jurists and Kings: Law and Custom in the Late Roman and Early Medieval West," *Past and Present* 168 (2000): 6–29, employs mainly the concepts of provincial law and custom, though antecedent debt to Levy, while obscured, seems clear. Considerable use of modal verbs, or their equivalents, tends to be used in broad attempts such as these. Guy Halsall, *Barbarian Migrations and the Roman West* (Cambridge: Cambridge University Press, 2007), 376–568 (462–66 deals forthrightly in vulgar law, but the tentative nature of the subject is still apparent).

Roman Law

As Levy's criticism made clear, the general literature on this subject has tended to suppose a uniform Roman law, basically classical, unless recourse is had to Justinian, and then generally invoking approvingly his classicizing tendencies. Roman law was much more than that, and if one has doubts, not only the codifications of the successor kingdoms but also the everyday documents of their cities should be consulted, as well as everyday texts from the eastern parts in the late imperial and Byzantine periods.

Moreover, not always appreciated are the social and cultural evolution and even technological changes that overlie the ancient law of Rome. The originally archaic law, performative and oral in its expression, was for a long time vigorously maintained by the jurists and cleverly manipulated and modified by the law of the *praetor*, called the *ius honorarium*. But time does pass, and even clever tricks have to give way to new political, ethnic, and technical developments. It is hard, for instance, to overrate the role writing played over time (a long time) in reconfiguring the formal expression of classical law. Some formal terms, living on in new contexts in the overwhelmingly written and sometimes oddly conservative legal culture of the early Middle Ages, are often taken as signs of that cliché of scholarship on Late Antiquity, degeneration, whereas the language has just been acclimatized, adapted, and subsumed to the new conventions of written instruments; the genuine invocation of the ancient line of Roman legislation and practice has generally at some point been discarded. Shocked expectation of anything else is misplaced.

Another example of the inevitable and hardly to be lamented historical processes working upon Roman law can be found in procedure in the late Empire where the two-stage formulary procedure involving first a magistrate and then a private judge gave way to the originally extraordinary (*extra ordinem*) procedure of *cognitio*, where the entire proceedings were handled by a single judge (usually an imperial official or delegate) and his tribunal. *Cognitio* and its ready adaptation of writing in all phases of procedure were two of the many late developments that stamped themselves upon the law of the successor kingdoms.

One peculiar characteristic of the study of classical Roman law as a juristic enterprise has, I think, rather misled scholars of the early Middle Ages. To the ancient jurists, and indeed to the modern scholars who study them, their subject has been largely private law. Even given the fairly extensive dimension of Roman private law, which included the delicts of the law of obligations, much was left out of consideration – public law, criminal law (in a public not delictual sense), and the wide range of administrative practices, sometimes coercive, sanctioned by the State, but likely nevertheless to be contentious among those who had to put up with them. Scholars of the late Empire are naturally well aware of these areas, but legal scholars of the early medieval kingdoms, taking their cues from the Romanist focus on private law, have often cast a rather narrow gaze upon their sources; modern Roman legal handbooks here are generally of limited use as a point of comparison. The implications of this lapse will be considered below with respect to the administrative laws of the Merovingian kings.

Ancient Roman law thus is a broad subject covering the conventional areas of private, public, criminal, and administrative law, and extending for over a millennium from the Twelve Tables to Justinian. Its practice and application in the last centuries of the Western Empire and the East until at least the time of Justinian would seem to be the focus upon which scholars of the post-Roman kingdoms should concentrate, though an understanding of classical institutions will add depth and perspective to our grasp of legal culture and practice.

This part of the discussion was prefaced with the question of whether the term "vulgar law" illuminates this period. The pejorative implications of the term – and here I speak as an historian – are I think inherent if not in the term itself, at least in its definition, and are regrettable. Moreover, it hardly describes all Roman law of the age and for that reason its use should be limited (I avoid the question whether it influences imperial legislation). The concept has also had a checkered history and is sometimes interpreted inconsistently, sometimes in reference to style, sometimes to content; its detection in the sources is often controversial. The term has its uses (following Brunner and Levy's definition) but the concept hardly captures a period or some hidden stratum of provincial law. The sources are there to be read for the imperial period and its successor states and they cover far more than the focus on classical-style juristic literature ever envisaged. Vulgar law should be left by the various types of historians of the post-Roman kingdoms as a term for Romanists to figure out, one day. It is a term that originated in, and applies to, modern juristic thinking about Roman law. The term is not without its uses, but I would endorse, as a general approach to the period, the view expressed at the outset of this volume by Jill Harries that "Roman law spoke with many voices." Each of these has to be distinguished in its own terms and examined in its own right.

Germanic Law

The term "Germanic law" is the binary opposed to "Roman law," in the usage of the specialist literature and in standard histories of Western law and institutions dealing with the early Middle Ages. Often resembling ideal types, the terms in conjunction are supposed to sum up the legal content of the age. As ideal types they are often used to supply elements deemed to be missing from texts and social circumstances.

To generation upon generation of scholars and readers of historical literature, "Germanic" has seemed like a plain, self-evident, and indisputable term meant to reify the obvious. The term is not so obvious, and it is loaded.[18] But even the severest misgivings about its usage have not yet dispelled its prevalence as an essential part of

[18] Cf. Walter Goffart, *Barbarian Tides*, esp. 4–6 (cited previously).

conceptualizing the field. Readers may have noticed that up to this point I have generally used it. That is because it is impossible to deal with historiography without the term. It is a standard and ubiquitous feature of the discourse and not really avoidable when such is the subject under examination. I will continue to use it as an historiographic term, and I will try where possible not to put quotation marks around it. But voice is important for readers and authors to remember and distinguish. As unavoidable as the term is in retrospective contexts, it is nevertheless in present circumstances misleading and usually inaccurate.

The origins of the term are ancient and go back to Caesar's "discovery" of the *Germani* in his wars in Gaul. Whatever the original context of the term *Germani*, which is debated, the Romans used it (and its adjectival form, Germanic) in a generic fashion to apply to a variety of peoples with their own separate ethnic identifiers; the counterpart geographical form *Germania* was applied to vast territories beyond the Rhine and Danube, as well as to two provinces on the left bank of the Rhine. *Germani*, and Germanic were in this usage exonymic; they did not reflect the self-consciousness of their subjects but were abstract classifications of ancient ethnography, whose inner meanings in particular instances were generally opaque. The problem is not the ancient terms (they are what they are) but their modern interpretation and role in historical discourse. I pass over the erroneous penchant for assimilating the terms to modern Germans (*Deutsche*) and Germany (*Deutschland*) – see for example the genre *Deutsche Rechtsgeschichte*, which generally starts with the ancient and Merovingian sources. The now common scholarly acknowledgment that "Germanic" does not equal "deutsch," however, only deals with half the difficulty. The problem for legal history is the following. In modern scholarship Germanic has become, on one hand, a linguistic term for a group of related languages; the beginnings of this classification go back to the Carolingian period. In modern linguistics, the Germanic group constitutes a branch of the Indo-European family of languages – a classification that is not about to change soon. There would be no problem if the term were used in a generic sense only for this related family of languages (which includes English) and even, formally, the speakers of them if the context is linguistic. The difficulty that compromises such a linguistic generalization has arisen because scholars have long assumed – confounding the independent variables of social existence and employing an inflated sense of the power of philology – that behind the resemblances in speech that justify the notion of a Germanic family of languages, there once existed a common culture, a common approach to life, a common body of legal ideas, and even, in some versions, a common racial substrate. And it is not quite right to think of this culture as only existing in an indefinite and localized distant past; for its main traits were generally assumed to be an immutable aspect of language and the culture it was thought to support, stretching over time and space.

"Germanic" thus became a term to describe an abstract, coherent, alternative world to that of the Roman Empire. Indeed, the encounter of the "two worlds" is still a common metaphor and dramatic device for picturing the rise of the post-Roman kingdoms. In a legal context, this was conceived to mean, on one hand, a Roman legal tradition, written, urbane, and sophisticated, if (in common renditions of the view) enervated or degenerate by the time of the late empire (compare vulgar law) – and, on the other hand, a Germanic one, rural, primitive in one way or another, and sharing across the various peoples who established regimes in the Roman provinces a common heritage of legal traits marked by orality, simplicity, and crude energy. This concatenation of dubious tropes forms the basis of the perspectives outlined in the opening paragraph of this chapter. In one configuration or another, with deletions when the times deemed them inappropriate, it has passed easily from one historical school to another or to those of no particular historical school. It has been assumed by those searching for primitive democratic institutions, as well as by those discovering a putative Germanic order based on aristocratic houses; and it is taken for granted by traditionalists convinced of the fall of civilization with the end of Roman power, and by those suspicious of the capacity of early medieval states to organize society at all by means of institutions and directed, literate, administrations.

The misconceptions can pile up other terms thought to be suitable. For instance, part of this scholarly vocabulary of Germanic law is the frequent use of the modifier "tribal" to characterize the groups creating new kingdoms in the provinces. It is meant to establish the primitive character of their legal institutions. Its noun, tribe, is, like all such terms in social science, contested. I will not pretend to disentangle the viewpoints here (nor to touch the apparently German equivalent *Stamm* and its derivatives). It can be said that its use in the literature dealing with early Europe, and common enough in other literature, means societies organized by descent groups, that is to say clans (unilineal usually, but with room by modern lights for cognatic varieties). It has served as a central element in evolutionary paradigms of human development on a global level. "Tribal" is meant to suggest pre-state kinship-based forms of social organization with conservative, long-standing social practices. Though the clan has, until recently, been a common element in traditional accounts of early European and Germanic society (and still in general and reference sources where its ghost hangs on), there is, nevertheless, no evidence at all that the peoples who occupied the Roman provinces were ever organized along those lines. Indeed, the so-called Germanic laws rather show they were not.[19] Invented "tribes" and clans are just another way to suggest a grand encounter between a primitive Germanic law and a sophisticated Roman law in the Western provinces.

To speak of "tribes" and ethnic groups inevitably means touching on the makeup of the peoples (led by kings) who supplanted Roman power in the provinces and whose ethnic names grace the codes and legislation in modern collections of early European law. Traditional literature that speaks of "tribal law" and "Germanic law" tends to presuppose homogeneous groups with deep traditional roots, going back

[19] Alexander C. Murray, *Kinship Structure*, cited earlier.

great temporal and geographical distances to imaginary times and lands far away. There is no reason to see these peoples that way. There is a long and respected, but until recently not dominant, tradition in Western historical scholarship of seeing them as composed of various, disparate, and fragmented groups, united under kings in the times of their encounter with Rome. The self-styled Vienna school has made hay on this perception, arguing with reason for the artificial, that is political, character of Western barbarian ethnic groups; with much less reason it has relocated distant continuity (still a desideratum in its view) to the realms of myth, genealogy, and the so-called *Traditionskern*, often translated as "nucleus of tradition." This was first conceived of as the core of nobles around the king and then slyly morphed into merely enduring cultural attributes of myth and genealogy.[20]

While the origins of the laws bearing the monikers of barbarian peoples have still to be worked out in a general way based on detailed understanding of their contents, it is clear at this point that the concept Germanic is a thoroughly inapt description. Even the linguistic criterion fails. The Continental sources are all in Latin (with occasional Germanic terms, but relying on a common Roman law vocabulary, some of it technical); the insular Anglo-Saxon laws in the vernacular lie outside the scope of the present discussion, though they tend to imitate their Continental models. The philological despair caused Germanists by the Latinity of the Continental sources has not prevented linguists (nor should it have) from ransacking the sources for traces of Germanic terms and speech. At least to begin with, the societies for whom the laws were intended were in various ways bilingual. But the pickings for Germanists are disappointing. Even a set of Frankish glosses attached at some point to the (Latin) Merovingian code *Lex Salica*, and apparently providing the forensic terms of the Frankish speaking population of north-Western Gaul, were badly understood by later scribes; in what is probably the second oldest manuscript of the law, the scribe famously commented that he was omitting the glosses he found in his exemplar because they were Greek. (He might be forgiven, for the common view by his time was that the Franks were in origin Trojans.)

How, then, should we characterize these laws closely connected with the settlements in the empire (or later reflecting the hegemonic kingdom of the Gallic Merovingian kings)? In a formal sense, the answer is fairly simple. There are ready terms, based on the regimes under which the codes were produced: Gothic (in two varieties), Burgundian, Frankish, Alamannian, Bavarian, and Lombard – and so on under Frankish hegemony beyond the area and the time-period dealt with here. From another perspective, some of the laws can be called Roman because they draw explicitly on late Roman collections and seem directed at provincial populations though not necessarily exclusively so. Such terms are descriptive, do not prejudge the source of particular laws, and limit their scope to historical conditions, even if these are not always well understood. The terms may seem a little awkward, for they

[20] Alexander C. Murray, "Reinhard Wenskus on 'Ethnogenesis,'" cited earlier.

have to do multiple duties referring to peoples, kingdoms, and the distinctive legal practices of the respective communities (whose ethnic names defined an ever-changing reality), but that is scarcely a hardship, and no different than Germanic as a term. Particular usages can always be made obvious. But even narrow legal and ethnic qualifications can be more complex than they first seem, though hardly requiring head scratching. The *Edict of Theoderic* was Gothic because such was the ethnicity of the king who issued it, and it applied to the Goths of Italy. Seen from a slightly different angle it was also Roman, since it applied to both the Goths *and* the Romans, and it was issued by a king presiding over a Roman administration in the name of a Byzantine (Roman) emperor. Its content happens to be Roman law. Even if the term be generously interpreted, the *Edict of Theoderic* was never Germanic.

LAW CODES

What are the sources for the study of law in this period? What is their general character? The sources for law in the broad sense in the successor kingdoms cover a range of source-types that is extensive, though the depth of the evidence they contain has often barely been plumbed. Much of the attention of modern scholarship on European law has been directed at legal collections, generally categorized as "codes" and usually defined by various (often retrospective) ethnic modifiers. We can begin with the codes – without attempting a fancy definition of the term. They have played an artificially large, even an exclusive, role in evaluations of the period and its position in legal history.

Accompanying these codes are scholarly terms for them that imply more than they should. The Latin term *leges barbarorum* ("laws of the barbarians"), which we owe to the humanists, is still popular in English-language scholarship. Whether they are all the product of royal legislation – a common assumption – is an unresolved question. The German terms *Volksrechte* and *Stammesrechte* are considered in much of German scholarship to be far superior to *leges barbarorum*; the English terms "national laws" (or "folk laws") and "tribal laws," respectively, are roughly equivalent.[21] The term "custom," which has an ethnic implication even without a modifier, is another common and fair equivalent of the German terms. Such terms seem to exclude Roman-law collections of the period, although apart from the *Breviary of Alaric* (a version of the *Theodosian Code*) and a similar Burgundian collection (discussed below), there has historically been no agreement as to which collections should fall under the broad designation of "Roman." All are nevertheless part of what constitutes the law codes of the post-Roman kingdoms.

[21] *Volksrechte* in current speech seems to refer to "popular" or citizens' rights, but this use is distinct from its meaning in historiography.

The laws in Continental codifications made before 750 can be listed in a variety of ways, depending on the pedagogical point the list is intended to achieve. I have chosen to classify the codes in two broad geographical groups: those of the southern kingdoms on one hand and those of the northern, Frankish-dominated territories on the other. At least to begin with, I give the conventional names of the codes according to the designation of their modern editions (mainly MGH), though readers will soon learn of the artificiality of many of these titles. Running the risk of inconsistency, I have nevertheless tended for historiographical and mnemonic purposes to use these modern Latin titles as the basis of an abbreviation, appearing in parentheses.

The Southern Codes

Visigothic Kingdom (418–711):

1) *Codex Euricianus* (CE), c. 476. Gallic Visigothic kingdom and beyond. The CE is the earliest of the codes and the name attributing it to King Euric (d. 484) is modern, though probably accurate enough in its way. The text gives no author or issuer because it is fragmentary. We are lucky to know of its existence, for it survives in a palimpsest, a text effaced and written over; only parts of it can be deciphered, and barely clauses 276–336 leave any traces. The code, which was substantial, looks as if it were intended for the Visigoths, but that does not exclude its general provisions having a wider application. It was a significant work, but its remnants have not elicited unanimity on the quality of its legislation, valuations ranging from very high to mediocre (much depends here on how one thinks law should be presented). It is by no stretch of the imagination *Stammesrecht*. Its Roman character in recent times is largely agreed upon. What is interesting is that the code seems to emend earlier written Gothic law that was essentially Roman, but now takes it in a direction that was more in tune with the concerns of the time in which it was issued.[22] It had influence on Burgundian law (item 5, below) and particularly on the, apparently, much later *Lex Baiuvariorum* (item 12, below), some of whose provisions have been used in reconstructing the original Visigothic text. A much greater general influence on subsequent Western laws can rightly be suspected, but the fragmentary nature of CE makes this likelihood hard to demonstrate.

2) *Lex Romana Visigothorum* (LRV), c. 506. Again, this is a modern name, "Roman Law of the Visigoths," and supposed to contrast its contents with the putative Gothic code of Euric. The name intended at the time is not clear. The code was issued as an edict (*auctoritas*) by King Alaric II and calls itself at one point *Liber legum*, "Book of Laws." Another common modern name for the LRV (since the sixteenth century) is

[22] Murray, *Kinship Structure*, 236 with n. 3. See further 238–41 for CE's temporary influence on the Roman-based inheritance elements of the *Lex Burgundionum*.

the Breviary of Alaric (*Breviarium Alarici*). It contains both legislation and juristic literature, namely: selected titles from all sixteen books of the *Codex Theodosianus* (these laws are the ones in the Mommsen edition and the Clyde Pharr translation that have *interpretationes* attached to them), plus excerpts from the earlier private collections of imperial constitutions, the *Codices Gregorianus* and *Hermogenianus*; in addition there are excerpts from the post-Theodosian *Novels*, the *Sentences* attributed to Paul, an abbreviation of Gaius's *Institutes*, and one title from Papinian's *Responsa*. A valuable addition to the *Theodosian Code* are the above-mentioned interpretations (*interpretationes*), or juristic summaries, which reflect conditions and legal understanding close in time to the LRV codification. Interpretations are also attached to *Paul's Sentences* and have been a major source for the concept of Roman vulgar law. The work was probably issued at Toulouse, before the Visigothic kings were forced to retrench further south after the Frankish conquest. The LRV was often copied, and abbreviated, and constituted a major source of Roman law in the Merovingian kingdom, and ultimately in France, though it was not the only source of Roman law available (see below).

3) *Lex/Leges Visgothorum* (LV). These are modern names for the *Liber iudiciorum* ("Book of Judgments") of Recceswinth (653–72), a work of twelve books, like the *Codex Justinianus*, and perhaps published in 654. It draws upon, among other sources, previously mentioned Visigothic legislation, CE and LRV, and encapsulates a lawbook of Leovigild (568–86), called the *Antiqua*, and substantial work by Chindasvinth (642–53). A revised edition was issued by Ervig in 681, later supplemented by *novellae* (new laws) of Egica (687–702) and other laws.

Ostrogothic Kingdom (493–553):

4) *Edictum Theodorici* (ET), c. 500. The date given here supposes that the Theoderic in question is the Ostrogoth of that name, the ruler of Italy (c. 493–526), though a Visigothic, pre-Eurician king of the same name has also been suggested. As the law itself says, the code was designed for both Goths and Romans. The substance of the law, as already noted, is Roman throughout. Modern editions point out the Roman-law text analogues.

Burgundian Kingdom (c. 443–534):

5) *Lex Burgundionum* (LB), c. 500, "Law of the Burgundians." Again, a modern name. Its original name seems to be *Liber Constitutionum*, "Book of Constitutions," a designation that already shows that its legislators operated within the thought world of imperial legislation, though this impression may not always seem justified by some of its provisions. As to the legislators, the complicated and contrary manuscript tradition provides two possibilities: either Gundobad, former Master of the Soldiers for Gaul, Patrician and emperor maker in Italy, and the king of the Burgundians (c. 474–516); or his son, King Sigismund (516–523). The usual resolution is to suppose a Gundobadian recension around 500 and a reissue by Sigismund in 517, with additions; the reissue is the version that survives.

6) *Lex Romana Burgundionum* (LRB), early sixth century, "Roman Law of the Burgundians." This modern name is supposed to establish the code as an (official) partner of the LB, which it may have been, but unlike the latter no preface or grand name for the collection is given in the rather sparse traces of its survival. At one point it is modestly described as *capitula legis Romanae*, chapters of Roman law. It mirrors the LB to a significant extent, including laws of Sigismund, a circumstance suggesting it belongs to his reign. Its sources appear similar to those of the LRV – whether it used another version of its *interpretationes* is contested.

Lombard Kingdom (568–774):

7) *Leges Langobardorum*, "Laws of the Lombards," a general term for the sequence of laws that begin with the edict of King Rothair (*Edictum Rothari*) in 643 and proceed, intermittently, with the legislation of various kings: Grimwald in 668; Liutprand from 712 to 735, issued at various intervals; Ratchis in 745/6; and finally, Aistulf in 750 and 755. The laws of the Lombard Kingdom continued to accumulate under the Franks after the conquest in 774 and under the early German emperors, the sequence being collected in the eleventh century in a form that shows they had been for some time cultivated, and finally used for teaching and as subjects of learned glosses and expositions (*Liber Papiensis, Lombarda*, and *Expositio ad librum Papiensem*, which included references to what will come to be understood as the *Corpus Iuris Civilis*).

The Northern, Frankish-Based Codes

As in southern Gaul and Italy, the beginning of the sixth century seems to be the beginning of Frankish, and Frankish-directed, codification (below, items 8–12). Text problems and attribution difficulties are a common denominator of *all* of the collections. The usual scholarly attribution of state (meaning Merovingian) direction to the earliest codifications (and sometimes the later ones as well) is not necessarily wrong, but it is also driven by wishful thinking.

8) *Lex Salica* (LS), "Salic Law." Supposing an early sixth-century date for this codification is harmless enough, though much earlier dates are now suggested, but without, I think, sufficient basis. The earliest manuscripts are Carolingian, providing grounds for the complex interrelation of the various redactions that present themselves and date from the Merovingian to the Carolingian period. The earliest redaction, A, also called the sixty-five-title text (and possibly called *Pactus Legis Salicae* originally), has overwhelmingly been attributed by scholarship to Clovis at some imagined, convenient spot in his reign. The text is unaccompanied by any marks of official promulgation, though later redactions (C and D) add imaginative attributions of its origins. The traditional scholarly attribution to Clovis can only be considered possible. The original text is supplemented by various additions, often

identifiable as Merovingian legislation. The existence of a *lex Salica*, a body of customary law associated with the Neustrian Franks though not coterminous with the codification of the same name (which I capitalize as *Lex Salica*), like its counterpart *lex Romana* (see below) complicates our grasp of the actual influence of the code on the law of the period. The currency of the codification *Lex Salica* as a written source of law before the Carolingian period and even after is in dispute.[23] The common view that the major recensions of the work are official products of the monarchy (bringing LS, incidentally, into line with the practice of southern legislation) is a supposition of the modern edition and modern commentators, not a product of research.

9) *Lex Ribvaria* (*LRib.*), early seventh century. Intended for the Austrasian Franks of the Cologne area, in significant parts *LRib.* is clearly a revised version of *Lex Salica*, though it presupposes the widespread use of writing to modify the oral procedures of its model. It is the best evidence we have of the currency of a *Lex Salica* before the Carolingian period, as opposed simply to a body of customary law called *lex Salica*. Despite the typical northern lack of signs of official promulgation, the redaction of the text tends to be attributed by scholars to Dagobert I (623–39), possibly at the moment when his son Sigibert III was established as king of Austrasia in 633/4. Arguments have been made for Carolingian interpolations. Provisions in the first part of the code (*LRib.* 61.1 and 2) with self-references in the first-person plural are thought to point to earlier laws by Chlothar II after 614.

The Frankish area also yields laws from the more southerly trans-Rhenan lands, regions never integrated into the Roman provincial system. The three laws listed here (10–12) are united at the very least by similar problems of dating, attribution, and material interconnections. Their prefatory introductions – not necessarily reliable – seem to assume great Frankish assemblies in their promulgation. The overlordship of the Merovingian kings is presumed in parts of the texts, though there is room in the redactions for an autonomous ducal role as the public authority.

The law of the Alamannians consists of two texts:

10) A fragmentary one, *Pactus Alamannorum* (PA), from one manuscript; and 11) *Lex Alamannorum* (LA). The PA (*pactus* means something like "agreement") is partly reproduced in titles 92–98, added to manuscripts of the LA. Though there is agreement that the PA belongs to at least the first part of the seventh century and the LA to the early part of the eighth, precise dating, and its political implications, tend to hinge on the question of the value of the various introductions.

12) *Lex Baiuvariorum* (*LBai.*), "Law of the Bavarians." Its prologue (with selections from Isidore of Seville) places the code in a world-historical context of famous

[23] Hermann Nehlsen, "Aktualität und Effektivität der ältesten germanischen Rechtsaufzeichnungen," in Peter Classen (ed.), *Recht und Schrift im Mittelalter*, Vorträge und Forschungen 23 (Sigmaringen, 1977), 449–502. This is the most circumstantial account. With focus on a narrower group of texts, see Murray, *Kinship Structure*, 122–33.

legislation and is the most circumstantial of the introductions to the trans-Rhenan codes. As far as its origins are concerned, scholarship is divided as to whether the code is an accumulation of layers from the sixth to mid-eighth century, or a late, mainly unified, composition in the last decade or so of that period. *LBai.*, despite its often-assumed late milieu and dating, is notable in using selected laws from the Visigothic CE; it also shows close correspondences to the LA, but the determination of priority here tends to founder on the dating problems of the laws in question and the possibility of a common intermediary.

The Character of the Codes

Much could be said about LRV and LRB regarding their selection of Roman texts and their form, but I shall limit my comments here to the other codes that have historically been connected in scholarship with the concept of national, Germanic law and so-called tribal custom, the *leges barbarorum*. Two features of these codes are worth noting here.

The first is the heterogeneity of their contents. As already noted, CE and ET consist basically of Roman and Roman-derived law, despite the ethnicities of those bound by their provisions. The other codes too, in varying degrees, contain rules based on Roman law or on practices arguably derived from Roman thinking and provincial norms. Since Savigny (who pretty much gives the ur-list), scholars have suggested many examples of such features, even proposing in post-Levy historical scholarship provincial origins for broad areas of practice. The subject, including procedure, currently needs a comprehensive compilation and consideration of these at present isolated propositions, especially when they are based on specialized historical and legal research. The same codes also contain law recognizably based on Christian and ecclesiastical norms, either directly derivative of known texts of Roman law or canonical regulation, or based on Christian norms and biblical precedent. (Even the original redaction of LS may not lack for examples.)[24] Whole sections of the LA and *LBai*. are given over to essentially public law regulating the right of clerics and the relation of the church to its dependents. LS 45, at an earlier date, regulates the vicinage groups of landholders (*vicini*) in a fashion that echoes regulations for corporate and rural fiscal associations in the *Theodosian Code*. It is a fair assumption too that some of the law in the codes was *sui generis*, that is specific responses to immediate concerns of the day and based on contemporary thinking without much reference to long tradition.

And naturally customary law of various ethnic communities also makes its way into most of the codes, without in itself telling us much about its antiquity or its

[24] For the use of biblical sources, see Hermann Nehlsen's survey of his own work, "Der Einfluß des Alten und Neuen Testaments auf die Rechtsentwickelung in der Spätantike und im frühen Mittelalter bei den germanischen Stämme," in Gerhard Dilcher and Eva-Marie Distler (eds.), *Leges – Gentes – Regna: Zur Rolle von germanischen Rechtsgewohnheiten und lateinischer Schrifttradition bei the Ausbildung der frühmittelalterlichen Rechtskultur* (Berlin: Erich Schmidt Verlag, 2006), 203–18.

ultimate source.[25] Scholars have often supposed that they could identify the character or subject matter of such customary law. Levy, for instance, thought that family law was the least likely to be influenced by Roman and provincial norms, retaining instead its supposedly Germanic character. This seems to be a mistake. Family law was in fact in flux by the late Empire (the Eastern reforms of Justinian were only one solution), and Western law and legislation in the new kingdoms reflect focused efforts to balance competing interests as regards authority, inheritance, and property rights.[26]

Scholars have also usually pointed to apparently primitive features in the laws as common Germanic practices. Judicial duel is a prime example. But though this form of proof is not Roman, it is also not found in Visigothic law, perhaps unsurprisingly; but neither is it found in Salic or Anglo-Saxon law, the usual exhibits for Germanic practices. The duel joins a list including oath-helping and ordeal, the latter generally a court's admission of defeat or suspicion of the litigants, that have until recently been stamped unproblematically with a Germanic provenance.[27] Detailed lists of penalties for homicide, wounding, and injuries of various kinds sometimes excite the derision of modern commentators for the primitive world of Germanic legal thinking, but the contents of the provisions have a rational cold logic that a modern actuary would hardly despise in his calculations. Colorful and quaint procedural points too arouse the conviction that we stand before primitive Germanic custom. But caution is required. For example, Bavarian law (and later documents from the region) require that witnesses be designated by having their ears tugged. But the practice looks as if it goes back to early Roman law, though its legal context is only first attested in literary sources of the late Republic and early Empire. It was never the stuff of jurists or indeed legislation but was intrinsic to actual practice. It seems to make its last appearance in legal sources in the Dubrovnik region during the late Middle Ages.[28]

Alongside customary laws and practices, scholars have long recognized that the codes contain provisions that originated in royal enactments. Indeed, this observation provides the old and misleading bipartite classification of the laws into

25 Alan Watson, *The Evolution of Law* (Baltimore: Johns Hopkins University Press, 1985), 43–97 (ch. 2), has important observations on the character of customary law that challenge common assumptions about the subject.

26 Murray, *Kinship Structure*, Appendix III, "The Succession Right of the Mother in Roman, Visigothic and Burgundian Law," 235–42. Cf. Antti Arjava, *Women and Law in Late Antiquity* (Oxford: Clarendon Press, 1996), esp. ch. 3.

27 For an interesting and early attempt to push back on some of this, under the apparent influence of Levy's disruption of standard models, see Wood, "Disputes," esp. 15–20.

28 Reinhard Selinger, "Das Ohrläppchenziehen als Rechtgeste," *Forschungen zür Rechtsarchälogie und Rechtlichen Volkskunde* 18 (2000): 201–15; Nella Lonza, "Pulling the Witness by the Ear: A Riddle from the Medieval Ragusan Sources," *Dubrovnik Annals* (2009): 25–35. Savigny noted the connection (2: §31), although he was not the first to do so. He makes it with a perplexing reticence, however, perhaps betraying awareness of incipient Indo-European studies. Rivers' translation of *LBai.* (see Sources at end) misinterprets the action as referring to "hearsay" evidence.

Volksrecht and *Königsrecht* (i.e., popular law and royal law). The origins of particular provisions in enactments are sometimes obvious, but scholars do not always agree as to the range of laws that should be classified as royal enactments.

The codes were not only heterogeneous, drawing elements from various sources, but they were also interconnected, with shared features. These are not drawn from some hypothetical Germanic prehistory but from borrowings and shared sources, whether textual or legislative, or common practices of the period. CE, even in the depleted state we have it, clearly left its mark, not only on the later Visigothic laws but also on Burgundian and Bavarian law. *LRib.* was built on LS. Alamannian and Bavarian law share provisions, whether through textual borrowing or shared Frankish legislation.

Given the profiles and interrelation of the codes, it seems difficult to maintain the notion that most of them constitute a body of Germanic law or represent the ancient and ethnically distinctive customs of tribal societies. There are good reasons why among historians working on the period the tide appears to have turned away from the traditional model outlined at the beginning of this chapter.

BEYOND THE CODES I: THE SOURCES AND PRACTICES OF ROMAN LAW

I said above that the codes tend to play an outsize role in evaluations of the law of the post Roman kingdoms. Beyond the codes, other sources exist that rarely get much attention outside specialized studies. For example, West Roman legal sources have come down to us that passed through Merovingian and Italian scriptoria but so far as we know thus far did not necessarily leave a mark on practice.[29] One of these that did leave a mark, however, not just on legal sources but on legal and learned culture of the period, is the *Theodosian Code* itself. It needs to be considered alongside its slightly later companion the LRV (see the list above, item 3).

The *Theodosian Code*, and not just in its LRV version, proved influential in the early Middle Ages, at first mainly in Gaul, the original center of the Visigothic kingdom, but later elsewhere thanks to the Franks. In Spain and Italy, the practice of supplanting early codes with later ones seems to have depressed the value and diffusion of the *Theodosian Code*. But it flourished in Gaul, especially in educated culture, where it was a well-attested and important resource of learning in both ecclesiastical and lay circles. When legal and narrative sources refer to the *Theodosian Code*, it is often unclear whether they are referring to the original version or to the LRV (or its abbreviated offshoots).

[29] Fritz Schultz, *History of Roman Legal Science* (Oxford: Clarendon Press, 1946), ch. 3, surveys the Eastern and Western literature. For more detail on Gaul, see Detlef Liebs, *Römische Jurisprudenz in Gallien (2. bis 8. Jahrhundert)*, Freiburger Rechtsgeschichtliche Abhandlungen n. F. 38 (Berlin: Duncker & Humblot, 2002).

Nevertheless, the Gallic manuscript record of the *Theodosian Code* itself is solidly attested.[30]

The period has also preserved a small but important collection of imperial laws, the so-called *Sirmondian Constitutions*, named after their Jesuit editor, Jacques Sirmond. Distinct from the *Theodosian Code* and transmitted separately, the collection provides not only fuller versions of laws found in the *Theodosian Code* but also constitutions that the Theodosian redactors either missed or omitted. The ecclesiastical focus of the collection, with an emphasis on rights and jurisdiction, explains its preservation and transmission but also arouses suspicion of authenticity in its parts.

The last example suggests there could have existed collections of Roman sources whose impact might go unnoticed because in the course of things they failed to leave manuscript traces. A curious indication of this appears in *LBai.* 2.1. The law, dealing with plots against the life of the duke (as it notes, appointed by the Merovingian king), cites verbatim language of the jurist Modestinus as repeated in Justinian's *Digest*. Savigny (2 §29) spotted this, acknowledging that it might come from a source lying behind the *Digest*. Commentators have speculated on the nature of such a collection and the source-type that might have provided the text of the Bavarian-law provision.[31]

As to the Justinianic corpus (i.e., the *Institutes, Code, Novels,* and *Digest*): This was certainly received in Italy, where sixth-century manuscript fragments attest to its presence, and where a unique intact ancient manuscript of the *Digest* was preserved. But it appears that even here the *Novels* were more widely and seriously cultivated in the Latin *Epitome Juliani*. Justinian's laws even imprinted themselves on royal Visigothic and Lombard conceptions of the legislator's function.[32] For the Frankish awareness of Justinian's Pragmatic Sanction, see below.

It is worth noting that in the early Middle Ages, especially in Gaul, the term *lex Romana* did not necessarily refer to specific, identifiable statutes or juristic texts, or to one of the versions of the *Theodosian Code* (which was not a comprehensive summary of law anyway but just a particular, if important, collection of imperial constitutions). The term *lex Romana*, thus, often seems to refer to Roman law as generally known among the Roman population, as Savigny long ago noted.[33] (Levy rather hastily characterized such law, unrooted in a surviving text, as vulgar law, though just calling it Roman law or practice would seem sufficient).[34]

30 Ian Wood, "The Code in Merovingian Gaul," in J. Harries and I. N. Wood (eds.), *The Theodosian Code: Studies in the Imperial Law of Late Antiquity* (London: Duckworth, 1993), 164–66.

31 See Stefan Esders, "Late Roman Military Law in the Bavarian Code," in *Clio@Themis: Revue électronique d'histoire du droit* 10 (2016), regarding this and a number of other passages in the *LBai.*

32 Gerhart B. Ladner, "Justinian's Theory of Law and the Renewal Ideology of the 'Leges Barbarorum'," *Proceedings of the American Philosophical Society* 119.3 (1975): 191–200.

33 Savigny 1 §§37–38 (Eng. trans. 1:115–22). The term *lex Salica* (see list above, item 8) presents a comparable problem.

34 Levy, *West-Roman Vulgar Law*, 16 n. 69.

BEYOND THE CODES II: PUBLIC LAW, ROYAL ENACTMENTS, LEGAL PRACTICE, AND LEGAL DOCUMENTS IN THE MEROVINGIAN KINGDOM

There are still broader questions regarding law and the sources that support its interpretation to be considered. To understand the law of the post-Roman kingdoms, one has to consider sources that reflect actual administrative practices and legal conceptions on a wider scale than the codifications of the period could ever encapsulate. This huge subject, with multiple source-types spread over a wide expanse of time and space, is fundamental to forming an idea of the legal contours of the kingdoms. The following comments are limited to the Merovingian kingdom – or rather to that part of it on the Gallic side of the Rhine in the old Roman provinces. This limitation will provide focus while allowing us to draw on the broadest range of specimens that record legal activity in the period. The approach followed here will emphasize the Roman background, because oddly, or so it seems to me, the Frankish kingdom is commonly and spuriously held up (in comparison to Spain and Italy) as some bastion of Germanic institutions in an idealized form, imported into the body politic of the Roman provinces. I assume that readers will understand that Frankish practices and procedures can accompany some of the features that I outline below.[35]

I begin with the administrative forms of the Frankish kingdom, which were the basic structures in which the law functioned and was dispensed and adjudicated. Law operated in the countryside as it always had: sometimes in patrimonial courts of landlords, and sometimes in public fora over which appointees of the central courts and their deputies presided. In a formal sense the jurisdictional order in Gaul was still based, at least through the seventh century, on the *civitas*: the old Roman regional unit based on an urban center (the city in a narrow sense), which was often surrounded by late Roman walls. (The final demise of these walls came much later, sometimes not until the modernizations of the nineteenth century.)[36] The persistence of such long-standing administrative units might tell us, I should think, something about the deep-rooted expectations of their legal communities. Administering this city, both the urban center and its regional extension, were a count (*comes*), representing the king, and a bishop.

Who was the bishop representing? The bishop represented in the first instance the Christian community, which was the *civitas* construed as a diocese, although the last term was slow to acquire specialized significance. A bishop's actual appointment,

35 For a more circumstantial but still fairly concise account, see Alexander C. Murray, "The Merovingian State and Administration in the Times of Gregory of Tours," in Alexander C. Murray (ed.), *A Companion to Gregory of Tours*, Brill's Companions to the Christian Tradition 63 (Leiden: Brill, 2016), 191–231.

36 Michael Greenhalgh, *Destruction of Cultural Heritage in 19th-Century France: Old Stones Versus Modern Identities* (Leiden: Brill, 2015), suggests just how long the monuments of this world lasted in significant quantities.

however, often contentious in its politics, rested in the sixth and seventh centuries ultimately upon the approval of the king. If the community sent to the king a document, called a *consensus*, recommending a particular candidate to a vacancy, the king might designate this candidate; or he might choose to ignore the local input of the *consensus* and to appoint a candidate more to his liking or attuned to his interests. The metropolitan of the province and his suffragan bishops had to accept the royal instruction to consecrate whomever the king designated (with rare protestations and usurpations of the royal right in evidence). Both count and bishop were in fact creatures of the king. The ecclesiastical provinces, under the metropolitans, corresponded in large part with the secular groupings of *civitates* and their provinces of the late Empire, with readjustments especially in the southeast caused by the episcopal rivalries of the late fifth and early sixth centuries.

We have some idea of the law practiced in these cities because of the survival of formularies. These were essentially books of *formulae* recording legal transactions and even specimens of royal privileges, based it seems on previous models at the disposal of notaries. Formularies survive from the Merovingian through the Carolingian periods, although the surviving specimens hardly encompass all the regions of the kingdom. Their survival, like all the documents to which we have made reference up to this point, has depended on ecclesiastical archives and a good measure of serendipity. It should not be controversial to say that they largely contain Roman-based practices, as well as late Roman institutions, with extensive dependence on written instruments and even access to public archives. Distinctively Frankish rules are also recognized and integrated into the formularies' literate form. Sometimes only fine distinctions can separate Roman from Frankish norms.[37] Here, too, a systematic survey would be useful.

Both count and bishop exercised jurisdictions over the *civitas*, which eventually became the *comitatus*, or county. (The term originally denoted a count's office or command, but it eventually took on territorial connotations.) The count and his subordinates, especially the *centenarii* responsible for subdistricts, presided not only over policing and criminal matters but also, as *Lex Salica* shows, over noncriminal cases, especially those requiring public attestation. As to the matters coming before the comital tribunal itself, in addition to criminal cases, much probably depended on the type of suits to which the count opened his court. (The same could be said of an even higher local official, the duke [*dux*], who presided over several counts and their jurisdictions.) These royal officials were accompanied on the tribunal by local notables, both lay and clerical. Others participated in the proceedings as experts in

37 See Murray, *Kinship Structure*, 194 n. 4, on the confusion among scholars caused by similar but not identical wording in formulas dealing with representation in the direct line: Marculf 2.10 and Tours 22 – the former representing Frankish and the latter Roman practice, and both modified by *epistolae hereditariae*.

the law or as reliable witnesses, and were called *rachinburgs*, a Frankish term, or *boni homines* ("good men"), an old Roman term.[38]

The jurisdiction of the bishop and the church is well documented, but its exact profile is hard to determine.[39] Bishops exercised the voluntary jurisdiction that went back to the Constantinian period, and that might handle serious cases indeed, but impose milder, healing, penalties relying on compensation. Clerics and their descendants for three generations were supposed to be subject to church jurisdiction as were dependents of the churches as well as freed persons for whose status the church became a guarantor. These jurisdictions were not always to go unchallenged by royal officials, and even individual clerics had their own idea of where their interests might be better served, though bishops and councils strove to channel their cases into ecclesiastical courts. Bishops claimed exemption from secular courts and seem to have been successful in maintaining their right to be tried by episcopal peers before a synod, in the presence of the king if he were party to a complaint. Mixed tribunals before an episcopal and a royal representative are also attested in matters where both the spiritual and the temporal authorities had interests. Such issues had a long history ahead of them. In the *Edict of Paris* (614), a number of the claims of clerical exemption and the right to episcopal jurisdiction received formal acknowledgement, at least for the time being. Here, too, both secular and ecclesiastical authorities were enjoined to protect widows, orphans, and the poor. The effect of such injunctions, though obviously part of the ideology of the period, is impossible to judge and was hardly an absolute separated from other interests and social views.

Complicating these already overlapping jurisdictions, there also existed on lay and ecclesiastical landed estates patrimonial courts, a customary institution with roots in the late Empire. Their authority by the late sixth century could be bolstered by grants of immunity from the monarchy that seem designed to contribute to a monopoly on the part of the landlord-recipient. The immunity, however, did not in itself establish jurisdiction, which was pre-existing. Nor did it exempt patrimonial courts or jurisdictions from claims by the royal authorities to produce parties of interest to the public tribunals. Perhaps this situation accounts for abbots presiding over courts in some of the *formulae*. Judges could be appointed by ecclesiastical and lay possessors to preside over the judicial affairs of their tenants but, as reaffirmed in the early seventh century, only under the prescriptions of the public law.[40]

Much seems to have depended on the confidence, cunning, and persistence of litigants, including their access to patrons, as to where their cases would be heard and what their chances of success might be in the various fora. The potential

38 Karin Nehlsen-von Stryck, *Die boni homines des frühen Mittelalters: unter besonderer Berücksichtigung der fränkischen Quellen*, Freiburger rechtsgeschichtliche Abhandlungen nF 2 (Berlin: Duncker & Humblot, 1981).

39 Cf. Edward James, "*Beati pacifici*: Bishops and the Law in Sixth-Century Gaul," in J. Bossy (ed.), *Disputes and Settlements: Law and Human Relations in the West* (Cambridge: Cambridge University Press, 1983), 25–46.

40 Alexander C. Murray, "Immunity, Nobility and the *Edict of Paris*," *Speculum* 69.1 (1994): 18–39.

executive powers that these courts might deploy were surely another consideration, making the royal court the preferred venue for churches and elites. Written records, as known from *formulae* and *placita* (see below), were made at various stages in the proceedings. Even the earliest recension of LS notes that royal officials issued written receipts for fines paid to the state.

Sources of law extend well beyond the books of *formulae* and the codes. The edicts of the Merovingian kings are well attested for the sixth and early seventh centuries, and we know from narrative sources that they continued after that, although no examples of these later edicts have survived.[41] Seven sixth-century kings have left an example of an edict and sometimes more than one under their names, making a total of nine separate "capitularies," as they are called in the MGH edition. Capitulary, for edict, is a long-standing recognized misnomer, persisting it seems because it is enshrined by the MGH. The word capitulary in origin was a Carolingian term for what the Merovingians, following precedent, called a *constitutio, auctoritas, edictum, praeceptio/praeceptum, decretio/decretum* – in sum, directives of a general or specific kind in the Roman mode. Some attest the participation of magnates and bishops in their promulgation. As general edicts, they tend to be, as a whole, a motley collection, as one would expect of ad hoc legislation.

Summarizing their content adequately in a short space is not really possible. Much is in support of the church, including recognizing privileges, supporting the clerical view of asylum (for malefactors and runaway slaves) and confirming prohibitions against alleged pagan (or better, non-Christian) practices, work on Sunday, and forced marriages with religious. An inordinate amount of the content deals with law as commonly experienced, that is, with public safety. Thus, there are various provisions on criminal law, including homicide, abduction, and what might be called incorrigible or professional criminals (who must have been numerous in a society with large numbers of mobile animal stock); and on summary procedure, some of it hard (if hardly unusual), including passing recognition of an established non-Roman and decisive proof: the ordeal of the lot (to be distinguished from the cauldron ordeal in the earliest redaction of LS). Despite this curiosity, most of these provisions fall readily within late-antique patterns, but little of the harsh stuff is of the type that would ever have engaged jurists of important centers. Some measures are somewhat closer to the themes of juristic literature, such as Roman-law representation in the direct line (in aid of emending Frankish inheritance) and confirmation of rights of prescription (as defenses against dispossession). There are even signs of borrowing from the contemporaneous Byzantine world. The famous and constitutionally significant chapter 12 of Chlothar II's *Edict of Paris* (614), requiring that counts be recruited from the region in which they served, appears to be modeled on a provision from Justinian's Pragmatic Sanction for Italy (554) regarding governors.

41 Alexander C. Murray, "The New MGH Edition of the Charters of the Merovingian Kings," *Journal of Medieval Latin* 15 (2005): 246–78, surveys the character of the legal evidence.

The aim in both cases was to facilitate the ability of subjects to sue the chief official set over them.

I will mention two sequences of this body of legislation. The first is the *Constitution of Chlothar II* (584–629).[42] Issued on an unknown occasion, this guaranteed to the provincials the operation of the ancient law (*antiqua lex*), with more than sufficient context to leave no doubt that this refers to Roman law. Even without a text before us, we might expect such affirmations, but what is more interesting is that the edict acknowledges an important Roman constitutional idea: that directives solicited against the law, even if they come from the prince, are invalid.[43] This principle is casually attested in literary sources, and it stands against a whole tradition of Germanist interpretations of early Frankish royal charters, including the *placita*, mentioned below.

The second is a series of provisions in the edicts regarding the regulation of police associations, composed of landholders obligated to act as watches and to mobilize against and to pursue thieves, seemingly rustlers of stock. Borders provided fertile ground for such activities, and the Merovingian kings took measures to check them, sometimes acting in collaboration. The means adopted recognize the existence of local associations on the ground even before the kings in question felt the need to get involved and replicate to a remarkable degree enduring late-Roman provincial measures to control the countryside. Merovingian legislation on these matters illustrates the subterranean and largely unacknowledged forces of Roman provincial culture upon the legal framework of their kingdoms.[44]

The general directives (i.e., legislation) I have just referred to are complemented in the seventh century by records of specific directives, namely grants, privileges, and exemptions as issued by kings, in our sources to churches, but quite clearly also dispensed to lay recipients. These documents generally go under the modern name of royal charters or diplomas, *diplomata* (s. *diploma*); their model is the imperial rescript.[45] The phenomenon of privilege or exemption is hardly new, but the contents of the seventh-century varieties are distinctive, especially that type bearing the ancient name "immunity," which became a model for legal privileges, including those of the ecclesiastical/episcopal variety that had nothing to do with the essentially secular, fiscal exemptions of the Merovingian kings. Immunity is a Roman concept of public law (and ancient beyond that). It grants exemption (which is what the term immunity means) from public burdens to those who can claim to be providing socially significant contributions deserving of recompense in some way through state exemptions (readers can readily think of modern analogies, generally

42 The alternative view that the king to which the title refers is Chlothar I (511–561) is not relevant to the following commentary.

43 See Esder's edition and commentary, cited under Sources at the end.

44 Alexander C. Murray, "From Roman to Frankish Gaul: *Centenarii* and *Centenae* in the Administration of the Merovingian Kingdom" (cited previously).

45 See Murray, "The New MGH Edition of the Charters of the Merovingian Kings" (cited previously), which provides direction on the German work of Peter Classen.

of the business/corporate-taxation variety). The earliest Merovingian immunities followed pretty much the lines of Roman ones: granting tax exemptions along with grants to clerics on the understanding that they would somehow contribute to the mission of the church and by implication the health of the state; charity, prayer, and liturgical services were readily so conceived in antiquity and the Merovingian kingdom as state services, and thus deserving of exemptions to support their performance. The later seventh-century Merovingian charter record is clear that the early fiscal tax exemption was reconfigured into an exemption also from judicial intervention and thus from the (still) fiscal collection of judicial fines, which now redounded to the benefit of the immunist, the receiver of the immunity grant, and assisted his control over a patrimonial court.[46]

A special type of *diploma* needs to be noted: the records of judicial decisions before the royal court covering disputes but also public conveyances. The modern name for these documents is *placita*. The modalities are clearly derived from Roman practice, including the recording of minutes, no matter what precise track is thought to have produced them. For example, one elaborate inquiry involving multiple stages, and the rights of the fisc under the Mayor of the Palace, portrays clearly the use of the fiscal inquest – a mainstay of Roman administration.[47]

Incidentally, analogous powers of inquiry, requiring testimony to questions under oath, were also employed by Roman security officials as a tool to manage peacekeeping in the countryside (though they were unlikely to be an imperial invention). The same process can be spotted in the police measures mentioned above and was even used to indict incorrigible malefactors. An addition to *Lex Salica* provides another example involving the investigation of a suspicious death.[48] Merovingian sources are an important waystation in the long and influential history of the inquest.

Finally, what of "private" charters? Merovingian Gaul does not have its equivalent to the trove of Italian Ravenna papyri. It does, however, have its books of *formulae*, as already noted, based on actual practice. A few authentic, stand-alone charters and wills have also survived. Far more come down to us in still mainly suspicious, copied versions. Their contents confirm the themes above, but, with some exceptions (those associated with Le Mans, for example) they have not on the whole received the same attention as the royal *diplomata*, apart from that species of charter recording supposed episcopal privileges granted to monasteries that show the same problems of authenticity bedeviling diploma copies.

46 Alexander C. Murray, "Merovingian Immunity Revisited." *History Compass* 8/8 (2010): 913–28 surveys the issues.

47 Alexander C. Murray, "So-called Fictitious Trials in the Merovingian *Placita*," in S. Diefenbach and G. M. Müller (eds.), *Gallien in Spätantike und Frühmittelalter. Kulturgeschichte einer Region* (Berlin: De Gruyter, 2013), 297–330. Appendix III, 319–22 is a translation of diploma 157 of the new MGH edition.

48 *Childeberti secundi Decretio*, c. 7 (Boretius edition). LS 102.

CONCLUSIONS

It is time to bring this story to a halt. It is by necessity a short story. But what is it a story of? I began by commenting on current surveys of European and medieval European law and then looked at some of the standard historiographical interpretations, from which these modern accounts derive and that emphasize a putative Germanic order that supposedly stamped itself on the post-Roman kingdoms. In one form or another this perspective still lies behind widespread scholarly and popular conceptions. Seen this way it is a story of deep misunderstanding.

The work of Ernst Levy marks an important turning point at least as far as specialists in the period are concerned. Though he is not the hero of the tale (there are none), he did dispel the illusion that Roman law reflected a narrow slice of classical texts and legislation and, at the same time, broke down the reflexive distinctions between Roman and Germanic codes. Much of this kind of thinking had been elaborated much earlier for sources of the eastern parts of the Empire and even adumbrated tentatively for the West by the arch-Germanist Heinrich Brunner. But it was Levy who broke through the inertia in thinking about the Western sources – though the effect has been limited to a few specialists and historians of the post-Roman kingdoms. This occurred even as his broader assertions about late Roman law in a juristic sense were being assailed by Romanists. At the same time, his method, particular interests, and presuppositions never quite caught on among early medievalists, who were not trained in the tradition that Levy represented. While he has always been ignored by those sticking to Germanic-law tracks (especially translators), there is still noticeably a pre-Levy and post-Levy period in the way the sources have been approached by those early medievalists attuned to the period's connection to the late Roman Empire.

This brings us to another part of the story – the focus on sources. The codes and, among them, the West Roman sources, are valuable testaments of legal thinking and have long attracted the attention of scholars attempting to capture the essential legal character of the period. The successor kingdoms, however, preserve source-types that provide other ways of understanding the legal world of the post-Roman kingdoms, especially the recurrent products of cities (*civitates*) and kings: *formulae*, charters, and edicts. These often provide connections to late imperial practices, especially, as highlighted here, administrative law, but also other legal institutions well beyond the ken of traditional legal history. These institutions also undoubtedly look forward to future developments of fundamental importance to European history. The institutional approach, now in disrepute, is certainly not new (though there are always new ways to carry it out) and has driven forward a significant part of European historiography since the early modern period. Its days are not over.

To conclude, the story presented here is in the end, as readers must have noticed, programmatic. The period is fascinating; its character is elusive and demonstrably important; it takes diverse skills to get at its reality. It should not be dealt with in tired clichés. There is, in short, much to be done, from systematic explications of historiography to new, detailed research on law and institutions. Perhaps one day even general histories will be persuaded to recast their portrayal of the legal foundations of the post-Roman kingdoms.

SOURCES

The diverse sources of late Roman law should form the basic point of comparison for the law of the post-Roman Continental kingdoms. The standard edition of the *Codex Theodosianus* is by Theodore Mommsen (Berlin: Weidmann, 1905). It includes large parts of LRV (including its *interpretationes*), because Mommsen used it for reconstructing the *Cod. Theod.* Theodore Mommsen, Paul Krueger, and Rudolph Schoell edited Justinian's *Institutes, Digest, Code*, and *Novels*, which together comprise the *Corpus Iuris Civilis*, in 3 vols. (Berlin and Hildesheim: Weidmann, 1872–95). The *Epitome Juliani*, a Latin digest of the *Novels* (most of which were issued in Greek), is edited by Gustav Haenel, *Epitome Latina Novellarum Justiniani* (Leipzig: Hinrichsius, 1873). There is an online version at the Volterra Project, www.ucl.ac.uk/volterra (accessed April 3, 2018). The edition of the Visgothic LRV is still that of Gustav Haenel, *Lex Romana Visigothorum* (Berlin: 1849).

The range of Roman source types for the late empire (and before) is found in FIRA = *Fontes Iuris Romani Anteiustiniani*, 2nd edition by S. Riccobono et al., 3 vols. (Florence: Barbèra, 1943–1968). ET and LRB are found here in vol. 2 (ed. J. Baviera, and J. Furlani); there are also editions in MGH, below.

Most of the sources referred to in the chapter as *leges, capitularia, formulae*, and *diplomata* are edited in the Leges and Diplomata sections of MGH, available online (www.dmgh.de/, accessed April 3, 2018). Readers should compare in the series older and later editions of individual works. CE (found with *Leges Visigothorum* in MGH, Leges nationum Germanicarum 1) should be compared to the edition and commentary by Alvaro D'Ors, *El codigo de Eurico*, Cuadernos del Instituto Juridico Español 12, Estudios Visígoticos 2 (Rome: CSIC, 1960). There is a new edition of what can properly be called the *Constitution of Chlothar* (Boretius, the MGH editor of the capitularies, called it *Chlotharii II Praeceptio*) by Stefan Esders, *Römische Rechtstradition und merowingisches Königtum: zum Rechtscharakter politischer Herrschaft in Burgund im 6. und 7. Jahrhundert* (Göttingen: Vandenhoeck & Ruprecht, 1997), 109–267, which includes extensive commentary.

The remarkable Ravenna collection of papyri is edited (with a German translation) by Olof Tjäder, *Die nichtliterarischen lateinischen Papyri Italiens aus der Zeit 445–700*, Acta Instituti Romani Regni Sueciae, series in 4° 19, 2 vols. (Lund: C.W.K Gleerup, 1955; Stockholm: Paul Åströms Förlag, 1982). For the Lombard charters, see L. Schiaparelli et al., *Codice Diplomatico Longobardo*, 5 vols. (Rome: Tipografia del Senato, 1929–2003).

Although some Gallic private charters claiming to be from the period can be found in particular editions of cartularies, the comprehensive and standard edition remains Jean-Marie Pardessus, *Diplomata, chartae, epistolae, leges aliaeque instrumenta ad res gallo-francicas spectantia*, 2 vols. (Paris, 1843, 1849; repr. Aalen: Scientia, 1969), which depended on a 1791 edition by Brequigny. Two new editions of important authentic materials are edited by Margarete Weidemann: *Das Testament des Bischofs Berthramn von Le Mans vom 27. März 616: Untersuchungen zu Besitz und Geschichte einer Fränkischen Familie im 6. und 7. Jahrhundert*, Monographien 9 (Mainz: Römisch-Germanisches Zentralmuseum, 1986); and Margarete Weidemann, *Geschichte des Bistums Le Mans von der Spätantike bis zur Karolingerzeit: Actus Pontificum Cenommanis in urbe degentium und Gesta Alderici*, 3 vols. (Mainz: Römisch-Germanisches Zentralmuseum 2002).

Original charters can be found in the series edited by Albert Bruckner and Robert Marichal, *Chartae Latinae Antiquiores: Facsimile Edition of the Latin Charters Prior to the Ninth Century*, 49 vols. (Olten: U. Graf, 1954–98). A second series for post-800 charters is scheduled for completion in 2020.

English-language translations exist for much, but by no means all, of this material. Readers should regard translations as an aid to the Latin text, not a replacement for it. Circumspection is required in the use of them, even the best; and if readers remember this caution, the following translations (most but not all English-language) will prove useful.

Clyde Pharr's *The Theodosian Code* (Princeton: Princeton University Press, 1952) is invaluable and includes the *interpretationes* from the LRV version of the text. The *Digest*, a point of comparison for West-Roman sources, is translated by Alan Watson, *Digest of Justinian*, 4 vols. (Philadelphia: University Press, 1985). This edition includes the Latin text of the Mommsen/Krueger edition on facing pages. It is currently available in e-book formats, without the Latin text. An earlier, partial translation (first fifteen books) under the same title by Charles Henry Monro exists as well, 2 vols. (Cambridge: Cambridge University Press, 1904–10). The *Codex Justinianus* is translated by S. P. Scott (though not according to the divisions of the modern edition), along with the entire Justinianic *Corpus Iuris Civilis* in seventeen vols., under the title *The Civil Law* (Cincinnati, 1932; rpr. New York 1973). Scott's translations do not always elicit approval. The translations of Justinian's *Code* and *Novels* by Fred H. Blume are available online at the law library of the University of Wyoming: www.uwyo.edu/lawlib/blume-justinian/ (accessed April 3, 2018). Bluhme's translation of the *Code* with parallel ancient text and annotations is now published separately in 3 vols. (Cambridge: Cambridge University Press, 2016) under the general editorship of Bruce W. Frier.

For CE, see the Spanish translation of the D'Ors edition (cited above). LV is translated by S. P. Scott under the title *Visigothic Code (Forum Iudicum)* (first published Boston: Boston Book Co., 1910) and is available online at http://libro.uca.edu/vcode/visigoths.htm (accessed May 21, 2018).

A translation of ET can be found in Sean Lafferty, *Law and Society in the Age of Theoderic the Great* (Cambridge: Cambridge University Press, 2013), Appendix, 243–94.

Several codes are translated by Katherine Fischer Drew: (1) *The Burgundian Code* (Philadelphia: University of Pennsylvania Press, 1949); (2) *The Laws of the Salian Franks* (Philadelphia: University of Pennsylvania Press, 1991) – presenting a synthesized text that needs to be read against the edition and the various redactions and manuscripts; and (3) the pre-Frankish Italian royal laws of the Lombards: *The Lombard Laws* (Philadelphia: University of Pennsylvania Press, 1973). Some Frankish laws and east-Rhenan codes are translated by Theodore John Rivers: *Laws of the Salian and Ripuarian Franks* (New York: AMS Press, 1986), with the same caveat as for the Drew translation; and Theodore John Rivers, *Laws of the Alamans and Bavarians*, based on particular versions (Philadelphia: University of Pennsylvania Press, 1977).

Two basic and tricky Merovingian formularies are translated by Alice Rio, *The Formularies of Angers and Marculf: Two Merovingian Legal Handbooks* (Liverpool: Liverpool University Press, 2008).

Various items – parts of *Lex Salica*, a few *formulae*, a fair selection of so-called capitularies, and some conciliar canons on the subject of ecclesiastical privilege – are translated by Alexander C. Murray, *From Roman to Merovingian Gaul: A Reader*, Readings in Medieval Civilizations and Culture (Peterborough, Ont.: Broadview, 2000), 533–87; on the *Constitution of Chlothar*, a revision of c. 2 is found in Alexander C. Murray, "The New MGH Edition of the Charters of the Merovingian Kings." *Journal of Medieval Latin* 15 (2005): 258, n. 37. A translation of two *placita*, one a conveyance and the other a true dispute, can be found in Alexander C. Murray, "So-called Fictitious Trials in the Merovingian *Placita*," in S. Diefenbach and G. M. Müller (eds.), *Gallien in Spätantike und Frühmittelalter. Kulturgeschichte einer Region* (Berlin: De Gruyter, 2013), Appendices II and III, 319–24.

FURTHER READING

General Guides

The best general guide to the various laws and related subject matter, though weighted heavily toward traditional German scholarship, is the *Handwörterbuch zur deutschen Rechtsgeschichte*, ed. A. Erler, E. Kaufmann, and D. Werkmueller, 5 vols. (Berlin: E. Schmidt, 1964–98), abbreviated *HRG*. A second edition appeared in 2004, ed. Albrecht Cordes et al. Thus far, three of a projected six volumes have appeared. Items of the 2nd edition can be acquired on line at a hefty per-page rate: www.hrgdigital.de/ (accessed May 14, 2018).

Other Secondary Works

Mainly English-language titles that supplement works cited in the footnotes:

Arjava, Antti. "The Survival of Roman Family Law after the Barbarian Settlement." In *Law, Society, and Authority in Late Antiquity*, edited by Ralph Mathisen, 33–51. Oxford: Oxford University Press, 2001. [Based on the author's book of 1996, which is cited in the notes.]

Bibliotheca Legum: A Database on Secular Carolingian Law Texts. www.leges.uni-koeln.de/en/, accessed May 14, 2018. [Despite the subtitle, also covers pre-Carolingian legal collections.]

Dilcher, Gerhard and Eva-Marie Distler. *Leges – Gentes – Regna: Zur Rolle von germanischen Rechtsgewohnheiten und lateinischer Schrifttradition bei the Ausbildung der frühmittelalterlichen Rechtskultur*. Berlin: E. Schmidt, 2006. [Papers reflecting the state of research and controversy among German legal scholars, linguists, and at least one faction of the history fraternity. On the term "Germanic," see the contribution by Jörg Jarnut, p. 69. For general guidance, see the review by Karin Nehlsen-von Stryck in ZRG Germanistische Abteilung 124/1 (2007): 426–36.]

Goebel, Julius. *Felony and Misdemeanor: A Study in the History of Criminal Law*. Philadelphia: University of Pennsylvania Press, 1976 (orig. published New York, 1937). [Dated classic, notable for its critique of the Germanist "peace theory."]

Harries, Jill. "Not the Theodosian Code: Euric's Law and Late Fifth-Century Gaul." In *Society and Culture in Late Antique Gaul: Revisiting the Sources*, edited by Ralph W. Mathisen and Danuta Shanzer, 39–51. Burlington, VT: Ashgate, 2001. [*CE* is Roman law but, as the article title suggests, not to be rated highly as legislation.]

Jurasinski, Stefan. *Ancient Privileges:* Beowulf, *Law, and the Making of Germanic Antiquity*. Morgantown: West Virginia University Press, 2006. [Nineteenth-century philology, ancient poetry, and the concept of Germanic law.]

Matthews, John F. "Interpreting the *Interpretationes* of the *Breviarium*." In *Law, Society and Authority in Late Antiquity*, edited by Ralph Mathisen, 11–32. Oxford: Oxford University Press, 2001. [Influential, but the method developed here is arguably less than it seems.]

Rio, Alice. *Legal Practice and the Written Word in the Early Middle Ages: Frankish Formulae, c. 500–100*. Cambridge: Cambridge University Press, 2009. [The most comprehensive discussion of the *formulae* in English.]

Volterra Project. www.ucl.ac.uk/volterra, accessed May 14, 2018. [Online resources for both Roman and Early Medieval law.]

Wormald, Patrick. "*Lex Scripta* and *Verbum Regis*: Legislation and Germanic Kingship from Euric to Cnut." In P. H. Sawyer and I. N. Wood (eds.), *Early Medieval Kingship*, 105–138. Leeds: Leeds, University of Leeds, School of History, 1977. [An influential article.]

4

Ecclesiastical Councils

Gregory I. Halfond

The history of ecclesiastical councils does not lend itself easily to summary or generalization. This is in part because of the sheer quantity of meetings held during the first millennium: we have reports of over five hundred councils held in the Latin West alone (including North Africa) between the third and tenth centuries. But it is the diversity of these meetings, as much as their quantity, which discourages generalization. Councils engaged in a wide range of activities, often even in the course of a single meeting, including the crafting of canonical regulations, confirming gifts or privileges granted to ecclesiastical institutions, and serving as venues for episcopal ordinations or for judicial hearings for offending clerics and sometimes even laymen.

Although Western councils often shared certain procedural and ideological influences as well as similar legislative priorities, it was the unique personalities of both the convokers and the attendees that assured the distinctiveness of every assembly. At their core, councils constituted gatherings of individuals whose consensus was thought to imbue their collective decisions with authority. While their identities are in most cases unrecoverable, the collaborative engagement of these unique personalities was the single most significant factor in determining the priorities, judgments, and ultimately the influence, of individual councils. Progress in canonical regulation during the first millennium was the work of countless skilled "jurists," most of whom were bishops. Sometimes their names are recorded in subscriptions, but even then we rarely know who they were: their personalities, and how they lived their lives. Nor do we know how each contributed to the end result.

CONCILIAR ORIGINS, TYPOLOGY, AND PROTOCOL

While participation in conciliar business in the first millennium was never limited solely to the episcopate, it was bishops whose presence assured that councils represented the corporate authority of the ecclesiastical leadership. It is for this reason, despite both Eastern and Western antecedents stretching back as far as the apostolic age, that Christianity's conciliar tradition proper can be said to have begun only in the third century, following the emergence of monarchical episcopacy, in which bishops assumed full authority over the ecclesiastical institutions and staff within their cities at the same time that they began identifying themselves as members of an elite corporate body within the church. And it was only in the fourth century, with Christianity's new protected status under the Christian Roman emperors, that what Gaudemet called "*une époque d'intense vie conciliaire*" was able to flourish.[1] By this time, an episcopal hierarchy had emerged that mirrored Roman provincial organization. Within each province, one bishop exercised a special administrative, metropolitan authority over his subordinate colleagues (his suffragan bishops), including the obligation to call them together regularly in council. In the Latin West, the words *concilium* and *synodus* were used interchangeably from a relatively early date to describe episcopal conferences, with the former term initially the more common.[2] The designation of certain councils as ecumenical is first attested in 338 CE in reference to the earlier Council of Nicaea (325 CE), although it probably did not indicate then a uniquely eminent form of ecclesiastical assembly.[3]

Modern studies of early conciliar history have superimposed onto this spare contemporaneous typology distinctions between types of council that are often anachronistic in nomenclature if not necessarily in accuracy. In his monumental *Das Kirchenrecht der Katholiken und Protestanten in Deutschland* (1869–97), Paul Hinschius systematically distinguished among four primary forms of conciliar assembly: (1) general or ecumenical; (2) provincial and plenary; (3) interprovincial, national, or imperial; and (4) diocesan.[4] Despite the relative simplicity of this schema, its terminology has never been universally adopted, and actual councils cannot always be easily classified in these terms. Scholars have introduced categories that do not fit Hinschius's categories, such as the Carolingian-era mixed councils, or *concilia mixta*. This modern typological confusion results largely from the fluidity and imprecision of conciliar constitutions, definitions, and terminology in late-antique and early-medieval Europe.[5]

Conciliar protocol was similarly fluid in these centuries. The procedures adopted by early councils were grounded not in a uniform liturgical tradition but rather in parliamentary procedures common to the Roman world. The protocol of the more than half a dozen councils convoked by Cyprian of Carthage (d. 258), an early and innovative advocate of conciliar governance in the 250s, was influenced – whether directly or indirectly remains a matter of debate – by Roman senatorial procedure

1 Jean Gaudemet, *Les sources du droit de l'Eglise en Occident, du IIe au VIIe siècle* (Paris: Cerf, 1985), 41.

2 Adolf Lumpe, "Zur Geschichte der Wörter *Concilium* und *Synodus* in der antiken christlichen Latinität," AHC 2.1 (1970): 1–21. Unless otherwise indicated, I use the two terms synonymously here.

3 Henry Chadwick, "The Origin of the Title 'Oecumenical Council'," JTS 23.1 (1972): 132–35.

4 Paul Hinschius, *Kirchenrecht* (Berlin: I. Guttentag, 1869–97), 3:328.

5 Jean Gaudemet, *L'Église dans l'Empire Romain (IVe–Ve siècles)* (Paris: Sirey, 1958), 223.

(Cyprian *Epp*. 55–57, 59, 64, 67, 70, and 72; *Sententiae episcoporum*).[6] This protocol dictated that the council's president would introduce an issue before the assembled body (his *relatio*), after which the other members were permitted to respond with their own positions on the question (their *sententiae*). A formal vote would follow, and then the approved resolution would be transcribed and publicized.[7]

Evidence that variations of this standard protocol were subsequently adopted by councils of the fourth century and later can be found in those many late-antique conciliar acts (*acta*) that employ what Hamilton Hess has labeled the "*placuit*-form," modeled on the senate's *liber sententiarum* (book of resolutions). In this form of conciliar acts, an introductory *praefatio* (preface) precedes individual prescriptive pronouncements, following which the subscriptions of the participants are appended. The pronouncements themselves (*canones*) employ stock Roman legal phrases indicating the reaching of decision, such as *placuit nobis* ("it pleased us"), *decrevimus* ("we determined"), and *censuimus* ("we judged").[8]

The first council known to have issued canons was the Iberian Council of Elvira (c. 305/6), although it is possible that only the first twenty-one of the eighty-one credited canons were composed at the meeting.[9] In what sense were these canons considered to be binding? There is more than a little truth in the observation that late-antique conciliar canons "represented the expression of an ideology more than an enforceable program of law."[10] The episcopal authors of conciliar legislation sometimes lacked the ability to enforce their own decrees, and secular promotion was at best inconsistent. Nevertheless, while conciliar regulators might distinguish their decrees from secular *leges* (written legal statutes), they regularly classified canons as binding rules (*regulae*) that defined proper action. This definition would be popularized by bishop Isidore of Seville (c. 560–636) in his influential *Etymologiae* (VI.16.1). As rules, canons were classified as enforceable prescriptions whose authority was grounded in their compositional context. As early as Cyprian of Carthage, the *consensus* (agreement) of conciliar participants was identified as the ideal basis for conciliar decision-making. Subsequent efforts to champion the authority of councils, most significantly the Council of Nicaea (325), emphasized multiple forms of *consensus*, both intra-ecclesiastical (i.e., among the conciliar participants themselves as well as the larger Christian community) and with

6 Cf. Pierre Batiffol, "Le règlement des premiers conciles africains et le règlement du sénat romain," *Bulletin d'ancienne littérature et d'archéologie chrétiennes* 3 (1913): 3–19; Philip R. Amidon, "The Procedure of St. Cyprian's Synods," *Vigiliae Christianae* 37 (1983): 328–39.

7 Hermann J. Sieben, *Die Konzilsidee in der Alten Kirche* (Paderborn: Schöningh, 1979), 476–82.

8 Hamilton Hess, *The Early Development of Canon Law and the Council of Serdica*, Oxford Early Christian Studies (Oxford: Oxford University Press, 2002), 69–75.

9 Maurice Meigne, "Concile ou collection d'Elvire?" RHE 70 (1975): 361–87.

10 William E. Klingshirn, *Caesarius of Arles: The Making of a Christian Community in Late Antique Gaul*, Cambridge Studies in Medieval Life and Thought (Cambridge: Cambridge University Press, 1994), 103.

Scripture and tradition (patristic and conciliar), which H. J. Sieben has identified respectively as horizontal and vertical consensus.[11]

Justifications of conciliar authority such as these did not necessarily ensure enforcement. For canonical rules to be functional, they first had to be disseminated – initially by the conciliar participants themselves – and preserved. Preservation was not limited solely to producing and maintaining written copies of whole acts or individual canons, but could also include the oral recitation of canons in local churches and the implicit or explicit citation of old rules by new councils. Canons in many cases prescribed specific penalties against transgressors, such as excommunication, but the practical execution of penalties was presumably dependent more on the authority and will of an enforcer (such as a bishop, abbot, or secular officeholder) than on that of the original authors. Particularly in those instances when intra-ecclesiastical *consensus* was lacking, the endorsement and enforcement of conciliar *auctoritas* by civil authorities could be the determining factor in the implementation of synodal decrees.

Councils were religious as well as decision-making assemblies, at which ordained clerics, mainly bishops, sought guidance from the Holy Spirit. Part of the procedure, therefore, was liturgical, involving prayer and ritual.[12] But while Roman administrative and legal traditions continued to inform conciliar protocol in the Latin West long after the disappearance of an active imperial government, it only was in the seventh century that an effort was made to craft a uniform liturgy for councils. The earliest of the conciliar *ordines* (liturgical scripts), which was intended for a provincial council and unsurprisingly was reflective of Roman procedural influence, originated as the fourth canon of the acts of the Fourth Council of Toledo (633), held in Visigothic Spain and presided over by bishop Isidore of Seville (*Die Konzilordines des Früh- und Hochmittelalters* no. 1). A subsequent version of this *ordo*, likely composed in late-seventh-century Toledo, became widely known beyond Iberia thanks to its inclusion in the late eighth-century *Collectio Hispana Gallica* and subsequently the Pseudo-Isidorian corpus (*Die Konzilordines des Früh- und Hochmittelalters* no. 2). Despite the spread of this and variant *ordines* in the early-medieval West, it is difficult to gauge how much influence this Visigothic-derived conciliar liturgy had on protocol beyond Iberia. There is no strong evidence to suggest, for example, that it had much of a practical influence in the Frankish Kingdom to the north, where there already was a well-established conciliar tradition, although it would serve as the basis for a Frankish-composed *ordo* c. 800 (*Die Konzilordines des Früh- und Hochmittelalters* no. 7). Additionally, an illustration of bishops in council included in the ninth-century Utrecht Psalter (Utrecht, Bibl. der Rijksuniversiteit 32, f. 90 v) may be reflective of the *ordo*'s protocol.[13] But even if

[11] Sieben, *Die Konzilsidee in der Alten Kirche*, 25–380.

[12] Giuseppe Alberigo, "Sinodo come liturgia?" *Cristianesimo nella storia* 28.1 (2007): 1–14.

[13] Roger E. Reynolds, "Rites and Signs of Conciliar Decisions in the Early Middle Ages," in *Segni e riti nella chiesa altomedievale occidentale, = Settimane di studio del Centro italiano di studi sull'alto*

the direct impact of the Visigothic-derived *ordines* may have been limited, their fairly rapid dissemination and multiplication speaks both to a common episcopal interest in formalizing conciliar protocol as well as in emphasizing the ritualistic component of conciliar assemblies.

Along with the protocol of the assemblies themselves, there also was considerable variability in Late Antiquity as to the identity of conciliar convokers. Contemporaneous canons – most influentially Nicaea (325), c. 5 and Chalcedon (451), c. 19 – tasked metropolitan bishops with the regular convocation of provincial councils. But as early as the Council of Arles (314) – a meeting convoked by Constantine the Great for the purpose of settling the Donatist schism – Roman emperors themselves assumed the responsibility for inaugurating episcopal synods. This imperial prerogative was rarely questioned, despite the fact that the involvement of emperors in conciliar affairs seldom brought about a quick resolution to intra-ecclesiastical disputes and often exacerbated tensions. Imperial involvement could extend well beyond the formal convocation; on various occasions emperors facilitated episcopal travel to councils, mandated attendance, announced agendas, enforced rulings, and supervised proceedings either directly or indirectly via their subordinates. Nevertheless, the extent of imperial involvement varied from council to council, and meetings could and did assemble without any input from Roman emperors. Beginning in the early sixth century, following the breakup of the Western Roman Empire, barbarian kings, too, began to involve themselves regularly in conciliar activity, while never exercising a monopoly on either the convocation of participants or the determination of agendas. In particular, Visigothic kings and Frankish kings and emperors assumed a role in protecting the church and overseeing councils akin to that of the Byzantine emperors.

BISHOPS AND COUNCILS IN THE POST-ROMAN WEST

The disintegration of the Western Roman Empire may have contributed to the diversity of conciliar practices found in the barbarian kingdoms of the early Middle Ages, but variation had always been the norm. In some parts of the former Western Empire, there was no immediate break in conciliar activity despite concurrent political transformations. The rulers of the Gallic successor kingdoms c. 500, for example, collectively embraced conciliar convocation both as a form of symbolic *imitatio imperii* (imitation of imperial rule) and as a practical tool for encouraging productive collaboration with the ecclesiastical administrators of their respective realms. In the Visigothic kingdom of Toulouse, the Arian king Alaric II (d. 507) promoted conciliarism – with the cooperation of Caesarius, metropolitan bishop of Arles – to express to the catholic population his legitimacy as a promoter of

medioevo 33 (Spoleto: Fondazione Centro Italiano di studi sull'alto medioevo, 1985), 207–44, at 221–25.

ecclesiastical and political unity.[14] Alaric's Gallic contemporaries, the Frankish Clovis (d. 511) and the Burgundian Sigismund (d. 523), were similarly supportive of episcopal assemblies, with the former personally addressing *tituli* (chapters) to the attendees of the Council of Orléans (511) to assist them in the determination of their agenda. This council's location, attendance, and legislative priorities all suggest a conscious royal initiative to integrate recently annexed dioceses into a united Gallo-Frankish *ecclesia*. Sigismund, a convert to the catholic (pro-Nicene) faith from Arianism, never personally convoked a synod as far as we know, but he did permit several to assemble during his relatively brief reign. These included the Council of Lyons (518/22), at which eleven prelates broke with the king in their push to convict one of Sigismund's officials with incest, threatening to cloister themselves in monasteries if the king did not support their condemnation (*Concilia Galliae: A.511–A.695*, 38–41).

The most vociferous Gallic proponent of conciliarism in the early decades of the sixth century was not a barbarian king but Caesarius, metropolitan bishop of Arles. Although, following the Council of Agde (506), Caesarius personally convoked those synods over which he presided, he was able to pursue his conciliar agenda only thanks to the eventual peace brought about by the Ostrogothic occupation of Provence (508–37), which followed Clovis's defeat of the Visigoths in 507. During the politically tumultuous years that immediately followed the defeat of his sometime-patron, sometime-persecutor, Alaric II, Caesarius was unable to convoke any councils at all. But beginning in the 520s, Caesarius organized a rapid sequence of provincial synods: Arles (524), Carpentras (527), Orange (529), Vaison (529), and Marseilles (533). Among these, the Council of Orange proved particularly influential for its rejection of what is now known as semi-Pelagianism, but the canons of several of these meetings circulated in a number of sixth- and seventh-century canonical collections (*Concilia Galliae: A.511–A.695*, 53–76). Like his fifth-century predecessors in the episcopal see of Arles, Caesarius exploited councils as a means to accentuate and assert his regional authority in southern Gaul. His colleagues did not always willingly accede to his agenda. At the Council of Marseilles (533), Caesarius's suffragan bishops balked at his harsh treatment of their colleague Contumeliosus of Riez, who stood accused of many moral infractions (*multa turpia et inhonesta*). Caesarius felt compelled to solicit the support of the papacy: first John II (533–35), and then his successor Agapitus I (535–36). Agapitus supported Contumeliosus's right of appeal. The Contumeliosus affair suggests that despite Caesarius's vigorous exercise of his metropolitan authority at his councils, the fraternal consensus among

[14] Ralph Mathisen, "The 'Second Council of Arles' and the Spirit of Compilation and Codification in Late Roman Gaul," JECS 5.4 (1997): 511–54. I use the term "conciliarism" here and elsewhere following the definition of Paul Valliere, *Conciliarism: A History of Decision-Making in the Church* (Cambridge: Cambridge University Press, 2012), 7: "Decision-making by means of . . . formally constituted, trans-local leadership assemblies called together to resolve issues affecting the life and ministry of the church."

the Provençal attendees may have exceeded their metropolitan's own ability to impose from above conformity in council (*Concilia Galliae: A.511–A.695*, 85–97).[15]

The Contumeliosus episode is also an important reminder of the at-best inconsistent influence of the papacy on conciliar activity beyond Rome during this early period. While prelates might seek papal intervention in local disputes, the bishop of Rome's ability directly to influence foreign affairs was limited.[16] Even Pope Gregory I (590–604), whose prodigious correspondence helped him to stay relatively informed about local ecclesiastical affairs beyond Italy, posted numerous letters over the course of several years to Gallic prelates and monarchs in an effort to encourage them stamp out simony, that is, the selling, purchase, or bartering of ecclesiastical offices and positions (Gregory I *Registrum epistularum* 5.58–60, 8.4, 9.214, 9.216, 9.219–20, 9.223). Gregory proposed a *synodus* as the proper venue to inaugurate this campaign, but as far as we know this synod was never held, and certainly simony did not immediately cease in the Frankish Kingdom.

While the Gallic bishops appear to have been the most active conciliar attendees at the turn of the sixth century, ecclesiastical synods continued to be convoked in other parts of the former Western Empire during these same decades. In the Ostrogothic kingdom, Theodoric the Great, despite his own Arian faith, sought a conciliar resolution to the Laurentian schism, which had been instigated by the contested election of Symmachus (498–514) as bishop of Rome. Unfortunately, this rift engendered hostilities and unresolved issues that ultimately required more direct royal intervention.[17] In an even less successful act of royal interference in conciliar affairs, the Vandal king Huneric convoked a synod of both Arian and pro-Nicene bishops in 484, which proved to be less a sincere effort at arbitration than a staged debate in which the Arians were expected to triumph (Victor of Vita, *Historia* 2.38–44 and 2.52–55). No purely Nicene councils would be held again in Vandal North Africa until the mid-520s, following King Hilderic's recall of exiled bishops in 523. In Iberia, only three synods are known to have assembled in the first three decades of the sixth century, namely, the provincial councils of Tarragona (516), Gerona (517), and Toledo (527/31). While provincial meetings would continue to be held sporadically through the remainder of the century, it was the Third Council of Toledo (589), convoked by the catholic convert King Reccared (d. 601), that marked a new beginning for Iberian conciliarism. It took even longer for conciliarism to take root in Anglo-Saxon England; synods were not held with any regularity until the late seventh century, more than half a century after the missionary bishop Augustine of

15 Klingshirn, *Caesarius of Arles*, 247–50.

16 Ralph W. Mathisen, *Ecclesiastical Factionalism and Religious Controversy in Fifth-Century Gaul* (Washington, DC: Catholic University of America Press, 1989), 44–68, 141–72, and 228–34.

17 Eckhard *Wirbelauer, Zwei Papste in Rom: Der Konflict zwischen Laurentius und Symmachus* (Munich: Tuduv-Verlagsgesellschaft, 1993). John Moorhead, *Theodoric in Italy* (Oxford: Clarendon Press, 1992), 114–39.

Canterbury (d. 604) supposedly met in council with British bishops and teachers (*doctores*) (Bede *Historia Ecclesiastica* 2.2).

While the intensity of conciliar activity varied considerably across the former Roman West at the turn of the sixth century, therefore, the disappearance of imperial rule did not necessarily instigate a sudden or dramatic break in prior conciliar practice. Although a number of the barbarian kings of the early sixth century helped to facilitate continuity with the synodal traditions of previous centuries, it was the episcopal attendees of these councils who ensured links with previous practice. It is as dangerous to generalize about these bishops as it is about the councils they attended. Even within single regions, bishops could vary as to wealth, political involvement, and degree of piety. Recent prosopographical research has also suggested that old assumptions about the common familial backgrounds of bishops may obscure a more diverse reality.[18] Nevertheless, several general observations can be made. First, there was notable continuity in Western provincial organization between the fifth and sixth centuries, with the most notable exceptions occurring in outlying regions of the former empire. While the imposition of new political borders on a traditional ecclesiastical organization complicated not only the exercise of metropolitan authority but also the convocation of interprovincial councils, provincial membership nevertheless remained an important factor in synodal planning and business. Second, while they could in some cases exercise significant local authority, bishops also frequently transcended any theoretical divisions between local and central politics by, among other means, their participation in councils convoked by secular authorities. Finally, through their ordination, common pastoral responsibilities, and their conciliar activities, Western prelates embraced a corporate identity that transcended local, regional, and national borders. While in this period it is more accurate to speak of regional churches than to speak of "the church" as a single corporation, the members of the episcopate nevertheless recognized themselves as belonging to a common order.

These diverse prelates brought with them to councils a shared reverence for tradition. To ensure adherence to accepted norms, conciliar attendees consulted and cited in their acts collections of conciliar canons (*libri canonum*) as well as of Scripture, patristic texts, and Roman secular laws (*leges*). Past canons were read out at councils: a practice that served not only to aid memory but also as a justification for new or revised canonical rules. Conciliar acts often describe this review of older canons as a means of renewing (*renovanda*) ecclesiastical standards, but such conservative claims can obscure a real willingness by conciliar participants to elaborate upon precedent. For example, nearly a dozen Western councils, primarily

18 Steffen Patzold, "Zur Sozialstruktur des Episkopats und zur Ausbildung bischöflicher Herrschaft in Gallien zwischen Spätantike und Frühmittelalter," in M. Becher and S. Dick (eds.), *Völker, Reiche und Namen im frühen Mittelalter* (Munich: W. Fink, 2010), 121–40. On prosopography, see George Beech, "Prosopography," in J. M. Powell (ed.), *Medieval Studies: An Introduction*, 2nd ed. (Syracuse: Syracuse University Press, 1992), 185–226.

Gallic, between the fourth and eleventh centuries promulgated bans against commensality (meal sharing) between Jews and Christians (Elvira [c. 305/6], c. 50; Vannes [461/91], c. 12; Agde [506], c. 40; Epaone [517], c. 15; Orleans [538], c. 14; Mâcon [581/3], c. 15; Clichy [626/7), c. 13; Meaux-Paris [845–6], c. 73; Metz [893], c. 7; Benevento [c. 900], c. 9; Oviedo [1050], c. 6). Despite their shared concern over interfaith dining, the participants of these synods responded to canonical precedent in new and innovative ways, addressing in their canons different populations, threatening a variety of penalties, and providing different justifications for the ban.[19] Explicit reference to canonical tradition could also validate potentially divisive proposals. In 577, for instance, the Frankish king Chilperic I personally supplied a *liber canonum* (book of canons), with supplementary pages, to the forty-five bishops assembled in the Basilica of St. Peter in Paris to hear charges against their colleague, bishop Praetextatus of Rouen (Gregory of Tours, *Decem Libri Historiarum* 5.18). Aware that some of the assembled bishops were hesitant to convict their colleague, Chilperic hoped that the apostolic authority of these canons would convince the prelates to remove Praetextatus from office, which they ultimately voted to do despite the protests of some of those present.

COUNCILS IN THE FRANKISH AND VISIGOTHIC KINGDOMS, c. 511–768

While councils remained an integral part of ecclesiastical governance in the former Roman West, it was in the Frankish and Visigothic Kingdoms between the sixth and eighth centuries where they became most closely integrated with royal administration. Incidents such as Praetextatus's conciliar trial have encouraged the view that councils were little more than royal instruments in both of these regimes. There is little question that the Frankish and post-conversion Visigothic monarchies were heavily invested in conciliarism. Individual kings convoked councils, provided space for their sessions, helped to determine their legislative or judicial agendas, and subsequently promulgated their decrees. But the view that Frankish and Visigothic synods were merely royal instruments ignores the complexity and diversity of conciliar activity in these respective *regna*.

We have knowledge of nearly eighty councils convoked in the Frankish Kingdom between 511 and 768. Of these, there is evidence of royal convocation for only a little more than 60 percent. Moreover, the Frankish monarchy never made any concerted or sustained efforts to monopolize conciliar convocation. Provincial councils continued to be held – although their frequency is difficult to gauge – throughout this period without any royal involvement whatsoever. We must be wary, too, about assuming what the extent of royal involvement was even in those councils known to

[19] Gregory I. Halfond, "A Hermeneutical Feast: Interreligious Dining in Early Medieval Conciliar Legislation," *Haskins Society Journal* 26 (2014): 31–46.

have been convoked on royal authority. For example, while Chilperic I succeeded in his push to have Praetextatus of Rouen removed from office in 577, he failed to convince the bishops assembled at his villa at Berny three years later to convict bishop Gregory of Tours on charges of slandering Chilperic's queen, Fredegund. According to Gregory's own account of the proceedings, Chilperic realized that the accused enjoyed wide episcopal and possibly even popular support, and so allowed the council to dismiss the charges against Gregory (Gregory of Tours, *Decem libri historiarum* 5.49).

In several cases, Frankish councils directly challenged royal interests. When the Council of Saints (561/67) deposed bishop Emerius of Saintes against the wishes of Chilperic's brother, Charibert, the furious king ordered the council's president, bishop Leontius of Bordeaux, to be fined (Gregory of Tours, *Decem libri historiarum* 4.26). The Council of Tours (567) similarly failed to convince Charibert of the canonical necessity of putting aside his wife Marcovefa, a former nun and sister-in-law of the king. As a result, one of the council's participants, bishop Germanus of Paris, later excommunicated the king (*Concilia Galliae: A.511–A.695*, 175–94; Gregory of Tours *Decem libri historiarum* 4.26).

Anecdotes such as these are suggestive less of conciliar independence in the Frankish kingdom than of the role of councils as institutions that mediated, not always successfully, between royal and episcopal agendas. We should recall that when councils such as Paris (577) and Berny (580) assembled to purge episcopal enemies of the regime, they did so with the support of many of the assembled prelates. The Council of Mâcon (585), for instance, penalized those bishops who supported the territorial claims of the royal pretender Gundovald against those of the council's convoker, Guntram of Burgundy (Gregory of Tours, *Decem libri historiarum* 8.20). The powerful seventh-century Neustrian mayor Ebroin similarly enjoyed episcopal support when he sought conciliar condemnations of ecclesiastical nemeses including Chramlinus of Embrun and Leudegar of Autun (*Die Urkunden der Merowinger* no. 122; *Passio Leudegarii I* 33).

Without generalizing the extent of Gallo-Frankish bishops' involvement in the political machinations of the court, we may say that the corporate episcopate certainly was invested in and attempted to influence royal policy. To this end, Frankish councils assembled not only to dictate intra-ecclesiastical policy, but also to settle public matters (*pro causis publicis*), addressing issues related to public welfare, peace, and administrative order. It was not uncommon, for instance, for synods to meet following the cessation of military conflicts to address territorial and property disputes, the partisan activities of ecclesiastics, and the charitable obligations of the episcopate. Additionally, councils such as Orléans (511) and Paris (614) – the latter convoked by the triumphant Chlothar II following the execution of his longtime political foe, Brunhild – facilitated the assimilation of Gallic bishops into newly expanded kingdoms. Inspired by their belief that domestic peace impacted the ability of Christians to enjoy the *pax ecclesiae* (i.e., the unity and tranquility of the Church), bishops in council sought *consensus* among themselves and with the monarchy.

In short, the legislative agenda of Frankish councils were intended to complement or inform royal policy rather than to compete with it. While sometimes canons explicitly called for the assistance of secular judges (*iudices*) in the enforcement of the new rule within their jurisdictions (e.g., Orléans [538], c. 34; Tours [567], c. 16; Mâcon [581/83], c. 7 Clichy [626/67], c. 27), many others with no such instructions still required royal support if they were ever to be implemented, such as those canons excluding Jews from public office (Clermont [535], c. 9; Mâcon [581/83], c. 13). In the preamble (*praefatio*) of the acts of the Council of Clichy (626/67), the bishops requested the assistance of Chlothar II in the promulgation of those canons produced more than a decade earlier at the Council of Paris (614). The Merovingian rulers were probably selective in their enforcement of conciliar canons, just as they were selective in their use of such canons as the basis for their own legislation. And in those cases when royal legislation did derive its inspiration from conciliar antecedents – as was the case with Chlothar's edict issued at the conclusion of the Council of Paris – the language and even intent of the original canons could be dramatically altered to align more closely with royal interests (*Capitularia regum Francorum* no. 9). The Frankish kingdom, which generally embraced pluralism in its acceptance of legitimate sources of regulation, maintained in this way a traditional distinction between canonical *regulae* and secular *leges* while still recognizing the binding authority of each.[20]

The integration of conciliar rules and secular legislation in the Frankish Kingdom became even more pronounced in the mid-eighth century, when the Pippinid mayors, whose power by now surpassed that of the Merovingians themselves, took responsibility for promulgating conciliar canons in their own capitularies, which lacked the episcopal subscriptions that traditionally had evidenced the consensus of the episcopal participants.[21] When *consensus* is referenced in these documents it is not in reference to intra-episcopal agreement, but rather to the consensus between the Pippinid convoker with the conciliar participants. The proof of orthodoxy lay in the canons' contents, rather than the identities of their authors. It is possible that the growing influence of systematic canonical collections, such as the early seventh-century *Vetus Gallica*, may already have acculturated the Gallo-Frankish bishops to this notion that canonical authority could be gauged without knowledge of the legislators' identities. Additionally, this evolving conception of conciliar consensus, as well as the new medium of canon publication, derives in part from the nature of those councils that promulgated these canons: Following a Merovingian precedent, the early Pippinid councils typically met alongside or in conjunction with an

20 Olivier Guillot, "La justice dans le royaume franc à l'époque mérovingienne," in *La giustizia nell'alto medioevo, secoli V–VIII*, Settimane di Studio del Centro Italiano di Studi sull'alto medioevo 42 (Spoleto: Fondazione Centro Italiano di studi sull'alto medioevo, 1994), 653–731.

21 On the rise of the Pippinids, see Paul Fouracre, *The Age of Charles Martel* (Harlow: Pearson, 2000).

assembly of secular magnates. The term *concilia mixta* is sometimes used by modern scholars to describe this model of conciliar organization. But it is unlikely that all of the councils of the 740s and 750s took this precise form. Similarly, as regards their legislative agendas, these councils did not represent a dramatic break with prior Frankish conciliar precedent, despite their foreshadowing of a subsequent Carolingian conception of the role of synods in royal governance.

While the Franks were quick to embrace conciliarism as an effective medium for coordinating episcopal and royal agendas, this realization did not find common acceptance in Visigothic Spain until the conversion of Reccared from Arian to Catholic Christianity in 587. On one level, this is somewhat surprising, if one considers the sponsorship of conciliarism by Alaric II in the Visigothic kingdom of Toulouse at the beginning of the century. But the political uncertainty following Alaric's death (which included a period of Ostrogothic intervention in Iberia), the doctrinal divisions between the royal regime and the Iberian episcopate, and the possible paucity of even provincial conciliar activity in the intervening decades, were all probable factors in delaying this process. Only six provincial councils are attested in Visigothic Iberia between 515 and 587, not including the Councils of Braga of 561 and 572 convoked in the Suevic Kingdom.

Nevertheless, between the Third and Fourth Councils of Toledo (589 and 633), both of which were convened on royal authority, a new Visigothic conception of conciliarism emerged, grounded in an expanded and ultimately coercive notion of Christian consensus. This consensus went far beyond the conciliar attendees themselves to include the entirety of the kingdom.[22] The subsequent seventh-century councils of Toledo expanded on this notion, threatening harsh sanctions against those who challenged the ecclesio-political unity of the kingdom. Beginning with Toledo (633), c. 75, canons regularly threatened persons who challenged royal authority (e.g., Toledo [636], cc. 2–5 and 7; Toledo [638], cc. 12, 17–18; Toledo [646], c. 1; Toledo [656], c. 2; Toledo [683], c. 4, Toledo [693], cc. 9–10), while others restricted the rights of perceived social and religious deviants, notably the Jews. Indeed, in their severity, the Visigothic anti-Jewish legislation has no parallel anywhere else in the early medieval Latin West. Additionally, the Visigothic councils, with greater regularity than even near-contemporary Frankish canonical legislation, addressed issues of direct political consequence, such as royal succession, rebellion, and loyalty oaths. This unusual degree of concern with secular affairs was the consequence of several factors, including Toledan councils' royal convocation, the attendance of kings and/or their delegates, and the regular provision (after 653) by convoking monarchs of written instructions (*tomi*) intended to inform conciliar agendas.

[22] Rachel L. Stocking, *Bishops, Councils and Consensus in the Visigothic Kingdom*, 589–633 (Ann Arbor: The University of Michigan Press, 2000).

In light of this close attention to temporal concerns, it is not at all surprising that the seventh-century Councils of Toledo frequently have been characterized as uniquely national or political institutions, even as proto-parliaments, and Visigothic political ideology as a form of Iberian caesaropapism, in which the head of state also dominated the church.[23] Yet, while there is little question that Visigothic kings recognized councils as venues for promoting their own ecclesio-political agendas, the actual business conducted in these assemblies did not always precisely conform to these agendas. Moreover, the convocation of national councils did not necessarily coincide with moments of royal strength. At the Council of Toledo (653), for instance, the bishops and lay courtiers seem to have worked collaboratively to win concessions from the recently crowned King Reccesuinth, who had just put down an uprising against his power. A similar alliance reemerged in the early 680s in the aftermath of Wamba's deposition.[24] Such moments may give some credence to a view of the Visigothic program of conciliar-imposed consensus as a practical failure.[25] Nonetheless, a failure to reach true consensus at specific moments, particularly moments of political stress or transformation, did not negate the mutual recognition by the Visigothic monarchy, nobility, and episcopate that councils were an ideal venue for articulating, if not always enforcing, a shared vision of a kingdom unified under God. In general, as Roger Collins has observed, "the Church in Visigothic Spain was a redoubtable supporter of kingship ... but it did not commit itself to the fortunes of individual kings."[26] And while it is true that national councils were not held at regular intervals between 589 and 711, and that they varied in scale of attendance, councils remained an integral institution of the realm during virtually the entirety of the Visigothic period. It is no coincidence that it was in Iberia that the earliest conciliar *ordines* were composed.

[23] For some characterizations of the councils, see E. A. Thompson, *The Goths in Spain* (Oxford: Clarendon Press, 1969), 279; Jeremy duQuesnay Adams, "The Eighth Council of Toledo (653): Precursor of Medieval Parliaments?" in T. F. X. Noble and J. J. Contreni (eds.), *Religion, Culture, and Society in the Early Middle Ages: Studies in Honor of Richard E. Sullivan*, Studies in Medieval Culture 23 (Kalamazoo: Medieval Institute Publications, 1987), 41–54. On Visigothic caesaropapism, see P. D. King, *Law and Society in the Visigothic Kingdom*, Cambridge Studies in Medieval Life and Thought (Cambridge: Cambridge University Press, 1972), 125; A. T. Fear, "God and Caesar: The Dynamics of Visigothic Monarchy," in L. Mitchell and C. Melville (eds.), *Every Inch a King: Comparative Studies on Kings and Kingship in the Ancient and Medieval Worlds*, Rulers & Elites 2 (Leiden: Brill, 2013), 285–302.

[24] Roger Collins, *Visigothic Spain, 409–711* (Oxford: Blackwell Publishing, 2004), 86–90, 95–96, and 103–04.

[25] Stocking, *Bishops, Councils and Consensus*, 189–91.

[26] Roger Collins, *Early Medieval Spain: Unity in Diversity, 400–1000*, 2nd ed., New Studies in Medieval History (London: Palgrave, 1995), 121.

BISHOPS AND COUNCILS IN THE CAROLINGIAN ERA

While the Pippinid Councils of mid-eighth-century Francia drew much of their inspiration from the synods of preceding centuries, they also served as a prelude to a new era of conciliarism in Western Europe, one that properly began with the royal coronation of Charlemagne in 768. Like his father and uncle before him, Charlemagne assumed personal responsibility for the publication of conciliar canons in his own capitularies, but he went even further in his integration of the ecclesiastical and royal agendas. Embracing his own ministerial duty (*ministerium*) to safeguard the spiritual health of his realm, he promoted conciliarism – perhaps most notably at the Council of Frankfurt (794), in whose deliberations he personally participated – while never relying exclusively on councils as the means to ensure this goal. Capitularies like the *Admonitio generalis* (789) promulgated ecclesiastical rules on the authority of the king, not on the fraternal consensus of his bishops. Charlemagne did not intend to undermine the legislative authority of the Frankish episcopate; on the contrary, his program of reform (*correctio*) embraced both corporate and individual episcopal rulemaking, the latter in the form of episcopal capitularies.[27] Furthermore, in his own legislation, Charlemagne drew heavily on episcopal guidance, both venerable and contemporary. Not only did the *Admonitio generalis* draw heavily on the contents of the *Dionysio-Hadriana* (a chronologically arranged collection of conciliar canons and papal decretals commissioned by Pope Hadrian I before 774), but its germination may lie in the counsel proffered to Charlemagne by his religious advisors.[28] Yet the *Admonitio* ultimately did not derive its compulsory authority from episcopal deliberation, but rather from the ministerial power of the king himself. Charlemagne treated the royal assembly over which he personally presided as an organ of religious legislation that was as legitimate as purely episcopal councils had been in the past.

Charlemagne's practice of absorbing matters traditionally addressed in church councils into royal law, such as the protection of churches, orphans, and widows, did not render ecclesiastical councils superfluous. Nevertheless, following his imperial coronation in 800, the emperor seems to have convoked only a handful of councils in the years prior to his so-called reform councils of 813. Possibly drawing inspiration from the program of Bavarian councils convoked a little over a decade earlier by Arn of Salzburg, Charlemagne organized the five reform synods, which met respectively in Arles, Rheims, Mainz, Chalon, and Tours, in order to implement on a regional level the program of *correctio* that he had begun over two decades earlier.[29] But it remains a matter of debate as to the extent to which these councils also marked a revival of episcopally driven conciliarism in the Frankish realm.

27 Jennifer R. Davis, *Charlemagne's Practice of Empire* (Cambridge: Cambridge University Press, 2015), 211–15.

28 Rosamond McKitterick, *Charlemagne: The Formation of a European Identity* (Cambridge: Cambridge University Press, 2008), 239–40.

29 Davis, *Charlemagne's Practice of Empire*, 243–59 and 373–74.

During the imperial reign of Louis the Pious (814–40), the Frankish emperor maintained his responsibility to minister to his people while recognizing the bishops as active partners in this task, as suggested by the regularity of conciliar meetings. From the episcopal perspective, such collaboration was naturally desirable, but increasingly the Frankish bishops maintained that it had to be predicated on a recognition of their own unique and separate (some even argued superior) authority, in what has been dubbed by Steffen Patzold the "Paris Model" (after the Council of Paris of 829). This fluid ideological construct may have found early expression in the Pseudo-Isidorian forgeries (see Chapter 19).[30]

The program of ecclesiastical reform (*correctio*) sponsored by the Carolingians and the Frankish bishops influenced conciliar activities beyond the borders of the empire, most notably in Anglo-Saxon England. Conciliarism in Anglo-Saxon England, as already noted, only began in earnest in the late seventh century. It continued intensely over the next several centuries. While the evidence for synodal activity in England becomes increasingly sparse in the late ninth century, royal assemblies attended by both ecclesiastics and secular magnates, akin to the Carolingian *concilia mixta*, seem to have retained their significance into the tenth century.[31] Not surprisingly, papal influence on the English conciliar protocol and priorities was strong, but this influence was partly filtered through the Frankish kingdom, where seventh-, eighth-, and ninth-century English prelates sought consecration and monastic cloister, as well as manuscripts. On very rare occasions, English prelates even crossed the channel to attend Frankish synods, such as Paris (614) and Frankfurt (794). The Franks, for their part, did not make much of an effort to attend English synods, although Charlemagne, from a distance, played a role in the Legatine Councils of 786.[32] Frankish influence on Anglo-Saxon canonical legislation can be seen in the acts of the Council of Clofesho (747), the Legatine Councils of 786, and the Council of Chelsea (816).[33]

Books proved to be the greatest transmitter of Continental influence. These manuscripts included canonical collections, which documented the Mediterranean conciliar tradition. Among those early medieval collections that were brought to England from abroad, only a small number survive in English copies, such as the *Collectio Quadripartita*, a late ninth-century compilation from Rheims, copied in revised form in a tenth- or eleventh-century manuscript from Exeter (Oxford, Bodl. 718 [2632]). The

30 Steffen Patzold, *Episcopus. Wissen über Bischöfe im Frankenreich des späten 8. bis frühen 10. Jahrhunderts* (Stuttgart: Thorbecke, 2008).

31 Catherine Cubitt, "Bishops and Councils in Late Saxon England," in W. Hartmann (ed.), *Recht und Gericht in Kirche und Welt um 900*, Schriften des Historischen Kollegs 69 (Munich: Oldenbourg 2007), 151–67. R. H. Helmholz, *The Oxford History of the Laws of England*, vol. 1 (Oxford: Oxford University Press, 2004), 17–19.

32 Hanna Vollrath, *Die Synoden Englands bis 1066* (Paderborn: Schöningh, 1985), 165. Joanna Story, *Carolingian Connections: Anglo-Saxon England and Carolingian Francia, c. 750–870* (Aldershot: Ashgate, 2002), 90.

33 Catherine Cubitt, *Anglo-Saxon Church Councils c. 650 – c. 850, Studies in the Early History of Britain* (London: Leicester University Press, 1995), 102–04, 160–85, 200–02.

identities of additional canonical collections known to English clerics can be inferred from citations that appear in English manuscripts. For example, excerpts from Ansegisus's early ninth-century collection of Frankish capitulary articles – most frequently *De festivitatibus anni* (2.33) – were included in several tenth- and eleventh-century English manuscripts (e.g., Cambridge, Corpus Christi 57; Cambridge, Corpus Christi 265; London, BL Cotton Tiberius A.III; and London, BL Cotton Titus A.IV). At the turn of the millennium, Frankish influence was filtered through Archbishop Wulfstan II of York (d. 1023) – whom Patrick Wormald once described as a "Carolingian ideologue" – and his circle, who drew heavily upon Carolingian canons and collections, including Ansegisus, the *Admonitio Generalis*, and the *Capitula* of Theodulf of Orléans.[34] The early years of the Norman period would see the popularization in England of the Carolingian era's most notorious intellectual achievement, the Pseudo-Isidorian corpus (see Chapter 19), through the compilation and dissemination of the *Collectio Lanfranci*.

On the Continent, the second half of the ninth century did not witness any notable diminishment of conciliar activity despite gradual political fragmentation within the Frankish empire. In Italy, conciliar activity seems actually to have increased, despite the receding of Carolingian influence, with at least two dozen Roman synods alone attested for the years between 850 and 900. The pontificate of John VIII (872–82) was a particularly busy period for episcopal meetings in Rome and in Northern Italy, with more than half a dozen recorded synods, including two held in Rome in 876 at which the pontiff condemned the ambitious bishop and future pontiff, Formosus of Porto (d. 896). These synods would by no means be the last conciliar tribunals to judge Formosus. Certainly, the most infamous of the late ninth-century Italian councils was the "Cadaver Synod" of 897, at which Pope Stephan VI (896–97) ordered the body of Formosus, his now-deceased predecessor, to be dug up and placed on trial. Although Formosus was thrown into the Tiber following his conviction, the posthumous miracles attributed to him helped lead to an overturned conviction and the murder of his papal prosecutor. By the tenth century, synodal activity in Italy had slowed somewhat, with only two major clusters of papal synods roughly coinciding with the imperial reigns of Otto I (962–73) and Otto III (996–1002). Not surprisingly, the bulk of these councils responded in various ways to the involvement of the German emperors in Italian and papal affairs.

In the Frankish heartland, as well, the Carolingians and their bishops continued to pursue ecclesiastical *correctio* through conciliarism into the tenth century. Recent scholarship has demonstrated in particular the conciliar and canonical productivity in the late ninth century and the beginning of the tenth, with nearly two dozen canonical *acta* surviving from this period, whose contents demonstrate innovative

[34] Patrick Wormald, *The Making of English Law: King Alfred to the Twelfth Century*, Legislation and Its Limits 1 (Oxford: Wiley, 1999), 211–19, 341–45, and 465.

approaches to new and traditional issues of conciliar concern. Additionally, these decades saw the popularization of the itinerant synodal court (*Sendgericht*), which heard cases involving both clerics and laymen.[35] While conciliar activity in the aggregate did not dramatically diminish in frequency in subsequent decades of the tenth century, comparatively more councils are recorded for the western kingdom than the eastern, and there were fewer large reform councils comparable to those of Charlemagne and Louis the Pious. Additionally, there was a significant decline in canonical legislating, initially in the west, and by mid-century in the east as well.[36] Nevertheless, both the conciliar acts and the canonical collections of the tenth century suggest that bishops in these years prioritized many of the same legislative concerns as their Carolingian-era predecessors.[37] They similarly inherited a conception of their own ministerial responsibilities from these precursors, with whom they also shared a substantial public status and influence that transcended any simple divisions between political periphery and center, spiritual and earthly authority, and individual charisma and corporate identity.[38]

The Reception of Conciliar Canons at the End of the Millennium and Beyond

The fundamental irony of canonical transmission is that conciliar canons, in order to retain their relevancy over time, had to be detached (and detachable) from the circumstances that prompted their composition. While the compilers of canonical collections made their selections on the basis, in no small part, of the manuscripts that happened to be available to them locally, the contents of systematic collections in particular reflected the conscious choices made by the compilers. And while the status awarded to certain synods, most notably the eastern ecumenical councils of Late Antiquity (see, e.g., Isidore of Seville *Etymologiae* 6.16.5–10), was certainly a factor, so too was relevancy. In his preface to his *Libri Duo de Synodalibus Causis*, Regino of Prüm famously defended his decision "to include those decisions

35 Wilfried Hartmann, *Kirche und Kirchenrecht um 900: die Bedeutung der spätkarolingischen Zeit für Tradition und Innovation im kirchlichen Recht* (Hannover: Hahn, 2008).

36 Ernst-Dieter Hehl, "Die Synoden des ostfränkisch-deutschen und des westfränkischen Reichs im 10. Jahrhundert Karolingische Traditionen und Neuansätze," in Hartmann, *Recht und Gericht in Kirche und Welt um 900*, 125–50.

37 Rosemond McKitterick, "The Church," in T. Reuter (ed.), *The New Cambridge Medieval History*, vol. 3 (Cambridge: Cambridge University Press, 2015), 130–62, at 153–56.

38 John S. Ott and Anna Trumbore Jones, "Introduction: The Bishop Reformed," in J. S. Ott and A. Trumbore Jones (eds.), *The Bishop Reformed: Studies of Episcopal Power and Culture in the Central Middle Ages*, Church, Faith, and Culture in the Medieval West (Aldershot: Routledge, 2007), 1–20, at 1–12. John Eldevik, *Episcopal Power and Ecclesiastical Reform in the German Empire: Tithes, Lordship, and Community*, 950–1150 (Cambridge: Cambridge University Press, 2012), 7–10. Timothy Reuter, "A Europe of Bishops. The Age of Wulfstan of York and Burchard of Worms," in L. Körntgen and D. Waßenhoven (eds.), *Patterns of Episcopal Power, Bishops in 10th and 11th Century Western Europe* (Berlin: De Gruyter 2011), 17–38.

I believed more relevant to our dangerous age, and which seemed to pertain to matters of concern" (Regino of Prüm, *Libri Duo de Synodalibus Causis, praefatio*). Additionally, not only did many councils and individual canons fail to make any significant impact on the canon law of the central and late Middle Ages, but also in the process of transmission councils could be misidentified and authorship of their acts could be misattributed. For example, the Council of Tours (567), c. 21 misattributed Carthage (416), c. 26, to a fictional Milevitan synod, a mistake repeated in several sixth- and seventh-century Gallic and Iberian canonical collections. In a similar case of mistaken identity, the council of Metz (893), c. 7, credited the legislation of Mâcon (581/3) to bishop Syagrius of Autun, who had indeed attended that council, but whose identity as the author of its acts is not indicated by any contemporary source. And then there were the outright forgeries and canons edited or rewritten to suit a copyist's needs. The legacy of individual councils thus was at best uneven, with the memory of many meetings preserved only through references, often brief, in other sources.

That said, while many individual synods failed to make any appreciable impact outside of their own immediate context, collectively they still contributed to a living tradition of ecclesiastical regulation that had yet to be codified, with its inconsistencies ironed out, but that would eventually be incorporated into the canon law of the central Middle Ages. The conciliar participants of Late Antiquity and the early Middle Ages, most of whose identities either were forgotten or reduced to mere names by subsequent canonists, consciously participated in this tradition through the publication of their own acts, in which they legislated for the present, with an eye to the past rather than to the future. And while their acts reflect a common effort to instill administrative and moral order within the Church, they were the product of hundreds of meetings and thousands of authors. They were the sources of that discord out of which Gratian, author of the influential *Concordance of Discordant Canons* (usually known as the *Decretum*) in the 1140s, and subsequent canon lawyers wrought harmony.

SOURCES

Bede. *Historia Ecclesiastica Gentis Anglorum*. Ed. Bertram Colgrave and R. A. B. Mynors. Revised ed. Oxford, 1992. [English translation: *The Ecclesiastical History of the English People*, trans. Bertram Colgrave, ed. Judith McClure and Roger Collins (Oxford: Clarendon Press, 1999).]

Capitularia regum Francorum. MGH LL, Sectio II, 1–2. Ed. Alfred Boretius and Viktor Krause (1883–97).

Concilia aevi Karolini 742–842. MGH Conc. (=MGH LL, Sectio III), 2: 1–2. Ed. Albert Werminghoff (1906–08).

Concilia Africae: A.345–A.525. CCL 149. Ed. Charles Munier (1974).

Concilia Galliae: A.314–A.506. CCL 148. Ed. Charles Munier (1963).

Concilia Galliae: A.511–A.695. CCL 148A. Ed. Charles de Clercq (1963).

Concilios visigóticos e hispano-romanos. Ed. José Vives. Barcelona and Madrid: Instituto Enrique Flórez, 1963.

Councils and Ecclesiastical Documents Relating to Great Britain and Ireland. Vol. 3. Ed. Arthur West Haddan and William Stubbs. Oxford: Clarendon Press, 1871.

Councils and Synods with Other Documents Relating to the English Church I (A.D. 871–1204). Ed. Dorothy Whitelock, Martin Brett, and Christopher Brooke. Oxford: Clarendon Press, 1981.

Cyprian of Carthage. *Epistularium*. Ed. G. F. Diercks. CCL 3B-D (1994–99).

Cyprian of Carthage. *Sententiae episcoporum numero LXXXVII de haereticis baptizandis*. Ed. G. F. Diercks. CCL 3E (2004).

Gregory I, Pope. *Registrum Epistularum*. CCL 140. Ed. Dag Norberg (1972). [English translation: *The Letters of Gregory the Great*, trans. John R. C. Martyn, 3 vols., Mediaeval Sources in Translation (Toronto: PIMS, 2004).

Gregory of Tours. *Decem Libri Historiarum*. MGH SRM 1.1. Ed. by Bruno Krusch and Wilhelm Levison. Hanover: Hahn, 1937–51. English translation: *History of the Franks*. Trans. Lewis Thorpe. London: Penguin, 1974.

Isidore of Seville. *Etymologiae*. Ed. by W. M. Lindsay. Oxford: Clarendon Press, 1911. [English translation: *The Etymologies of Isidore of Seville*, trans. S. A. Barney, W. J. Lewis, J. A. Beach, and O. Berghof (Cambridge: Cambridge University Press, 2006).

Die Konzilien der Karolingischen Teilreiche 843–859. MGH LL, Sectio III, tom. 3. Ed. Wilfried Hartmann (1984).

Die Konzilien der Karolingischen Teilreiche 860–874. MGH Conc. (= MGH LL, Sectio III), tom. 4. Ed. Wilfried Hartmann (1998).

Die Konzilien der Karolingischen Teilreiche 875–911. MGH Conc. (=MGH LL, Sectio III), tom. 5. Ed. W. Hartmann, Isolde Schröder, and Gerhard Schmitz (2014).

Die Konzilien Deutschlands und Reichsitaliens 916–1001. MGH Conc. (= MGH LL, Sectio III), tom. 6. Ed. Ernst-Dieter Hehl, H. Fuhrmann, and C. Servatius (1987–2007).

Die Konzilordines des Früh- und Hochmittelalters. Ed. Herbert Schneider. Hanover: Hahn, 1996.

Passio Leudegarii Episcopi et Martyris Augustodunensis I. MGH SRM 5. Ed. Bruno Krusch (1910) [English translation in *Late Merovingian France: History and Hagiography, 640–720*, trans. P. Fouracre and R. A. Gerberding (Manchester: Manchester University Press, 1996).]

Regino of Prüm. *Das Sendhandbuch des Regino von Prüm*. Ed. and trans. F. W. H. Wasserschleben and Wilfried Hartmann. Darmstadt: Wissenschaftliche Buchgesellschaft, 2004.

Die Urkunden der Merowinger. Ed. C. Brühl, T. Kölzer, M. Hartmann, and A. Stieldorf. Hanover: Hahn, 2001.

Victor of Vita. *Historia persecutiones Africanae provinciae*. MGH AA 3.1. Ed. Karl Halm (1879).

TRANSLATIONS

For English translations of the canons of those councils considered ecumenical in the Roman tradition, see Norman P. Tanner, *Decrees of the Ecumenical Councils*, 2 vols. (Washington, DC: Georgetown University Press, 1990). This has the Latin edition of Guiseppe Alberigo et al. with English translations by Tanner on facing pages.

The acts of most of the Western councils discussed in this chapter have never been translated into English in their entirety. Nevertheless, there are some translations and many paraphrases of numerous canons in Karl Joseph von Hefele, *Conciliengeschichte nach den Quellen bearbeitet*, 9 vols. (Freiburg im Breisgau: Herder, 1873–90). The first four volumes of Hefele's *Conciliengeschichte* cover church councils of the first millennium. A revised edition in French, translated initially by Henri Leclercq and continued by others, is now a standard work of reference: *Histoire des conciles d'après les documents originaux*, 11 vols. (Paris: Letouzey: 1907–52). There is also a partial English translation from the German by William R. Clark, A *History of the Christian Councils from the Original Documents*, 5 vols. (Edinburgh: T. & T. Clark, 1872–96), although this lacks the expanded commentary and reliability of the French edition. All three of these resources are readily available online.

Also translated into English by Richard Price are *The Acts of the Lateran Synod of* 649, Translated Texts for Historians (Liverpool: Liverpool University Press, 2014), which includes extensive and informative commentary.

FURTHER READING

Brundage, James A. *Medieval Canon Law*. New York: Routledge, 1995.

Cubitt, Catherine. *Anglo-Saxon Church Councils c. 650–c. 850*. London: Leicester University Press, 1995.

Halfond, Gregory I. *The Archaeology of Frankish Church Councils, AD 511–768*. Leiden: Brill, 2010.

Hess, Hamilton. *The Early Development of Canon Law and the Council of Serdica. Oxford Early Christian Studies*. Oxford: Oxford University Press, 2002.

Louth, Andrew. "Conciliar Records and Canons." In F. Young et al. (eds.), *The Cambridge History of Early Christian Literature* (Cambridge: Cambridge University Press, 2004), 391–95.

MacMullen, Ramsay. *Voting About God in Early Church Councils*. New Haven, CT: Yale University Press, 2006.

Mathisen, Ralph W. *Ecclesiastical Factionalism and Religious Controversy in Fifth-Century Gaul*. Washington, DC: Catholic University of America Press, 1989.

McKitterick, Rosamond. *The Frankish Church and the Carolingian Reforms, 789–895*. London: Royal Historical Society, 1977.

Rapp, Claudia. *Holy Bishops in Late Antiquity: The Nature of Christian Leadership in an Age of Transition*. Berkeley: University of California Press, 2005.

Reuter, Timothy. "A Europe of Bishops. The Age of Wulfstan of York and Burchard of Worms." In L. Körntgen and D. Waßenhoven (eds.), *Patterns of Episcopal Power: Bishops in 10th and 11th Century Western Europe* (Berlin: De Gruyter, 2011), 17–38.

Reynolds, Roger. "The Organization, Law and Liturgy of the Western Church, 700–900." In R. McKitterick (ed.), *The New Cambridge Medieval History*, vol. 2, 587–621. Cambridge: Cambridge University Press, 1995.

Stocking, Rachel L. *Bishops, Councils, and Consensus in the Visigothic Kingdom, 589–633*. History, Languages, and Cultures of the Spanish and Portuguese Worlds. Ann Arbor: The University of Michigan Press, 2000.

Ullmann, Walter. "Public Welfare and Social Legislation in the Early Medieval Councils." *Studies in Church History* 7 (1971): 1–39.

5

The Papacy

Clemens Gantner and Stefan Schima

The papacy is connected to the office of the bishop of Rome. During the central Middle Ages, by around 1050, the papacy was at the center of a well-integrated juridical and bureaucratic institution encompassing all of Western Europe. And by the middle of the thirteenth century, decretal letters, in which the popes spoke authoritatively both as jurists and as judges, had become the chief basis of canon law. This chapter considers the emergence of the papacy during the first millennium.

Which bishop of Rome was the first to merit the title "pope" (*papa*) in the medieval and modern sense of that term – for this was originally a title of respect used to address any bishop – is disputable. Only from the early second century may we even speak of a "Roman Church" in the sense of a community identified as being that of the capital of the empire. By around the middle of the second century, this community was headed by a single bishop. The idea of double "apostolicity" – i.e., that two Apostles, Peter and Paul, had founded the Roman see – can be traced to the second half of the second century.[1] But Paul shows in his letter to the Romans, written in the middle of the first century, that there were already Christians in Rome before he visited the city (e.g., Rom 1:7). It is clear, therefore, that Paul was not responsible for bringing Christianity to Rome. Moreover, Paul says nothing about Peter's visiting the city. That Peter did so may be surmised for a later date, but it cannot be proved.[2]

Peter has a special role among the Apostles in New Testament writings, although it would be difficult to define this role precisely.[3] Two sayings of Jesus have

1 On the concept of "apostolocity," see G. G. Blum, *Tradition und Sukzession. Studien zum Normbegriff des Apostolischen von Paulus bis Irenäus*, Arbeiten zur Geschichte und Theologie des Luthertums 9 (Berlin: Lutherisches Verlagshaus, 1963), especially 208–13 on the Roman church's claim to apostolicity.

2 On Peter and Paul in Rome and their supposed burial places, see S. Heid (ed.), *Petrus und Paulus in Rom. Eine interdisziplinäre Debatte* (Freiburg i. Br.: Herder, 2012); and O. Zwierlein, *Petrus und Paulus in Jerusalem und Rom. Vom Neuen Testament zu den apokryphen Apostelakten* (Berlin: De Gruyter, 2013).

3 S. Schima, *Caput Occidentis? Die römische Kirche und der Westen von den Anfängen bis Konstantin*, Kirche und Recht 23 (Vienna: Plöchl, 2000), 18–19.

traditionally been used to justify Roman primacy on the basis of Peter's association with the city: Matthew 16:18–19 (the rock passage) and John 21:15–17 (the charge to Peter to care for the sheep). In academic biblical exegesis today, however, these are not seen as historical references to a universal church, still less as allusions to papal primacy.[4]

Paul did not know Jesus personally and was not an apostle in the strict sense of being a companion of Jesus. Nevertheless, the large quantity of Pauline writings included in the New Testament is a sign that Paul enjoyed high standing in early Christianity, alongside Peter and other Apostles who held special significance in the early church, such as James "the brother of our Lord" (Gal 1:19).

THE STATUS OF ROME BEFORE THE CONVERSION OF CONSTANTINE

The importance and relevance of Rome for the pagan world must have influenced the special status of the Roman church in Christianity. This is hard to prove, but there are many clues. For example, the imperial cult was rooted in the cult of Rome as a city, and the pagan High Priest (*pontifex maximus*) held an important office in Rome and was not allowed to leave *Terra Italia*. The most important Pantheon of the whole empire, the center of the veneration of the Capitoline Triad, was in Rome, and the city was the center of the *Pax Romana*. That said, only a few sources provide concrete evidence that the special position of Roman Christianity was underpinned not only by the apostolic tradition but also by the city's supreme position in pagan Antiquity.

The Roman church was (and still is) the only local church claiming to be situated at the site of the martyrdom and burial of *two* Apostles. This put Rome in a singular position. Although the presence of an apostolic grave did not in itself constitute a decisive marker of apostolic authority for local churches,[5] it could nevertheless be used as evidence that an opinion held by a local church was authentic and authoritative.

The so-called *First Epistle of Clement*, dating from the end of the first century, holds up the example of the apostles Peter and Paul, who are said to have "persevered" until their deaths (5.2; FC 15, 75–76) and to have died confessing their faith (5.4–7; FC 15, 77). This might refer to their ministry and eventual martyrdom at Rome. The letter was dispatched by a church in Rome. Although no author is mentioned, analysis of the text suggests that it was the work of a single individual. Remarkably, the letter assumes a certain air of authority, perhaps because it was sent from the imperial capital, although this supposition would still leave many questions unanswered. The letter is addressed to the church in Corinth, where a conflict

4 Cf. N. Brox, *Kirchengeschichte des Altertums*, 5th edition (Düsseldorf: Patmos, 2008), 105.

5 N. Brox, "Probleme einer Frühdatierung des römischen Primats," *Kairos* 18 (1976): 81–99, at 89.

among the members of the community has made the letter necessary. A few younger members have risen against the presbyters, ousting them from their positions. The letter advises the Corinthians that these actions are wrong and encourages contrition and repentance. The *First Epistle of Clement* is an admonitory letter, but it is not characterized by any sense that the author was hierarchically superior to those he is addressing, although later commentators reasonably construed it as an early example of Roman primacy in jurisdiction. The letter treats the conduct of the younger community members in Corinth as an insurrection (1.1, 46.9, 51.1; FC 15, pp. 65, 179, and 191), and the tenor of the letter is the idea of the *Pax Romana*.[6] We cannot be entirely certain that the letter really dates from the first century,[7] but its reception history is more important than the date of its origin. In view of the eschatological expectations prevailing in early Christianity, we need not interpret *First Clement* as a canonical or legal text, yet the history of its interpretation underlines and secures the high authority of the Roman church, construed as legal supremacy.

The *Epistle to the Romans* ascribed to Ignatius of Antioch is another literary witness to the prestige of the Roman church in early Christianity. Whether this letter was written in the early second century or half a century later is still contested.[8] It seems unlikely that the letter was, as it claims, written by a bishop of Antioch, but the fact that the author presented himself as such was important for the impact of the text. In the narrative, the author is brought to Rome as a captive in order to be put on trial. He expresses the wish to suffer martyrdom in a city famous for the many martyrs who died there, and he asks those to whom he writes not to intervene on his behalf. The letter is directed to the "church that presides over the territory of the Romans" (SC 10, 124), but there is no mention of a bishop. The term "territory" is clearly meant to include the city of Rome, but perhaps it extends to Rome's hinterland as well. This church is presented as pre-eminent because it holds the office of "presiding over love" (*prokathēmenē tēs agapēs*, SC 10, 24). There are many interpretations of this phrase, but the general opinion today is that it did not refer to any juridical supremacy over other churches.[9]

In a letter of AD 170 to the Roman community, bishop Dionysius of Corinth stated that Peter and Paul had "sown the seed" at Rome and Corinth, had taught in Italy, and had both suffered martyrdom at the same time (Eusebius, *Church History*, II.25.8, Schwartz 73). Dionysius acknowledges in this way that the two apostles were the founders of Roman Christianity. He also reveals that the *First Epistle of Clement*

6 K. Wengst, *Pax Romana. Anspruch und Wirklichkeit. Erfahrungen und Wahrnehmungen des Friedens bei Jesus und im Urchristentum* (München: Kaiser, 1986), 131–46.

7 S. Schima, "Der Heilige Stuhl und die Päpste," in M. Gehler and R. Rollinger (eds.), *Imperien und Reiche in der Weltgeschichte. Epochenübergreifende und globalhistorische Vergleiche*, vol. 1: *Imperien des Altertums, Mittelalterliche und frühneuzeitliche Imperien* (Wiesbaden: Harrassowitz, 2014), 725–60, at 730.

8 Schima, *Caput occidentis?*, 47.

9 Cf. W. R. Schoedel, *Ignatius of Antioch: A Commentary on the Letters of Ignatius of Antioch* (Philadelphia: Fortress Press, 1985), 165–66.

was customarily read before the Roman community at gatherings, although it is clear that this *Epistle* was still not interpreted as a juridical document containing a stringent list of legal requirements.

Hegesippus, who died around AD 180 and about whom we have no biographical details, wrote an account of a journey to Rome that includes a list of its bishops (Eusebius, *Church History* IV.22.2–3, Schwartz 156). That does not necessarily mean that there had already been a single bishop of the city since the first century. The list was supposed to provide a succession of persons who had transmitted the correct teachings.[10] Around the mid-second century, several presbyters held collateral leadership over the community, which consisted of small house churches.[11] Monoepiscopacy (the leadership of a single bishop in each city, each presiding over several presbyters) seems to have become fully established in Rome only during the decades following Hegesippus's visit.

In his *Adversus haereses*, written against gnostic sects in the eighties of the second century, Irenaeus of Lyon praises the Roman church, which he claims had been founded by both Peter and Paul. He describes the Roman church as *maxima* and *antiquissima*, according to the Latin translation of the lost Greek original. These terms do not have to be interpreted as superlatives ("greatest" and "oldest"). They may instead mean only that this was a "very big" and "very old" church. Nevertheless, Irenaeus claims that every local church must be in concord with the Roman church because of its pre-eminence (*propter potentiorem principalitatem*). Moreover, he says that the faithful coming to Rome from everywhere have kept the important traditions (III.3.2; FC 8/3, 30). To put this special status of the Roman church in its proper perspective, however, we should remember that this was a tradition associated with the two apostles. It is likely that *every* church founded by an apostle was entitled to the same privileges and authority as Rome enjoyed. What was special about Rome was that it was the only church able to claim apostolic foundation, presence, and ministry *in the West*. That said, we may discern here the beginnings of the idea that the Roman church held universal importance, as well as the basis of the later Roman or Western patriarchate.[12]

We encounter an engagement of the Roman church at the episcopal level in the context of the so-called Easter controversy (Eusebius, *Church History* V.23–25, Schwartz 209–14), regarding the correct date for the festival. This issue was all the more important because Easter was still the only universally observed Christian holiday at that time. Bishop Victor I of Rome (189–199) was directly challenged by people residing in the city who celebrated Easter on 14 Nisan, that is, on the full moon after the vernal equinox, regardless of what day of the week this was. Victor

[10] P. Lampe, *Die stadtrömischen Christen in den ersten beiden Jahrhunderten*, Wissenschaftliche Untersuchungen zum Neuen Testament II.18, 2nd edition (Tübingen: Mohr Siebeck, 1989), 342.

[11] On the sources see Lampe, ibid., 334–39.

[12] N. Brox, "Rom und 'jede Kirche' im 2. Jahrhundert (Zu Irenäus, *adv. Haer.* III 3,2)," *Annuarium Historiae Conciliorum* 7 (1975): 42–78, emphasizes the special Western dimension of this passage, whereas K. Schatz, *Der päpstliche Primat. Seine Geschichte von den Ursprüngen bis zur Gegenwart* (Würzburg: Echter, 1990), 22–24, weakens this Western character in favor of universality.

tried to suppress this custom, which stemmed from Judeo-Christian traditions. Several synods were held in the Roman Empire to address the same issue, and it is possible that Victor was speaking on behalf of the universal church when he took the initiative. In his conflict in Asia Minor with bishop Polykrates of Ephesus over this matter, bishop Victor invoked Rome's apostolic tradition, as we can infer from a letter by Polykrates (Eusebius, *Church History* V.24.2–8, Schwartz 211–12). Victor then tried to exclude communities of Asia Minor from the communion of churches. This earned him a reproof from Irenaeus of Lyon. Irenaeus probably agreed with Victor regarding the Easter question, but he criticized him for taking a relentless stance in a matter that did not affect doctrine and was capable, therefore, of varying practices. That said, we cannot exclude the possibility that Irenaeus saw the Roman church as especially responsible for regional practice in the West.[13]

It is also possible that the Roman church had a prominent role during this early period in the decisions as to which Christian writings constituted the canon, although we cannot be certain of this.[14] It was important for the integrity of the entire church to decide which writings were to be counted in the canon of the New Testament and thus read in the communities.

Another source indicating that the Roman church had a special status in the West is the *De praescriptione haereticorum* (*On the Prescription of Heretics*) by Tertullian of Carthage (d. 225). This work was completed before Tertullian became drawn to the New Prophecy movement, also known as Montanism, which tended to put less emphasis on the episcopal system, although differences between the earlier "orthodox" Tertullian and the later "Montanist" are much less clear than scholars used to think.[15] For Tertullian, the Roman church had authority (*auctoritas*) over the North African church. He recommended a general adherence to the teachings of the apostolic churches as far as doctrine was concerned (36.1–2; FC 42, 304), and he reasoned that this implied adherence to the Roman church in the West. A certain western pride was certainly part of his thinking when he showered Rome with praise, but we should not overlook entirely his sense that the Roman church had a uniquely universal character. Not only did Tertullian know of the martyrdom of Peter and Paul in Rome, but we also find another tradition in his claim that John the Apostle was also put on trial there. The Romans tossed John into boiling oil, according to this account, but he emerged unharmed, so they banished him to an island (presumably Patmos).

In the mid-third century, we have, with at least a high degree of probability, the first case of a Roman bishop, Stephen I (254–257), appealing to the proof text about the rock (Matt 16:18–19) to support a claim of special authority.[16] The circumstances were

[13] Brox, "Rom und 'jede Kirche'," 72–78.

[14] Schima, *Caput occidentis?*, 40–41. The so-called *Canon Muratori*, which originated from Rome from the late second century, is presumably the oldest known canon list.

[15] Schima, *Caput occidentis?*, 76–77.

[16] For the following, see G. W. Clarke, *The Letters of St. Cyprian of Carthage*, vol. 4, *Letters* 67–82, ACW 47 (New York: Newman Press, 1989), 270. See also Schima, *Caput occidentis?*, 23–24.

complicated. In the context of a controversy over Christians who had lapsed under persecution, Stephen and his Carthaginian counterpart, Cyprian, held opposing views regarding persons who had been baptized in communities that were now seen as heretical or schismatic. Cyprian was of the opinion that a mere act of penitence would not suffice, and that these people would have to be re-baptized in order to be admitted into the catholic community. Cyprian was supported by Firmilian, bishop of Cappadocian Caesarea, among others. Firmilian reports in a letter included in Cyprian's corpus that Stephen underscored his argument by invoking his succession from St. Peter, who had laid the foundations of the church.[17] It is clear that Cyprian himself attributed high status to the Roman church, although he did not connect this with the idea of any mandatory juridical supremacy.[18]

FROM THE CONVERSION OF CONSTANTINE TO INNOCENT I

Constantine I (r. 306–337) was the first Roman emperor to embrace Christianity in a lasting and personal fashion, although we assume today that he received baptism only on his deathbed. Although he made Constantinople, rather than Rome, his imperial residence in 330, Rome remained the capital of the empire. Already under Constantine, we can see a symbiosis between a universal imperial ideal and Christian universal aspirations. A Christian conception of Rome became manifest during the second half of the fourth century, when the idea of *Pax Romana* was transformed into that of *Pax Christiana*.[19]

Constantine surrounded himself with Christian advisers, and it is not surprising that when he convened an episcopal court in 313 to deal with the Donatist controversy in North Africa, he chose Rome as the venue. This Roman court was presided over by the local bishop Miltiades (311–314). An assembly of bishops at Arles dealt with the same issues in the following year. Although the delegates at Arles did not vote entirely in line with the decisions of the Roman synod, their letter to the Roman bishop Silvester I (314–335) shows the highest respect for his office (*Optatus*, App. IV, CSEL 26, 206–08). Moreover, they addressed the Roman bishop as *papa* ("father"). This title could still be applied, as a mark of respect, to any bishop by his subjects, but this is the first known instance of bishops addressing a fellow bishop by the title. This suggests that they held the bishop of Rome in special regard.[20]

17 *Ep.* 75, 17, CCL 3/1, 581–604, at 596–97: "qui sic de episcopatus sui loco gloriatur et se successionem Petri tendere contendit, super quem fundamenta ecclesiae collocata sunt."

18 M. Wojtowytsch, *Papsttum und Konzile von den Anfängen bis zu Leo I. (440–461), Studien zur Entstehung der Überordnung des Papstes über Konzile*. Päpste und Papsttum 17 (Stuttgart: Hiersemann, 1981), 392.

19 Schatz, *Der päpstliche Primat*, 46–47.

20 For further references, as well as for detail on Silvester's title *papa* and its implications for Rome's apostolicity, see Schima, *Caput occidentis?*, 128.

In 325, Constantine convened an assembly of bishops on an unprecedented scale in Nicaea, in Asia Minor.[21] The Roman bishop, Silvester I, was represented there by two presbyters, while Constantine himself presided. The way in which the attendees were listed is notable. Ossius of Cordoba is always mentioned first, for he was the most important theological adviser of Constantine at the time. Next on the list, however, are always the names of the two Roman presbyters, who signed themselves "on behalf of our *papa* and bishop Silvester (*pro papa et episcopo Silvestro*). As well as dealing with the heterodox teachings of the Alexandrian presbyter Arius regarding the Godhead, the council sought to establish a mutually acceptable date for Easter and addressed supra-regional church organization. Canon 6 records the established custom whereby the bishops of Rome, Alexandria, and Antioch were responsible for special and vast territories of jurisdiction, and the Roman church was to serve as a model in this respect (COD I, 8–9). Although the Roman church demonstrated at Nicaea, not for the first time, that she was not an ideal protagonist in the conduct of dogmatic reflection and debate, Rome was clearly assigned important tasks in the context of calculating the date of Easter (Athanasius, ed. Opitz 3.1, nos. 23, 12, and 26.10). Although a decree "discovered" in the nineteenth century regarding this topic now appears to have been forged,[22] it is clear that the Roman church held a position at least coequal with that of the church of Alexandria as regards the Easter question.

Even though contemporaries were aware that the episcopal assembly at Nicaea of 325 was special in many respects, the category of "ecumenical" councils, reserved for exceptionally significant councils considered to speak for the entire church, was established only later.[23] Nearly half a century after the council, the Roman bishop Damasus I (366–384) emphasized the importance of the presence of Roman emissaries there (JK 232; ed. Sieben, FC 58.1, 196). Indeed, Roman participation was already seen as essential when it came to the general commitment to any articles of faith issued by an episcopal assembly.[24] While none of the early councils that were deemed ecumenical during the patristic period conformed to the standards that Western canon law has required for a "general" council since the late Middle Ages, where papal authority is, indeed, crucial, the involvement of the Roman bishop during this period already provided the requisite authority for important conciliar decisions.

By the 420s, at the latest, churchmen assumed that the Roman bishop had *approved* the decisions of the council of Nicaea (Turner I, 173). At Chalcedon in 451, the Roman legate recited a version of the Nicene canon affirming that the Roman church had always held primacy (ACO 2, 3, 3, 109).[25]

21 On the status of the Roman church and its bishop concerning assemblies, see Schima, *Caput occidentis?*, 135–55.

22 Schima, *Caput occidentis?*, 143–44.

23 For the later reception of this episcopal assembly as an ecumenical council, see H. Hess, *The Early Development of Canon Law and the Council of Serdica* (Oxford: Oxford University Press, 2002), 46–47.

24 Wojtowytsch, *Papsttum und Konzile*, 85–87.

25 Ibid., 88–89.

A letter of Julius I in 341, issued in the context of the Arian controversy, is the first by a Roman bishop that has been preserved (JK 186; FC 58.1, 88–135). It was written to accompany a Roman synod, and it is important in documenting Roman episcopal ideas about primacy. Because the crisis of Arianism directly affected the Alexandrian church, Julius insisted vigorously on Roman participation in any doctrinal deliberations over this issue. Julius invokes the apostles Peter and Paul as the source of the special Roman responsibility for the Christian community, although he does not claim that Rome had authority in any strictly legal sense.[26]

During the reign of Julius I, an episcopal assembly was convened at Serdica (modern-day Sofia) to deal with the Arian dispute (342).[27] Nearly all of the Eastern participants soon left the assembly, but the Western participants remained, revealing a rift within the church between East and West. The synod finally issued regulations that appointed the Roman bishop as a court of review, albeit probably not a court of appeal in the strict sense. Canon 3 includes the possibility that a bishop convicted by his neighboring bishops could declare this fact to the Roman bishop, who in turn could refer the matter to bishops of an adjacent ecclesiastical province. The latter bishops were free to reach a different judgment. Canon 4 reserves judgment to the Roman bishop in cases in which a bishop has been deposed by his neighboring bishops. No new bishop was to be appointed before this judgment from Rome. According to canon 5, if the bishop in question then wanted to appeal his case to Rome again, the Roman bishop could do what he deemed best. These canons did not presume that the Roman bishop would have the final decision in such matters. The regulations seem not to have had any practical relevance at the time, but Julius's successor, Liberius (352–366), tried to extend the scope of Rome's authority in such matters beyond the Western dioceses.[28]

Damasus I (366–384), Liberius's successor, was the Roman bishop in whose pontificate emperor Theodosius I issued the edict *Cunctos populos* (380) (*Cod. Theod.* 16.1.2, ed. Mommsen 1.2, 833). Theodosius declared that Christianity in the form received by the Romans from St. Peter and adhered to by the bishops Damasus of Rome and Peter of Alexandria was binding for all Christians. This edict is often interpreted as a declaration that Christianity was to be the state religion, although this is inaccurate for reasons that cannot be discussed here. We are interested, rather, in the notion that Rome and Alexandria were of equal standing. Already in the following year, the synod at Constantinople, later seen as the second ecumenical council, issued in canon 3 a clause whereby the bishop of Constantinople would have precedence in honor second only to the Roman bishop, since Constantinople was the New Rome

26 Schatz, *Der päpstliche Primat*, 39.

27 See H. Hess, *The Canons of the Council of Sardica, A.D. 343: A Landmark in the Early Development of Canon Law* (Oxford: Clarendon Press, 1958), passim. For the content of the canons addressed below, see Hess, *The Early Development of Canon Law*, 190–97. On the Arian controversy, see G. M. Berndt and R. Steinacher (eds.), *Arianism: Roman Heresy and Barbarian Creed* (Farnham: Ashgate, 2014).

28 H. C. Brennecke, "Rom und der dritte Kanon von Serdika (342)," ZRG Kan. Abt. 69 (1983): 15–45, at 25–45.

(COD I, 32). Only one year later, reacting against this, a Roman synod proclaimed the doctrine of the Petrine Triad, whereby Rome, Alexandria, and Antioch were the preeminent churches of Christianity because all three cities were traditionally associated with St. Peter (Dobschütz 29–33). The concern in Rome was that Constantinople might eventually ascend to become the imperial capital. But Rome did not wish to concede equality with Alexandria and Antioch. After all, Rome could boast not only of St. Peter's ministry but also of his grave, and it enjoyed the tradition of *two* founding Apostles.

From the fifth century onward, Eastern emperors supported the idea that there was one universal church in which primacy was determined by the special honor of certain sees. The most honorable sees were those of Rome, Constantinople, Alexandria, Antioch, and Jerusalem. This idea was formulated at the Council of Chalcedon (451) in canon 28 (COD I, 99–100). This idea of a Pentarchy ("rule of five") supplanted that of the Petrine Triad (Rome, Alexandria, and Antioch).[29] The teaching would later be expressed in the laws for the church issued by emperor Justinian (527–565), which generally presupposed that the church was divided into the five patriarchates (*Nov.* 109 pr. and 123.3; ed. Schoell and Kroll 518 and 597).

Already in 450, a year before the Council of Chalcedon, the Eastern emperor Theodosius II had addressed Leo I as patriarch.[30] The bishop of Rome was to be seen as "patriarch of the West" – in other words, as the only patriarch *in the West*. On the one hand, from the emperor's point of view, the Roman bishop's unique position as Western patriarch did not necessarily entail special authority even over the entirety of the West, let alone over the universal church. On the other hand, the status of "patriarch of the West" would never play a large role in the self-perception of the Roman bishops.[31] Western bishops of the first millennium, including metropolitans, did not see themselves as subject to the Roman church in the framework of a special Western church community. Even in regions that now make up modern Italy, conflicts among bishops were the order of the day, especially during the sixth and seventh centuries.[32]

Supremacy of the Roman bishop over the West would seem at first glance to be implied by a rescript issued by the Western emperor Gratian in 378 (*Collectio Avellana* no. 13, CSEL 35.1, 54–58). In response to a request by a Roman synod, Gratian assigned to the bishop of Rome general responsibility for criminal charges involving all Western bishops. The rescript seems to have been applied only in Italy, but it was no doubt used to bolster the self-confidence of the Roman bishops.[33]

29 On the Pentarchy in Late Antiquity, see F. R. Gahbauer, *Die Pentarchietheorie: Ein Modell der Kirchenleitung von den Anfängen bis zur Gegenwart*, Frankfurter Theologische Studien 42 (Frankfurt a.M.: Knecht, 1993), 65–75.

30 R. Schieffer, "Der Papst als Pontifex Maximus," ZRG Kan. Abt. 57 (1971): 300–309, 437.

31 A. Garuti, *Patriarca d'Occidente? Storia e attualità* (Bologna: Edizioni Studio Domenicano, 2007), 139–46. Benedict XVI ceased using this title in 2006.

32 See, e.g., B. Schimmelpfennig, *Das Papsttum. Von der Antike bis zur Renaissance*, 6th edition (Darmstadt: Wissenschaftliche Buchgesellschaft, 2009), 80–81.

33 J. Speigl, "Die Päpste in der Reichskirche des 4. und frühen 5. Jahrhunderts von Silvester I. bis Sixtus III," in M. Greschat (ed.), *Das Papsttum*, vol. 1: *Von den Anfängen bis zu den Päpsten in Avignon* (Stuttgart: Kohlhammer, 1985), 43–55, at 48.

Another factor to be taken into account is that the metropolitan structure was still not fully developed in the fourth century in the West.[34] Milan had the status of being a metropolitan see at that time: a perception possibly connected with the authority of St. Ambrose, who was bishop there. But Aquileia held metropolitan power only from the early fifth century onward, and Ravenna reached the status of a metropolitan see in 430. Henceforth, the metropolitan sees gained an ever-stronger position. Their influence was curtailed only in the ninth century, as we shall see below.

During the reign of Damasus I (366–384), the label "Apostolic See" (*Sedes apostolica*), which had originally designated every episcopal see with an apostolic tradition, was now exclusively employed in the West for Rome.[35] In this period, too, we find the first use of the title *pontifex* for the Roman bishop. At that time, Roman emperors still assumed the title *pontifex maximus*, alluding to the pagan, high-priestly function of their office. Even after this period, however, several non-Roman bishops continued to be called *summus pontifex* ("supreme pontiff"). The popes seem not to have employed the title *pontifex maximus* before the fifteenth century.[36]

Either Damasus or his successor, Siricius (384–399), was responsible for the first papal decretal.[37] Decretals were individual decisions sent in response to queries put before the Roman bishop, mainly by other bishops. Most decretals concerned questions of church discipline. The decretals of Roman bishops were written in the style of imperial letters; more precisely, of imperial rescripts. Before the late fourth century, the letters of Roman bishops had taken the form of brotherly admonitions, but now their approach was marked more by prescriptions and prohibitions. In due course, papal decretals often included remarks that the recipient was to inform neighboring bishops about the letter, so that decretals acquired wider significance. It is not surprising, therefore, that they would eventually attain the

[34] S. Schima, "Innozenz I. – Ein Zeitgenosse des Johannes Chrysostomus und sein Kirchenbild," in G. Crisostomo (ed.), *Oriente e occidente tra IV e V secolo (XXXIII Incontro di studiosi dell'antichità cristiana, Roma, 6–8 maggio 2004*, Studia Ephemeridis Augustinianum 93.2 (Rome: Institutum Patristicum Augustinianum, 2005), 665–86, at 669.

[35] Y. Congar, "Titel, welche für den Papst verwendet werden," *Concilium* 11 (1975): 538–44, at 539–40.

[36] Schieffer, "Papst als Pontifex Maximus"; R. Dijkstra and D. Van Espelo "Anchoring Pontifical Authority: A Reconsideration of the Papal Employment of the Title Pontifex Maximus," *Journal of Religious History* 41.3 (2017): 312–25.

[37] That is, according to interpretation, either Damasus's *Canones Romanorum ad Gallos* (JK after 285; FC 58.1, 238–262) or Siricius's *Letter* 385 to bishop Himerius of Tarragona (JK 255; FC 58.2, 302–326). See C. Hornung, *Directa ad decessorem. Ein kirchenhistorisch-philologischer Kommentar zur ersten Dekretale des Siricius von Rom*, Jahrbuch für Antike und Christentum, Ergänzungsband, Kleine Reihe 8 (Münster: Aschendorff, 2011), passim; A. Ferreiro, "Pope Siricius and Himerius of Tarragona (385): Provincial Papal Intervention in the Fourth Century," in G. D. Dunn (ed.), *The Bishop of Rome in Late Antiquity* (Farnham, UK: Ashgate, 2015), 773–85; Christian Hornung, "Siricius and the Rise of the Papacy," in Dunn, *The Bishop of Rome*, 57–72, at 61–72; L. Kéry, "Das Kirchenrecht als Instrument päpstlichen Führungsanspruchs," in B. Schneidmüller et al. (eds.), *Die Päpste. Amt und Herrschaft in Antike, Mittelalter und Renaissance*. Die Päpste, Bd. 1, Publikation der Reiss-Engelhorn-Museen, Bd. 74 (Regensburg: Schnell & Steiner, 2016), 275–98, at 277–78.

character of *decreta generalia* ("general decrees"), and thus of universal church law, having the same juridical value as the "canons" of synods and councils. Siricius expressed this thought already when he told bishop Himerius that no one should feel free to disregard the "statutes of the apostolic see and the venerable decrees of the canons" (*statuta sedis apostolicae vel canonum venerabilia definite*, c. 20, FC 58.2, 326). Nevertheless, we should keep in mind that the distinction between decretals and papal letters of other kinds is not always clear.

FROM INNOCENT I TO SYMMACHUS

Because there are good reasons to regard Innocent I (401–417) as the first bishop of Rome who was pope, he merits a fuller discussion here. It is significant that the sacking and looting of Rome by Alaric, a Visigoth, in 410 occurred during Innocent's pontificate. Hitherto, no external power had managed to take control of the city for eight hundred years. Innocent was not residing in Rome at the time, and we do not know what his immediate reaction was to these events, but he realigned the papacy so that it would take the place of declining imperial power in the West. This pattern was to be repeated with Leo I and Gregory I. All three led the Roman people during periods of tribulation and invasion. Another factor that strengthened the ecclesiastical standing of Rome during Innocent's reign may have been the move of the western imperial residence from Milan, which had been destroyed, to Ravenna. The see of Milan, associated with the famous bishop Ambrose and formerly prominent, was condemned henceforth to prolonged insignificance.

Innocent issued numerous decretals, and he was the first Roman bishop to send such a letter to an Eastern addressee: namely, to bishop Alexander of Antioch in 415 (JK 310; FC 58.2, 482–86).[38] This attempt to exert Roman episcopal authority in the East is another reason to regard Innocent as the "first pope." His decretal to Alexander proves that he did not rely solely on secular models for his authority. Innocent points out that the church of Antioch owes its special importance not so much to the size of the city as to its apostolic tradition. He was clearly arguing along the lines of the Roman synod of 382.

Already in 404, Innocent directed a letter to bishop Victricius of Rouen (JK 286; FC 58.2, 372–86), in which he demanded that Rome should be responsible for all important cases (*causae maiores*) in the church (c. 6; FC 58.2, 378).[39] Innocent did not define what constituted a major case, but he was evidently inspired by Exodus 18:21–22, where Jethro advised Moses, who was about to leave Egypt, to appoint judges who would adjudicate minor matters themselves while passing on major ones to Moses. Likewise, therefore, the *causae maiores* were to be passed on to the Apostolic See of Rome and not handled by the local authorities. Innocent probably

[38] See also E. Caspar, *Geschichte des Papsttums von den Anfängen bis zur Höhe der Weltherrschaft*, vol. 1: *Römische Kirche und Imperium Romanum* (Tübingen: Mohr, 1930), 322.

[39] Wojtowytsch, *Papsttum und Konzile*, 207–209.

intended only to supervise the Gallic synods, since making such a claim in respect of the Eastern churches would have been unrealistic.

It is with Innocent, too, that we first encounter the idea that the bishop of Rome has care over all the churches (*sollicitudo omnium ecclesiarum*). This becomes evident in his letter to the participants of the synod of Mileve in North Africa in 417 (JK 322; FC 58/2, 544–552, hier c. 2, 546). The letter was written under the pressure of the Pelagian controversy, and Innocent cites 2 Corinthians 11:28, where Paul claims responsibility for all communities. This use of this passage is later mainly associated with Leo I (440–461), which demonstrates how much Innocent shaped important features of his famous successor's pontificate.

The Pelagian controversy shows again that the Roman church was still not at the vanguard of dogmatic disputation. Instead, bishop Augustine of Hippo (395–430) was the leading figure in the opposition to Pelagius and his followers, and Augustine demanded more vigorous action against the Pelagians than Innocent did.[40] Innocent intervened shortly before his death, however, prompting a famous response from Augustine. This dictum is usually remembered in a misleadingly abbreviated form: "Rome has spoken, the case is closed" ("*Roma locuta causa finita*"). In fact, what Augustine said was this: "For now two councils have sent reports to the Apostolic See, and two replies have come back. The case is finished. Would that the error might end soon."[41] In praising the Apostolic See, Augustine was probably thinking of Zosimus (417–418), Innocent's immediate successor, who cleared Pelagius of all accusations in the summer of 417. Augustine apparently meant to praise Innocent while by implication rebuking Zosimus, who had failed to follow his predecessor's decisions.[42]

Innocent I's decretal to Decentius, bishop of Gubbio, in 416 is also significant in relation to the emergence of papal authority (JK 311; FC 58.2, 488–502).[43] The letter deals with liturgical customs. The pope emphasizes that Decentius has often traveled to Rome, where he has seen the liturgy for himself. But in that case, why did Innocent need to send written instructions to Decentius? It is likely that this letter was an exercise in promulgation – that Innocent intended Decentius to share the content of the decretal with all the clerics in his sphere of influence.

The decretal to Decentius is intriguing for another reason as well. In the context of a discussion of ordinations, Innocent says that it was commonly acknowledged that everyone should adhere to the traditions given to the Roman church by Peter, Prince of the Apostles, for nothing should be added or introduced that is contrary to Peter's instructions. It is evident, Innocent claims, that in all Italy, Gaul, Spain, Africa,

40 S. Schima, "Carthagine locuta – causa finita? Afrikanisches Selbstbewusstsein und römischer Eigensinn," in J. van Oort and W. Wischmeyer (eds.), *Die spätantike Kirche Nordafrikas im Umbruch*, Studien der Patristischen Arbeitsgemeinschaft 10 (Leuven: Peeters, 2011), 59–91.

41 Augustine, *Sermo 131*, c. 10, PL 38:754: "Iam enim de hac causa duo concilia missa sunt ad sedem apostolicam; inde etiam rescripta venerunt. Causa finita est; utinam aliquando finiatur error."

42 Schima, *Carthagine locuta*, 89–90.

43 Schima, *Innozenz I*, 674–78.

Sicily, and the islands in between, no one but Peter or the presbyters appointed by his successors have ever founded churches (c. 2, FC 58.2, 488–490). No other sources coming from the Roman episcopate or the papacy before Innocent claimed suzerainty for the Roman church in this fashion, and we may wonder whether Innocent had thought this argument through. Since he was the first pope to send a decretal to an Eastern addressee, perhaps this claim was largely rhetorical.

Innocent I acted as a Roman patriarch when he founded the vicariate of Thessalonica. By claiming special rights over the churches in eastern Illyricum, he clearly wanted to show his Roman colors to the bishop of Constantinople.[44] While this was probably not his main reason for establishing the vicariate, the opposition to Constantinople is plain. The Milanese church had enjoyed greater influence in Illyricum than Rome for a long time. Temporarily in 379 and indefinitely in 395, Illyricum Orientale had been allotted to the eastern part of the empire. Damasus I had already revealed his interest in the region, and Siricius had enacted episcopal ordinations there under the supervision of the bishop of Thessalonica (*Ep.* 4, JK 259; FC 58.2, 343). Innocent's letter of 412 to bishop Rufus of Thessalonica (*Ep.* 13, JK 303; FC 58.2, 442–460) may be seen as the foundation of the vicariate of Thessalonica. Rufus was to care for the churches of eastern Illyricum in the sender's stead, and the churches were to have written communication with Innocent only under Rufus's supervision. Innocent cited here the example of St. Paul, who had delegated the supervision over Crete and Asia Minor to his disciples.

Innocent's immediate successor, Zosimus, was remembered unfavorably in Rome not only because of his stance in the Pelagian controversy but also because of his policy toward Gaul. He conferred upon bishop Patroclus of Arles supreme episcopal rights that effectively made him metropolitan of Gaul. These rights restricted the powers of other regional bishops, and they enabled Patroclus to question papal authority. Perhaps Zosimus took these actions because Patroclus had helped him to become pope.[45] Boniface I (418–422) had a more self-confident interpretation of his office. He resolutely aimed to keep eastern Illyricum under the influence of the Roman church. In the course of these quarrels, he claimed that the Council of Nicaea had already acknowledged that St. Peter was the head of his community, and that separation of the diocese from Rome would amount to its exclusion from the Christian religion (*Ep.* 9, JK 364; FC 58.3, 702).

Celestine I (422–432), successor to Boniface, acted self-confidently as well. He repeatedly pointed out that he, as St. Peter's vicar, had responsibility for supervision of the universal church. This claim paved the way for Leo I. In Celestine's imagination, Peter and his successors had all been bishops of Rome.[46] Celestine had to

44 J. Macdonald, "Who Instituted the Papal Vicariate of Thessalonica?" *Studia Patristica* 4 (1961): 478–82, at 481. Schima, *Innozenz I.*, 680–82.

45 V. Reinhardt, *Pontifex. Die Geschichte der Päpste. Von Petrus bis Franziskus* (München: C. H. Beck, 2018), 69.

46 J. Fellermayr, *Tradition und Sukzession im Lichte des römisch-antiken Erbdenkens: Untersuchungen zu den lateinischen Vätern bis zu Leo dem Großen* (München: Minerva, 1979), 378–79.

demonstrate his authority against the overly self-confident African bishops, and he was also successful in his Illyrian policy. His pontificate saw the beginning of the dispute between Nestorius of Constantinople and Cyril of Alexandria over the question of the human and divine natures in Christ, which turned on whether Mary could be addressed as *theotokos* ("God bearer," or mother of God). Cyril argued in favor of *theotokos* and prevailed at the council of Ephesus (431). This assembly is counted as an ecumenical council despite the fact that the decisions were made before the Roman envoys arrived. Celestine's successor, Sixtus III (432–440), supported reconciliation with Nestorius and his followers, and in this he was successful at first. Regarding eastern Illyricum, he was defensive. It was becoming clear that this region would sooner or later come under the influence of Constantinople.

Even more than Innocent, Leo I, also known as Leo the Great (440–461), shaped the history of the Roman church. We shall not go into detail here because he is dealt with in depth elsewhere in this volume (Chapter 13). It should be noted, however, that during Leo's reign the invocation of St. Peter reached a new high point and even gained the approval of the fathers of the Council of Chalcedon (451). In many respects, Leo shaped the terminology of papal reform in the eleventh century.

We should be careful not to overestimate the impact of the end of the Western Roman Empire in 476, but it is significant, nevertheless, that the secular power vacuum brought about by the changing authority of various secular rulers encouraged the popes to enhance their claims of dominance over the universal church. The divergence between Eastern and Western traditions soon became apparent through the so-called Acacian schism, which lasted from 484 until 519. This made visible a rift between the two churches, represented mainly by Constantinople and Rome respectively. In the 490s, the Ostrogothic king Theoderic the Great (r. 493–526), who had acted as master of soldiers of the Eastern Roman emperor and was thereafter recognized as ruler (*rex*) in the West, gained control of the largest part of the Apennine peninsula.[47] Because Theodoric was an Arian Christian, the Roman church was notably more free from interventions by the secular ruler than the Eastern church was. Only in the final years of his rule was Theoderic inclined to interfere in the ecclesiastical sphere. This new interest was perhaps less connected with the end of the Acacian schism or with dread of a closer alliance between Byzantium and the papacy than it was a reaction to the anti-Arian measures taken by the Eastern Roman emperor Justin I (518–527).

Among the popes upholding the idea of papal authority in this period, Gelasius I (492–496) stands out above all (see Chapter 14 in this volume). Gelasius stressed the divine origins of both the ecclesiastical and the secular power. The latter should be

47 On the relations between Theoderic and the papacy, see T. F. X. Noble, "Theodoric and the Papacy," in *Teoderico il Grande e i Goti d'Italia: Atti del 13°Congresso internazionale di studi sull'Alto Medioevo, Milano 2–6 novembre 1992*, 2 vols. (Spoleto: Centro Italiano di Studi sull'alto Medioevo, 1993), 1:395–423.

subordinate to the former as far as spiritual responsibility before God was concerned. In retrospect, we can see here an important movement toward the binary models of church and state that would flourish in the second millennium, such as the "Two Swords" theory.

We should also mention the pontificate of Symmachus (498–514).[48] The title of cardinal is first attested for the Roman church during his reign. Symmachus emerged from a highly contested double election. Laurentius, too, was elected pope, and a schism lasting for several years ensued. This situation led to the adoption in 499 of rules for electing the pope at a Roman synod (MGH AA 12, 403–04): the first such regulations known to have been issued by the church. The rules that were passed at that time are the only ones known to us that include the right of "designation," whereby a sitting pope is entitled to choose, or "designate," his successor. This implies that the synodal regulations would be relevant only if a pope had not nominated anyone.[49] That said, we know of only one successful designation of a pope by his predecessor, when Felix IV proposed Boniface II, who was consecrated, albeit with severe difficulties, in 530. It is possible that in claiming this right Symmachus was only expressing an enhanced consciousness of papal primacy. The times were very insecure indeed, and designations in both the ecclesiastical and the secular spheres seem to have been in vogue during the early sixth century. The early sixth-century *Regula magistri*, for example, assigns the right of designation in the strict sense to abbots.[50]

It is not surprising, therefore, that Symmachus was acting according to his own conception of papal primacy. For the same reason, he tried to limit secular influence in the dispute that followed his election. He and his followers produced documents, some of them supposedly dating to the era of Constantine's conversion, that explicitly adhered to the principle that the primary see may not be judged by anyone else ("*prima sedes a nemine iudicatur*"). Although these documents were spurious, this principle is held in high esteem in current Catholic canon law.

The so-called *Liber Pontificalis*, a collection of papal biographies, first appeared in the context of the schism of 498 and the pontificate of Symmachus. The final draft, which goes up to the sixth century, was completed in the 530s. The *Liber Pontificalis* was modeled chiefly on Roman imperial biographies and to a lesser degree on biblical biographies.[51] This work strengthened the claims of papal primacy.

48 On his pontificate and the schism, see J. Richards, *The Popes and the Papacy in the Early Middle Ages, 476–752* (London: Routledge & Kegan Paul, 1979), 69–99; E. Wirbelauer, *Zwei Päpste in Rom. Der Konflikt zwischen Laurentius und Symmachus (498–514). Studien und Texte,* Quellen und Forschungen zur antiken Welt 16 (München: Tuduv, 1993), passim (includes editions of numerous primary texts).

49 On the importance of the designation of successors at that time, see Schima, "Der Heilige Stuhl und die Päpste," 120–25.

50 S. Schima, *Papsttum und Nachfolgebeeinflussung. Von den Anfängen bis zur Papstwahlordnung von 1179*, Kirche und Recht 26 (Freistadt: Plöchl, 2011), 122–24.

51 R. McKitterick, "La place du *Liber pontificalis* dans les genres historiographiques du haut Moyen Âge," in F. Bougard and M. Sot (eds.), *Liber, Gesta, histoire. Écrire l'histoire des évêques et des papes de l'Antiquité au XXIe siècle* (Turnhout: Brepols, 2009), 23–35, at 29. See also D. M. Deliyannis,

The Scythian monk Dionysius Exiguus was active in Rome during Symmachus's pontificate (see Chapter 15 in this volume). Around the year 500, Dionysius produced a collection of thirty-eight papal decretals together with a collection of synodal decrees, or canons. Known as the *Dionysiana*,[52] the collection was intended to enhance the status of the papacy. The version of the *Dionysiana* that included the papal decretals was an important source for many pre-Carolingian collections of canon law, such as the *Concordia canonum* of Cresconius and the *Vetus Gallica*. All the papal decretals from the *Dionysiana* were also inserted into the chronological version of the *Collectio Hispana*. Nevertheless, it seems that Dionysius did not get the decretals of the *Dionysiana* directly from the papal archives,[53] which makes it less likely that the texts were transmitted in a form that was free from corruption.

Although the patriarchal rank of the popes was of only marginal importance as regards the pope's own self-perception, it did play an important role in relation to the legal reality of the Byzantine Empire.[54] Even though they were the heads of the most prominent church in the world, the Roman bishops were expected to bow to the emperor's will. Byzantine religious policy was to affect the fate of papal Rome fairly often, at times posing a critical threat to its status.

GREGORY I AND THE PROLONGED CONFLICT BETWEEN THE PAPACY AND BYZANTIUM

Gregory I, also known as Gregory the Great (590–604), was in constant communication with the Byzantine East. In this respect, however, he inherited the problems experienced by his predecessors. The Roman church and its chief representatives had been at odds with the emperors since the reign of Justinian (527–565). When they recovered parts of Italy, including Rome, from Gothic dominance in 536, the Byzantines had deposed the sitting pope, Silverius. In his place they installed Vigilius as pope (537–555), although he lacked the support of the Roman clergy. Nevertheless, the new pope did not act as a mere puppet of Constantinople. Vigilius was weary of the so-called Three-Chapter Controversy that Justinian had started: an attempt to reconcile the Coptic and Syrian miaphysites with Chalcedonian

"A Biblical Model for Serial Biography: the Books of Kings and the Roman Liber Pontificalis," *Revue Bénédictine* 107 (1997): 15–23.

52 L. Kéry, "Kanonessammlungen als Fundorte für päpstliche Schreiben," in J. Johrendt and H. Klaus (eds.), *Das Papsttum und das vielgestaltige Italien. Hundert Jahre Italia Pontificia*, Abhandlungen der Akademie der Wissenschaften zu Göttingen, Neue Folge, Bd. 5 (Berlin: De Gruyter, 2009), 275–97, at 280. On the *Dionysiana*, see also L. Fowler-Magerl, *Clavis Canonum: Selected Canon Law Collections Before 1140*, MGH Hilfsmittel 21 (2005), 29–32.

53 H. Wurm, *Studien und Texte zur Dekretalensammlung des Dionysius Exiguus*, Kanonistische Studien und Texte 16 (Bonn: Rohrscheid, 1939), 190–91, 227–230. Fowler-Magerl, *Clavis Canonum*, 31.

54 R. Schieffer, "Der Papst als Patriarch von Rom," in M. Maccarrone (ed.), *Il primato del vescovo di Roma nel primo millennio. Ricerche e testimonianze. Atti del Symposium storico-teologico Roma, 9–13 Ottobre 1989*, Pontificio Comitato di scienze storiche, Atti e documenti 4 (Città del Vaticano: Libreria Editrice Vaticana, 1991) 433–51, at 440–41.

orthodoxy by condemning some writings, known as the "Three Chapters," that were deemed to be Nestorian. Vigilius did not adopt the imperial view of the matter at first. Instead, he had to be seized by Byzantine troops in 546 and brought to Constantinople, where he was detained until 554. Only then did he finally accept the view imposed by the emperor. This final adoption of the condemnation of the Three Chapters led to a rift among the Italian bishops, for many could not accept the new "orthodox" point of view, especially those in the northern dioceses, which had been under Lombard control since the early 570s.[55]

As a result of the unexpected and rapid expansion of Islam during the seventh century, the patriarchal sees of Alexandria, Antioch, and Jerusalem rapidly declined in significance and influence. This decline led to a certain bipolarity between Rome and Constantinople, although Constantinople, too, was somewhat weakened by the expansion of Islam.

The pontificate of Gregory I (see Chapter 17 in this volume) may be seen as a landmark. There is good reason for situating it both in Late Antiquity and in the Middle Ages. Gregory descended from the esteemed house of the Anicii, from which at least one and possibly several of his papal predecessors had come. His family's wealth may well have provided an important basis for the formation of the later Papal State. His introduction of a missal provided part of the groundwork for the unity of the Latin church. His missionary policy differed from that of the earlier Roman bishops insofar as it was well organized and precisely targeted. His pontificate paved the way for later developments that proved to be decisive, such as the establishment of a greater distance from Byzantium and a stronger interest in the kingdoms of the West and their peoples.

The antagonism between papacy and empire was a persistent feature that shaped papal policy for centuries to come. In 638, the Byzantine emperor Herakleios (610–641), who had been the great anti-Persian hero in the 630s but had since lost large parts of his empire to the Arabs, issued a decree that marked the official recognition of Monothelitism by an emperor. According to this doctrine, which for the time being was officially that of Constantinople, there were two natures but only one (divine) will in Christ. The first careful formulations of this new doctrine, which was designed as a kind of doctrinal peace offering to the anti-Chalcedonian Monophysites (more precisely, miaphysites) in Armenia, Syria, and Egypt, were accepted by Pope Honorius (625–638). Soon after Honorius's death, however, opposition to this Christological novelty began to form, and Rome soon became one of the main strongholds of the traditionalists, who rallied around Maximus the Confessor. In 649, a synod gathered in Rome under the nominal leadership of Pope Martin I (r. 649–653, d. 655) condemned Monothelitism. Olympus, imperial exarch of Ravenna, was sent to Rome to get the pope back in line. He failed, however, and instead rebelled

55 J. Herrin, *The Formation of Christendom* (Princeton: Princeton University Press, 1987), 106–27.

against the emperor, although he died of an illness while trying to control southern Italy with his army. Martin I was subsequently apprehended by other Byzantine troops and tried for high treason in Constantinople.[56] Rome remained steadfast in its opposition against Monothelitism, which was eventually condemned at the Third Council of Constantinople (680–81) under the auspices of emperor Constantine IV (668–685). Rome was treated with all due honors on this occasion, but good relations were not to last.

In 691, the so-called Quinisext council was held under emperor Justinian II. There, canons were agreed upon that were in stark contrast to Roman or Latin customs of the time and unacceptable to Pope Sergius I (687–701). When the pope declined to subscribe to the acts of this council, the Byzantines again tried to seize a pope from Rome, although on this occasion they were repelled and humiliated by a combined Lombard-Roman force.[57]

The estrangement between Rome and Byzantium became even more marked under Gregory II (715–731).[58] First, according to Roman sources, high-ranking Byzantine officials in Rome tried to assassinate Gregory with the consent of the reigning exarch of emperor Leo III (717–741). When this plot was discovered and foiled, imperial troops marched on Rome again, but in 729 the two sides reached a truce that preserved the status quo: a semi-autonomous papal Rome on the one side, and Ravenna, dominated by the East, on the other. The origins of this dispute were of a different nature than hitherto. Although the authors of the *Liber Pontificalis* wanted their audience to believe that incipient iconoclasm was at the root of papal dissent, research has shown that this is highly unlikely. The main reason for hostilities was rather that the pope, together with the central Italian imperial subjects, was unwilling to pay the dramatically increased taxes imposed by Constantinople. This resulted in what has been called an outright tax war.[59]

Once the hostilities had ceased, iconoclasm (opposition to the veneration of images) became an issue in Byzantium (around 730) and shortly thereafter in Rome.[60] Popes Gregory III (731–741) and Zacharias (741–752) worked in opposition to iconoclasm in the East, convening councils, sending letters of protest, and commissioning a high-profile program of images in the Eternal City. When the

56 R. Price et al. (ed. and trans.), *The Acts of the Lateran Synod of 649*, Translated Texts for Historians 61 (Liverpool: Liverpool University Press, 2014), 5–86.

57 Herrin, *Formation of Christendom*, 284–90.

58 E. Lipperts, "Papst Gregor II. und Kaiser Leon III. Die Abtretung Siziliens im Licht der neueren Forschung," in D. Engels et al. (eds.), *Zwischen Ideal und Wirklichkeit. Herrschaft auf Sizilien von der Antike bis zum Spätmittelalter* (Stuttgart: Franz Steiner, 2010), 231–45.

59 W. Brandes, *Finanzverwaltung in Krisenzeiten. Untersuchungen zur byzantinischen Administration im 6.-9. Jahrhundert*, Forschungen zur byzantinischen Rechtsgeschichte 25 (Frankfurt am Main: Löwenklau, 2002), 368–84.

60 L. Brubaker and J. Haldon, *Byzantium in the Iconoclast Era, c. 680–850: A History* (Cambridge: Cambridge University Press, 2011).

iconoclastic movement was made official at the Council of Hiereia in 754, another schism ensued. At the Roman council of 769, Pope Stephen III (768–772) had iconoclasm officially condemned.[61] Stephen's successor, Hadrian I (772–795), seized the opportunity presented by the death of emperor Constantine V in 775 and refused to recognize Byzantine supremacy. The papacy now began to date its documents by the pontifical years of the popes and to mint its own coins. The religio-political divide was overcome when the Second Council of Nicaea condemned iconoclasm in 787, but the political separation from the East remained a reality in Italy.[62]

THE ALLIANCE WITH THE FRANKS AND THE "BIRTH OF THE PAPAL STATE"

As well as the breach between the papacy and the Byzantine empire, the eighth century saw the beginning of the Franco-papal alliance, which was to prove decisive for the history of the Roman pontificate. Contacts between the Franks – especially the Carolingians, the new dynasty of that kingdom – and the papacy had been intensifying throughout the eighth century. From the Roman point of view, the search for a militarily potent ally became far more urgent when the Lombard king Aistulf took Ravenna in 750. Even though he did not attack Rome itself, his army posed a considerable threat to the immediate papal sphere of interest in central Italy.[63] In 753, after several failed negotiations, Pope Stephen II (752–757) traveled to the Frankish kingdom to meet King Pippin I (751–768). This momentous event has been treated extensively in the literature on European history, but some remarks about it are relevant here.

In 751, Pippin III, son of Charles Martel and *major domus* of the entire Frankish kingdom except for Aquitania, had deposed the last Merovingian king of Francia. Pippin received a favorable assessment of his actions from Pope Zacharias (741–752), who, according to Frankish sources, confirmed that it was better if the person who was really in power also bore the royal title.[64] In 753, Zacharias's successor, Stephen II, traveled northward. He stopped first at the Lombard capital, Pavia, where he negotiated again with king Aistulf in the presence of Frankish envoys. When these proceedings came to nothing, he traveled further north, becoming the first pope ever to cross the Alps. At meetings with the pope at Quierzy, Pippin agreed to help. In the

61 C. Gantner, *Freunde Roms und Völker der Finsternis. Die päpstliche Konstruktion von Anderen im 8. und 9. Jahrhundert* (Vienna: Böhlau, 2014), 102–118.

62 F. Hartmann, *Hadrian I. (772–795): Frühmittelalterliches Adelspapsttum und die Lösung Roms vom byzantinischen Kaiser,* Päpste und Papsttum 34 (Stuttgart: Hiersemann, 2006), 157–81.

63 W. Pohl, "*Das Papsttum und die Langobarden,*" in M. Becher and J. Jarnut (eds.), *Der Dynastiewechsel von 751. Vorgeschichte, Legitimationsstrategien und Erinnerung* (Münster: Scriptorium, 2004), 145–61.

64 Thomas F. X. Noble, *The Republic of St. Peter: The Birth of the Papal State, 680–825* (Philadelphia: University of Pennsylvania Press, 1984), 67 ff.

event that the Lombard kingdom happened to fall in the process, Pippin promised that the Roman church would have suzerainty of some kind over sizable parts of central and southern Italy.

Pope Stephen crowned and anointed Pippin as king of the Franks in Spring 754. He also bestowed the title "Patrician of the Romans" (*patricius Romanorum*) on him, which gave him some form of theoretical overlordship over the Eternal City's worldly affairs. Pippin never used the title for himself, however, and his son and successor Charlemagne (768–814) did so only after he had annexed the Lombard kingdom in 774. By then, he probably felt worthy of the title. The popes addressed every male Carolingian with whom they corresponded from 754 onward by this title, probably to invoke the Franco-papal alliance forged between Stephen and Pippin.[65]

Pippin had some trouble getting his army to intervene in the Lombard kingdom, which had been essentially allied with the Franks since the rule of his father, Charles Martel. With the help of urgent papal letters, he managed to get an expedition going, swiftly defeating Aistulf's forces and compelling the Lombards to agree to a peace treaty. This treaty did not keep the Lombards from attacking Roman territory in 755, leading to a papal diplomatic mission in the same year and another Frankish campaign in northern Italy in 756. On this occasion, Pavia was taken by force, and Aistulf was obliged to sign another peace treaty. This was the basis for the famous Donation of Pippin, which has been associated with the "birth of the Papal State" in central Italy ever since. As Thomas Noble explains, however, this state was "really a parcel of land – actually several widely scattered parcels – that [Pippin] forced Aistulf to donate to the papacy. If [Pippin] had deposed Aistulf and taken his kingdom by right of conquest, then the Donation of [Pippin] would have followed the terms of the Quierzy document, but in 756 ... [Pippin] stopped far short of wreaking maximum devastation on the Lombards."[66] Thus, contrary both to popular belief and to later papal claims, this series of events did not lead to a large papal state in the region but rather restored to the pope, with a few additions here and there, lands that he had controlled for decades.

The nomination of a Carolingian as (at least theoretical) overseer of Roman affairs was of far more immediate relevance, for it would soon shape political reality – certainly by the year 774, but probably even earlier, as we shall see.

Pope Stephen II died in 757. His pontificate had lasted for only five years, but these had been decisive. He was succeeded by his brother Paul I (757–767), under whose pontificate the current status quo was more or less preserved. At Paul's death, however, there was turmoil in Rome. The local aristocrat Toto of Nepi managed to get his brother consecrated as pope Constantine II against severe opposition from the Lateran clergy and officials. This resulted in a veritable putsch in 768, when the high-ranking officers Christopher and his son Sergius invaded Rome with the help of

65 Gantner, *Freunde Roms*, 66–67 and 240–41.
66 Noble, *Republic of St. Peter*, 93.

a Lombard army and had their candidate Stephen III (768–772) elected pope. Stephen convened a synod at Rome in April 769. During the synod's four sessions, the iconoclast Council of Hiereia (held in 754) was condemned and pope Constantine II was deposed. New rules for papal elections were drawn up. These excluded the Roman aristocracy from the process, placing the election solely in the hands of the local clergy. Even though these prescriptions seem not to have been observed immediately, they did help to articulate an ideal that would eventually prevail.[67]

The pontificate of Hadrian I (772–795) saw the next big political changes for the papacy. In 774, Charlemagne invaded Italy and seized the Lombard throne. Contrary to papal aspirations, the central and southern Italian Lombard dukes also accepted Charlemagne's rule. Nevertheless, the pope took advantage of this situation by asserting political independence from the Byzantine Empire during the 770s. Charters now were dated by Hadrian's pontifical years, and the papacy struck its own coins.

The Second Council of Nicaea in 787 proved to be a major turning point in religious affairs. The papacy was awarded the highest-ranking position at this council, which condemned iconoclasm. But the small papal realm in central Italy, which the popes sometimes called the "republic of the church" in their letters, remained *de facto* autonomous from the eastern empire. Throughout his pontificate, Hadrian seems also to have maintained a de facto autonomy in relation to Frankish influence, but the alliance worked well.[68] In the field of canon law, for example, Rome provided the Franks with a reworked and augmented version of Dionysius Exiguus's canon-law collection, known as the *Dionysio-Hadriana*. This collection was very successful. It was frequently copied throughout the Latin West, especially in the areas controlled by Charlemagne and his successors.[69]

THE NEW WESTERN EMPERORS AND THEIR ROLE IN ROME

This situation changed after the death of Hadrian I. The Roman clergy speedily elected Leo III pope, a choice that inspired the equally swift formation of opposition against that pope, mostly, it seems, from the ranks of the old administration and of relatives of the deceased pope. The situation culminated in an attempted coup in 799, when Leo III barely escaped from Rome. He returned with Frankish support in 800 and was cleared of the numerous charges that had been brought against him in a public trial for his conduct in office. Leo then crowned Charlemagne as Emperor of the Romans in Rome on Christmas day 800, probably at Old

67 S. Scholz, *Politik – Selbstverständnis – Selbstdarstellung. Die Päpste in karolingischer und ottonischer Zeit*, Historische Forschungen 26 (Stuttgart: Franz Steiner, 2006), 74–77.

68 Hartmann, *Hadrian I.*

69 Fowler-Magerl, *Clavis*, 44–45. Hartmann, *Hadrian I*, 267–72.

St. Peter's. This effectuated another major change in the legal position of the Roman bishop. Henceforth, the Carolingians could, at least in theory, rule over Rome. And while these imperial rights were seldom enforced, the situation lay at the core of the repeated struggles between popes and emperors during the central Middle Ages.

The significance of Charlemagne's coronation in Rome has been much discussed in scholarship over the centuries. It is clear that the crowning must have been negotiated beforehand, even though Charlemagne's biographer Einhard claimed that the king was taken by surprise. It is very likely, however, that the pope contrived to acquire a far more prominent role for himself, the Roman church, and the Roman elites than had been agreed beforehand.[70] The role of the pope in determining who would be Western emperor remained in force ever after. Leo's successor, Stephen IV (816–817), even went to Reims in 816 to crown Charlemagne's successor, Louis the Pious. A contract was drawn up on that occasion, known today as the *(Pactum) Ludovicianum*. This essentially codified the Franco-papal alliance and laid down the rights and obligations on each side.[71] Even more importantly, perhaps, following Stephen's urgent intervention, most emperors would be crowned in Rome by the pope. Stephen had secured a very important prerogative for the papacy, which was to last until the Habsburg emperor Ferdinand I set it aside as obsolete in 1558.[72]

The relationship with the Franks was even further strengthened in 824, when Lothar I, at that time co-emperor with his father, Louis the Pious, drew up the *Constitutio Romana* and made Pope Eugene II (824–827) accept its terms. These new rules were based on the *Ludovicianum*, but they greatly strengthened the imperial position in Rome. New popes could be elected by the Romans, but their rightful election had to be confirmed by the emperor. What is more, the Carolingians received wide-ranging judicial rights in the city of Rome. And the popes and the people of Rome were required to swear an oath of allegiance to the reigning emperor. The papal side seems to have agreed to these terms because there had been upheaval in Rome under the previous pope, Paschal I (817–824).[73] As with all medieval legislation, it is hard to say whether the laws were ever followed. For example, while the *Constitutio Romana* prescribes that there must be an imperial envoy residing in Rome at all times, this seems not to have been the case until emperor Louis II of Italy, Lothar's son and heir, appointed an envoy in 864.[74]

70 J. L. Nelson, "*Why Are There So Many Different Accounts of Charlemagne's Imperial Coronation?*" in Nelson, *Courts, Elites, and Gendered Power in the Early Middle Ages: Charlemagne and Others*, Variorum Collected Studies series (Aldershot: Ashgate, 2007).

71 Noble, *Republic of St. Peter*, 300–05.

72 K. Herbers and H. Neuhaus, *Das Heilige Römische Reich: Schauplätze einer tausendjährigen Geschichte (843–1806)* (Cologne: Böhlau, 2006), 215–16.

73 C. J. Goodson, *The Rome of Pope Paschal I: Papal Power, Urban Renovation, Church Rebuilding and Relic Translation, 817–824* (Cambridge: Cambridge University Press, 2010), 269–73.

74 J. Haller, *Nikolaus I. und Pseudo-Isidor* (Stuttgart: J.G. Cotta, 1936), 47–52. C. Gantner, "Louis II and Rome: On the Relationship of the Carolingian Emperor of Italy with 'His' Popes Nicholas I and Hadrian II," forthcoming in G. Vocino et al., *Through the Papal Lens: Shaping History and Memory in Late Antique and Early Medieval Rome, 300–900*.

Nevertheless, the *Constitutio Romana* attests that there was a strong Carolingian overlordship in Rome during the ninth century, at least until the death of Louis II in 875.[75]

A POWERFUL PAPACY: THE PECULIAR CASE OF NICHOLAS THE GREAT

The ninth-century papacy remained involved in politics regarding the East. It opposed a second movement of iconoclasm, albeit perhaps not with as much vigor as it had in the eighth century. And the papacy intervened conspicuously in the church of Constantinople. When Patriarch Ignatius was deposed by emperor Michael III in 858 and replaced by Photios, an erudite churchman who had been ordained uncanonically, Ignatius's followers appealed to Pope Nicholas I (858–867), who officially deposed Photios and reinstated Ignatios. This papal decree was not enforced, but it seems to have exacerbated poor relations with the East, and it led to a bitter exchange of letters among Pope Nicholas, emperor Michael III, and patriarch Photios. One result was the so-called Photian Schism, separating the papacy from the Eastern church. This was ended only by Photios's deposition in the autumn of 867, following the murder of emperor Michael III.

Although this putsch in Constantinople led to reconciliation between the papacy and the Eastern empire, there was no lasting peace. First, there was bitter strife about the obedience of the new Bulgarian church. In the course of this controversy, Pope Nicholas wrote a long letter to the Bulgar khan Boris-Michael (the famous *Responsa Bulgarorum*), articulating the important differences between the Latin and the Greek churches. The *Responsa* are an invaluable source for the customs of the Roman church in the early Middle Ages. It is very likely that the pope answered more questions than had been put to him and was effectively acting on his initiative in this instance. In other words, he was legislating for the Bulgarian church of his own accord.[76] Nevertheless, the Byzantine side established irreversible domination over Bulgaria in the course of the 870s. To add insult to injury, Photios was reinstated as patriarch in 877, after Ignatios's death. Pope John VIII (872–882) grudgingly accepted him, for he needed Byzantine military assistance against the south Italian Saracens.[77]

75 Arnold, *Johannes VIII*, 67–115. M. Costambeys, M. Innes, and S. MacLean, *The Carolingian World* (Cambridge: Cambridge University Press, 2011), 405–35. This account of the late Carolingians north of the Alps does not show how detached the politics already were from any papal influence.

76 Rudolf Schieffer, "Motu proprio. Über die papstgeschichtliche Wende im 11. Jahrhundert," *Historisches Jahrbuch* 122 (2002): 27–41, at 29.

77 C. Gantner, "New Visions of Community in Ninth-Century Rome: The Impact of the Saracen Threat on the Papal World View," in Walter Pohl et al. (eds.), *Visions of Community in the Post-Roman World: The West, Byzantium and the Islamic World, 300–1100* (Farnham, UK: Ashgate, 2012), 403–21, at 409–11.

The main focus of the papacy was now on the Western Empire. While the papacy had to accept Carolingian overlordship in worldly matters, it expanded its influence in all matters related to religion and Christian discipline. The pontificate of Nicholas I stands out in this respect, too. Nicholas intervened in cases concerning canon law in Italy and north of the Alps, often revising the judgments of metropolitan bishops, even including Hincmar of Reims, arguably the most influential bishop in the second half of the ninth century. Nicholas's most famous intervention was in the divorce case of King Lothar II. Nicholas rescinded a divorce that had already been agreed upon by the bishops of the Carolingian middle kingdom (Lotharingia, later Lorraine), including the archbishops of Cologne and Trier. And he forced the king to take back his wife and to repudiate the woman whom he had intended to marry. Nicholas also deposed several bishops. A comparable process had never before been litigated by the papacy, but the parties involved respected the pope's authority, and his judgement was eventually upheld.[78]

This was not a one-sided or one-dimensional development. In the ninth century, there were many people outside Rome, even outside Italy, who believed that the pope should be the highest authority in all questions concerning the church and the Christian religion. A written statement of this position has been transmitted to us in the forged Pseudo-Isidorian collection (see Chapter 19 in this volume). This compilation of texts, which was made around the middle of the ninth century in the west Frankish kingdom, is an artful mix of mostly false or falsified canon-law texts, and it contains many forged papal decretals. One of its aims was to raise the standing of the papacy in the Frankish realms and in the universal church. Although this text did not come from the papal chancellery, it still shaped the thinking about the role of Roman pontiffs in the church for decades and centuries to come.[79] It also helped the papacy to obtain a stronger position in the Western church. At the same time, the papacy was beginning to push back against the strong position that metropolitan bishops had held in the West for centuries.

The forged decretals already contained another text that was to become very important for the papacy and its adversaries during the high Middle Ages: the so-called *Constitutum Constantini*, often known, with reference to the central event that it records, as the Donation of Constantine. When and even where, exactly, this programmatic text was drafted are contested issues.[80] Suffice to say that it claimed for

78 Thomas F. X. Noble, "Pope Nicholas I and the Franks: Politics and Ecclesiology in the Ninth Century," in R. Meens et al. (eds), *Religious Franks. Religion and Power in the Frankish Kingdoms: Studies in Honour of Mayke de Jong* (Manchester: Manchester University Press, 2016), 472–88.

79 C. Harder, *Pseudoisidor und das Papsttum. Funktion und Bedeutung des apostolischen Stuhls in den pseudoisidorischen Fälschungen* (Cologne: Böhlau, 2014). See also Harder's Chapter 19 in this volume.

80 C. J. Goodson and J. L. Nelson, Review article: "The Roman Contexts of the 'Donation of Constantine'," *Early Medieval Europe* 18 (2010): 446–67. M. Edwards, *Constantine and Christendom: The Oration to the Saints, the Greek and Latin Accounts of the Discovery of the Cross, The Edict of Constantine to Pope Silvester*, Translated Texts for Historians 39 (Liverpool: Liverpool University Press, 2003), xl–xlvii.

the papacy suzerainty over the whole Latin West. When it was drafted, however, it was probably only an "apprentice piece," not designed to prove any real legal point.

A CHAOTIC CENTURY OR A PRELUDE TO NEW GREATNESS?

The late ninth century saw a decline in papal power in the West, not least because of internal conflict in Rome. This decline reached its sad nadir in the so-called "Cadaver Synod" of 897, when Pope Formosus (891–896), who had been dead for several months, was exhumed and posthumously tried and convicted. His ascension to the papal throne was retroactively declared uncanonical on the grounds that he had previously been bishop of the suburbicarian see of Portus, thereby violating the ban on the translation of a bishop from one see to another. This deposition also nullified all ordinations and consecrations that Formosus had performed, leading to a prolonged crisis in the Roman clergy. Some popes upheld the decisions of the Synod of 897, but others condemned them.[81]

Around the same time, lay aristocrats of the house of Theophylact rose to prominence in Rome. Notable among them were Theodora the Elder and her daughter Marozia, who were to play an important role in Roman politics. At times, they even controlled the popes. Marozia seems to have ruled Rome quite independently for a few years under the title of Senatrix, until she was deposed by her own son, Alberic II, in 932. Alberic then ruled the Eternal City himself until he died in 954. His rule is important for the Roman church, for he fostered the Cluniac Reform.[82] His son Octavian held the papal throne from 955 to 964 as John XII. He was also the pope who crowned the Saxon, east-Frankish king Otto I emperor in 962. Upon this occasion, the new emperor had a charter drawn up for the papacy, known as the *Privilegium Ottonianum*, which is extant in the Vatican archives.[83] This document aligned the new Ottonian regime with the old Carolingian one. On the one hand, the privileges of the Roman church were confirmed, as were Rome's territorial claims, which, as by tradition at this point, far exceeded the actual borders of the papal state. On the other hand, the rules set in the *Constitutio Romana* were also upheld, so that the Ottonian dynasty acquired considerable judicial rights in Rome, at least in theory.[84]

While the *Privilegium Ottonianum* restored to some extent a situation that had been in place a century earlier, it was also the starting point for new Ottonian projects in Italy. Otto's grandson Otto III (983/996–1002) even attempted to make

81 M.-L. Heckmann, "Der Fall Formosus – ungerechtfertigte Anklage gegen einen Toten, Leichenfrevel oder inszenierte Entheiligung des Sakralen?" in S. Weinfurter (ed.), *Päpstliche Herrschaft im Mittelalter. Funktionsweisen, Strategien, Darstellungsformen*. Mittelalter-Forschungen 38 (Ostfildern: Jan Thorbecke, 2012), 223–38.

82 See V. West-Harling, "The Roman Past in the Consciousness of the Roman Elites in the Ninth and Tenth Centuries," in Walter Pohl et al. (eds.), *Transformations of Romanness* (Berlin: De Gruyter, 2018), 173–94.

83 Ed. Sickel, 322–27.

84 H. Zimmermann, *Regesta imperii* II.5.2, no. 305, p. 93.

Rome his capital city, which would have made him the first emperor actually to rule from the Eternal City since the fourth century. This initiative was furthered by two successive popes, Gregory V (Bruno of Carinthia, 996–999) and Silvester II (Gerbert of Aurillac, 999–1003). They had been close associates of the emperor and, like Otto, they were outsiders in Rome. The project ultimately failed in the face of strong resistance from the Roman aristocracy. When the insurrections from the clan of the Crescentii had finally been violently crushed, Otto succumbed to an illness while marching back to Rome to retake the city.[85] With his death, the plan for imperial domination in the city was abandoned for good, and Rome reverted to the ways in which it had been governed during the ninth and part of the tenth centuries, with a strong papacy heavily influenced by a handful of local powerful families.

Although this aspect of the papacy would not change fundamentally for centuries, there would soon be major changes involving the so-called reform papacy, starting in the mid-eleventh century. That development goes beyond the scope of this volume, but we should note that many of the ideas formulated during this papal, or "Gregorian," reform had their roots in the early medieval centuries described in this chapter. Aspects of the new papal confidence, too, had been prefigured earlier, not least by Nicholas I in the ninth century. It is no coincidence that his writings began to be cited frequently again during the era of the reform papacy.

SOURCES AND ABBREVIATIONS

Primary Sources Cited in Abbreviated Form

COD I — *Dekrete der ökumenischen Konzilien*, vol. 1: *Konzilien des Ersten Jahrtausends*. Ed. Giuseppe Alberigo et al., trans. Josef Wohlmuth. 2nd edition. Paderborn: Schöningh, 1998.

FC 58.1–3: — Hermann-Josef Sieben (ed.), *Vetustissimae epistulae Romanorum Pontificum. Die ältesten Papstbriefe*. FC 58.1 (Freiburg i. Br.: Herder, 2014), 58.2 (Freiburg i. Br.: Herder, 2014), 58.3 (Freiburg i. Br.: Herder, 2015).

Other Primary Sources

Athanasius. *Werke*, vol. 3, *part 1. Urkunden zur Geschichte des arianischen Streites 318–328*. Ed. Hans-Georg Opitz. Berlin: De Gruyter, 1934–35.

Collectio Avellana. Ed. Otto Guenther. CSEL 35.1 (1895).

Dobschütz, Ernst von (ed.). *Das Decretum Gelasianum de Libris recipiendis et non recipiendis*. Leipzig: Hinrichs, 1912.

Eusebius, *Church History: Eusebius, Kirchengeschichte*. Ed. Eduard Schwartz. Kleine Ausgabe 5. Berlin, 1952.

First Epistle of Clement: Klemens von Rom, Epistola ad Corinthios. Brief an die Korinther. Ed. Gerhard Schneider. FC 15. Freiburg im Br.: Herder, 1994.

85 Scholz, *Politik*, 267–395.

Ignatius of Antioch, *Lettres*. Ed. Pierre Thomas Camelot, SC 10 (1958).
Irenaeus of Lyon, *Adversus haereses: Gegen die Häresien, Liber III. Buch III*. Ed. Norbert Brox. FC 8/3. Freiburg i. Br.: Herder, 1995.
Iustinianus, *Novellae*. Ed. Rudolf Schoell and Wilhelm Kroll. CIC 3. Berlin: Weidmann, 1895.
Liber Pontificalis. Ed. Louis Duchesne. 3 vols. Second Edition. Paris: E. de Boccard, 1955–57.
Sickel, Theodore von (ed.). MGH Diplomata, *Die Urkunden der deutschen Könige und Kaiser*, vol. 1: *Konrad I., Heinrich I. und Otto I* (1879–84).
Tertullian, *De praescriptione haereticorum: Vom prinzipiellen Einspruch gegen die Hôretiker*. Ed. D. Schleyer. FC 42. Turnhout: Brepols, 2002.
Turner, Cuthbert H. (ed.). *Ecclesiae Occidentalis Monumenta Iuris Antiquissima*. 2 vols. in 7. Oxford: Clarendon Press, 1899–1939. [Turner I = vol. 1, 1899.]
Zimmermann, Harald (ed.). *Regesta Imperii II. sächsische Zeit, 5, Papstregesten 911–1024*, Bd. 2: *verbesserte und ergänzte Auflage*. Vienna: Böhlau, 1998.

FURTHER READING

Demacopoulos, George E. *The Invention of Peter: Apostolic Discourse and Papal Authority in Late Antiquity*. Philadelphia: University of Pennsylvania Press, 2013.
Duffey, Eamon. *Saints and Sinners: A History of the Popes*. Fourth edition. New Haven, CT: Yale University Press, 2015.
Dunn, Geoffrey D. (ed.). *The Bishop of Rome in Late Antiquity*. Farnham, UK: Ashgate, 2015.
Ferreiro, Alberto. "Pope Siricius and Himerius of Tarragona (385): Provincial Papal Intervention in the Fourth Century." In Dunn, *The Bishop of Rome*, 73–85.
Gantner, Clemens. "New Visions of Community in Ninth-Century Rome: The Impact of the Saracen Threat on the Papal World View." In Walter Pohl, Clemens Gantner, and Richard Payne (eds.), *Visions of Community in the Post-Roman World: The West, Byzantium and the Islamic World, 300–1100* (Farnham, UK: Ashgate, 2012), 403–21.
Goodson, Caroline J. *The Rome of Pope Paschal I: Papal Power, Urban Renovation, Church Rebuilding and Relic Translation, 817–824*. Cambridge: Cambridge University Press, 2010.
Hornung, Christian. "Siricius and the Rise of the Papacy." In Dunn, *The Bishop of Rome*, 57–72.
Noble, Thomas F. X. "Morbidity and Vitality in the History of the Early Medieval Papacy." *Catholic Historical Review* 81 (1995): 505–40.
"The Papacy in the Eighth and Ninth Centuries." In Rosamond McKitterick (ed.), *New Cambridge Medieval History*, vol. 2: *c.* 700–*c.* 900 (Cambridge: Cambridge University Press, 2008), 561–86.
The Republic of St. Peter: The Birth of the Papal State, 680–825. Philadelphia: University of Pennsylvania Press, 1984.
Richards, Jeffrey. *The Popes and the Papacy in the Early Middle Ages 476–752*. London: Routledge & Kegan Paul, 1979.
Schimmelpfennig, Bernhard. Trans. James Sievert. *The Papacy*. New York: Columbia University Press, 1992.
Seppelt, Franz Xaver and Klemens Löffler. *A Short History of the Popes*. St. Louis, MO: Herder, 1932.
Sessa, Kristina. *The Formation of Papal Authority in Late Antique Italy: Roman Bishops and the Domestic Sphere*. Cambridge: Cambridge University Press, 2012.
Wickham, Chris. *Medieval Rome: Stability and Crisis of a City, 900–1150*. Oxford: Oxford University Press, 2015.

6

The Sacred Palace, Public Penance, and the Carolingian Polity[1]

Mayke de Jong

The concept of the "sacred palace" provides us with a key to understanding how Carolingian kings and emperors understood their role as rulers and legislators in relation to religion and the church. They did not consider church and state to be fundamentally separate or mutually antagonistic domains. Moreover, without understanding royal religious power in this era, we cannot properly interpret the role of public and royal penance during the reign of emperor Louis, Charlemagne's son and successor.

The expression *sacrum palatium* as denoting the Carolingian palace first emerged in the context of the synod of Frankfurt (794), where Charlemagne, king and future emperor, presided over a gathering of bishops convened to deal with the supposed heresy of Adoptionism. Afterward, bishop Paulinus of Aquileia vividly evoked these discussions in the presence of the ruler, "when all were seated in the hall of the sacred palace [*aula sacri palatii*], with priests, deacons, and the entire clergy standing around us in a circle," presided over by Charlemagne.[2] The expression *sacrum palatium* had gained some currency by the end of Charlemagne's reign in 814. In 813, Hildebold of Cologne was referred to as the "archbishop of the sacred palace" (*archiepiscopus sacri palatii*), and his successor Hilduin, the abbot of Saint-Denis and the most powerful man at the court of emperor Louis, carried the title "archchaplain of the sacred palace" (*archicapelleanus sacri palatii*).[3] When in 813 a synod

[1] Editorial note: This chapter is an English version of a paper published in French in *Annales*: Mayke de Jong, "*Sacrum palatium et ecclesia.* L'autorité religieuse royale sous les Carolingiens (790–840)," *Annales HSS*, 58.6 (2003): 1243–69, © Éd. de l'Ehess, Paris. It is included here by permission of the editors of *Annales* as well as of the author. Author and editor have made minor revisions and adjustments, but we have made no attempt to update the contents or to modify the style of the paper, which illustrates the approach typical for an academic journal.

[2] Paulinus of Aquileia, *Libellus sacrosyllabus episcoporum Italiae*, MGH Conc. 2.1 (1906), 131. On this gathering, see Rainer Berndt (ed.), *Das Frankfurter Konzil von 794. Kristallisationspunkt karolingischer Kultur*, 2 vols. (Mainz: Selbstverlag der Gesellschaft für mittelrheinische Kirchengeschichte, 1997). On the controversy over Adoptionism, see John C. Cavadini, *The Last Christology of the West: Adoptionism in Spain and Gaul, 785–820* (Philadelphia: University of Pennsylvania Press, 1993).

[3] Thomas Zotz, "*Palatium* et *curtis*. Aspects de la terminologie palatiale au Moyen Âge," in A. Renoux (ed.), *Palais royaux et princiers au Moyen Âge* (Le Mans: Centre d'édition et de publication de l'Université du Maine, 1996), 7–15, at 9.

in Tours could not decide on which book of penance should be used, the bishops decided to wait for further instruction when they would be "gathered with all the bishops in the sacred palace."[4] In the same year, Charlemagne's biographer archbishop Leidrad of Lyon provided his "constant and sacred emperor" with a proud account of the success of reform in his own archdiocese, thanking him for sending books as well as an expert in singing. As a consequence of Leidrad's efforts and of the emperor's support, the chant of Lyon's divine office was now performed according to "the usage of the sacred palace" (*ritus sacri palatii*).[5]

The emergence of a Carolingian *sacrum palatium* has been interpreted as the result of Byzantine influence,[6] yet there was more to Charlemagne's sacred palace than a mere borrowing of late-Roman and Byzantine terminology in order to lend imperial glamour to a Frankish court hierarchy increasingly conscious of governing an empire. Even if Roman and Byzantine models played a part in shaping Western notions of the sacredness of the palace, these notions still functioned in a different cultural context: one that invested them with new and specific meaning. When Leidrad referred to the "usage of the sacred palace" (*ritus sacri palatii*), he had Aachen in mind, not Constantinople. Charlemagne's palace at Aachen was called "sacred" because it had become the place where royal religious authority was embedded, enhanced, and articulated. For Leidrad, as well as for his colleagues gathered in Tours, the *sacrum palatium* was a source of authoritative liturgy and doctrine: a religious center to which bishops looked for guidance, and where they would find what in their eyes counted as genuine orthodoxy.[7]

As explanations in terms of "Byzantine influence" suggest, the Carolingian notion of the sacred palace transgresses a still-pervasive Western paradigm that has defined the spheres of religion and politics as fundamentally separate and opposed to each

[4] Council of Tours (813), c. 22, MGH Conc. 2.1, 289: "Ideo necessarium videbatur nobis, cum omnes episcopi ad sacrum palatium congregati fuerint, ab eis edoceri, cuius antiquorum liber poenitentialem potissimus sit sequendus."

[5] Alfred Coville, *Recherches sur l'histoire de Lyon du Ve siècle au IXe siècle (450–800)* (Paris: Picard, 1928), 283–87. E. Dümmler (ed.), MGH Epist. 4 (*Epist. Kar. Aevi* 2), 542–45. On Leidrad's biography and the date of the letter, see Coville, *Recherches*, 294–96, who proposes a date between 809 and 812. In 816, Leidrad retired to the monastery of Saint-Médard in Soissons. See also Otto G. Oexle, *Forschungen zu monastischen und geistlichen Gemeinschaften im westfränkischen Bereich*, Münstersche Mittelalter-Schriften 31 (München: Wilhelm Fink, 1978), 134–35.

[6] Joseph Fleckenstein, *Die Hofkapelle der deutschen Könige, vol 1: Grundlegung. Die karolingische Hofkapelle* (Stuttgart: Anton Hiersemann, 1959), 49. See also Otto Treitinger, *Die oströmische Kaiser- und Reichsidee nach ihrer Gestaltung im höfischen Zeremoniell. Vom oströmischen Staats- und Reichsgedanken* (Darmstadt: Gentner, 1956.) For a broader approach that also takes the Merovingian period into account, see Josiane Barbier, "Le sacré dans le palais Franc," in M. Kaplan (ed.), *Le sacré et son inscription dans l'espace à Byzance et en Occident. Études comparées, Byzantina Sorbonensia* 18 (Paris: Publications de la Sorbonne, 2001), 27–41. On the court and entourage of Louis the Pious, see Philippe Depreux, *Prosopographie de l'entourage de Louis le Pieux (781–840)* (Sigmaringen: Thorbecke, 1997), esp. 9–64.

[7] On the authority of the Carolingian court regarding liturgy, see Yitzhak Hen, *The Royal Patronage of Liturgy in Frankish Gaul to the Death of Charles the Bald (877)* (London: Henry Bradshaw Society, 2001).

other. This long tradition of construing clerical and secular domains in terms of an antagonistic dualism between Church and State, with one inevitably posing a threat to the autonomy of the other, has turned the religious authority of Byzantine emperors into an anomaly called "caesaropapism."[8] This same intellectual heritage has deeply influenced the historiography of politics and religion in the early-medieval West, and particularly that of the first two Carolingian emperors, Charlemagne and Louis the Pious. Charlemagne is credited with wielding a too-extensive religious authority, and, therefore, with having been caesaropapist and even aspiring to a "royal theocracy," for this was a powerful ruler who kept his bishops well in check.[9] By contrast, the reign of his son Louis supposedly saw a transgression in the other direction, in which clerics massively and illegitimately invaded the domain of secular power. Instead of keeping itself to its proper priestly and pastoral functions, on this view, "the church" increasingly turned its religious authority into a political leadership based on the superiority of episcopal authority (*auctoritas*) over royal power (*potestas*). This so-called *Augustinisme politique* supposedly dominated the reign of Charles's successor, Louis the Pious.[10] In recent scholarship, Louis's reign has been the subject of increasingly positive reassessment,[11] yet the view that bishops undermined Louis's effectiveness as a ruler and ultimately the Carolingian empire has been remarkably tenacious. Emperor Louis's public penance in 833, recently characterized as the first Stalinist trial in history, still counts in historiography as clear evidence of a bid for an "episcopal theocracy," which set the scene for the disintegration of the Carolingian empire after Louis's death.[12]

The nature of the Carolingian state has been the subject of much reflection and debate,[13] but the same does not hold true for "the church," which still tends to be

8 Gilbert Dagron, *Empereur et prêtre. Étude sur le "césaro-papisme byzantin"* (Paris, Gallimard, 1996), 290–322. For discussion of this groundbreaking study, see Evelyne Patlagean, "Byzance et la question du roi-prêtre," *Annales HSS* 55.4 (2000): 871–78; and Alain Boureau, "Des politiques tirées de l'Écriture. Byzance et l'Occident," ibid., 879–87.

9 Boureau, "Des politiques tirées de l'Écriture," 883.

10 The two classic statements of this view are Henri-Xavier Arquillière, *L'Augustinisme politique* (Paris: Vrin, 1934); and Étienne Delaruelle, "En relisant le *De institutione regia* de Jonas d'Orléans," in *Mélanges d'histoire du Moyen Âge, dédiés à la mémoire de Louis Halphen* (Paris: Presses Universitaires de France, 1951), 185–93. The intellectual background and context of the concept of *Augustinisme politique* is outlined in Boureau, "Des politiques tirées de l'Écriture."

11 See the collected articles in Peter Godman and Roger Collins (eds.), *Charlemagne's Heir: New Perspectives on the Reign of Louis the Pious (814–840)* (Oxford: Clarendon Press, 1990), and the excellent survey of Philippe Depreux, "Louis le Pieux reconsidéré? À propos des travaux récents consacrés à l'héritier de Charlemagne et son règne," *Francia* 21.1 (1994): 181–212.

12 Élisabeth Magnou-Nortier, "La tentative de subversion de l'État sous Louis le Pieux et l'oeuvre des falsificateurs," *Le Moyen Âge* 105 (1999): 331–65 and 615–41, at 640. See also Monika Suchan, "Kirchenpolitik des Königs oder Königspolitik der Kirche? Zum Verhältnis Ludwigs des Frommen und des Episkopates während der Herrschaftskrisen um 830," *Zeitschrift für Kirchengeschichte* 111.1 (2000): 1–27, who takes a similar view.

13 Johannes Fried, "Der karolingische Herrschaftsverband im 9. Jahrhundert zwischen Kirche und Königshaus," *Historische Zeitschrift* 235 (1982): 1–43. For a critical response, see Hans-Werner

perceived as an entity that supersedes time and change. The term *ecclesia*, which looms large in Carolingian royal legislation, evokes two basic connotations today: it is either a clearly defined and separate clerical hierarchy pursuing its own interests, or a "real church" considered to be universal: a society of the elect not bound up with earthly polities. Deviations from these modern conceptions of "the church," such as when kings cooperated with bishops and ruled with their help – a widespread early-medieval pattern – or when the term *ecclesia* was used to denote a polity, tend to be either ignored or treated as anomalous. In spite of a growing body of scholarship that argues differently,[14] historians still suppose that "royal theocracy" characterized the reign of Charles, whereas "episcopal theocracy" came to prevail under his son Louis.[15]

In what follows, I intend to show that this supposed contrast between the two regimes is anachronistic and misleading. Both in Charlemagne's and in Louis's reign, the palace embodied *royal religious authority*, above all because the ruler was perceived as the leader of an empire that was also an *ecclesia*. Together with his bishops, the ruler was responsible for the salvation of the Christian people (*populus christianus*) over which he ruled, and he was accountable to God for its sins. This aspect of royal and episcopal leadership was further articulated after 814. Whereas Charlemagne had repeatedly instigated collective and public acts of atonement without taking a prominent part in them himself, Louis played a leading role in collective efforts to placate an offended deity, evincing a truly imperial humility that was reminiscent of the emperor Theodosius I (also known as Theodosius the Great), who did penance in 390 at Ambrose's behest. This developing "penitential state" was the background to Louis's public penance in 833, for it created the context within which political conflict could be conceptualized in terms of sin and penance.

Goetz, "*Regnum*: zum politischen Denken der Karolingerzeit," *Zeitschrift der Savigny-Stiftung für Rechtsgeschichte, Germanische Abteilung* 104 (1987): 110–89. See also Janet L. Nelson, "Kingship and Empire," in J. H. Burns (ed.), *The Cambridge History of Medieval Political Thought c. 350–c. 1450* (Cambridge: Cambridge University Press, 1988), 211–51.

14 Rosamond McKitterick, *The Frankish Church and Carolingian Reforms, 789–895* (London: Royal Historical Society, 1977). Nikolaus Staubach, "*Cultus divinus* und karolingischen Reform," *Frühmittelalterliche Studien* 18 (1984): 546–81; Nikolaus Staubach, *Rex christianus. Hofkultur und Herrschaftspropaganda im Reich Karls des Kahlen, II: Die Grundlegung der* religion royale, Pictura et poesis 2 (Cologne: Böhlau, 1993). Karl-Ferdinand Werner, "*Hludovicus Augustus.* Gouverneur l'empire Chrétien – Idées et réalités," in Godman and Collins, *Charlemagne's Heir*, 3–124. Matthew Innes, "Charlemagne's Will: Inheritance, Ideology and the Imperial Succession," *English Historical Review* 112 (1997): 833–55. Mayke de Jong, "The Empire as *ecclesia*: Hrabanus Maurus and Biblical *Historia* for Rulers," in Y. Hen and M. Innes (eds.), *The Uses of the Past in the Early Middle Ages* (Cambridge: Cambridge University Press, 2000), 191–226.

15 This is a standard opinion in textbooks. Cf. Geneviève Bührer-Thierry, *L'Europe carolingienne (714–888)* (Paris: Armand Colin, 2001), 74–78.

PALACE AND CLOISTER

Leidrad and his colleagues in Tours did not have just any of Charlemagne's many palaces in mind, but rather the royal residence that came to be called the "senior palace," namely, Aachen.[16] From the winter of 774/75, this new palace became Charlemagne's preferred winter residence. From the winter of 801–02 onward, he resided there more or less permanently, with breaks only for summer campaigns and autumn hunting. Contemporaries were deeply impressed by its magnificent buildings, particularly its *opus mirabile*, the church dedicated to the Virgin, adorned with pillars brought from Rome and Ravenna. Once Charlemagne's residence had become permanent, Aachen grew into a busy hub with a thriving settlement (*vicus*), a market, and a mint. Aachen's sacred character was drawn from many different sources. Its church, dedicated to the Virgin, was likened to Solomon's temple – and understandably so, for, like Aachen, this biblical model of a cultic center had encompassed an interconnected temple and royal residence. But there were other sources of inspiration as well: notably Byzantium, late-antique imperial Rome, and, above all, the Rome of pristine and authentic Christianity, represented by the Acts of the Apostles and the martyrs. No single model from an authoritative past dominated the physical structure of the palace at Aachen and the meanings attached to it by contemporaries and subsequent generations.[17] Instead, drawing eclectically upon the symbolic resources of an authoritative past, the palace in Aachen resembled Carolingian culture in general.

The undiminished importance of this palace as a seat of royal authority after Charlemagne's death is revealed by the way in which Louis's succession was portrayed in contemporary sources. His taking over the empire from his father in 814 meant, first of all, that Louis took possession of Aachen.[18] Similarly, when the empress Judith was accused of adultery in 830 and sent to the monastery of Sainte-Croix in Poitiers to atone for her sins, her subsequent rehabilitation was depicted as readmission to Aachen. The empress was ceremonially welcomed to her rightful seat of power, with her son and other great men riding out from the palace to meet her, in the manner of a Roman *adventus*.[19]

16 The literature on Aachen is vast. See especially J. L. Nelson, "Aachen as a Place of Power," in M. de Jong and F. Theuws (eds.), *Topographies of Power in Early Medieval Europe* (Leiden: Brill, 2001), 217–42; J. L. Nelson, "La cour impériale de Charlemagne," in R. Le Jan (ed.), *La royauté et les élites dans l'Europe carolingienne (du début du IXe aux environs de 920)* (Lille: Université Charles-de-Gaulle/Lille, 1998), 181–82, repr. in J. L. Nelson, *Rulers and Ruling Families in Early Medieval Europe: Alfred, Charles the Bald, and Others* (Aldershot: Brookfield, 1999), ch. XIV; Ludwig Falkenstein, "Charlemagne et Aix-la-Chapelle," *Byzantion* 61 (1991): 231–89; Barbier, "Le sacré dans le palais Franc."

17 Nelson, "Aachen as a place of power," rightly emphasizes this point. For a brief but illuminating discussion of the eclectic symbolism of the Aachen palace and chapel complex, see Mary Garrison, "The Franks as the New Israel? Education for an identity from Pippin to Charlemagne," in Hen and Innes, *The Uses of the Past*, 154–56.

18 Astronomus, Vita Hludowici, cc. 21–23, ed. E. Tremp, *Thegan, Die Taten Ludwigs des Frommen; Astronomus, Das Leben Kaiser Ludwigs*, MGH SRG 64 (1995), 348–52.

19 *Annales Mettenses priores*, s.a. 830, ed. B. von Simson, MGH SRG 10 (1905), 97–98.

Despite this palace's undoubted prominence, Carolingian royal rule remained multifocal. Aachen became the central node in a network and hierarchy of palaces that created interconnecting royal landscapes. Even the most peripheral palaces that kings hardly ever visited became infused with royal presence, for those living in them had vivid memories of having visited the great palaces, such as Aachen. As Stuart Airlie put it, there was an enduring "palace of memory" invested with a royal authority that depended not merely on the accidental presence of the king and his court but more on the memories and experiences of those who had visited the most prominent royal seats and had basked in the reflected glory of the ruler's proximity. Such central palaces embodied a shared ideal of the palace that could be transmitted to more peripheral royal spaces.[20] As a result of changing political constellations, the geographical location of central palaces shifted over time, but royal authority, nevertheless, came to be associated with specific locations, rather than being dependent upon the mere presence of the king in whatever palace he happened to be residing. Even palaces that he hardly ever visited became infused with royal authority.

The network of palaces of which Aachen was the central node consisted not only of *palatia* in the strict sense of the word but also of royal monasteries. In the course of the seventh century, Merovingian kings and queens had favored select religious communities with privileges of immunity, which created a direct link between the ruler and sacred spaces. Their Carolingian successors depended upon direct access to monastic resources to a much greater extent. Such resources consisted not only of a vast landed wealth of which kings might dispose to reward their faithful men, but also of the prayer that was necessary for the stability of the realm (*stabilitas regni*) and for the victory of the armies: in short, the "right worship" that would ensure God's favor. Carolingian royal protection (*tuitio*) turned these monasteries into a distinct but integral part of royal space.[21] As with palaces, the hierarchy within this network of royal monasteries was determined by royal favor and presence. The most prominent among them were entrusted to abbots and abbesses who were closely connected to

20 Stuart Airlie, "The Palace of Memory: The Carolingian Court as a Political Centre," in S. Rees Jones, R. Marks, and A. J. Minnis (eds.), *Courts and Regions in Medieval Europe* (Rochester: York Medieval Press, 2000), 1–20. See also Thomas Zotz, "Le palais et les élites dans le royaume de Germanie," in Le Jan, *La royauté et les élites dans l'Europe carolingienne*, 233–47.

21 See Mayke de Jong, "Carolingian Monasticism: The Power of Prayer," in R. McKitterick (ed.), *The New Cambridge Medieval History II, c. 700–c. 900* (Cambridge: Cambridge University Press, 1995), 622–53, which includes extensive references to the older literature. For an innovative perspective on the concept of Carolingian royal protection (*tuitio*) as distinct from that of Merovingian immunity, see Barbara H. Rosenwein, *Negotiating Space: Power, Restraint and Privileges of Immunity in Early Medieval Europe* (Ithaca: Cornell University Press, 1999). On monasteries as mediators of royal power in the Carolingian empire, see Anne-Marie Helvétius, "L'abbatiat laïque comme relais du pouvoir royal au frontières du royaume: le cas du Nord de la Neustrie au IXe siècle," in R. Le Jan (ed.), *La royauté et les élites dans l'Europe carolingienne (du début du IXe siècle aux environs de* 929 (Lille: Centre d'Histoire de l'Europe de Nord-Ouest, 1998), 285–300; and Matthew Innes, "Kings, Monks and Patrons: Political Identities and the Abbey of Lorsch," ibid., 310–24.

the royal household. Such communities were, in effect, parallel palaces that served to a large extent as dependencies of the court.[22] They were "sacred places" (*loci sancti*), the status of which contributed to the notion of the sacred character of the palace. This was true of male as well as of female communities. Charlemagne entrusted a precious relic collection to his sister Gisela, abbess of the royal nunnery of Chelles.[23] The abbess of Remiremont, thanking Louis the Pious for his generosity, assured the emperor that over the past year her community had sung a thousand Psalms and celebrated eight hundred masses for his well-being and for that of his queen and their children.[24]

Royal monasteries served other distinctive purposes: They were temporary residences for the royal household, which regularly visited the most privileged of these sacred spaces; they were sources of human talent recruited by the palace in the shape of young monks and clerics sent to the court by their abbots for further training and future royal service; and they were places where prominent royal opponents, be they lay aristocrats or high-ranking clerics, might lie low, doing penance for their political sins until the tide had turned and they enjoyed royal favor once more.[25] As Fulda's monks knew well in 816 when they had to elect a new abbot, good connections with the palace were of crucial importance. Thus, some argued in favor of electing an aristocratic abbot. "You know why? Because he will enjoy generosity in the palace."[26] A balance had to be struck. Much of Carolingian monastic reform was designed to curtail excessive proximity to the world of the court, but too much distance would mean a loss of the royal patronage (*generositas in palatio*), which was essential to the survival of the community. Moreover, it was the ruler who was the final court of appeal in situations of conflict and who served as the ultimate guarantee of the monastery's *regularitas* (i.e., adherence to the precepts of the *Rule of Benedict*). Thus, disgruntled monks from Fulda appealed first to Charlemagne (812) and then to Louis (816/17), calling for a restoration of the community's *regularitas*.[27] Reflecting on these turbulent times two decades later, Brun Candidus recorded that Louis the Pious himself outlined the basic principles

[22] Airlie, "The palace of memory," 18, makes this point in passing, but it deserves more emphasis in the present context than the author had occasion to give to it.

[23] Janet L. Nelson, "Women at the Court of Charlemagne: A Case of Monstrous Regiment?" in J. L. Nelson (ed.), *The Frankish World, 750–900* (London and Rio Grande: Hambleton Press, 1996), 223–24, at 236. On the relics of Chelles, see J.-P. Laporte, *Le trésor des saints de Chelles* (Chelles: Société archéologique et historique de Chelles, 1988), 115–50.

[24] MGH *Formulae Merowingici et Karolini Aevi* (=MGH Leges, Sectio 5), ed. K. Zeumer (1882–86), 525–26.

[25] *Annales S. Bertiniani*, s.a. 834, ed. R. Rau, *Quellen zur karolingischen Reichsgeschichte* II (Darmstadt: Wissenschaftlichte Buchgesellschaft, 1972), 22.

[26] Bruno Candidus, *Vita Aegil*, c. 5, ed. Gereon Bercht-Jördens, *Vita Aegil abbatis Fuldensis a - Candido ad Modestuum edita prosa et versibus. Ein opus geminatum des IX. Jahrhunderts* (Frankfurt-am-Main: Knecht, 1994), 6.

[27] Cf. Steffen Patzold, "Konflikte im Kloster Fulda zur Zeit der Karolinger," *Fuldaer Geschichtsblätter* 76 (2000): 69–162, with extensive references to older literature.

of monastic discipline in a long sermon. In Fulda's attempt to overcome a troubled past, the emperor was the ultimate source of religious authority.[28]

Palaces, with their constant flow and ebb of people, were different from monasteries, which anxiously guarded the boundaries of the cloister (*claustrum*): the inner enclosure into which only full members of the community and a few privileged guests had access.[29] Nonetheless, monastic life was part of the self-definition of many "men of the palace" (*palatini*), who belonged to the inner circle of the royal household, for some members of this charmed circle were men with prior monastic experience, sent to the court by their abbots for further training and in view of future royal service.[30] Einhard is an interesting case in point. His celebrated *Life of Charlemagne* (*Vita Karoli*) has often been characterized as "secular," and even as "anti-clerical."[31] The notion that Einhard was a "secular" author is influenced by his use of classical models – notably Suetonius and Cicero – but it also follows from the erroneous premise that he wrote his *Vita Karoli* as an implicit critique of the overly "monastic" emperor Louis the Pious. In fact, Einhard's career is not unlike that of many courtiers whose lives constantly crossed the boundary between cloister and palace. Raised in Fulda before he came to Aachen in 794 as an adolescent or young adult, Einhard was first Charlemagne's tutor (*nutritus*) and then Louis's faithful courtier. When Einhard's wife Imma died in 836, he retired to the religious community of Seeligenstadt, which he had founded with her on land given by emperor Louis.[32] There is no contradiction between Einhard's impressive classical scholarship, on the one hand, and his imperial virtues with a monastic resonance, on the other. The Charlemagne of the *Vita Karoli* is not only a victorious warrior but also the embodiment of a royal religious authority that is characterized by humility. This holds true not only for the ruler's appropriate reluctance to be crowned emperor,[33] but also for his punctilious attendance at services in Aachen's palace chapel, where

28 Bruno Candidus, *Vita Aegil*, cc. 9–10, pp. 9–11.

29 For a further discussion of the concept of the *claustrum*, see M. de Jong, "Carolingian Monasticism," at 636–40; and M. de Jong, "Internal Cloisters: The Case of Ekkehard's Casus Sancti Galli," in W. Pohl and H. Reimitz (eds.), *Grenze und Differenz im frühen Mittelalter*, Forschungen zur Geschichte des Mittelalters 1 (Vienna: Verlag der österreichische Akademie der Wissenschaften, 2000), 209–22.

30 Matthew Innes, "A Place of Discipline: Carolingian Courts and Aristocratic Youths," in C. Cubitt (ed.), *Court Culture in the Early Middle Ages. The Proceedings of the First Alcuin Conference* (Turnhout: Brepols, 2003), 59–76.

31 Matthias M. Tischler, *Einharts "Vita Karoli": Studien zur Entstehung, Überlieferung und Rezeption*, MGH Schriften 48 (Hannover: Hahnsche, 2001), 157, with reference to Helmut Beumann, *Ideengeschichtliche Studien zu Einhard und anderen Geschichtsschreibern des früheren Mittelalters* (Darmstadt: Wissenschaftliche Buchgesellschaft, 1969), 49–52.

32 On Einhard's biography, see Paul E. Dutton (ed. and trans.), *Charlemagne's Courtier: The Complete Einhard* (Peterborough, Ontario: Broadview Press, 1998); and Julia M. H. Smith, "Einhard: The Sinner and the Saints," *Transactions of the Royal Historical Society* (Cambridge: Cambridge University Press, 2003), 55–77.

33 Einhard, *Vita Karoli*, c. 28, ed. Reinhold Rau, *Quellen zur karolingischen Reichsgeschichte* I, Ausgewählte Quellen zur deutschen Geschichte des Mittelalters 5 (Darmstadt: Wissenschaftliche Buchgesellschaft, 1974), 198–200.

Charles the Great carefully corrected the way the Psalms were sung, although he took care never to sing or read publicly and loudly himself. The emperor personally supervised the liturgy in its most precise details, making sure that nothing impure might contaminate these sacred precincts.[34] The juxtaposition of Charles's construction of the chapel with his concern with the purity and correctness of its services in Einhard's account is reminiscent of the history of Solomon, another great ruler whose completion of the temple was followed by God's warnings about ritual correctness and obedience.[35] The Hebrew king and his people should keep God's "commandments and ceremonies," lest Israel would be "cut off out of the land I have given them, and this house, which I have hallowed" would be cast out of God's sight.[36] Einhard portrayed a typically royal kind of regularity, based on both monastic and classical templates.[37] This regularity included moderation in food, albeit only to an extent suitable to an emperor. The daily reading (*lectio*) at the royal table included not only selections from Augustine's *City of God* but also the "histories and the deeds of the ancients" (*historiae et antiquorum res gestae*). Like monks, this emperor regularly interrupted his sleep, even four or five times a night, although he did so not to pray but to dispense justice. Einhard wrote about Charlemagne's *vita interior et domestica*. The expression is difficult to translate, but it amounts to "the king's ordered life in the palace."[38]

CHURCHMEN AND THE CHURCH

In Notker's *Gesta Karoli*, written in the mid-880s in the royal monastery of Saint-Gall, vainglorious or downright silly bishops were the author's favorite target of ridicule. Unlike kings, abbots, and monks, bishops did not really belong to the sacred space represented by monasteries and palaces.[39] Reading Notker, one is reminded of Alcuin, who wrote thus to the archbishop of Canterbury in 801 with regard to his imminent visit to the palace:

34 Ibid., cc. 24–25, pp. 194–216.

35 M. Garrison, "The Franks as the New Israel?" 156.

36 III Kgs 9:6–7: "custodientes mandata mea et caeremonias quas proposui vobis."

37 On the classical models, see Martin Kempsall, "Some Ciceronian Models for Einhard's Life of Charlemagne," *Viator* 26 (1995): 11–37. For a recent and cautious attempt at dating this work, see Karl-Heinrich Krüger, "Neue Beobachtungen zur Datierung von Einhards Karlsvita," *Frühmittelalterliche Studien* 32 (1998): 124–45. For a study of the text, see David Ganz, "Einhard's Charlemagne: The Characterization of Greatness," in J. Storey (ed.), *Charlemagne: Empire and Society* (Manchester: Manchester University Press, 2005), 38–51. On the convergence of classical and monastic traditions in Carolingian biographies of rulers, see Matthew Innes, "'He never even allowed his white teeth to be bared in laughter': The Politics of Humour in the Carolingian Renaissance," in G. Halsall (ed.), *Humour, History and Politics in Late Antiquity and the Early Middle Ages* (Cambridge: Cambridge University Press, 2002), 131–57.

38 Einhard, *Vita Karoli*, c. 18, p. 188.

39 On Notker's *Gesta Karoli*, see Matthew Innes, "Memory, Orality and Literacy in an Early Medieval Society," *Past & Present* 158 (1998): 3–36.

> If you come to my lord the King, warn your companions and particularly the clergy to conduct themselves respectfully in all religious observances, in dress and in church order, so that you always set a good example wherever you go. Do not let them wear gold ornaments or silk clothes in the king's sight; they should go humbly dressed as befits servants of God.[40]

As well as being the target of Notker's jokes, medieval bishops are often the black sheep of historians today, who believe that by defining kingship as a divinely bestowed "ministry" (*ministerium*), for which the ruler would be held accountable to God in the Final Judgment, bishops in the late 820s and 830s relegated the ruler to the status of an ordinary sinner. Kingship became a conditional office, on this view, divinely conferred on good kings but withheld from bad ones. By virtue of their "power of the keys," bishops were now the ultimate judges of the kings, and so in a position to undermine royal power.[41] In the absence of a clear distinction between office and incumbent, the ruler was a "son of the Church," whose moral conduct was subject to episcopal judgment: not as the king, but rather "only as an individual, as a father or a lord."[42] This was the Carolingian "dualism" that supposedly emerged in the reign of Louis the Pious, with bishops assuming ultimate moral responsibility for the realm. But this depiction of the situation is at best one-sided.

One should keep in mind that the joint governance by kings and bishops had been the norm in late-antique and early-medieval history.[43] In Merovingian Gaul and Visigothic Spain, the new rulers relied on an already existing infrastructure of local episcopal leadership and on a late-antique tradition that had considered the Christian emperor to be the "real leader of the bishops." This is not to say that there were no conflicts between rulers and bishops, but the prevailing pattern that gradually grew more pronounced in Merovingian conciliar acts was one of a "synergic-binary structure,"[44] whereby the king and the bishops jointly shared the responsibility for the well-being of the Christian people (*populus christianus*). This dual authority among the Merovingians was clearly expressed at the Neustro-Burgundian council of Mâcon convened by King Guntram in 585. Bishops were aware of being leaders of an ecclesial body (an *ecclesia*) that surpassed the boundaries of kingdoms (*regna*), but they also voiced the need for a new political unity

40 Alcuin, *Epistolae*, no. 230, MGH Epist. 4 (1895), 374–75.

41 Compare the comments of Alain Dubreucq (ed. and trans.), Jonas d'Órléans, *Le métier du roi*, SC 407 (1995), 85–90.

42 Nelson, "Kingship and Empire," 211–51, at 224.

43 On Gregory of Tours's vision of the cooperation between bishops and the Christian ruler (*christianus princeps*) within the framework of the *ecclesia*, see Martin Heinzelmann, *Gregor von Tours (538–594)* (Darmstadt: Wissenschaftliche Buchgesellschaft, 1994); and, with a broader chronological and geographical scope, Aloys Suntrup, *Studien zur politischen Theologie im frühmittelalterlichen Okzident. Die Aussage konziliarer Texte des gallischen und iberischen Raumes*, Spanische Forschungen der Görresgesellschaft 36 (Münster: Aschendorf, 2001).

44 Suntrup, Studien zur politischen Theologie, p. 76, speaks of a synergisch-binäre Struktur. He derived this concept from Karl-Ferdinand Werner, *Naissance de la noblesse. L'essor des élites politiques en Europe* (Paris: Fayard, 1998), 150.

under one ruler, who would embody and strengthen this church.[45] When Chlotar II convened a synod in Paris in 614, which many leading laymen as well as clergy attended, this new political unity had been achieved. It was conceptualized as a tripartite ecclesiastical body (*corpus ecclesiae*) consisting of the people (*populus christianus*), the clergy (*ordo ecclesiasticus*), and the ruler (*princeps*). This *ecclesia* was ruled by a king who was supported by the bishops and his leading men (*proceres*). The synod discussed "what is most useful [*utilis*] to the king and to the salvation of the people, and what the ecclesiastical order should observe for its own benefit."[46] A later gathering in Clichy (626/7), also dominated by Chlotar II, hailed the king as David, because he governed his realm with divine providence and fulfilled a prophetic ministry.[47]

This is the context in which the notion of Frankish kingship as a divinely bestowed "ministry" first emerged. The notion was further articulated among the Carolingians in the 820s, but its contours are already visible in the Merovingian period. At least from the early seventh century onward, kings and bishops were seen as jointly responsible for the salvation of the Christian community (*populus christianus*) and for the right worship of God. The bishops who compared Chlotar II to David and credited him with a "prophetic ministry" (*ministratio prophetica*) were referring to this dual responsibility. Basing themselves on older structures and traditions, the new rulers used synods as public forums for the business of the realm in the widest sense, including worship and the clergy. In 742, Carloman, as mayor of the Merovingian palace, convened the so-called German Council (*Concilium Germanicum*) with his "bishops and magnates" (*episcopi et optimates*), calling for the "restoration of the Law of God [*lex Dei*] and ecclesiastical discipline [*aecclesiastica religio*], which have fallen into ruin under past rulers of bygone days." He wondered "how the Christian people [*populus Christianus*] can reach salvation and will not perish because of false priests."[48]

By assuming royal authority, the mayors of the Merovingian palace (the future Carolingian dynasty) made themselves accountable to God for the salvation of the people, and thereby for the worship of God (*cultus divinus*). This had to be performed correctly and regularly, for the good fortune of the Frankish kingdom (and later of the empire) was dependent on right worship as well as on divine

45 Suntrup, *Studien zur politischen Theologie*, 103–05.

46 Council of Paris (614) prologue, ed. Jean Gaudemet and Brigitte Basdevant, *Les canons der conciles mérovingiens (V^e–VIIe siècles)*, SC 354 (1989), 508: "quid quommodo principis, quid saluti populi utilius conpeteret vel quid ecclesiasticus ordo salubriter observaret."

47 Council of Clichy (626/627), prologue, ed. Gaudemet and Basdevant, SC 354, 528.

48 *Concilium Germanicum*, prologue, MGH Conc. 2.1 (1906), 2: "quomodo lex Dei et aecclesiastica religio recuperetur, que in diebus preteritorum principum dissipata corruit, et qualiter populus Christianus ad salutem animae pervenire possit et per falsos sacerdotes deceptus non pereat." On Merovingian royal involvement in synods as a model for the religious authority of Carolingian rulers, see Philippe Depreux, "L'Expression 'statutum est a domno rege et sancta synodo' annonçant certaines dispositions du capitulaire de Francfort (794)," in Berndt, *Das Frankfurter Konzil von 794*, 1:80–101.

benevolence and obedience to divine precepts. The notion that true Christian kingship was defined by the ruler's ultimate responsibility for the "worship of the true God" (*cultus veri dei*) was explicitly and famously formulated in the prologue to Charlemagne's *Admonitio generalis*, issued in Aachen in 789:

> For we read in the Books of Kings how the saintly Josiah, by visitation, correction, and admonition, strove to recall the kingdom that God had given him to the worship of the true God. I say this not to compare myself with his holiness, but because it is our duty, at all times and in all places, to follow the examples of the saints, and necessary for us to gather together whomever we can to apply themselves to a good life in praise and glory of our Lord Jesus Christ.[49]

The ruler's responsibility for "worship of the true God" and for his people's salvation is fully articulated in the biblical text itself. Josiah, upon discovering God's law in the Temple that he was engaged in rebuilding and realizing how far the conduct of God's people had become removed from what was demanded by God's law (*lex dei*), tore his clothes in a gesture of penance (IV Kgs 22:11–13). Disobedience to God's law (i.e., to Scripture) called for atonement, first of all by the ruler who had failed in his duty to visit, correct, and admonish his subjects. Charlemagne presented himself in the *Admonitio generalis* as the "rector of the kingdom of the Franks and the devout defender and adjuvant of the holy church [*sancta ecclesia*]."[50] The kingdom (*regnum*) and the church (*ecclesia*) were not perceived as identical, but the king's leading role in both domains drew the two spheres together.

In order to guarantee right worship of God, successive synods and assemblies, mostly initiated by the rulers, insisted on ever stricter distinctions within the "ecclesiastical order" (*ordo ecclesiasticus*), which mediated between God and mankind. This pattern is already visible in the *Admonitio generalis*, which addressed a broad category of priestly men (*sacerdotes*) that included not only the leading priests, especially bishops, but also monks and canons. The two classes were related but separate entities. It also addressed nuns and those virgins who were dedicated to God but not leading a regular life in a religious community. Finally, the *Admonitio* was directed at "all," that is, to the *populus Dei* that the ruler was to visit, correct, and admonish. This differentiation between the various "orders" comprising the church became increasingly complex. Churchmen (*ecclesiastici*) comprised a distinct category by virtue of their sacerdotal ministry, but this does not mean that Carolingian reform can accurately be described as "ecclesiastical."[51] It was Charlemagne who, in

49 *Admonitio generalis*, prologue, MGH Capit. 1 (1883), 54. On the religious nature of this capitulary and on Charlemagne's important role in its conception, see Thomas M. Buck, *Admonitio und Praedicatio. Zur religiös-pastoralen Dimension von Kapitularien und kapitulariennahen Texten (507–814)* (Frankfurt am Main: Peter Lang, 1997).

50 *Admonitio generalis*, prologue, 53: "Ego Karolus, gratia Dei eiusque misericordia donante rex et rector regni Francorum, et devotus sanctae aecclesiae defensor humilis adiutor . . . "

51 For an excellent recent reassessment of Carolingian reform, see Philippe Depreux, "Ambitions et limites des réformes culturelles à l'époque carolingienne," *Revue historique* 307.3 (2002): 721–51.

809, initiated an inquiry into the correct form of baptism, eliciting a wide response from his bishops, of which over sixty answers are still extant.[52] During a penetrating interrogation of his leading men in 811, when he engaged them in collective and individual self-examination, the emperor himself asked the crucial question: "Are we really Christians?"[53] On this occasion, bishops, abbots, and counts had to sit in distinct blocs, so that they were recognizable as separate orders with their distinct ministries. Nevertheless, the agenda of the meeting was a common one, as was the exposure of individual failure in the presence of the entire gathering.

The ninth-century *ecclesia* was not the church as later understood, consisting of the clergy as a separate domain. Nor was this the universal Church of theology, which transcended political boundaries. Already at an early stage, the expression *ecclesia* had come to denote and define the Carolingian polity. According to the Royal Frankish Annals of 791, Charlemagne, having consulted the Franks, the Saxons, and the Frisians, set out to avenge the "unbearable evil" committed by the Avars against "the Holy Church and the Christian people" (*sancta ecclesia vel populus christianus*).[54] The term *ecclesia* was not used here to refer to the church as a separate institution. Nor was it a premodern society's way to refer to the body politic in the absence of more abstract terms.[55] Rather, it was an articulation of the identity of an expanding Frankish polity that was derived from the same "worship of the true God" as was mentioned in the *Admonitio generalis*. In 796, when the Avar khaganate had fallen, Carolingian bishops gathered at the new frontier – not only to convert the heathens, but also to eradicate deviant forms of baptism dispensed by "illiterate clerics," that is, by Avar priests pronouncing baptismal formulas that were incorrect in the eyes of the bishops who followed in the wake of Carolingian armies. This concept of the "holy church" (*sancta ecclesia*) was both inclusive and exclusive. It defined the boundaries of the polity by including as the entire "people of God" all those who lived according to "correct" religious worship and doctrine, whereas it excluded those who did not do so.[56]

52 Susan A. Keefe, *Water and the Word: Baptism and the Education of the Clergy in the Carolingian Empire*, 2 vols. (Notre Dame: University of Notre Dame Press, 2002).

53 For an illuminating analysis of two capitularies from 811, with references to older literature, see J. L. Nelson, "The Voice of Charlemagne," in R. Gameson and H. Leyser (eds.), *Belief and Culture in the Middle Ages: Studies Presented to Henry Mayr-Harting* (Oxford: Oxford University Press, 2001), 76–88. On Charlemagne's urgent concern with religious unity during the last years of his reign (but here interpreted from the traditional perspective of a sharp discontinuity between the reigns of Charles and Louis), see also Johannes Fried, "Elite und Ideologie oder die Nachfolgeordnung Karls des Großen vom Jahre 813," in Le Jan, *La royauté et les élites*, 71–109.

54 *Annales regni Francorum* s.a. 791, ed. Rau, *Quellen zur karolingischen Reichsgeschichte* I, p. 58: "propter nimiam malitiam et intollerabilem, quam fecerunt Avari contra sanctam ecclesiam vel populum christianum."

55 As Fried assumes in "Der karolingische Herrschaftsverband im 9. Jhdt."

56 Helmut Reimitz, "Grenzen und Grenzüberschreitungen im karolingischen Mitteleuropa," in H. Reimitz and W. Pohl (eds.), *Grenze und Differenz im frühen Mittelalter*, 105–66. Helmut Reimitz, "Conversion and Control: The Establishment of Liturgical Frontiers in Carolingian Pannonia," in

Because of the ruler's religious authority, the palace itself transcended such divisions. The synod of Frankfurt (794), where the expression *sacrum palatium* was first used to designate Charlemagne's palace, decreed that all archbishops should reside in their respective dioceses, but with one notable exception. With the express consent of Pope Hadrian, it had been decided that Archbishop Hildebold of Cologne, later designated as "archbishop of the sacred palace," should reside at the palace.[57] He did so, allegedly, "in view of ecclesiastical affairs": a phrase that should be construed as "being in charge of the worship of God." The sacred palace was meant to be the center of an *ecclesia*. As Janet Nelson put it, Aachen became "a new kind of religious center, a theatre for the rites of rulership." But the question remains whether the absence of a local bishop who might steal the royal show made all that much difference.[58] The palace enforced ecclesiastical structures and distinctions between the social and ecclesiastical classes (*ordines*), but these did not govern the palace community itself, which was the center of the *ecclesia*. Bishops such as Leidrad of Lyon looked to the palace for models of the right worship of God.

This vision of the Frankish body politic as an *ecclesia* was elaborated in liturgical texts, and above all in biblical commentaries commissioned by or dedicated to rulers. Works of history commissioned by Carolingian kings are rare, and whether Carolingian rulers ever read the royal Frankish Annals remains unknown, but royal appreciation of biblical exegesis is crystal clear. Charlemagne surrounded himself with superb biblical scholars such as Theodulf and Alcuin, and he commissioned a commentary on Genesis from the otherwise unknown cleric Wigbod.[59] Working within an authoritative tradition of spiritual exegesis established by Augustine, Jerome, Ambrose, Gregory the Great, and Bede, these biblical scholars created a lively Carolingian exegetical tradition that lasted for at least three generations. Kings and queens were among the main recipients of such commentaries, especially of those on Old Testament books.[60] This was not the result of a simplistic equation of

W. Pohl, I. Wood, and H. Reimitz (eds.), *The Transformation of Frontiers from Late Antiquity to the Carolingians* (Leiden: Brill, 2000), 189–207.

57 *Concilium Francofurtense* (794), c. 56, MGH Conc. 2.1, 171.

58 Nelson, "Aachen as a Place of Power," 224–25.

59 Michael Gorman: "The Encyclopedic Commentary on Genesis Prepared for Charlemagne by Wigbod," *Recherches Augustiniennes* 17 (1982): 173–201. Michael Gorman, "Wigbod and Biblical Studies under Charlemagne," *Revue Bénédictine* 107 (1997): 40–76; and "Theodulf of Orléans and the Exegetical Miscellany in Paris. Lat. 15679," *Revue Bénédictine* 109 (1999): 278–323. The *Libri carolini* provide evidence of biblical scholarship at Charlemagne's court and of the ruler's personal involvement in it. For an edition, see Ann Freeman with Paul Meyvaert (eds.), *Opus Caroli contra synodum (Libri Carolini)*, MGH Conc. 2, supplement (Hannover: Hahnsche Buchhandlung, 1998).

60 On exegesis for rulers, see De Jong, "The Empire as ecclesia," 191–226; and De Jong, "Exegesis for an Empress," in E. Cohen and M. de Jong (eds.), *Medieval Transformations: Texts, Power and Gifts in Context* (Leiden: Brill, 2001), 69–100, with further references. On the Carolingian image of the *rex sapiens* and its consequences for royal involvement in theological debates, see Staubach, *Rex christianus*, 21–104 (esp. 12 n. 45, on biblical commentary for rulers and the royal preference for allegory).

the Franks with the "New Israel."[61] What mattered was the allegorical or spiritual level of exegesis that transformed the history of the "earlier people" – of the Synagogue that had forfeited its right to be God's elect by not having acknowledged Christ as a Savior – into the deeper truth of a victorious *ecclesia* that had succeeded Israel as God's Elect. The deeper meaning of the Old Testament could be grasped only if it was read allegorically, or spiritually. A thorough knowledge of Scripture was of the utmost importance for rulers who were in charge of correcting their *ecclesia*. Thus, Louis's biographer Thegan portrayed Charlemagne as correcting the Gospels on his death bed, and Louis as an expert on the allegorical sense of Scripture.[62]

Only the truly wise ruler (*rex sapientissimus*), who was capable of grasping the multiple levels of meaning in Scripture, could be a true leader (*rector*) of his Christian people. This became an integral part of definitions of good kingship, but there is also much evidence for rulers taking an active interest in exegetical work. When it came to the orthodoxy of such texts, authors awaited the royal judgment with trepidation. Hraban Maur, abbot of Fulda and archbishop of Mainz (d. 856), became the main provider of Old Testament exegesis to Louis the Pious, to his sons Lothar and Louis the German, and to the empresses Judith and Ermengard. His dedicatory letters evoke a lively image of rulers attempting to complete their essential exegetical library and sitting down with their "most learned readers" (*sapientissimi lectores*) at the court in order to digest and judge its contents. To Hraban, Old Testament *historia* (the literal level) was itself sacred history, but its true significance was revealed at the spiritual level, where the "earlier people" became a victorious church of all peoples and nations (*ecclesia gentium*). In the context of an expanding Carolingian empire, such time-honored themes of patristic exegesis gained a new meaning.[63] In Hraban Maur's biblical commentary for kings and queens, the *ecclesia gentium* that included all the peoples ready to recognize Christ, in contrast to the Synagogue, figured as a powerful image of the contemporary polity. In 830, when the Empress Judith was accused of adultery, Hraban dedicated two commentaries on the Books of Judith and Esther to her, likening the empress in distress to two biblical heroines, both of whom were interpreted as "types" of the *ecclesia*. The author called himself "a particle of the people governed by you."[64] This close association of the empress Judith with an *ecclesia* and with the *populus christianus* that she ought rightfully to "govern" was powerful ammunition indeed. It also provides us with an example of the ways in which Carolingian polity could be defined in exegetical terms. Some supposedly political texts used similarly religious language. For example, according to the *Ordinatio Imperii* of 817, by which Louis the Pious and his *fideles* (his entourage of ministers and defenders) attempted

61 For a perceptive discussion of this issue, see Garrison, "The Franks as the New Israel?"

62 Thegan, *Gesta Hludowici* cc. 7 et 19, ed. E. Tremp, *Thegan, Die Taten Ludwigs des Frommen*, 184–86 and 200.

63 De Jong, "The Empire as *ecclesia*," 223–26. Staubach, "*Cultus divinus*," 555–57.

64 Hrabanus Maurus, MGH Epist. 5, no. 17a, p. 420. De Jong, "Exegesis for an Empress."

to safeguard both the unity of the realm and the aspirations of his sons, the unity of the empire was to be preserved by God. It should not be torn apart by human division, "lest this cause scandal in holy church and we incur the wrath of him in whose power all the rights to kingdoms remain."[65] It is to this fear of God's wrath that we now turn.

PURITY AND DANGER

The ruler was responsible for restoring order in the realm by placating God's wrath. A capitulary issued in 806 and addressed "to all," which discusses what action should be undertaken in the case of famine, mortality, pestilence, bad weather, or any other tribulation, warned "that men are not to wait for our decree but are straightway to pray for God's mercy."[66] Apparently, the "all" to which this warning was addressed had become accustomed to a ruler and a court who identified "tribulations" and then took the lead in any empire-wide intensification of prayer. It seems that one could not initiate fasts and litanies *without* having received proper instructions from the palace. From the 790s onward, episodes of collective atonement by fasting, almsgiving, and litanies appear in the sources.[67] During the campaign against the Avars, for example, the Carolingians implored God for victory in this way not only before the army crossed the frontier but even at Regensburg, where Queen Fastrada and her entourage (*fideles*), at Charlemagne's request, organized the appropriate litanies.[68] Again, in 805, when famine raged, a general royal call for fasting and prayer was directed to bishops and possibly also to the counts. Charlemagne's letter to Bishop Ghaerbald of Liège on this subject has survived. After due consultation with his liegemen (*fideles*), both spiritual and secular, Charlemagne urged Ghaerbald to organize three-day fasts, which were "to be observed by all of us, without exception."[69]

The most striking feature of such palace-initiated acts of atonement is their collective nature. All persons were to be involved, according to their position within the structure of complimentary classes (*ordines*). Those incapable of fasting for reasons of infirmity were allowed to find another suitable atonement, but all were expected to gather at the ninth hour in their local church and, if the light and location permitted, to go in procession singing litanies, before returning to church to

65 *Capitulare missorum in Theodonis villa datum secundem generale*, c. 4, MGH Capit. 1, no. 44, pp. 122–23.

66 *Karoli ad Ghaerbaldum episcopum epistola*, MGH Capit. 1, no. 124, pp. 245–46.

67 *Capitulare episcoporum* (780?), MGH Capit. 1, no. 21, pp. 51–52, which is probably connected with the Avar campaign.

68 E. Dümmler (ed.), MGH Epist. 4, no. 20, pp. 528–29. Cf. Janet L. Nelson, "The Siting of the Council at Frankfurt: Some Reflections on Family and Politics," in Berndt, *Das Frankfurter Konzil von 794*, 149–66. For Charlemagne's letter to Fastrada, see E. Dümmler (ed.), MGH Epist. 4, no. 20, pp. 528–29. On intercessory prayer in wartime, see Michael McCormick, "The Liturgy of War in the Early Middle Ages: Crisis, Litanies and the Carolingian Monarchy," *Viator* 15 (1984): 1–23.

69 *Karoli ad Ghaerbaldum episcopum epistola*, 244–46.

sing psalms and hear the mass. Every priest was to celebrate mass, and all clerics, monks, and women consecrated to God who were capable of doing so should sing fifty psalms. Churchmen and religious had special duties, but it was the entire people of God, defined in this letter as "parts of the body of the holy church," who were called upon to appease God's wrath by doing penance. For this reason, the letter was to be read out in all monasteries and baptismal churches (i.e., churches maintained by the episcopal diocese). God's displeasure had manifested itself in abnormal and extraordinary phenomena that were reported across the entire empire, such as barren soils causing famine, intemperate weather causing crop failure, and pestilence and incursions of pagan enemies on an unprecedented scale. It was God's people who had sinned, and who should therefore atone collectively:

> And we can most certainly conclude from these external signs that we who are obliged to suffer such ills outwardly are in every way displeasing inwardly to the Lord. Wherefore it seems to us wholly right that each of us should strive to humble his heart in truth and on whatever occasion he should discover that he has offended God, whether in deed or in thought, should atone by doing penance, should lament by weeping, and in the future should guard and protect himself to the best of his ability against these ills.[70]

Such collective penitential action at times of crisis remained a feature of Louis's reign, but in assuming the burden of sin and the responsibility for atonement, the ruler and the palace played an even more central role. For example, the capitulary that resulted from the assembly at Attigny (822), where Louis reconciled himself with his enemies, depicted the emperor as taking the lead in a public confession of his sins, giving a "most salubrious example" to his bishops.[71] Following suit, the bishops also confessed publicly, admitting their negligence in fulfilling their episcopal duties (*ministerium*). This was a further expression of the notion that the ruler was accountable for the salvation of "the people committed to us by God," with the bishops in the role of his "helpers" (*adiutores*). One of Louis's biographers, known as Astronomer, emphasized the spontaneous and voluntary nature of the ruler's atonement, comparing this Carolingian emperor to his Roman predecessor Theodosius the Great, for this was humility of a truly imperial kind.[72]

In 811, as we have seen, Charlemagne had discussed the crucial issue with his bishops and leading laymen: "Are we really Christians?" In the winter of 828/29, when Louis's inner circle met in Aachen, the question was now: "How have we offended God?" A series of military defeats, famines, and ominous portents, duly recorded in the Royal Frankish Annals, induced a call for concerted prayer and reform. Some in the palace were treated as scapegoats and ousted, blamed with

70 Ibid., 245–46.

71 *Capitula ab episcopis ad Attiniaci data* (822), prologue, MGH Capit. 1, no. 174, p. 357.

72 Astronomus, *Vita Hludowici*, c. 35, MGH SRG 64, 406.

misfortunes that were perceived as God's punishment. Earlier, in February 828, counts Matfrid of Orleans and Hugh of Tours had been deprived of their *honores* (offices and the property that went with it) for the alleged mismanagement of a campaign against the Saracens: a controversial measure that was to cost Louis dearly in the years thereafter.

Two subsequent political and religious upheavals have dominated interpretations of the preceding years. In 830, the empress Judith was accused of adultery with Bernard of Septimania. In 833, a public penance was imposed on emperor Louis himself. Whenever texts from this period reveal anxiety about a lack of purity among the *populus christianus* and express a sense of the imminent danger of God's retribution, modern historians have read them as religiously veiled criticisms of a weak emperor.

Einhard's *Translatio Marcelli et Petri* is a case in point. This narrative about the successful theft of Roman martyrs and their transfer to Francia features the demon Wiggo, who lists the people's sins that have brought on plagues and pestilence in the realm over the past years. Einhard also mentions a written communication from the archangel Gabriel, concerning matters to be urgently known about martyrs. He brought this to the emperor Louis, who read it throughout, albeit without implementing all of its precepts. Clearly, Einhard was deeply concerned about the disasters that had struck the realm, identifying disobedience of divine precepts as the cause of adversity. Moreover, he attributed a special responsibility to the ruler, who was accountable to God for the sins of his people.[73] Yet this text is not the blatant indictment of the emperor that some scholars have made it out to be. Nor should Einhard's celebrated Life of Charlemagne (*Vita Karoli*) be interpreted as presenting a "counterimage" as an implicit critique of Louis. Scholars have deduced from this interpretation that the Life should be dated to the troubled years 828–829.[74] But such interpretations are based on the assumption that the urgent call for religious reform was a one-sided clerical attack on royal authority. This ignores the possibility that the emperor himself played a leading role in the anxious search for ways to placate God, with strategies that included confession and self-incrimination. Louis had led his bishops in a public confession of sin at the assembly of Attigny in 822.

Scholarly interpretations of the royal missive that followed the anxious winter assembly of 828–829 provide us with another example of the modern tendency to confuse collective anxiety with clerical critique of the ruler.[75] This letter exists in two versions. The shorter one, written by emperor Louis, called for a new three-day fast

73 Einhard, *Translatio Marcellini et Petri* II, cc. 13–14, ed. O. Holder-Egger, MGH SS (in Folio) 15.1 (1887), 252–54. Trans. Paul E. Dutton, *Charlemagne's Courtier: The Complete Einhard* (Peterborough, Ontario: Broadview Press, 1998), 100–05.

74 For the image of Einhard as a fierce critic of Louis, see Tischler, *Vita Karoli*, 167–87; and Paul E. Dutton, *The Politics of Dreaming in the Carolingian Empire* (Lincoln, NE: University of Nebraska Press, 1994), 91–101.

75 *Hludowici et Hlotharii epistola generalis*, MGH Conc. 2.2, 599–601.

after the octave of Pentecost that was "to be observed by all with the utmost devotion." Then, in order to combat the enemies that had upset the holy church (*sancta ecclesia*) and infested "the realm committed to us by God," all men with military duty had to prepare themselves for fighting. Furthermore, after consultation with the bishops and with the lay magnates, it was decided that four synods would meet in the spring of 829: in Mainz, Paris, Lyon, and Toulouse. The longer version of the letter was jointly issued by the emperors Louis and Lothar. This includes an extensive digression about God's wrath, the trials and tribulations that were inflicted upon God's people, and about the reasons for all this. One reason was that "scandals caused by tyrants had occurred in this realm" ("*scandala per tyrannos in hoc regno exsurgunt*"). This idea reveals the influence of an Irish treatise, Pseudo-Cyprian's *Twelve Abominations of the World*, the ninth abomination in which was an unjust king (*rex iniquus*), whose errors would bring trials and tribulations of cosmic dimensions on the people: barren soils causing famine, intemperate weather, crop failure, pestilence, and incursions of pagan enemies (also mentioned in Charlemagne's letter to Ghaerbald of Liège).[76] Bishop Jonas of Orléans cited this section of Pseudo-Cyprian in his edition of the acts of the Council of Paris (829). He did so again in his *Via regia*, written in 831 for Pippin of Aquitaine.[77]

Modern scholars have made much of the accusation of being an unjust king (*rex iniquus*) as an instrument by which bishops criticized the emperor Louis. The reference to the "scandals caused by tyrants" has led to the conclusion that the longer version of the imperial letter, which called for atonement, was "a bishop's forgery."[78] Others have argued that Pseudo-Cyprian's idea of the unjust king became an Irish building block for new Frankish "episcopal models" of Christian kingship.[79] This particular vision of unjust kingship and of its cosmic consequences for the people and the realm did indeed originate in Ireland, but one should keep in mind that the Irish treatise drew upon biblical texts that were also available and intensely read on the Continent. This was one of the reasons why its argument fell on fertile ground there. The idea of a ruler whose iniquities spelled ruin for his people was

76 On the *De duodecim abusivis saeculi* of Pseudo-Cyprian, see Michael E. Moore, "La monarchie Carolingienne et les anciens modèles Irlandais," *Annales HSS* 51 (1996): 307–24; and Rob Meens, "Politics, Mirrors of Princes and the Bible: Sins, Kings and the Well-Being of the Realm," *Early Medieval Europe* 7 (1998): 345–57.

77 Jonas, *De institutione regia*, c. 3, SC 407, 188.

78 Dutton, *The Politics of Dreaming*, 99–100, with reference to A. Werminghoff's assessment in his introduction to the two versions of the letter (MGH Conc. 2.2 [1908], 597–98).

79 Moore, "La monarchie Carolingienne," also stresses that this was a model that primarily served episcopal ideology and its critique of the ruler: "Pour Jonas, c'était la justice du roi at son adhesion au modèles episcopaux qui garantissait la paix de royaume, la vigeur de la nature et la capacité de rois a regner" (p. 323). But cf. Martina Blattmann, "'Ein Unglück für sein Volk.' Der Zusammenhang zwischen Fehlverhalten des Königs und Volkswohl in Quellen des 7.-12. Jahrhunderts," *Frühmittelalterliche Studien* 30 (1996): 80–102, who argues convincingly that the theme of the immoral king who ruins his people is a much more general early-medieval theme derived mostly from the Old Testament.

a familiar Old Testament theme. Moreover, rather than automatically assuming that any reference to the *rex iniquus* or variations on this theme is an instance of episcopal criticism of errant kings, one should take into account the possibility of royal self-criticism in accordance with the example of David, whose humility and penance were an integral part of this biblical ruler's authority. The longer version of the imperial letter presents the image of two penitent rulers declaring that they had "sinned all the more because we should have been the embodiment of salvation [*forma salutis*] for all and should have had the care [for the salvation] of all [*cura omnium*] because of our imperial authority."[80] If this was indeed a forgery produced by a bishop (which one may well doubt on the grounds of manuscript transmission), it was also an eloquent statement of royal religious authority.

The synod that gathered in Paris in 829 as a result of the imperial call for collective atonement has become well known in the history of political ideas because Jonas of Orléans cited in his summary a short passage from the celebrated letter of Pope Gelasius to the emperor Anastasius (see Chapter 14 in this volume). In the late eleventh century, this letter became one of the key texts supporting the superiority of pontifical authority (*auctoritas*) over imperial coercive power (*potestas*). As a result, the synod of Paris has become in modern scholarship the classic case of an emerging dualism of secular power and episcopal authority, wherein both lords were supreme within their own sphere of competence, but the bishop was just a little more supreme than the ruler.[81] This synod supposedly was the first concerted effort "to erect ecclesiastical government irrefrangibly as an integral political entity apart from secular institutions."[82] Yet the contention that the central aim of this gathering was the separation (*Abgrenzung*) of kingdom (*regnum*) and priesthood (*sacerdotium*) is the result of an excessive concentration on the phrase "two august empresses by whom the world is ruled": a garbled quotation of Gelasius's letter.[83] Moreover, the interpretation totally disregards the rest of this long text as well as the context within which it was drawn up.

The synod of Paris was convened in 829 in order to identify the sins of the leaders and the people, and thereby to pacify an offended God. According to a time-honored tradition of Carolingian "correction," the aim of the synod of Paris was to combat "confusion," that is, to restore order by clarifying and reimposing distinctions among the social classes and offices (*ordines*). The ecclesiastical and royal spheres had to be clearly distinguished, therefore, but these two legal "persons," respectively sacerdotal and royal,

80 *Hludowici et Hlotharii epistola generalis*, MGH Conc. 2.2, 600.

81 Jonas, *De institutione regia*, SC 407, 175. *Concilium Parisiense* (829), MGH Conc. 2.2, c. 55 [1], 649: "Duae sunt, inquit [Gelasius], imperatrices augustae, quibus principaliter hic regitur mundus: auctoritas sacra pontificum et regalis potestas. In quibus tanto est gravius pondus sacerdotum, quanto etiam pro regibus hominum in divino sunt examine rationem reddituri."

82 Karl F. Morrison, *The Two Kingdoms: Ecclesiology in Carolingian Political Thought* (Princeton: Princeton University Press, 1964), 45.

83 For "Abgrenzung," see Egon Boshof, *Ludwig der Fromme* (Darmstadt: Wissenschaftliche Buchgesellschaft, 1996), 176.

were integral parts of an all-embracing *ecclesia*, which was equivalent to the "Christian people." Unlike the original letter of Gelasius and its later interpretations, the ruler and the bishops at the synod of Paris were perceived as being both part of the *ecclesia* and directly accountable to God. There was, indeed, a certain "dualism" here, but it was one in which the ordering was mutual and complementary. Bishops and rulers are portrayed as responsible for each other's well-being and salvation, with the ruler having a right to correct his bishops by virtue of his own "ministry." Rather than the hierocratic vision of episcopal leadership that a superficial reading of Jonas's citation of Gelasius's letter might suggest, the acts of the synod of Paris reflect anxiety on the part of bishops faced with formidable imperial might, who were trying to defend their rights against a ruler who had freely helped himself to ecclesiastical property in order to reward his followers. More importantly, the complementary "ministries" of the ruler and of the bishops, who had mutually invaded each other's spheres of competence, should be disentangled and more clearly defined, for it was this disorder that was perceived as the root of all the evils that had assailed the *populus christianus*.[84] This, as we have seen, was part and parcel of an older Frankish tradition, as was construing kingship as a form of "ministry." In the *Admonitio generalis*, Charlemagne had been portrayed as the *adiutor sanctae ecclesiae*: the one who aided Holy Church. All modern authorities agree that this had nothing to do with subservience, but when Jonas did the same with regard to Louis, historians explain this as an instance of royal subservience to bishops, typical of this particular age and emperor.[85] Yet the notion that a *ministerium* was divinely conferred on kings did not necessarily imply an enfeeblement of royal power (*affaiblissement du pouvoir royal*). On the contrary, the concept of ministry was derived from a long tradition of reflection upon the sacerdotal office, and to apply this notion consistently to kingship meant a recognition and articulation of royal religious authority.

What was at stake in 828–829 was that both "persons," royal and priestly, perceived themselves as having neglected their God-given *ministerium* and as being in need of correction.[86] It was not only the rulers who were to blame but also the bishops. Indeed, the first and by far the largest section of the synodal proceedings (*acta*) deals with the many ways in which the bishops themselves felt that they had failed. It consists of a long litany of the bishops' sins: simony, avarice, cupidity, vanity, lack of hospitality, using church property for their own glory, oppressing the faithful, leading less than chaste lives. In short, it was better to have no bishops at all than negligent ones. The second section is devoted to "kings and princes and, more generally, to all the faithful," as Jonas put it. This is where we find the "unjust king," but Pseudo-Cyprian pales into insignificance compared to many other authoritative texts cited, particularly biblical ones, for Scripture contained all that kings needed to

84 *Concilium Parisiense*, c. 93 [26], p. 679.

85 Jonas d'Orléans, *Le métier du roi*, SC 407, 88. Magnou-Nortier, "La tentative de subversion de l'État."

86 See Hans Hubert Anton, "Zum politischen Konzept karolingischer Synoden und zur karolingischen Brüdergemeinschaft," *Historisches Jahrbuch* 99 (1979): 55–132.

know about fulfilling their ministry.[87] Above all, the acts of the synod of Paris were a statement about the joint need of the two "persons" to identify their sins and do penance for the scandal that they had caused in the sacred church (*sancta ecclesia*). In this setting, the term *scandalum* refers to public and scandalous sins that disturbed a divinely inspired social order, and that should therefore be expiated by an equally public form of penance. "Scandal" of the kind that prompted divine retribution is often mentioned in the acts of the synod of Paris – which is not surprising, given that the central issue on this meeting's agenda was the question how God had been offended. Still, because this synod is often perceived in terms of bishops imposing their superior authority on the ruler, it is worth pointing out that the term *scandalum* occurs most frequently in the "ecclesiastical" section of this text, in which the bishops outlined their *own* manifold sins.[88] That the sacred palace, too, was a potential source of scandal comes to light only toward the end of a summary of the deliberations that the bishops had presented to their ruler: "It is fitting that your sacred house should appear admirable and imitable, and that its good reputation should spread abundantly to others subjected to your government, as well as to foreign nations."[89] Here, the potential danger that might threaten the reputation (*fama*) of the palace – and, by proxy, of the realm – is identified more generally as dissension and discord. Soon, however, the palace was to become the very center of a scandal of the most dangerous kind. An empress was accused of adultery, and thereby of contaminating the order and well-being of the political community.

SCANDAL

The preceding years of soul-searching, mutual blame, and self-incrimination go a long way toward explaining why empress Judith (d. 843), Louis's second wife, could become a scapegoat upon whom the fears of an anxiety-ridden court community were temporarily concentrated. The empress was made to atone not only for her own sins but also for her alleged contamination of the polity. This was the crux of the scandal, for it was the leaders of Carolingian polity – those who were tasked with a special "ministry" – who were most capable of offending God and the *ecclesia*. For similar reasons, the public atonement of kings, queens, bishops, and other "leading men" was considered to be most effective in placating an irate deity.[90] Judith was

87 *Concilium Parisiense*, cc. 8–9, pp. 659–61.

88 *Concilium Parisiense*, cc. 16, 19, 25, 53.

89 *Concilium Parisiense* c. 91 [c. 24], p. 678: "Decet quippe, ut sacra domus vestra cunctis spectabilis appareat et imitabilis existat et fama suae opinionis sive alios imperii vestri subiectos sive exteras nationes habundantissime perfundat. Ubi igitur omnes dissensions et discordias dirimende et omnis malitia imperiali auctoritate est comprimenda, necesse est ut quod maliis corrigere decernit in ea minime reperiatur."

90 Mayke de Jong, "Power and Humility in Carolingian Society: The Public Penance of Louis the Pious," *Early Medieval Europe* 1 (1992): 29–51. Mayke de Jong, "What Was Public About Public Penance? Paenitentia publica and Justice in the Carolingian World," in *La giustizia ne'll alto*

accused of adultery because she was considered crucial to the well-being of the polity: both as the guardian of the honor and purity of the palace, and as a queen who also had a "ministry," namely, the duty of governing the empire, or *ecclesia*, with her husband. As archbishop Agobard of Lyon put it, "If the queen is incapable of governing herself, how then can she guard the honor [*honestas*] of the palace, or how can she effectively handle the reins of the realm?"[91] In the 820s and 830s, anyone with "ministry" was likely to become a scapegoat, but one should not perceive a ministry bestowed on the rulers by God as an ecclesiastical straightjacket on royal power. One should remember that clerics defined their own office as a ministry as well: the *ministerium sacerdotale*. They surely did not think of this role as subservient or dishonorable. On the contrary, humility elevated both bishops and rulers.

In 833, Louis's eldest son and co-emperor Lothar took charge of the situation. As a result, in October, the large crowd that had gathered in the church of Saint-Médard in Soissons witnessed an emperor, Louis, lying prostrate before the main altar, tearfully confessing his crimes and asking for a public penance, for he had scandalized the *ecclesia*. Following this public confession, Louis handed a written list of his sins to the bishops, who laid this on the altar. The emperor in turn laid his weapons (*cingulum militiae*), signifying his royal ministry, on the altar, and he exchanged his royal attire for the robes of a public penitent.[92] We owe this account of what Halphen has called an "odious comedy"[93] to the bishops who administered the penance. In a joint statement, they defended the legitimacy of the proceedings, stressing that this was an entirely voluntary penance. But Louis's biographers, reflecting on the matter after Louis had regained power, argued that this penance was imposed on the ruler for sins for which he had already atoned in Attigny in 822, and they emphasized the involuntary nature of the penance, which in their view had rendered it invalid. All in all, this revolt was as short-lived as the one of 830, for already on March 1 of 834, Louis was solemnly rehabilitated in the abbey church of Saint-Denis. Nevertheless, the mainstream view in modern historiography has been that the shameful humiliation in Soissons had rendered the emperor politically impotent for the rest of his reign.[94]

There is no doubt that Louis had acted under duress, but this does not mean that the bishops engineered his deposition by turning the ruler into a private sinner

medioevo (secoli IX-XI) II, Settimane di studio sull' alto medio evo 42 (Spoleto: Centro Italiano di studi sull'alto medioevo, 1997), 863–902.

91 Agobard of Lyon, *Liber apologeticus* I, c. 4, ed. L. van Acker, *Agobardi opera comnia*, CCM 52, 311: "si qua regina semetipsam regere non novit, quomodo de honestate palatii curam habebit? aut quomodo gubernacula regni diligenter exercet?"

92 *Episcoporum de poenitentia quam Hludowicus imperator professus est, relation Compiendensis*, MGH Capit. 2, no. 195, pp. 51–55. *Agobardi cartula de poenitentia ab imperatore acta*, ibid., no. 198, pp. 56–57

93 Louis Halphen, *Charlemagne et l'Empire carolingien* (Paris: Albin Michel, 1947), 291: "odieuse comedie."

94 The discussion is summarized in Depreux, "Louis le Pieux reconsidéré," 184–86.

subject to their ecclesiastical jurisdiction, nor that they had organized the first Stalinist trial in history. Bishops who sided with Lothar, notably Ebbo of Reims and Agobard of Lyon, had imposed the public penance on the emperor, whereas bishops who rallied to Louis's cause reconciled him in Saint-Denis, restoring his royal garb and armor to him. Thus, "the bishops" did not present a united front in an effort to undermine imperial authority or "the State." Nor was the public penance of 833 the infamous humiliation that it has been made out to be. At the time, the controversial question was not whether an emperor could or should atone publicly for sins that had affected the well-being of his realm – Louis had done this in 822, to great acclaim – but rather whether he had done so voluntarily or not. Furthermore, whether a penance of this sort would render the emperor permanently incapable of ruling was a matter for debate, which was why his adversaries tried to press him to take monastic vows. The public penance of 833, therefore, was not a simple act of deposition. This was not an ecclesiastical discipline by which "the clergy succeeded in imposing new standards of conduct on laymen whom penance hit where it hurt, namely, in the zone of military and sexual activity."[95] First and foremost, public penance was an instrument of royal authority.

Public penance, as distinct from its private counterpart imposed for sins that had not created scandal, first re-emerges around 800 in texts closely connected to the royal court.[96] It was one of the key issues on the agenda of Charlemagne's synods of 813, and it was the issue that the bishops gathered in Tours to consider, hoping for further instruction from the *sacrum palatium*.[97] Its more eloquent advocates presented public penance Carolingian-style as a return to an ancient canonical discipline that had flourished in the pristine Christianity of the early church, but this supposed revival of an ancient discipline really represented a new kind of penitential discipline: one directed primarily against flagrant crimes of a violent or sexual nature – rebellion, rape, robbery, incest – that had upset the order of Christian society. The key word was *scandalum*, which denoted dangerous dissension, strife, and confusion of the kind that contaminated the entire Christian community (*ecclesia*), offending a divinely inspired social order and, ultimately, God Himself. Because leadership of the *ecclesia* was more capable of causing such dangerous offense than others, public penance was especially appropriate for members of the elite, whose sins, because of their leading position and their ministry, tended to be notorious and scandalous.

Churchmen were not excepted from this regime of public penance. There was a clerical version called "canonical penance," which also required a withdrawal

95 Janet L. Nelson, "Rituals of Power: By Way of Conclusion," in F. Theuws and J. L. Nelson (eds.), *Rituals of Power: From Late Antiquity to the Early Middle Ages* (Leiden: Brill, 2000), 477–86, at 484.

96 *Paenitentiale Remense* IV, cc. 50–51, ed. F. Asbach, *Das Poenitentiale Remense und der sogenannte Excarpsus Cummeani* (doctoral dissertation, Regensburg, 1975), 30. Theodulf of Orléans, *Capitulare II*, c. VII, 8, ed. P. Brommer, MGH Capit. Episc. 1 (1984), 166–67.

97 See de Jong, "What Was *Public* About Public Penance?" 893–98, for a fuller discussion of these texts.

from public office and an atonement that was, as in other cases, usually carried out within the confines of a religious community. One leading cleric punished in this way was archbishop Ebbo of Reims, the scapegoat of the rebellion of 833. After seven years of atonement in the monastery of Fulda, Ebbo felt that he should now rightfully return to his archepiscopal see. Arguing his case, the archbishop remarked: "Clearly, the modern authority of the palace has compelled the laity, both men and women, to assume the monastic habit of the penitent only to allow them to return to their former secular status once peace has returned. There is nothing unseemly, therefore, in a lapsed cleric who after humble satisfaction reclaims his rightful office."[98] The practice this lapsed bishop referred to scathingly as the "modern authority of the palace" (*moderna auctoritas palatii*), – i.e., withdrawal to a monastery as a temporary atonement that could be ended "once the peace had returned" – was a reflection on the many instances in which Louis had used public penance as a key instrument of royal discipline. In the wake of the rebellions of 818 and 830, political adversaries, clerics as well as laymen, disappeared into monasteries to atone for their political sins, re-emerging again once the tide had turned. The public penance of prominent lay and clerical opponents of royal authority, who were those most likely to cause scandal, was a temporary act of atonement, the duration of which depended on when "peace" was restored: peace in this case being the willingness of the ruler to terminate the penance.[99]

It was this public penance, administered by bishops but as an instrument of royal authority, that Lothar employed against his father in October 833. Rather than regarding this episode as a bid for episcopal theocracy or as a political deposition masked by a deeply humiliating ecclesiastical ritual, one should take its potential open-endedness into consideration. With hindsight, the Astronomer depicted Louis as an emperor with one foot in the monastery, who was kept from following his religious inclinations only by the duties of governance, and whose public confession in 822 turned the emperor into a new Theodosius the Great. Such images were meant to enhance the emperor's reputation, not to diminish his stature. As in the case of Visigothic kings who became penitents when their sons made a successful bid for succession, the penance of 833 may have been perceived by Louis's adversaries as an honorable way out for the old emperor, for whom humility and atonement had become part of an imperial idiom.[100] Louis himself, for all we know, may well have taken the ritual in Soissons in his stride, knowing that a public penance was as temporary as the ruler on whom it was imposed. He stopped short of making a subsequent monastic profession, for this would have meant a definitive farewell to his active governing of his empire.[101]

98 Ebbo of Reims, *Apologeticum, forma 1*, MGH Conc. 2.2, 799.

99 Mayke de Jong, "Monastic Prisoners or Opting Out? Political Coercion and Honour in the Frankish Kingdoms," in De Jong and Theuws (eds.), *Topographies of Power*, 291–328, at 291–92.

100 *Annales S. Bertiniani*, s.a. 834, ed. R. Rau, *Quellen zur karolingischen Reichsgeschichte* II (Darmstadt: Wissenschaftlichte Buchgesellschaft, 1972), 22.

101 De Jong, "Monastic Prisoners."

CONCLUSION

In 885/86, the monk Notker Balbulus wrote of an emperor whom he had never personally known in a palace that he had never visited: Charlemagne and Aachen. In this palace, Notker explained, the emperor could always see what his resident nobles were up to from the vantage point of his private quarters (*solarium*) overlooking the court. Not even the servants escaped Charles's eagle eye:

> All the dwellings of the magnates were situated on the second floor, so that underneath not only all their retainers and their servants but anyone might find shelter from rain or snow, cold or heat, without ever being able to hide themselves from the eyes of the most acute Charles.[102]

Was this merely a figment of Notker's monastic imagination, seventy years after Charlemagne's death – a projection of his ideals of monastic discipline onto a court and palace of the past, or, as one historian observed ironically, a monastic author who anticipated Michel Foucault's Panopticon?[103] Or was this vision of the palace as a place of near-monastic discipline – a legacy of Louis the Pious, the emperor who had turned the monastery into a "model for empire"?[104] I should interpret Notker's description as an image that had become familiar among Charlemagne's grandchildren and their contemporaries: that of a ruler who kept a keen eye on his sacred palace and his realm, inspecting his courtiers as well as his *populus christianus*. As Hincmar and his fellow bishops wrote to King Louis the German in 856, "your palace should be sacred, not sacrilegious."[105] The authors of this letter were "men of the palace," who knew all about what palaces should be like, as did the royal recipient of their admonition. For bishops and kings alike, the question was still the one that Charlemagne had posed: "Are we really Christians?" Three generations later, the answer was still one to be sought and found in the palace.

FURTHER READING

First published in French in 2003, this essay was a pilot study for Mayke de Jong, *The Penitential State: Authority and Atonement in the Age of Louis the Pious (814–840)* (Cambridge: Cambridge University Press, 2009): one of a series of recent English-language monographs on Carolingian rulers that take into account the religious aspects of kingship. Others include: Simon MacLean, *Kingship and Politics in the Late Ninth Century: Charles the Fat and the End of the Carolingian Empire* (Cambridge: Cambridge University Press, 2003); Eric J. Goldberg, *Struggle for*

[102] Notker, *Gesta Karoli* I, 30, ed. H. F. Haefele, MGH SRG (Berlin: Hahnsche Buchhandlung, 1962), 41.

[103] Airlie, "The palace of memory," 5.

[104] Thomas F. X. Noble, "The Monastic Ideal as a Model for Empire: The Case of Louis the Pious," *Revue Bénédictine* 86 (1976): 235–50.

[105] *Epistola synodi Carisacensis ad Hludowicum regem Germaniae directa* (Nov. 858), c. 5, MGH Conc. 3, 411–12: "quoniam palatium vestrum debet esse sacrum et non sacrilegium."

Empire: Kingship and Conflict under Louis the German, 817–876 (Ithaca: Cornell University Press, 2006); Rosamond McKitterick, *Charlemagne: The Formation of a European Identity* (Cambridge: Cambridge University Press, 2008); and Courtney M. Booker, *Past Convictions: The Penance of Louis the Pious and the Decline of the Carolingians* (Philadelphia: University of Pennsylvania Press, 2009). For an excellent general introduction to the Carolingians, which includes extensive references to further literature, see Marios Costambeys, Matthew Innes, and Simon MacLean, *The Carolingian World* (Cambridge: Cambridge University Press, 2011). See now also the themed issue of *Early Medieval Europe* 25 (2017), edited by Mayke de Jong and Irene van Renswoude, on Carolingian cultures of dialogue, debate, and disputation; and Mayke de Jong, *Epitaph for an Era: Politics and Rhetoric in the Carolingian World* (Cambridge: Cambridge University Press, 2019)

7

Canonical Collections

Roy Flechner

Canonical collections from Late Antiquity and the early Middle Ages, consisting chiefly of conciliar canons and papal decretals, far outnumber the law codes issued by kings, which are commonly regarded as "secular." A crude measure of the scale of surviving canonical collections from the Latin West can be obtained from the latest standard reference book, which lists approximately seventy collections before the eleventh-century Gregorian Reform.[1] Unlike royal legislation, these collections never played a significant part in the process of identity formation of barbarian successor states, nor were they incorporated into modern grand narratives of nationhood. This partly explains why early canonical collections, unlike royal legislation, have mostly been relegated to the margins of history textbooks. But they are of great value, nevertheless, as historical sources, and their significance ranges beyond their intrinsic relevance to legal history. By their very nature, these miscellaneous collections, which exhibit a wide and diverse range of excerpted material, are important witnesses to the reception and transmission of texts, as well as to cross-cultural interactions. Likewise, the changes that these collections underwent in their transmission offer unique evidence for regional variation in doctrinal observance and ecclesiastical governance. And the preoccupation of many collections with matters of social significance, such as marriage, landholding, and the socially disadvantaged, is an important complement to contemporaneous accounts of social realities.

The present chapter will offer an introductory sketch of the development of these important sources in the Latin West, insofar as a clear trajectory of development can be observed. It is not my aim to replace existing historical surveys of canonical collections from Late Antiquity and the early Middle Ages, which have been instrumental in compiling the present chapter. Rather, my intention is to give an account that is broadly chronological, with reflection on central themes that have punctuated the study of collections, such as their sources, their authority, their main concerns, the motivations for their compilation, and their impact. The account will open, however, by considering the vexed question of identifying and classifying

[1] Kéry, *Collections*.

canonical collections and determining what distinguishes one canonical collection from another and gives it a discrete identity.

IDENTIFYING AND CLASSIFYING COLLECTIONS

Fluidity and mutability have been, from an early date, the hallmarks of canonical collections. Some texts, such as the *Collectio Hispana*, mutated frequently, mostly as a result of augmentation, and they left a trail of manuscript copies that allow us to trace (more or less) the phases of change that they underwent. Other collections, such as the *Collectio Hibernensis*, appear to have existed in multiple forms from their inception, continuing to morph as they were transmitted throughout Europe.[2] Yet other collections, such as the *Vetus Gallica*, seem to have matured gradually and lineally. The original version of the *Vetus Gallica* is believed to have been conceived in late sixth- or early seventh-century Lyon. Thereafter, the collection grew steadily until it assumed its final shape in eighth-century Corbie.[3] Hubert Mordek, the *Vetus Gallica*'s editor, has inferred the stages leading up to the Corbie version, primarily from text-critical analysis.

The three foregoing examples illustrate several largely unresolved challenges to identifying canonical collections. These include questions such as whether the recensions of the *Collectio Hispana* – designated by scholars as *Hispana Gallica*, *Hispana Gallica Augustodunensis*, and *Hispana Systematica* – should be considered as variations of the same text or as different texts that share certain affinities. Likewise, should the two main branches of the *Hibernensis* (which are commonly referred to as recensions A and B) and its later abridged or augmented versions be considered as several collections or as variations of a single collection? And is the supposed linear development of the *Vetus Gallica* no more than a teleology imposed by modern scholars? In addressing such questions, scholars acknowledge that the transformations that a text underwent could be either deliberate or random. On the one hand, changes might have been responses to the specific requirements of the community for which the collection was copied, or the result of adding canons that were not hitherto available. On the other hand, changes might have resulted from such arbitrary factors as the limited space of a manuscript or scribal incompetence. Whatever the reason, the mutable nature of collections hinders our ability to distinguish among them clearly and to classify them.

Scholarship commonly upholds one major division in classifying early canonical collections: that between systematic and chronological collections. As these descriptive labels suggest, systematic collections observe a thematic division of their

2 Roy Flechner, "The Problem of Originality in Early Medieval Canon Law: Legislating by Means of Contradictions in the *Collectio Hibernensis*," *Viator* 43 (2012): 29–47.

3 Hubert Mordek, *Kirchenrecht und Reform im Frankenreich: Die Collectio Vetus Gallica, die älteste systematische Kanonessammlung des fränkischen Gallien: Studien und Edition*, =*Beiträge zur Geschichte und Quellenkunde des Mittelalters* 1 (Berlin: De Gruyter, 1975), 62–94.

material, in which canons are separated from their original contexts and placed under thematic headings or titles, whereas chronological collections are primarily records of the *acta* (decisions) of church councils, copied in their entirety and placed one after the other in chronological order. In both cases, collections contain attributions, either genuine or spurious, which direct the reader to their material sources (*fontes materiales*), namely the original sources upon which they draw, such as conciliar *acta* or papal letters. In thematic collections, the attributions tend to be prefixed to individual canons, while in chronological collections each attribution precedes a large block of incorporated text, which usually consists of a complete set of *acta* from a council. Although this is the most prevalent division for classifying early collections today, it cannot be neatly applied to all collections. Structures were not fixed but variable, and some collections can be placed under more than one category. For example, the *Hispana* has both a chronological and a systematic version, and Cresconius's mid-sixth-century adaptation of the chronologically ordered *Dionysiana* essentially transformed this source into a systematic collection, which is known by the title *Concordia Canonum*.

Other variables used for classification include: sanctioning by authority (rare) *versus* absence of sanctioning by authority (the norm); collections drawing almost exclusively on church councils and papal decretals *versus* collections that are more eclectic, using sources such as wisdom texts, local customary law, the pronouncements of local church leaders, or even works of history and myth; collections attributed to named compilers *versus* anonymous collections; and provincial collections concentrating on material drawn from a particular place or intended to serve a particular area *versus* collections aiming for a "universal" horizon. Local collections are not as common as collections that were intended to have a wider application. Nevertheless, the surviving examples of canonical collections (*libri canonum*) from Gaul show a good deal of regional variation with respect to themes and sources, sometimes even incorporating royal letters and legislation.[4]

The variability of canonical collections may also be regarded as part and parcel of a protracted dialectical process, which over the centuries contributed to the shaping of ecclesiastical doctrine, principles of church government, ecclesiastical administrative procedures, and protocols for dispute settlement. The most conspicuous expression of this dialectic is to be found in the debate culture of councils, the rulings from which constitute the main body of material incorporated into canonical collections. Indeed, some collections preserve for us the vestiges of debates through which the conciliar canons or papal decretals came into being. Compilers of canonical collections themselves can be seen to contribute to the process through which ecclesiastical regulation and measures of penance were formed by exercising a certain interpretative license

4 Ralph W. Mathisen, "Church Councils and Local Authority: The Development of Gallic *Libri canonum* During Late Antiquity," in C. Harrison, C. Humfress, and I. Sandwell (eds.), *Being Christian in Late Antiquity: A Festschrift for Gillian Clark* (Oxford: Oxford University Press, 2014), 175–91.

either subtly, by choosing what to include and what not to include, or, more heavy-handedly, by modifying the content. It is not uncommon to find compilers assuring readers that they did not modify any of the material that they included, but then on closer inspection to discover that their disclaimer is no more than a deprecatory trope disguising an interventionist editorial policy. Compilers tended to present themselves as curators of an ecclesiastical normative tradition or, at most, as interpreters of tradition. They would not admit to creating anything new, for the power to regulate for the church lay exclusively in the hands of councils and popes, the two indisputable sources of normative authority within the church.

Nevertheless, canonical collections were rarely promulgated by authority, and even when they were, there is rarely evidence that they were treated as binding for the laity or the community at large, let alone enforced. In fact, whether there was such a thing as binding church law during the first millennium and, if so, on whom such law was binding, are debatable issues. There are, nevertheless, certain papal pronouncements that suggest an awareness that canonical decisions could have the binding quality of laws. The *Libellus responsionum*, a papal decretal (J³ 2970) by Gregory the Great (d. 604), may be the earliest source to treat canons as binding church law, albeit not necessarily as a requisite for defining Christian identity. In *responsio* §5, Gregory stipulates that one would be punished by excommunication for knowingly breaking the law, although there is no indication that one would cease to be considered a Christian. Notwithstanding isolated references such as these, there are few explicit statements by late-antique popes to tell us how they understood the force of ecclesiastical legislation in relation to Christian society more generally.

We are better informed about the place of conciliar canons within the ecclesiastical sphere. Gregory the Great proclaimed the first four Ecumenical Councils to be on a par with the four Gospels in settling major doctrinal disputes (J³ 2099), while he and other bishops also recognized the value of such canons as a device for addressing routine doctrinal questions, for moderating forces within the church, for establishing hierarchies, for introducing mechanisms of dispute settlement, for regulating liturgical practice, and for safeguarding ecclesiastical property. There are also several fifth- and sixth-century examples in which conciliar and papal pronouncements can be shown to have been considered binding upon the clergy.[5] Clearly, ecclesiastical decisions were seen to have their own special, quasi-legal utility. As the material emanating from councils and decretals accrued, so collections began to play a more vital role.

THE EVOLUTION OF COLLECTIONS: BEGINNINGS

The origins of canonical collections in the Latin West are often traced to Greek texts spuriously attributed to the teachings of the Apostles, in particular the first- or

[5] Detlev Jasper and Horst Fuhrmann, *Papal Letters in the Early Middle Ages* (Washington, DC: Catholic University of America Press, 2001), 16–18.

early second-century *Didache*, a text of unknown origin consisting of sixteen brief chapters that mostly address moral and liturgical issues. The *Didache* was included as the seventh book of the fourth-century *Apostolic Constitutions*, the first six books of which were drawn from another pseudo-apostolic text, the third-century Syrian *Didascalia Apostolorum*. The *Didascalia* dealt with themes that would become a staple of canonical collections thereafter, such as ordination, the duties of bishops, liturgical observance (broadly defined), women in the church, dispute settlement, and the distribution of church funds. Even more important to the canonical tradition in the West is the concluding text (VIII.47) of the *Apostolic Constitutions*. This section came to be known in the early Middle Ages as the *Apostolic Canons*. These are concerned primarily with the ordination and duties of the clergy and their moral standards. Fifty of its eighty-five canons were translated into Latin by Dionysius Exiguus (see Chapter 15) in the early sixth century and incorporated into his *Dionysiana*, on which more anon. Thereafter, the *Apostolic Canons* were frequently excerpted by subsequent collections that drew on the *Dionysiana* or on parts thereof. The *Dionysiana* provided a table of contents for the Apostolic Canons (as it did for all the texts that it contained), from which I cite a selection below as an example of a typical list of concerns addressed by canonical collections:[6]

i. *De ordinatione episcopi* ("Concerning the ordination of the bishop")
ii. *De ordinatione presbiteri, diaconis et ceterorum* ("Concerning the ordination of the priest, deacon and the other [clerical grades]")
iii. *Nihil aliud in sacrificio praeter quod Dominus statuit offerendum* ("That nothing should be offered in sacrifice beyond that which the Lord ordained")
iv. *Ut episcopus aut presbyter uxorem suam, quam debet caste regere, non relinquat* ("Let a bishop or priest not leave his wife, whom he ought to guide chastely")
v. *Ut sacerdotes et ministri altaris saecularibus curis abstineant* ("Let the priests and those who minister at the altar refrain from worldly pursuits")
vi. *Quo tempore pascha celebretur* ("At what time Easter ought to be celebrated")

The *Dionysiana* itself is seen today as a watershed in the Western canonical tradition. It constituted the first concentrated attempt to draw together both a large variety of canons from Eastern councils – among them the ecumenical councils of Nicaea (325), Constantinople (381), and Chalcedon (451) – and papal decretals, thereby bridging Eastern and Western teachings on ecclesiastical order and discipline and providing the church with its first substantial compendium of rules. Dionysius compiled three versions of the text, the third of which could claim papal authority because it was commissioned by Hormisdas, bishop of Rome from 514 to 523, to whom it is dedicated. (Only the preface of this third version survives today.)

6 Ed. Adolf Strewe, *Die Canonessammlung des Dionysius Exiguus in der ersten Redaktion* (Berlin: De Gruyter, 1931), 2.

Other influential early collections are the *Statuta ecclesiae antiqua* (c. 475) and the (probably) late fifth-century *Quesnelliana*, both of which, it has been argued, were compiled in Gaul, although it has also been suggested that the latter might have originated from Rome.[7] The most recent editor of the *Statuta*, Charles Munier, believes that it was compiled by Gennadius of Marseille. This relatively short systematic collection – comprising 102 canons derived mainly from the *Apostolic Canons*, the Council of Nicaea (325), Innocent I, Leo I, and Gallic councils (e.g. Riez, Orange, Vaison) – is devoted primarily to matters of clerical ordination and discipline. In contrast, the *Quesnelliana*, a chronological collection, contains considerably more material and covers Christological doctrine. Some of its ninety-eight chapters consist of documents incorporated in their entirety, especially letters associated with the Council of Chalcedon in 451 and letters of Leo I, bishop of Rome from 440 to 461. The *Quesnelliana* is an example of a collection compiled for a single specific purpose rather than as a comprehensive code. It was conceived in the context of the Acacian schism (482–519), which was sparked by the so-called *Henōtikon*. Formulated by Acacius, the patriarch of Constantinople from 471 to 489, the *Henōtikon* was issued as part of emperor Zeno's plan to reach a theological compromise between the Monophysites, who maintained that in Christ there was only one, divine nature, and the adherents of the two-nature doctrine of Chalcedon. It accepted the Niceno-Constantinopolitan creed but disregarded the Christological rulings of the Council of Chalcedon. The selection of texts that comprise the *Quesnelliana*, including Leo's Christological writings, constitute an affirmation of Chalcedonian orthodoxy vis-à-vis the Acacian compromise.

Of importance to the development of collections of the systematic variety are the *Breviatio Canonum* (c. 535) by the Carthagenian deacon Fulgentius Ferrandus and the aforementioned *Concordia Canonum* (mid-sixth century) by Cresconius. Although the former is counted among the systematic collections of canons, it might be interpreted as a summary or digest because it consists of 232 titles, without the content of the corresponding canons. The canons to which the titles allude are from the Councils of Nicaea, Ancyra, Neocaesarea, Gangra, Antioch, Laodicea, and Constantinople – the very same councils as those covered by the *Dionysiana*. The two texts were probably intended to be used side by side, therefore, with the *Breviatio* serving as a reading guide or index to the *Dionysiana*. The two were finally merged in Cresconius's collection. He used Fulgentius's titles to form a skeletal structure that he fleshed out with material from the *Dionysiana*. Cresconius explains the purpose of his collection in the prologue:

> From such a work, furthermore, with God's help, this benefit results: when an exceedingly fair judge personally ascertains that every canonical decree by which a proceeding at a given moment is conducted is applicable in various ways, he can

[7] Joseph Van der Speeten, "Le dossier de Nicée dans la Quesnelliana," *Sacris Erudiri* 28 (1985): 383–450.

> learn by careful examination whether he ought to form his opinion according to severity or leniency.[8]

This suggests that Cresconius intended the collection primarily to serve as an authoritative tool for ecclesiastical judges, although we have no information as to what kinds of tribunals or procedures Cresconius might have envisaged.

A similar interplay between a systematic list of titles and an earlier unsystematic collection can be observed in a recension of the *Hispana* commonly known as the *Excerpta Hispana*, which dates from between 656 and 675. The *Excerpta* is a systematic index of canons from the *Hispana*, a chronological collection compiled earlier in the same century. The *Excerpta* was to be used in conjunction with the chronological *Hispana*, but for anyone who did not possess the latter a new version was compiled, known as *Hispana Systematica*. Here, the titles of the *Excerpta* were matched with corresponding canons from the chronological version. In its earliest form the *Hispana* drew upon the second redaction of the *Dionysiana*, but in the course of the seventh century it accrued additional material from Spanish councils. The latest such material in the first version is from the fourth Council of Toledo of 633; the latest in the second version is from the twelfth Council of Toledo of 681; and the latest in the most recent version of the *Hispana*, the so-called *Vulgata*, is from the seventeenth Council of Toledo of 694. The hypothesis that bishop Isidore of Seville (d. 636) was responsible for the original compilation of the *Hispana* is doubtful. By the end of the seventh century, the *Hispana* also circulated in two modified versions in Gaul, known respectively as *Hispana Gallica* and *Hispana Gallica Augustodunensis*.

SYSTEMATIC COLLECTIONS AND THE AUTHORITY OF COLLECTIONS

The pinnacle of systematic compiling in the early-medieval period is the *Hibernensis*, which originated in late seventh- or early eighth-century Ireland. It was probably compiled by two ecclesiastical scholars: Ruben of Dairinis (d. 725) and Cú Chuimne of Iona (d. 747). These scholars were based, respectively, in the southernmost and northernmost ends of the Gaelic-speaking insular world. Although no copy from Ireland survives, the *Hibernensis* circulated widely in Continental Europe, where several derivative collections were also made. It is by far the most comprehensive of the early systematic collections, and it also contains the most diverse selection of sources, on which more below. Among its most significant innovations was the expansion of the remit of concerns addressed by canonical collections. It encompassed such ostensibly secular matters as kingship, theft, inheritance, treason, and even fair wages for workmen. The following example illustrates how a novel topic of this kind, theft, was addressed with support from

8 *Prefaces*, 52–53.

a new type of source, a history – in this case by Orosius (*Histories Against the Pagans*, 4.13.17–18):

> Concerning the matter that a thief is not deserving of death, but of retribution, Orosius says: "Here emerged a little of that ancient Roman appetite for excessive praise, even for kin-slaying. For Fabius Censorius slew his son Fabius Buteo, who was accused of theft. Indeed, the offence that the father deemed worthy of punishing by kin-slaying, not even the laws [*leges*] punished in the case of anyone, except by a large fine, or the remotest exile."[9]

The comprehensive range of the *Hibernensis*, considered in light of the wide variety of sources that it employs, has been interpreted variously as an attempt to create a law code for Christian society as a whole, or as a text of Christian jurisprudence designed to provide adjudicators with an all-encompassing blueprint for interpreting law.[10] Indeed, theoretical questions concerning law and its application loom large in the *Hibernensis*. In books entitled *De lege*, *De testimonio*, *De ordine inquisitionis causarum*, *De prouincia*, *De iudicio*, *De sceleribus et uindictis*, and *De contrariis causis*, the compilers cite excerpts from various sources (e.g., the Bible, unnamed Irish councils, Isidore) concerning legal procedure as well as conceptual questions about law and authority. Among the issues being debated are by what order should authoritative sources be consulted in dispute settlement, how should judges cope with the problem of conflicting authoritative sources, and, more fundamentally, what should be considered law, who has the power to legislate, and who ought to judge. Many of these questions are given conflicting answers and are left unresolved, suggesting that their presence in the *Hibernensis* was intended as a snapshot of a contemporaneous debate going on between clerical scholars.

Among the collections of the Carolingian era that drew upon the *Hibernensis* for some of their material is the Corbie version of the *Vetus Gallica*, completed c. 748. According to its editor, Mordek, it went through a three-stage process of development, beginning in early seventh-century Lyon – which was then gaining a reputation as a center for canonical learning – continuing at Autun, and culminating with the Corbie redaction. Like the *Hibernensis*, and probably because of its influence, the Corbie *Vetus Gallica* also deployed a pool of sources more varied than the standard combination of conciliar *acta* and papal decretals.[11] Its thematic scope, although not as broad as that of the *Hibernensis*, was nevertheless impressive,

9 Cited from the B-recension of the *Hibernensis*, Oxford, Bodleian Library, MS Hatton 42, fol. 55r. My translation.

10 The two are not mutually exclusive. See, respectively, T. M. Charles-Edwards, "Early Irish Law," in Dáibhí Ó Cróinín (ed.), *A New History of Ireland I* (Oxford: Oxford University Press, 2005): 331–370, at 353; and Roy Flechner, "The Problem of Originality," 43.

11 On these two texts in comparison, see Rob Meens, "The uses of the Old Testament in Early Medieval Canon Law: The *Collectio Vetus Gallica* and the *Collectio Hibernensis*," in Y. Hen and M. Innes (eds.), *The Uses of the Past in the Early Middle Ages* (Cambridge: Cambridge University Press, 2000): 67–77.

with concerns ranging from authority within the church to episcopal government, to behavioral standards expected of clerics, to liturgical matters, to pastoral care.

The scope and objectives of the earliest form of the *Vetus Gallica* were more focused. It was first compiled as a reforming text, perhaps in response to the rising power of abbots in Gaul and the growing trend among Gallic aristocrats to patronize monasteries.[12] The compiler was either bishop Etherius of Lyon (d. 602) or his successor, Aridius (d. 614).[13] It seems to have been concerned chiefly with defending and sustaining episcopal authority and with the mechanisms of ecclesiastical government in which bishops were prominent, as is clear in the following example:

> Concerning the ordination of a metropolitan [bishop], it behooves that a metropolitan be ordained by a metropolitan in the presence of all fellow-provincials, if this is possible . . . Let the same metropolitan be elected by the fellow-provincial bishops, just as the decretals of the Apostolic See hold, with the consent of the clerics and the citizens; for this is right, just as the same Apostolic See said: "He who has been placed above all others, ought to be elected by all."[14]

Here, the election of a metropolitan bishop is described as a process that requires both broad consensus and legitimation by high authority.

Both the *Vetus Gallica* and the *Hibernensis* circulated widely in Carolingian Europe in multiple versions made at different times, with no evidence that any particular version was given priority over others.[15] It was not unusual for different versions of a canonical collection to continue to be copied simultaneously, so that the later version did not replace the earlier one but rather coincided with it. This could raise practical problems. Sometimes contradictions arose between earlier and later texts, without there being any established principle for giving precedence to the most recent version, even if a chronological sequence could be established. Such contradictions are attested, for example, in different recensions of the so-called *Canons of Theodore*, archbishop of Canterbury from 669 to 690. This is a series of texts best described as a combination of primary legislation and a collection of derivative material.[16] The various recensions of the collection were formed on the basis of Theodore's teachings and his responses to both canonical and penitential material. Comparison yields a number of contradictory rulings attributed to Theodore, such as those on whether a man could lawfully remarry after divorcing a fornicating wife. In three recensions of the *Canons of Theodore*, the archbishop is

12 Its reforming objectives were suggested by Mordek, *Kirchenrecht und Reform*, 35, while the stress on the political context is mine.

13 For authorship, see Mordek, *Kirchenrecht und Reform*, 62–82.

14 Cited from *Vetus Gallica*, V.4a, ed. Mordek, *Kirchenrecht und Reform*, 386–87. My translation. The source is canon §3 of the Council of Orléans in 538. The phrase "Apostolic See" refers to Pope Leo I.

15 Roger E. Reynolds, "*Unity and Diversity in Carolingian Canon Law Collections: The Case of the Collectio canonum Hibernensis and Its Derivatives*," in Uta-Renate Blumenthal (ed.), *Carolingian Essays* (Washington DC: Catholic University of America Press, 1983), 99–135.

16 Discussed by Roy Flechner, "The Making of the Canons of Theodore," *Peritia* 17–18 (2003/04): 121–43.

said to have approved of remarriage after divorce, following the teachings of St. Basil: "If one's wife has committed adultery, he may expel her and take another."[17] But two recensions forbid remarriage after a man's divorce of a fornicating wife. Another recension is self-contradictory, both permitting and forbidding remarriage in these circumstances.[18] Why there should be such variance in the judgments attributed to Theodore on this matter is unclear. Perhaps certain copyists manipulated the archbishop's sayings to suit their own views or the views of their patrons. Or perhaps this is merely a result of corruption through copying, which is something that the *Canons of Theodore* warn against in one recension.

One way that a collection could stand a better chance of being transmitted in a fixed form, or of being at least temporarily immune from mutation, was by receiving papal sanction. We have already considered one such text: the third version of the *Dionysiana*, of which only the preface survives. But by far the best known papally sanctioned collection from the Carolingian period is the *Collectio Dionysio-Hadriana*, which is commonly understood to have been commissioned by Charlemagne from Pope Hadrian. As such, it is the earliest canonical collection believed to have been endorsed by both a pope and a monarch. As its title suggests, it was based on a version of the *Dionysiana*, but this was augmented with – among other sources – creeds, papal decretals, and a number of letters by Pope Gregory II (r. 715–731). The *Dionysio-Hadriana* can boast the highest survival rate of all contemporary canonical collections, with more than ninety extant manuscript copies. The circumstances in which the collection was compiled, as well as its date, have largely been inferred from a dedicatory acrostic text, embedded in an opaque eulogizing poem. This reads: "To the most excellent son lord Charles, the great king, from Pope Hadrian."[19] It has been argued recently, however, that the evidence of the acrostic ought not be considered conclusive, as formerly thought. While the case for a papal or royal involvement in the compilation has not been entirely lost, other interpretations remain to be explored.[20]

Although formal promulgation by diocesan bishops is not well attested, indications of direct or indirect involvement by bishops in the process of compilation are

17 See P. W. Finsterwalder, *Die Canones Theodori Cantuariensis und ihre Überlieferungsformen* (Weimar: Böhlaus, 1929), 251, 277, 326. Cf. Basil's *Letter* 188, to Amphilochus, c. 9, ed. Yves Courtonne, *Saint Basile, Lettres*, 3 vols. (Paris: Les Belles Lettres, 1957–1961), 2:128–29. For Theodore's debt to Basil's teachings on remarriage, see T. M. Charles-Edwards, "The Penitential of Theodore and the Iudicia Theodori," in M. Lapidge (ed.), *Archbishop Theodore: Commemorative Studies on His Life and Influence* (Cambridge: Cambridge University Press, 1995), 141–74, at 158–9. Remarriage under other circumstances is mentioned in Finsterwalder, *Die Canones Theodori*, 247, 251, 277, 307, 327–29.

18 For details see Flechner, "The Making of the Canons of Theodore," 121–24.

19 Translation by Abigail Firey, "Mutating Monsters: Approaches to 'Living Texts' of the Carolingian Era," *Digital Proceedings of the Lawrence J. Schoenberg Symposium on Manuscript Studies in the Digital Age* 2 (2010): 1–14, at 6.

20 Florian Hartmann, *Hadrian I. (772–795): Frühmittelalterliches Adelspapsttum und die Lösung Roms vom byzantinischen Kaiser*, = *Päpste und Papsttum* 34 (Stuttgart: Hiersemann, 2006), 267–72. Firey, "Mutating Monsters," 3–9.

more common. I offer three examples. The first is, again, the *Vetus Gallica*, which was either commissioned or compiled by an early seventh-century bishop of Lyon, probably Etherius or Aridius. The second is the group of texts known collectively as the *Canons of Theodore*, discussed earlier. And the third is a collection for clerics compiled by bishop Atto of Vercelli (d. 961), who embarked on a reform program in his diocese supported by canonical precepts on clerical discipline. The attribution of a collection to a bishop would invariably endow it with authority, but later versions may omit the attribution or, as we have seen already, they may introduce revisions that are inconsistent with that bishop's teachings.

Another means by which authority could be conferred on a collection was by association with its constituent canons, provided that these were enacted by councils or popes. But what of a collection that also included sources whose authority could not easily be determined? Such borderline sources can be found in collections such as the *Hibernensis* and Regino of Prüm's *Libri Duo de Synodalibus Causis* (on which more below), which applied, in addition to the usual roster of conciliar and papal rulings, material that did not appear to be ecclesiastical at all, such as Roman or vernacular law. When the *Hibernensis* was put before Pope Leo IV (847–845), he dismissed it as unauthoritative.[21] Instead, he endorsed the *Dionysio-Hadriana*, which he referred to not by its title (for it did not have one then) but by referring to the sources that it comprised:

> the rulings [*iudicia*] ... of the apostles, of Nicaea, of Ancyra, of Neocaesarea, of Gangra, of Antioch, of Laodicea, of Chalcedon, of Sardica, of Carthage, of Africa, and alongside these the rules [*regulae*] of the Roman pontiffs Sylvester, Siricius, Innocent, Zosimus, Celestine, Leo, Gelasius, Hilarius, Symmachus, Simplicius, Hormisdas, and Gregory the younger. These are the ones without exception; and bishops judge by them, and bishops and likewise clerics are judged by them.[22]

It would appear, therefore, that for Leo IV, at least, a collection was the sum of its parts. If the parts individually had legal or quasi-legal force, so also did the collection. Some compilers, skeptical of certain sources and concerned that their entire project may be tainted by them, went so far as to omit doubtful texts when they copied earlier collections. For example, the compiler of the second version of the *Hispana* omitted the *Apostolic Canons*, which (via the *Dionysiana*) had formed part of the first version of the *Hispana*. He explained in his prologue that he considered them to be both spurious and heretical, for their authority could not be securely established:

> But the canons which are called "of the apostles," because neither the apostolic see receives them nor the holy Fathers offered approval of them, since they are known

[21] Roy Flechner, "*Libelli et commentarii aliorum*: The *Hibernensis* and the Breton Bishops," in K. Ritari and A. Bergholm (eds.), *Approaches to Religion and Mythology in Celtic Studies* (Newcastle: Cambridge Scholars Publishing, 2008): 100–119.

[22] Ed. W. Hartmann, MGH Conc. 3 (1984): 187–188, at 189. My translation.

to have been written by heretics under the name of the apostles ... are to be relegated among the apocrypha.[23]

FROM THE CAROLINGIAN ERA TO THE ELEVENTH CENTURY

Many collections of the Carolingian era were no more than ad hoc compilations designed to address matters of the hour. Their interrelationships are notoriously difficult to untangle, raising further problems of text identity. More focused in their aims, but just as textually complicated, are the mid-ninth-century False Decretals of Pseudo-Isidore and their associated texts, which are the subject of another chapter in this volume (Chapter 19).

The *Collectio Anselmo Dedicata*, a popular collection from the late ninth century, drew upon material from both Pseudo-Isidore and the *Dionysio-Hadriana*. It was compiled under the aegis of Anselm, bishop of Milan from 882 to 896. It is a systematic collection in twelve books, dealing especially with the ecclesiastical hierarchy, church government, and liturgical matters. It may be contrasted with the collection of abbot Abbo of Fleury, which drew primarily on the *Dionysiana* and *Hispana*. Commonly dated 995 or 996, Abbo's is regarded as a monastic collection because of its preoccupation with safeguarding monastic privileges and property rights from encroachment by bishops and powerful laymen.[24] Abbo himself stated that his collection was meant *ad defensionem monastici ordinis* ("in defense of the monastic order").

In the ninth and early tenth centuries, one begins to witness a more pronounced presence of penitential prescriptions in canonical collections. Among the most influential collections to have incorporated penitential material extensively are the *Collectio Dacheriana* (c. 800), the *Collectio canonum quadripartita* (c. 850), and the *Libri Duo de Synodalibus Causis* compiled by Regino of Prüm c. 906. Circulating widely in two recensions, the *Dacheriana* is based in the main on the *Dionysio-Hadriana* and the *Hispana*. It comprises three books, the first of which is devoted exclusively to penance and addressed chiefly to the laity. The *Collectio Quadripartita* (also known as the *Quadripartitus*) is an episcopal compendium of canons and penitential rulings in four books. It circulated widely in Continental Europe and influenced several canonical collections, including Regino's *Libri Duo*. The *Libri Duo* were, likewise, intended primarily for bishops, but secondarily for those participating in church government through councils, and for clergy dispensing pastoral care. Regino's use of penitentials was of a piece with his predilection, already mentioned, for tapping sources not usually found in canonical collections,

23 *Prefaces*, 56–57.

24 Theo Kölzer, "Mönchtum und Kirchenrecht: Bemerkungen zu monastischen Kanonessammlungen der vorgratianischen Zeit," ZRG Kan. Abt. 69.1 (1983): 121–42.

which included Frankish capitularies and even Roman laws of the *Codex Theodosianus* (cited via the *Lex Romana Visigothorum*, or *Breviary of Alaric*). Not only did he draw upon new sources, but he also did not shy away from modifying the material that he cited.

Penance also figures prominently in a dependent and equally influential collection compiled between 1012 and 1022: the *Liber Decretorum* of Burchard of Worms (see Chapter 23).[25] Divided into twenty books, its nineteenth book, concerning penance, achieved the greatest renown and was often copied independently. The texts on penance are elaborate, sometimes describing at length the circumstances in which a sin was committed, and they treat of a great variety of sins, some pertaining to clerics alone, others to the laity at large. For example, in a chapter on homicide, one text reads:

> Have you committed manslaughter in battle, by the command of a legitimate ruler, who commanded this for the sake of peace, and have you killed a tyrant who strove to pervert peace? You should do penance on each and every appointed day of the three forty-day periods. But if it happened otherwise, namely without the command of a legitimate ruler, you should do penance for voluntary manslaughter, namely, a fast of seven weeks [*carina*], with seven subsequent years.[26]

Like Regino, Burchard also engaged in modifying received canons. Among his reasons for doing so was his wish to harmonize discordant canons, such as the ones that he found in the *Libri Duo*.[27] He even changed the attributions of certain sources, especially when he reiterated material from derivative sources that cited lesser-known authorities. For example, "Ferrandus the Deacon" became "Augustine."[28] He also used spurious attributions to cover his tracks when drawing upon secular sources or citing secular forms of punishment, such as fines paid to secular lords or incarceration.

Unlike most early-medieval collections, there is direct evidence for the use of Burchard's *Liber decretorum* in councils, and the dissemination of its manuscript copies shows that it was widely diffused. Approximately eighty copies survive, making it the second best attested collection after the *Dionysio-Hadriana*. Its sources were varied, and most notably it drew on a good number of previous collections, including, as well as Regino's *Libri Duo*, the *Hibernensis* and the *Anselmo Dedicata*, and even Roman law. By drawing on Roman law, it resembles both Regino's collection and the *Anselmo Dedicata*, which cites a *florilegium* containing texts from Justinian's Code.

25 The most comprehensive study of the *Liber Decretorum*'s manuscript tradition is Hartmut Hoffmann and Rudolf Pokorny, *Das Dekret des Bischofs Burchard von Worms: Textstufen, frühe Verbreitung, Vorlagen* (Munich: MGH, 1991).

26 PL 140:952C. My translation.

27 Greta Austin, *Shaping Church Law Around the Year 1000: The Decretum of Burchard of Worms* (Farnham: Ashgate, 2009), 141.

28 Austin, *Shaping Church Law*, 114.

The *Anselmo Dedicata* and Burchard's *Liber decretorum* are among compilations that used formal sources (*fontes formales*, i.e., other collections, which served as secondary, intermediate sources) as well as material sources. As we have seen, there were precedents for this practice from as early as Cresconius's *Concordia Canonum*, but it is more in evidence from the eighth century onward. A very partial roster of collections that drew from prior collections includes the *Hibernensis* (which drew upon the *Statuta ecclesiae antiqua* and the *Dionysiana*), the *Dacheriana* (*Dionysiana* and *Hispana*), and the early tenth-century *Collectio IV librorum* (Regino's *Libri duo* and Cresconius's *Concordia canonum*). It would appear that as the store of canonical collections increased over time, so the *fontes formales* gained as much currency as the *fontes materiales* in the formation of new collections.

Does the growth of the genre of canonical collections attest to a rise in their influence? Outside the realm of intertextual connections between various collections, it is nearly impossible to assess the impact that canonical collections actually had on, say, dispute settlement, judicial proceedings, clerical discipline, or, more broadly, on the conduct of Christians. Most of our direct evidence for the use of canonical collections comes from the invocation of "books of canons" at church councils, such as the Council of Carthage in 525 (which refers to a "*liber canonum*"), the Council of Tours in 567 ("*canonici libri*"), the Council of Clichy in 626/7 ("*diuersi canonum libri*"), or the Council of Hertford in 672 ("*liber canonum*").[29] Obviously, this use does not tell us how canons were put to use beyond conciliar settings. Otherwise, we depend on sporadic and rather rare anecdotes for evidence, for example: the testimony of Gregory of Tours that a canon from the *Apostolic Canons* was quoted through a *liber canonum* in the deposition of Bishop Praetextatus of Rouen (d. 586); the citations from the *Hibernensis* in a letter (c. 801) by Alcuin, in which he defends his decision to give shelter at Tours to a delinquent monk; and the eleventh- and twelfth-century testimonies to the use of Burchard's collection by councils.[30] The extensive copying and broad dissemination of certain collections is often interpreted as evidence for use, which is reasonable, but the circumstances in which this use occurred and exactly how this resource was used remain obscure. The frequent copying of collections in the same manuscripts alongside other canonical material may also suggest another kind of use, namely, jurisprudential learning, although most canonical collections of the first

[29] See, respectively, CCL 149, p. 263; CCL 148A, p. 187; CCL 148A, p. 291; A. W. Haddan and W. Stubbs, *Councils and Ecclesiastical Documents Relating to Great Britain and Ireland*, 3 vols. (Oxford, 1869–1878), vol 3, 119.

[30] Gregory of Tours, *Histories*, 5.18, ed. B. Krusch and W. Levison, *Gregorii Episcopi Turonensis Libri Historiarum X*, MGH SRM 1.1 (Hannover, 1951), 222. The canon (§25) is not in the first recension of the *Dionysiana* but may have been known through another Latin translation of the Greek text, such as the *Sanblasiana*. On Alcuin, see MGH Epist. 3, ed. E. Dümmler (1895), 396, lines 8–12; and Luitpold Wallach, *Alcuin and Charlemagne: Studies in Carolingian History and Literature, Cornell Studies in Classical Philology* 32 (Ithaca: Cornell University Press, 1959), 129–30. On Burchard, see the notes by Eberhardt of Constance (d. 1046) in a copy of the *Liber* and the *De scriptoribus* by Sigebert of Gembloux's (d. 1112) §142. Austin discusses both in *Shaping Church Law*, 26, 30, 42.

millennium do not treat issues of jurisprudence explicitly. The exception is the *Hibernensis*, which, as we have seen, includes discussions of questions such as "What is law?" and "What purpose does it serve?" Its material is organized in such a way as deliberately to draw attention to the perennial problem of contradictions between legal authorities. For a more developed engagement with jurisprudence, and a measurable influence on the subsequent practical application of canon law, one must leap beyond the chronological limits of the present narrative to Gratian's *Decretum* in the mid-twelfth century. This rendered nearly all previous collections obsolete at the time, although they have found a new life today as valuable historical documents.

SOURCES

Selected modern editions of major collections:

Burchard of Worms. *Liber Decretorum*. PL 140:537–1058.

Collectio Hibernensis. Ed. Hermann Wasserschleben, *Die irische Kanonensammlung*. Giessen, 1874. 2nd ed. Leipzig, 1885. [A new edition with translation by Roy Flechner will appear soon in the series Studies in Medieval and Early Modern Canon Law, published by the Catholic University of America Press.]

Cresconius. *Concordia canonum*. Ed. Klaus Zechiel-Eckes. *Die concordia canonum des Cresconius: Studien und Edition*. 2 vols. Frankfurt: Lang, 1992.

Dionysiana [first recension]. Ed. Adolf Strewe. *Die Canonessammlung des Dionysius Exiguus in der ersten Redaktion*. Berlin: De Gruyter, 1931.

Dionysio-Hadriana. Transcribed by Michael Elliot from Oxford, Bodleian Library, MS Hatton 42, fols. 142 v–188 v. Available at: http://individual.utoronto.ca/michaelelliot/manuscripts/texts/transcriptions/hadriana.pdf (accessed December 14, 2016).

Fulgentius Ferrandus. *Breuiatio canonum*. Ed. C. Munier, CCL 149 (1974), 287–306.

Hispana Collectio. Ed. G. Martínez Díez (ed.), *La colección canónica Hispana*. 5 vols. Madrid: Instituto Enrique Flórez, 1966–1992.

Regino of Prüm. *Libri Duo de Synodalibus Causis*. Ed. F. G. A. Wasserschleben. *Regionis abbatis Prumiensis libri duo de synodalibus causis et de disciplinis ecclesiasticis*. Leipzig: Engelmann, 1840. [Republished with a facing German translation by W. Hartmann, *Das Sendhandbuch des Regino von Prüm* (Darmstadt: Wissenschaftliche Buchgesellschaft, 2004).]

Statuta ecclesiae antiqua. In Charles Munier (ed.), *Les statuta ecclesiae antiqua*. Édition, Études critiques. Paris: Presses Universitaires de France, 1960.

Vetus Gallica. In H. Mordek. *Kirchenrecht und Reform im Frankenreich: Die Collectio vetus Gallica, die älteste systematische Kanonessammlung des fränkischen Gallien: Studien und Edition, = Beiträge zur Geschichte und Quellenkunde des Mittelalters 1* (Berlin: De Gruyter, 1975), 343–617.

For English translations of selected prefaces to canon law collections, see Somerville and Brasington, *Prefaces*.

FURTHER READING

Article-Length Introductions to the History of Collections

Roger E. Reynolds, "Law, Canon: To Gratian." In Joseph R. Strayer et al. (eds.), *Dictionary of the Middle Ages*, 13 vols. (New York: Scribner, 1982–1989), 6:395–413.

Kenneth Pennington, "The Growth of Church Law." In A. Casiday and F. W. Norris (eds.), *Cambridge History of Christianity II: Constantine to c. 600* (Cambridge: Cambridge University Press, 2007), 386–402.

Repertories and General Studies

Friedrich Maassen, *Geschichte der Quellen und der Literatur des canonischen Rechts im Abendlande bis zum Ausgange des Mittelalters*. Graz: Leuschner & Lubensky, 1870.

Paul Fournier and Gabriel Le Bras, *Histoire des collections canoniques en Occident, depuis les Fausses Décrétales jusqu'au Décret de Gratien*. 2 vols. Paris: Sirey, 1931–32.

Lotte Kéry, *Canonical Collections of the Early Middle Ages (ca. 400–1140): A Bibliographical Guide to the Manuscripts and Literature*. Washington, DC: Catholic University of America Press, 1999.

Linda Fowler-Magerl, *Clavis Canonum: Selected Canon Law Collections Before 1140*. Hannover: Hahnsche, 2005.

Internet Resources, A Partial List of a Constantly Expanding Field

See Michael Elliot's excellent Wikipedia entries on collections, for which links can be found in the parent entry, "Collections of ancient canons," at https://en.wikipedia.org/wiki/Collections_of_ancient_canons (accessed Dec 14, 2016).

The Carolingian Canon Law Project, overseen by Abigail Firey, is an important portal for expertly transcribed or edited collections, many of which have no modern edition or have never been printed: http://ccl.rch.uky.edu (accessed Dec 14, 2016).

For recent reliable editions and transcriptions, see Michael Elliot's Anglo-Saxon Canon Law, at http://individual.utoronto.ca/michaelelliot (accessed Dec 14, 2016).

Links to early modern editions and transcriptions are available at the Medieval Canon Law Virtual Library, curated by David Freidenreich, at http://web.colby.edu/canonlaw/2009/10/01/resources (accessed Dec 14, 2016).

8

The Practice and Literature of Penance

Rob Meens

Christianity is a religion that from its beginnings demanded specific forms of behavior from its adherents, and this made it necessary to think about what to do with those believers who broke the moral code.

The forms of behavior that the religion demanded from its followers changed over time. Early Christians, for example, worried about adhering to Jewish dietary rules, but this issue did not become a dominant concern in Christianity. Nevertheless, it did come to the surface occasionally in the Middle Ages. For example, in the eighth century, the Anglo-Saxon missionary Boniface worried whether Christians could eat hare or horsemeat; Pope Nicolas I (r. 858–867) had to reassure the Bulgarians that they could continue to eat whatever animals they wanted if they joined the church of Rome; and the inhabitants of Iceland decided to convert to Christianity only if they could continue to eat horsemeat.[1]

The formulation of moral norms had to be accompanied by regulations for dealing with those believers who failed to adhere to such a code of conduct, and who were regarded, therefore, as erring or sinning. In essence, there were two ways of dealing with sinners: They could be excluded from the Christian community, and thus from the path of salvation; or they could be reconciled with that community: with the church in the official sense. Exclusion from the Christian community may be regarded as a punishment – a terrible one, if one thinks of its supernatural consequences. It was effected by a sentence pronounced by a high authority, be it a council or an individual bishop.[2] Reconciliation with the community, on the contrary, was achieved through what was seen as a voluntary act of penance, although this could be less voluntary in practice than it was in theory. Through confessing the wrongs committed and making up for these by specific acts of

1 For a brief discussion of dietary rules, see Rob Meens, "Eating Animals in the Early Middle Ages: Classifying the Animal World and Building Group Identities," in A. Craeger and W. C. Jordan (eds.), *The Animal-Human Boundary: Historical Perspectives* (Rochester, NY: University of Rochester Press, 2002), 3–28. For abbreviated titles, see the section on Sources, below.

2 For a recent volume dedicated to the practice of excommunication, see Geneviève Bührer-Thierry and Stéphane Gioanni (eds.), *Exclure de la communauté chrétienne. Sens et pratiques sociales de l'anathème et de l'excommunication (IV–XII siècle)* (Turnhout: Brepols, 2015).

mortification, the sinner re-established relations with God as well as with the Christian community. Penance, the process through which a sinner was reconciled with God and the church, could take many different forms. It could be formal, in the sense that the sinner was ceremonially acquitted of guilt through an ecclesiastical ritual, or it could be informal, consisting of various forms of mortification without mediation by the official church.[3]

Formal ways of proceeding are found in canons pronounced by early Christian councils. According to these canons, sinners would be reconciled with the community after long periods of penance, in which the errant are only gradually readmitted as full members of the Christian community. At the council of Ancyra (314), for example, the bishops decided that a Christian who had sinned in a sexual way with an animal should live fifteen years as a supplicant. After that period, the penitent was allowed to pray in church, but without partaking of communion. After another five years, the supplicant gained admission to "simple communion" – apparently indicating attendance at the eucharist without reception – and eventually he or she would be admitted to full communion.[4] Such rules imply some kind of formal ecclesiastical control over the process by which a Christian made up for sins, and it usually fell to the bishop to oversee the process. But it is hard to know how regularly these rules were applied and whether this was done in a uniform way. Augustine informs us that "penitents abounded" in Hippo around the year 400 and were clearly visible to the community.[5] Decisions of the Council of Ancyra and other councils, which assigned a particular form or period of penance for specific sins, entered medieval canonical collections and so became regarded as authoritative statements. But how these early rulings were interpreted and applied, for example, in ninth-century Francia, is another question, and one that is not easy to answer.

Conciliar decisions assigning periods of penance regarded certain sins, such as apostasy, adultery, and murder, as serious deviations from Christian norms, requiring a formal procedure. For example, Caesarius of Arles in the sixth century distinguished between capital sins (*peccata capitalia*) and venial sins (*peccata minuta*, or *peccata quotidiana*). Among the former he reckoned murder, adultery, honoring pagan gods, false testimony, theft, pride, envy, avarice, anger, heavy drinking, fornication, and abortion. One could atone for such sins through a formal procedure supervised by the bishop. Venial sins such as immoderate eating

3 R. Price, "Informal Penance in Early Medieval Christendom," in K. Cooper and J. Gregory (eds.), *Retribution, Repentance, and Reconciliation*, Studies in Church History 40 (Woodbridge, UK: Boydell Press, 2004): 29–39.

4 Council of Ancyra, c. 16, in C. H. Turner (ed.), *Ecclesiae occidentalis monumenta iuris antiquissima canonum et conciliorum graecorum interpretationes Latinae*, vol. 2.1 (Oxford: Clarendon Press, 1907), 92–99.

5 Augustine, Tractatus habitus tertia feria (Sermo 232), 8, ed. Suzanne Poque, Augustin d'Hippone, Sermons pour la Pâque. Introduction, texte critique, traduction et notes, SC 116, 274–78. For general background, see Kevin Uhalde, *Expectations of Justice in the Age of Augustine* (Philadelphia: University of Pennsylvania Press, 2007), 105–34.

or drinking, harsh treatment of beggars, nonobservance of fasting periods, idle talk in church, or evil thoughts, on the contrary, could be absolved through various forms of virtuous behavior, such as fasting, distributing alms, or forgiving one's enemies.[6] In such cases, although spiritual direction by a priest or monk might be helpful, it was not essential. But this expectation would change. In the period from the seventh to the ninth century, ever more sins would require a formal ecclesiastical ritual to make up for the trespass.

MONASTIC PENANCE AND PENITENTIAL BOOKS

In monasteries, it was essential for monks to seek spiritual advice from more experienced members of the community to combat sin and temptation. Benedict of Nursia (d. c. 540), for example, demanded that his monks confess their sins not only to God but also to the abbot. In order to receive proper spiritual direction, the monks needed to reveal their inner thoughts, as well as their actions.[7] Other early monastic authors, such as John Cassian (d. 433), showed similar concerns. We are not very well informed about some early Western forms of monasticism, especially those in the British Isles, but monasticism was a central ecclesiastical institution in Ireland by the seventh century at the latest, when monasteries such as Kildare, Armagh, and Iona became influential ecclesiastical centers. In these communities, penance was an important part of monastic discipline, as demonstrated by the Rule of Columbanus (d. 615), the Irishman who in the late sixth and early seventh centuries founded influential monastic communities in Gaul and northern Italy. Although his *Regula Coenobialis* was included in the compilation of monastic rules that Benedict of Aniane made in the ninth century and was regarded as a rule of monastic discipline,[8] Benedict refers to it there as a "penitential book," demonstrating the importance of the penitential aspect of the rule. The rule begins by discussing the need to confess one's sins every day before a meal or going to bed, "because confession and penance liberate from death." Columbanus went on to say that even small sins should be confessed, since from overlooking small matters a decline can set in.[9] The actual form of penance assigned was usually physical, consisting of corporal punishments.

This monastic practice of confessing sins became available to lay people as well, perhaps at first only to those closely attached to a monastery as patrons or tenants. The central position of monasteries in the Insular churches probably played a role in this opening up of monastic forms of confession and penance to sectors of the laity.

6 Caesarius, *Sermo* 60 and 179, ed. G. Morin, *Sancti Caesarii Arelatensis Sermones*, CCL 103–104, 1:275–76 and 2:725–26.

7 RB 4, 57–58 and 44–48, ed. A. De Vogüé and J. Neufville, *La Règle de Saint Benoît*, SC 181–82, vol. 181, pp. 460 and 484.

8 See Chapter 9 by Albrecht Diem in this volume.

9 Columbanus, *Regula Coenobialis*, 1, ed. G. S. M. Walker, *Sancti Columbani Opera*, Scriptores Latini Hiberniae 2, 2nd edition (Dublin: Dublin Institute for Advanced Studies, 1970), 144–46.

Another factor contributing to this process was probably the intermediary role that religious persons could play in conflicts. When sins such as homicide or adultery had serious social repercussions, monks or clerics acted as intermediaries in the ensuing conflicts, so that confession and penance were part of a process of reconciling the conflicting parties. This is evident from the books written at the time to instruct confessors how to deal with sinners: books generally referred to as penitential books, or simply penitentials. The earliest specimens of this genre were composed in the Insular world. They contain fairly detailed descriptions of sinful behavior and give advice on the proper form of penance that a confessor should assign to reconcile the sinner with God and the Christian community. Apart from the anonymous *Paenitentiale Ambrosianum*, these early Insular texts were attributed to local ecclesiastical authorities of the period, such as Finnian, Cummean, and Columbanus.

The fact that many Insular works include material forms of compensation for injuries corroborates the claim that confession and penance could be part of a mediating process between opposing parties. For example, Finnian's penitential, a sixth-century text, requires that a cleric who has committed murder should live in exile for ten years and then, on his return to his homeland, should come to an agreement with the friends of the victim and serve the victim's parents, if they are still alive, as if he were their child (*Paenitentiale Vinniani*, 23, Bieler, 80–82). Such a process seems hard to imagine without some form of mediation by the confessor. This approach was not peculiar to Finnian. Columbanus adopted the clause from Finnian with little alteration but elaborated the aspect of material compensation. He required, for example, that an adulterer should pay the cheated husband a "price of chastity," probably a form of the financial compensation that is also found in secular legislation of the period (*P. Columbani B* 14, Bieler, 102). Such evidence strongly suggests that confessing one's sins and fulfilling a particular form of penance were not purely ecclesiastical matters but rather could be part of a wider social process of reconciliation between two parties.[10]

We know these early Insular penitential books only from a handful of manuscripts written on the European mainland. These are found in manuscripts written in the monastic foundations of Bobbio, Salzburg, and Saint-Gall. The texts must have been brought over to the Continent, probably by Irish ascetical wanderers (*peregrini*) such as Columbanus or Virgil of Salzburg. Such texts were also known in Anglo-Saxon England in the seventh century, as a result of the close connections with Irish forms of monasticism. Later Anglo-Saxon missionaries such as Willibrord and Boniface were familiar with these works and used them during their long period of activity in the kingdoms of the Franks and beyond. Theodore, archbishop of Canterbury (d. 690), who was of Byzantine Greek descent, contributed to the

[10] See Rob Meens, *Penance in Medieval* Europe, 600–1200 (Cambridge: Cambridge University Press, 2014), 45–69.

penitential literature in Anglo-Saxon England during the second half of the seventh century. We know of five traditions of texts referred to as *Iudicia Theodori*, or the *Canons of Theodore*, which reflect his teachings on penance and law. They not only deal with matters pertaining to sins and their remedies but also provide rules for ordination, the authority of an abbot, and the age at which a son or daughter could choose to enter a monastery without parental consent. These texts illustrate the ambiguous character of penitential rulings as a form of regulation, or perhaps better their fluid nature, for they sometimes included authoritative statements and are similar in this respect to canonical texts. As a consequence, several manuscripts have penitential texts attached to canonical collections, and compilers of such collections included material from penitential books. The fluid nature of the *Iudicia Theodori* is suggested by their inclusion in Roy Flechner's chapter on canonical collections in this volume (Chapter 7). The compiler of a version of the *Iudicia Theodori* known as the *Discipulus Umbrensium*[11] tried to separate penitential from regulatory material by dividing the collection into two books. All Theodorian versions contain a core that reflects Theodore's teachings, but the five extant versions were most probably compiled by some of his pupils, or by others who were somehow related to him. That Irish penitential books were circulating in Anglo-Saxon England at the time is demonstrated by Theodore's mentioning a *libellus Scottorum* ("little book of the Scots"), probably referring to Cummean's work.

Following the Irish penitentials, Theodore saw in penitential procedure room for material compensation to an offended party. He ruled, for example, that if a murderer paid compensation, which Theodore calls the estimated price (*pecuniam aestimationis*), to the victim's family, the penance would be halved (*Paenitentiale Theodori U* I, 4, 1, Finsterwalder, 294). This implies, however, that he foresaw that some would not pay compensation: that it was possible to confess one's sins and do penance without coming to an agreement with the offended party. For Theodore, moreover, confession even among the laity was no longer confined to sins of a public nature, as it had been in the Irish penitentials. This is apparent in his discussions of minor sins that did not harm other people and, therefore, must have had very limited or no social impact. Theodore provided penances for persons who had indulged in eating to the point of vomiting, and he even discussed whether consuming blood because of bleeding gums was a sin that required penance. Theodore was also the first to discuss sexual behavior of spouses, censuring practices such as having sex during menstruation, on Sundays, or in improper positions (*Paenitentiale Theodori U* I, 14, 18–23, Finsterwalder, 309). This suggests that in Theodore's time, laypersons were expected to confess their sins not only when these caused scandal or social disruption, but also when they wanted to cleanse themselves of the burden of guilt, even if there was no major social pressure to do so.

11 "Disciple of the Umbrenses," a people of northeastern England.

Like the early Insular penitentials, Theodore's work is known today mainly from manuscripts written on the Continent. As the surviving manuscripts indicate, however, the *Iudicia Theodori* were disseminated much more widely than the early Insular penitential texts. More than forty manuscripts of *Iudicia Theodori* are still extant.

Penance remained important in Columbanus's monastic foundations in Gaul and Lombardy, as demonstrated by the *Life of Columbanus*, which Jonas of Bobbio put to parchment between 639 and 642. We also know a number of early Frankish penitential books that drew their inspiration from Columbanus's work, enriching it with conciliar decisions not only from the late-antique councils of Ancyra and Nicaea but also from the more recent Merovingian council of Auxerre. This group of eight texts, known as the "simple Frankish penitentials," not only indicates the influence of Columbanus on penitential practice in Merovingian Francia but also testifies to the ease with which Irish penitential material could be combined with more traditional canonical provisions. The close relationship between penitential material and canonical regulation is again clearly visible in the second quarter of the eighth century. At that time, the monks of the northern French monastery of Corbie reworked and updated the systematic canonical collection that we know as the *Collectio Vetus Gallica* (*Old Gallic Collection*), first put together around the year 600. In updating it, the compilers included material not only from the Irish *Collectio Hibernensis* but also from the *Iudicia Theodori*.

DEALING WITH VARIETY

An important comprehensive penitential book based on the Frankish penitentials inspired by Columbanus, on the *Iudicia Theodori*, and on the Irish penitential of Cummean, probably originated from the same workshop as the *Collectio Vetus Gallica*. This penitential book, known as an "excerpt" of Cummean (*Excarpsus Cummeani*), incorporated a good deal of material from these three traditions, but only after a careful process of selection.

The work's treatment of perjury is a case in point. The simple Frankish penitentials had required a penance of seven years for this crime, three of them on a diet of bread and water, and they stipulated that the culprit should never swear an oath thereafter. If he had perjured himself under pressure or without knowing that he swore a false oath, he should do penance for three years, one of them on bread and water.[12] But Cummean considered perjury to be less serious and demanded only a four-year penance. The versions of *Iudicia Theodori* are inconsistent. In the *Discipulus Umbrensium* version, a whole chapter containing five *sententiae* (judgments or prescriptions on particular topics) is devoted to this subject. It starts with

[12] See *Paenitentiale Burgundense*, 5–6 and the parallels in the other texts of this group, in Kottje, *Paenitentialia minora*, 9–16.

assigning an eleven-year penance to anyone who broke an oath sworn in a church. If, however, someone did so under pressure (*necessitate coactus*), three fasting periods of forty days each would suffice. Theodore adds, citing his Greek experience, that if someone has pledged an oath merely "in the hands of a man" (i.e., rather than with something sacred), "this is nothing." But if someone swears in the hands of a bishop, a priest, or a deacon, or on the altar or on a consecrated cross, he should do penance for a year. The short section ends with the imposition of a three-year penance for perjurers (*Paenitentiale Theodori U* I, VI, 1–5, Finsterwalder, 297–98). A confessor having access to these three traditions would have found diverse penances assigned to perjury.

The *Excarpsus* apparently tried to clear up the confusion. It starts with a ruling that differentiates among penances according to the status of the sinner. For a layperson, a three-year penance would suffice, while a cleric should remain in penance for five years, a subdeacon for six, a deacon for seven, a priest for ten, and a bishop for twelve. The *Excarpsus* leaves out Theodore's reference to Greek custom, whereby an oath in the hands of a man is regarded as nothing, but it adds that an oath on an unconsecrated cross deserves one year of penance. It also looks at the motivation of the sinner. If moved to perjury by greed, the perjurer should give away all his belongings and enter a monastery. If moved by mortal danger, he should do penance for three years, but if out of need, only for three fasting periods. Anyone who has caused someone to swear a false oath should do penance for seven years. One who committed perjury unknowingly and found out about it afterward should fast for three years, while someone already doubtful at the time of his oath should fast for twice as long (*Excarpsus Cummeani*, V, 1–8, ed. Schmitz II, 621). Thus, while leaving some ambiguities and possibilities for interpretation in the hands of the confessor, the compiler of the *Excarpsus* tried to refine the treatment of perjury and to make it more systematic. This is typical of the way he dealt with his sources.

The *Excarpsus* was an early effort to harmonize the different traditions of penitential books circulating in Francia. The number of surviving copies and its employment in other texts indicates that this effort was successful. Part of its wide dissemination may be attributed to the fact that it was combined with the other product of the monastery of Corbie, the *Collectio Vetus Gallica*. Other texts followed suit, many of them using the same set of basic sources as the *Excarpsus Cummeani*, namely, the simple Frankish penitentials, the *Iudicia Theodori*, and the penitential of Cummean. The *Paenitentiale Sangallense tripartitum* (*Penitential of Saint-Gall in Three Parts*), probably composed at the end of the eighth century, distinguishes among three series of penances on the basis of these sources, but it rearranged these according to the order of the simple Frankish penitentials, facilitating a comparison between the different traditions. The *Paenitentiale Capitula Iudiciorum*, written a little later on the basis of the *Sangallense tripartitum*, made comparison still less complicated by presenting the three traditions separately for each sin. The chapter on perjury, for example, first discusses the sentences on the topic from the simple Frankish penitentials, then those of Theodore, and finally Cummean's rulings.

These texts convey a desire to be comprehensive and to distinguish among the circumstances of people's sins and among their motivations. They also convey a certain unease about the varying scales of penance assigned for similar (or seemingly similar) cases. This attempt at differentiation was all the more urgent since there were other traditions circulating in the Frankish kingdoms as well, in addition to the three just mentioned. An important tradition was associated with the English authorities Bede and Egbert. Whereas the penitential handbook attributed to Bede was probably written in the Frankish lands, the text attributed to Egbert was possibly composed in England. Its textual transmission, however, is almost entirely Continental, and it was on the Continent that these two texts were combined in different stages, eventually coming together as a single integrated work.

The unease regarding the diverging ways of dealing with penitents that we observe in these texts was clearly expressed at the Carolingian reform councils convened by the emperor Charlemagne in 813.[13] In the field of penance, these councils did not succeed in formulating a unified and clear program of reform. On the contrary, the five councils convening in that year at the behest of the aging Charlemagne (d. 814) all expressed different views or expressed their views differently. The council of Mainz did not discuss the problem, whereas the council of Arles was anxious to emphasize that whoever had committed a public crime should be judged in public and should perform penance in public. At the councils gathering in Reims, Chalon-sur-Saône, and Tours, the bishops addressed the varying ways in which priests judged sinners. The council at Reims admonished priests and bishops to examine how they judged penitents and how they decided the length of penance, but the council did not go into this further. At Tours, the bishops clearly spoke out against priests assigning penances in varying degrees and without proper discernment of each case. Here, the bishops decided to meet at the royal palace to decide which of the ancient penitential books should be followed, but there is no evidence that a decision was ever reached. At Chalon-sur-Saône, the bishops were very outspoken about penitential books. They complained most of all about the books' anonymity and consequent lack of authority, and they decided that these should be abolished because "their errors were as certain as their authors were uncertain."[14]

From the late eighth century onward, the importance of penance in a religious, social, and political context seems to have increased substantially. This is not only reflected in the number of texts and manuscripts dealing with penance that were produced in this period, but also in the fact that these texts addressed more and more minor sins, which suggests that penance had become a routine for many of the laity. Confessing one's sins and doing penance for them was regularly linked to receiving

13 For these councils, see Chapter 4 by Gregory I. Halfond in this volume.

14 Council of Arles, c. 26; Tours, c. 22; Reims, c. 16; Chalon-sur-Saône, c. 38, in MGH Conc. 2.1, 253, 289, 255, 281.

holy communion, which Christians were obliged to do on the three important festivals of Christmas, Easter, and Pentecost.

A PENITENTIAL STATE

The importance of penance in the Carolingian period is further illustrated in the influential canonical collection called the *Collectio Dacheriana*, with its stress on the topic of penance (also discussed by Roy Flechner in Chapter 7 of this volume). As we have seen, Charlemagne put penance on the agenda for the five reform councils that he convened in 813, demonstrating thereby that the topic concerned him. Under his son and successor, Louis the Pious (d. 840), penance became a matter of political strife as well as a focus of political discourse. Thus, a recent historian has characterized Louis's reign as a "penitential state."[15] In 822, the emperor Louis the Pious did penance in a very public way at the royal palace in Attigny, an event that was recorded in the *Royal Frankish Annals* and thereby reached a wide audience. Through this public ritual, Louis reconciled himself with members of his family and their supporters, who had fallen out of royal favor in the early years of his reign. By opting for a public penitential rite, Louis put himself in the tradition of the great Roman emperor Theodosius, enhancing his prestige by his association with this most Christian ruler. Later, Louis was confronted by a serious rebellion by his sons. As a result, he was forced to do penance again in the year 833, but this time he did not gain prestige through the humiliating ritual. On the contrary, the emperor underwent the ritual this time only reluctantly, and he was forced to abdicate. A year later, the tables were turned. After regaining his throne, Louis forced one of his most outspoken opponents – Ebo, the archbishop of Reims, who had presided over Louis's penance of 833 – to resign after confessing his sins in public. Such high-profile cases, in which penitential rituals and the ensuing interpretation of their intent were an essential component of political strife in the highest circles, made penance a central topic in political and ecclesiastical discourse in Carolingian Francia.

Under Louis the Pious, churchmen who were closely involved in these political issues were also instrumental in the composition of new handbooks for penance. Ebo of Reims prompted bishop Halitgar of Cambrai to compile a book of this sort from the sayings of the Church Fathers and the sentences of the canons. This work was meant to remedy a situation in which the judgments of the penitents were confused, diverse, and contradictory, as Ebo noted.[16] Hrabanus Maurus, who resigned as abbot of Fulda because of his entanglement in the revolt against Louis the Pious and its consequences, wrote two penitential books in the form of elaborate

[15] Mayke de Jong, *The Penitential State: Authority and Atonement in the Age of Louis the Pious, 814–840* (Cambridge: Cambridge University Press, 2009). See also Courtney Booker, *Past Convictions: The Penance of Louis the Pious and the Decline of the Carolingians* (Philadelphia: University of Pennsylvania Press, 2009).

[16] Letter of Ebo to Hrabanus, MGH Epist. 5, 617.

letters to two bishops. The first was addressed to Otgar, the bishop of Mainz, and it is therefore known as the *Paenitentiale ad Otgarium*. Much more influential was the later *Paenitentiale ad Heribaldum*, addressed to Heribald, bishop of Auxerre. To make these handbooks more authoritative, Hrabanus and Halitgar both preferred to avoid traditional penitential books and to refer instead to established sources of authority, such as conciliar legislation and the works of the Church Fathers. Other authors followed suit. Quite a few new books were meant to meet these new expectations, but ideas of what exactly constituted authoritative sources were far from uniform. Texts such as the pseudo-Theodorian and the pseudo-Gregorian penitentials continued to use traditional material, although they subscribed to the reform program in their prologues and stressed that they relied on established and trustworthy canonical sources. Manuscript evidence, moreover, demonstrates that earlier works continued to be copied and used, and that works attributed to Bede and Theodore gradually became accepted as reliably authoritative.

SPREADING THE MESSAGE

As far as the sources allow us to judge, this new upsurge of interest in things penitential occurred in Carolingian realms during the Carolingian period. From there, however, Carolingian penitential books were introduced into adjacent regions. In England, for example, Carolingian penitential books and manuscripts containing literature of this kind were available from the time of King Aelfred the Great (d. 899). Wulfstan, a towering figure who was bishop of London and Worcester and archbishop of York in the years 996 to 1023, employed Carolingian penitential books along with canonical material, secular law tracts, prayers, and homilies in his so-called commonplace books. In the tenth and eleventh centuries, vernacular penitential books were written in England, based mainly on Continental models but sometimes adapted to English circumstances.[17] Carolingian texts were the basis for new penitential books also in Spain and Italy. In Spain, three books of this kind were written in the period between the late ninth century and the middle of the eleventh century, all of them using either the eighth-century Frankish *Excarpsus Cummeani* or the so-called *Paenitentiale Remense*, a text closely related to it. One of these, the Cordoba penitential, is peculiarly interesting in that it includes rules that seem to have been originally devised to accommodate a community of Christians living in a Muslim environment. These texts were composed and copied in important monastic communities such as those of St. Martin in Albelda and of San Millán de la Cogolla, and they are closely related to royal policy.[18]

[17] S. Jurasinski, *The Old English Penitentials and Anglo-Saxon Law* (Cambridge: Cambridge University Press, 2015).

[18] Francis Bezler, *Les Pénitentiels Espagnols. Contribution à l'étude de la civilisation de l'Espagne chrétienne du haut Moyen Âge*, Spanische Forschungen der Görresgesellschaft 2, Reihe, Bd. 30 (Münster: Aschendorff, 1994).

Penitentials were known in northern Italy from the time when Columbanus settled in Bobbio, in the early seventh century, but they were copied in the central and southern parts only from the tenth century onward. Quite a few texts written in the latter regions from the late tenth to the early twelfth century were based on the Frankish *Paenitentiale Capitula Iudiciorum*, but they were also related to two influential Italian canonical collections: the *Collection in Five Books* and the *Collection in Nine Books*. Penitential books shared with these canonical collections not only the same sources but also the same techniques of using them. As in Spain, monasteries played a role in the production and distribution of these texts. In Italy, the monasteries of Montecassino and Farfa, in particular, were involved in their production.[19]

CANONICAL REGULATION AND PENITENTIAL RULINGS

As the Italian texts just discussed demonstrate, there was a close connection between canonical rules and penitential sentences. Thus, penitential judgments entered canonical collections, while material from canonical collections entered penitential handbooks. This should not come as a surprise, for both texts formulated rules for Christian behavior and defined ways to enforce these rules. How these texts were used in practice is very hard to determine, but the fact that we frequently find canonical collections and penitential books together in the same manuscript suggests that they were sometimes employed in a similar environment. Priests were expected to know the canonical rules, although it remains unclear what exactly was regarded as standard knowledge in this field. Local priests were expected to possess a penitential book, and we have evidence that they did; whether they also owned a copy of a canonical collection is less evident, though not implausible. Bishops judging in ecclesiastical courts could consult penitential books in cases where their collection of canons did not suffice. While in some periods or regions the fluid boundary between canons and penitential decisions was unproblematic, in others, as evidenced by the Carolingian reform councils discussed above, the relationship between canonical material and penitential handbooks could be rather strained.

When Regino, abbot of Prüm, had to resign from office in the year 899, he took refuge in the monastery of St. Martin in Trier, where he was appointed abbot by bishop Radbod. As abbot in Trier, Regino composed between 906 and 913 a practical handbook for episcopal visitations.[20] In this work in two books, dedicated to Archbishop Hatto of Mainz, Regino assembled a rich collection of material to provide the archbishop with the necessary legal and disciplinary background when travelling around his diocese, taking care of ecclesiastical discipline

19 See Adriaan Gaastra, *Between Liturgy and Canon Law: A Study of Books of Confession and Penance in Eleventh- and Twelfth-Century Italy* (doctoral dissertation, University of Utrecht, 2007) and his edition of some of these texts in *Paenitentialia Italiae Saeculi XI–XII*, CCL 156C.

20 See Chapter 7 by Roy Flechner and Chapter 22 by Greta Austin in this volume.

in the local communities that he visited. Regino claimed that he took his material from the councils of the fathers and papal decisions, yet in practice he used a much wider range of sources, including royal capitularies and penitential handbooks. In the first book, dealing mainly with clerical discipline, Regino included an elaborate discussion of penance and confession. It appears from this discussion that Regino expected parishioners to confess their sins every year before Lent to their parish priest (*ad proprium sacerdotem*). Regino includes here not only liturgical instruction on how to receive and absolve a penitent but also a long list of questions for interrogating the sinner about his behavior, which amounts to a small penitential book. In the beginning of the second book of his collection, Regino describes the procedure of episcopal visitations in considerable detail. He includes a list of questions that the bishop should put to trusted members of the locality he is visiting. This list, too, is inspired by penitential literature. In the remainder of the book, when dealing with the ways to remedy sinful behavior, Regino regularly cites the penitentials of Theodore of Canterbury, the penitential attributed to Bede, and Halitgar's work. He evidently regarded these works as proper sources of ecclesiastical authority and used them to enhance the authority of the bishop when touring his diocese.

Regino's list of questions was a source of inspiration for Burchard, bishop of Worms from 1000 to 1025.[21] Burchard compiled a hugely influential canonical collection in twenty books, known as the *Decretum*, and he devoted the nineteenth book to penance. Burchard regarded this book not merely as a useful addition to his collection but rather as its culmination. His immense knowledge of the canonical tradition was put "in the service of pastoral care."[22] Burchard included in the nineteenth book a long catalogue of questions that could be put to a confessing Christian, and by so doing he demonstrated his intimate knowledge of human behavior. That his efforts in the field of penance were appreciated becomes clear from the fact that the nineteenth book was often transmitted on its own. In some manuscripts, Burchard's material is rearranged so as to put more stress on its penitential character. The earliest manuscripts produced in Worms under Burchard's supervision demonstrate that he was assisted by a considerable team of scribes. His work was widely distributed, especially in the regions that made up the Ottonian empire, but it also inspired Ivo of Chartres in France. Burchard's work remained popular in Italy, and Gratian used it in turn when composing his own *Decretum*.

21 See Greta Austin's Chapter 23 in this volume.

22 Greta Austin, "Jurisprudence in the Service of Pastoral Care: The Decretum of Burchard of Worms," *Speculum* 79 (2004): 929–59. Greta Austin, *Shaping Church Law Around the Year 1000: The Decretum of Burchard of Worms* (Farnham, UK: Ashgate, 2009). Ludger Körntgen, "Canon law and the Practice of Penance: Burchard of Worms's Penitential," EME 14 (2006): 103–17.

CONCLUSIONS

This brief overview of the development of penitential books reveals their close relationship with canonical collections. As with the latter, it is not always clear how the penitential books were used.[23] The early Insular books of this genre suggest a monastic background, and it was monastic founders such as Columbanus who brought such compositions to the European mainland. These early books deal with lay sinners, too, but mainly with regard to serious sins such as murder, adultery, or theft – sins that caused a major social scandal and thus could lead to serious conflicts. The forms of penance devised in these cases often included some material compensation for the offended party, which suggests that penance formed part of a process of reconciliation between two parties, in which a person invested with religious authority – a priest, bishop, abbot, or even an abbess – played a mediating role. We can imagine that in such circumstances, social pressure was utilized to bring the sinner to confession. Since men were normally held accountable for the social consequences of their behavior and of that of their female relatives, penitentials in general address male perpetrators.

In later texts, forms of material compensation become less prominent. This change is clearly visible in the eighth- and ninth-century texts written in Francia. We also see that these later works gradually begin to deal with sins of a socially less visible nature. This suggests that confession of sins was becoming a way for Christians to cleanse their souls, even in cases where there was no social pressure to do so. References to women penitents as a distinct group are more frequent in these later penitential books. Confession of sins is sometimes linked as a prerequisite to receiving the eucharist, a liturgical ritual in which the laity participated only at the major Christian festivals of Easter, Pentecost, and Christmas. Like the penitential season of Lent itself, confession and penance were preparation for such holy occasions. In the Carolingian realms, this seems already to have been a generally accepted phenomenon, though we should probably reckon with considerable geographical diversity. Carolingian episcopal statutes expected priests to own a penitential book, and church inventories from Bavaria and the Reims area show that such precepts did not remain a dead letter. Regino of Prüm expected Christians to confess their sins at the start of the Lenten season to their own parish priest – a rule that would gain wider application with the famous decree *Omnis utriusque* (canon 21) of the Fourth Lateran Council in 1215.

The evidence suggests, therefore, that starting from quite modest beginnings in monasteries, the practice of regular yearly confession as part of a general Christian round of duties was developed within the Carolingian realms from the late eighth or early ninth century onward. Because there is no hard evidence regarding the frequency of confession, there is room for doubt regarding the general acceptance of this practice among the laity, but the fact that many manuscripts contain

[23] See Roy Flechner's chapter in this volume.

penitential books suggests regular and frequent confession.[24] The close connections with canonical rules have persuaded some historians to see confession and penance as a practice still in the hands of bishops during this early period. It is only in the eleventh century, with the chronicle of Ekkehard IV of Saint-Gall, that we have a description of a local priest hearing confession and assigning penance. Nevertheless, the evidence of parish libraries in the Carolingian period, the pastoral or liturgical content of some manuscripts containing penitential books, and descriptions of priestly duties, all indicate that confession was part of a fairly widespread practice of pastoral care.[25] The diffusion of Carolingian penitential handbooks may be interpreted as a sign of the dispersion of this Carolingian ideal and its practice later to Anglo-Saxon England, to Spain, and to Italy.

Yet we also see that bishops worried about the variety of prescriptions in the handbooks that they encountered, and some of them tried to remedy this situation by compiling new texts for the priests in their diocese. Moreover, we encounter penitential books also in manuscripts that contain canonical collections, sometimes even accompanied by secular law texts. In such cases, we must assume that such codices were meant for episcopal use, and it seems that the borders between canons proper and penitential rulings were not always meticulously drawn. It is possible that canonical rulings were used in a confessional setting, while penitential prescriptions could serve in dealing with cases that came to the episcopal court. In the *Collectio Dacheriana* and in the Italian Collections in Five and in Nine Books, as well as in the works of Regino of Prüm and Burchard of Worms discussed above, penitential and canonical works are so closely intertwined that they actually form a real symbiosis. Such evidence suggests that in practice, judgment in ecclesiastical courts and the hearing of confessions by priests and bishops were closely related.

In the past, scholars have distinguished categorically between canon law and penance during the early Middle Ages. Canon law, according to this view, was associated especially with ecclesiastical courts and with forms of public penance (the external forum), whereas penitential books were linked to private penance (the internal forum). But such a clear distinction is not warranted by the sources. Already in Late Antiquity, many different forms of doing penance existed, some more and some less public. When penitential books were first being composed in Wales and Ireland, they were not regarded as a novelty to be distinguished from the practice of

24 Alexander Murray expresses doubts regarding the frequency of confession among the laity in "Confession Before 1215," *Transactions of the Royal Historical Society*, 6th series, 3 (1993): 51–81; and more recently in Alexander Murray, *Conscience and Authority in the Medieval Church* (Oxford: Oxford University Press, 2015). See the responses to Murray's minimalistic stance by Rob Meens, "The Frequency and Nature of Early Medieval Penance," in P. Biller and A. J. Minnis (eds.), *Handling Sin: Confession in the Middle Ages*, York Studies in Medieval Theology 2 (Woodbridge, UK: York Medieval Press, 1998): 35–61; and David S. Bachrach, "Confession in the Regnum Francorum (742–900): The Sources Revisited," JEH 54 (2003): 3–22.

25 For Ekkehard see Mayke de Jong, "Pollution, Penance and Sanctity: Ekkehard's *Life* of Iso of St Gall," in Joyce M. Hill and Mary Swan (eds.), *The Community, the Family, and the Saint: Patterns of Power in Early Medieval Europe*, International Medieval Research 4 (Turnhout: Brepols, 1998): 145–58.

public penance, and the same can be said about their introduction in Francia. Only the Carolingians started to worry about the different procedures, and it was they who introduced the distinction between public and secret penance, but there is no way of linking one or the other practice to a specific penitential text. In 813, the Council of Chalon-sur-Saône decreed that whoever sinned in public should do penance in public, and the councils convening in that year in Arles and Reims decided in a similar way.[26] An earlier penitential, the *Remense*, had already formulated a similar rule: Whoever sinned in public should do penance in public, and whoever sinned in secret should do penance secretly.[27] But it would have been difficult to apply such general regulation consistently in practice, particularly since several rulings entailed a form of compensation for the offended party. If the offended had to be compensated, the whole process of confession and atonement must have been more or less public, for only in this way could opposing parties be reconciled. The case of the royal public penance undertaken by Louis the Pious in 822 demonstrates on a grand scale how penance could be employed as a means of reconciliation, but his penance of 833 warns us that it could also be used as a highly politicized instrument of division.

In general, the relationship between penitential books and canonical collections before 1100 seems intricate and complex. The same can be said about the practice of confession and penance on the one hand, and ecclesiastical regulation and jurisdiction on the other. Distinctions are not always easy to draw, and scholars working in this era should be careful not to employ concepts that developed later too readily. Moreover, one should not assume that theoretical or normative distinctions were straightforwardly applicable in practice. The sources do not allow us to get a clear picture of what priests, bishops, and monks actually did as regards the ministry of penance during the first millennium, but they do suggest that they had considerable flexibility when dealing with the sins of their fellow Christians.

SOURCES AND ABBREVIATIONS

The modern scholarly study of penitential books started in the nineteenth century, when Friedrich Wilhelm Hermann Wasserschleben published the majority of such texts in *Die Bussordnungen der abendländischen Kirche* (Halle, 1851). His work was supplemented by Hermann Joseph Schmitz with two important books: *Die Bussbücher und die Bussdisciplin der Kirche. Nach handschriftlichen Quellen dargestellt* (Mainz, 1883); and *Die Bussbücher und das kanonische Bussverfahren* (Düsseldorf, 1898) [abbreviation: Schmitz II]. Both are reprinted in Graz, 1958. The versions of the penitential of

[26] Council of Chalon, c. 25, in MGH Conc. 2.1, 278; Arles, c. 26, ibid., 278; and Reims, c. 31, ibid., 256.

[27] *Paenitentiale Remense* IV, 50–51, ed. Franz-Bernd Asbach, "Das Poenitentiale Remense und der sogen. Excarpus Cummeani: Überlieferung, Quellen und Entwicklung zweier kontinentaler Bußbücher aus der 1. Hälfte des 8. Jahrhunderts," unpublished inaugural dissertation, University of Regensburg (1975), Anhang, 30.

Theodore of Canterbury were edited by Paul Willem Finsterwalder, *Die Canones Theodori Cantuariensis und ihre Überlieferungsformen*, Untersuchungen zu den Bußbüchern des 7., 8. und 9. Jahrhunderts, 1 (Weimar: Böhlaus,1929) [Finsterwalder]. The Insular penitentials, with the exception of the *Paenitentiale Ambrosianum*, are now best consulted in Ludwig Bieler (ed.), *The Irish Penitentials*, with an appendix by D. A. Binchy, Scriptores Latini Hiberniae 5 (Dublin: Dublin Institute of Advanced Studies, 1963) [Bieler]. The tripartite penitentials are edited in Rob Meens, *Het tripartite boeteboek. Overlevering en betekenis van vroegmiddeleeuwse biechtvoorschriften (met editie en vertaling van vier tripartita)*, Middeleeuwse Studies en Bronnen 41 (Hilversum: Verloren, 1994). Since the 1990s, the Continental penitentials are edited in *Corpus Christianorum Series Latina* 156. To date, the following editions have appeared there: R. Kottje (ed.), *Paenitentialia minora Franciae et Italiae saeculi VIII–IX*, CCL 156 (1994) [Kottje, *Paenitentialia minora*]; F. Bezler (ed.), *Paenitentialia Hispaniae*, CCL 156A (1998); C. van Rhijn (ed.), *Paenitentiale Pseudo-Theodori*, CCL 156B (2009); and A. Gaastra (ed.), *Paenitentialia Italiae Saeculi XI–XII*, CCL 156 C (2016). Only Bieler's edition contains a translation in English. Meens provides a translation in Dutch. A selection of these sources is translated in J. T. McNeill and H. Gamer, *Medieval Handbooks of Penance: A Translation of the Principal* Libri Poenitentiales *and Selections from Related Documents* (New York: Columbia University Press, 1938; repr. 1990).

FURTHER READING

For a general introduction to early medieval penance and penitential books, see Rob Meens, *Penance in Medieval Europe, 600–1200* (Cambridge: Cambridge University Press, 2014), a study to which I refer readers for more detail. See further Allen J. Frantzen, *The Literature of Penance in Anglo-Saxon England* (New Brunswick, NJ: Rutgers University Press, 1983); Sarah Hamilton, *The Practice of Penance, 900–1050* (Woodbridge, UK: Boydell and Brewer, 2001) (with an emphasis on the liturgy of penance); and the relevant sections in Abigail Firey (ed.), *A New History of Penance* (Leiden: Brill, 2008). For a broader context, consult Peter Brown, *The Ransom of the Soul: Afterlife and Wealth in Early Western Christianity* (Cambridge, MA: Harvard University Press, 2015); Abigail Firey, *A Contrite Heart: Prosecution and Redemption in the Carolingian Empire* (Leiden: Brill, 2009); Mayke de Jong, *The Penitential State: Authority and Atonement in the Age of Louis the Pious, 814–840* (Cambridge: Cambridge University Press, 2009); and Stefan Jurasinski, *The Old English Penitentials and Anglo-Saxon Law* (Cambridge: Cambridge University Press, 2015). For a very different view, see Alexander Murray, *Conscience and Authority in the Medieval Church* (Oxford: Oxford University Press, 2015).

9

Monastic Rules

Albrecht Diem[1]

Monastic rules functioned as normative texts, but in what sense? We have tended to assume that following a rule has been a stable feature of monastic life since the beginning of coenobitic (communal) monasticism – that most early communities that outlasted the lifetime of their founders and charismatic leaders would have observed a particular rule, such as one of the roughly thirty surviving Latin monastic rules that were written before the *Rule of Benedict* (*Regula Benedicti*) became the guiding norm for monks and nuns.[2] Living in obedience to a particular written rule, according to this understanding, was what distinguished monks and nuns in the proper sense from others who lived more loosely defined, arguably inferior forms of religious or ascetic life.[3] The content of the rule, according to this narrative, was what defined a monastic community's form of life.

Scholars of monasticism have recognized that the very notion of a monastic rule as normative text developed in stages during the early Middle Ages, and in response to specific circumstances, although they have not always drawn some of the conclusions that follow this premise. Our received notion of a rule depends on the *Rule of Benedict* (see Chapter 16 in this volume), but the notion arguably depends even more on Benedict of Aniane (d. 821), the abbot and monastic reformer who in the early ninth century instigated a monastic reform project that not only submitted all

1 I should like to thank Matthieu van der Meer and Scott Bruce for their suggestions and corrections. This chapter has been written as a contribution to the Spezialforschungsbereich F 4202 *Visions of Community*, funded by the *Fonds zur Förderung der wissenschaftlichen Forschung* (FWF), the Faculty of History and Cultural Sciences of the University of Vienna and the Austrian Academy of Science.

2 For surveys of monastic rules, see Adalbert de Vogüé, *Les règles monastiques anciennes (400–700)*, Typologie des sources 46 (Turnhout: Brepols, 1985); and Albrecht Diem and Philip Rousseau, "Monastic Rules, 4th–9th c.," in Alison Beach and Isabelle Cochelin (eds.), *The Cambridge History of Western Medieval Monasticism*, vol. 1 (Cambridge: Cambridge University Press, in press).

3 Karl S. Frank, *Grundzüge des christlichen Mönchtums*, 5th ed. (Darmstadt: Wissenschaftliche Buchgesellschaft, 1993), 49–65. Clifford H. Lawrence, *Medieval Monasticism: Forms of Religious Life in Western Europe in the Middle Ages* (London: Longman, 1984), 1–17. Gert Melville, *The World of Medieval Monasticism: Its History and Forms of Life* (Collegeville, MN: Liturgical Press, 2016), 7–23. Marilyn Dunn, *The Emergence of Monasticism: From the Desert Fathers to the Early Middle Ages* (Oxford: Blackwell, 2000), 25–73.

Frankish monasteries to the *Regula Benedicti* but also implemented a particular way of understanding the monastic rule as a normative text.

Historians of early monasticism in recent years have found it necessary to challenge the working assumption, however convenient in some contexts, that monasticism generally entailed a stable, "regular life" (*vita regularis*), defined by a particular written rule. Early monasticism included a multiplicity of diverse and often experimental forms of religious life, which refuse to be captured under a single category.[4] Written rules may initially have played only a marginal role within this monastic diversity. Early-medieval monasteries created, almost as a by-product, both the concept of monastic life as a *vita regularis* and the idea that a single text could provide the internal laws and guidelines for a monastic community's discipline. The practice of organizing communal life according to written norms would eventually extend far beyond the boundaries of the cloister. Thus, the *Regula Benedicti*, the rule that prevailed, is in some sense the ancestor of every rule of life, whether religious or secular.[5]

This chapter explores the developments that led to the medieval Western notion of regular observance. It traces the unexpectedly complicated history of the relations among text, norm, and life in monasticism.[6] If we recognize their diversity, early monastic communities appear as multifaceted mirrors reflecting what was going on in their respective political, social, and cultural surroundings. Quite often these mirrors reveal what would otherwise have remained invisible.

Late-antique and early-medieval monastic communities played a double role within the "Transformation of the Roman World." On the one hand, the roughly thirty early rules that have survived can be read as reflections of the legal concepts and practices of the world around them. On the other hand, monastic communities were not only shaped by societal change. At least some of the early rules played an active role as agents of transformation. The communities that used them were cradles of new, and sometimes lasting, institutional forms and models of the Christian life.[7] By historicizing "regular observance" and questioning the notion of the *vita regularis* as a continuous unifying marker of monastic life, we can generate a methodological "surplus" that is beneficial for the study of legal systems in general.

4 The best access to the diversity of early medieval monastic life and to the current state of research will be the first volume of A. Beach and I. Cochelin (eds.), *Cambridge History of Western Monasticism*, Cambridge University Press, in press.

5 Compare Giorgio Agamben, *The Highest Poverty. Monastic Rules and Form-of-Life* (Stanford: Stanford University Press, 2013).

6 For an analysis of RB as a legal text, see Uwe K. Jacobs, *Die Regula Benedicti als Rechtsbuch. Eine rechtshistorische und rechtstheologische Untersuchung* (Köln: Böhlau, 1987).

7 For a case study of a late-antique monastery as "mirror" and "agent," see Albrecht Diem, "Who Is Allowed to Pray for the King? Saint-Maurice d'Agaune and the Creation of a Burgundian Identity," in G. Heydemann and W. Pohl (eds.), *Post-Roman Transitions: Christian and Barbarian Identities in the Early Medieval West* (Turnhout: Brepols, 2013), 47–88.

BENEDICT OF ANIANE AND THE INVENTION OF REGULAR OBSERVANCE

The paradigm of monastic life as a *vita regularis* was largely based on a single textual witness: the famous *Codex Regularum* compiled around the beginning of the ninth century by Benedict of Aniane. Known as the "Second Benedict," he is credited with turning the rule ascribed to his namesake, Benedict of Nursia (d. c. 550), into the norm to be followed by all Frankish monasteries, and subsequently by virtually all monasteries in the Latin Medieval West for centuries.[8]

Benedict of Aniane's *Codex Regularum* is preserved in a single early-medieval manuscript: Munich, *Bayerische Staatsbibliothek*, Clm 28118.[9] It contains almost the entire corpus of surviving late-antique and early-medieval Latin monastic rules.[10] About a third of these rules would have been lost if Benedict of Aniane had not collected and preserved them.[11] His *Codex Regularum* describes monastic history as a long chain of regular observance. After presenting the text of the *Regula Benedicti* as the summa of all monastic rules, Benedict of Aniane documents, first, the *Regulae patrum* (the rules allegedly written by famous Desert Fathers). Then come the rules of Pachomius, Basil, Augustine, and Columbanus, other rules from Gaul, rules from Visigothic Spain, the *Rule of the Master* (*Regula magistri*), and a set of female monastic rules.

Benedict of Aniane presents the *Rule of Benedict* as the best of all monastic rules because it incorporates, in his view, the best norms from *all* these rules.[12] As a result, the Carolingian monastic reforms have generally been understood as a process by which the diversity of rules that monastics followed before Benedict of Nursia was reduced to observance of a single rule.[13] It is noteworthy, however, that Benedict of

8 Josef Semmler, "Benedictus II: una regula – una consuetudo," in W. Lourdaux and D. Verhelst (eds.), *Benedictine Culture 750–1050* (Leuven: Leuven University Press, 1983), 1–49. Albrecht Diem, "Inventing the Holy Rule: Some Observations on the History of Monastic Normative Observance in the Early Medieval West," in H. Dey and E. Fentress (eds.), *Western Monasticism ante litteram: The Spaces of Monastic Observance in Late Antiquity and the Early Middle Ages*, Disciplina Monastica 8 (Turnhout: Brepols, 2011), 53–84.

9 For a facsimile with extensive description of the Munich manuscript, see Pius Engelbert, *Der Codex Regularum des Benedikt von Aniane* (St. Ottilien: Eos Editions, 2016).

10 Among the early rules known to us, only the *Rules* for monks of Eugippius and Caesarius of Arles and the *Rule* for virgins by Leander of Seville do not appear in the *Codex Regularum*. For editions, translations, and the manuscript transmission of all monastic rules written before the ninth century, see www.earlymedievalmonasticism.org (accessed March 20, 2019).

11 Ardo, *Vita Benedicti Anianensis*, cc. 18 and 38, MGH Scriptores (in Folio) 15.1, 206 and 217, describe how Benedict of Aniane collected and compiled all the monastic rules that he could find.

12 Benedict of Aniane, *Concordia Regularum*, prologue, CCM 168A, 3–7.

13 On the Carolingian monastic reforms, see Mayke de Jong, "Carolingian Monasticism: The Power of Prayer," in R. McKitterick (ed.), *The New Cambridge Medieval History*, vol. 2: *c. 700–c. 900* (Cambridge: Cambridge University Press, 1995), 622–53 and 995–1002; Albrecht Diem, "The Carolingians and the *Regula Benedicti*," in D. van Espelo et al. (eds.), *Religious Franks: Religion and Power in the Frankish Kingdoms: Studies in Honour of Mayke de Jong* (Manchester: Manchester University Press, 2016), 243–61.

Aniane in his collection not only *assembled* monastic rules. He also established a new textual genre, turning a heterogeneous assemblage of texts of various sorts into the ancestors and siblings, as it were, of the *Rule of Benedict*. Some of the texts in the collection do indeed have similarities in content and style to the *Regula Benedicti*, but others do not. They range from succinct lists of organizational instructions, which sometimes fill barely one folio, to the *Rule of the Master*, which includes more than a hundred questions (with lengthy answers) on grand spiritual and theological questions as well as such details as how the monks should make pancakes once a week from the breadcrumbs that the monks left at the table.[14] The Master's work extends over forty-three densely written folios: several hundred pages in a modern edition.

It is significant that only about half of the texts in the *Codex Regularum* have the term *regula* in their titles. Other terms used include *instituta, praeceptum, lex, iudicium, verbum, consensorium, titulum, sententiae, tractatus, epistola, doctrina, pactum*, and *excarpsum*: terms that arguably imply diverse understandings of the intended use, function, and normative character of the texts. Benedict of Aniane not only construed diverse monastic exhortations, guidelines, instructions, spiritual reflections, and so forth as rules. He also presented his collection – or at least all the rules for monks therein – as a single all-encompassing "*Rule of the Holy Fathers*" (*Regula sanctorum patrum*).

His collection begins with the words: "Here begins the prologue of the *regula* (singular!) of the holy monks" ("*Incipit prologus sanctorum regulae monachorum*"). After this incipit comes a text that we know as the prologue of the *Rule of Benedict*, which serves here as prologue of the entire collection. The last rule for monks in his collection, the *Rule of the Master*, concludes with the words: "Here ends the rule of the holy fathers" ("*Explicit regula sanctorum patrum*").[15] Benedict of Aniane presented the entire collection, therefore, as if it was a single enormous rule of which the *Regula Benedicti* was only a small part. This all-encompassing *regula* of "the holy monks" or "holy fathers" consists of hundreds of diverse and sometimes contradictory regulations along with various admonitions, exhortations, instructions, sanctions, recommendations, and so forth.

In what follows, I shall suggest, on the basis of four texts included in Benedict of Aniane's *Codex Regularum*, that the notion of "following a rule" in the "pre-Benedictine" world, when closely examined, falls apart into several distinct phenomena. Not only were the rules in Benedict's *Codex Regularum* diverse in content, but each text originally functioned differently, developing a distinct notion of normativity and legitimizing its authority in its own way.

14 *Regula magistri*, ed. Adalbert de Vogüé, SC 105 and 106. On the pancakes, see c. 23.34–39, SC 106, p. 118.

15 Munich, Bayerische Staatsbibliothek Clm 28118, fols. 1r and 184v.

Each rule in the *Codex Regularum* can tell us two different stories: one about the circumstances of its origin, and the other about its use, reception, and impact. We may assume that most, perhaps all, of the monastic rules in Benedict of Aniane's work were the products of some sort of crisis that required a community either to deviate from existing norms or to "textualize," and hence to codify and monopolize, some already established tradition. None of these texts would have been written down without a specific reason – and these reasons in and of themselves may elucidate important turning points in monastic history. Either their authors considered the existing textual repertoire to be inadequate, or monastic communities (or their leaders) saw a need to step away from unwritten codes of practice – from orally transmitted teachings of monastic leaders or long-established practices and traditions – and to establish their form of life on a textual, codified basis. The reason for producing a new text, we must assume, lay in some conflict, whether within the community, between the community and its leader, or between the community and the surrounding world.[16]

The four rules, or sets of monastic norms, to be discussed here have been chosen not only because they rank among the best known, but also because we know about each of them through several different narrative sources. Hagiographic texts, too, provide us in these cases with important information about the origins of these rules, and they also played a crucial historical role in the dissemination of the rules, enhancing their authority.

PACHOMIUS AND THE ANGELIC RULE

The Egyptian monk Pachomius (d. 348), whom hagiographic tradition regards as the founding father of coenobitic (communal) monasticism, received his rule from an angel, as several versions of his *Vita* and other biographical sources attest. Some of these sources describe a dramatic event in which Pachomius, like Moses, received the precepts for his community on a tablet (*tabula*): in this case, one of bronze. A few of them also provide the text or a summary of the angel's instructions.[17]

[16] On rules as markers of conflicts, see Diem and Rousseau, "Monastic Rules."

[17] The "Angelic Rule" is mentioned in the following: the second Greek *Vita Pachomii*, c. 12, ed. François Halkin, *Sancti Pachomii Vitae Graecae* (Brussels: Societé des Bollandistes 1932); Dionysius Exiguus, *Vita Pachomii*, cc. 12, 21–22, 24, 28, ed. H. van Cranenburgh, *La Vie Latine de Saint Pachôme* (Brussels: Societé des Bollandistes, 1969), 104–06, 126–28, 134–38, 150; *Historia Lausiaca*, c. 32.2–8, ed. Adelheid Wellhausen, *De lateinische Übersetzung der Historia Lausiaca des Palladius* (Berlin: De Gruyter, 2003), 591–92; Gennadius of Marseille, *De viris inlustribus*, c. 142 (7), ed. Carl Albrecht Bernoulli (Freiburg: Hinrichs, 1895), 63; *Vita Pacomii (iunioris)*, ed. Albrecht Diem and Hildegund Müller, "Vita, Regula, Sermo: Eine unbekannte lateinische Vita Pacomii als Lehrtext für ungebildete Mönche und als Traktat über das Sprechen," in R. Corradini et al. (eds.), *Zwischen Niederschrift und Wiederschrift. Frühmittelalterliche Hagiographie und Historiographie im Spannungsfeld von Kompendienüberlieferung und Editionstechnik* (Vienna: Verlag der Österreichischen Akademie der Wissenschaften, 2010), 223–72. Dionysius Exiguus, the *Historia*

It is striking that none of these narrative accounts of this "angelic" rule corresponds to the text of the *Regula Pachomii* that exists both in Coptic and Greek fragments and as a complete text in Jerome's Latin translation (the version included in Benedict of Aniane's *Codex Regularum*).[18] The *Regula Pachomii* as we know it through Benedict of Aniane consists of more than two hundred short practical precepts (*praecepta*), many of which deal with the minutiae of monastic life: topics such as the requirement to wear a belt around one's goatskin habit, the prohibition against oiling one's shoes, and the rule that two monks should not sit together on an unsaddled donkey or on a wagon shaft (*Regula Pachomii, Praecepta* 99, 104, 109). These texts are largely devoid of spiritual reflections and biblical references. It seems unlikely that any angel would have inscribed on a bronze tablet the detailed, often mundane text that is now considered to be the authentic *Regula Pachomii*.

Philip Rousseau argues in his study of Pachomian monasticism that the text that formed the basis of Jerome's translation was most likely not written down during Pachomius's own lifetime but rather evolved over a longer period in reaction to problems arising in Pachomius's foundations.[19] Rousseau's assumption about the genesis of the collection of Pachomian precepts is consistent with the role that the *Regula Pachomii* played in the numerous Coptic, Arabic, Greek, and Latin *Vitae* written in the first two centuries after Pachomius's death.[20]

Neither the most extensive version of *Vita Pachomii*, which was written in the Bohairic dialect of Coptic, nor the oldest surviving Greek version, refer to an "angelic" rule, although they do say that what motivated Pachomius to found his first monastery was the appearance of an angel.[21] Moreover, rather than referring to any written *regula*, these two early hagiographies convey Pachomius's monastic ideals by paraphrasing his teachings and describing his exemplary behavior. We find the story of the *Angelic Rule* for the first time in the second Greek *Vita Pachomii*, which may have been written in the early sixth century. We also find it in the Latin *Vita Pachomii* by Dionysius Exiguus (d. 544), which is apparently a translation of a Greek version that was similar to the second Greek *Vita Pachomii*.[22]

Lausiaca, and the *Vita Pacomii (iunioris)* provide different accounts of the contents of the "Angelic Rule."

18 Amand Boon (ed.), *Pachomiana Latina. Règle et épitres de S. Pachome, épitre de S. Théodore et "liber" de S. Orsiesius* (Leuven: Bureaux de la Revue, 1932), 3–74. For the Coptic and Greek fragments, see ibid., 155–182.

19 Philip Rousseau, *Pachomius: The Making of a Community in Fourth-Century Egypt* (Berkeley: University of California Press, 1999), 48–53.

20 On the hagiographic tradition regarding Pachomius, with its chronology and interdependences, see Amand Veilleux, *Pachomian Koinonia*, vol. 1: *The life of Saint Pachomius and His Disciples* (Kalamazoo: Cistercian Publications, 1980), 1–21; and Rousseau, *Pachomius*, 37–48.

21 Bohairic, *Vita Pachomii*, trans. Veilleux, *Pachomian Koinonia* 1:23–295, at 39. First Greek *Vita Pachomii*, c. 12, ed. Halkin, *Sancti Pachomii*, trans. Veilleux, *Pachomian Koinonia* 1:305.

22 Second Greek *Vita Pachomii*, c. 12, ed. Halkin (using the term *typos*); Dionysius Exiguus, *Vita Pachomii*, c. 12, ed. Cranenburgh, 104–06.

Both the second Greek *Vita Pachomii* and Dionysius's Latin version emphasize at several points in the narrative that Pachomius composed *written* guidelines, which included a rule for his female community. They also give examples how Pachomius's monks followed or violated the rule of their monastery. In several places, Dionysius Exiguus's version takes the idea of Pachomian monastic life as a *vita regularis* even further than the second Greek *Vita Pachomii*.[23] It must have seemed logical to Dionysius, a scholar of canon law, that Pachomius's foundation adhered strictly to a written rule, which he had received from an angel and written down for his monks.[24]

Comparison of the different versions of the *Vita Pachomii* shows how a notion of monastic life as a *vita regularis* emerged slowly out of a narrative tradition in which monastic discipline was based chiefly on the teachings and the exemplary life of Pachomius and his successors. The idea that monks and nuns should follow a written, codified rule was superimposed onto an older hagiographic tradition long after Pachomius's lifetime. Latin monks, unaware of the complicated genealogy of the *Lives* of Pachomius, saw him not only as the founding father of coenobitic monasticism but also as an abbot who organized his monasteries on the basis of his own divinely sanctioned written rule.[25]

Nevertheless, even monks in the Latin West did not necessarily consider the version that Jerome translated to be the only valid version of Pachomius's "angelic" rule. They may also have known about the angelic guidelines through their inclusion in Dionysius's *Life of Pachomius* and in the *Historia Lausiaca*, a collection of Lives of Egyptian saints that included extensive sections on Pachomius and the communities he founded. Moreover, there existed another Latin *Vita Pachomii*, as well as that of Dionysius Exiguus, which culminated in a long address that Pachomius delivered to his community, the text of which was dictated by an angel. It was this version of the Life that Benedict of Aniane included in his *Codex Regularum*. Because the address was presented as a speech embedded in a narrative framework, scholars failed to notice until recently that this was, in effect, yet another Pachomian rule.[26]

Ardo Smaragdus tells how Benedict of Aniane initially dismissed the *Regula Benedicti* as a rule only for beginners. Instead, he wanted to follow the much stricter guidelines of Basil and Pachomius.[27] It is surely unlikely that Smaragdus had Jerome's two hundred rather pedantic Pachomian precepts in mind when he

[23] I am drawing here on research in progress, as yet unpublished. Details of these variations and correspondences will appear in forthcoming publications on monastic normativity.

[24] Compare Dionysius Exiguus, *Vita Pachomii*, prologue, ed. Cranenburgh, 78–79.

[25] A major source of information for Latin monks was the bio-bibliography of Gennadius of Marseille, *De viris inlustribus*, written toward the end of the fifth century. See c. 142 (7), ed. Bernoulli, 63.

[26] Munich, Bayerische Staatsbibliothek, Clm 28118, fols. 24–41v, ed. in Diem and Müller, "Vita, Regula, Sermo."

[27] *Vita Benedicti Anianensis*, c. 2, MGH Scriptores (in Folio) 15.1, 202, alluding to RB 73.4–6 (SC 182, 672–74).

described Pachomius's rule as the summit of ascetic strictness. Perhaps in his mind Basil and Pachomius were living embodiments of the allegedly much stricter forms of ascetic life that prevailed in the East.

Although the *Regula Pachomii* ranks high on the list of important pre-Benedictine monastic rules, it was not a normative text in any straightforward sense. Jerome's translation, the text usually identified as *Regula Pachomii*, was only obliquely related to the historical Pachomius. In fact, several texts and paraphrases claiming to represent Pachomius's rule share nothing more than the idea of an angelic intervention as a source of authority. There is no indication that any monastic community in the Latin West tried to use the *Regula Pachomii* as the legal or normative basis of their way of life. Instead, Jerome's translation served as a textual quarry, from which material could be mined and then inserted, with appropriate modifications, into later monastic rules, such as the *Regula Orientalis*, Caesarius's *Regula ad virgines*, the *Regula Tarnatensis*, the *Regula Pauli et Stephani*, and probably also the *Regula Benedicti*.[28]

The foregoing observations regarding the *Regula Pachomii* provide us with an analytical framework for approaching other monastic rules. Questions about their authorship, their relation to hagiographical and to other narrative and traditions, the source of their authority, their character and function as normative texts, their level of codification, and their textual form, use, afterlife, and reception, can be productively asked about any monastic rule. From this point of view, the term "rule" is equivocal, for these texts regulated monastic life in diverse ways and different senses. By considering early monastic rules in relation to such questions, we can better appreciate the progression toward a "Benedictine" understanding of the regular life.

CAESARIUS: A HOLY RULE FOR A HOLY COMMUNITY

Bishop Caesarius of Arles (d. 542) lived two hundred years after Pachomius, but he was a contemporary of some of Pachomius's later hagiographers. Early in his career, Caesarius founded a community of religious women outside the city walls of Arles. When this monastery was destroyed during a siege in 508, Caesarius moved his nuns within the city and built for them a strictly enclosed dwelling close to his own cathedral church.[29] Total enclosure would be the hallmark of Caesarius's community. His nuns were strictly prohibited from leaving the confines of the monastery for the rest of their lives.[30]

28 On the reception of the *Regula Pachomii* in other monastic rules, see De Vogüé, *Les règles monastique anciennes*, 14.

29 *Vita Caesarii* I, c. 28, MGH SRM 3, 467; I, c. 35, 470.

30 On monastic enclosure, see Jane T. Schulenburg, "Strict Active Enclosure and Its Effects on the Female Monastic Experience (ca. 500–1200)," in J. A. Nichols and L. T. Shank (eds.), *Medieval Religious Women*, vol. 1: *Distant Echoes* (Kalamazoo: Cistercian Publications, 1984), 51–86; and

At some time before moving his nuns into an enclosed space within the city, Caesarius had addressed them in a long exhortatory letter in which he described the spiritual basis of their life and warned them against engaging in any contact with outsiders. This letter, named after its opening word *Vereor*, exists also in a version addressing monks. It could be considered as a "proto-rule," for which Caesarius chose a non-normative textual form. As an epistolary rule, Caesarius's letter was not unusual. Especially in the fourth and fifth centuries, we find several guidelines for monastic life that were phrased as letters rather than as lists of precepts organized in paragraphs and chapters.[31]

The *Life of Caesarius*, which was written shortly after his death, recounts that he started writing a rule for his foundation after he transferred the community into the city (*Vita Caesarii* I, c. 28), and that he elaborated and amended this text over a period of at least twenty years, taking changing circumstances and the problems arising within community into account. It is this text that Benedict of Aniane included in his collection. The different stages of production of Caesarius's *Rule for Nuns* can still be discerned in its text. They document the genesis and transformation not only of the *Regula* itself but also of his understanding of its normativity.[32]

The first step in this transformation, as already noted, was the move from exhortatory letter to a guide to monastic life written as a list of precepts. In the latter form, it became the first rule written exclusively for a female community. It begins with the requirement of total enclosure:

> If a girl, leaving her parents, desires to renounce the world and enter the holy fold to escape the jaws of the spiritual wolves by the help of God, she must never, up to the time of her death, go out of the monastery, nor into the basilica, where there is a door.[33]

At this point, Caesarius does not yet call his text a *regula*. He describes it rather as "admonishments according to the statutes of the ancient fathers" (*monita secundum statua antiquorum patrum*), and he explains that the differences between the male and female forms of religious life prompted him to select "some of the many things"

Maaike van Rossem, "De poort in de muur. Vrouwenkloosters onder de Regel van Caesarius," *Jaarboek voor vrouwengeschiedenis* 4 (1983): 41–91.

31 Caesarius of Arles, *Epistola "Vereor,"* ed. Adalbert de Vogüé and Joël Courreau, SC 345, 294–337. Other examples of "epistolary Rule" include Jerome's *Epistola* 22 and 125, CSEL 56, 118–42; Ps.-Macharius, *Epistola*, ed. A. Wilmart, "La fausse lettre latine de Macaire," *Revue d'ascéticisme et de mystique* 3 (1922): 411–19; and Evagrios Pontikos, *Epistola ad virginem directa*, ed. André Wilmart, "Les versions latines des sentences d'Evagre pour les vierges," *Revue Bénédictine* 28 (1911): 143–53.

32 On the different phases of the production of Caesarius's *Rule*, see Albrecht Diem, *Das Monastische Experiment. Die Rolle der Keuschheit bei der Entstehung des westlichen Klosterwesens* (Münster: LIT-Verlag, 2005), 154–93.

33 Caesarius, *Regula ad virgines*, c. 2.2 (SC 345, 180), trans. Maria C. McCarthy, *The Rule for Nuns of St. Caesarius of Arles: A Translation with a Critical Introduction* (Washington, DC: Catholic University of America Press, 1960), 170.

(*pauca de pluribus*) pertaining to monks and to adapt them for use with a female community (Caesarius, *Rule for Nuns*, c. 1.2). This characterization is fairly accurate for the first thirty-five chapters of his rule, which consist of practical provisions (especially on enclosure and entry into the monastic life) and of adaptations from older rules written for monks. Chapters 17–35 constitute a long, slightly revised excerpt of the *Rule of Augustine*. The expression *regula* appears only three times in these first thirty-five chapters, and then it refers only in a general way to a regular way of life (*institutio regulae*), not to the text itself.

The tone of chapters 36–47 is profoundly different. These must have been added when the community had already been in existence for some time. They address various practical aspects of organizing and maintaining monastic enclosure. Some of them aim to resolve or prevent conflicts within the community. Several of these chapters contain phrases such as "first and foremost" (*ante omnia*) or "I admonish and charge you ("*ammoneo et contestor*"), which indicate the urgency of the matters addressed and show that Caesarius was getting increasingly anxious about the reputation and success of his project (cc. 36.1, 42.1, 43.1, 47.1). We may assume that these chapters were written in response to challenges arising in the daily life of a community that was still in the process of inventing itself. Chapters from this part of Caesarius's *Rule for Nuns*, for example, prohibit the sisters from doing laundry for outsiders, regulate how craftsmen should enter the monastery for repairs, and aim to prevent nuns from starving themselves (cc. 36, 42, 46).

Unlike the previous chapters, chapters 36–47 are not simply admonishments (*monita*). Instead, Caesarius now calls his work a "holy rule" (*sancta regula*). At one point, he states that nuns transgressing his *Holy Rule* need to be severely punished, for they "should know that they shall have to defend themselves with me before God" (c. 43.4; trans. McCarthy, 185). Moreover, the text now presents itself as a binding norm for a holy community (*grex sancta, congregatio sancta*). Such a community is able to reach salvation through strict adherence to the *Holy Rule* and by maintaining total enclosure. Obedience to the rule becomes a matter of eternal life and death. In the last chapter of this section, which is an admonishment to the abbess, the term "holy" (*sancta*) occurs four times. The tone is remarkably anxious:

> I admonish and I charge you before God and the angels, holy and highly venerated mother of the monastery, and you, the prioress of the holy congregation, let no one's threats or persuasions or flattery ever relax your spirit, and do not yourselves take away anything from the established form of the holy and spiritual rule. I trust, moreover, by the mercy of God, that you will not incur guilt for any negligence, but rather, through your obedience, which is holy and pleasing to God, will be able happily to attain eternal beatitude.[34]

[34] Caesarius, *Regula ad virgines*, c. 47 (232), trans. McCarthy, 187.

For Caesarius, the rule and total enclosure had become the two most important tools to create and maintain a state of collective sanctity, and to ensure that each member of this holy community should attain eternal salvation.

At a later stage, Caesarius added a third section to his rule: a *recapitulatio* in which he declares that this current version, after many changes and improvements, is to be definitive, and that all other versions are henceforth invalid (cc. 48–49). This declaration marks another important transformation: the monastic rule has become a canonical text. Caesarius's *recapitulatio* returns, time and again, to two central topics: to maintaining total enclosure, and to adhering to the unchangeable rule (*institutio sanctae regula*). The rule must not be altered by anyone: not by the abbess, the prioress, or the community; not by any outsider; and especially not by Caesarius's successors to the episcopal see (cc. 62–65). Caesarius mentions in the text that he has received confirmation of his *sancta regula* from the Roman Pontiff (c. 64.1), and his rule bears the signatures of six of his fellow bishops, who confirm its validity (c. 73).

Caesarius not only created, therefore, a new and (as we know from various sources) rather controversial institutional model.[35] He also shaped a new, even revolutionary concept of monastic normativity. He turned the admonitions (*monita*) that he had initially drafted for his community into an unchangeable, legally binding text, and even into a *holy* rule: an instrument for attaining salvation. It is no surprise that Caesarius's *Regula ad virgines* had a profound impact on later developments of regular observance. Several sixth-century monastic rules, for monks as well as for nuns, are based on Caesarius's *Rule*, including the *Regula Tarnatensis*, the *Regula Ferrioli*, and rules of his successor Aurelianus of Arles (d. 551).[36] Aurelianus composed a revised version of Caesarius's text, in which unconditional submission to the *regula* becomes the core of monastic conversion. For Aurelianus, adherence to the *regula* is even more important than monastic enclosure.[37] A hundred years later, bishop Donatus of Besançon (d. c. 660) used Caesarius's *Regula ad virgines* as the basis for his own *Rule for Nuns*, which expands the text with excerpts of the rules of Benedict and Columbanus. Jonas of Bobbio, whom we will encounter in the next section, drafted another *Regula ad*

35 See William E. Klingshirn, "Caesarius's Monastery for Women in Arles and the Composition of the *Vita Caesarii*," *Revue Bénédictine* 100 (1990): 441–81.

36 Albrecht Diem, "… ut si professus fuerit se omnia impleturum, tunc excipiatur. Observations on the Rules for Monks and Nuns of Caesarius and Aurelianus of Arles," in V. Zimmerl-Panagl et al. (eds.), *Edition und Erforschung lateinischer patristischer Texte* (Berlin: De Gruyter, 2014), 191–224.

37 Caesarius's *Rule for Nuns* begins and ends with two chapters addressing the requirement of total enclosure. The first and the last chapter (as it were the alpha and omega) of Aurelianus' *Rule* require unconditional submission under the *Regula*. See Aurelianus of Arles, *Regula ad monachos*, c. 1 and c. 55, ed. Albert Schmidt, "Zur Komposition der Mönchsregel des heiligen Aurelian von Arles," in *Studia Monastica* 17 (1975): 240 and 256.

virgines, and this, too, was probably composed as an extended version of Caesarius's *Rule*.[38]

Two narrative sources confirm the legally binding character of Caesarius's *Rule*. From these we learn that Queen Radegund (d. 587) imported Caesarius's rule into her monastic foundation in Poitiers in order to protect the monastery from external interference, and that Gregory of Tours used the text as a legal basis for suppressing nuns who rebelled in Radegund's monastery after the foundress's death.[39]

Caesarius's *Rule for Nuns* fell out of use after the seventh century, but the idea of a monastic rule as a *sancta regula* – a salvific instrument, and a canonical and legally binding text – survived and took on a life of its own. Another rule, the one allegedly written by Benedict of Nursia around the same time as Caesarius's rule, would become the new, definitive *sancta regula*.

REGULA COLUMBANI

Before turning to the *Regula Benedicti*, I shall briefly address another famous rule with a complicated story: the *Regula Columbani*. This emerged later than the *Regula Benedicti*, but it gained influence more than a century before the *Rule of Benedict* became the binding norm of monastic life in the medieval West.

According to the received narrative, the *Regula Columbani* (as it appears in Benedict of Aniane's *Codex Regularum*) was written by the Irish missionary and monastic founder Columbanus (d. c. 615), and it was initially followed in his three monastic foundations, Luxeuil, Annegray, and Bobbio, as well as later in the various communities affiliated to Luxeuil, which became in effect the "headquarters" of Columbanian monasticism. About a generation after Columbanus's death, the *Regula Columbani* was allegedly combined with the *Regula Benedicti*, which spread throughout Merovingian Francia along with Columbanus's rule. Eventually the *Regula Benedicti* was recognized as more moderate and practicable than Columbanus's harsh precepts, which were left on the wayside. Toward the end of the seventh century, the *Regula Columbani* disappeared from narrative sources.[40]

In fact, the history of Columbanus's rule was more complicated than that narrative implies and reveals yet another way of understanding normativity. Jonas of Bobbio describes in his *Life of Columbanus* how Columbanus composed a rule for his monks at Luxeuil that would serve as their guide whenever his vocation as a hermit or his responsibilities to his other foundations required him to be absent.

38 Albrecht Diem, "Columbanian Monastic Rules: Dissent and Experiment," in R. Flechner and S. Meeder (eds.), *The Irish in Early Medieval Europe: Identity, Culture and Religion* (London: Palgrave Macmillan, 2016), 68–85, at 77–79 (with references).

39 *Letter of Abbess Caesaria to Richildis and Radegund*, 63–73, SC 345, 686. Gregory of Tours, *Decem libri historiarum* IX, c. 39, MGH SRM 1, 463.

40 Friedrich Prinz, *Frühes Mönchtum im Frankenreich. Kultur und Gesellschaft in Gallien, den Rheinlanden und Bayern am Beispiel der monastischen Entwicklung (4. bis 8. Jhd.)*, 2nd ed. (Munich: Oldenbourg, 1988), 263–92.

Here we have an example of another rationale for a written rule: to serve as a substitute for an absent (or sometimes deceased) charismatic leader. Jonas writes:

> After he had settled the community of monks in these places, he divided his time between them, and filled with the Holy Spirit he set down a rule which they were to follow. The sensible reader or listener [*prudens lector vel auditor*] realizes in this the excellence of the holy man and the extent of his religious instruction.[41]

Just as in the several *Lives* of Pachomius and in the *Life of Benedict* (which I shall discuss in the next section), so here there is a striking discrepancy between the hagiographic narrative and the evidence provided in the rule itself. The text that has come down to us as the *Rule of Columbanus* consists of two parts that were transmitted under the titles *Regula Columbani, Regula monachorum*, or *Regula coenobialis*. Both parts appear, sometimes conjoined and sometimes separately, in the manuscripts in numerous variants that differ in size and content, indicating that the rule was considered a "living text," which could be adapted to circumstances, rather than as a codified set of norms.[42]

This "monastic rule of the abbot and confessor saint Columbanus" (*Regula coenobialis sancti Columbani abbatis et confessoris*), as it is called in Benedict of Aniane's *Codex Regularum*, shows little resemblance to the other rules in Benedict's collection. The first part, entitled *Regula monachorum* in its (problematic) modern edition, is an ascetic treatise about several monastic virtues and ideals – obedience, silence, fasting, poverty, chastity, *discretio, mortificatio*, and *perfectio* – combined with an outline of monastic liturgy. The second part, which modern editors call *Regula coenobialis*, is a penitential handbook addressing ritual and social transgressions in a monastic community. Neither part can properly be called a normative text. These texts make sense neither as a substitute for an absent leader (as Jonas would have it) nor as a program for the "Columbanian" monastic reform movement, which would profoundly change the monastic landscape in Gaul and shape what we now know as "medieval monasticism."

Aside from describing the genesis of Columbanus's *Rule*, Jonas of Bobbio refers to the *Regula Columbani* in other respects at several points throughout his *Life of Columbanus:* mostly in the context of the foundations of Luxeuil's affiliations, but also twice when describing conflicts pertaining to Luxeuil itself. It is striking, therefore, that Jonas, apart from two very vague allusions to the *Regula coenobialis*, entirely ignores and content of Columbanus's *Regula monachorum* and *Regula*

41 Jonas, Vita Columbani I, c. 10, MGH Scriptores rerum Germanicarum in usum scholarum separatim editi 37, 170. Trans. by Ian Wood and Alexander O'Hara, *Jonas of Bobbio Life of Columbanus, Life of John of Réomé, and Life of Vedast*, Translated Texts for Historians (Liverpool: Liverpool University Press, 2016), 117–18.

42 *Regula monachorum and Regula coenobialis*, ed. G. S. M. Walker, *Columbani opera* (Dublin: Dublin Institute for Advanced Studies, 1957), 122–69. On these texts, see Diem, "Columbanian Monastic Rules," 68–71 (with references).

coenobialis.[43] Jonas's work contains numerous outlines of the guidelines prescribed by Columbanus and his successors as well as descriptions of monastic practices in Luxeuil, Bobbio, and Faremoutiers (the first Columbanian monastery for women), but none of these matches the content of Columbanus's rules as they have come down to us.[44] Rather than quotations of or allusions to parts of the *Regula Columbani*, what we find in Jonas's Life are numerous passages that have parallels, as regards both content and language, to another work included in the *Codex Regularum*: an anonymous female monastic rule that Benedict of Aniane describes merely as *Someone's Rule for Nuns* (*Regula cuiusdam ad virgines*). The sheer number of parallels – there are more than a hundred – makes it likely that Jonas himself was the "someone" (*quidam*) who composed this anonymously transmitted rule.[45] It is unlikely, therefore, that Jonas had Columbanus's *Regula monachorum* or *Regula coenobialis* in mind when he referred to the *Regula Columbani*. Instead, he may have considered his own writings, both his *Vita* and the *Regula ad virgines*, as the most authentic textual representation of Columbanus's ideals or way of life. I suggest, therefore, that the so-called *Regula Columbani* should be understood not as a single specific written text but rather as heavily contested representations of Columbanus's monastic ideal, which could manifest themselves in a variety of texts: in Columbanus's own works, in his *Life*, in other "Columbanian" monastic rules, and in the Lives of Columbanus's followers.[46] The rule as an ideal has been "textualized" differently by each party who claimed to profess its most authentic understanding.

Jonas does not conceal the fact that Columbanus's legacy was highly contested. In his *Life of Columbanus*, God's favor eventually determined who could rightfully claim to follow the "true" *Regula Columbani*. According to the *Vita Columbani*, all opponents of Columbanus and his successors fell prey to God's vengeance. Hardly any other saint's Life recounts as many casualties as Jonas of Bobbio's *Vita Columbani*.[47]

The *Vita Columbani* points toward another innovation, which may seem at first glance to contradict the idea of the *Regula Columbani* as a contested monastic program. Jonas lists a number of monasteries that were founded with the support of Luxeuil after Columbanus's death. All of them were, as Jonas emphasizes, founded

43 The allusions are in Jonas, *Vita Columbani* II, c. 9, 250–51.

44 See especially Jonas, *Vita Columbani* I, c. 5, 161–62 – a short description of the way of life of Columbanus's community.

45 This aspect will be discussed in my forthcoming edition of the *Regula cuiusdam ad virgines*. See also Albrecht Diem and Matthieu van der Meer, *Columbanische Klosterregeln* (St. Ottilien: EOS, 2016), 51–66.

46 This argument is developed more extensively in Albrecht Diem, "Was bedeutet Regula Columbani?" in Maximilian Diesenberger and Walter Pohl (eds.), *Integration und Herrschaft. Ethnische Identitäten und soziale Organisation im Frühmittelalter* (Vienna: Verlag der Österreichischen Akademie der Wissenschaften, 2002), 63–89.

47 Albrecht Diem, "Monks, Kings and the Transformation of Sanctity: Jonas of Bobbio and the End of the Holy Man," *Speculum* 82 (2007): 521–59.

on the basis of Columbanus's rule (*ex regula Columbani*: Jonas, *Vita Columbani* I, cc. 24, 26; II, cc. 9–11). As we know not only from Jonas himself but also from other hagiographic and diplomatic sources, most of the earliest Columbanian monastic foundations, such as Rebais, Solignac, Remiremont, and Grandvalle, were founded on royal fiscal land by members of aristocratic families that had supported Columbanus, in collaboration with the abbots of Luxeuil and with support from local bishops, who often were members of the same aristocratic families. These monasteries were usually headed by an abbot who had been a monk at Luxeuil.[48] The term *Regula Columbani* here seems to refer primarily to a very specific legal construction: one that involves all of these different parties and is designed to ensure (albeit with little success in the end) that the abbots of Luxeuil, as Columbanus's successors, would retain the ultimate control over the newly founded monasteries. Yet another textual manifestation of this *Regula Columbani*, construed as a legal construction, may be found in the few preserved episcopal privileges for Columbanian monasteries, which describe the process of monastic foundation in great detail. Eventually, however, the *Regula Benedicti* would supersede the *Regula Columbani* in Carolingian monastic foundation charters and royal privileges.

THE *RULE OF BENEDICT*

Gregory the Great describes in the second book of his *Dialogues* (the *Vita Benedicti*) how Benedict of Nursia, the founder of Montecassino, wrote down toward the end of his life a rule that was "both excellent for its discretion and eloquent for its style."[49] Scholars generally assume that it was Benedict of Nursia's work that became, in the course of monastic reforms at the beginning of the ninth century, the guiding norm for monastic life. Thus, monasticism became "Benedictine" under Carolingian rule. But, as in the other cases I have described, there are several problems with this deceptively straightforward narrative.

Whether the rule mentioned in Gregory's *Life of Benedict* was indeed the text that we know as *Regula Benedicti* should be treated as an open question, although in the received tradition each was a lens for interpreting the other.[50] The narrative that connects the alleged origin of the *Regula Benedicti* with its triumph during the Carolingian period is largely based on sources describing events that happened centuries before they were recorded. The text of the *Regula Benedicti*, as we know it, left no traces in Gregory the Great's work, so it is unlikely that Gregory himself knew it.[51] We find its earliest traces in the first decades of the seventh century in Gaul

[48] See Yaniv Fox, *Power and Religion in Merovingian Gaul. Columbanian Monasticism and the Frankish Elites* (Cambridge: Cambridge University Press, 2014); and Jamie Kreiner, *The Social Life of Hagiography in the Merovingian Kingdom* (Cambridge: Cambridge University Press, 2014).

[49] Gregory the Great, *Dialogi* II, c. 36, ed. Adalbert de Vogüé and Paul Antin, SC 260, 242.

[50] See Diem, "Inventing the Holy Rule," 72–76.

[51] Kassius Hallinger, "Papst Gregor der Große und der hl. Benedikt," in Basilius Steidle (ed.), *Commentationes in Regulam S. Benedicti* (Rome: Herder, 1957), 231–319, at 269–77.

and, somewhat later, in Anglo-Saxon England. The oldest surviving manuscript of the *Regula Benedicti* was produced in Anglo-Saxon England, probably at the beginning of the eighth century – more than 150 years after it was supposedly written.[52] The first source that links the "blessed" (*benedictus*) author of this rule with the protagonist of Gregory's *Life of Benedict* is Bede's *Historia Abbatum*, which was written roughly 180 years after Benedict's death (if we assume that the latter died around 550).[53] Montecassino, the alleged place of origin of the *Regula Benedicti*, had been destroyed by Lombard warriors and was rebuilt around 718, after an absence of some 150 years. It was an Anglo-Saxon monk, Willibald, who taught his newly founded community how to live according to the *Regula Benedicti*. It is not unlikely that it was Willibald who brought the text from Anglo-Saxon England to Montecassino.[54] The widely accepted narrative that the autograph of the *Regula Benedicti* was saved after the Lombards had raided Montecassino and returned to the monks there under Pope Zachary (d. 752) was first told by the monk and historiographer Paul the Deacon (d. 799), toward the end of the eighth century.[55] We shall probably never know for sure whether the *Regula Benedicti* as we know it came originally from Montecassino or from elsewhere in Italy – or even from Gaul or from Anglo-Saxon England.

It is unclear, too, whether the rule known as the *Regula Benedicti* was the work of a single author. It is evidently composite, and there are parts that could stand on their own, such as the prologue, chapter 4 (The Instruments of Good Works), chapter 7 (The Twelve Steps of Humility), and the outline of the Divine Office in chapters 8–18.[56] The oldest textual witnesses of the *Regula Benedicti* are the two Columbanian rules for nuns that I mentioned in the previous section: the *Rule of Donatus* and the anonymous *Regula cuiusdam ad virgines*. Both of these rules used large parts of the *Regula Benedicti*, but they show no traces either of its prologue or of chapter 8–18. Perhaps the authors used a version of the *Regula Benedicti* that did not contain these parts. If it was in fact composed from several pre-existing texts, the *Regula Benedicti* would not be exceptional. Several rules combine texts written by different authors or at different times.[57]

52 Oxford, Bodleian Library, Hatton 48. See Ludwig Traube, *Textgeschichte der Regula S. Benedicti*, 2nd edition, ed. Heribert Plenkers (Munich: Verlag der Königlich-Bayerischen Akadademie der Wissenschaften, 1910).

53 Bede, *Historia abbatum*, c. 11, ed. Charles Plummer, *Venerabilis Baedae Opera Historica* (Oxford: Oxford University Press, 1896), 375.

54 Hugeburc, *Vita Willibaldi*, c. 5, MGH Scriptores (in Folio) 15.1 (1887), 102–03.

55 Paulus Diaconus, *Historia Langobardorum* IV, c. 17, MGH *Scriptores rerum Langobardicarum et Italicarum*, 122; IV, c. 40, 178–79.

56 For example, Würzburg, Universitätsbibliothek, M.p.th.q.22, s. IX$^{1/4}$.

57 See, e.g., *Regula quattuor patrum*, ed. Adalbert de Vogüé, SC 297, 180–204 (four different addresses to a monastic community); *Regula orientalis*, SC 298, 462–95 (excerpts of the *Regula patrum secunda* and the *Regula Pachomii*); *Regula Eugipii*, ed. Fernando Villégas and Adalbert de Vogüé, CSEL 87 (excerpts from the *Rules* of Augustine, Basil, Pachomius, Cassian's *Institutiones*, and other texts).

The heterogeneity of the *Regula Benedicti* manifests itself especially when one looks at the use of the term *regula* – a consideration that brings us back to the question of how the notion of *vita regularis* evolved.[58] The prologue to the *Regula Benedicti* presents itself as the commands of a *praecepta magistri* (master) and an *admonitio* (admonitory counsel) addressed to an individual disciple who should listen with the ears of his heart (RB, prologue, 1). The term *regula* does not appear at all in this part of the text. Chapter 7 of the *Regula Benedicti* identifies observing a *regula* as the eighth of twelve steps of humility – placing this virtue rather low on the list. Previous steps include, for example, revealing evil thoughts, being content with anything shabby, and judging oneself as unworthy. This is a far cry from Caesarius's idea of the *Sancta Regula* as a salvific instrument. The epilogue of the *Regula Benedicti* (c. 71) describes the text simply as a "rule for beginners" – a point of departure for religious who are aspiring to higher goals. Benedict recommends as ideal companions the works of the "holy catholic fathers" (*sanctorum catholicorum patrum*), John Cassian's *Conferences*, and the Scriptures, in both the Old and the New Testaments, which are the truest "norm of human life."

Benedict also uses the noun *regula* and the adjective *regularis* in the context of punishments for various transgressions. Thus, he speaks of the "discipline of a rule" (*disciplina regulae*) and of discipline, correction or reproof, and punishment as being "regular," that is, done according to a rule (*disciplina regularis, correptio regularis, vindicta regularis*; see cc. 3.10, 32.5, 48.20, 54.5, 65.19, 67.6, 70.6). There is no indication, however, that these phrases refer to the written rule itself, which for the most part leaves the abbot to decide what punishments a monk should receive for his transgressions. Here, it seems, the rule to which Benedict refers is probably the monastery's regime or way of life.

The *Regula Benedicti* contains several references to a *Regula* that can only be this written rule itself. Usually, Benedict talks in these contexts about "this rule" (*haec regula*) or "the present rule" (*praesens regula*), implying a distinction between monastic rules in general and this rule in particular. All monks, including ordained monks, the prior, and the abbot are bound to follow "this rule" (*haec regula*), which is to be read out to the community routinely and during mealtimes, so that no one has the excuse of ignorance. (cc. 3.7, 11; 60.2, 5, 9; 62.2–3; 64.20; 65.17; 66.8). Postulants have to listen to the entire rule three times, after two, six, and ten months; and they need to understand this rule as the law (*lex*) under which they ought to serve. A monk is admitted if he promises to observe and to fulfill everything, being aware that everything is determined by the law of the rule (*lege regulae constitutum*). From that day forth, he is not allowed to leave the monastery or to shake off from his

58 Christoph Dartmann, "Normative Schriftlichkeit im früheren Mittelalter: das benediktinische Mönchtum," *Zeitschrift der Savigny-Stiftung für Rechtsgeschichte, Kanonistische Abteilung* 100 (2004): 1–61, at 21–28, makes similar observations about the various meanings of *regula* and the various concepts of normativity within RB.

neck the yoke of the rule, to which he has freely committed himself (58.9–16). On three occasions, Benedict refers to what his own *regula* says about a specific issue: regarding disobedience, silence, and diet (23.1–2, 37.1, 42.9).

Thus, the *Regula Benedicti* develops no less than eight different concepts of *regula*: as teachings of the master to a disciple; as a *disciplina regularis* that goes beyond the written text, which by implication is only a part of a larger, not wholly written rule; as the monastic law (*lex*) that needs to be professed and read out; as a particular regulation contained in the rule; as a guideline for beginners; as the practical application of Scripture, which is the truest *regula*; as a tool for exercising humility; and as the formal and legal basis for monastic conversion. Each of these meanings has different implications regarding the function of the text itself.

The diverse meanings of the term *regula* in the *Regula Benedicti* may have posed a particular challenge at the time when Carolingian reformers tried to turn this rule into a binding norm for all monasteries. The text was at this point roughly 250 years old and not up to date. It had been written for a community of ascetic enthusiasts living in the fractured, late-Roman world, and not for Carolingian monasteries, which played a prominent economic and political role: as places of recruitment for a new political elite; as places of learning and the preservation of knowledge; as sources of moral correction (*correctio, emendatio*) for the entire Frankish people; as shrines of saints and places of pilgrimage; and, above all, as powerhouses of intercessory prayer.[59] Living entirely according to the organizational precepts of the *Regula Benedicti* was hardly possible in a Carolingian context, where the social composition and duties of monks in relation to society at large required a system of values and monastic practices for which the *Regula Benedicti* could at most serve as a source of inspiration.[60]

This does not mean that Carolingian monastic reformers did not take the text of the *Regula Benedicti* seriously, or that they regarded its title as a "rule" only as a convenient label. On the contrary, in order to give this rule a place within the broader society, Carolingian monastic scholars developed a number of different, often barely compatible or even contradictory ways of interpreting and applying it. Perhaps led by the various understandings of the term *regula* within the *Regula Benedicti* itself, Carolingian monks created, as it were, a number of different rules out of the same text. Many of these different ways of reading the *Regula Benedicti* are similar to, and perhaps inspired by, the concepts and uses of rules that we encountered in our exploration of other early-medieval monastic norms. The *Regula Benedicti* functioned as a *sancta regula*, following the model of Caesarius's *Rule for Nuns*.[61] Carolingian councils uses it as a quarry to be mined for regulations, as

59 Renie S. Choy, *Intercessory Prayer and the Monastic Ideal in the Time of the Carolingian Reforms* (Oxford: Oxford University Press, 2017). Dartmann, "Normative Schriftlichkeit," 42–46, makes a similar point about the anachronistic character of RB.

60 This issue is discussed more fully in Diem, "The Carolingians and the *Regula Benedicti*."

61 The term *Regula sancta* appears frequently in the acts of Carolingian councils, *Capitularia*, and royal charters. For a list, see Diem, "Inventing the Holy Rule," 64 n. 66.

their predecessors had done with the *Regula Pachomii*.[62] Excerpts from the text were used for pastoral purposes outside the monastery.[63] The text was elaborated with new regulations reflecting changed circumstances and current problems.[64] It was used as a spiritual text and as the object of exegesis[65] – a privilege otherwise reserved for the Scriptures. The text was the basis for granting legal rights in royal charters, as was the *Regula Columbani*. It was inscribed in narratives and especially in hagiographic texts, as Jonas had done with the *Regula Columbani* in his *Vita Columbani*.[66] It became a precious, representative object.[67] Like a liturgical text, it was read out to an audience on a regular basis.[68] It was reduced to certain aspects, such as its liturgical program, or the right of the monks to choose their own abbot (which may have been one of the main incentives for monasteries to adopt the *Regula Benedicti*). It was even used to train novices in the Latin language.[69] Thus, while the *Rule of Benedict* became the legal basis of medieval monasticism, it was always a multifunctional, adaptable text, with special meanings for particular communities and in particular situations.

THE MONASTIC RULE AS NORMATIVE TEXT

Considered independently, the rules of Pachomius, Caesarius, Columbanus, and Benedict represent four different concepts of normativity, none of which entirely matches any post-Carolingian notion of regular observance. The differences manifest themselves not only in the content of each rule but also in such aspects as their sources of authority (angelic, rule of a charismatic founder, "textualized" teaching, legal confirmation, holy rule, and so forth); the ways in which they were used (as textual quarry, salvific tool, theological program, legal text, juridical basis for a foundation or precondition of granting rights and privileges); and their degree of

62 For example, *Capitula ad lectionem canonum et regulae S. Benedicti pertinentia* (802), c. 23, MGH Capitularia 1, 109.

63 Diem, "The Carolingians," 253–54.

64 As with the *Regula Pachomii*, Benedict of Aniane's expansion of RB exists in different versions: as inserted in his Ardo Smaragdus's *Vita Benedicti Anianensis*, cc. 37–38, 216–17; and as a list of very specific, arguably pedantic regulations, ed. Josef Semmler, *Corpus Consuetudinum Monasticarum* 1 (Siegburg: Schmitt, 1963), 515–36.

65 Especially in the commentaries of Smaragdus and Hildemar: See Diem, "The Carolingians and the *Regula Benedicti*," 246–51.

66 For a case study on inscribing a *Regula* into a hagiographic text, see Albrecht Diem, "Die 'Regula Columbani' und die 'Regula Sancti Galli'. Überlegungen zu den Gallusviten in ihrem karolingischen Kontext," in F. Schnoor et al. (eds.), *Gallus und seine Zeit. Leben, Wirken, Nachleben* (St. Gallen: Verlag am Klosterhof, 2015), 65–97.

67 It is treated thus in, e.g., Munich, Bayerische Staatsbibliothek, Clm. 19408, s. VIII^{ex}; Stiftsbibliothek St. Gallen, 914 and 915; Würzburg, Universitätsbibliothek, M.p.th.q.22; and New York, Pierpont Morgan Library, M. 642.

68 Ardo, *Vita Benedicti Anianensis*, c. 38, 207–08. Smaragdus, *Expositio Regulae* c. 3.66.8, ed. Pius Engelbert and Adalbert Spannagel, *Corpus Consuetudinum Monasticarum* 8 (Siegburg: Schmitt, 1974), 325. See also Dartmann, "Normative Schriftlichkeit im früheren Mittelalter," 32.

69 *Glosae in Regula Sancti Benedicti Abbatis*, ed. Matthieu van der Meer, CCM 282.

textualization (a list of ad hoc regulations, excerpts of the works of the "holy fathers," a *florilegium* of excerpts drawn from other rules, a codified, unchangeable text, the textual manifestation of an abstract rule). If we broadened the pool by adding, for example, Augustine's *Praeceptum*, the *Ordo monasterii*, the *Regula magistri*, the four other "Columbanian" monastic rules, and the four Visigothic monastic rules, we should complicate the meaning of the term *regula* and the concept of regular observance even more.[70]

Nevertheless, there were some important developments. We noted above that the term *regula* is used in the *Regula Benedicti* in diverse ways. The first chapter of this rule, like the *Rule of the Master*, contains a remarkable statement: that coenobitic monks in a properly disciplined community live "under a rule and an abbot" (*sub regula vel abbate*).[71] This statement occurs in a four-fold typology of monks that contrasts the two acceptable forms of monastic life with two false ones. There are two acceptable types: the coenobites, and the hermits who have first been trained as coenobites. The unacceptable types are the sarabaites, who are not living according to any rule or obedience, and the gyrovagues: vagrants who freeload at the expense of properly constituted monastic communities.

The Master and Benedict adapted in their opening chapters older typologies of monks, such as we find them, for example, in a letter of Jerome or in John Cassian's *Conferences*,[72] but they added, crucially, the premise that a rule is what determines whether a monk or a monastic community is living an acceptable life. Two of the other three monastic rules discussed in this essay make similar but less radical claims. In the case of Pachomius, it is the hagiographic tradition that retroactively transforms Pachomius into the founder of "regular" coenobitic monasticism. Caesarius defines the *sancta regula* as a salvific instrument within his own specific monastic experiment.

The first half of the sixth century seems to have been a period in which the notion that a normative text was the basis for monastic life was promoted with increasing vigor. The "invention" and propagation of regular observance does not mean, however, that Benedict's claim that true monks live "under a rule and an abbot" (*sub regula vel abbate*) was already generally accepted around the middle of the sixth century. On the contrary, there is overwhelming evidence that most monastic communities still operated without a written or unwritten rule and continued to do so until the Carolingian period. Aristocratic family monasteries such as those of Cassiodorus, Sulpicius Severus, and Paulinus of Nola continued to function without codified or textual rules, as did numerous communities of various forms that

70 For an overview of texts, editions, and manuscripts for these rules, see www.earlymedievalmonasticism.org (accessed March 27, 2018).

71 RB c. 1.1–2, 436: "Monachorum quattuor esse genera manifestum est. Primum coenobitarum, hoc est monasteriale, militans *sub regula vel abate*" (italics mine). Cf. RM 1.2, SC 105, 328.

72 Jerome, *Ep.* 22, c. 34, CSEL 54, 196–97. Cassian, *Collationes* XVIII, c. 4, CSEL 13, 209. See also Adalbert de Vogüé, "Le 'De Generibus Monachorum' du Maître et de Benoît. Sa source – son auteur," *Regulae Benedicti Studia* 2 (1973): 1–25.

emerged beside the burial places of saints and martyrs or were founded by living charismatic ascetics, many of which did not turn into permanent institutions.[73] Hagiographic sources indicating that rules were being followed are scarce. Neither Gregory the Great (d. 604) nor Gregory of Tours (d. c. 594), our main witnesses to the diversity of sixth-century monastic life, expected that monasteries would follow a rule. Nor did they assume that the written *regula* was a distinctively monastic genre. Pope Gregory's *Regula pastoralis*, for example, one of his most important works, was addressed to clerics, not monks, and it is largely a guide to preaching, not a normative text.

It is not until the 670s that we find episcopal councils in Gaul and in the Frankish kingdoms requiring monastic communities live "under a rule" (*sub regula*).[74] In the acts of earlier Merovingian episcopal councils, we find the term *regula* being used more often in the context of clerics than of monks and nuns.[75] But there was an important change in this respect during the course of the seventh century. Foundation narratives of monasteries that emerged in the aftermath of Columbanus's arrival in Gaul began to describe the monastic life as one self-evidently lived *sub regula*.[76] To what extent these post-Columbanian rules were written down remains an open question, as does how much of the "unregulated" monastic diversity survived this innovation.

None of the sources pertaining to the Carolingian monastic reforms and to the triumph of the *Regula Benedicti* in that context indicate that monasteries abandoned prior written rules in order to follow the *Regula Benedicti*. It is likely that for most monasteries, adoption of the *Regula Benedicti* entailed not transferring their allegiance from one normative text to another, but rather adhering to some written rule – in other words, pursuing a text-based *vita regularis* – for the first time. Nor did this shift imply that henceforth these communities would sail in the calm waters of "Benedictine monasticism." The question of the meaning, function, and the legal character of the *Regula Benedicti* would remain a matter of variance and even strife and contention throughout and even beyond the medieval period.

73 Compare Roberto Alciati, "And the Villa Became a Monastery: Sulpicius Severus' Community of Primuliacum," in Dey and Fentress, *Western Monasticism ante litteram*, 85–98. On sixth-century monastic diversity, see Albrecht Diem, "Gregory's Chess Board: Monastic Conflict and Competition in Early Medieval Gaul," in Philippe Depreux et al. (eds.), *Compétition et sacré au haut Moyen Âge: entre médiation et exclusion* (Turnhout: Brepols, 2015), 165–91.

74 Hubert Mordek and Roger E. Reynolds, "Bischof Leodegar und das Konzil von Autun," in H. Mordek (ed.), *Aus Archiven und Bibliotheken. Festschrift für Raymund Kottje zum 65. Geburtstag* (Frankfurt am Main: Peter Lang, 1992), 71–92.

75 The evidence may be found in the *indices verborum* of CCL 148 and 148a (*Concilia Galliae*).

76 For example, *Vita Walarici*, c. 3, MGH SRM 4, 162; Walahfrid, *Vita Galli* I, c. 1, 285; II, c. 10, 319–20; *Vita Desiderii*, c. 23, 580; *Virtutes Fursei*, c. 3, 441; *Vita Geremari*, c. 6, 629; *Vita Eligii* I, cc. 16–17, 682–84; *Vita Wandregisili*, cc. 11 and 14, MGH SRM 18–19; *Vita Germani Grandivallensis*, c. 5, 35; *Vita Sadalbergae*, c. 2, 51; *Vita Remacli*, c. 6, 108; *Passio Praeiecti*, c. 34, 245; *Vita Ansberti*, c. 5, 622; *Vita Filiberti*, c. 5, 587.

SOURCES

Ardo, *Vita Benedicti Anianensis*. Ed. G. Waitz, MGH Scriptores (in Folio) 15.1 (1887), 198–220. [English translation by Allen Cabaniss in Thomas F. X. Noble and Thomas Head (eds.), *Soldiers of Christ. Saints and Saints' Lives from Late Antiquity and the Early Middle Ages* (University Park, PA: Pennsylvania State University Press, 1995), 213–54.]

Aurelianus of Arles, Regula ad monachos. Ed. Albert Schmidt, "Zur Komposition der Mönchsregel des heiligen Aurelian von Arles," *Studia Monastica* 17 (1975): 237–56.

Benedict of Aniane, Codex Regularum, PL 103 (selections). [See also *Codex Regularum des Benedikt von Aniane: Faksimile der Handschrift Clm 28118 der Bayerischen Staatsbibliothek München*, ed. Pius Engelbert (Sankt Ottilien: EOS Editions, 2016).]

Benedict of Aniane, *Concordia Regularum*. CCM 168A (1999).

Boon, Amand. *Pachomiana Latina. Règle et épitres de S. Pachome, épitre de S. Théodore et "liber" de S. Orsiesius*. Leuven: Bureaux de la Revue, 1932.

Caesarius of Arles, *Oeuvres Monastiques*. Ed. A. de Vogüé and J. Courreau, SC 345 and 398 (1988, 1994).

Caesarius of Arles, *Regula ad virgines*. Ed. A. de Vogüé and J. Courreau, SC 345 (1988), 170–272. [English translation by Maria C. McCarthy, *The Rule for Nuns of St. Caesarius of Arles: A Translation with a Critical Introduction* (Washington, DC: Catholic University of America Press, 1960).]

Columbanus, *Regula monachorum* and *Regula coenobialis*. Ed. and trans. G. S. M. Walker, *Columbani opera* (Dublin: Dublin Institute for Advanced Studies, 1957), 122–69.

Dionysius Exiguus, *Vita Pachomii*. Ed. H. van Cranenburgh, *La Vie Latine de Saint Pachôme*. Brussels: Societé des Bollandistes, 1969.

Halkin, François. *Sancti Pachomii Vitae Graecae*. Brussels: Societé des Bollandistes, 1932.

Jonas of Bobbio, *Vita Columbani*. Ed. Bruno Krusch, MGH *Scritpores rerum Germanicarum in usum scholarum separatim editi* 37 (1905). [English translation by Ian Wood and Alexander O'Hara, *Jonas of Bobbio Life of Columbanus, Life of John of Réomé, and Life of Vedast*, Translated Texts for Historians (Liverpool: Liverpool University Press, 2016).]

Mordek, Hubert, and Roger E. Reynolds. "Bischof Leodegar und das Konzil von Autun." In H. Mordek (ed.), *Aus Archiven und Bibliotheken. Festschrift für Raymund Kottje zum 65. Geburtstag* (Frankfurt am Main: Peter Lang, 1992), 71–92.

Regula Benedicti. Ed. Jean Neufville and Adalbert de Vogüé. SC 181 and 182 (1971, 1972).

Regula Donati. Ed. Victoria Zimmerl-Panagl, CSEL 98 (2015).

Regula Eugipii. Ed. Fernando Villégas and Adalbert de Vogüé. CSEL 87 (1976).

Regula magistri. Ed. Adalbert de Vogüé. SC 105 and 106 (1964, 1965).

Regula orientalis. Ed. Adalbert de Vogüé, SC 298 (1982), 462–95.

Regula quattuor patrum. Ed. Adalbert de Vogüé, SC 297 (1982), 180–204.

Veilleux, Amand. *Pachomian Koinonia*, vol. 1. Kalamazoo: Cistercian Publications, 1980.

FURTHER READING

Agamben, Giorgio. *The Highest Poverty: Monastic Rules and Form-of-Life*. Palo Alto: Stanford University Press, 2013.

Choy, Renie S. *Intercessory Prayer and the Monastic Ideal in the Time of the Carolingian Reforms*. Oxford: Oxford University Press, 2017.

Dartmann, Christoph. "Normative Schriftlichkeit im früheren Mittelalter: das benediktinische Mönchtum." ZRG Kan. Abt. 100 (2004): 1–61

De Jong, Mayke. "Carolingian Monasticism: The Power of Prayer." In Rosamond McKitterick (ed.), *The New Cambridge Medieval History*, vol. 2: *c.* 700–*c.* 900 (Cambridge: Cambridge University Press, 1995), 622–53, 995–1002.

Dey, Hendrik, and Elizabeth Fentress (eds.). *Western Monasticism ante litteram. The Spaces of Monastic Observance in Late Antiquity and the Early Middle Ages*. Disciplina Monastica 8. Turnhout: Brepols, 2011.

Diem, Albrecht. "Columbanian Monastic Rules: Dissent and Experiment." In R. Flechner and S. Meeder (eds.), *The Irish in Early Medieval Europe: Identity, Culture and Religion* (London: Palgrave Macmillan, 2016), 68–85.

"The Carolingians and the *Regula Benedicti*." In D. van Espelo et al. (eds.), *Religious Franks Religion and Power in the Frankish Kingdoms: Studies in Honour of Mayke de Jong* (Manchester: Manchester University Press, 2016), 243–61.

"... ut si professus fuerit se omnia impleturum, tunc excipiatur. Observations on the Rules for Monks and Nuns of Caesarius and Aurelianus of Arles." In V. Zimmerl-Panagl et al. (eds.), *Edition und Erforschung lateinischer patristischer Texte* (Berlin: De Gruyter, 2014), 191–224.

"Die 'Regula Columbani' und die 'Regula Sancti Galli'. Überlegungen zu den Gallusviten in ihrem karolingischen Kontext." In Franziska Schnoor et al. (eds.), *Gallus und seine Zeit. Leben, Wirken, Nachleben* (St. Gallen: Verlag am Klosterhof, 2015), 65–97.

"Inventing the Holy Rule: Some Observations on the History of Monastic Normative Observance in the Early Medieval West." In H. Dey and E. Fentress (eds.), *Western Monasticism ante litteram: The Spaces of Monastic Observance in Late Antiquity and the Early Middle Ages*, Disciplina Monastica 8 (Turnhout: Brepols, 2011), 53–84.

"Was bedeutet Regula Columbani?" In M. Diesenberger and W. Pohl (eds.), *Integration und Herrschaft. Ethnische Identitäten und soziale Organisation im Frühmittelalter* (Vienna: Verlag der Österreichischen Akademie der Wissenschaften, 2002), 63–89.

Diem, Albrecht, and Philip Rousseau. "Monastic Rules, 4th–9th c." in Alison Beach and Isabelle Cochelin (eds.), *The Cambridge History of Western Medieval Monasticism*, vol. 1 (in press).

Hallinger, Kassius, "Papst Gregor der Große und der hl. Benedikt." In B. Steidle (ed.), *Commentationes in Regulam S. Benedicti* (Rome: Herder, 1957), 231–319.

Schulenburg, Jane Tibbetts. "Strict Active Enclosure and Its Effects on the Female Monastic Experience (ca. 500–1100)." In J. A. Nichols and L. T. Shank (eds.), *Medieval Religious Women*, vol. 1: *Distant Echoes* (Kalamazoo: Cistercian Publications, 1984), 51–86.

Semmler, Josef. "Benedictus II: una regula – una consuetudo." In W. Lourdaux and D. Verhelst (eds.), *Benedictine Culture 750–1050* (Leuven: Leuven University Press, 1983), 1–49.

PART II

10

Lactantius

Elizabeth DePalma Digeser

L. Caelius Firmianus Lactantius developed the first systematic argument for Christian *patientia* in the face of religious difference. To show patience, in this sense, was to refrain from enforcing what is due in matters of religious observance. His position is consonant with notions of religious toleration or concord that philosophers such as John Locke set out in the context of the Protestant Reformation. The emperor Constantine (r. 306–337 CE), to whose court in Trier (southwestern Germany) Lactantius belonged, was receptive to this concept. And it was a core tenet of Lactantius's seven-volume treatise, *The Divine Institutes*, for which he took inspiration from texts designed to teach Roman legal principles. The *Divine Institutes* is the chief source for the account of Lactantius on law and religious diversity that follows.

Lactantius was a North African professor of rhetoric, whom the emperor Diocletian (r. 284–305) had summoned to his court in Nicomedia (Izmit, Turkey) shortly before issuing the edicts that initiated what became known as the "Great Persecution" (303–311). Lactantius's work drew on the concept of *libertas religionis* (freedom of religion) that the Christian Apologist Tertullian of Carthage (*Ad Scapulam* 2.2) had briefly articulated a century before.[1] Unlike his predecessor, however, Lactantius made this tenet the cornerstone of his work in *The Divine Institutes*, a treatise whose aim was to define and advocate for justice. In his view, the Roman state could not achieve justice until people were free to pursue true wisdom and true reverence (*cultus*), qualities that Lactantius found in Christianity. Persecution had motivated him to write, for he believed that people could no longer exercise the free will (*voluntas*) that choosing this way of life required.

LIFE AND WORKS

According to a short account that the late fourth-century Christian author Jerome compiled (*De viris illustribus* 80), Lactantius's origins were in North Africa. The date

[1] For abbreviations used in parenthetic citations, see the list at the end of this chapter.

of his birth is unknown. He studied with Arnobius of Sicca, a professor of rhetoric, probably in Carthage. As a young man, Lactantius wrote a *Symposium* and presumably taught rhetoric in North Africa until Diocletian enjoined him to teach in the new administrative capitol, Nicomedia. Recording his journey in a poem, he arrived in Nicomedia not long before Diocletian issued edicts disenfranchising Christians, who had enjoyed freedom of worship since the reign of Gallienus (260–268). Constantine, the future emperor, also frequented Diocletian's court, and it is possible that he met Lactantius there. After Diocletian condemned Christian churches and Scripture and erased the community's legal standing (February 303), Lactantius remained in Nicomedia for at least two years.

In 306, Constantine succeeded his father to the northwestern throne in Trier (Diocletian had apportioned the early fourth-century Roman imperial administration between himself and three other colleagues). By 314, if not before, Lactantius had joined Constantine's court and had written *De opificio dei* (*On the Work of God*), *Divinae institutiones*, and probably *De mortibus persecutionum* (*On the Deaths of the Persecutors*). Historians argue over where Lactantius was between 305 and 314, with some thinking that he went directly to Trier, possibly as early as 306, and others thinking that he arrived in 314, perhaps after spending time in North Africa. After writing *De mortibus persecutionum*, Lactantius authored *De ira dei* and *Epitome divinarum institutionum*. The precise dates for these are unknown. At some point in his career he also wrote the poem, *De ave phoenicam* (*On the Phoenix*).[2]

The date of Lacantius's death is unknown. Nothing in the record suggests that Lactantius had any religious affiliation other than Christianity. Later theologians disputed his Christology and his views on the Holy Spirit.

THE HISTORICAL CONTEXT

Many historians once supposed that Christian practice was not fully legal in the Roman Empire until Constantine, together with his imperial colleague Licinius, established freedom of religious worship in 313. This assumption, however, defies the testimony of the church historian Eusebius. Not only does he indicate that in 260 the emperor Gallienus recognized the church as a legal association, but he also explicitly states that Christians had religious freedom before Diocletian's edicts (*HE* 8.1). Christians had been able to come out into the open, build their churches, assemble, and even participate in civic life and government. Diocletian's legislation, then, is best understood as a backlash that occurred forty years after Christian practice had entered the Roman public sphere.

Although the text of Diocletian's ruling is no longer extant, clues to his motivations survive in Lactantius's *De mortibus persecutorum*, a polemical tract aiming to

[2] Most historians distinguish Firmianus Lactantius from Lactantius "Placidus," the author of a commentary on Statius's *Thebaid*.

demonstrate how God had punished every emperor who had assaulted Christian churches, and giving special attention to his own day. In particular, the emperor Galerius's law (311) repealing Diocletian's anti-Christian decrees indicates that their intent was to address a situation in which "by virtue of their own authority [*pro arbitrio suo*] and in their own interest, [Christians] were making up for themselves the laws that they were to observe and were assembling a multitude of diverse peoples [*populos*] together for different things [*per diversa*]." Introducing his own account of Diocletian's measures, Eusebius contextualizes Galerius's edict. "The emperors [*kratountōn*]," he says, "committed to [our people] the government of provinces, and ... released them from anxiety in regard to sacrificing." Moreover, "all officers [*epitropois*] and governors [*hēgemosin*]" accorded "the greatest favor" to "the leaders [*archontas*] in every church," who built large new meeting places to accommodate the "famous gatherings," the "vast assemblies, and the multitude that crowded together in every city."

Eusebius blames heated conflict between these church leaders for a persecution that he views as God's justified punishment. Given Galerius's reference to laws and assemblies in his ruling, however, we should pay special attention to what Eusebius says about the situation in the cities and provinces at the turn of the fourth century. On the one hand, we see the tremendous political power that a bishop of a city potentially wielded in attracting a congregation that, in theory at least, cut across traditional ethnic and other social boundaries. On the other hand, we see Christians serving as provincial governors who did not perform the rituals long associated with that office, deciding for themselves which parts of their legal responsibilities they could perform. Galerius's edict thus indicates potential concerns about the extent to which a Christian provincial governor would feel bound by the legal precedents of his province if he was supported by a popular bishop.

When Diocletian assumed the throne in 284, the administration of the legal system had also been upended for some time. Half a century earlier, the Severan dynasty had made the application of Roman law much more uniform throughout the provinces by granting nearly universal citizenship and by codifying provincial law and standardizing its application across the Empire. The assassination of Alexander Severus in 235, however, inaugurated fifty years of upheaval marked by pandemic disease, conflict with a new, aggressive Persian dynasty, frequent Germanic raids into borderland provinces, and recurrent usurpations that also led to political and territorial divisions. Under these circumstances, the Severan legal reforms must surely have languished and grown obsolete.

Diocletian's first task was to restore political order and integrity to the Roman frontiers, which he did by the power-sharing arrangement mentioned earlier, and by an aggressive series of forays against Germanic confederacies and the Persians. As a man who had seized power and not inherited it, Diocletian had nothing but violence upon which to stake his legitimacy, and perhaps for that reason he devised an elaborate political theology advertising himself as the son of Jupiter, or Jovius. His

Eastern subordinate, Galerius, shared this surname, and he dubbed Maxentius, his co-regent in the West, as son of Hercules, or Herculius. Constantius I (Constantine's father) also assumed the latter surname. The emperors' subjects developed the implications of these titles. Disparate fourth-century sources refer to the emperors as incarnate gods or as "lords and gods" (*domini et dei*), and palace protocol came to require full body prostration, as one would perform before a deity. Notwithstanding the silence in these sources regarding how the imperial cult reflected these changes, the conclusion that their effect became more significant within the army, the palace, and the cities is hard to escape.

Of these three settings, most historians have focused on the army as the first locus of conflict between Diocletian's claim to Jovian descent and Christian monotheistic scruples. Indeed, Eusebius says that the persecution began in the army. Even though that may have been the first community in which the emperors chose to enforce obeisance to their new conception of sovereign power, historians tend to overlook the role of urban communities in developing the momentum against the empire's Christian citizens. Nevertheless, it is important to recognize that emperors since the time of Gallienus had not had the luxury of residing in a city for any extended period of time, as they responded to frequent border incursions from Germanic tribes and Persian armies. Moreover, the significance of the *limes* (boundaries) with Persia and the Germanic Danube frontier meant that when Diocletian was finally able to restore peace, he resided not in Rome but in Nicomedia, closer to both arenas. Here, Lactantius tells us, a large church stood facing the palace. The new administrative center, therefore, was home to one of those bishops whose congregation likely brought together formerly disparate ethnic and social groups, offering the prelate a uniquely inclusive clientele: a populus likely averse to the new political theology. The prominence of Nicomedia's church also hints at a long-standing Christian community of some means, whose members, serving as decurions or other civic magistrates, had bent the rules about performing and observing traditional rituals, including those of the imperial cult. Thus, there was a gap between what law and tradition required of civic officials, and what some of them, at least, were willing to enforce. The community that stood apart from law and tradition also represented a cross-section of Nicomedia's population.

That gap between law and tradition on the one hand, and contemporary practice on the other, would also have been apparent to the jurists and philosophers active under Diocletian and his colleagues. In the 290s, two compilations of imperial edicts appeared, the *Codex Gregorianus* and the *Codex Hermogenianus*. Although neither is extant, their traces in later compilations such as the *Visigothic Code* and Justinian's *Code* disclose that their authors aimed to restore the level of organization and provincial standardization that the Severan jurists had accomplished. The *Codex Gregorianus*, in particular, endeavored to collect and organize imperial rescripts since Hadrian's reign (117–138). Although it focused primarily, though not exclusively, on private law, the codex would have embraced efforts by the emperors

Decius (249–251) and Valerian (253–260) to compel citizens to perform ritual sacrifice,[3] as well as Gallienus's recognition of the church as a legal corporation.

The rift separating contemporary practice from law and tradition may also have worried late third-century philosophers, especially those in the circle of the most eminent Platonist, Plotinus. Although historians of philosophy once assumed that "Neoplatonists" avoided both political theory and involvement in public affairs, recent scholarship challenges this view.[4] Plotinus and his student, Porphyry of Tyre, considered that the regulation of worship through legislation was, in practice, a feature of the best regimes. They found their justification for these tenets in Plato's *Laws*, which imagines, not the ideal regime (as in the *Republic*), but rather the best possible state. According to Plato, a community's happiness depends on the diligent pursuit of justice, which in turn requires piety, for the people should regard God, and not other human beings, as their example. Piety consists in "the reverence of gods, spirits, heroes, and ancestors," Plato says, and the lawgiver "should not tamper" with it (*Leg.* 716a–718a; 738). Impiety undermines the regime; piety strengthens it (*Leg.* 889b–e). A government properly constituted along these lines will cultivate virtue (*Leg.* 906) by supporting a cosmic system of justice, allowing each soul after death to live in a region appropriate to its character.

This is the context, then, in which Diocletian issued the first edicts stripping Christians of their civil rights, razing their churches, and incinerating the Scriptures. Historians sometimes wonder why he waited almost twenty years into his reign to move against those opposed to the way his political theology had brought a new spirit to the imperial cult. But the pressure of his campaigns meant that he did not have a settled residence until 300.[5] Moreover, the first city in which he spent any significant length of time was Antioch, home since the first century to a significant Christian community whose prominent members were known to Eusebius and were likely among those who had neglected the imperial cult, some as officials in charge of its observance. In the early fourth century, the emperor's deputy was Sossianus Hierocles. He had close connections to Antioch's Platonist community, who, in turn, wanted to reinvigorate traditional pagan ritual and divination. Hierocles' responsibilities would also have forced him to confront the gap between the civic imperial cult observances for which magistrates were responsible, and what they had actually been doing. Diocletian initially resisted the pressure that Hierocles and the philosophical community brought to bear, and he was willing at first only to force his troops to sacrifice (and this only after a diviner blamed his inability to take the auspices on the presence of Christians at the ritual). Soon, his junior colleague,

3 According to Paul Schubert, "On the Form and Content of the Certificates of Pagan Sacrifice," *Journal of Roman Studies* 106 (2016): 172–98 at 187–89, the emperors required people to taste meat from a blood sacrifice.

4 Dominic J. O'Meara, *Platonopolis: Platonic Political Philosophy in Late Antiquity* (Oxford: Clarendon Press, 2003).

5 Timothy D. Barnes, *The New Empire of Diocletian and Constantine* (Cambridge, MA: Harvard University Press, 1982), 55.

Galerius, assumed leadership of the faction seeking to roll back Christian influence. Through a variety of machinations, they achieved their aim in February 303, when Diocletian issued the first set of edicts from Nicomedia, where Lactantius was residing. Lactantius, therefore, was an eyewitness observer.

The legal targeting of Christians often distracts the gaze of historians writing about this period from the political turbulence that quickly ensued after the emperors issued the edicts. By 310, by which time Lactantius had finished his *Divine Institutes*, Diocletian had retired (305), and Galerius and Constantius had assumed the rank of senior emperors. Galerius had appointed new junior colleagues, Severus and Maximin Daia, ostentatiously overlooking the sons both of Maximian (co-Augustus with Diocletian) and of Constantius. In 306, Constantius died, and his soldiers acclaimed Constantine. In the same year, Maximian's son, Maxentius, seized power at Rome; and within a year, Severus had died attempting to unseat Maxentius. Galerius appointed Licinius to replace Severus.

It makes sense that Lactantius would have written the sort of treatise that he did in this context. Christianity, in his view, was unjustly under siege. He was writing in an era when the educated elite believed that Roman law should be uniform and standardized, and in which a number of prominent intellectuals had argued that the political system should in some way reflect or reinforce fundamental metaphysical truths. In Lactantius's view, Diocletian's system did not do this, for it seemed to smack too much of polytheism. And so he set out, as Plato had done, to imagine a new ideal political association, founded on his own conception of divine law. He dedicated the *Divine Institutes* to Constantine, indicating that his audience included those of the Roman educated elite best equipped to put his ideas into practice. For that reason, he based his arguments not on Scripture but on a host of testimonies from Greek and Roman poets, oracles, and philosophers: precisely those sources most prized by his opposition.

LACTANTIUS AND ROMAN LAW

By revoking privileges from Christians in 303 and 304, Diocletian interrupted four decades during which Christians had practiced their faith while fulfilling their responsibilities as Roman citizens and enjoying the legal protections that came with that status. This caused Lactantius to think deeply about the legal foundation of Rome's government, the role of Christians within it, and what ought to be the case in the future. Lactantius followed the examples of Plato and Cicero: philosophers who had responded to the crises of the Athenian democracy and the Roman Republic, respectively. He also addressed third-century Platonist efforts to theorize about what was the best regime in practice. Mindful of the risks that proposing political change under a hostile government entailed (e.g., Lact. *Inst.* 1.19, 2.3), however, Lactantius made a case that rested as much on allusions and insinuations as it did on straightforward argument.

First, Lactantius argues in the *Divine Institutes* that Christians become a people with a distinct identity through obeying divine law. He does this by flagging the link between his own divine institutes and what the jurist Ulpian had characterized as the *ius publicum*. This comprised the foundation or identity of the Roman state, with laws covering religious affairs playing a key role (Lact. *Inst.* 1.1.2–17; Justinian, *Dig.* 1.1.1.2 and *Inst.* 1.1.1). For Lactantius, God has issued a new law through Christ as a teacher of justice (4.13.1). This divine law (*divina ius*) is not only the basis of the *Divine Institutes*, in his view, but also the defining aspect of the Christian polity, and thus a fundamental element of the identity of Christians as a people. Those who uphold Christ's law are a *populus* apart, for the law has been revealed to them and to no others. Accordingly, only among this *populus* is justice to be found (5.15.1).

Next, having established his intention to educate his readers about public law and its intimate connection to worship, Lactantius invokes Cicero to help imagine a legal foundation that would unite Christians and other Romans in the same political community. According to Lactantius, the "first principle" of divine law is to know God, and to obey and worship only the "author and ruler [*imperator*] of all" (6.8.12; 6.9.1), which echoes Exodus 20:2–3.[6] The second is that man must join himself with his fellow man (6.10.1). Whereas the first law is equivalent to piety (*pietas*) (5.14.12), which Lactantius often equates with cult (*religio*) (4.3.2; 5.14.7–11), the second is equivalent to equity (*aequitas*) (5.14.15). On the one hand, Lactantius's principles echoed the two commandments upon which Jesus based Christian law (Matt 22:36–40).[7] On the other hand, in asserting that piety and equity were the first two principles of divine law, rather than love of God and love of neighbor, Lactantius adopted Cicero's conception of natural law, with "the force of [divine law] being cult [*religio*] and that of [human law] being equity [*aequitas*]" (*Part.* 37.129; Wilkins). Cicero believed that true justice would naturally occur in a *res publica* founded on the principles of natural law, which he saw as comprising both divine law and the dictates of reason (*Leg.* 1.6; *Rep.* 3.22). Lactantius agreed, but for him natural law was grounded in the Gospel.

Thoroughly condemning the rule of the persecuting emperors as illegitimate (Lact. *Inst.* 5.14.19), Lactantius imagined a *res publica* under which Christians – and anyone else revering the One God – could live as full citizens, but under which polytheists had nothing to fear. To accomplish this end, Lactantius divorced public religious observance from good citizenship. Drawing on Cicero again, Lactantius denies that the state has responsibility for policing "impiety." Cicero believed that the gods should be approached chastely, "by people offering piety and laying aside wealth," with God punishing "the one who does differently" (*Leg.* 28. in *Inst.* 5.20.3).

6 "I am the Lord your God . . . you shall have no other gods before me" (NRSV).

7 "When a lawyer asked Jesus, Teacher, which commandment in the law is the greatest? Jesus answered: You shall love the Lord your God with all your heart, with all your soul, and with all your mind. This is the greatest and first commandment. And the second is like it: You shall love your neighbor as yourself. On these two commandments hang all the law and the prophets" (NRSV).

Lactantius takes Cicero to mean that a true deity would reject human coercion to obtain worship (5.20.5). Following Cicero, therefore, Lactantius argued that coercive force was inconsistent with the true spirit of religion (5.19.9). "We put up with practices that should be prohibited," he claims. "We do not resist even verbally, but concede revenge to God" (5.20.9–10). True veneration, Lactantius claims, cannot be forced, for each person must be able to exercise free will (*voluntas*) (5.19.11). And the only way to defend a religious system is through *patientia* (forbearance), that is, by declining to redress a harm (5.19.22). Although he believed that Christianity was the only true religion, he also asserted that one who had chosen this faith without the exercise of reason was useless to God (5.19.12–13). This *res publica*, then, would, as in Cicero, return the populace to a condition of *libertas* in which deliberative reason could prevail. Accordingly, polytheists in this *res publica* would have – indeed *had* to have – their full citizen rights. Otherwise, they could not choose freely to be Christian.

No one who reads the *Divine Institutes* can miss Lactantius's appeal for religious toleration on behalf of the empire's Christian inhabitants. Nevertheless, some scholars have pointed to Lactantius's condemnations of traditional cults as evidence that, if the tables were turned, he would not advocate tolerance of religious diversity under a Christian emperor. This position, however, misunderstands the logic of Lactantius's argument. He maintains that "worship cannot be forced; it is a matter achieved by works, not violence, so that there may be free will" (5.19.11). And he claims that virtue is possible only where evil also exists (2.18; 3.12, 29; 4.24; 5.7). These two principles together require that a Christian sovereign should refrain from coercion. If a Christian emperor forbade traditional religion, for example, he would annul the possibility for free will. This constraint means that Christian subjects of a Christian emperor would continue to live, at least for the short term, among what Lactantius saw as so many evils, for these are precisely the conditions that are the proving ground for Christian virtue. Lactantius certainly looks forward to the day when all people will choose to be Christian, and he imagines that over time, persuasion will achieve this goal. But to suppose that in his view such tolerance is required only of non-Christian emperors in relation to their Christian subjects would be a serious misunderstanding of his argument about *patientia* and *voluntas*.

Finally, Lactantius imagines law as a divinizing agent in the best possible *res publica*. Here, he displays his awareness of the Platonist political theory that helped to justify Diocletian's edicts of 303–304. For Lactantius, the Christians' ancestors, the ancient Hebrews, had created a just society founded on monotheistic piety (Lact. *Inst.* 4.10.5). But like the rest of the world, the Hebrews moved away from monotheism; their descendants became the Jews (4.10.7–11; 14). In Lactantius's view, God repudiated the Jews, but he sent Christ to restore justice, at least for a few (4.11.7). Like a late-Platonist philosopher-lawgiver, Christ – whom Lactantius portrays wearing the philosophers' tunic and pallium (4.18.8) – communicates to humanity a new law that fosters monotheistic piety (4.17.6–7; 11.8).

For Lactantius, the law of Moses is an image of God's divine law. It cryptically embodies the "true precepts of justice" that only Christians can discern because they know the divine law (4.20.1). Here Christians play a role analogous to that of Platonist philosophers in their ability to find what is true within an image of the intelligible world. "All the precepts of the Jewish law," Lactantius argues, "look toward the working of justice because they were given enigmatically, so that through the figure of carnal things, the spiritual things might be understood" (4.17.21). The unique polity that Moses' law defines has the same relationship to the realm defined by divine law as the unique polities crafted by lawgivers under Zeus' inspiration have to the realm of Kronos (5.8.6–9). In short, Lactantius rejects the notion that the pagan Roman polity, even with the guidance of a Platonist philosopher, could possibly be the best regime in practice (5.12.1). Instead, Lactantius sees the Jewish community under Moses' law as fulfilling a preparatory role. As Eusebius also construes the law of Moses as the image of the divine, it seems very likely that Lactantius developed this legal and political understanding of Christianity in response to contemporary challenges from Platonist philosophers.

RECEPTION AND SIGNIFICANCE

As tutor to Constantine's son Crispus in the northwestern capital Trier, Lactantius was uniquely well situated to circulate his ideas to the emperor's court and to the emperor himself. Textual parallels between an imperial edict issued in 314 as well as Constantine's speech *To the Assembly of the Saints* indicate that people in the Western court and the emperor himself were open to Lactantius's input and ideas. Indeed, the history of Constantine's reign indicates that the emperor long promoted a policy of religious tolerance, even after his own decision to count himself among the number of Christians, which may have been as early as 312 and the Battle of the Milvian Bridge. This is certainly the case with his policy toward Jews throughout his reign. With respect to the rest of Roman religious diversity, the emperor was equally tolerant – so far as the sources reveal – while he ruled in the West. Once he defeated his Eastern colleague Licinius, however, the tone of his rhetoric changed. Like Lactantius before him, he began to speak harshly about what he termed the "temples of lies." The emperor's biographer, Eusebius, also claims that Constantine outlawed sacrifice sometime after 324. But if so, it is curious that nothing survives of this edict, despite the fact that Eusebius includes many others verbatim and the *Theodosian Code* preserves still more. (One possibility is that Constantine allowed Christian magistrates to refrain from an obligation to sacrifice, thus returning the empire to the state of affairs before Diocletian's edicts, although Eusebius claims that he outlawed the practice.)

Although to our eyes Constantine may not have practiced *patientia* (as Lactantius understood it) toward diverse religious practices as consistently as we might have wished, the emperor did seem to endorse Lactantius's political theory overall.[8] For example, Constantine equated Christian law with justice when he argued that the judgment of Christian priests, in some cases, "should be regarded as if God himself were in the judge's seat. For these have no power either to think or to judge except as they are instructed by Christ's teaching" (Optatus, *App.* 5).

Constantine's successors carried forward his legal policy toward religious diversity for the next half century. The *Theodosian Code*, compiled under Theodosius II (r. 408–450), does include several edicts outlawing sacrifice, but these do not necessarily indicate repression of traditional cults. First, "pagan" authors from Porphyry of Tyre, writing in the third century, to Ammianus Marcellinus, in the late fourth, indicate that blood sacrifice may no longer have been a central ritual (a development that might also explain why emperors and governors waived this requirement for Christian magistrates even before Diocletian's edicts of 303). Next, edicts collated in the *Theodosian Code* lack all of their introductory language, describing the occasion that prompted the legislation. For this reason, whether an emperor intended an edict or rescript to be generally applicable is impossible to ascertain. Finally, Roman emperors did not enforce law through agencies such as police forces, as happens in modern states. To be enforced, a law required citizens to bring its infringement to the attention of authorities. Thus, an emperor could legislate, but a citizen would have to have had a vested interest in applying a law against sacrifice for change to have happened.

From a legal point of view, however, the toleration of religious diversity ended under Theodosius I, who decreed in 392 that Christianity (in its Nicene form) was the only religion with legal standing in the Roman Empire – even if later emperors and their magistrates did not uniformly enforce this edict.[9] Legislation against traditional ritual would have also had a more forceful impact after the publication of the *Theodosian Code*. With that effort, all relevant legislation by emperors from Constantine to Theodosius II was not only collected and organized, but also disseminated to the Eastern provinces and the Western empire. Governors (and soon Germanic kings) thus had at their fingertips a systematic compilation of laws against sacrifice and traditional cult. The same pattern of behavior would repeat in the sixth century with the *Codex* and *Digest* of Justinian.

With the exception of Augustine of Hippo, the patristic tradition remembered Lactantius primarily as an Apologist. Among late-ancient authors, Jerome (d. 420) was the best informed. His accounts of Lactantius in *De viris illustribus* (18, 58, 80, 111) and his *Chronicle* show deep familiarity with Lactantius's work, most likely

[8] We might note in passing that Jean-Jacques Aubert, "Christianisme antique, droit romaine et homosexualité," in Michael Groneberg (ed.), *Der Mann als sexuelles Wesen / L'homme – créature sexuelle: Zur Normierung mänlicher Erotik / La normation de l'érotisme masculin* (Fribourg: Academic Press, 2006), 103–25, argues that subsequent emperors agreed with Lactantius's condemnation of same-sex intercourse.

[9] *Cod. Theod.* 16.10.12. See also the constitutions of *Cod. Theod.* 16.1, "on the catholic faith."

acquired (along with the texts themselves) when Jerome was a student in Trier. In several letters (*Epp.* 48, 58, 60, 84), Jerome praises Lactantius's eloquence and knowledge, but in his Commentaries (*On Isaiah* 8; *On Ezekiel* 4, 11; *On Ephesians* prol.; and *On Galatians* 6), he criticizes him for denying the Holy Spirit and for his view that the Book of Revelation was literally true. Through Jerome, Pope Damasus and Rufinus of Aquileia also discovered Lactantius, and their remarks make it clear that Jerome gave them copies of some of his works (letters, for example) that are no longer extant. Later authors who refer to Lactantius by name acknowledge him for similar reasons: They admire him as an Apologist (Sidonius Apollinaris, Aldhelm of Sherborne, Jonas of Orleans, and Berengar of Tours), or they respect his attitude toward the Liberal Arts (Cassiodorus), or they engage with his views on Revelation (Gennadius of Marseilles, Rabanus Maurus, and Peter Abelard), or they are aware that he was an eminent Christian author (Gelasius I, Hormisdas I, Alcuin, Atto of Vercelli, Liutprand of Cremona, Honorius of Autun, and Wibaldus of Stavelot). Frecult of Liseaux and the *Annales Francici* are familiar with his *De mortibus persecutorum*. But not one of them refers to his ideas about law in general or religious tolerance in particular.

This neglect of the legal character and thrust of Lactantius's *Divine Institutes* probably derives from his treatment by the great theologian and political theorist, Augustine of Hippo (see Chapter 12). Early in his career, Augustine had praised Lactantius as an apologist who found "gold" and "silver" among the ore of pagan poets and philosophers (*Ep.* 55, *De doctrina christiana* 2.40.61). Augustine observes in *On Nature and Grace* (61), however, that his Pelagian opponents had cited Lactantius in their defense, a circumstance that would not have boosted his reputation in the Middle Ages. Moreover, Augustine's *City of God* departs dramatically from the project of the *Divine Institutes*. Where Lactantius had argued forcefully that earthly government should reflect the divine government of the cosmos, with the emperor as the image of God, Augustine, in full consciousness of Lactantius's work, posited a fundamental difference between the city of God and the human commonwealth, with each pursuing its own ends. As a bishop, Augustine rejected the virtue of *patientia* in the face of religious diversity that Lactantius had defended, especially during the Donatist crisis. Such was Augustine's authority in the Western Middle Ages that the political and legal import of the *Divine Institutes* fell into oblivion. And when humanists rediscovered his works in the fifteenth century, they admired his gorgeous Latin prose more than his political theory.

In the mid-twentieth century, however, Lactantius's advocacy for freedom of religion gained currency once again when the Second Vatican Council drew attention to his ideas. In the Declaration *Dignitatis humanae* (1965), the Council asserted that "the human person has a right to religious liberty,"[10] a doctrine that,

[10] Concilium Vaticanum II, *Declaratio de libertate religiosa "Dignitatis humanae"* 2: "personam humanam jus habere ad libertatem religiosam." Cf. Anthony P. Coleman, "Lactantius and

they said, stemmed from the earliest traditions of the church, citing Lactantius as support.[11] Moreover, even such disparate figures as Benedict XVI and John XXIII recognized the link between the Council's advocacy of religious liberty and the church's most ancient patrimony, especially that of Lactantius.[12]

ABBREVIATIONS

Augustine, *Ep.*	Augustinus, *Epistola*
Cic. *Leg.*	Cicero, *De legibus*
Cic. *Part.*	Cicero, *Partitiones oratoriae*
Cicero, *Rep.*	Cicero, *De republica*
Eusebius, *HE*	Eusebius, *Historia ecclesiastica*
Jerome, *Ep.*	Hieronymus, *Epistola*
Justinian, *Dig.*	Justinianus, *Digesta*
Justinian *Inst.*	Justinianus, *Institutiones*
Lactantius, *Inst.*	Lactantius, *Divinae institutiones*
Optatus, *App.*	Optatus, *Appendix* to *Contra Parmenianum Donatistum*, in *Urkunden zur Entstehungsgeschichte des Donatismus* (von Soden, 1913)
Plato, *Leg.*	Plato, *Leges*

SOURCES

L. Caelius Firmianus Lactantius. *Divinarum institutionum libri septem. Fasc. 1; Libri I–II*. Ed. Eberhard Heck and Antonie Wlosok. Munich: K. G. Saur, 2005.

Divinarum institutionum libri septem. Fasc. 2; Libri III–IV. Ed. Eberhard Heck and Antonie Wlosok. Berlin: De Gruyter, 2007.

Divinarum institutionum libri septem. Fasc. 3; Libri V–VI. Ed. Eberhard Heck and Antonie Wlosok. Berlin: De Gruyter, 2009.

Divinarum institutionum libri septem. Fasc. 4; Liber VII, appendix, indices. Ed. Eberhard Heck and Antonie Wlosok. Berlin: De Gruyter, 2011.

Epitome divinarum institutionum. Ed. Eberhard Heck and Antonie Wlosok. Stuttgart: Teubner, 1994.

Divine Institutes. Trans. Anthony Bowen and Peter Garnsey. Translated Texts for Historians, LUP 40. Liverpool: Liverpool University Press, 2003.

Epitome of the Divine Institutes. Trans. E. H. Blakeney. London: S.P.C.K., 1950.

'Ressourcement': Going to the Sources of Religious Liberty in the Civic Order," *Vox Patrum* 34 (2014): 209–219 at 209.

[11] *"Dignitatis humanae"* 10: "expraecipuis doctrinae catholicae, . . . a Patribus constanter praedicatum, hominem debere Deo volunatie respondere credendo." Cf. Coleman, "Lactantius and 'Ressourcement'," 210, 216.

[12] Benedict XVI, *Ad Romanam Curiam ob omnia natalicia*, in *Acta Apostolicae Sedis* 98 (2006): 50; John XXII, *Pacem in terris*, in *Acta Apostolicae Sedis* 55 (1963): 260–61. Cf. Coleman, "Lactantius and 'Ressourcement,'" 210, 217.

FURTHER READING

Aubert, Jean-Jacques. "Christianisme antique, droit romain et homosexualité." In Michael Groneberg (ed.), *Der Mann als sexuelles Wesen / L'homme – créature sexuelle: Zur Normierung männlicher Erotik / La normation de l'érotisme masculine* (Fribourg: Academic Press, 2006), 103–25.

Cain, Andrew Jason. "Three Further Echoes of Lactantius in Jerome." *Philologus* 154.1 (2010): 88–96.

Coleman, Anthony P. "Lactantius and 'Ressourcement': Going to the Sources of Religious Liberty in the Civic Order." *Vox Patrum* 34 (2014): 209–19.

Corbo, Chiara. "Tra Italia e Africa: La legislazione di Costantino sugli 'inopes parentes'." *Koinonia* 36 (2012): 37–55.

Digeser, Elizabeth DePalma. "Lactantius on Religious Liberty and His Influence on Constantine." In Timothy Samuel Shah and Allen D. Hertzke (eds.), *Christianity and Freedom*, vol. 1: *Historical Perspectives*, Cambridge Studies in Law and Christianity (Cambridge: Cambridge University Press, 2016), 90–102.

"Religion, Law and the Roman Polity: The Era of the Great Persecution." In Clifford Ando and Jörg Rüpke (eds.), *Religion and Law in Classical and Christian Rome* (Stuttgart: Franz Steiner Verlag, 2006), 68–84.

"Citizenship and the Roman *Res publica*: Cicero and a Christian Corollary." *Critical Review of International Social and Political Philosophy* 6 (2003): 5–21.

The Making of a Christian Empire: Lactantius and Rome. Ithaca: Cornell University Press, 2000.

Garnsey, Peter D.A. "Lactantius and Augustine." In A. K. Bowman, H. M. Cotton, M. Goodman, and S. Price (eds.), *Representations of Empire: Rome and the Mediterranean World*, Proceedings of the British Academy 114 (Oxford: Oxford University Press, 2002), 153–79.

Girardet, Klaus Martin. "*Libertas religionis*: 'Religionsfreiheit' bei Tertullian und Laktanz: Zwei Skizzen." In Karlheinz Muscheler (ed.), *Römische Jurisprudenz: Dogmatik, Überlieferung, Rezeption: Festschrift für Detlef Liebs zum 75. Geburtstag* (Berlin: Duncker und Humblot, 2011), 205–26.

Grossmann, Christiane. "Die neutestamentlichen Grundlagen der Gerechtigkeitsdefinition im 5. Buch der *Institutionen* des Laktanz." *Mittellateinisches Jahrbuch* 37 (2002): 395–403.

Ingremeau, Christiane. "Lactance et la justice: Du livre V au livre VI des 'Institutions divines'." In J.-Y. Guillaumin and S. Ratti (eds.), *Autour de Lactance: Hommages à Pierre Monat* (Paris: Presses Universitaires de Franche-Comté, 2003), 43–52.

Kahlos, Maijastina. "The Rhetoric of Tolerance and Intolerance: From Lactantius to Firmicus Maternus." In J. Ulrich, A.-Ch. Jacobsen, and M. Kahlos (eds.), *Continuity and Discontinuity in Early Christian Apologetics*, Early Christianity in the Context of Antiquity 5 (Bern: Peter Lang, 2009), 79–95.

Moreschini, Claudio. "L'intellettuale cristiano e l'impero da Tertulliano a Costantino." In Renato Uglione (ed.), *Atti del convegno nazionale di studi "Intellettuali e potere nel mondo antico"* (Alessandria: Ed. dell'Orso, 2003), 237–256.

Rivière, Yann. "Constantin, le crime et le christianisme: Contribution à l'étude des lois et des moeurs de l'Antiquité tardive." *Antiquité Tardive* 10 (2002): 327–61.

Walter, Jochen. *Pagane Texte und Wertvorstellungen bei Lactanz*. Göttingen: Vandenhoeck und Ruprecht, 2006.

11

Ambrosiaster

David G. Hunter

"Ambrosiaster" is the name given to an anonymous Latin biblical commentator who wrote in Rome during the final decades of the fourth century. He was the author of the first complete Latin commentary on the letters of Paul, extant in multiple versions or recensions, as well as a collection of *Questions on the Old and New Testament* (*Quaestiones ueteris et noui testamenti*), which also survives in multiple versions. The Pauline commentary was attributed to Ambrose throughout most of the Middle Ages, although Augustine at one point referred to its author as Hilary.[1] The *Quaestiones* are ascribed to Augustine in most of the manuscript witnesses. Partly because of the dual attribution to Ambrose and Augustine, this anonymous author acquired considerable influence in the Middle Ages, although the medieval reception of Ambrosiaster's work has never been fully explored. The designation "Ambrosiaster" was coined in the early modern period when the pseudonymous character of the Pauline commentary was established.[2] In the early twentieth century, Alexander Souter definitively proved that the same author produced both the commentary and the *Quaestiones*.[3]

The commentary and *Quaestiones* seem to have been issued anonymously at the beginning. The identity of the author, therefore, has escaped the grasp of modern scholars, as well as the knowledge of Ambrosiaster's ancient readers. Nevertheless, significant information about him can be gleaned from the texts themselves. The author states that he is writing in Rome during the pontificate of Damasus I, that is, between 366 and 384. In his Pauline commentary, he refers to the church "whose

[1] In *c. duas epist. Pelagianorum*. 4.4.7 (CSEL 60:528), Augustine referred to the view of "Hilary," but he quoted from Ambrosiaster, *In Rom* 5:12 (CSEL 81.1:165). Cf. *Ep*. 82.24 (CSEL 34.2:376), where Augustine referred to the views of *noster Ambrosius*, apparently in reference to Ambrosiaster, *In Gal.* 2:11–14 (CSEL 81.3:25–27).

[2] Jan Krans, "Who Coined the Name 'Ambrosiaster'?" in Jan Krans et al. (eds.), *Paul, John, and Apocalyptic Eschatology: Studies in Honour of Martinus C. de Boer*, Novum Testamentum, Supplement 149 (Leiden: Brill, 2013), 274–81.

[3] *A Study of Ambrosiaster*, Texts and Studies 7.4 (Cambridge: Cambridge University Press, 1905), building on the work of Joseph Langen, *De commentariorum in epistulas paulinas, qui Ambrosii, et quaestionum biblicarum, quae Augustini nomine feruntur scriptore dissertatio* (Bonn, 1880).

rector at present is Damasus" (*In 1 Tim* 3:15; CSEL 81.3:270). In one of his *Quaestiones*, Ambrosiaster speaks of being "here in the city of Rome and its environs" (*Quaest.* 115.16; SC 512:168), and in one of the versions of his commentary on Romans he mentions being "here, that is, in Rome" (*In Rom* 16:3–5; CSEL 81.1:479). There is no doubt, therefore, that both the *Commentary* and the *Quaestiones* were produced at Rome sometime during the pontificate of Damasus.

Some scholars have sought greater precision and have argued that portions of the *Commentary* and the *Quaestiones* were composed in the early to mid-380s, at least in their later recensions. In 1956, Heinrich Vogels published an article that demonstrated connections between a letter of Jerome, written in 384, and the commentary on Romans by Ambrosiaster.[4] In *Letter* 127, addressed to Marcella, Jerome complained of certain "two-legged asses" who were criticizing his revision of the New Testament gospels based on Greek codices, citing a handful of disputed readings. Vogels showed that these were taken from Ambrosiaster's commentary on Romans. Vogels also demonstrated that one of the later recensions of Ambrosiaster's Romans commentary contains a more elaborate defense of his preference for the Old Latin versions of the Bible (*Vetus Latina*) and an explicit defense of the readings that Jerome had criticized. Vogels concluded that Ambrosiaster must have criticized Jerome in the first edition of his Romans commentary, that Jerome responded in *Letter* 127, and that Ambrosiaster revised and reissued the Romans commentary to respond to Jerome.

More recently, several scholars have confirmed Vogels's thesis that Ambrosiaster was active in Rome during the years of Jerome's sojourn there, that is, between 382 and 385. In her monograph on Ambrosiaster's political theology, Sophie Lunn-Rockliffe has suggested a date of c. 384 for *Quaest.* 115, and a date of no later than the mid-380s for the rest of his work.[5] A collection of articles examining Ambrosiaster's revisions of his own writings by Marie-Pierre Bussières, Theodore de Bruyn, Stephen Cooper, and David Hunter has presented evidence suggesting the influence of the Council of Constantinople I (381) and of a Roman synod of 382 on Ambrosiaster's theology of the Holy Spirit.[6] Cooper and Hunter have also argued for further literary encounters between Ambrosiaster and Jerome. The emerging consensus is that the later revisions of the *Commentary* and the *Quaestiones* date

4 "Ambrosiaster und Hieronymus," *Revue Bénédictine* 66 (1956): 14–19.

5 *Ambrosiaster's Political Theology*, OECS (Oxford: Oxford University Press, 2007), 12–17. As Lunn-Rockliffe observes (p. 15), the existence of multiple versions of both the *Quaestiones* and the *Commentary* complicates the question of dating. We cannot be sure how much time elapsed between the recensions, and some *quaestiones* may have circulated independently.

6 "L'Ambrosiaster révise l'Ambrosiaster/ Ambrosiaster Revising Ambrosiaster," *Revue d'études augustiniennes et patristiques* 56 (2010): 21–91. The importance of the councils of 381 and 382 for the development of Ambrosiaster's pneumatology had already been noted in regard to the *Quaestiones* by Bussières, "L'influence du synode tenu à Rome en 382 sur l'exégèse de l'Ambrosiaster," *Sacris Erudiri* 45 (2006): 107–24.

from the mid-380s. The earlier versions would have been written in the early 380s, or perhaps at some time in the later 370s.

While little can be known about the details of Ambrosiaster's life, his works reveal significant information about him. It is virtually certain that he was a presbyter in the church at Rome. His writings show extensive knowledge of ecclesiastical customs in Rome, especially those pertaining to church office.[7] For example, he had a special interest in the origins of the office of bishop, and he provides a historically nuanced account of the distinction between presbyters and bishops.[8] In several places, Ambrosiaster referred to liturgical practices such as the singing of hymns, fasting, and the bestowal of nuptial blessings at marriages of Christians.[9] His writings also offer early evidence for the requirement of permanent sexual continence for the higher clergy, a practice he strongly supported.[10] In one of the *Quaestiones* (*Quaest.* 101, "The Boasting of the Roman Deacons"), Ambrosiaster developed a lively apology for the authority of presbyters, their nearly equal rank with bishops, and their superior status over deacons. It is difficult to imagine anyone but a Roman presbyter expressing such concern over these issues.

Perhaps the most compelling argument for Ambrosiaster's status as presbyter is that several of his *Quaestiones* appear to be sermons directed to an audience of "beloved brethren," and in one he even referred to the speaker (almost certainly himself) as a "priest" (*sacerdos*) (*Quaest.* 120; CSEL 50:361).[11] Sophie Lunn-Rockliffe has proposed that Ambrosiaster may have been a presbyter attached to one of the great cemetery churches at Rome outside the city walls. These Roman presbyters, unlike those within the city proper, had the right to preside, preach, and consecrate the eucharistic elements.[12] This suggestion is quite plausible and would explain Ambrosiaster's status as both an insider and an outsider to clerical culture at Rome. He was deeply involved in pastoral and liturgical activities, yet he sometimes cast a critical eye at the behavior of his confreres in church office. Nevertheless, he offered strong arguments for the authority of clerical office and, in particular, for the prerogatives of presbyters. While none of these arguments in itself is conclusive, the cumulative evidence strongly suggests that Ambrosiaster was a Roman presbyter, most likely at one of the suburban churches.

Beyond his role as a Roman presbyter, little more can be ascertained by way of the biography of Ambrosiaster. Some earlier scholars offered ingenious attempts to

[7] See the extensive discussion in Lunn-Rocliffe, *Ambrosiaster's Political Theology*, 106–26.

[8] *In Eph* 4:11–12 (CSEL 81.3:99–100). See the discussion in Maurice Bévenot, "Ambrosiaster's Thoughts on Christian Priesthood," *Heythrop Journal* 18 (1977): 152–64.

[9] *In 1 Cor* 14:14 (CSEL 81.2:153): on Latin Christians singing hymns in Greek; *Quaest.* 120 (CSEL 50:361–63): on fasting; *Quaest.* 127.3 (CSEL 50:400), *In 1 Cor* 7:40 (CSEL 81.2:90), and *In 1 Tim* 3:12 (CSEL 81.3:268): on nuptial blessings.

[10] *Quaest.* 127.35–36 (CSEL 50:414–16). Cf. *In 1 Cor* 7:5 (CSEL 81.2:71–72).

[11] Lunn-Rockliffe, *Ambrosiaster's Political Theology*, 74–75, provides an extensive list of the sermonic elements in Ambrosiaster's *Quaestiones*.

[12] Lunn-Rockliffe, *Ambrosiaster's Political Theology*, 80–86.

identify Ambrosiaster with a known personage in the church at Rome. The distinguished Benedictine, Dom Germain Morin, offered no less than five different hypotheses over the course of nearly thirty years, none of which has carried the day. The most popular theory was that the anonymous Ambrosiaster was the Jewish convert Isaac, who is said to have brought a capital charge against Damasus and later to have turned away from the Christian faith.[13] While some scholars have continued to be intrigued by Ambrosiaster's numerous observations about Judaism, the identification with Isaac is not tenable. Equally inconclusive was Souter's effort to identify Ambrosiaster with Decimus Hilarianus Hilarius, a Roman official who served as proconsul of Africa in 377 and later as the Prefect of Rome (*praefectus urbi Romae*).[14]

VARIETIES OF SACRED AND SECULAR LAW

Ambrosiaster features in this volume as an author who spoke about law and justice. In fact, he was a thinker whose mind was shaped by notions of law in several different ways. He was interested in theoretical questions about the origin and nature of the different forms of regulation under which human beings have lived: the natural law, the Mosaic law, ecclesiastical canons, and the laws of nations, such as the Roman Empire. As a biblical commentator, especially of the Pauline corpus, he devoted special attention to the relation between the Mosaic law – sometimes dubbed the "law of deeds" (*lex factorum*) – and the Christian "law of faith" (*lex fidei*) that superseded it. But Ambrosiaster also showed an unusual degree of interest in Roman legal procedures, and at times he used these to illustrate Christian doctrines and practices. While scholars have concluded that the anonymous author did not have a highly specialized knowledge of law, he did evince an unusual degree of interest in the varieties of law present in both scriptural and secular contexts.[15] I shall examine here both his theoretical discussions of the nature and origin of the different kinds of law (natural, Mosaic, and Roman) and the ways in which his preoccupation with Roman law shaped his presentation of Christian doctrine and practice.

13 Morin's arguments for Isaac were summarized and expanded by A. E. Burn, "The Ambrosiaster and Isaac the Converted Jew," *Expositor* 2 (1989): 368–75.

14 Souter, *Study of Ambrosiaster*, 183–85. Souter was pursuing a suggestion of Germain Morin, "Hilarius l'Ambrosiaster," *Revue Bénédictine* 20 (1903): 113–31.

15 Several previous studies of Ambrosiaster's ideas about law have appeared. The oldest and most thorough is Othmar Heggelbacher, *Vom römischen zum christlichen Recht: Iuristische Elemente in den Schriften des sog. Ambrosiaster* (Freiburg: Universitätsverlag Freiburg Schweiz, 1959). See also Wilhelm Geerlings, "Das Verständnis von Gesetz im Galaterbriefkommentar des Ambrosiaster," in B. Aland et al. (eds.), *Die Weltlichkeit des Glaubens in der Alten Kirche: Festschrift für Ulrich Wickert zum siebsigsten Geburtstag* (Berlin: de Gruyter, 1997), 101–13; Lunn-Rockliffe, *Ambrosiaster's Political Theology*, 50–57; Souter, *Study of Ambrosiaster*, 23–31.

FROM NATURAL LAW TO MOSAIC LAW

The starting point of Ambrosiaster's reflections on what he calls the "natural law" or the "law of nature" (he used both terms) was Paul's discussion in his Letter to the Romans, especially Romans 1:20 ("Ever since the creation of the world God's invisible nature, namely, his eternal power and deity, has been clearly perceived in the things that have been made") and Romans 2:14–15 ("When Gentiles who have not the law do by nature what the law requires, they are a law to themselves ... They show that what the law requires is written on their hearts"). For Ambrosiaster, the natural law entailed both a basic knowledge of God and a sense of upright moral behavior, both of which were accessible, in principle, to all human beings. As he put it in one of his *Quaestiones*:

> At first there was no need for the law to be given in letters, because it was inserted into nature itself in some way, and knowledge of the creator was not hidden from transmission, for who does not know what befits a good life, or who is not aware that one should not do to another what one does not wish to be done to oneself? (*Quaest.* 4.1; CSEL 50:24)[16]

As Ambrosiaster saw it, human beings had the natural ability to recognize the existence of God and to acknowledge that God should be worshipped: "Therefore, nature itself by its own discernment acknowledges its creator, not through the [written] law, but by reason of nature. A thing that is made perceives its maker within itself" (*In Rom* 2:14; CSEL 81.1:75).[17] Ambrosiaster could even speak of "seeds of righteousness" (*iustitiae semina*) having been sown in human nature: A "natural capacity for righteousness" (*naturale iustitiae ingenium*) exists, which was created to produce the "fruit of righteousness" (*fructum iustitiae*) when given the assistance of the written law (*In Rom* 5:20; CSEL 81.1:185).

The foregoing statement raises the question of a relationship between the natural law and the Mosaic law. Ambrosiaster's views on this point went in several directions. On the one hand, he sometimes spoke as if the Mosaic law was given simply as an "aid" (*adiutorium*) to bring the natural seeds of righteousness to fruition:

> This is why the prophet Isaiah says: *The law was given as an aid* (Isa 8:20). That is, since the seeds of righteousness were somehow implanted in nature itself, the law was added so that by its authority and instruction the natural capacity might develop to produce the fruit of righteousness. Just as a newborn dies unless it has the nourishment by which, having been fostered, it matures,

[16] Cf. *In Rom* 2:13 (CSEL 81.1:169), where Ambrosiaster suggested that there are three parts to the natural law: the knowledge of God, the moral life, and the communication of the knowledge of God and the moral life to other people by example.

[17] My translations of the Pauline commentary are taken from *Ambrosiaster's Commentary on the Pauline Epistles: Romans*, translated with notes by Theodore S. de Bruyn, with an introduction by Stephen A. Cooper, Theodore S. de Bruyn, and David G. Hunter (Atlanta: SBL, 2017). Translations from the *Quaest.* are my own.

> so too the natural capacity for righteousness does not readily develop, but becomes diseased and gives in to sins that overcome it, unless it has something to be mindful of and to revere. It is overwhelmed by the habit of transgressing so that it does not develop fruit, and in this way it is extinguished. (*In Rom* 5:20; CSEL 81.1:185)

This passage would suggest that for Ambrosiaster the law of Moses functioned in an essentially supplementary way, that is, to assist in the development of the "seeds of righteousness" that were already present in the natural constitution of human beings, especially in their capacity to know God and the fundamentals of the moral life.

In other places, however, Ambrosiaster tended to emphasize a more corrective function of the Mosaic law, which was to bring about a greater awareness of sin and to inform people that they would be judged not only by human beings but also, ultimately, by God. For example, in his comment on Romans 5:13 ("Until the time of the law sin indeed was in the world. But sin was not reckoned as long as there was no law"), Ambrosiaster observed that although the natural law could never be completely unknown, it did not clearly teach that God would hold people accountable for their sins. Therefore, the Mosaic law was needed to inform people about rewards and punishments after death: "However, when the law was given through Moses, it was plainly revealed that God cares about human affairs and that there will be punishment for those evildoers who for whatever reason escape at the present time" (*In Rom* 5:13; CSEL 81.1:167–168). Ambrosiaster noted that the Mosaic law was given only because people treated the natural law with contempt, as if it had no authority (*In 1 Tim* 1:11; CSEL 81.3:254). The purpose of the written law of Moses, then, was to serve as a reminder of the natural law and to bolster its authority by warning that there would be ultimate penalties to pay for sin: "It showed that God's judgment would come, so that no sinner is free from punishment, lest perhaps someone who eluded punishment for a time be thought to have made a mockery of the law. This is what the law showed, that sin was imputed before God" (*In Rom* 3:20; CSEL 81.1:117).

FROM MOSAIC LAW TO THE "LAW OF FAITH"

Although the law of Moses was given to reinforce the law of nature and to make sin known, it, too, had its deficiencies, according to Ambrosiaster. Foremost among these was its inability, in itself, to provide forgiveness:

> For although the law of Moses was given to be advantageous, it nonetheless became a law of death when it was despised. Therefore, since it was unable to provide for sinners, the law of faith came, a law of the sort to save them, not only pardoning but even justifying them. (*In 2 Cor* 3:7–8; CSEL 81.2:215)

Now that Christ has come, a "new law" has been given. This is the law of faith, which brings life through the Spirit. Commenting on 2 Corinthians 3:6 ("The letter kills, but the Spirit gives life") Ambrosiaster observed:

> For the books of Moses were given to this end: so that the law would kill, by its native right, those who were despising it. *But the Spirit* – that is, the law of faith which is not written down but is contained in the heart – *gives life* to those condemned to death, at any rate, to those who turn themselves around, so that having been justified they would henceforth not sin. (*In 2 Cor* 3:6; CSEL 81.2:214)

Not written in letters but "insinuated into hearts," this new law brings freedom because it enables people to believe in things unseen: "This law, requiring faith alone (*solam fidem*), grants freedom, so that since faith believes things it does not see, one would deserve to be rescued from one's situation" (*In 2 Cor.* 3:17; CSEL 81.2:219).[18]

It is noteworthy that while Ambrosiaster could use the phrase "faith alone" (*sola fides*) in the context of justification and salvation, elsewhere he described this faith as "supplemented by the natural law" (*addita lege naturali*):

> In fact, however, God's mercy was given so that the burdens of the law might end, as I have already said several times. For out of consideration for human weakness God decreed that that the human race should be saved by faith alone, supplemented by natural law. (*In Rom* 1:11; CSEL 81.1:29)

As Ambrosiaster saw it, the *lex naturalis* remained intact and was even restored to its prior prominence by the gift of salvation brought through faith.

FROM NATURAL LAW TO ROMAN LAW

Given the prominence of the *lex naturalis* or *lex naturae* in Ambrosiaster's thought, it is not surprising that he acknowledged its role in the formation of Roman law. Commenting on Romans 7:1 ("Do you not know, brethren – for I am speaking to those who know the law – that the law is binding on a person only during his life?"), he observed that Roman law was formed partly on the basis of the natural law, partly under the influence of the Mosaic law, and partially from Greek sources:

> Because the Romans are not barbarians, they know about the law. But they grasped natural justice [*naturalem iustitiam*] partly by themselves, partly from the Greeks, and partly from the Hebrews. Although the law was not hidden prior to Moses, it was nevertheless without arrangement and authority. For the arrangement of the law was conveyed to the Romans from Athens. (*In Rom* 7:1; CSEL 81.1:211)

18 Ambrosiaster is commenting on the verse, "Now the Lord is the Spirit, and where the Spirit of the Lord is, there is freedom."

Ambrosiaster's mention of "Athens" here is an allusion to the tradition preserved in Livy (3.31.8) that several men were sent to Athens by the *decemuiri* "with orders to copy the famous laws of Solon, and to acquaint themselves with the institutions, customs, and laws of the other Greek states."[19] Since Ambrosiaster believed that Roman law was based partly on the natural law and partly on the Mosaic law, he was comfortable drawing lessons for Christians from Roman law, as well as parallels from Roman legal concepts, to illustrate Christian practice.[20]

On several occasions, Ambrosiaster referred to specific Roman laws. He was aware that several edicts had been issued against the Manicheans, and he cited a portion of Diocletian's law against them: "Obviously the Manichaeans did not live during the time of the apostles, just as the Arians did not, a fact which the emperor Diocletian points out in his own constitution when he says: 'this filthy and impure heresy, which has just recently come out of Persia.'"[21] In *Quaest.* 115, "Concerning Fate," Ambrosiaster also cited variations in Roman law as an argument against astral fatalism. Thus, he mentioned the expulsion of astrologers from the city of Rome (*Quaest.* 115.63),[22] a law of the emperor Julian allowing women to divorce their husbands (*Quaest.* 115.12), the law of Constantine prohibiting crucifixion (*Quaest.* 115.67), and the prohibition of eunuchs in the Roman Empire (*Quaest.* 115.17). In another of the *Quaestiones*, he mentioned that convicted thieves were required to provide fourfold restitution "according to the law" (*iuxta legem*), a specification found in the *Institutiones* of the jurist Gaius (*Quaest.* 83.5; CSEL 50:142). Ambrosiaster also made frequent references to the Emperor and his ministers and officials (*imperator, comites, praefecti, senatores, officiales*).[23]

ROMAN LAW AND CHRISTIAN DOCTRINE AND DISCIPLINE

Perhaps the most significant feature of Ambrosiaster's interest in law is the way in which he viewed Christian practices and doctrines through the lens of Roman legal practice and political structures. To an unusual degree, legal language infused his

19 See also *Quaest.* 75.2 in the appendix in Souter (CSEL 50:468), where Ambrosiaster provided further details.

20 In this respect, Ambrosiaster shows an outlook similar to that of the anonymous compiler of the contemporaneous *Collatio legum Mosaicarum et Romanarum*. See the recent examination by Robert M. Frakes, *Compiling the Collatio Legum Mosaicarum et Romanarum in Late Antiquity* (Oxford: Oxford University Press, 2011). The *Collatio* has sometimes been attributed to Ambrosiaster. See the recent discussion by Andrew S. Jacobs, "'Papinian Commands One Thing, Our Paul Another': Roman Christians and Jewish Law in the *Collatio Legum Mosaicarum et Romanarum*," in Clifford Ando and Jörg Rüpke (eds.), *Religion and Law in Classical and Christian Rome*, Potsdamer Altertumswissenschaftliche Beiträge 15 (Stuttgart: Franz Steiner Verlag, 2006), 85–99.

21 *In 2 Tim* 3:7 (CSEL 81.3:312). The full text of Diocletian's edict is found in the *Collatio legum Mosaicarum et Romanarum* 15.3. *Quaest.* 127.18 (CSEL 50:407) mentions several "edicts of the emperors" against the Manichaeans.

22 There had been numerous attempts to ban astrologers from Rome. See the note in Marie-Pierre Bussières (ed.), *Ambrosiaster: Contre les païens et Sur le destin*, SC 512 (2007), 241–42.

23 Detailed in Souter, *Study of Ambrosiaster*, 23–27.

discussion of several topics, ranging from gender relations to church structure to Trinitarian doctrine. For example, he frequently used terms such as *legatus* and *uicarius*, which had a variety of connotations in the realms of civic and imperial administration. The former signified the role of an ambassador or of an official appointed for a special task by the Roman emperor or senate. The latter designated a "substitute," or someone who acted in place of another (e.g., *uice agens*), such as the administrative head of a diocese or, in the case of a *uicarius iudex*, a judge who acted in the place of a provincial governor.[24] Ambrosiaster regularly employed these terms to describe the role of clerics, such as bishops and presbyters, who acted as the "legates" or "vicars" of Christ. For example, when commenting on a passage from 1 Timothy 5:19 ("Never admit a charge against an elder"), Ambrosiaster observed:

> Because the honor of this office is exalted – for men of this rank are vicars [*uicarii*] of Christ – for this reason an accusation against this person should not be easily received. For it ought to seem implausible that a man who is the overseer [*antistes*] of God would be engaged in criminal behavior, just as it is quite plausible that an actor would live a disreputable life. (*In 1 Tim* 5:19; CSEL 81.3:284)[25]

Ambrosiaster also invoked these official terms to endorse the discipline of permanent sexual continence, which the church at Rome had begun to impose on the higher clergy:

> Is everything that is permitted in the presence of other people also permitted in the presence of the emperor? How much more in matters that concern God! This is why God's overseer [*antestitem eius*] must be purer than other people, for he has the role [*personam habere*] of God. He is God's representative [*uicarius*], so that what is permissible for others is not permissible for him, because every day he must act in the place of Christ [*Christi uicem*], either by praying for the people, or by offering the sacrifice, or by baptizing. (*Quaest.* 127.36; CSEL 50:415)[26]

Ambrosiaster proceeded to extend the analogy, comparing the sexual continence of the clergy to the clothing that was appropriate to emperors and senators: "Isn't it the case that the tunic of an ordinary person, even though it is clean, is foul and unlawful for an emperor? And isn't it the same with the clothing of a Saxon and that of a senator? . . . For no one serves the emperor unless he is properly attired" (*Quaest.* 127.36; CSEL 50:415–416).

In other contexts, Ambrosiaster invoked the terms *uicarius* and *legatus* to describe the authority of bishops, specifically over women in the Christian community. This

24 Adolf Berger, *Encyclopedic Dictionary of Roman Law*, transactions of the American Philosophical Society, new series 43, pt. 2 (Philadelphia: American Philosophical Society, 1952), 539 (*legati*), 763–64 (*uicarius*).

25 The term *antistes* is difficult to translate. It could mean priest, magistrate, or administrator, but it was already a technical term for bishop among Christians by the fourth century.

26 The expression *personam habere* also had legal connotations: In the Roman Empire, a *persona* was any being with legal rights, including the state.

usage was closely connected with his understanding of the "image" of God, which Ambrosiaster believed belonged only to men, not to women:

> This is the image of God in man: that he was made one lord [*dominus*], as it were, from whom all the others would arise, holding the *imperium* of God as his vicar [*uicarius*] since every ruler has the image of God. And for this reason woman was not made in the image of God . . . That is why the apostle said: "The man should not veil his head because he is the image and glory of God" (1 Cor 11:7), but the woman veils because she is not the image and glory of God. (*Quaest.* 106.17; CSEL 50:243)[27]

As Ambrosiaster saw it, both the imperial hierarchy and the ecclesiastical hierarchy were founded on the created order of God. To be created in the image of God, therefore, was to be a *dominus* and thereby to exercise dominion as God's *uicarius*. Hence, women were to be excluded from any roles in which they might exercise authority over men. For Ambrosiaster, Roman legal practice illustrated this "natural" hierarchy: "For how can it be said of woman that she is the image of God when it is clear that she is subject to the dominion of the man and that she has no authority? For she is not able to teach, nor to be a witness, nor to make a contract [*fidem dicere*], nor to be a judge. How much less is she able to give commands" (*Quaest.* 45.3; CSEL 50:83).[28]

It is clear that Ambrosiaster employed the terms *legatus* and *uicarius* to characterize the roles of the higher clergy and their superior status over women, but, more surprisingly, he also used these concepts to illustrate distinctions within the Trinity. In one of the *Quaestiones* dedicated to the topic of the identity of Melchisedek, Ambrosiaster offered the somewhat idiosyncratic suggestion that this Old Testament priest was actually the Holy Spirit. This led him to reflect on how both Christ and the Holy Spirit could be considered "priests" (*sacerdotes*) of God the Father, a notion that he then interpreted in terms of their role as *uicarii* of God:

> Since in every way the authority of the one God must be preserved, for this reason the second and third persons are subordinated to the name of the Father. Now Christ is the vicar [*uicarius*] of the Father and his overseer [*antestes*], and for this reason he is also called "priest" [*sacerdos*]. Likewise, the Holy Spirit who has been sent as the overseer [*antestes*] of the Most-High God is called "priest," but not the "highest priest" . . . since, although Christ and the Holy Spirit are of one substance, the rank of each must be preserved. Therefore, they are called "priests" or "legates" [*legati*] because in themselves they reveal that One whose legates they are. So, then, Christ and the Holy Spirit, who have by nature the image of God, are called his "priests." God is seen in them, just as the Lord said: "The one who has seen me has seen the Father." (John 14:9; *Quaest.* 109.21; CSEL 50:268)

27 For a more detailed discussion of this topic, see David G. Hunter, "The Paradise of Patriarchy: Ambrosiaster on Woman as (Not) God's Image," *Journal of Theological Studies* n.s. 43 (1992): 447–69.

28 See also Ambrosiaster's comments on 1 Cor 11:8–10 and 1 Cor 14: 34, where he further emphasized the subordination of women to the clergy.

For Ambrosiaster, the hierarchies evident in Roman society provided a model for hierarchy not only within the church, but also within the divine being.

A final example of Ambrosiaster's use of Roman legal practice to illustrate Christian practice can be found in his discussion of the role of the clergy in administering the sacraments. In his lengthy *Quaest.* 102, *Contra Novatianum*, Ambrosiaster argued that the efficacy of a priest's sacramental actions did not depend on his personal holiness. When a person comes to a priest to receive the faith or to be baptized, it is the faith of the believer that is crucial, not the moral status of the priest. "One should regard priests [*antistites*] as one regards legal advocates [*aduocatorum ... more*]." Ambrosiaster continues:

> If an advocate lives wickedly, will the judgment go against his client? The duty of the advocate is to plead the case of his client according to the rule of law. If his life is shameful, will this impede his client's case? The advocate's character can be neither an impediment nor an asset. It is the nature of the case that will determine its outcome. (*Quaest.* 102.31; CSEL 50:223)

Such is the situation of people who want to become Christian. They come to the priest (*antistes*) and say their vows, and he speaks the words of ecclesiastical law (*iuris ecclesiastici*). If their vows are true, the judge will accept them. Only God, the judge, knows the true character of human beings, that is, the frame of mind in which they have approached him. "It is for the priest to perform the office assigned to him," Ambrosiaster writes, "it is for the judge to accept or reject the petition of the client" (*Quaest.* 102.31; CSEL 50:223–24).

Ambrosiaster's argument here was directed against the Novatianist[29] claim that clergy who were morally compromised could not perform the duties of their office, but the framework of his argument was derived from the model of legal advocacy in a Roman courtroom. Ambrosiaster's numerous references to legal practice and his use of legal terminology indicate that he had at least a rudimentary education in forensic rhetoric. As Sophie Lunn-Rockliffe has suggested:

> A knowledge of and interest in law are not sure signs of a writer's having been a *iurisconsultus* or an advocate. The prominence of legal language and argumentation in the writings of ecclesiastics in this period is testimony to the fact that many had benefited from a career-oriented education in forensic rhetoric ... Few historians would now suggest that Ambrosiaster had actually practiced as a jurist or advocate, but he almost certainly received an education befitting one, and this explains the remnants of legal language and argumentation in his works.[30]

[29] Novatian was a presbyter at Rome in the mid-third century. After the persecution of Emperor Decius (251), he formed a rigorist sect in opposition to the Roman bishop Cornelius, rejecting the possibility of penance for serious sins, such as apostasy. Followers of Novatian remained active at Rome well into the fifth century.

[30] *Ambrosiaster's Political Theology*, 57.

Whatever the extent of Ambrosiaster's education, it is clear that he was a Christian thinker whose mind was profoundly shaped by legal terminology and categories. He was confident that the world around him reflected a created order that derived from God and that was accessible to all human beings through the natural law. As a result, he believed that the legal practices and political structures of Roman society provided appropriate analogies for ecclesiastical offices and activities.

RECEPTION AND SIGNIFICANCE

As noted above, Ambrosiaster's writings seem to have circulated from the start either anonymously or under the names of other authors, but they were immediately read by some of his most prominent contemporaries, such as Jerome and Augustine. It has also been established that Pelagius knew both the *Quaestiones* and Ambrosiaster's commentaries on the Pauline epistles and used them in his own writings on Paul.[31] In the sixth century Cassiodorus had heard of a commentary on Paul's letters attributed to Ambrose, which was probably the work of Ambrosiaster, although he had not been able to acquire a copy (*Inst.* 1.8.10). Numerous ninth-century writers used the commentary and referred to it as a work of Ambrose: among them, Claudius of Turin, Hatto of Vercelli, Amalarius of Metz, Haymo of Halberstadt, Sedulius Scottus, Hrabanus Maurus, Prudentius of Troyes, and Hincmar of Reims.[32] Citations of both the Pauline commentary and the *Quaestiones* have been discovered in the *Libri Carolini*, a late eighth-century response, composed at the request of Charlemagne, to the teaching on icons of the Seventh Ecumenical Council, Nicaea II (787).[33]

Because the *Quaestiones* were usually attributed to Augustine and the Pauline commentaries to Ambrose, they enjoyed considerable authority in the Middle Ages. Recent studies have drawn attention to Ambrosiaster's influence especially on the development of canon law. For example, in his discussion of the so-called Pauline Privilege, where Paul argued that "if the unbelieving partner desires to separate, let it be so; in such a case the brother or sister is not bound" (1 Cor 7:15), Ambrosiaster had claimed that "a marriage is not valid [*ratum*], if it lacks devotion to God, and therefore there is no sin if the person who is divorced for the sake of God marries another" (*In 1 Cor* 7:15; CSEL 81.2:77). Several twelfth-century canonists and

[31] A. J. Smith, "The Latin Sources of the Commentary of Pelagius on the Epistles of St. Paul to the Romans," *Journal of Theological Studies* 19 (1918): 162–230. Georges de Plinval, *Pélage: Ses écrits, sa vie et sa réforme* (Lausanne: Librairie Payot, 1943), 86–92.

[32] Further details in Heinrich Joseph Vogels, "Die Überlieferung des Ambrosiasterkommentars zu den Paulinischen Briefen," *Nachrichten von der Akademie der Wissenschaften in Göttingen* 7 (1959): 107–42; and Theodore de Bruyn, "Ambrosiaster: *Commentarius in xiii epistulas Paulinas*," in *Traditio Patrum: The Transmission of the Latin Fathers in the Middle Ages*, Emanuela Colombi et al. (eds.) (Turnhout: Brepols, forthcoming). I am grateful to Professor de Bruyn for making a draft of his article available to me prior to its publication.

[33] Luitpold Wallach, "Ambrosiaster und die Libri Carolini," *Deutsches Archiv für Erforschung des Mittelalters* 29 (1973): 197–205.

theologians cited and discussed this dictum, including Vacarius, Gratian, Hugh of Saint-Victor, and Peter Lombard.[34] Similarly, Ambrosiaster's teaching on the image of God as belonging to men and not women entered the medieval canonical tradition through the writings of Ivo of Chartres and Gratian.[35] Ambrosiaster represents a distinctive voice within the patristic tradition, especially on matters pertaining to law and political theology. His covert influence on the subsequent Christian tradition, under the names of Augustine and Ambrose, remains a rich field for further exploration.

SOURCES

Ambrosiaster. *Commentarius in epistulas paulinas*. Ed. Heinrich J. Vogels. CSEL 81.1–3 (1966–69).

Quaestiones Veteris et Novi Testamenti CXXVII. Ed. Alexander Souter. CSEL 50 (1908). [A full critical addition of the *Quaestiones* is currently being prepared by Marie-Pierre Bussières for the CCL series.]

Contre les païens et *Sur le destin*. Ed. / trans. Marie-Pierre Bussières. SC 512 (2007). [A critical edition and French translation of *Quaestiones* 114 and 115.]

Commentaries on Romans and 1–2 Corinthians and Commentaries on Galatians-Philemon. Trans. / ed. Gerald L. Bray. Downers Grove, IL: InterVarsity Press, 2009. [This translation must be read with caution, for it is idiosyncratic and does not properly distinguish the different versions of the Commentaries. A new English translation by Theodore de Bruyn, Stephen Cooper, and David G. Hunter has begun to appear in the series Writings from the Greco-Roman World series from the SBL Press. See note 17 above.]

FURTHER READING

Di Santo, Emanuele. *L'apologetica dell'Ambrosiaster. Cristiani, pagani e Giudei nella Roma tardoantica*. Studia Ephemeridis Augustinianum 112. Rome: Institutum Patristicum Augustinianum, 2008.

"La lex Christiana nell'apologetica romana di fine IV secolo: L'Ambrosiaster e le Consultationes Zacchaei et Apollonii." In *Lex et religio: XL Incontro di Studiosi dell'Antichità Cristiana (Roma, 10–12 maggio 2012)*, Studia Ephemeridis Augustinianum 135 (Rome: Institutum Patristicum Augustinianum, 2013), 535–56.

Frakes, Robert M. *Compiling the Collatio Legum Mosaicarum et Romanarum in Late Antiquity*. Oxford Studies in Roman Society and Law.Oxford: Oxford University Press, 2011.

34 See Philip L. Reynolds, *How Marriage Became one of the Sacraments: The Sacramental Theology of Marriage from Its Medieval Origins to the Council of Trent*. Cambridge Studies in Law and Christianity (Cambridge: Cambridge University Press, 2016), 93 (Vacarius), 241 (Gratian), 396–97 (Hugh of Saint-Victor), 423–24 (Peter Lombard).

35 Maryanne C. Horowitz, "The Image of God in Man—Is Woman Included?" *Harvard Theological Review* 72 (1979): 175–206. Kari Elisabeth Børresen, "Imago dei, privilège masculin? Interprétation augustinienne et pseudo-augustinienne de Gen 1,27 et 1 Cor 11,7," *Augustinianum* 25 (1985): 213–34. In this careful study, Børresen argues that a more egalitarian view of the image of God, found in the authentic writings of Augustine, eventually found favor with the great scholastics, whereas Ambrosiaster's view persisted in the legal tradition.

Geerlings, Wilhelm. “Das Verständnis von Gesetz im Galaterbriefkommentar des Ambrosiaster.” in Dietmar Wyrwa (ed.), *Die Weitlichkeit des Glaubens in der Alten Kirche. Festschrift für Ulrich Wickert zum siebezigsten Geburtstag*, Zeitschrift für die neutestamentliche Wissenschaft und die Kunde der älteren Kirche, Beihefte 85 (Berlin: De Gruyter, 1997), 101–13.

Heggelbacher, Othmar. *Vom römischen zum christlichen Recht. Iuristische Elemente in des Schriften des sog. Ambrosiaster*. Arbeiten aus dem iuristischen Seminar der Universität Freiburg Schweiz 19. Freiburg: Universitätsverlag, 1959.

Hunter, David G. “The Paradise of Patriarchy: Ambrosiaster on Woman as (Not) God’s Image,” JTS n.s. 43 (1992): 447–69.

“The Significance of Ambrosiaster.” JECS 17 (2009): 1–26.

Lunn-Rockliffe, Sophie. *Ambrosiaster’s Political Theology*. Oxford Early Christian Studies. Oxford: Oxford University Press, 2007.

Souter, Alexander. A *Study of Ambrosiaster*. Texts and Studies 7.4. Cambridge: Cambridge University Press, 1905.

12

Augustine of Hippo

Brian Gronewoller

Augustine (AD 354–430) was bishop of Hippo Regius (Annaba, Algeria), a port city in Roman North Africa, from 396 until he died. At the time of his death, Vandal pirates were besieging Hippo Regius and taking control of Roman North Africa, separating it from the easy passage across the Mediterranean to Rome that had made it a thoroughly Romanized province of the empire. Augustine's spiritual autobiography, the *Confessions*, provides us with most of our knowledge of his early life and spiritual journey.

Aurelius Augustinus was born into a family of moderate means in the small town of Thagaste (Souk Ahras, Algeria). His mother, Monica, was a pious Christian, but his father, Patricius, did not "believe" until he was nearing death in AD 372 (*Confessions* I.11.17; cf. IX.9.19).[1] As a young adult, Augustine became a follower of Manichaeism, a radically dualistic religion similar in some respects to second-century Gnosticism. Trained in the art of oratory, Augustine worked as a teacher of rhetoric and sometimes engaged in public debates with Christians, using his superior skills to ridicule their beliefs and to argue for the veracity of Manichaeism. Augustine became disillusioned with his newfound religion, however, after meeting the Manichaean bishop Faustus, who was unable to provide satisfactory answers to Augustine's searching questions. Now in his thirties, Augustine made his way from Manichaeism to Christianity with the help of insights from Neoplatonism.

During this unsettled and transitional period of his life, Augustine's career had taken him from Carthage (near modern-day Tunis, Tunisia) to Rome, and eventually to Milan. Augustine converted to Christianity while living in Milan in 386. He returned to North Africa soon after his conversion and baptism and remained there, fervently pursuing his Christian faith, until his death in 430.

Augustine interacted with late-antique Roman law in several ways throughout his life. As a Roman citizen, he lived under the umbrella of Roman law on a daily basis, and law and rhetoric were closely related disciplines in Roman culture. Augustine's

[1] Both Augustine and his mother, Monica, are venerated as saints in traditions within Eastern and Western Christianity. Peter Brown offers 372 as the year of Patricius's death. Peter Brown, *Augustine of Hippo: A Biography*, new ed. (Berkeley: University of California Press, 2000), 3.

early career in rhetoric, moreover, brought him into contact with several people who played roles in making and enforcing the laws of the Roman Empire. While teaching rhetoric in Rome, Augustine was noticed by Symmachus, a powerful senator who recommended him to his next position as professor of rhetoric in Milan. Milan was the imperial seat in the West at that time, and in late 384 Augustine gave the panegyric (a speech of praise) before the young Western Emperor, Valentinian II. In 385, Augustine delivered another panegyric, this time to Flavius Bauto, Valentinian's *magister militum* (Master of Soldiers). Augustine's move to Milan also brought him into the circle of Ambrose, bishop of Milan and a profoundly learned Christian scholar. Formerly governor of Liguria and Emilia in northwestern Italy, Ambrose was the first bishop to deny the Eucharist to a sitting Roman emperor.[2] (After Theodosius I sanctioned the massacre of several thousand rioters in Thessalonica in 390, Ambrose would not allow him to enter the church or receive the sacraments until he had performed public penance.) Beside such interactions with leading figures, Augustine's position as a teacher of rhetoric probably brought him into contact with students who would eventually serve in some capacity within the Roman Empire. Rhetoric was an art prized by the wealthy and by the ambitious alike, since it provided them with the skills of persuasion necessary for success in law courts, councils, and meetings of the Senate.

Augustine's position as bishop of Hippo Regius – he was ordained co-bishop in 395 and bishop in 396 – also brought him into contact with various aspects of Roman law and legal practice. His duties as bishop included the *episcopalis audientia* ("audience of the bishop"). Bishops were authorized to act as judges in arbitrating disputes, including disputes over merely civil matters (see Chapter 2 in this volume).[3] Augustine's friend, fellow priest, and biographer Possidius tells us that Augustine would often spend his mornings and sometimes even entire days fulfilling his duty as episcopal judge.[4] Augustine's episcopacy also brought Roman law into his purview during the Donatist controversy, and again in the wake of the sacking of the city of Rome by Alaric and the Visigoths in AD 410. I shall discuss his thinking about law in relation to these two periods later in this chapter.

[2] See Ambrose, *Ep.* 51, in Ambrose, *Letters 1–91*, ed. R. J. Deferrari et al., trans. M. M. Beyenka, Fathers of the Church 26 (New York: Fathers of the Church, 1954), 20–26, esp. 24; Paulinus of Milan, *The Life of Ambrose* 24, in C. Harrison (ed.) and B. Ramsey (trans.), *Ambrose*, The Early Church Fathers (London: Routledge, 1997), 205–06; Theodoret, *Ecclesiastical History* V.17, NPNF 2.3, 143–45.

[3] There is disagreement among scholars concerning the genesis of the *episcopalis audientia*. John Lamoreaux, "Episcopal Courts in Late Antiquity," JECS 3.2 (1995): 143–67, at 143, frames it as "a new stage in the development of the late antique episcopal office." But Caroline Humfress, "Bishops and Law Courts in Late Antiquity: How (Not) to Make Sense of the Legal Evidence," JECS 19.3 (2011): 375–40, at 396, argues that what came to be known as the *episcopalis audientia* was merely one instantiation of the traditional Roman practice whereby private citizens could act as delegated judges, mediators, or arbitrators.

[4] Possidius of Calama, *The Life of Augustine* 19, in Possidius, *The Life of Saint Augustine*, trans. H. T. Weiskotten, Christian Roman Empire Series 6 (Merchantville: Evolution, 2008), 28.

We should be careful not to overstate Augustine's influence in the political realm of his era. He spent most of his days after his return from Milan and Rome in a small region of Roman North Africa: mainly in Hippo Regius, but sometimes in Carthage. In fact, Augustine spent only six years of his life outside of Roman North Africa, which was somewhat removed from the main currents of Roman and imperial culture. (He had sailed for Rome in 383, converted to Christianity in Milan near the end of 386, was baptized on Easter Sunday 387, and returned home to North Africa late in 388. He had intended to return earlier, but his journey was delayed by the campaign of the usurper Magnus Maximus against Valentinian II, which failed in August 388.)

Despite his immense erudition, therefore, Augustine led a provincial life. He had little in common with Christian thinkers who had direct access to the highest levels of government, such as John Chrysostom in Constantinople and Alcuin in Charlemagne's court. We might compare him rather with a figure such as Jonathan Edwards, inasmuch as both spent most of their lives removed geographically from the centers of political power and cultural energy. Because of this geographic separation, Augustine's attempts to influence the Roman government were usually made via letters sent to government officials (e.g., *Ep.* 100) or to friends who might influence such figures (e.g., *Ep.* 10*).

Moreover, unlike Aristotle (in the *Politics*) and Cicero (in *On the Republic*), Augustine did not write a treatise on politics or law. Instead, his ideas about these topics are scattered throughout his corpus and must be understood within the context of his theological projects, his engagement with religious crises and controversies, and his duties as a bishop. For example, one of Augustine's most important treatments of law is in his work *On Free Choice*, but this discussion is part of a theological argument concerning the source of evil. Scholars must reconstruct his views about law and politics from remarks throughout his corpus, therefore, keeping in mind their specific contexts.

Nevertheless, it would be difficult to overstate Augustine's enduring influence on Western legal thinking. He died as the Western Roman Empire was beginning to fail, and his extensive writings became a prominent point of reference for Christians living in the uncertain centuries that followed. In appropriating Augustine's writings for their own circumstances, his readers also interacted with the ideas on law contained within those writings.

In this chapter, I shall outline four aspects of Augustine's Christian understanding of both law and politics, for politics is the framework within which law operates. First, I shall consider Augustine's thought on the nature of law and, in particular, his division of law into four main species: eternal, temporal, natural, and divine. Second, I shall present Augustine's two-cities model of history, which he used to explicate the relationship between the Christian religion and the secular government. Third, I shall consider his thoughts on the Christian use of government-sponsored coercion, especially during the Donatist controversy. Finally, I shall outline his theory of the just war.

THE NATURE AND SPECIES OF LAW: ETERNAL, TEMPORAL, NATURAL, AND DIVINE

Augustine thought that every just temporal law (*lex temporalis*) was derived from the eternal law (*lex aeterna*). He establishes this dependence in his earliest extensive discussion of the nature of law, which is in Book I of his dialogue *On Free Choice* (AD 387–391). Here, Augustine illustrates how temporal law functions by considering a hypothetical case involving two different laws, both of which address who has the right to appoint government officials (*On Free Choice*, I.6.15). The two laws, which have been enacted in the same society at different times and in different circumstances, are mutually incompatible but equally just. One law was made during a period when the society was well ordered and the citizens placed public above private interest. In such a society, a law that gives to the people themselves the right to name the officials who will govern them is just. Later, however, this society becomes corrupt, and the people place private above public interest. Now, a different law is just: one that takes away the right to choose government officials from the people and vests it either in a single person or in a small group of persons. Although both laws cannot rightly be enacted simultaneously, Augustine argues, they are both just in relation to their respective epochs. Such contingency is part of the very essence of temporal law, which varies over time.[5]

After describing temporal law by means of this illustration, the dialogue distinguishes between temporal and eternal law and explains how they are related to each other:

AUGUSTINE: Therefore, if it pleases you, let us call that law temporal which, although it is just, can nevertheless be justly changed through time.

EVODIUS: Let us do so.

AUGUSTINE: What [else]? That law which is called the highest reason [*summa ratio*] – which should always be obeyed, through which evil [persons] earn a miserable life and the good [earn] a happy life, [and] finally through which the [law] that we said should be called temporal is rightly brought and rightly changed – cannot any intelligent [persons] see that [it is] unchangeable and eternal? (*On Free Choice* I.6.14–15; CCL 29: 220.42–51[6])

Over and above temporal law, therefore, Augustine posits a law that exists outside of time, and through which temporal law "is rightly brought and rightly changed." A few lines later, Augustine calls this law eternal and describes its relationship with temporal law:

[5] In a later chapter, Augustine adds that temporal law is what brings individuals together to form diverse societies. He writes: "For a people consists of human beings joined together by one law – the law which, as I said, is temporal." *De libero arbitrio* I.7.15 (CCL 29, 221, lines 2–3). All translations from Latin in this chapter are my own.

[6] For details of the editions of Augustine cited in this chapter, see the section at the end titled Sources.

EVODIUS: I see that this is an eternal and unchangeable law.
AUGUSTINE: Likewise, I also judge that you see in that temporal [law] nothing just and lawful that human beings did not derive from this eternal [law] (I.6.15; CCL 29: 220.55–58).

All temporal laws that are "just and lawful," Augustine claims, are derived from the eternal law (cf. *On True Religion* 31.58). Eternal law, therefore, is the source of every just temporal law.[7]

Up to this point, Augustine has established that the law in question is eternal, and that it is the source of just temporal laws. Augustine now posits three more characteristics of the eternal law:

> I want to explain briefly with words, inasmuch as I can, the notion of the eternal law that has been impressed on us – it is that by which it is just that all things may be most ordered . . . Since this law, therefore, from which all those temporal [laws] are altered for the purpose of ruling human beings, is one, it surely cannot be altered in any way (I.6.15; CCL 29: 220.64–66, 69–71).

Augustine has now revealed five characteristics of this first species of law: It is eternal, it is the source of just temporal laws, it is one, it is unalterable, and some "notion" of it has been impressed upon human beings.

What is not yet clear is the relationship between the eternal law and God in Augustine's mind. Alois Schubert has proposed in passing that Augustine understood the eternal law to be "God Himself" (*Gott selber*).[8] As I shall demonstrate in a moment, this was indeed Augustine's position by the middle of his career; but perhaps it was already his position in *On Free Choice*, where he refers to the eternal law as the "highest reason" (*summa ratio*; I.6.14–15; CCL 29: 220.46). It is possible that what Augustine denotes by the phrase "highest reason" here is God. In *On True Religion* (AD 390–91), written while he was completing Book I of *On Free Choice*, Augustine describes God as "the unchangeable nature that is above the rational soul [*supra rationalem animam*]" (*On True Religion* 31.57; CCL 32: 224.2). The Latin term for "rational" (*rationalis*) is the adjectival form of the term for "reason" (*ratio*). If Augustine, therefore, held that what is above the rational soul is also rational, then God must be "highest reason." Augustine places God above the rational soul as the source of reason in *On True Religion* (31.57), and nothing is higher than God. But

7 On Augustine's understanding of justice, see the following works by Robert Dodaro: "*Iustitia*," in C. Mayer (ed.), *Augustinus-Lexikon* (Basel: Schwabe, 2004–10), 3:865–82; *Christ and the Just Society in the Thought of Augustine* (Cambridge: Cambridge University Press, 2004), 4–5; and "Justice," in A. D. Fitzgerald et al. (eds.), *Augustine Through the Ages: An Encyclopedia* (Grand Rapids: Eerdmans, 1999), 481–83. Augustine accepts the classical philosophical doctrine that justice is the virtue of giving to each what is due while integrating that with the Great Commandment of Matt 22:37–40, since what is primarily due to God and to neighbor is love.

8 Alois Schubert, *Augustinus Lex-Aeterna-Lehre nach Inhalt und Quellen*, Beiträge zur Geschichte der Philosophie des Mittelalters 24.2 (Münster: Aschendorffschen Verlagsbuchhandlung, 1924), 5 n. 21. Schubert justifies his proposal by referring the reader to *On True Religion* 31.57.

although this reading of *On Free Choice* (I.6.14–15) is plausible, it remains only one possible reading of the text among others. James Wetzel, for example, suggests that the eternal law of *On Free Choice* is something merely "impersonal."[9]

That the eternal law is identical with God is clearer, however, in Augustine's treatment of God's will in two works written around the middle of his career. In *Confessions* VII (4.5; CCL 27: 95.17–18; AD 397–401), Augustine states: "For God Himself is the will and power of God" (*"uoluntas enim et potentia dei deus ipse est"*). This statement is consistent with his early understanding of divine simplicity. Lewis Ayres has demonstrated that by the time Augustine wrote *On Faith and the Creed* (9.20) in AD 393, he had developed a way of speaking consistent with the premise that nothing in God is accidental.[10] From this perspective, therefore, Augustine's statement in *Confessions* VII (4.5) should be understood as it is written: God's will is God. Either at the same time or shortly after writing *Confessions* VII (4.5), Augustine states twice in *Against Faustus the Manichaean* (XXII.27 and XXII.30; AD 398–400 or 408–10) that the terms "eternal law" and "the will of God" are, in effect, synonyms.[11] Taken together, these three texts show that Augustine understands the eternal law to be the same as the will of God, and the will of God to be the same as God. In short, the eternal law is God.

We cannot be certain whether this understanding of the eternal law as God was already present, albeit implicit, in Augustine's earlier thought, or rather resulted from a development that occurred between *On Free Choice* (I.6.14–15) and *Against Faustus* (XXII.27 and XXII.30). Nevertheless, we may be confident that by the time Augustine wrote *Against Faustus* in AD 398–400 or 408–10, he thought that the eternal law was God.

If we now return to the characteristics of eternal law that Augustine named in *On Free Will*, we find that two of them offer us insight into his understanding of the relationship between God and law. First, since God *is* the eternal law, all just temporal laws derive from God. Second, since God is the eternal law, a "notion" of God has been impressed upon human beings. This second insight introduces us to Augustine's third species of law – natural law.

The term "natural law" in Augustine describes the product of impressing the eternal law on to human beings. We have already encountered this idea in Augustine's discussion of the eternal law in *On Free Choice* (I.6.15). It is important to notice the precise language that Augustine uses there. What exists in human beings is not the eternal law itself, according to Augustine, but rather a certain impression or "notion" of the eternal law (*aeternae legis notionem*). Augustine,

9 James Wetzel, *Augustine and the Limits of Virtue* (Cambridge: Cambridge University Press, 1992), 72.

10 Lewis Ayres, *Augustine and the Trinity* (Cambridge: Cambridge University Press, 2010), 208–17.

11 In 22.27 (CSEL 25.1, p. 621, lines 13–14), Augustine equates the eternal law with both the reason and the will of God: "Truly the eternal law is the divine reason or the will of God, commanding the natural order to be preserved . . . " In 22.30 (p. 624, line 12), Augustine refers to "that eternal law, i.e., the will of God . . . "

moreover, explains how the notion and the eternal law itself are related. The notion "has been impressed" (*inpressa est*) upon human beings. In commonplace, non-theological discourse, the verb *inprimere* ("to impress") was used to describe the process of making coins by stamping an image onto heated metal. In that process, an unchanging original image (the stamp) was used to impress a likeness of that image on to some metal. The impression, therefore, is not the original stamp but rather a representation of it, which conveys a likeness. Augustine's use of the verb "to impress" in describing the natural law in *On Free Choice* (I.6.15) is consistent with this commonplace usage. When God creates a human being, the eternal law (the original archetype: God) impresses a notion of the eternal law (an image of the archetype) on to what is created.

A few years later, in *On the Lord's Sermon on the Mount* (2.32; AD 393–395), Augustine uses the term "natural law" explicitly to denote something that is innate in each human being. He asks: "Who wrote the natural law in the hearts of men if not God?" Augustine is thinking of Romans 2:15, where Paul refers to a law "written in their hearts," which manifests itself as conscience even among the Gentiles.[12] Following Paul, Augustine uses the verb "to write" (*scribere*) here, rather than "to impress" (*inprimere*), but they convey the same idea. In *On Free Choice* (I.6.15), Augustine describes the product by reference to its source: The natural law is a "notion of the eternal law." In *On the Lord's Sermon on the Mount* (2.32), Augustine describes the product itself, calling it simply the "natural law."

A passage in *On the Spirit and the Letter* (AD 412), too, shows that the natural law is a created impression of the eternal law. Augustine is discussing Romans 2:14–15, where Paul mentions how the Gentiles (which Augustine takes to be nonbelievers, or pagans) "naturally do those things which are of the law," even though they do not possess the revealed law of God. To be sure, sin has obscured this original, innate law, but not entirely:

> Yet the image of God is not completely rubbed away in the human soul by the blows of the earthly affections, so that no outlines remain there. Hence one may rightly say that [the soul], even in the very impiety of its life, does or at least understands something of the law, if this is what was written: "that the Gentiles who do not have the law" (this is the law of God) "naturally do those things which are of the law," and that "in the same manner, human beings themselves are a law to themselves, and they have the work of the law written on their hearts" (Rom 2:14–15), then what was impressed [*inpressum est*] there through the image of God when they were created is not entirely destroyed in every respect (*On the Spirit and the Letter* 28.48; CSEL 60: 202.12–20).

12 Rom 2:14–15 would become the proof text of natural law theory in scholastic theology. See, e.g., Thomas Aquinas, *Summa theol.* I–II.94.6, corpus and *sed contra* (citing Augustine). What Paul meant by the "Gentiles" in Rom 2:14 and by the law "written in their hearts" in 2:15, however, has been a matter of debate since the Reformation, and it continues to be contested today. See, e.g., Simon J. Gathercole, "A Law unto Themselves: The Gentiles in Romans 2.14–15 Revisited," *Journal for the Study of the New Testament* 24.3 (2002): 27–49.

Augustine distinguishes here between the law that God gave to the Jews, and another law "that was impressed [*inpressum est*] there through the image of God when they [both Jews and Gentiles] were created." This second type of law matches Augustine's description of the natural law throughout his corpus – he consistently refers to the natural law as a law written on the hearts of human beings, often with reference to Romans 2:14–15 (e.g., *Ep.* 157.3.15). Moreover, he again uses the verb "to impress" to explain how the natural law is derived from the eternal law (cf. *On Free Choice* I.6.15). But here he adds another detail: The impressed natural law belongs to the created image of God. Since God is the eternal law, and since human beings are made in the image of God (Gen 1:26–27), human beings bear the image of the eternal law.

In texts such as *Ep.* 157 (3.15), Augustine distinguishes between the overarching law that judges all human beings as guilty (presumably the natural law as an impression of the eternal law) and the special law that the Israelites received through Moses. The latter is Augustine's fourth species of law, which he variously refers to as the "law of God," "divine law," or simply "law." Unfortunately, Augustine's use of the phrase "divine law" is not entirely consistent. For example, in his twenty-fifth *Exposition on Psalm* 118 (4), Augustine uses "divine law" to refer to the Mosaic law, to which the Jews alone had access, whereas both Jews and Gentiles had access to the natural law. But in *On the Greatness of the Soul* (33.76), Augustine uses the term "divine law" to express a broader concept: that of all law that has been passed down by God.

To sum up, Augustine held that there were at least four species of law: first, the eternal law, which is God; second, the natural law, which is a "notion" of the eternal law "impressed" on human beings, and an aspect of the innate image of God; third, the temporal law, wherein particular laws change over time and vary according to circumstance, and which includes what we should call civil or secular law (and Thomas Aquinas will characterize both as "human law" and as "positive law"); and, fourth, divine law: a term that sometimes refers narrowly to the Mosaic law but can also express a broader concept of any laws passed down by God.

CHRISTIANITY'S RELATIONSHIP TO EARTHLY GOVERNMENT: THE TWO CITIES

Augustine wrote his *City of God* over a period of fourteen years (413–427). He began to write it partly in response to the sack of Rome by the Goths in 410, which had revived anxiety about traditional civic piety. Some worried that the calamity occurred because citizens had turned away from worship of the pagan and civic gods. Although the traditional cults were not demanding, the Romans had historically considered such piety to be necessary for the peace and prosperity of the community: the "peace of the gods" (*pax deorum*) established the well-being of the political community (*salus publica*). The *City of God* is primarily a theological work, therefore, in which Augustine interprets world history and earthly politics from the perspective of Scripture.

Augustine's *City of God* is a massive and complex work, impossible to summarize. The aspect of the work that is of particular interest here is his idea of the two concurrent cities, respectively earthly and heavenly. This is not exactly a theory. It is an exercise, rather, in theological reflection on the course of history, especially the human story of Rome and the divine story of God's people. Thus, it is an interpretation of history in light of theological and especially biblical ideas.

Augustine frames the story of the human condition here as one that begins with the fall from original bliss and will culminate in the eschaton: the end of the world and final judgment. During this long interim, the two cities, earthly and heavenly, are inextricably mixed together. Until the eschaton, they cannot be disentangled or manifestly distinguished. Consequently, the two communities have no perfect or manifest physical representation in time and space (XV.1). Nevertheless, the two cities are differentiated by their respective beginnings, loves, and ends.

With regard to their beginnings, or at least their human beginnings (for the separation and fall of the angels is in the background), Augustine offers Cain and Abel as the human sources of the two cities (*City of God* XV.1). He focuses on the order of their births, interpreting it in light of 1 Corinthians 15:46: "Yet that was not first which is spiritual, but that which is natural." Just as Cain was begotten first and then Abel, so the carnal, earthly city came first after the expulsion from the earthly paradise, whereas it will be followed by the spiritual, heavenly city. Moreover, whereas Cain was born as a citizen of this post-lapsarian world, Abel was born merely as a pilgrim in the earthly city, sojourning there until the advent of the heavenly city.

As a community of human beings, any "city" (i.e., a political community, or *polis*) is defined by the common purpose of its citizens, which Augustine characteristically identifies as their shared love. In Book XIV of the *City of God* (28), Augustine describes the two chief loves that differentiate the two cities. The earthly city is founded on love of self, which entails contempt for God. Conversely, the heavenly city is founded on love of God, which entails contempt of self. The citizens of the earthly city share a lust for dominating others, which pervades not only their leaders but also those under their leadership. It infects all this city's institutions of law and government. Because the earthly city loves its own strength, it honors and elevates its powerful human leaders. The citizens of the heavenly city, on the contrary, are led by an authentic love that is founded on the love of God. Here, both leaders and followers serve one another, and their mutual service is an expression of their love of God.

As regards their respective ends, the earthly city is predestined to eternal punishment with the devil, whereas the heavenly city is predestined to reign with God for all eternity (XV.1). Thus, although Rome was known as the eternal city, Augustine asserts that it is the heavenly city, or the City of God, which is truly the eternal city.

Augustine understood the two cities as having an intermingled existence until the eschaton, a view that affected his thought on law and politics. His model of intermingled existence draws on Jesus' parable of the wheat and the tares (Matt 13:24–30), which are inextricably mixed together until they are separated at the final judgment (e.g., *City of God* XX.9). Reference to this parable adds another layer of complexity to Augustine's understanding of how the two cities are related to each other. Although the two populations are intermingled for the time being, like the wheat and the tares in the field, people who appear to be citizens of one city may, in due course, reveal themselves as citizens of the other city. We might take Augustine's own life to illustrate this observation. At the age of twenty-five, the still-unconverted Augustine would have seemed to be a citizen of the earthly city. But after his conversion at the age of thirty-two, it became apparent that he was really a leading citizen of the heavenly city. Augustine's model is designed, therefore, to discourage the reader from wholly differentiating or separating the two cities. Moreover, because the two cities are intermingled for the time being, every political community is necessarily composed of citizens from both cities attempting to make common cause with one another. And this is presumably as true of the visible church as it is of the civil government.

In Book XIX of the *City of God* (15–17), Augustine construes human, man-made political structures – the authority that some human beings wield over others – as a temporal reality that emerged in response to sin.[13] He begins this discussion by arguing that slavery is an unnatural human condition. The argument depends on an exegesis of the creation story in Genesis. Augustine notes that at the time of their creation, before sin had entered into the world, human beings had dominion over the irrational animals (Gen 1:28), but not over other human beings. The "first just men" (*primi iusti*), therefore, were (literally) shepherds of flocks rather than kings of men. But with sin came slavery. In the following passage (XIX.16), Augustine implies that the Roman institution of the *paterfamilias* – a male head of household who dominates his extended family – is another result of the entry of sin into the world. Later (XIX.17), he extends the idea that domination results from sin to civic modes of authority. Whereas the heavenly city seeks eternal peace, the earthly city seeks only an earthly peace. This is achieved, according to Augustine, by a harmony of command and obedience, which results in a limited unity of human wills as regards the things necessary for mortal life.

It is here that Augustine makes one of his clearest statements regarding the relationship between the two cities. He writes:

> Moreover, it is necessary that the heavenly city, or rather the part of it that is sojourning in this [state of] mortality and living by faith, also uses that peace,

[13] Compare Paul Weithman, "Augustine's Political Philosophy," in D. V. Meconi and E. Stump (eds.), *The Cambridge Companion to Augustine*, 2nd edition (Cambridge: Cambridge University Press, 2014), 234–52, at 238–39.

> until that mortality, for which such peace is necessary, passes away. And on account of this, as long as it leads a captive life of sojourning, so to speak, among the earthly city – the promise of redemption and the spiritual gift as a pledge having been already received – it does not hesitate to obey the laws of the earthly city, by which those things which are suitable for sustaining mortal lives are administered. So, since it is common [to citizens of both cities], that mortality is protected by a harmony among both cities in things pertaining to it (*City of God*, XIX.17; CCL 48: 684.15–25).

Augustine understands that, because mortality is common to both cities for the time being, the two cities should work harmoniously together as regards the matters pertaining to their mortal existence.

Augustine does not maintain, therefore, that Christians should separate themselves entirely from the civil government. On the contrary, as long as the two cities are intermingled, Christians should work to live in harmony with the earthly city and should obey "the laws of the earthly city, by which those things which are suitable for sustaining mortal lives are administered." Augustine regards government as a feature of the earthly city, therefore, which Christians cannot avoid. In Augustine's day, the "laws of the earthly city" were to a large extent the laws of the Roman Empire, even when the emperor was a Christian who protected the church and convened ecclesiastical councils. But Augustine also set limits for this harmony and obedience. For example, he notes that Roman religious laws were formerly inconsistent with what the Scriptures tell us about God. In such circumstances, Christians are obliged to disobey the laws of the civil government – which was in fact, in Augustine's view, how Christians had historically behaved (XIX.17).

CHRISTIANITY'S USE OF THE IMPERIAL GOVERNMENT: THE DONATIST CONTROVERSY

Augustine's writings pertaining to the Donatist controversy provide us with insight into his view of the church's use of government resources to accomplish its own ecclesiastical purposes. The policies in question are often construed today as religious coercion. The Donatists, whose movement emerged after a disagreement over the contested election of the bishop of Carthage in AD 311, were members of an uncompromising, rigorist North African sect that claimed to be the continuation of authentic Christianity. The movement spread elsewhere, but it was strongest and most successful in North Africa, and Augustine spent a significant portion of his first decades as bishop addressing the controversy.

Augustine's participation in the Donatist controversy took place in the context of a Roman legal culture that was quite different than it had been a century before. In February of AD 380, the emperor Theodosius I (r. 379–395) circulated the Edict of Thessalonica (*Cod. Theod.* XVI.1.2). The edict recognized catholic Christianity as the only fully licit religion of the empire, although it did not require citizens to convert to Christianity or force them to receive baptism (as the Visigoths would do to the Jews in Spain in the sixth century, and Charlemagne would to the Saxons in the eighth century). Whether it made Christianity in some sense the "state church" of the empire is debatable, but it did confirm the role of the emperors as protectors overseeing the conduct of the Christian religion.

From the point of view both of the imperial government and of most mainstream, or "catholic," bishops, divisions within Christianity were more threatening than residual non-Christian religions.[14] Catholic bishops, therefore, collaborated with the imperial government to make a series of laws that attempted to restore Christian unity by coercing Donatist clerics and lay persons to return to the catholic church.[15] Although the laws did not permit the use of physical violence against citizens on religious grounds, by AD 407 the Donatists lost certain individual rights, such as the right to make a contract and the right to receive an inheritance (*Cod. Theod.* XVI.5.40.3–4). In 407/08, Donatist churches were confiscated and handed over to their catholic adversaries (*Cod. Theod.* XVI.5.43). By 412, heavy fines were imposed on Donatists who refused to rejoin the catholic church (*Cod. Theod.* XVI.5.52). Such, at least, was the position in law, although how effective these measures were in practice is unclear. The reality on the ground in North Africa did not always match the surviving legal texts, and the absence of any strong military presence in the province often meant that imperial laws were left to local bodies to enforce, with only mixed enthusiasm and success.[16] Donatist sentiments, moreover, were deeply entrenched in North African culture. The extent to which anti-Donatist laws and decrees were carried out to the letter in North Africa, therefore, probably varied from time to time and from place to place.

Earlier in his career, Augustine had not supported the use of law to enforce orthodoxy. In *Ep.* 93.5.17 (AD 407/08), he describes his original position as "that no one should be compelled to the unity of Christ if he were not led by a word, fought with an argument, and conquered by reason." He explains that he was concerned lest coerced conversions produce "false catholics" (*fictos catholicos*), who underwent an external conversion without a change of heart. But he notes that his opinion shifted after he observed several examples of people who had truly converted in response to unfavorable laws (see also *Ep.* 185.7.25–26; AD 416/17). Augustine, therefore, eventually accepted the use of laws and even of physical violence to coerce the Donatists back into the catholic fold.

14 I use the terminology of "catholic" vs. "Donatist" here because it was that of Augustine and of those who agreed with him, as well as of the *Theodosian Code*. There is debate among scholars over how best to frame the Donatist conflict. For example, Maureen A. Tilley, "Redefining Donatism: Moving Forward," *Augustinian Studies* 42.1 (2011): 21–32, argues that historians should speak about Donatism in its own terms, and not as a heresy.

15 The Donatists are named in such laws beginning in AD 405 (e.g., *Cod. Theod.* XVI.5.37ff).

16 Peter Brown, "Religious Coercion in the Later Roman Empire: The Case of North Africa," *History* 48 (1963): 283–305, at 288.

Augustine's rationale for this position was theological. Injury to the soul, he reasoned, was far worse than injury to the body. He outlined his new position in his *Tractates on the Gospel of John* (11.13; after AD 406). Because the Donatists are injuring souls, Augustine argues, God sometimes uses physical suffering to correct them for the sake of their own souls. In the case of the Donatists, from Augustine's perspective, God sometimes uses the laws and coercive means of the Roman government to save their souls. To justify this position, Augustine employs a figurative interpretation of the story of Sarah and Hagar in Genesis 16, where an angel instructs Hagar to return to Sarah even though Sarah was the source of Hagar's suffering (Gen 16:7–11).

Augustine does not clearly delineate what kinds of physical coercion are appropriate in this *Tractate*, but elsewhere he excludes the death penalty. In *Ep.* 100 (AD 408), Augustine writes to the proconsul of Roman North Africa, Donatus (who was not affiliated with the Donatists), to ask that he refrain from using the death penalty against Donatists who are brought into his courts. Augustine follows this plea with a polite ultimatum: If the death penalty is used in such cases, then the catholic bishops will stop referring these cases to Donatus's courts, preferring to face the threat of death at the hands of violent (but living) Donatists rather than send perpetrators to face death. In a letter written a few years later, Augustine even argues against the death penalty in the case of Donatists who had confessed to mutilating and murdering a catholic priest (*Ep.* 139.2; AD 411/12).

CHRISTIANITY, WAR, AND JUSTICE

Notwithstanding Augustine's objections to the use of the death penalty during the Donatist controversy, he was no pacifist. He articulates his position on lawful violence most fully in relation to what is known today as the just-war theory.[17] Augustine did not think that war was natural, but he believed that persons of good will must recognize that it is sometimes a necessary evil (*City of God* IV.15). Augustine's concept of the "just war" had two main pillars – prior wrongdoing and legitimate authority – as well as several ancillary aspects.

The first pillar is that wars are just only if they are waged to punish prior evil. He makes this claim in his only concise description of the just war, stated in *Questions on the Heptateuch* (6.10; CCL 33: 319.59–60; AD 419/20): "Just wars themselves are

[17] E. M. Atkins and Robert Dodaro argue that it is misleading to label Augustine the "first Christian just war theorist" because Christians had assumed that war was permissible for a long time prior to Augustine's engagement of the topic, and because Augustine had "no systematic theory of what would count as a just war." See their introduction to E. M. Atkins and R. Dodaro (eds.), *Augustine: Political Writings*, Cambridge Texts in the History of Political Thought (Cambridge: Cambridge University Press, 2004), xxiv. John McGuckin, however, sees Augustine as changing the position of his predecessors such as Tertullian, who "had severely warned against the military life outright as a profession that radically endangered one's church membership." *The Ascent of Christian Law: Patristic and Byzantine Formulations of a New Civilization* (Yonkers: St. Vladimir's Seminary Press, 2012), 143–44.

customarily defined as those which punish wrongdoings." In the *City of God* (III.10), Augustine offers an example of this pillar of just war: the Roman use of military force to defend themselves against invaders. Earlier, in *Ep.* 47.5 (before AD 399), Augustine had provided further details regarding this position. There he had stated that while no individual human being should kill another solely out of self-defense, soldiers may kill, even to defend themselves, if the killing meets two criteria: It is done on behalf of others, and it is done under lawful authority.

The second criterion introduces Augustine's second pillar, which is that just wars can only occur under legitimate authority. Augustine claims that there are two types of legitimate authority, both of which originate in God. In the *Questions on the Heptateuch* (6.10) and in *Against Faustus* (XXII.73), Augustine points out that wars waged at God's command, of which there are several examples in the Scriptures, must be just. Augustine there invokes Romans 13:1 to show that human rulers receive their authority from God (e.g., *Against Faustus* XXII.74–75). Thus, wars are just only inasmuch as they are waged under legitimate authority, that is, either directly under God's authority or under the authority of a human ruler, who in turn receives his authority from God. The role of the soldier in the just war, then, is to fight in obedience to that legitimate authority, and not on his own account.

Augustine's thought on just war also focuses on intention and attitude. Throughout his writing on war, Augustine is concerned more with the higher things of the soul than with the lower things of the body. The fault in unjust wars is not in killing per se, therefore, but rather in the bad intentions or motives of those who wage war: intentions that are incompatible with the well-ordered soul. Augustine writes in *Against Faustus* (XXII.74) that true culpability in war exists in "the desire to do harm, cruelty in punishing, an implacable soul [that is] without peace, savageness in rebelling, a lust for dominating, and any similar things." Motives are central, therefore, to whether a war is just, "for it makes a difference for which causes and by which authorities human beings undertake the waging of wars" (*Against Faustus* XXII.75). Augustine does not provide us with any specific criteria for right intention here, but we may infer from his broader theological agenda that the right reasons for waging war pertain to love of God and love of other human beings, whereas the wrong reasons pertain to love of self.

In the *City of God* (IX.7), Augustine outlines three general criteria for the manner in which the wise ruler will approach war. First, while wise persons recognize the necessity of war, they will also grieve that war is necessary. Second, the only wars that the wise will wage are just wars. Third, the wise are obligated to wage just wars only because of the wrongdoing of their opponents, and they regard even this iniquity less with anger than with sorrow.

RECEPTION AND SIGNIFICANCE

Augustine's works have remained widely read since his death in AD 430. Indeed, no Christian author in the West has been more widely read or widely quoted, from Late

Antiquity at least until the sixteenth-century Reformations, and his work continues to attract scholars, perhaps especially Christian ethicists. Christian thinkers from every Western era, furthermore, have engaged his ideas about law and politics, which are spread throughout his corpus.

Nevertheless, Augustine's ideas about law and politics have enjoyed varying degrees of influence, according to circumstance and receptivity. The ideas outlined in this chapter provide us with two contrasting examples. On the one hand, Augustine's four types of law are the basis for Thomas Aquinas's fourfold division of law in the *Summa theologiae* (I–II.91), although Aquinas modifies and develops Augustine's account for his own purposes, incorporating insights from many other sources, ranging from Aristotle and Cicero to Jerome and Albertus Magnus. On the other hand, Western Christianity after Augustine's death had little use for his dualistic theory of two intermingled and invisible cities, one destined for damnation and the other to salvation. Instead, political theology in the medieval West has showed a marked preference for models that divided Christendom (the *res publica christiana*) into two interdependent and equally Godly realms, respectively spiritual and temporal. Unlike Augustine's two cities, such realms were "visible" and clearly differentiated, not mysteriously commingled and separable only in the final judgment. Two-realm political theologies flourished in the central Middle Ages after the so-called Gregorian Reform and the establishment of the papal monarchy, but they drew less on Augustine than on ideas found in Leo I (d. 461), Gelasius I (d. 496), Isidore of Seville (d. 636), and the fraudulent Carolingian document known as the *Donation of Constantine*.[18] Charlemagne is said to have loved no book more than the *City of God* and to have had it read to him at meals,[19] but if so he seems to have either misunderstood or deliberately ignored some aspects of Augustine's model, for he understood the aggregated Christian community over which he ruled as forming a concrete manifestation of Augustine's heavenly city.[20] The heavenly city, in Charlemagne's view, was a discernible, "visible" structure even in his own time: a view foreign to Augustine's more pessimistic perspective. Later generations selectively took from Augustine's fertile mind and massive corpus precisely what they wanted and needed, adapting it to meet current needs and circumstances.

[18] See Walter Ullmann, *The Growth of Papal Government in the Middle Ages: A Study in the Ideological Relation of Clerical to Lay Power*, 2nd edition, Routledge Library Editions, Political Science 35 (London: Methuen & Co., 1962), 1–42.

[19] Einhard, *Vita Karoli Magni*, c. 24, MGH SRG (1911), 29. Cf. Thomas K. Sidey, "The Government of Charlemagne as Influenced by Augustine's *City of God*," *Classical Journal* 14.2 (1918): 119–27.

[20] See Alcuin's letter to Charlemagne, in which he both refers to Charlemagne as "David (*Dauid*)" and states that Charlemagne "rules Jerusalem (*imperare Hierusalem*)." Alcuin, *Ep.* 198 (MGH Epist. IV: 327.1, 3). See also Mayke de Jong's discussion of the Carolingian concepts of the "sacred palace" and of the empire as *ecclesia* in this volume (Chapter 6).

SOURCES

Confessiones, or *Confessionum libri XIII* [397–401] (*Confessions*): CCL 27 (ed. L. Verheijen, 1981). Henry Chadwick's translation remains the most widely read and arguably the most reliable of the several English translations, which have varying merits: Augustine, *Confessions*, trans. Henry Chadwick, Oxford World's Classics (Oxford: Oxford University Press, 2008).

De ciuitate dei [413–427] (*City of God*): CCL 47–48 (ed. B. Dombart and A. Kalb, 1955). Among several English translations, Dyson's is the most sensitive to concepts of law and politics: Augustine, *The City of God Against the Pagans*, ed. and trans. R. W. Dyson, Cambridge Texts in the History of Political Thought (Cambridge: Cambridge University Press, 1998).

Contra Faustum Manichaeum [397–399] (*Against Faustus the Manichaean*): CSEL 25.1 (ed. J. Zycha, 1891). English translation: *Answer to Faustus, a Manichean*, trans. Roland Teske, ed. Boniface Ramsay, The Works of Saint Augustine: A Translation for the 21st Century [WSA], 1.20 (2007).

De libero arbitrio [387/88–395] (usually rendered in English as *On Free Choice* or *On Free Will*): CCL 29 (ed. K. D. Daur, 1970). English translation: *On Free Will*, in Augustine, *Earlier Writings*, ed. and trans. J. H. S. Burleigh; repr. in The Library of Christian Classics (Louisville: Westminister John Knox, 2006).

Quaestionum in Heptateuchum [419/420] (*Questions on the Heptateuch*): CCL 33 (eds. J. Fraipont and D. De Bruyne, 1958). English translation: *Questions on the Heptateuch*, trans. Joseph T. Lienhard and Sean Doyle, in *Writings on the Old Testament*, ed. Boniface Ramsay, The Works of Saint Augustine: A Translation for the 21st Century [WSA], 1.14 (2016).

Latin editions of Augustine's letters are dispersed across several volumes, including the following: CCL 31 (for *Epp.* 1–50); CCL 31A (for *Epp.* 51–100); CCL 31B (for *Epp.* 101–139); and CSEL 34, 44, 57, and 88. English translations of his letters can be found in volumes 2.1–4 of WSA.

FURTHER READING

Atkins, E. M., and Robert Dodaro (eds.). Augustine, *Political Writings*. Cambridge Texts in the History of Political Thought. Cambridge: Cambridge University Press, 2004. [See the editorial introduction, xi–xxvii.]

Brown, Peter R. L. *Augustine of Hippo: A Biography*. New edition. Berkeley: University of California Press, 2000.

"St. Augustine's Attitude to Religious Coercion." *Journal of Roman Studies* 54.1/2 (1964): 107–16.

Fitzgerald, Allan D. et al. (eds.). *Augustine Through the Ages: An Encyclopedia*. Grand Rapids: Eerdmans, 1999.

Langan, John. "The Elements of St. Augustine's Just War Theory." *The Journal of Religious Ethics* 12.1 (1984): 19–38.

Lenski, Noel E. "Evidence for the *Audientia episcopalis* in the New Letters of Augustine." In R. W. Mathisen (ed.), *Law, Society, and Authority in Late Antiquity* (Oxford: Oxford University Press, 2001), 83–97.

Markus, R. A. *Saeculum: History and Society in the Theology of St. Augustine*. Revised edition. Cambridge: Cambridge University Press, 1988.

"Saint Augustine's Views on the 'Just War.'" In W. J. Sheils (ed.), *The Church and War: Papers Read at the Twenty-First Summer Meeting and the Twenty-Second Winter Meeting of the Ecclesiastical History Society*, Studies in Church History 20 (Oxford: Blackwell, 1983), 1–13.

McGuckin, John A. *The Ascent of Christian Law: Patristic and Byzantine Formulations of a New Civilization*. Yonkers: St. Vladimir's Seminary Press, 2012. [See ch. 6 (pp. 127–66), "A Theology of Politics and Law in the Latin West: St. Augustine of Hippo."]

O'Donovan, Oliver. "Augustine's City of God XIX and Western Political Thought." *Dionysius* 16 (1987): 89–110.

O'Donovan, Oliver, and Joan Lockwood O'Donovan. "Augustine of Hippo." In Oliver O'Donovan and Joan Lockwood O'Donovan (eds.), *From Irenaeus to Grotius: A Sourcebook in Christian Political Thought, 100–1625* (Grand Rapids: Eerdmans, 1999), 104–63.

TeSelle, Eugene. "Toward an Augustinian Politics." *Journal of Religious Ethics* 16.1 (1988): 87–108.

13

Leo the Great

Susan Wessel

LIFE AND WORK

Tradition has it that Leo the Great was the son of a Tuscan man named Quintianus.[1] We know nothing about the place of his birth or the circumstances of his upbringing. The quality and extent of his education can be surmised only from his literary output. The succinct Latin style of his letters and sermons reveals a good, general education in rhetoric, while the rhythm of his prose suggests a certain familiarity with the style of writing used by the imperial chancery. Missing from his writings are the allusions to pagan literature and philosophy that we find in the most sophisticated theologians of the early church, such as Augustine and Ambrose. Also missing are the elaborate rhetorical flourishes that were common among the educated elite of the Greek-speaking Eastern churches. Instead, we are treated to a balanced and terse prose stylist whose education consisted in the typical school exercises in which the elite of the late Roman world participated. Generally, these emphasized the rules of rhetoric, which were gathered from examples drawn from pagan literature and courtroom speeches. The pagan literature and culture that Leo must have met during the course of his education did not find its way into the content of his prose.

Most of the over 170 extant letters that Leo wrote to emperors, bishops, and clergy can be assigned to one or the other of two groups.[2] Some negotiated the relationship between Rome and the Western churches of Arles, Spain, North Africa, Italy, and the vicariate of Illyricum, whereas others articulated Rome's intention to influence the debates about the connection between the human and divine natures of Christ that were taking place among the bishops and clergy of the eastern Roman world. The importance of the letters goes well beyond their stated purpose. Interspersed with comments about social and political life and its circumstances, they include windows onto the shifting contexts and untold challenges that Christians

1 A more complete treatment of the material discussed here can be found in S. Wessel, *Leo the Great and the Spiritual Rebuilding of a Universal Rome*, Vigiliae Christianae Supplements 93 (Leiden: Brill, 2008).

2 On the manuscript collections and early editions of Leo's letters and sermons, see Charles L. Feltoe, in NPNF 2/12 (Edinburgh: T & T Clark, repr. 1989), xiii–xiv.

encountered while living in the late Roman world. It is here in the letters, nestled among the developing relationships of power, that Leo's legal material appears.

The extant corpus also includes ninety-six sermons. Although these do not contain explicit legal material, they are relevant for understanding the theology of law and justice that emerged in the context of his pastoral commitments.

Leo's ecclesiastical career began when he served as an acolyte for Zosimus, the bishop of Rome from 417 to 418. During that time, he delivered a letter condemning the teachings of the monk Pelagius (c. 360–418) on divine grace to Aurelius of Carthage (d. c. 430). Some five to ten years later, when Caelestine was the bishop of Rome (r. 422–432), Leo was promoted to the office of archdeacon. His responsibilities included administering church finances and making distributions to the poor. During the bishopric of Sixtus III (r. 432–440), he offered advice regarding the treatment of those who subscribed to Pelagianism. We also hear about Leo's duties as archdeacon during the course of the Christological controversy involving Cyril of Alexandria and Nestorius, then metropolitan bishop of Constantinople. Leo took a stand by commissioning the monk and spiritual leader John Cassian to write a treatise condemning Nestorius's Christology. In a letter that foretold Leo's later commitment as the bishop of Rome to shaping the relative distribution of patriarchal authority, Cyril complained that Juvenal of Jerusalem had attempted improperly to elevate the see of Jerusalem.[3] He requested Leo's political intervention in Rome to scale back the jurisdictional encroachment.

While still an archdeacon, Leo also served in a secular diplomatic mission to settle a controversy between Albinus, the Italian praetorian prefect, and Aetius, the Gallic *magister militum* (commander of soldiers).[4] Tension had been growing between the Italian and Gallic aristocracies because of Aetius's new policy of equitable taxation among the landholding Italians. It would have resulted in their bearing a greater percentage of the tax burden. Leo was chosen for the mission even though members of the court of Western emperor Valentinian could have intervened, having just returned to Rome from a stay at the imperial residence in Ravenna. We may conclude from Leo's participation in the mission that he was not merely filling a power vacuum in Rome, but rather was uniquely qualified to represent the interests of the Italian aristocracy. While Leo was serving as a diplomat in Gaul, Sixtus III, the bishop of Rome, died. Upon Leo's return to Rome, he was consecrated priest and bishop on 29 September 440, becoming the forty-seventh bishop of Rome.

As bishop, Leo expanded the same policies and cultivated similar priorities as he had pursued as an archdeacon. For example, in accordance with his prior recommendations to Sixtus III, he regulated the reentry into orthodoxy of Pelagian priests, deacons, and lower clergy in the province of Aquileia. The Pelagians were known for their controversial view that divine grace was not necessary to attain spiritual

[3] Leo, *Ep.* 119.4, 11 June 453.

[4] Briggs L. Twyman, "Aetius and the Aristocracy," *Historia* 19.4 (1970): 480–503, at 490–91.

perfection. Against the heresy known as Manicheanism, a dualist sect that challenged Leo's view of the Incarnation, he orchestrated what might be considered the first inquisition in Rome.[5] Leaders of the sect were examined before a panel of ecclesiastical and secular officials over which Leo presided. The trial resulted in the burning of their books and the banishment of their members. After the trial, bishops and clergy were instructed to seek out those who had left Rome to hide in the countryside. In support of these disciplinary measures, emperor Valentinian withdrew the Manicheans' rights of citizenship. Leo used the same collaborative approach as he had used to suppress the Manicheans, in which he involved the Christian aristocracy and imperial court as well as the provincial bishops, more generally to enact his other policies.

With respect to Leo's relationship with the Western churches, his reputation as an ambitious architect of Roman hegemony has perhaps been overstated. The situation in Gaul is a case in point. Leo's interest there was not merely to extend Roman leadership into Gaul but rather to preserve the relative autonomy of its provincial bishops. Hilary, the bishop of Arles (d. 449), was a well-educated aristocrat with ties to the ascetic spirituality centered on the island of Lerins, off the southern coast of Gaul. It came to Leo's attention that Hilary had deposed Celidonius, the bishop of Besançon in northern Gaul, for having violated canonical regulations. Celidonius traveled to Rome to appeal against his deposition (445). In the presence of Hilary, Leo conducted a hearing at which Celidonius was absolved of the charges against him, and Hilary's authority was limited to Arles.[6] We know that Leo was at least open to the idea of Gallic bishops' expanding their sphere of activity, because five years later (450) he divided the authority of the metropolitan between the new bishop of Arles and the bishop of Vienne.[7] His objection had been to Hilary's intervention in the affairs of outlying bishoprics. This was not an attempt to radiate power unilaterally from the Roman see.[8]

Apart from Hilary, the Western provincial churches generally acknowledged the authority of Rome to issue decisions and prescribe regulations that applied to their internal administration. During these same years (443–446), for instance, a certain willingness to listen to Rome was apparent in the province of Mauritania Caesariensis in North Africa. Leo issued a number of decretals that were meant to provide guidelines for the administration of this province.[9] Many of the rulings were

[5] See Bronwen Neil's chapter on Gelasius I in this volume.

[6] Leo, *Ep.* 10.3. Leo thought the proceedings in Rome were legitimate because he was merely responding to an appeal that Celidonius's supporters in Gaul had sent to him.

[7] The people apparently reported that at one time the bishoprics of Arles and Vienne were under a common jurisdiction. Leo decided that the bishop of Vienne was to preside over the neighboring cities of Valence, Tarentaise, Geneva, and Grenoble, while the bishop of Arles was to govern the remaining cities of the province. See Leo, *Ep.* 66.2, 5 May 450, *Lectis dilectionis vestrae*.

[8] On the later reception and development of Leo's view of papal authority, see Neil's chapter on Gelasius I in this volume.

[9] Leo, *Ep.* 12, August 446, *Cum de ordinationibus*.

familiar from other contexts and would not have been controversial. Widowers and twice-married men were not to serve as priests; usury was forbidden for both clergy and laity; the multiplication of bishoprics was to be avoided; ecclesiastical promotions were not to be hasty; and there were rules to govern the appointment of bishops. A cursory view of the matter might suggest that Leo conspired to interfere in the governance of the provincial churches. Yet it is worth mentioning that the African province had initiated contact with Rome in order to resolve certain administrative problems that had arisen in the context of the Vandal invasions. Leo's decretals provided the guidelines within which provincial bishops were to operate, and they perhaps offered a sense of order amid the chaos of the Vandals. Although this model of ecclesiastical authority was hierarchical, it drew its inspiration from the fluid notion of power that operated in the secular administration where provincial officials carried out their duties autonomously. They were expected to resolve most problems independently of the central administration.

The patriarchal churches of the East had their own way of understanding the circumstances under which Rome might intervene in their administration. Their model of ecclesiastical decision-making recognized the exercise of Roman episcopal authority only within the context of an ecumenical council. Such a council was thought to be legitimate when an emperor convoked it and large numbers of clergy and bishops attended. Constantinople argued further that its standing among the patriarchal sees should reflect its political distinction as the new Rome. As the Eastern center of imperial and senatorial power, Constantinople's political stability rivaled the shifting political landscape in Rome. In contrast, Leo understood the Roman primacy to originate directly from its unique authority as the Apostolic See of St. Peter. These divergent models contributed to the disagreements that unfolded over the course of the Nestorian controversy and the subsequent Council of Chalcedon (449–454). During the Council, for instance, the see of Constantinople confirmed its place of honor alongside Rome and secured the jurisdictional privileges it had been exercising over the Eastern dioceses of Pontus, Asia, and Thrace.[10] This extension of jurisdictional boundaries was perhaps modeled on Rome's relationship to the metropolitan district in southern Italy and to the provincial churches of the North. Whereas Constantinople drew its jurisdictional boundaries to reflect the current state of its ecclesiastical responsibilities, Rome saw the move as an intentional slight against Roman hegemony.

At the same time as the Christological controversies were unfolding in the East (450–455), the Huns and then the Vandals were threatening the Western empire. With respect to the Huns, their leader, Attila, had launched an unsuccessful military campaign against Gaul (451). On retreat from their losses, Attila and his men plundered the cities and towns of northern Italy, which the imperial army had

[10] See Leo, *Ep.* 98; *Epistula concilii Chalcedonensis ad Leonem*, ACO II.3.2, 93–96, at 93. For an English translation, see Richard Price and Michael Gaddis, *The Acts of the Council of Chalcedon* (Liverpool: Liverpool University Press, 2005), vol. 3, 120–27, at 121.

abandoned. To spare the destruction of Rome, Leo, accompanied by two ex-officials, undertook a diplomatic mission to convince Attila to withdraw his troops peacefully beyond the Danube river. Attila complied. Leo's secretary, Prosper of Aquitaine, attributed the success of the mission to the sacerdotal power of the Roman episcopal office.[11] Although this explanation cannot be trusted, there is no doubt that Leo, seasoned by his earlier mission in Gaul, was the most qualified person left in Rome to undertake the embassy. It was a compelling rebuke of the political situation.

When the Vandal king Geiseric learned that the imperial succession was in disarray, he marched on Rome (454).[12] Loyal supporters of Aetius had recently assassinated Valentinian in revenge for his murder. Less than three months later, the imperial servants murdered his successor, Petronius Maximus, whom they perceived as an illegitimate usurper. The Vandals easily captured Rome. Leo intervened by meeting with Geiseric outside the city gates. In exchange for sparing the city from ruin, the Vandals abducted Valentinian's widow and daughter, took thousands of Roman prisoners, and looted Rome for its treasures. The most Leo could do was replace the consecrated vessels that the Vandals had stolen by melting down silver water-jars for the parish churches. He negotiated with the Vandal king without the objections either of the imperial court or of the aristocracy, with whom he had formed an alliance. Yet there is no evidence that Leo's diplomacy in this regard was interpreted in anything other than political terms. Not even Prosper claimed that divine intervention had redirected the Vandals. The cautious intervention of a bishop seemed to imply that Rome was more than its imperial territories, that it could exist without the presence of the Western emperor, and that its boundaries could be defended in normal, linear time. Rome was not fading away; it was simply changing. Prosper was determined to show that Leo and the sacerdotal office that he represented were destined to guide the transformation.

THE DEVELOPMENT OF ECCLESIASTICAL REGULATION

Leo inherited a view of justice drawn from the Old Testament, where the virtuous were rewarded and the sinful punished, as well as from the New Testament, which emphasized divine mercy and forgiveness. Both theologies were combined with the Stoic ethics and metaphysics that Leo would have absorbed through such predecessors as Ambrose and Augustine. The Stoic principles with which he and other educated Christians were familiar looked something like the following: First, the natural impulse of parents to love their children led to the formation of human associations and then of societies. Second, law, being the practical embodiment of

11 "Ita summi sacerdotis praesentia rex gavisus est" ("So the king rejoiced in the presence of the highest priest"). Prosper of Aquitaine, *Epitoma Chronicorum*, a. 452, 1367, in Theodore Mommsen (ed.), *Chronica Minora*, MGH AA 9:385–485.

12 Prosper, *Epitoma Chronicorum*, a. 455, 1375.

divine reason, was instrumental even in the creation of human beings and of the universe. Stoic rationality guided the ethical movement from parental love of children to the widespread love of humanity. This Stoic humanitarian vision was rooted in the utilitarian desire to bring about certain social ends,[13] but it had nothing to do with the Christian commitment to a universal altruism. The Stoic sage was the perfect embodiment of the rationality of the cosmos, which he expressed in his moral actions.[14] Among the early Christians, however, such perfection was held as an ideal that could never be attained. Because the human mind was only an image and not a replica of the perfect divine rationality, even the model Christian could not fully grasp God's moral plan. Over time, the ecclesiastical regulations acknowledged this truth about human imperfection and the limits of human knowledge. The circumstances of individual cases shaped the development of canonical regulation, even while certain universal principles continued to function.

Early in his episcopacy (c. 442), Leo identified two main sources of ecclesiastical regulation: canons and decretals. Canons were rulings promulgated in the context of ecumenical and provincial councils, while decretals were decisions that the bishops of Rome made in response to questions posed by members of the church hierarchy.[15] As in Roman law, both resources recognized prior decisions as binding legal precedent. For example, when the members of a council developed new canons, they examined the circumstances before them in the context of earlier canons. Likewise, the bishop of Rome issued decisions that applied scriptural ordinances, conciliar canons, and prior decretals to particular cases. The legitimacy of the regulation depended on this sense of continuity. In terms of jurisprudence, continuity held the promise of fairness and guarded against the development of ad hoc and arbitrary rules. It was consistent with the traditional nature of Christian doctrine and its rejection of innovation. Yet the commitment to continuity was not such that it prevented the Christian ideals of mercy and kindness from functioning in the legal context.

The Christians departed from the Stoics in the way they made the principles of justice and equity enter canonical regulation. Among the Stoics, the wise man was an extension of the same moral law as that rooted in the natural universe. Among Christians, however, the evolving character of the good man took the place of the universal reason of Stoic moral theory. Leo was instrumental in this transformation.

13 Malcolm Schofield, "Two Stoic Approaches to Justice," in André Laks and Malcolm Schofield (eds.), *Justice and Generosity: Studies in Hellenistic Social and Political Philosophy*, Proceedings of the Sixth Symposium Hellenisticum (Cambridge: Cambridge University Press, 1995), 193, 203, and 206.

14 Phillip Mitsis, "Natural Law and Natural Right in Post-Aristotelian Philosophy: The Stoics and Their Critics," in *Aufstieg und Niedergang der römischen Welt* II.36.7 (1994): 4812–50, at 4813 and 4843. On law as the "supreme reason" that generates positive laws, see Jill Harries, *Cicero and the Jurists: From Citizen's Law to the Lawful State* (London: Duckworth, 2006), 53–58.

15 On imperial rescripts, see Jill Harries, *Law and Empire in Late Antiquity* (Cambridge: Cambridge University Press, 1999), 26–31, as well as Harries' chapter in this volume (ch. 2), passim, and esp. the section on "Thinking Law."

He thought that the character of the righteous Christian should be cultivated in the context of human imperfection. It was not a natural extension of the universal law. "The law had not been set down for the righteous" (1 Tim 1:9), he pointed out, for the just man fulfilled the norms of legal precepts by a discernment of his will, and the true love of justice contained the authority both of the Apostles and of the canons.[16] Instead of the sage who embodied legal principles by virtue of his nature, there was the Christian just man whose character "fulfilled the norms of legal precepts" with his moral effort. Through cautious attention to his spiritual development, the Christian cultivated Christian virtues so that he might become just. The intention of the interpreter and the quality of his moral character, therefore, influenced the process, as well as the outcome, of legal interpretation. Following the rules strictly did not guarantee their just application, as it might have for the Stoic sage. Leo thought that human beings, in their fallen nature, could neither embody nor implement divine justice perfectly. The most they could do was approximate it through the just man's application of the law.

Those whom Leo disparaged as heretics undermined this understanding of justice by being too much like the Stoics. The Priscillians, followers of a Christian sect known for their rigorous asceticism and dualist beliefs, are a case in point.[17] Just as the Stoics posited a reason that pervaded the universe, so the Priscillians saw divine universalism everywhere. Leo thought that this view led inexorably to a kind of astrological fatalism, in which the rationality of astral movements controlled the correspondingly rational decisions of human beings. Astrological fatalism diminished the gulf between humanity and the divine because it made human moral action dependent on the cosmos. Leo thought that this weakened the justice of rewards and punishments, thereby destroying "all the decrees not only of human laws, but also of the divine constitutions." The possibility of moral failure had been accounted for in the narrative of the Fall and in the transgressions of Adam and Eve. It was the reason for the fully human nature of Christ that Leo articulated in his theology of the Incarnation. Only a Christ who had truly suffered and died as a human being was capable of saving the human race. Astrological fatalism challenged the necessity of the Incarnation because it assumed that human beings were endowed with the perfect rationality of the cosmos and did not need to be saved.

The reality of suffering in the late Roman world was, as far as Leo was concerned, inconsistent with the view that human actions mirrored the stars. Suffering existed because human beings were imperfect and incapable of perceiving the rationality of the divine law. They could not understand why God did not compensate according to individual merit. Yet, for Leo, the unequal distribution of heavenly gifts was not a fact to be lamented. It mirrored the grace in Christ that God had freely bestowed. Just as Christ had received grace without regard to his merit, so had human beings

16 Leo, *Ep.* 41, c. 22, August 449, *Provectionem dilectionis.*

17 Leo, *Ep.* 15.11, 21 July 447, *Quam laudabiliter pro.*

been rewarded and punished without regard to merit. Likewise, Paul had taught that it was grace that saved people, not works. Grace was the principle of righteousness, the source of goodness, and the origin of charitable acts.[18] Leo incorporated such Pauline ideas when he said that divine preparation (*praeparatio*), not innate diligence (*naturalis industria*), bestowed good works. In making this claim he challenged the anthropology both of astrological fatalism and of Pelagianism. Both had imagined the possibility of human perfection in the context of justice. Leo, in contrast, saw that human beings were only an image and not a copy of the divine, wholly rational mind, and that their moral actions required divine assistance.

Leo's notion of justice presumed that human beings were autonomous individuals who achieved virtuous acts and carried out transgressions in the context of the Christian narrative of redemption. Free will was both the precondition for the Fall and integral to the divine, salvific plan. Like his predecessors in the West, Leo believed that "the devil had not dealt with the first man [i.e., Adam] so violently as to bring him over to his side without the consent of free will [*sine liberi arbitrii consensione*]."[19] Humanity inherited this sin from Adam and received the punishment of death. Insofar as the sin had been voluntary, Leo thought that the punishment should be remedied according to equitable principles. He was certain that justice would not have been served by the unilateral application of divine power. The Incarnation brought about the just restoration of the human race because it respected the rationality of divine justice. It redeemed humanity through the very substance (*per ipsam materiam*) by which the "universal captivity" of the human race had come about.[20] The human nature that had sinned in Adam was restored in Christ, whose intermingling of the human and the divine healed the fallen human race. The perfect justice of Christ paid the debt that humanity owed because of original sin. For Leo, this equitable process preserved human dignity by acknowledging the individual as a flawed, though rational, decision-maker. It then transformed humanity into the divine in two ways: The payment of Adam's debt restored immortality to human beings, and the internal logic of the narrative of redemption reflected the divine rationality. The paradox was that human beings approached perfection only when the rationality of justice unfolded in the fully human context of freedom.

Leo applied this theology of justice to concrete cases. Yet his view that justice came about in the context of human frailty and imperfection did not necessarily result in lenient regulations or judgments. Consider, for instance, the wandering Pelagians. They were the priests, deacons, and lower clergy who had left their native province of Aquileia to travel to the neighboring cities and regions of northern Italy. Septimus, the bishop of one such city, Altino, reported them to Leo.[21] Several

18 Leo, *Ep.* 1.3, 442 (?), *Relatione sancti*.

19 Leo, *Serm.* 28.3, 452, *Cum semper nos*, December 452.

20 Leo, *Serm.* 63.1, 19 March 452, *Gloria, dilectissimi, dominicae passionis*.

21 Leo, *Ep.* 1.1, 442 (?). *Ep.* 14.9, 14.10, c. 6, January 446, *Quanta fraternitati*.

conciliar canons applied to traveling clerics: canon 15 of the Council of Nicaea made it unlawful for bishops, presbyters, or deacons to leave the church where they had been ordained; the Council of Sardica (342/3) excommunicated bishops who transferred their sees; canon 38 of the third Council of Carthage (397) held the governor of the province responsible for returning a transferred bishop to his original see. (An exception to this general rule was later recognized by the fourth Council of Carthage in 475, which said that bishops were permitted to transfer sees if a provincial synod determined that doing so would benefit the church.)[22] Leo reasoned that canons preventing the orthodox from leaving their churches should be applied even more strictly to Pelagians who had left their diocese. They, as well as the orthodox bishops who had received them, had violated the canons. Leo expanded this ruling four years later when he decided that bishops were not to receive the clergy of another diocese without the consent of both dioceses.[23] His successor, Hilary I, interpreted this rule in the strict manner in which it was intended. Thus, Hilary denied the transfer of a Spanish bishop, despite the fact that the people and clergy of the province supported the change and considered it beneficial.

Leo also contributed to the developing body of rules governing the election of clergy and bishops. These were supposed to embody the ideal just man whose discernment of the will imbued legal norms with the principles of justice. Leo articulated several criteria to identify suitable candidates: They were supposed to be (i) citizens and freed men, (ii) who had been instructed in the ecclesiastical discipline, (iii) over the course of many years.[24] Slaves and serfs who had not been freed by their masters were prohibited from serving in the priesthood. Leo thought that ordaining persons still in servitude compromised their loyalty to the church and infringed upon the rights of masters. The idea that servitude was incompatible with the responsibilities of church office had been established among the early Christians. The Apostle Paul, for example, never questioned that his friend and co-worker Philemon, a slave-owning master, must free his slave, Onesimus, according to Roman law before Onesimus could be of service to the church. By no later than the mid-fourth century, this example found its way into the *Apostolic Canons*, a collection of early canons that purported to derive its authority from the Apostles. Canon 82 decreed: "[I]f any servant should appear worthy of receiving an order, as our Onesimus appeared, and his masters agree, and liberate him, and send him out of their house, he may be ordained." The canon was construed narrowly by the Council of Elvira (c. 309), which prohibited freedmen whose former

22 Council of Nicaea, canon 15, in P.-P. Joannou (ed.), *Fonti. Discipline générale antique* (IVe–IXe s.) (Grottaferrata [Roma]: Tipografia Italo-Orientale "S. Nilo," 1962–1964), I, 1, 36–37. Council of Sardica, canons 1 and 2, in Joannou, I, 2, 175–76. Council of Carthage 3, August 397, canon 38, in Charles Munier (ed.), *Concilia Africae*, a. 345 – a. 525, CCL 149, 335–36. Council of Carthage 4, c. 475, canon 27, ibid., 346.

23 Leo, *Ep.* 14.10, c. 6 January 446.

24 Leo, *Ep.* 6.3, 12 January 444, *Omnium quidem litteras*. They were to avoid swift ordinations: see Leo, *Ep.* 12.2, 10 August 446.

patrons were still alive from being ordained to the clergy. In supposing that the master-slave relationship continued until the master's death, the council perhaps reasoned that ecclesiastical canons should be more rigorous than the secular laws. A former slave became eligible for ecclesiastical office only when he was severed from all earthly ties to his master. But it is unlikely that Leo either knew or approved of this narrow interpretation by the council. Rather, his ruling implied that slaves who had been freed according to Roman law could be ordained to the clergy, and that such an ordination would not compromise any presumed duty of a freedman to his prior master.

Several canons addressed the disruption to social and familial life caused by the Vandals and Huns. When the Huns invaded northern Italy, for example, they carried off men as prisoners of war. Women were left to manage the family alone. Believing their husbands would never return, some remarried. When several men returned unexpectedly, Leo responded with a series of decretals. He reasoned that legal obligations should be honored to restore life to conditions prior to the invasions. Marriage, being a contract like any other, he said, rendered the wife the property of the husband. The first husband was, therefore, entitled to recover his property and his marriage at his discretion. Yet Leo believed that such a man was not obligated to rejoin his wife unless he still felt affection toward her. The second husband, who had contracted a marriage that was legal at the time, had neither legal claim against the first husband nor liability for violating the former marriage. Such men were blameless, because, as Leo put it, "many things that belonged to those who were led into captivity could pass into the possession of another, and yet it is altogether just that, when these men return, their property should be restored."[25] In addition to slaves, lands, houses, and personal goods, personal property included wives. The preferences of women in such cases were irrelevant. If a woman refused to rejoin her first husband, then she was considered to be living in a state of incontinence and was excluded from communion. The Roman civil law had been more humane in permitting the original marriage to be reinstated only if both parties agreed. Prior to Leo, Innocent I had addressed the similar case of a woman who had returned from captivity to find that her husband had remarried in her absence. Because she, the first wife, was still alive, the marriage was declared valid, regardless of the husband's wishes.[26]

Another challenging case involved the consecrated virgins who had been raped by invaders.[27] No prior ruling addressed this situation precisely. Cyprian and Jerome

[25] Leo, *Ep.* 159.2, 1 March 458: "Sic enim multa quae ad eos qui incaptivitatem ducti sunt pertinebant in jus alienum transire potuerunt, et tamen plenum justitiae est ut eisdem reversis propria reformentur."

[26] Innocent, *Ep.* 36, PL 20:602B. Henri Crouzel, *L'église primitive face au divorce. Du premier au cinquième siècle* (Paris: Beauchesne, 1971), 303–04. Note that the secular law permitted women whose husbands had been missing for at least four years to remarry: See T. Mackin, *Divorce and Remarriage* (New York: Paulist Press, 1984), 98.

[27] Note that Leo distinguishes virgins who have taken the habit from those who have been consecrated. Even the former were guilty of wrongdoing if they married. René Metz, *La consécration des vierges dans l'église romaine, étude d'histoire de la liturgie* (Paris: Presses Universitaires de France, 1954), 89.

had said that virgins who had lost their virginity irresponsibly (as distinct, for example, from those raped by barbarians) were to be demoted to the status of widows; and the Council of Elvira (309) had ruled that consecrated virgins who married were guilty of adultery, because they were already married to Christ. Leo thought that this new case was different. He reasoned that the virgins who had been raped by invaders had not been defiled in their spirit (*animus*), because their mind (*mens*) had not acquiesced to the violence. Their status had changed, nonetheless, because of the defilement, and they were no longer counted among the holy virgins. Nevertheless, as long as they "persevered in the virgin life," they were allowed to partake of the sacraments.

The state of mind of a so-called sinner did not erase a transgression until Leo confronted the problem of rebaptism. In northern Italy, some had been taken captive by the Huns at such a young age that they could not recall whether they had been baptized.[28] The circumstances in southern Gaul were similar. Legal precedent in such cases was clear: as the Apostle Paul had said, "one Lord, one faith, one baptism." The injunction was later confirmed by Cyprian (except in the case of schismatic Christians) and then upheld by the Council of Carthage (397) and in the Canons of the Council of Carthage (419), which also forbade re-ordinations and the translation of bishops from one see to another.[29] Although Leo was aware of the precedent, he made an exception for prisoners of war who had returned home unable to recall whether they had received the rite as an infant. Where no memory of baptism existed, he reasoned, the rite could be performed without fear of repetition.[30] This case apparently differed from that of the consecrated virgins, because refusal to permit baptism would have prevented released captives from receiving the sacraments. The African Canons (419) had addressed a similar problem when the Vandals entered North Africa. Children who had been taken captive were, upon their return, to receive the rite of baptism, so that "failure to do so would not deprive them of the cleansing of the sacraments." Leo later decreed that baptism was acceptable for such children as long as no one could be found to testify that the rite had been performed earlier.[31]

See also Bryan Ward-Perkins, *The Fall of Rome and the End of Civilization* (Oxford: Oxford University Press, 2005), "The Horrors of War" (13–31) at 13.

28 Leo, *Ep.* 166.1, 24 October 458, *Frequenter quidem*.

29 On the canons promulgated at Carthage, known collectively as the African Canons, see F. L. Cross, "History and Fiction in the African Canons," *Journal of Theological Studies* 12.2 (1961): 227–47.

30 Leo, *Ep.* 167.16, 458/9 (?).

31 Note that Leo prohibited second baptism for those who had been baptized improperly by heretics. Such a person would not have received the Holy Spirit, but Leo reasoned the imposition of the bishop's hands, without baptism, would suffice to confer the Spirit. Leniency was still generally the rule when unintentional errors occurred. For example, someone who had mistakenly received a second baptism, and then later understood that this second baptism had violated the canons, would be received into full communion after receiving penitence and the laying on of the bishop's hands.

Penance excused former prisoners of war who had eaten the sacrificial food offered to them by their captors. Provided that they had taken the food because of fear (*metus*) or hunger (*indigentia*), and not as an expression of "religious devotion" (*pro religionis veneratione*), they were to be readmitted to communion after performing a sincere penance.[32] A stricter rule applied to those who had worshipped idols or committed murder or fornication while in captivity. They were to be admitted to communion only after performing public penance (*poenitentia publica*). Likewise, Gregory Thaumaturgus, the bishop of Neocaesarea, had earlier addressed the problems caused by the Goths' invasion of Asia Minor. Perhaps more forgiving than Leo, Gregory treated those who had unwillingly eaten sacrificial foods – assuming they had not worshipped idols – as if the incident had never occurred. Furthermore, women who had been raped by the Goths were not guilty of having engaged in sexual activity unless their prior life had been lascivious.

LATER INFLUENCE

The legal and canonical material that Leo drew upon, as well as the later reception of his decretals into the canon collections of the Middle Ages, presumes the existence of a papal bureaucracy. In the early period, the papal archive would have served this function. Known as the *scrinium*, such an office is, in fact, attested by the middle of the fourth century. It is then confirmed by Leo, who acknowledged having found "in our archives" (*in nostro scrinio*) a letter he had received from Cyril of Alexandria, presumably while he, Leo, was still a deacon. The archives contained the letters sent and received by the papal office and recorded in a register. The bureaucracy of the Roman Empire followed the same practice, although no such document from the early period has survived.

There are two document collections that suggest that the papal office made use of registers early on: a collection of decretals (c. 443), and the *Avellana collectio*, a compilation of four different registers starting from the papacy of Liberius (352–366).[33] Given that the prototype was the secular register, it is likely that the entire document, and not just the title and other epistolary features, was preserved in such registers. Also included in the archives were the notarial transcripts of councils from as early as the Council of Carthage (411), as well as copies of important letters and documents that the pope did not personally send or receive. The *florilegium* that Leo sent to educate the emperor Leo I regarding the Christological controversy attests to the range of documents at his disposal, whether from the archives or an adjacent library.[34] The office of the papal chancery, as it came to be known once the

[32] Leo, *Ep.* 159.5, 21 March 458.

[33] Reginald L. Poole, *Lectures on the History of the Papal Chancery down to the Time of Innocent* III (Cambridge: Cambridge University Press, 1915), 30. For the Avellana collectio, see *Epistulae Imperatorum Pontificum aliorum inde ab a. CCCLXVII usque ad a. DLIII datae*, CSEL 35.

[34] Leo, *Ep.* 109.3, 25 November 452, *Gravia sunt et. Ep.* 165, 17 August 458, *Promisisse me.*

title of chancellor was borrowed from the imperial bureaucracy in the eleventh century, was well on its way by the time of Leo.

Excerpts from the letters of Leo appear sporadically throughout collections from the early medieval period, though it is worth mentioning that sometimes the texts have been misattributed. The *Collectio Hispana* (c. 650) contains 123 excerpts from Leo; the *Collectio Dionysiano-Hadriano* (c. 774) has 5; the *Decretum* of Burchard of Worms (c. 1000) has 35; and the *Decretum* of Ivo of Chartres (c. 1100) has 115. Finally, Gratian's *Decretum* (c. 1140), the most important source collection for subsequent canonical and theological thought, includes approximately seventy-five texts attributed to Leo, excerpted from twenty different letters. It was chiefly through Gratian's *Decretum* that Leo influenced medieval and early-modern canon law.

SOURCES AND EDITIONS

For a catalogue of Leo's letters, see Philippus Jaffé (ed.), *Regesta Pontificum Romanorum ab condita ecclesia ad annum post Christum natum MCXCVIII* [abbreviated above as Jaffé] (Leipzig, 1885–1888). In the nineteenth century, Jacques-Paul Migne published an edition of the letters in the *Patrologia Latina*: PL 54:593–1218. Carlos Silva-Tarouca published an important critical edition of the letters pertaining to the Christological controversy surrounding the monk and archimandrite Eutyches in *S. Leonis Magni epistulae contra Eutychis haeresim*, Textus et documenta, Pontificia Università gregoriana, Series theologica 15, 20 (Rome, 1934–35). The monumental critical edition of the acts of the ecumenical councils, done under the editorial direction of Edward Schwartz, includes the letters of Leo that were relevant to the Council of Chalcedon. See E. Schwartz (ed.), *Acta Conciliorum Oecumenicorum*, vol. 2, parts 1–4 (Berlin, 1932–1935). Most of the letters have been translated in the following collections: Edmund Hunt, *St. Leo the Great. Letters*, Fathers of the Church 34 (Washington, DC: Catholic University of America Press, 1957); and Charles Lett Feltoe, *The Letters and Sermons of Leo the Great, Bishop of Rome*, in Philip Schaff and Henry Wace (eds.), *A Select Library of Nicene and Post-Nicene Fathers of the Christian Church*, vol. 12, 2nd series (Edinburgh: T & T Clark, repr. 1989), 1–114.

The Migne edition of the sermons can be found in PL 54:141–468. Antoine Chavasse published a modern critical edition of the extant sermons in his *Sancti Leonis Magni Romani pontificis tractatus septem et nonaginta*, CCL 138–138a (Turnhout: Brepols, 1973). The text also appears with accompanying introduction, translation, and commentary in Antoine Chavasse (ed.) and René Dolle (trans.), *Sermons. Léon le Grand*, SC 22, 49, 74, 200 (Paris, 1964, 1969, 1976, 1973). More recently, an expanded and corrected version of the second edition of the text appears in Antoine Chavasse (ed.) and René Dolle (trans.), *Sermons. Léon le Grand* (Paris, 2004–). A keyword concordance to the Latin text of the sermons can be found in Eddy Gouder, Michel Gueret, and Paul Tombeur (eds.), *Leo Magnus Tractatus*, Corpus Christianorum Instrumenta

Lexicologica Latina, Series B (Turnhout: Brepols, 1987). The sermons have been translated in the following volumes: Charles L. Feltoe, *The Letters and Sermons of Leo the Great, Bishop of Rome*, in NPNF 2/12 (repr. Edinburgh: T & T Clark, 1989), 115–205; Jane P. Freeland and Agnes J. Conway, *St. Leo the Great: Sermons*, Fathers of the Church 93 (Washington, DC: Catholic University of America Press, 1996); Hendrik G. Schipper and Johannes Van Oort, *Sermons and Letters Against the Manichaeans: Selected Fragments: St. Leo the Great* (Turnhout: Brepols, 2000).

FURTHER READING

Armitrage, J. Mark. *A Twofold Solidarity: Leo the Great's Theology of Redemption*. Strathfield NSW: Australian Catholic University, Centre for Early Christian Studies, 2005.

Gillett, Andrew. *Envoys and Political Communication in the Late Antique West, 411–533*. Cambridge: Cambridge University Press, 2003.

"Rome, Ravenna, and the Last Western Emperors." In *Papers of the British School at Rome* 69 (2001): 131–67.

Green, Bernard. *The Soteriology of Leo the Great*. Oxford: Oxford University Press, 2008.

Jalland, Trevor. *The Life and Times of St. Leo the Great*. London: SPCK, 1941.

Mathisen, Ralph W. *Ecclesiastical Factionalism and Religious Controversy in Fifth-Century Gaul*. Washington, DC: Catholic University of America Press, 1989.

McShane, Philip A. *La Romanitas et le Pape Léon le Grand. L'apport culturel des institutions impériales à la formation des structures ecclésiastiques*. Tournai: Desclée; Montréal: Bellarmin, 1979.

Neil, Bronwen. *Leo the Great*. The Early Church Fathers Series. Abingdon, UK: Routledge, 2009.

Reynolds, Philip L. *Marriage in the Western Church: The Christianization of Marriage During the Patristic and Early Medieval Periods*. Leiden: Brill, 1994.

Wessel, Susan. *Leo the Great and the Spiritual Rebuilding of a Universal Rome*. Supplements to Vigiliae Christianae Supplements 93. Leiden: Brill, 2008.

14

Gelasius I

Bronwen Neil

Gelasius I, bishop of Rome from 492 to 496, stands at the very peak of fifth-century bids for Roman primacy against the three largest churches of the Byzantine empire: those of Constantinople, Antioch, and Alexandria. His contribution to the collection of Dionysius Exiguus (see Chapter 15) would be of major significance for the development of Christian law during the Carolingian period, in Gratian's *Decretum* (1140s), and in the later Middle Ages. Gelasius's epistolary decretals reveal the ways in which Christianity shaped law generally, even secular or civil law, and the ways in which law was constitutive of Christian communities and guided Christian practices. Put simply, the authority of the bishop of Rome was paramount in Gelasius's view of how society was ordered by God, with the secular rulers and their laws coming a close second, but never before it.

This chapter surveys Gelasius, his letters and other works, and their importance for the development of a theology of law. It places his decretals in the context of Roman and Gothic interests in the canons and in civil law during the fifth and sixth centuries. It concludes with the reception of Gelasius's works in the medieval West, especially the lasting influence of his "two powers" theory and its significance for later ages.

GELASIUS'S LIFE AND WORKS

Born probably in North Africa, as the *Liber Pontificalis* claims (LP 1, 255), and the son of Valerius, Gelasius served as deacon under Felix III (483–496), who nominated him as his preferred successor. He penned at least one letter in Felix's name. As bishop of Rome, Gelasius was the author of many letters, of which forty-two have survived intact and another forty-nine as fragments. Over one-third of these pertained to church management or clerical discipline. In addition, there are six letter-treatises by Gelasius treating problems in the Roman church during his day. Four of these tracts are about the Acacian schism, that is, the schism between the bishops of Rome and the Byzantine emperors regarding Acacius, patriarch of Constantinople. (One of these, entitled *Against Eutyches and Nestorius, On Two Natures in Christ,* has been edited and translated by Ronzani.) Patriarch Acacius had been declared a heretic by Gelasius's predecessor, Felix III, for accepting the ordination of two other patriarchs who held purportedly Monophysite views on the nature of Christ – a Christology that the bishops of Rome had contested since the time of Leo I (440–461). The fifth tract is directed against Pelagianism in Italy and Dalmatia (*Against the Pelagian Heresy*), and the sixth tract, *Against Andromachus*, condemned the celebration of the pagan festival of Lupercalia in Rome.[1]

Most of the letters have not yet appeared in a modern Latin edition. The exception is *Letter* 42, on acceptable and non-acceptable books and the canon of Scripture, whose ascription to Gelasius has been disputed but was upheld by Ernst von Dobschütz with his edition of 1912.[2] Otherwise, various nineteenth-century editions have to suffice for the scholar of Gelasius. The earliest of these, edited by Thiel, was an artificial collection of papal letters from various ancient sources. All references to Gelasius's letters in what follows, unless otherwise specified, are taken from Thiel's 1867 edition. Four Gelasian letters were also contained in the 1895 edition of the sixth-century canon law collection known as the *Collectio Avellana* (CA).[3] In 1885, Löwenfeld published twenty-two "previously unedited" letters of Gelasius from the late eleventh-century *Collectio Britannica*. In fact, some of these letters had already been edited in Ewald's study of the British papal letter collection preserved in a single manuscript that is now held in the British Museum, where Ewald ascribed sixty-five letters to Gelasius.[4] Several of these do not appear in any other collection.[5] The authorship of several possibly Gelasian letters, such as *Fragment* 3, which Ewald attributed to Pope Pelagius I (556–561), is still unresolved. Forty letters that demonstrate Gelasius's contributions to pastoral care and his doctrinal concerns are now available in English translation, including *Letter* 12, his famous affirmation of papal primacy addressed to Emperor Anastasius I.[6] The last is the letter most relevant to our understanding of Gelasius as a lawmaker.

GELASIUS'S CONTEXT AS A LEGISLATOR

Although Gelasius's letters are usually studied in isolation as some of the earliest examples of Roman canon law, their content was largely prefigured in the letters of

[1] For the letter against Andromachus, see Gilbert Pomarès (ed. and trans.), *Lettre contre les Lupercales et dix-huit Messes du Sacramentaire Léonien*, SC 65. English translation: Neil and Allen, 211–21. For the abbreviations used here in citations of primary texts and translations, see Sources at the end of this chapter.

[2] E. von Dobschütz, *Das decretum Gelasianum de libris recipiendis et non recipiendis*, Texte und Untersuchungen 38.4 (Leipzig: Hinrichs, 1912). English translation: Neil and Allen, 157–69.

[3] CA nos. 95, 99, 101, and 103.

[4] For analysis of the contents of Brit. Mus. Addit. 8873 (c. 1090), which contains letters ascribed to Gelasius I and Pelagius I, see Ewald 505–26.

[5] Namely, Gelasius, *Ep.* 4 (Ewald 510), part of *Ep.* 14 (Ewald 514), *Ep.* 16 (Ewald 515), and *Ep.* 46, to Queen Hereleuva (Ewald 521–22).

[6] Neil and Allen, 73–207.

two earlier bishops of Rome: Innocent I (401–419) and Leo I (440–461; see Chapter 13 in this volume). These collections show the bishops of Rome struggling to assert their authority over ecclesiastical affairs against the secular rulers of Italy, Byzantium, and North Africa.

The "Two Powers" Theory

Gelasius made a fundamental distinction between the "laws of princes" and the "divine laws." This distinction underpinned his formulation of the "two powers" theory, which he laid out in a letter to the Eastern emperor Anastasius in 494 (*Ep.* 12).[7] The emperor in Constantinople was by then the sole ruler of Byzantine territories, whereas rule over Italy was at this point contested between the Byzantine emperor in the East and the newly arrived Gothic powers in the West. Gelasius sought to exploit this ambiguity by accepting Gothic rule in order to limit Constantinople's control of Rome. In the context of the Acacian schism, which had divided the Eastern and Western churches since 481, he explained to emperor Anastasius that no emperor had the right to lay down rules for the church to follow when it came to doctrine or the naming of heretics.

Letter 12 was Gelasius's first letter to the new emperor Anastasius. He had in 491 replaced Zeno, author of the problematic *Henōtikon* (482 CE), which sought to reunite the Eastern and Western churches after the vision resulting from the Council of Chalcedon. We do not have Anastasius's reply to Gelasius, but it seems that the pope's bid for universal authority was unsuccessful. Gelasius threatened that Anastasius would lose his rule if he did not comply, since God's protection rested upon his being faithful to the church – that is, to the Roman church, which was claiming universal authority in this matter. Anastasius nevertheless chose to uphold his predecessor's excommunication of the late Felix III, bishop of Rome, and he reigned for another twenty-four years, with the schism continuing beyond his death in 518.

Although Gelasius had no secular legislative power to restrain the emperor or any other ruler, his formulation of the "two powers" ideology was to enjoy a long life in Western Europe, especially during the central and late Middle Ages. (See below in the section on Reception and Significance.) The seminal passage excerpted in the central Middle Ages from *Letter* 12, known as *Duo sunt* ("There are two [realms]") from the first two words of the excerpt, begins as follows:

> In fact, august Emperor, there are two ways in which this world is chiefly ruled: the hallowed authority [*auctoritas*] of the pontiffs [*pontificum*], and the royal power [*potestas*]. In these two the responsibility of the priesthood [*sacerdotum*] is so much greater, to the extent at the time of divine judgement they will render an account

7 See especially chapters 2–3, translated by Matt Briel in George E. Demacopoulos, *The Invention of Peter: Apostolic Discourse and Papal Authority in Late Antiquity* (Philadelphia: University of Pennsylvania Press, 2013), 174–75; also translated in Neil and Allen, 74–75.

even for the very rulers of human beings. Indeed, my most indulgent son, you must know that you are permitted to superintend through high office of a human kind; however, in your devotedness you bow your head to the leaders of divine affairs, and from them you await the occasions of your salvation, and, in both taking the heavenly sacraments and being suitably disposed to them, you acknowledge that you must be subject to the order of religion, rather than be in control of it.[8]

Gelasius's Theory of Christian Law

As *Letter* 12 shows, Gelasius believed that the power of Christian (Roman) law lay in the strict adherence to orthodoxy, defined and maintained by the bishop of Rome, on which basis civilized society was built. As a corollary to this thesis, nonorthodox Christians were by definition "barbarians," and their laws were savage. We find this theory implicit also in Gelasius's letter to Succonius, orthodox bishop of North Africa who had taken refuge amongst the pro-Acacian "heretics" in Constantinople. Writing to Succonius, Gelasius made no attempt to disguise his contempt for the law of the Vandals ruling North Africa, demanding: "Are you not the one who, having spurned the threats of [Vandal] kings and disregarded the feral laws of the raging barbarians, put aside all at once your native land ... ?" (*Ep.* 9, 340). After the establishment of the Arian (more precisely, Homoian) church in North Africa by the Vandal Geiseric in 429, the catholic episcopate there would not be restored for seventy-four years.

Gelasius also tried to curtail the legislative powers of the Ostrogothic leader Theodoric, who from 493 assumed the title of king of Italy. He was more circumspect, however, toward the leader of his own country than he was about the North African Vandals. Gelasius made no reference to the fact that Theodoric, too, had adopted Homoian Christianity, and he politely refrained from mentioning his own two tracts against Arianism. He did, however, take Theodoric to task for summoning clergy to his court for trial on charges of property theft. The king must refer any clerics accused of misdemeanors to the bishop of Rome for examination (*frg.* 11; *frg.* 13; *Ep.* 46). The pope tried to ensure in this way that the "laws of princes" did not encroach on the domain of the church. Theodoric seems to have complied with this request, as Gelasius reported on three occasions, but he had plenty of other occasions to intervene in ecclesiastical affairs during his thirty-five-year rule, as the unfortunate demise of Pope John I (523–526) indicates. John was incarcerated by Theodoric in Ravenna on his way back from Constantinople, where, as the king's legate, he had failed to obtain Justin's approval for restoration of Eastern churches to Arian use. Instead, John I incensed Theodoric by crowning Justin as emperor.

8 Neil and Allen, 74, modified. The term "pontiffs" in this period might denote either the bishops of Rome (the popes) or bishops generally.

Gelasius, like John I, was forced to balance the interests of the papacy with the demands of two secular rulers, respectively of the Greek East and the Gothic West.

Gelasius enthusiastically suppressed two other heretical groups in Rome: the Manicheans and the Pelagians. Following the lead of Leo the Great, he exiled the Manicheans from Rome under the authority of emperor Valentinian III's *Constitution* of 445, and he instigated a public burning of their books in front of the church of St. Mary Major (LP 1, 255). His letter to bishop Honorius of Salona reveals that his persecution of Pelagian clergy extended beyond Italy to Dalmatia (CA 98; *Ep.* 4.3, 322). Gelasius justified his intervention by recourse to Christ's delegation of authority to the apostle Peter in John 21:17: "Peter, do you love me? Feed my sheep!" He also cited the precedents of predecessors in the Apostolic See: Innocent I, Zosimus, Boniface, Sixtus III, and Leo I. Three other writings by Gelasius deal with the Pelagian heresy: his letter to the bishops of Picenum (CA 94; *Ep.* 6), a second letter to the same Bishop Honorius (CA 96; *Ep.* 5), and *Tract* 5, *Against the Pelagian Heresy* (CA 97).

Rulings on Clerical and Social Abuses

Clerical and social abuses within the region of Rome's influence during this period included extortionate interest rates, people-trafficking, indentured labor of free children, and corruption in both secular and the ecclesiastical spheres. Gelasius often delegated to other bishops the task of investigating the claims of individuals against laypersons or clerics. Concern for papal property consumed much of his attention. In *Letter* 17, Gelasius reminds the bishops of Sicily to administer the powers of the church according to canonical decrees. He ruled that law of the *Codex Theodosianus*[9] imposing a statute of limitation on any case more than thirty years old should be upheld in the case of the bishops' occupation of churches, as also of dioceses.

Gelasius was fond of using the terms "law" and "ordinance" in his many letters regarding clerical discipline. These dealt with cases of rape, murder, abduction, disputes over family estates, theft of lay and church property, slaves who had absconded and bondsmen who had escaped to join the clergy, and the management of papal properties, which spread from Sicily in the south to Dalmatia in the northeast. Clergy were not allowed to appear before secular courts, as canon 9 of the Council of Chalcedon stipulated. Those doing penance were also forbidden to approach secular courts (Leo, *Ep.* 167, Response 10). It was common practice for the bishop of Rome to delegate judicial duties to other bishops, who would judge a dispute between members of the clergy. Roman bishops frequently tried to recover by legal process sacred vessels that had been stolen. For example, Gelasius tasked bishop Geruntius of Valva with investigating whether the bishop of Potentia had

[9] *Cod. Theod.* 4.14 (194–96), reiterated by Valentinian III (Nov 27, Pharr 538–39).

stolen a sacred paten and put it to his own private use, and he asked for a report on this matter.[10] In another allegation of episcopal theft (*Ep.* 20, Löwenfeld 10), Gelasius instructed three bishops to investigate the case of the cleric Festus, who had complained that the late bishop Urbanus had stolen property from him. Festus was Defender of the Church (*defensor ecclesiae*), that is, the official legal advocate tasked with representing the church in legal processes. Festus did not want to make his case before secular judges. The bishops were told to force the cleric Alexander to tell them what he knew about this matter, "so that you may decide everything that should be settled according to legal order." This probably gave them a mandate to extract information under torture if necessary: a legitimate practice under Roman law.

In the matter of Eucharistus, the would-be bishop of Volterra, and Faustus, the Defender of the Church of Rome, Gelasius wrote to a local count (*comes* or *teia*) urging him to stay out of ecclesiastical cases (*Ep.* 9, Löwenfeld 5–6). This is another example of Gelasius's insistence on the separation of powers. In a Roman synod held to judge the same case (*Ep.* 22, Löwenfeld 11–12), Gelasius dismissed the claim of Eucharistus, who wanted to reclaim the sixty-three *solidi* that he had paid to Faustus to acquire the bishopric of Volterra. What was at issue here was not the payment of an apparent bribe to secure a bishopric (surely a case of simony), but rather the principle that Eucharistus had no right to demand the return of his "bond." The clergy were not above conventional quid pro quo of the period. In a study of the recruitment of clergy in fifth and sixth centuries, Sabine Huebner noted that demanding or accepting payments in return for clerical offices was commonplace, and that the practice was eventually sanctioned by Justinian.[11] As Huebner observes, "The clergy . . . should be regarded as an institution that was tightly interwoven with the secular social structure of later Roman society."[12]

The Bishop's Court

Although clerics and laypersons could appeal to Rome, Gelasius preferred that most cases be settled by a local bishop's court known as the *audientia episcopalis*.[13] An extension of the Roman citizens' right to submit any dispute voluntarily to arbitration, this court, too, operated on a voluntary basis. Plaintiffs and defendants could not be forced to attend nor even to comply with the bishop's ruling, as stipulated in a *Novella* of Valentinian III (*Nov. Val.* 35, Pharr 545). Nevertheless, by placing the bishop's court on the same footing as the heavenly court of the Last Judgment,

10 In *Ep.* 7 (Löwenfeld 4). Cf. *Ep.* 21 (388), and Pelagius 1, *Ep.* 82 to Severus.

11 Sabine R. Huebner, "Currencies of Power: The Venality of Offices in the Later Roman Empire," in A. Cain and N. Lenski (eds.), *The Power of Religion in Late Antiquity* (Farnham, UK: Ashgate, 2009), 167–80, at 175–76 n. 46.

12 Huebner, "Currencies of Power," 179.

13 Jill Harries discusses the *audientia episcopalis* in the section on alternative law in Chapter 2 in this volume.

Gelasius elevated its authority so that it functioned effectively as a magistrate's court does today. Since the secular courts were overloaded, the bishop's court was often the best option for those in search of justice. The number of cases brought to the bishop's court far exceeded its capacity, however, and many people appealed to the bishop of Rome himself in desperation. On one such occasion, Gelasius asked two bishops, Respectus and Gerontius (*Ep.* 8, Löwenfeld 5), to settle a dispute between bishop Aufidianus and his clergy. Gelasius confessed that he was disturbed by the multitude of complaints that he was hearing. He would have liked to bring all of the plaintiffs to Rome, he explains, but because of the expense he judged that it was more useful for Respectus and Gerontius to hear and adjudicate the complaints locally, and to reach their own decision.

Matters of clerical discipline were often governed by the canons of provincial councils, which were held annually or twice a year in larger churches such as Rome, Arles, Carthage, and Toledo. Every bishop in a given province was invited to attend these councils, presided over by the metropolitan or the most senior bishop. Gelasius himself presided over the Synod of Rome in 495, which discussed the case of two papal legates who, under pressure in Constantinople, had abandoned their brief and declared their support for Acacius. Gelasius ensured that the legate Misenus, who had validated Acacius by receiving eucharist from him but had since regretted his actions, was pardoned after doing penance and making a written declaration of his errors. When faced with the collective might of a synod in Rome, most errant sinners found the threat of excommunication real enough to make them reconsider their position. In such cases, there were no comparable secular legal rulings, and the canons of each synod or council were useful as precedents. From the sixth century onward, these decisions were collated with pronouncements of the bishops of Rome in canonical collections.

GELASIUS'S DECRETALS

Papal responses to bishops and other senior churchmen on legal questions enjoyed wide circulation and became known as "decretals."[14] These letters were written in the style of imperial rescripts, by which Roman emperors had responded both to private citizens and to state officials regarding points of law that had arisen in actual cases.[15] Decretals were used to make dogmatic as well as disciplinary pronouncements, and they had quasi-legal force. Their language was juristic and authoritative, emphasizing the author's commanding position in relation to the enquirer or reader. Although decretals usually originated as responses to queries from individual bishops, they would later acquire universal application. The legal status of decretals was a matter of gradual evolution, and their later significance depended in large part

[14] See Detlev Jasper and Horst Fuhrmann, *Papal Letters in the Early Middle Ages*, History of Medieval Canon Law (Washington, DC: Catholic University of America Press, 2001), 12–19, with bibliography.

[15] *Cod. Theod.* 1.2 (trans. Pharr, 12–14).

on their preservation in medieval canonical collections. Two decretal letters of Gelasius deserve particular attention in view of their lasting impact. These are known respectively as the *Gelasian Decretal* (*Ep.* 42) and the *General Decretal Letter* (*Ep.* 14).

The Gelasian Decretal *(Ep. 42)*

Although Gelasius was not the first pope to issue decretals, he made the earliest extant description of the genre in *Letter* 42: an index of acceptable and forbidden books (*Libri recipiendi et non recipiendi*). Gelasius wrote: “Likewise, the decretal letters which the most blessed popes sent at different times from the city of Rome for the consultation of diverse fathers [i.e., bishops] are to be received with respect” (*Ep.* 42.3, 458).

The authenticity of *Letter* 42 has been questioned. Schwartz suggested that one section of the text (namely, chapters 4–5) was most likely composed in southern Gaul in the sixth century.[16] But a reference to the “Gelasian decretal” in a hostile prologue that was appended to it as early as the late fifth or the sixth century[17] makes it more likely that the attribution to Gelasius is correct, even if, as Eduard Schwartz argued, the first three chapters of the *Gelasian Decretal* were derived from Pope Damasus (366–384).[18] The first chapter begins with a justification of the authority of the bishop of Rome, for this see “is preferred to the other churches, since they have not been established by any synodical documents, whereas Rome obtained the primacy by the saying of our Lord” (i.e., Matt 16:18–19). The list of forbidden books in the Decretal included some apocryphal gospels (e.g., the *Gospel of Thomas*), forged letters (e.g., *King Abgar's Letter to Jesus*), and some early quasi-biblical texts that were at first included but later excluded from the canon of Scripture both in the West and in the Byzantine church, such as the *Shepherd of Hermas*. Books permitted to be read by Christians included the *Acts* of the ecumenical councils of Nicaea, Ephesus, and Chalcedon, the *Tome* of Leo I to Flavian, and the decretals of previous bishops of Rome. Gelasius treats the ancient conciliar canons and the papal writings as equally binding here, referring to them both as “canons.” This understanding was to persist from the sixth century onward.

Pope Hormisdas (514–23) reproduced the bulk of *Letter* 42 (chapters 4–9) and expanded it to include the canon of the Old and New Testaments (*Epp.* 125, 931–38). In this form, the letter was included in almost every canonical collection henceforth. It had become normative by the time of its inclusion in Gratian's *Decretum* in the twelfth century.[19]

16 Eduard Schwartz, “Zum Decretum Gelasianum,” *Zeitschrift für die neutestamentliche Wissenschaft und die Kunde der älteren Kirche* 29 (1930): 161–68, at 163.

17 Baudouin de Gaiffier, “Un prologue hagiographique hostile au décret de Gélase?” *Analecta Bollandiana* 82 (1964): 341–53, at 343–44.

18 Schwartz, “Zum Decretum Gelasianum,” 164–68.

19 Jasper and Fuhrmann, *Papal Letters in the Early Middle Ages*, 65.

The General Decretal Letter (*Ep.* 14)

Gelasius insisted on the authority of patristic tradition in the second of his decretals addressed to the bishops of Italy, which is known as the *General Decretal* (*Ep.* 14, 62–79). This letter was issued on 11 March 494, shortly after the triumph of Theodoric in Italy. It seeks to lay out ecclesiastical regulation but also strays into some areas of secular, or civil law. The closing statement of the letter (*Ep.* 14.28, 379) reveals Gelasius's lofty conception of his authority within the church hierarchy: "But by all means every single pontiff will be the destroyer of his own rank and office if he should think that these matters are to be kept from any one of the clergy or from the hearing of the whole church."

In his pronouncements on a variety of matters of discipline in the *General Decretal*, Gelasius refers frequently to the ancient canons of the church, although he allows for relaxations of these rules to meet current situations, such as an acute lack of clergy. The following examples illustrate this point: "Due deference to the ordinances of old remains, which it is appropriate to observe in accordance with the rules when there is no pressing emergency to do with circumstances or the times" (*Ep.* 14.2, 362). "Together the ancient tradition and the olden formulation of the apostolic see do not admit this" – i.e., the ordination of illiterates or amputees (*Ep.* 14.16, 371). "Concerning those who have castrated themselves, the canons of the fathers have clearly set down what ought to be followed" (*Ep.* 14.17, 372). "Any deserter ... will not escape the ordinances of the revered canons" (*Ep.* 14.23, 375). "Concerning monks and laypersons ... in the event that it is proved not to be a question of any exigency, only the ancient arrangement should be observed" (*Ep.* 14.24, 375). Gelasius notes in chapter 3 that a layman's suitability for ordination should be investigated more carefully in regard to his character and lifestyle than is prescribed for monks. Other matters under discussion included the marriage of previously consecrated virgins, clergy who have broken their vow of celibacy or committed theft, and clergy who have charged a fee for baptism or confirmation (an example of simony). Regarding marriage, the letter affirmed that the remarriage of lay persons was allowed but ruled that twice-married people could not be ordained as clerics. Likewise, because of their prior marriage, widows who became nuns should not be ceremonially veiled.

Pope Innocent's influence is perceptible in chapter 6, regarding chrism and confirmation. The separation of roles between priests and bishops meant that the first anointing, performed at baptism, and the second anointing, performed at confirmation, were separated in time, sometimes for an extended period. In 416, in a letter to Decentius of Gubbio, Innocent wrote: "For whether the bishop is present or not, presbyters are allowed to anoint the baptized with chrism, but they are not allowed to sign the forehead with the same oil consecrated by the bishop, for that is used by the bishops only when they give the Spirit [in confirmation]."[20]

20 Innocent I, *Ep.* 25.3, in Martin F. Connell, *Church and Worship in Fifth-Century Rome: The Letter of Innocent I to Decentius of Gubbio* (Cambridge: Grove Books, 2002), 28.

Gelasius confirms that anointing with chrism concluded the baptismal rite, but confirmation, of which anointing was the central feature, was reserved for bishops.

Chapter 20 of *Letter* 14 deals with the problem of men who live with holy virgins and of women who live with clerics in a "spiritual" (i.e., celibate) marriage. This practice was considered dangerous and had been condemned by several councils including Elvira (c. 306), Ancyra (314), and Nicaea (325).

Gelasius was not the first pope to make rulings on matters of civil, or secular law, but his *General Decretal* of 494 included a convenient collection of all previous rulings on secular and religious matters plus a few new ones, and it was the last of its kind. "The great age of the pontificates of Siricius, Celestine, Innocent I, and Leo I, which produced influential decretals and instructional letters with wide circulation, was over."[21]

Gelasius and the Acacian Schism

Under the protection of Odovacer's successor, Theodoric, Gelasius insisted that the condemnation of Acacius was the precondition for union between Rome and Constantinople, rejecting a proposed compromise in 494 regarding the autonomy of the bishop of Rome in theological matters.[22] Out of the total of twenty-six Gelasian letters pertaining to the Acacian schism, only three are included in *Collectio Avellana* (CA 81, CA 95, and CA 101). With these is a letter addressed to Gelasius from "the humble bishops" of Dardania (CA 80, Guenther 223). Another relevant text on the subject of the schism was the *Acts* of a Roman synod held in May 495 to absolve the erring papal legate Misenus (CA 103, Guenther 474–87; =Thiel, *Ep.* 30, 437–47).

The earliest and first tract on the topic in Gelasius's name, the *Gesta de nomine Acacii* (CA 99, Guenther 440–52), explains the reasons for the Roman excommunication of both Acacius and Peter, the anti-Chalcedonian patriarch of Alexandria. This was written during the first year of Gelasius's pontificate, or perhaps even before, while he was still a deacon under Felix III. The final chapter of the original version is Felix III's brief letter to the bishops in Egypt, Libya, the Thebaid, and Pentapolis, urging them to uphold his anathema against Peter of Alexandria (Felix III, *Ep.* 9 [250]). This fragment comes from the beginning of August 484: a date that provides a *terminus post quem* for Gelasius's *Gesta de nomine Acacii*.

Gelasius admonished the Dardanian bishops (or the Dacian bishops, according to another reading) to beware the tricks of Andreas, bishop of Thessalonica (CA 101). As long as Andreas refused to omit the name of Acacius from the diptychs, he did not deserve communion with the Holy See (*Ep.* 18, 382–85). Gelasius sent to the bishops of Dardania a dogmatic statement rendering a full account of why Acacius was

21 Jasper and Fuhrmann, *Papal Letters in the Early Middle Ages*, 59.

22 Patrick Amory, *People and Identity in Ostrogothic Italy*, 489–554 (Cambridge: Cambridge University Press, 1997), 221–27.

properly condemned by the Apostolic See (CA 95, 1 February 495). On 13 May 495, Gelasius and a Roman synod gathered in the basilica of St. Peter's to offer absolution to Misenus, the former papal emissary who had, under duress, supported the cause of Acacius (CA 103). Misenus, who by then was an elderly man, was suffering from chronic illness and was consumed by a wasting disease, and he had pleaded for the *viaticum* (*Ep.* 30.2, 438–39). Gelasius and forty-five other bishops signed the acts of the Roman council absolving him. Gelasius reported triumphantly that Misenus had renounced all heresies and was therefore restored to communion and to his episcopal office.

RECEPTION AND SIGNIFICANCE

Gelasius's *General Decretal* was incorporated into the *Collectio Dionysiana*, a canonical collection made by his Scythian contemporary, the monk Dionysius Exiguus (see Chapter 15 in this volume). Dionysius's selection of 173 papal pronouncements on subjects pertaining to ecclesiastical regulation and clerical discipline is among the earliest witnesses to the Roman canonical tradition. Dionysius divided Gelasius's *General Decretal* thematically into twenty-eight sections, which allowed it to be used as a handy reference to the various questions of discipline that continued to trouble bishops in later centuries. Dionysius also provided a heading for each chapter, and these were listed in his preface to the letter (Neil and Allen, 143–45). The inclusion of sixty-five letters of Gelasius in the *Collectio Britannica* (1090 or shortly thereafter) is further evidence that his influence was being felt beyond the shores of Italy. After a brief description of other collections that mediated Gelasian letters, I shall describe Gelasius's reception and the significance of his contribution in the Middle Ages, among the Carolingians in Francia, and in the Reformation.

The Avellana Collection and Other Early Canonical Collections

Prior to the twelfth century, the only texts of Gelasius commonly included in standard canonical collections, such as those of Anselm of Lucca, Deusdedit, and Ivo of Chartres, were excerpts from his *General Decretal*.[23] We have noted above, however, in connection with the Acacian Schism, that three letters of Gelasius were included in the sixth-century *Collectio Avellana*, whose collator limited his focus to Gelasius's correspondence with the bishops of Dardania.

Gelasius's letter to the Dardanian bishops (CA 95) is the only entry in the collection that also appears, albeit in epitomized form, in seven other collections of papal letters: (1) the *Quesnelliana*, (2) the Freising codex, (3) the Diessen codex, (4) the Verona codex (*Collectio Veronensis*), (5) the Augmented Hadrian Collection

[23] Jasper and Fuhrmann, *Papal Letters in the Early Middle Ages*, 64.

(Hadriana adaucta), (6) the Pseudo-Isidorian Collection, and (7) the Colbertine codex. A brief description of these suffices here. The *Quesnelliana* is the earliest of these seven collections. It was assembled around 496, toward the end of Gelasius's episcopate. Its offshoots include the Köln Collection (*Collectio Coloniensis*) and possibly the First Freising Collection (*Collectio Frisingensis prima*). The Verona codex dates to the end of the fifth century or the beginning of the sixth, and it is related to the Freising Collection. It is earlier than the sixth-century Italian *Collectio Avellana*, but there is no evidence for any direct relationship between the two. The Augmented Hadrian Collection (c. 850/72) is an expanded version of *Dionysiana Hadriana*: the version of Dionysius Exiguus that was sent to Charlemagne before 774 by order of Pope Hadrian I (772–95). The decretal collection pseudonymously ascribed to Isidore Mercator (see Chapter 19 in this volume), known as the *Pseudo-Isidoriana*, was composed in Gaul in the mid-ninth century. This contains many papal letters up to the eighth century, both genuine and forged. The Colbertine codex dates to the tenth century. It was through these early collections that Gelasius's letter to the Dardanian bishops reached the greater Western church, and in particular the Carolingian Franks.[24]

MEDIEVAL INTERPRETATIONS OF THE TWO POWERS THEORY

The Pseudo-Isidorian decretals were composed in the context of a power struggle between two Gallic bishops of the Carolingian era: Hincmar of Reims and his nephew, Hincmar of Laon (see Chapter 21 in this volume). The Gelasian theory was taken up in Carolingian times in the rhetoric of Two Realms, or Two Kingdoms, which operated independently and in parallel, but with the proviso that temporal power was subject in all spiritual matters to the divine rule of the clergy, who were subject to their supreme head, the bishop of Rome, or the pope.[25] Hincmar of Laon saw in the Gelasian formula support for his own view of papal monism, whereby the bishop of Rome was the supreme authority and the Carolingian emperor should be subject to him in all things. His uncle, Hincmar the archbishop of Reims, strongly contested this view. In his view, it compromised the authority of the Gallic church and its councils to determine and impose their own ecclesiastical rules, as well as his own authority as metropolitan over his suffragan bishops. Archbishop Hincmar sought successfully to have his nephew excommunicated and eventually arrested by Charles the Bald, king of the Western Franks, at which point the younger Hincmar appealed to the bishop of Rome, Hadrian II, to whom he attributed

[24] On the inclusion of Gelasian letters in various medieval collections and their offshoots, see Jasper and Fuhrmann, *Papal Letters in the Early Middle Ages*, 59–65; and Kéry, *Collections*, esp. 2–4, 9–21, 27–29, 31–32, 37–38, 44–45, and 100–14, with bibliography.

[25] Karl F. Morrison, *The Two Kingdoms: Ecclesiology in Carolingian Political Thought* (Princeton, NJ: Princeton University Press, 1964), 36–67.

plenary legislative power.[26] Hincmar of Laon's case collapsed after the death of Hadrian II, and conciliarism – the theory that ultimate ecclesiastical authority was vested not in a single pontiff but in church councils – was vindicated. Gelasius's decretals could not save Hincmar of Laon in the face of the archbishop's appeal to the sacred canons of the Gallic councils.

In later centuries, the Pseudo-Isidorian decretals took on a life of their own in Rome, whose bishops treated the collection as if it was entirely genuine.[27] Received thence, Gelasius's formulation of the two realms became a cornerstone of medieval political theology.

In his work *On the Sacraments of the Christian Faith*, written in the 1130s, Hugh of Saint-Victor (d. 1141) was the among the first to modify the Gelasian theory in order to defend the claim that the church, under the rule of the pope, had by right supreme authority in all matters but had delegated power over temporal matters to the king or to the secular state.[28] Hugh claims that the church, as the mystical body of Christ, who is its head, has two sides. The earthly, royal hierarchy constitutes the left side, whereas the spiritual, priestly hierarchy constitutes the right side. But Hugh goes on to claim that the spiritual power is prior to the secular power both historically and causally, since the latter owes its very existence to the former.[29] Hugh was arguably not able to articulate this theory convincingly in a thoroughly unitary way, whereby a superior spiritual power somehow encompassed the dualistic powers of both church and state, respectively spiritual and temporal, which were meant to support and reinforce each other.[30] The "Two Swords" theory provided an appropriate synthesis. It was originally based on an allegorical interpretation of the swords in Luke 22:38 and John 18:11. Although the Gelasian doctrine is often conflated with the Two Swords theory today, the allegory of the swords is absent from Gelasius's account, as is the absolute claim that all powers are ultimately subject to the church and its pope. Writing to Pope Eugenius III in 1150, Bernard of Clairvaux used the ancient allegory of the Two Swords[31] in a new way to defend the use of coercive, military power by kings and emperors to defend the church in the Crusades.[32] Although Bernard's allegory was designed narrowly to justify waging war on the church's behalf, it suggested a strictly hieratic view whereby secular power belonged by right to the pope as leader of the church. The priesthood, headed by the papacy,

26 Morrison, *Two Kingdoms*, 99–115.

27 See Jasper and Fuhrmann, *Papal Letters in the Early Middle Ages*, 170–95.

28 See J. A. Watt, "Spiritual and Temporal Powers," in J. H. Burns (ed.), *The Cambridge History of Medieval Political Thought c.350 – c.1450* (Cambridge: Cambridge University Press, 1988), 367–423, at 368–69.

29 Hugh of Saint-Victor, *De sacramentis christianae fidei*, II.2.1–4, II.2.7, PL 176:415B–418D. Trans. Roy J. Deferrari, *Hugh of Saint Victor on the Sacraments of the Christian Faith* (Cambridge, MA: Mediaeval Academy of America, 1951), 253–56, 258.

30 Watt, "Spiritual and Temporal Powers," 369–70.

31 See Gerard E. Caspary, *Politics and Exegesis: Origen and the Two Swords* (Berkeley: University of California Press, 1979).

32 Watt, "Spiritual and Temporal Powers," 372–73.

controlled both the material sword of coercion and the spiritual sword of counsel and penance (Luke 22:35–38) but declined to use the material sword (John 18:11), instead delegating that secular power to the princes and magistrates. Gelasius's idea, on the contrary, seems to have been strictly dualistic and separatist. In his view, neither power should intrude upon the other's domain, although the sacred power had greater dignity because it looked to eternal rather than to merely temporal welfare. The church should not interfere in strictly secular matters, just as the princes should not meddle in matters of doctrine or even attempt to administer justice to the clergy. Clergy should rather be judged by episcopal courts, or, if necessary, by the pope himself.

An elaborated synthesis of the Gelasian doctrine was subjected to an extreme interpretation in Pope Boniface VIII's bull, *Unam sanctam* (1302), which is considered to be a landmark in medieval political theology theory.[33] In an effort to assert the pope's authority over King Phillip IV of France (Phillip the Fair), Boniface combined Hugh of Saint-Victor's modified version of Gelasian theory, Bernard of Clairvaux's Two Swords allegory, and the Pseudo-Dionysius's hierarchical insight, from the *Ecclesiastical Hierarchy*, that divine laws lead the lowest to the highest through intermediaries. By this means, he arrives at a very "high" doctrine of papal supremacy, whereby the pope as Christ's only vicar has plenary power by right but delegates secular power to the princes.[34] Boniface claimed that both swords, the spiritual and the material, were in the power of the priesthood, but that whereas the former was to be administered by the priests, the latter was to be administered *for* the church *by* kings and their armies, albeit at the will of the priests. Thus, "one sword ought to be subordinated to the other," Boniface claims, and temporal authority subjected to spiritual power.

Later Interpretations of Gelasian Ideology

These later developments have made the proper interpretation of Gelasius's original model contested and unclear. The Two Swords theory proved useful in Protestant polemics against the Catholics in the Reformation, although it was soon eclipsed by the more flexible idea of the Three Estates. Luther himself used the phrase "two kingdoms" in three ways: for the distinction between God's rule and Satan's rule; for the distinction between church and state; and for the two ways in which God ruled the world: through the gospel of Christ and through (secular) law.[35] This last use of the phrase distinguished between the vertical relationship between God and human

33 E. Friedberg (ed.), *Corpus Iuris Canonici* (Leipzig: Tauchnitz, 1879–81), vol. 2, 1245–46. H. Denzinger and A. Schönmetzer (eds.), *Enchiridion Symbolorum*, 34th edition (1967), §§870–75. English translation: Brian Tierney, *The Crisis of Church and State 1050–1300* (Toronto: University of Toronto Press, 1988), 188–89.

34 Watt, "Spiritual and Temporal Powers," 368.

35 Robert Kolb, "Two-Kingdoms Doctrine," in *The Encyclopedia of Christianity*, ed. Erwin Fahlbusch et al., vol. 5 (Grand Rapids: Eerdmans, and Leiden: Brill, 2008), 569–75, at 571.

beings (the heavenly kingdom) and the horizontal relationships among human beings (the earthly kingdom).[36] Lutheran and Calvinist scholars writing about the Reformation have tended to read the Two Swords idea back into Gelasius.[37]

In the twentieth century, two main schools of thought developed regarding the theoretical underpinnings of Gelasius's understanding of his own power as bishop of Rome and vicar of the first apostle, Peter. The traditional view is that of Erich Caspar, who saw Gelasius as accepting a dualistic division between the coercive power (*potestas*) of the secular ruler and the spiritual authority (*auctoritas*) of the priestly ruler – power and authority being different modes of ruling.[38] But Walter Ullmann argued later that Leo I had conceived a much loftier conception of the papacy, and that Gelasius's model belonged to this tradition. Ullmann posited the development in late-antique Rome of an ideology whereby the pope as monarch enjoyed powers overarching those of any secular authority, including that of Gothic kings and Byzantine emperors.[39] Janet Nelson agrees with Ullmann's monarchic interpretation, citing the Roman law that made the *paterfamilias* responsible for all crimes of his sons and slaves.[40] The same line is taken by Kristina Sessa, who describes the fifth-century conception of the papacy as a dynastic institution that was domestic in nature.[41] An important qualification to Nelson's theory was the recognition that Gelasius's claim to power over the emperor in *Letter* 12 was based as much on the rights and responsibilities of a *tutor* under Roman tutelary law as on the model of the Roman *paterfamilias*.[42] Within this ideological framework, the emperor was in some sense the bishop of Rome's spiritual ward, for whom the pope would be held to account at the final judgment.

Contrary to Ullmann's argument that Gelasius adopted Leo I's ideology of the pope as monarch, other scholars have pointed out that Gelasius's claims in *Letter* 12 were unrealistic if understood literally, but above all a testament to his rhetorical skill. Subsequent generations have understood the pontiff to have claimed a measure of domestic and international influence that Gelasius could never actually have enjoyed at that time.[43] Beginning with its inclusion in the

36 Kolb, "Two-Kingdoms Doctrine," 571.
37 Ibid., 572.
38 Erich Caspar, *Geschichte des Papsttums von den Anfängen bis zur Höhe der Weltherrschaft*, vol. 2: *Das Papsttum unter byzantinischer Herrschaft* (Tübingen: Mohr, 1933), 70–71. Similarly, Francis Dvornik, "Pope Gelasius and Emperor Anastasius I," *Byzantinische Zeitschrift* 44 (1951): 111–16; and Wilhelm Ensslin, "*Auctoritas* und *potestas*: Zur Zweigewaltenlehre des Papstes Gelasius I.," *Historisches Jahrbuch* 74 (1955): 661–68.
39 Walter Ullmann, *The Growth of Papal Government in the Middle Ages: A Study in the Ideological Relation of Clerical to Lay Power*, 2nd edition (London: Methuen, 1962), 17–28.
40 Janet L. Nelson, "Gelasius I's Doctrine of Responsibility. A Note," JTS 18.1 (1967): 154–62.
41 Kristina Sessa, *The Formation of Papal Authority in Late Antique Italy: Roman Bishops and the Domestic Sphere* (Cambridge: Cambridge University Press, 2012), 201–02.
42 M. H. Hoeflich, "Gelasius I and Roman Law: One Further Word," JTS 26.1 (1975): 114–19.
43 George E. Demacopoulos, "Are All Universalist Politics Local?: Pope Gelasius I's International Ambition as a Tonic for Local Humiliation," in G. Dunn (ed.), *The Bishop of Rome in Late Antiquity* (Farnham, UK: Ashgate, 2015), 141–53, at 142.

decretal collection of the canonist Gratian in the 1140s, the letter has often been cited by medieval canonists and modern scholars alike as evidence that claims of papal primacy stretched back into antiquity. But the claims expressed in the letter are perhaps better read as attempts to mask both local and international humiliation: local ineffectiveness such as in the *Lupercalia* affair, if indeed Gelasius feared being mocked in public and scorned by senators at the Lupercalia festival, which he had failed to stop, as Demacopoulos suggests;[44] and international humiliation such as in the refusal of the East to recognize papal authority in the Acacian schism.[45]

CONCLUSION

In the letters and pronouncements that came from Gelasius's brief pontificate, we can see how this bishop of Rome laid claim to the power to dictate Christian faith and practice. He did not confine himself to disciplining clerics but extended his reach to all citizens of the Western Roman Empire, even up to King Theodoric. He also made pronouncements about noncitizen slaves. The scope of his responsibility embraced sexual morality, clerical discipline, ordinations and episcopal elections, the defining of heresy, and the anathematization of those who fell outside the definition of orthodoxy. Gelasius developed a quasi-legal ideology of Roman primacy based on the Petrine commission and the authority of previous popes, as handed down by their writings and the canons of earlier councils. Above all, he prized the canons of the first, third, and fourth ecumenical councils. In times of civil war, Gelasius was largely responsible for civic order in Rome. Such was the situation that Gelasius experienced at the beginning of his papacy, with the transition of Italian rule from Odovacer to Theodoric. The Roman church played an important role in maintaining civic order, as did the episcopal courts that took up the slack after the secular courts had become overloaded with secular disputes. In Gelasius, therefore, we can clearly see the operation of late-antique Christianity in the legal process. His impact on canonical regulation, and thus on medieval and especially Carolingian Christianity, was substantial. While the original version of the "two powers" theory may have been largely wishful thinking at the time, it grew in the telling until it became a way to understand church and civil government in the Middle Ages and beyond.

44 Demacopoulos, "Are All Universalist Politics Local?," 142–45; Demacopoulos, *The Invention of Peter*, 75–79.

45 Demacopoulos, *The Invention of Peter*, 94–95.

SOURCES

Sources Cited with Abbreviations

CA	Collectio Avellana: Otto Günther (ed.), Epistulae Imperatorum, Pontificum, aliorum inde ab anno 367 ad annum 553 datae Avellana quae dicitur collectio. 2 vols. CSEL 35.1–2 (1895–98).
CTh	Paul Krüger, Theodor Mommsen, and Paul M. Meyer (eds.), *Codex Theodosianus*. 2 vols. in 3. Hildesheim: Weidman, 1990.
Ewald	Paul Ewald, "Die Papstbriefe der Britischen Sammlung." *Neues Archiv der Gesellschaft für Ältere Deutsche Geschichtskunde* 5 (1880): 274–414, 505–96.
Löwenfeld	Samuel Löwenfeld (ed.), *Epistolae pontificum Romanorum ineditae*. Leipzig: Veit, 1885.
LP 1	Louis Duchesne and Cyril Vogel (eds.), *Le Liber pontificalis*. 2nd edition, vol. 1. Paris: Thorin, 1955.
Neil and Allen	Bronwen Neil and Pauline Allen, *The Letters of Gelasius I (492–496): Pastor and Micro-manager of the Church of Rome*. Adnotationes: Commentaries on Early Christian and Patristic Texts 1. Turnhout: Brepols, 2014.
Pharr	Clyde Pharr (trans.), *The Theodosian Code and Novels and the Sirmondian Constitutions*. Princeton, NJ: Princeton University Press, 1952.
Thiel	Andreas Thiel (ed.), *Epistulae Romanorum pontificum genuinae et quae ad eos scriptae sunt a s. Hilaro usque ad Pelagium II*. Braunsberg: Eduard Peter, 1867. Repr. New York: Olms, 2004.

Other Sources for Papal Letters

Connell, Martin F. *Church and Worship in Fifth-Century Rome: The Letter of Innocent I to Decentius of Gubbio; Text with Introduction, Translation and Notes*. Joint Liturgical Studies 52. Cambridge: Grove Books, 2002.

Demacopoulos, George E., with Matt Briel. *The Invention of Peter: Apostolic Discourse and Papal Authority in Late Antiquity*. Philadelphia: University of Pennsylvania Press, 2013. [See pp. 173–80 for Gelasius, *Letter* 12, and pp. 181–89 for *Against Andromachus*.]

Dobschütz, Ernst von (ed.). *Das decretum Gelasianum de libris recipiendis et non recipiendis. In kritischem Text hrsg. und untersucht von Ernst von Dobschütz*. Texte und Untersuchungen zur Geschichte der altchristlichen literatur 38.4. Leipzig: Hinrichs, 1912.

Gassó, M. and Columba M. Batlle (eds.), *Pelagii I Papae epistulae quae supersunt (556–561)*. Scripta et Documenta 8. Montserrat: Abatia Montisserrati, 1956.

Gelasius I, *Epistula de duabus naturis*:Rocco Ronzani (ed. and trans.), *Gelasio I*, Lettera sulle due nature. Biblioteca patristica 48. Bologna: EDB, 2012.

Innocent I, *Letter* 25 to Decentius of Gubbio: PL 20:551–61.

Pomarès, Gilbert (ed. and trans.). *Gélase Ier.* Lettre contre les Lupercales et dix-huit Messes du Sacramentaire Léonien. SC 65 (1959).

FURTHER READING

Charanis, Peter. *Church and State in the Later Roman Empire: The Religious Policy of Anastasius the First, 491–518*. 2nd edition. Thessalonikē: Kentron Vyzantinōn Ereunōn, 1974.

Dunn, Geoffrey D. (ed.). *The Bishop of Rome in Late Antiquity*. Farnham, UK: Ashgate, 2015.

Gallagher, Clarence. *Church Law and Church Order in Rome and Byzantium: A Comprehensive Study*. Birmingham Byzantine and Ottoman Monographs 8. Farnham, UK: Ashgate, 2002.

Hoeflich, M. H. "Gelasius I and Roman Law: One Further Word." JTS 26.1 (1975): 114–19.

Jasper, Detlev, and Horst Fuhrmann. *Papal Letters in the Early Middle Ages*. Washington, DC: Catholic University of America Press, 2001.

Kolb, Robert. "Two-Kingdoms Doctrine." *The Encyclopedia of Christianity*, ed. Erwin Fahlbusch et al., vol. 5 (Grand Rapids: Eerdmans, and Leiden: Brill, 2008), 569–75.

Moorhead, John. *The Popes and the Church of Rome in Late Antiquity*. London: Routledge, 2015.

Morrison, Karl F. *The Two Kingdoms: Ecclesiology in Carolingian Political Thought*. Princeton, NJ: Princeton University Press, 1964.

Neil, Bronwen. "The Decretals of Gelasius I: Making Canon Law in Late Antiquity." In *Lex et Religio in età tardoantica. XL incontro de studiosi dell'Antichità Cristiana*, Studium Ephemerides Augustinianum 135 (Rome: Institutum Patristicum Augustinianum, 2013), 657–68.

Taylor, Justin. "The Early Papacy at Work: Gelasius I (492–6)." *Journal of Religious History* 8.4 (1975): 317–32.

Ullmann, Walter. *The Growth of Papal Government in the Middle Ages*. 2nd edition. London: Methuen, 1962.

Watt, J. A., "Spiritual and Temporal Powers." In J. H. Burns (ed.), *The Cambridge History of Medieval Political Thought c.350 – c.1450* (Cambridge: Cambridge University Press, 1988), 367–423.

15

Dionysius Exiguus

David Heith-Stade

The monk Dionysius Exiguus, who came from Scythia Minor, was together with Boethius and Cassiodorus one of the great transmitters of the Greek patristic and classical heritage to Latin-speaking Christendom in the sixth century. The epithet *exiguus* ("the little") is neither a proper name nor a reference to the author's physical stature but rather a common formula of humility used in ecclesiastical circles during the period. Very few facts about Dionysius's life are known. We do not know when he was born or even when he died. The year 526 is the last known date in his life. He was already dead when his friend Cassiodorus wrote about him at some time between 551 and 562.

Dionysius's writings cover *computus* (the calculation of Easter), dogmatic theology, hagiography, and canon law. His most enduring legacy is perhaps the almost universally adopted Dionysian Era (also known today as the Common Era), which begins with the (miscalculated) year of the birth of Jesus Christ (*Anno Domini*), dividing the history of the world into BC and AD.

Dionysius's chief contribution to the canonical tradition was his two collections of sources: the *Liber canonum* and the *Liber decretalium*. The *Liber canonum* is a collection of canons (disciplinary decrees) from various church councils, primarily Eastern ones. Dionysius translated the Greek canons into Latin. The *Liber decretalium* is a collection of papal letters written in response to disciplinary questions, which were known as decretals. Subsequent generations combined these two collections into one, known as the *Collectio Dionysiana*. This served as the quasi-official collection of canon law of the Church of Rome. In a later recension, known as the *Collectio Dionysiana-Hadriana*, it served as the official collection of canon law of the Carolingian Empire.

The term "canon law" is conventionally used in English to render the Latin phrase *ius canonicum* (German: *kanonisches Recht*). In English, the word "law" is used to denote two or more distinct concepts that in many other languages are denoted by separate words, such as *Gesetz* and *Recht* in German, *loi* and *droit* in French, *legge* and *diritto* in Italian, and *zakon* and *parvo* in Russian. The first concept denoted here by the word "law" is a typically legislative act or statute (*lex*,

Gesetz, loi, legge, zakon). The other concept denoted here by the word "law" is a "legal order" or a "legal system" (*ius, Recht, droit, diritto, pravo*).[1] This second concept becomes apparent in English in phrases such as "public law," "criminal law," "private law," or "international law," which do not denote a single legislative act or statute (*lex*) but rather a legal order ("*ius est norma agenda*"). The phenomenon comprehended by the word "law" used in the second sense, may, in accordance with Sir Neil MacCormick's institutional theory of law, be minimally defined as an *institutionalized normative order*.[2] I use the term "canon law" in this chapter, therefore, to denote the institutionalized normative order of the church.

THE LIFE AND TIMES OF DIONYSIUS EXIGUUS[3]

Our primary sources of information about Dionysius's life are the short account by his friend Cassiodorus and his own writings.[4] Cassiodorus described him as a saint and famously characterized him as "Scythian in race but altogether Roman in customs" (*Scytha natione, sed moribus omnino Romanus*).[5] Dionysius studied philosophy with Cassiodorus, probably in Rome.

Dionysius came from the province Scythia Minor, which corresponds roughly to the transnational region of Dobruja (or Dobrudja) in today's Romania and Bulgaria. Latin was the main language of Scythia Minor, but Greek was also widely known. Cassiodorus describes Dionysius as completely bilingual and able to translate simultaneously from Greek into Latin and Latin into Greek.[6] Cassiodorus also praises Dionysius's knowledge and understanding of Sacred Scripture.

Some autobiographical information provided by Dionysius might be interpreted as meaning that he was abandoned in the wilderness as a child.[7] Schwartz and Wurm speculate that he was found and raised by monks. Wurm even speculates that Dionysius was raised by the bishop Peter to whom he dedicated his translation of Cyril's *Synodal Letter*.[8] Dionysius probably studied in Constantinople and perfected his skills in translation there.

1 On the distinction between a "legal system" and a "legal order," see Harold J. Berman, *Law and Revolution: The Formation of the Western Legal Tradition* (Cambridge, MA: Harvard University Press, 1983), 49–51.

2 Neil MacCormick, *Rhetoric and the Rule of Law: A Theory of Legal Reasoning* (Oxford: Oxford University Press, 2005), 2–7.

3 For the secondary literature on which this section is based, see Sources at the foot of this chapter.

4 Cassiodorus, *Institutiones divinarum et humanarum lectionum* 1.23.2–4, PL 70:1137–38.

5 Ibid., 1.23.2, 1137.

6 Ibid., 1137–38.

7 Cf. Hubert Wurm, *Studien und Texte zur Dekretalensammlung des Dionysius Exiguus* (Bonn: Röhrscheid, 1939), 11; Eduard Schwartz, "Die Kanonessammlungen der alten Reichskirche," in *Gesammelte Schriften*, 4: *Zur Geschichte der alten Kirche und ihres Rechts* (Berlin: De Gruyter, 1960), 159–275, at 269.

8 Wurm, *Studien und Texte*, 11.

Dionysius's work was shaped by the political developments and ecclesiastical controversies that divided the church during his lifetime. To set him in his historical context, we should mention the Council of Chalcedon, the Acacian Schism, the Laurentian Schism, and the Scythian Controversy.

The Council of Chalcedon and Its Aftermath

Dionysius lived during the aftermath of the Council of Chalcedon in 451. His work was shaped by three major ecclesiastical events: the Acacian Schism, the Laurentian Schism, and the Scythian Controversy. This was, however, a period of relative calm and stability during the reign of the benevolent Arian Ostrogoth king Theoderic the Great (r. 475–526), before Italy was plunged into chaos and despair following the Gothic War, the Lombardic invasion, and the plague pandemic of the sixth century.

The Council of Chalcedon was in many respects the defining event of the period. The first two councils considered to be ecumenical – Nicaea in 325 and Constantinople I in 381 – had established dogmas regarding the mystery of the Trinity. The debates about Christian doctrine then began to focus on the mystery of the incarnation. The main theological issue was how to reconcile the identities of the Logos of God and Jesus of Nazareth with the reality of the incarnation: in other words, to show how Jesus Christ was truly both the divine Logos and a human being. Discussion of this issue developed into a controversy about theological anthropology, which turned on the constitutive elements of a human being, such as body, mind, will, and agency. To what degree and how did Jesus Christ possess these constitutive elements of a human being? The debates that ensued were complicated and highly technical. They generated diverse shades of opinion and were fraught with misunderstandings. No attempt will be made here to survey these issues thoroughly. Instead, to place Dionysius in his context, a brief, schematic description must suffice, emphasizing the political and ethnic dimensions of the debates.

Christological controversy during the period focused initially on Nestorianism, a doctrinal position that seemed to separate the Logos of God and Jesus of Nazareth into two separate subjects, thus denying the reality of the incarnation. Although the controversy began with Nestorius, patriarch of Constantinople, Nestorianism was not necessarily the same as what Nestorius himself was teaching. Indeed, it is arguable that Nestorianism was to a large extent a theological straw man created by patriarch Cyril of Alexandria through a polemical misrepresentation of the theology of Nestorius. Be that as it may, patriarch Cyril was victorious at the Council of Ephesus in 431, which condemned patriarch Nestorius, and this council was later deemed ecumenical – as the Third Ecumenical Council.

Although patriarch Cyril of Alexandria was an astute theologian and became a hero to the anti-Chalcedonian Monophysites (or Miaphysites), he was an ambitious, divisive, and confrontational church leader whose legacy polarized the imperial church. His victory at Ephesus gave an impetus to various high Christological speculations that seemed to downplay or even to ignore the humanity of Jesus Christ. It also accentuated the differences between the Alexandrian and Antiochian traditions of the day, which had different focuses and practices of prayer and worship, and conflicting terminological usages. (Nestorius was Antiochian in his thinking.) A new balance was sought, therefore, and this effort resulted in the definition of the Council of Chalcedon in 451. The definition rehabilitated the Antiochian tradition and sought to find a synthesis between the two different Greek patristic traditions: one that could also guarantee a balanced Christology.

If the Council of Chalcedon was a triumph as regards Christological speculation, it was a spectacular failure as regards restoring unity in the universal church. Anti-Chalcedonianism established itself in Egypt, Syria, and parts of Palestine, while pro-Chalcedonianism established itself in the catholic West, the Balkans, Asia Minor, and other parts of Palestine. The anti-Chalcedonians, who became known as Monophysites, viewed the Christology of Chalcedon as, in effect, a form of Nestorianism, considered as heresy.[9]

Both Rome and Constantinople had vested interests in Chalcedon. Legates of the bishop of Rome had successfully lobbied to have Leo's *Tome* read in sessions of the council and had included it in the acts of the council, and Rome interpreted these actions as legitimizing its own claim to primacy in the universal church. The popes – if we may regard the bishops of Rome as popes by this time – came from then on to see themselves as the guardians of the Council of Chalcedon, whose Christology they interpreted primarily through Leo's theology, although this did not really address the finer points of the issues being debated in the East. Constantinople had managed to get the council to promulgate the so-called Canon 28 of Chalcedon at one of the last sessions. This canon, in effect, put Constantinople on an equal footing with Rome as regards primacy in the universal church, and it approved the jurisdictional claims of Constantinople. The popes, therefore, always rejected this canon.

In the wake of Chalcedon, sloganeering became an important tool in rallying popular support, which sometimes involved mob violence. This development had the unfortunate effect of tying the hands of the theologians of the competing post-Chalcedonian parties in the imperial church. Because they could not move beyond certain problematic formulas and slogans, they were unable constructively to address the actual theological issues without losing popular support, which was centered on these formulas and slogans. Otherwise, they risked becoming victims of their former supporters.

The concept of nature (in Greek, *physis*) became central in the subsequent debate, for it was understood differently in the Alexandrian and Antiochian traditions. The anti-Chalcedonians' main Christological slogan was "one incarnate

[9] W. H. C. Frend, *The Rise of the Monophysite Movement: Chapters in the History of the Church in the Fifth and Sixth Centuries* (Cambridge: Cambridge University Press, 1972).

nature," a formula derived from sayings and writings by Cyril of Alexandria. The pro-Chalcedonians' main Christological slogan was "one person in two natures." The pro-Chalcedonian slogan echoes the theology of Pope Leo the Great, but his theology was based on a separate Latin patristic tradition that only further contributed to the terminological confusion. The anti-Chalcedonians, therefore, were called Monophysites (i.e., adherents of the doctrine of one incarnate nature in Jesus Christ), while the pro-Chalcedonians are often called Dyophysites (i.e., adherents of the doctrine of two natures in Jesus Christ after the incarnation). During this period, thc anti-Chalcedonian Monophysites (more precisely, Miaphysites), pursuing Christologies based on Cyril's idea of "one nature" (*mia physis*) in Christ, prevailed in the East. The dogmatic formulas that defined the official doctrine of the imperial church also had political consequences. Concern for orthodoxy could be invoked by insurgents in order to gain legitimacy and even justify a *coup d'état.*

The Western Empire and the Acacian Schism

Things were further complicated by the cessation of the western Roman Empire. Imperial authority and administration waned rapidly during the first half of the fifth century, and in 476, the barbarian general Odoacer forced the nominal Western emperor, Romulus Augustulus, to retire. The only Roman emperor henceforth was in Constantinople. The barbarian conquerors of the West sought legitimacy as vassals of the emperor in Constantinople, but in reality they were only nominally subject to his power while pursuing a politically independent path. The Western parts of the empire were now outside the real power of the emperor. The interests of the government in Constantinople became increasingly focused on the Eastern part of the empire, which was for the moment dominated by anti-Chalcedonianism.

The policy of emperor Zeno (r. 474–475, 476–491), therefore, was focused on the East and its divisions. He sought to reconcile the anti-Chalcedonian establishment in the Eastern provinces with the imperial regime in Constantinople. The practical failure of Chalcedon seems to have convinced the emperor that the institution of church councils was ineffective. Without consulting a church council, he enacted his Decree of Union (*Henōticon*), aimed at silencing Christological controversy and restoring the status quo ante. The emperor had persuaded the patriarch of Constantinople, Acacius, to go along with this policy.

In the newfound ecclesiastical independence of the West under Arian Gothic rule, bishop Felix III of Rome and his archdeacon, the future Roman bishop Gelasius (see Chapter 14), rejected the *Henōticon* and the efforts of the emperor in Constantinople to placate the anti-Chalcedonians through doctrinal compromise. Rome had invested too much prestige in Chalcedon to let realpolitik win the day. Felix excommunicated patriarch Acacius of Constantinople and urged the emperor to abandon his ecclesiastical policy designed to settle the post-Chalcedonian disputes. Thus, a policy designed to reunite the ecclesiastical factions in the East was not only unsuccessful in that regard but also resulted in a schism with the West, known as the Acacian Schism.

With regard to the Acacian Schism, the Roman establishment was divided into hawks and doves. The hawks were dominated by the clergy and held to an uncompromising fidelity to Chalcedon, interpreted through the theology of Leo the Great. The doves were dominated by the senate and wanted reconciliation with the emperor and the Church of Constantinople. Gelasius, who succeeded Felix III as bishop of Rome, continued the hawkish policy that he had helped to formulate as archdeacon and secretary of his predecessor. Dionysius Exiguus became involved in this conflict as a dove.

Dionysius's Career in Rome: The Laurentian Schism

Gelasius (492–496) was succeeded as bishop of Rome by Anastasius II (496–498), who had a more dovish attitude toward the post-Chalcedonian disputes than his predecessor and began negotiations for reconciliation with Constantinople. Dionysius Exiguus came to Rome while Anastasius was bishop and was employed by him in 497 to translate a document stating the view of the Church of Alexandria on the issues relevant to the Acacian Schism.

When Anastasius II died suddenly in 498 with no obvious successor, his death put an end to the attempted reconciliation between Rome and Constantinople. Two separate electoral bodies assembled, electing and consecrating two different pretenders to the Roman See: the deacon Symmachus, and the archpriest Laurentius. Symmachus was supported by a majority of the Roman clergy, while Laurentius was supported by the senate. The two factions appealed to the Arian Gothic king, Theoderic, who approved the election of Symmachus because he had been elected and consecrated a couple of hours before Laurentius and by a majority of the clergy. Laurentius initially accepted Theoderic's decision, and he was given the see of Nocera. The episcopacy of Symmachus (498–514) was characterized by a renewed hostility against Constantinople.

In 501, the pro-Byzantine senatorial party was given a chance to get rid of the undiplomatic Symmachus and to install Laurentius as pope in his stead. Symmachus had decided to celebrate Easter according to the old Roman computation, which in that year prescribed a date different from that of the Alexandrian computation, used not only by the Eastern churches but also in some parts of Italy.

The senatorial party accused Symmachus before king Theoderic of not celebrating Easter with the rest of Christendom, of misusing church funds, and of keeping mistresses. After much ado, the king appointed a visitor to administer the Roman see, and he ordered that a synod of bishops be convened in Rome to judge the case of Symmachus. During this period, Symmachus took refuge at St. Peter's basilica on the outskirts of Rome, thus becoming the first pope to have his residence at the Vatican rather than at the Lateran Palace.

Both parties in this dispute harnessed the power of Christian charity and almsgiving in order to employ hooligans, who could promote their respective causes through intimidation and violence. The work of the synod was constantly obstructed by unrest in Rome. The bishops appealed repeatedly to the king, asking him to take the lead in the case. But the Arian king wisely kept away from the internal troubles of the catholics. Eventually, the bishops at the synod argued that they could not judge the pope and left the judgment to God. The Symmachian party took this as a victory and began to fabricate various pseudepigrapha, known as the Symmachian forgeries, to promote the idea that no one could judge the see of Rome because of its primacy (*prima sedes a nemine iudicatur*).

The senatorial party responded by bringing Laurentius back to Rome, who took possession of the Lateran and main urban churches. Thus, he is traditionally counted as an antipope. After a couple of years, king Theoderic intervened in favor of Symmachus, putting an end to the Laurentian Schism. The antipope Laurentius retired to a life of leisure at a country estate belonging to his senatorial patron, Festus. Some sectors of the Roman establishment refused to be reconciled with the episcopacy until the end of the reign of Symmachus.

It was during the reign of Symmachus that Dionysius compiled the first version of his collections of conciliar canons and papal decretals up to those of Anastasius II. Dionysius seems to have been sympathetic to the Laurentians. He mentions a Laurentius favorably in the preface to the collection of conciliar canons, and this may have been the antipope. But Dionysius did not have regular access to the papal archive during this period. His collection of papal decretals was based not on the official register of papal letters but on various private collections.

Hormisdas (514–523), who succeeded Symmachus as bishop of Rome, inherited the thankless task of cleaning up the mess left by his predecessors. In this, he succeeded, reconciling the Roman establishment with the church of Constantinople. Hormisdas's achievement was largely dependent on a change in the imperial regime in Constantinople. The new emperor, Justin, and his adviser and nephew, the future emperor Justinian, were pro-Chalcedonian and favorably disposed toward the West as regards policy. This new western orientation would reach its zenith in the pyrrhic reconquest of the West under emperor Justinian. A rapprochement between Rome and Constantinople was an initial stage in the new imperial policy. The third version of Dionysius's collection of conciliar canons was made in the context of this rapprochement. This version was made by order of Hormisdas, and it contained a bilingual collection of the Greek conciliar canons universally received by East and West, with a literal translation into Latin. Unfortunately, this version has been lost, and only the preface remains.

The Scythian Controversy

Rome and Constantinople were solemnly reconciled on Holy Thursday, March 28, 519 at the liturgy in the Hagia Sophia in Constantinople. A group of Scythian monks, compatriots of Dionysius, played a minor and indirect role in the rapprochement between Rome and Constantinople. They appeared in Constantinople in 519 with their leader John Maxentius, promoting a strictly Cyrillian interpretation of Chalcedon. They were equally opposed to Monophysitism and to Nestorianism, and they wanted to promote as dogma what became known as the Theopaschite formula: "One of the Trinity suffered for us." Although intended as a solution to the Christological debates, this anti-Nestorian formula was suspect because it had also been used by some of the anti-Chalcedonian Monophysites.

The emperor Justinian (r. 527–565), who did not want to jeopardize the reconciliation with Rome, referred the Scythian monks to Pope Hormisdas in Rome. Later in that year, some of the monks appeared in Rome in order to win over Hormisdas to their formula. They were not successful because he adhered to a Leonine understanding of Chalcedon, rather than a Cyrillian one. Hormisdas was further disturbed when he learnt that the formula of the Scythian monks had also been used by some anti-Chalcedonians. But the Scythian monks persisted. They staged public debates in Rome, accusing anyone who disagreed with them of being Nestorian. Finally, Hormisdas had them expelled from Rome in August, 520. In 521, he stated officially that, although their Theopaschite formula was not heretical in itself, it was problematic because it could be understood as anti-Chalcedonian.

Dionysius seems to have been sympathetic toward his Scythian compatriots. He translated Cyril's "synodal letter" against Nestorius into Latin in order to make the Cyrillian theology better known in the Latin West. And while the Scythian monks failed to win over Hormisdas, they did influence the great scholar Boethius, whose theological tracts show the influence of Theopaschitism. Through the influence of Boethius, therefore, the Scythian monks were to have an influence on medieval theology in the West.

Dionysius's Contribution to Christian Chronology

The issue of the computation of Easter, which had been at the source of the Laurentian Schism, came up again during the pontificate of John I, who turned to Dionysius for advice in 526. Dionysius composed a treatise on the computation of Easter, which settled the issue in favor of the Alexandrian method of computation. It was here, in the Easter table, that Dionysius introduced a new era, known as the Dionysian or Common Era, whereby each year was counted from the supposed date of the incarnation of Jesus Christ.

DIONYSIUS'S CONTRIBUTIONS TO THE CANONICAL TRADITION[10]

Dionysius is the first author of canonical collections in Latin who is known to us by name. Although his collections proved to be seminal and historically significant, his contribution to the canonical tradition was modest in itself. He did not arrange the canonical material systematically according to topics; he did not produce a doctrinal commentary on the laws and their sources; and he did not write any treatise on institutions of canonical regulation. As regards decretals, Dionysius compiled a collection that contained only letters on disciplinary issues, whereas some previous collections had included letters of dogmatic as well as of disciplinary content. But this last limitation was arguably an advance toward the identification of canon law or canonical regulation as a field of study.

Dionysius is historically important chiefly because he translated and compiled a collection of sources of canon law that laid claim to a certain degree of universality, but also because of some modest but useful advances in presentation. He gave the canons headings that stated their contents, and he prefixed a table of contents, making it possible to gain an overview of the subject matter of the canons. Likewise, he subdivided the decretals and introduced subheadings stating their contents. Dionysius's modest innovations seem to have been influenced by developments in Roman law, especially the early attempts at codifying the sources of Roman law in the *Theodosian Code*.

Although his contributions to the field may seem unimpressive in light of later developments in canon law, they represented a major advance in juridical technique in contrast to previous canonical collections.

The Liber canonum *and Its Sources*

The canonical collections of Dionysius Exiguus were part of a larger trend in the sixth century toward collections that stabilized the common sources of ancient canonical regulation (*ius antiquum*) and transcended regional churches. The canonical tradition had hitherto consisted largely of custom, pseudo-apostolic ecclesiastical decrees, and local regulation. Even the canons issued by the first ecumenical council, at Nicaea, were largely of a provincial nature and dealt with particular cases brought before the council by the attending bishops. Because such canons were largely focused on issues relevant to the church in the eastern Roman Empire, it took a long time even for the canons of Nicaea to be universally received.

Already in the fifth century, however, a universally accepted body of disciplinary canons (*corpus canonum*) was beginning to take shape through the fusion and distribution of earlier local collections of canons. The development of a common tradition of canonical regulation proceeded largely by the elevation of particular

10 For the secondary literature on which this section is based, see Sources at the foot of this chapter.

canons and decretals to the status of a universal resource through the expansion and reception of collections of canons.

Central to this emergence of a common fund of canons was an Antiochian collection of regional conciliar canons, known as the *Syntagma Canonum Antiochenum*. (This collection has been lost, although it can be at least partially reconstructed.) Compiled around the middle or latter half of the fourth century, the *Syntagma* provided the basis for later collections of conciliar canons in Greek, Latin, Syriac, and Coptic. The collection consisted of the canons of Ancyra (314), Neocaesarea (314–325), Antioch (341), Gangra (341), and Laodicea (343–380). To this material was prefixed the canons and creed of the first ecumenical council at Nicaea (325). In the original version of this collection, the canons were numbered continuously, rather than within each set or unit of canons, as in later versions. It was quoted and used in this earlier form at the Council of Chalcedon in 451. The collection was later expanded by the addition of canons from later councils, especially those considered to be ecumenical.

Dionysius Exiguus drew on the original version of the *Syntagma Canonum Antiochenum*. He prefixed fifty of the so-called apostolic canons to this corpus, and he added canons from Constantinople, Sardica (Serdica), Carthage, and Chalcedon.

As already noted, Dionysius made three recensions of his *Liber canonum*. The first recension is available today in a critical edition by Adolf Strewe.[11] The second edition has not been critically edited, but it is available in the vulgate form printed by Voellius and Justellus in the seventeenth century and reprinted by Migne in the nineteenth century.[12] Of the third recension, only the preface has survived.[13] From this preface, we learn that the third recension was a bilingual edition, with the original Greek texts and a literal Latin translation side by side. The third recension excluded the canons that could not claim universal reception at the time, namely, the Apostolic Canons, the Canons of Carthage, and the Canons of Sardica.

Thus, the *Liber canonum* includes in its first and second recensions the so-called Canons of the Apostles and the canons of the councils of Nicaea, Ancyra, Neocaesarea, Gangra, Antioch, Laodicea, Constantinople, Sardica (Serdica), and Carthage. Let us briefly consider each of these sources.

The Apostolic Canons are part of the corpus of pseudo-apostolic church ordinances, which played an important role in the development of canonical regulation until the fourth century. From that time, this pseudo-apostolic material was gradually displaced by conciliar canons and imperial laws, although it

[11] A. Strewe (ed.), *Die Canonessammlung des Dionysius Exiguus in der ersten Redaktion* (Berlin: De Gruyter, 1931).

[12] *Bibliotheca iuris canonici veteris*, vol. 1 (Paris, 1661), 101–174. PL 67:137–230.

[13] CCL 85, 35–42. Friedrich Maassen, Geschichte der Quellen und der Literatur des canonischen Rechts im Abendlande bis zum Ausgange des Mittelalters, vol. 1 (Graz, 1870; repr. Graz, 1956), 960–65.

continued to form part of the canonical regulation of the non-Chalcedonian churches, also known today as the Oriental Orthodox churches. The Apostolic Canons comprise the conclusion to the Apostolic Constitutions, the last major pseudo-apostolic church ordinances. The Apostolic Constitutions were compiled in Syria during the second half of the fourth century and consisted of a revised and expanded compilation of selections from three previous pseudo-apostolic church ordinances: the *Didascalia Apostolorum* (books 1–6), the *Didachē* (book 7), and the *Traditio Apostolica* (book 8). The eighty-five apostolic canons constitute the last chapter (47) of book 8 of the Apostolic Constitutions.

The sources of the Apostolic Canons include canons from the councils of Antioch, Laodicea, and Nicaea. The Apostolic Canons also summarize norms found in the rest of the Apostolic Constitutions. These are primarily concerned with regulating the life and duties of the clergy.

Dionysius translated only the first fifty of the Apostolic Canons, while the Greek *corpus canonum* contains eighty-five. It is unclear why Dionysius did not translate the remaining thirty-five. One explanation is that they contain norms that were contrary to the custom of the Roman Church at the time, but this is unconvincing because there are norms that are contrary to Roman custom even among the canons that Dionysius did include in translation. Another, arguably more plausible, explanation is that the Greek text that Dionysius used contained only the first fifty canons, although there were earlier Latin translations of all eighty-five canons.

Dionysius expressed doubt about the authenticity of the Apostolic Canons in the first preserved preface to his own collection (i.e., in the oldest surviving collection of councils, which was the second recension). Moreover, later recension of the so-called Decree of Pope Gelasius had dismissed the Apostolic Canons as apocryphal. Dionysius did not include them in the third and last version of his *Liber canonum*. Nevertheless, they passed from the first two recensions of his *Liber canonum* into central-medieval Latin collections of canon law, most notably the *Decretum* of Gratian. It should also be noted that emperor Justinian sanctioned the Apostolic Canons in *Novellae* 6 and 137. As a result, they are sometimes included in the sources of Byzantine law.

The Council of Nicaea, which the emperor Constantine convoked in 325, holds a special place in the history of the church. It was the first council that came to be considered as ecumenical (i.e., as speaking for the entire church), and it served as a model for later major councils. Its purpose was to address three main issues: the Arian controversy, the Melitian Schism in Egypt (regarding the treatment of Christians who had lapsed under persecution), and the date for the celebration of Easter. Only the creed, canons, a letter to the church of Alexandria, and the subscription list of bishops have been preserved. A summary of the Council of Nicaea's decision on the date of Easter has been transmitted in some Greek canonical collections.

In addition to doctrinal matters, Nicaea issued twenty disciplinary canons. One lasting influence of these canons was the introduction of the principle of accommodation in the organization of the church. The organization of the church should adapt itself to the organization of the empire. This led to the establishment of metropolitan provinces and synods corresponding to the provinces of civil administration as well as of supra-metropolitan regions corresponding to the dioceses into which the civil administration was divided. The canons on church organization were primarily adapted to the needs of the Eastern part of the empire, which differed from those in the West.

Dionysius eliminated some complications that had crept in regarding Nicene canons. In the original Greek record, there were twenty canons. But the Syriac, Ethiopian, and Arabic canonical traditions attributed various spurious canons to the Council of Nicaea (another indication of its importance). These pseudo-Nicaean canons are in many ways parallel to the pseudo-apostolic church ordinances. Moreover, the old Roman collection attributed the canons of Serdica to Nicaea (see below). And although Rufinus had translated only the genuine canons of Nicaea into Latin, he had divided both canon 6 and canon 8 into two, so that there were twenty-two canons of Nicaea in his version. Dionysius Exiguus separated the Canons of Serdica from the Canons of Nicaea and kept the original Greek numbering of the Nicene canons, so that in his collection there are twenty.

The SYNOD OF ANCYRA was held in 314, following the persecution of Christians under emperor Maximinus Daia. This council issued twenty-five canons. The major concern among them is how to rectify situations in the Christian community arising from the persecutions.

The SYNOD OF NEOCAESAREA was held between 315 and 319 in the province of Pontus Polemoniacus. It issued fifteen canons, which dealt with a variety of topics. These canons are important especially for the history of the institution of penance.

The SYNOD OF GANGRA was held around 340/42 in the province of Paphlagonia. The synod issued twenty canons against the rigorist ascetical movement of Eustathius of Sebaste and expressed disapproval of the ascetical excesses of this enthusiastic movement.

The manuscript tradition and old translations usually attributed the twenty-five "CANONS OF ANTIOCH" to the Synod of Antioch *in Encaeniis* ("in dedication"), held in 341. Already at the beginning of the fifth century, however, several authors argued that the canons were issued by an Arian (or more precisely Homoean) synod held around 330, and most scholars today accept the latter attribution. The canons are important for the history of the public regulation of the church. The major topics pertain to the relationships among bishops, between priests and their bishops, and between suffragan bishops and their metropolitan, and to the procedure to be used in cases against bishops. Some of these "Canons of Antioch" were quoted as authoritative canons at the Council of Chalcedon.

The Canons of Laodicea, from the fourth century, remain a mystery. According to a note prefixed to these canons, they originate from a synod of bishops in the province of Asia, convened in Phrygia Pacatiana. No date for this assembly is given. The canons must come from the fourth century but before the year 380. They give the impression of being epitomized and were perhaps compiled from the decisions from several synods. In the Greek tradition there are sixty canons, but the translation of Dionysius Exiguus has only the first fifty-nine canons, omitting the sixtieth, which is on the canon of Sacred Scripture.

The First Council of Constantinople in 381 was later considered ecumenical in relation to the doctrine of the Trinity, but it was convened chiefly in order to settle the situation that had arisen after the metropolitan of Alexandria had meddled in the affairs of the church of Constantinople and got Maximus the Cynic appointed as metropolitan there. The council annulled the appointment of Maximus (canon 4) and elected the Cappadocian theologian Gregory of Nazianzus in his stead, although the assembled bishops resisted Gregory's theological arguments, and he resigned.

Dionysius provides three canons from Constantinople I. The first ratifies the Creed of Nicaea and anathematizes various heretics. The second of Dionysius's canons corresponds to the second and third canons according to the Greek division. Canon 2 according to the Greek text decrees that the metropolitans of the imperial dioceses (i.e., supra-metropolitan regions) should not interfere in each other's affairs; and canon 3 according to the Greek text decrees that Constantinople, as the New Rome, comes second only to Rome in protocol and in precedence of honor. Canon 4 in the Greek (canon 3 according to Dionysius) deposes Maximus the Cynic as metropolitan of Constantinople.

It should be noted that Rome did not originally accept canons 2 and 3 (according to the Greek division), which infringed on Rome's claims to primacy. Nevertheless, Dionysius included these canons in his translation. The popes protested especially against canon 3. It was not until the Fourth Lateran Council of 1215 that the Papacy finally accepted canon 3 of Constantinople. After the Council of Chalcedon, the Council of Constantinople came to be viewed as an ecumenical council (i.e., as the second ecumenical council). Canon 2 and especially canon 3 (according to the Greek division) are still important for the public law of the Eastern Orthodox Churches.

We may note in passing two features of the Greek tradition that are absent from Dionysius's collection and from the Latin canonical tradition generally. First, the Greek tradition attributes three more canons to Constantinople I (381), although these are not found in the earliest canonical collections or in manuscript traditions. Canons 5 and 6 are probably derived from a council of Constantinople held in 382. Canon 7 is an excerpt from a letter by patriarch Gennadius I of Constantinople to Martyrius of Antioch on how to receive converts from various sects. Second, Latin sources, unlike Greek, do not attribute any canons to the

Council of Ephesus in 431. This council was later deemed to be the third ecumenical council, and it proved crucial in the history of Christology. It was convened to condemn Nestorianism, and it was here that Cyril of Alexandria proposed the ideas that later became the seeds of Monophysitism. In fact, the Council of Ephesus did not issue any canons as such, but the Byzantine canonists extracted some passages from the proceedings of the council, which passed into the Greek tradition as the eight canons of Ephesus.

The COUNCIL OF CHALCEDON was convened in 451 to resolve the Monophysite controversy. This council is important for scholars of canon law because an old Greek collection, the *Syntagma Canonum Antiochenum*, which was since lost, was quoted in the acts of the council, and these quotations are a resource for attempts to reconstruct the collection. The Council of Chalcedon enacted several canons, which covered a wide range of topics. The council provided the first comprehensive regulation of monasticism within the constitution of the church. Strictly speaking, the Council of Chalcedon enacted twenty-seven canons. In one of its last sessions, however, the council made a decision regarding the jurisdiction of the metropolitan of Constantinople, reiterating that this see had primacy of honor second only to Old Rome, and this decision made its way into the Byzantine canonical collections as canon 28 of Chalcedon. The popes vehemently opposed it. Two more decisions by the council were also excerpted from the acts by the Byzantine canonists and incorporated into the Byzantine canonical collections. Consequently, the Greek tradition attributes thirty canons to the Council of Chalcedon, whereas the Latin tradition only accepts twenty-seven, all of which are included in Dionysius Exiguus's collection.

The COUNCIL OF SERDICA (or Sardica: present-day Sofia in Bulgaria) was convened in 342 in the wake of the Council of Nicaea, but the council failed to resolve the controversial issues or to restore the peace of the church. The bishops from the Western and Eastern parts of the empire respectively split into two parties, anathematizing each other and carrying on two parallel councils. After the Eastern bishops had departed, the Western bishops continued and issued a number of canons, dealing primarily with the episcopacy (the office of bishops). The major innovation at the council was the approval of appellate review of decisions passed by provincial councils. This decision to allow appellate review was later used by the popes to support their claim that the Roman papacy held universal jurisdiction, although that was not the original intention.

Before Dionysius Exiguus, as already noted, a Roman collection had erroneously attributed the canons of Serdica to the Council of Nicaea. This error had already been discovered in the early fifth century, however, when Pope Zosimus appealed to these canons in order to intervene in the case of the priest Apiarius, who had been deposed by a council in Carthage. Protesting against the intervention of Rome, the African bishops pointed out that the supposedly Nicaean canons to which the pope appealed in order to justify his intervention were unknown in their own collections of canons. The African bishops sent the text of their collection of canons to Rome, including the genuine canons of Nicaea.

The canons of Serdica were not originally numbered, but the numbering used by Dionysius Exiguus has prevailed for the Latin tradition, which has twenty canons. The Latin text of the canons was probably the official version issued by the council. There is also a Greek version of the canons, which is independent of the Latin version, and there are differences between the two versions. A plausible theory promoted in recent scholarship is that there was a bilingual edition of canons, since the council was attended by Greek- and Latin-speaking bishops in roughly equal numbers. According to this theory, the Greek version of the canons was probably the work of interpreters at the council, and not a later translation of the official Latin. The Greek version of the Canons of Serdica was incorporated in the Byzantine canonical collections in the middle of the sixth century.

Finally, the COUNCIL OF CARTHAGE (419) was convened to consider the case of Apiarius (noted above). The council enacted thirty-three canons. Dionysius Exiguus records these in the first recension of his *Liber canonum*, together with documents from the church of Carthage relating to the case of Apiarius and to the canons accepted in Africa. In the second recension of his *Liber canonum*, Dionysius Exiguus incorporated a private collection of canons from previous councils held in Carthage. Consequently, all of these canons became known collectively as the 133 Canons of Carthage. These canons were translated into Greek in the late sixth century and in this form were ratified by the Quinisext Council in 691. This Greek translation was probably made from the *Liber canonum* of Dionysius Exiguus. If so, this is the only example of the influence of Dionysius Exiguus on the Eastern canonical tradition.

THE *LIBER DECRETALIUM*

Dionysius did not base his *Liber decretalium* on the registers of papal letters kept in the archive of the Roman Church, but rather on various other collections of papal letters. The chief innovation of Dionysius was that his *Liber decretalium* contained only papal letters on disciplinary matters, which were those most relevant to canonical regulation. He also introduced headings and subheadings in the material in order to make it more accessible. The *Liber decretalium* was appended at an early stage to the *Liber canonum*. Expanded, interpolated, and redacted versions were later made. The original *Liber decretalium* has been lost, but Wurm has reconstructed its content on the basis of later versions and other collections derived from the *Collectio Dionysiana*.[14] The original version contained thirty-eight decretals from Siricius, Innocentius, Zosimus, Bonifatius, Caelestinus, Leo, Gelasius, and Anastasius II, as well as an imperial rescript by emperor Honorius on papal elections.

[14] Wurm, *Studien und Texte*, 59–80.

The *Liber decretalium* is known today from versions found in or retrieved from the *Collectio Dionysiana-Hadriana* (see below).[15]

CONCLUDING OBSERVATIONS

Dionysius shows an affinity to the Eastern canonical tradition inasmuch as he deliberately tried to retain only authentic sources, eliminating pseudepigrapha and forgeries as sources of canonical material. The only pseudepigraphic texts in the canonical works of Dionysius are the so-called Apostolic Canons, and Dionysius acknowledged the questionable status of these Canons and excluded them from the third version of his collection of canons, commissioned by Pope Hormisdas. One might contrast his approach here to that of the contemporaneous supporters of Pope Symmachus, who resorted to forgeries (the *Symachian Forgeries*) in order to make their case within the canonical tradition.

Forgeries and false attributions have played a more important role in the development of the Western canonical tradition than in the East. Thus, the canons of Serdica were attributed to the Council of Nicaea and used to support papal claims. The most famous collection of forgeries is the influential Pseudo-Isidorian Decretals from the ninth century (see Chapter 19 in this volume).

One should not dismiss forged decretals and rules merely as examples of malicious opportunism. They were important means of legitimizing and articulating traditional convictions and customs by inventing written legal sources in absence of relevant written rules. Nevertheless, Dionysius characteristically represents a concern for authenticity in canonical regulation. He strove to use only conciliar canons that were universally accepted, translating them from the original Greek when they were not originally written in Latin.

It is significant, too, that Dionysius's selection of papal letters was limited to juridical, disciplinary material, unlike previous collections of papal letters, for this approach focuses more clearly on matters that are properly canonical. He also makes advances in technique by introducing subject indexes, headings, and subheadings, which provide an easily accessible overview of the juridical material despite its more or less chronological arrangement.

RECEPTION

The chief merit of Dionysius was to give the Latin church access to the Greek canonical sources. Through Dionysius, these profoundly influenced the development of canon law in the West.

[15] G. Voellus and J. Justellus (eds.), *Bibliotheca iuris canonici veteris*, vol. 1 (Paris, 1661), 183–248. Reprinted in PL 67:230–316.

There was no authorized, official collection (*collectio authentica*) of canonical regulation during the first millennium, but already Cassiodorus mentions that the *Liber canonum* of Dionysius Exiguus was being used by the church in Rome. Several other canonical collections were derived from the collection of Dionysius Exiguus. In 742, Pope Hadrian I gave a revised and augmented version of the *Collectio Dionysiana* to Charlemagne. This collection is known as the *Collectio Dionysiana-Hadriana*.[16] It served in effect as the code of canon regulation for the Frankish Empire and the Carolingian reforms. By this means, the collection of Dionysius Exiguus became one of the most influential canonical collections during the first millennium.

SOURCES

For the first recension of the *Collectio Dionysiana*, see A. Strewe (ed.), *Die Canonessamlung des Dionysius Exiguus in der ersten redaktion* (Berlin: De Gruyter, 1931).

For the second recension of the *Collectio Dionysiana*, see the edition printed by G. Voellius and H. Justellus, *Bibliotheca iuris canonici veteris*, vol. 1 (Paris, 1661), 101–174(conciliar canons) and 183–248 (decretals). Reproduced in PL 67:137–230 (conciliar canons) and 230–316 (decretals).

For Dionysius's prefaces, see Fr. Glorie, "Dionysii Exigui Praefationes," in *Scriptores 'Illyrici' Minores*, CCL 85, 29–51. There are English translations of these prefaces in Somerville and Brasington's *Prefaces*, 46–49.

Secondary Sources and Further Reading

The first section of this chapter, on Dionysius's life and times, is dependent on the following: Hubert Wurm, *Studien und Texte zur Dekretalensammlung des Dionysius Exiguus*, Kanonistische Studien und Texte, Bd. 16 (Bonn: Röhrscheid, 1939); Louis Duchesne, *L'Église au VIe siècle* (Paris: Boccard, 1925); Erich Caspar, *Geschichte des Papsttums von den Anfängen bis zur Höhe der Weltherrschaft, 2: Das Papsttum unter byzantinischer Herrschaft* (Tübingen: Mohr, 1933); Viktor Schurr, *Die Trinitätslehre des Boethius im Lichte der 'skythischen Kontroversen'* (Paderborn: Schöningh, 1935); E. Schwartz, "Die Kanonessamlungen der alten Reichskirche," in *Gesammelte Schriften, 4: Zur Geschichte der alten Kirche und ihres Rechts* (Berlin: De Gruyter 1960), 159–275; J.-M. Versanne, *Denys le Petit et le droit canonique dans l'Église latine au VIe siècle* (Villefranche: Réveil du Beaujolais, 1913); Jeffrey Richards, *The Popes and the Papacy in the Early Middle Ages, 476–752* (London: Routledge & Kegan Paul, 1979); John Moorhead, *Theoderic in Italy* (Oxford: Clarendon Press, 1992);

16 Printed editions: Johannes W. Cochlaeus, *Canones apostolorum, veterum conciliorum constitutions. Decreta Pontificum antiquiora* (Mainz, 1525); F. Pithou, *Codex canonum vetus Ecclesiae Romanae* (Paris, 1609, 1687).

H. Chadwick, *Boethius: The Consolations of Music, Logic, Theology, and Philosophy* (Oxford: Clarendon Press, 1981); James J. O'Donnell, *Cassiodorus* (Berkeley: University of California Press, 1979); W. H. C. Frend, *The Rise of the Monophysite Movement: Chapters in the History of the Church in the Fifth and Sixth Centuries* (Cambridge: Cambridge University Press, 1972); Leo Donald Davis, *The First Seven Ecumenical Councils (325–787): Their History and Theology* (Collegeville, MN: Liturgical Press, 1983); Hubert Jedin, *History of the Church, 2: The Imperial Church from Constantine to the Early Middle Ages* (New York: Crossroad, 1980); John Meyendorff, *Imperial Unity and Christian Divisions: The Church 450–680 AD* (Crestwood, NY: St. Vladimir's Seminary, 1989); S. Döpp and W. Geerlings (eds.), *Lexikon der antiken christlichen Literatur*, 3rd edition, Freiburg: Verlag Herder, 2002).

The second section of this chapter, on Dionysius's contributions to the canonical tradition, is dependent on the following: Wurm, *Studien und Texte*; Schwartz, "Die Kanonessamlungen der alten Reichskirche," 159–275; Willibald M. Plöchl, *Geschichte des Kirchenrechts, 1: Das Recht des ersten christlichen Jahrtausends von Urkirche bis zum großen Schisma, Geschichte des Kirchenrechts*, Bd. 1, 2nd edition (Vienna: Herold, 1960); Jean Gaudemet, *Les sources du droit de l'Église en occident du IIe au VIIe siècle* (Paris: Cerf, 1985); Alphonse Van Hove, *Prolegomena ad Codicem Iuris Canonici*, 2nd ed. (Rome: Dessain, 1945); Alphonsus M. Stickler, *Historia Iuris Canonici Latini, I: Historia Fontium* (Turin: Pontificium Athenaeum Salesianum, Facultas iuris canonici, 1950); Paul Fournier and Gabriel le Bras, *Histoire des collections canoniques en Occident depuis les Fausses Décrétales jusqu'au Décret de Gratien*, 1 (Paris: Sirey, 1931); Wilfried Hartmann and Kenneth Pennington (eds.), *The History of Byzantine and Eastern Canon Law to 1500* (Washington, DC: The Catholic University of America Press, 2012); Péter Erdö, *Storia delle fonti del diritto canonico* (Venice: Marcianum, 2008); P. Erdö, *Storia della scienza del diritto canonico: Una introduzione* (Rome: Editrice Pontificia Università gregoriana, 1999); Brian E. Ferme, *Introduction to the History of the Sources of Canon Law: The Ancient Law up to the Decretum of Gratian* (Montréal: Wilson and Lafleur, 2007).

On Rome and the papacy during Dionysius's lifetime, see Franca de Marini Avonzo, "Secular and Clerical Culture in Dionysius Exiguus' Rome," in Stephan Kuttner and Kenneth Pennington (eds.), *Proceedings of the Sixth International Congress of Medieval Canon Law, Berkeley, California, 28 July–2 August 1980* (Città del Vaticano: Biblioteca Apostolica Vaticana, 1985), 83–92; and Jeffrey Richards, *The Popes and the Papacy in the Early Middle Ages 476–752*. (London: Routledge & Kegan Paul, 1979).

On the development of theology and doctrine during the patristic period, see J. N. D. Kelly, *Early Christian Doctrines*, 5th edition (London: A. & C. Black, 1977); Jaroslav Pelikan, *The Christian Tradition: A History of the Development of Doctrine*, vol. 1: *The Emergence of the Catholic Tradition (100–600)* (Chicago: University of Chicago Press, 1973); and Angelo Di Berardino and Basil Studer, trans. M. J. O'Connell, *History of Theology*, vol. 1: *The Patristic Period*

(Collegeville, MN: Liturgical Press, 1996). On the ecumenical councils, see Leo Donald Davis, *The First Seven Ecumenical Councils (325–787): Their History and Theology* (Collegeville, MN: Liturgical Press, 1983).

For detailed information on the *Collectio Dionysiana*, including its manuscript traditions and its historical reception, see the online article by Abigail Firey, Carolingian Canon Law project, http://ccl.rch.uky.edu/dionysiana-article (accessed March 13, 2018).

16

Benedict's Rule

Hugh Feiss, OSB

The Benedictine tradition has been shaped by two documents: The *Regula Benedicti*, or *Rule of Benedict* (RB), and the saint's Life (*Vita*), which constitutes the second book of the *Dialogues* of Gregory the Great. The *Rule of Benedict* was probably written toward the middle of the sixth century, primarily for Benedict's community on Monte Cassino (although because it refers to monasteries, in the plural, Benedict must have envisaged a wider readership). The oldest surviving copy of RB is an English, or Anglo-Saxon, manuscript (in Latin) from the first half the eighth century.[1] The second-oldest but the most precious (because it is probably the most authentic) is a manuscript written in Aachen for Charlemagne after 810. This was copied from a text sent by the monks of Monte Cassino at Charlemagne's request, which was in turn supposedly a copy of the original.[2]

These two documents are connected by Gregory's statement that Benedict was renowned not just for his miracles but also for "his words of doctrine, for he wrote a rule for monks, remarkable for its discretion and elegant in its language. If anyone wishes to know more of his habits and life, he will find all the points of his teaching in the arrangements of this rule, for the holy man could in no way have taught other than he lived" (*Dial.* 2.36). How much of the biographical data about St. Benedict (d. c. 543) conveyed in Gregory's Life is factual and whether some parts of RB were added later, by others, are questions that need not concern us here. We know Benedict today, as his followers have always done over the centuries, primarily as the author of the *Rule of Benedict* ascribed to him and secondarily in light of Gregory's narrative, for there are really no other sources of information.

According to the Life, Benedict was born in the region of Nursia (modern Norcia) and educated in Rome but converted to the monastic life when he was still a young man. He lived as a hermit in several settings, including Subiaco, before yielding reluctantly to the urgings of some monks to be their superior. They found his regime too stringent – and perhaps it was – and tried to poison him. Benedict calmly left

[1] Oxford, Bodleian Library, MS Hatton 48 (c. 700/750), written in insular uncial (majuscule) script.

[2] MS Saint-Gall, Cod. Sang. 914, written in Caroline miniscule script.

them and "dwelt with himself" again as a hermit (*Dial.* 2.3.5–9). Then, when people were attracted by his miracles, he established twelve monasteries, each of which had a "father" and twelve monks. Their way of life had a favorable impact on the countryside (*Dial.* 8.1). A local priest became jealous and tried unsuccessfully first to poison Benedict and then to seduce the monks with seven naked dancing girls. Aware that the priest's hatred was directed only at himself, Benedict decided to go away quietly with a few of his monks. He had not gone far when it was reported to him that the priest had died, and Benedict was sorry for him (*Dial.* 2.8.5–7).

Having trained as a hermit and gained experience as an abbot, Benedict went to Monte Cassino, where he established a monastery, converted two pagan shrines into chapels of St. Martin and St. John, exercised gifts of miracle-working and prophecy, and distributed food to the populace during a famine. In his miraculous activities, he replicates patterns found in Old Testament heroes such as Elijah and Elisha and in the Life of St. Martin. After a final visit from his sister Scholastica (*Dial.* 2.32–33), Benedict had a vision in which the world appeared tiny in the light of God (*Dial.* 2.35).[3]

The Life of Benedict portrays the mature saint as charismatic wonder-worker, prophet, exorcist, and visionary, and one who (as an antiphon for his liturgical feast declares) exhibited the virtues of "all the just."

Just as the Life weaves together stories of many of the saints, so the *Rule of Benedict* weaves together many monastic texts and traditions. To this text we now turn. But Benedictine interpretation of that *Rule* will always be conditioned in some way by the Life written by Gregory, for there was more to him than a lawgiver, and being among Benedict's followers was and is more than observing his rule.

BENEDICT'S RULE IN CONTEXT

The notion of living under a rule (*regula*) is complex and evolved fundamentally during the first millennium, as explained elsewhere in this volume (Chapter 9). Moreover, documents that differ widely in character and purpose have been regarded and have functioned as monastic rules. Suffice it to say that there survive some thirty Latin documents traditionally categorized as monastic rules from the fourth through the seventh centuries. Benedict of Aniane (d. 821) assembled twenty-five of these rules in his *Book of Rules* (*Codex regularum*) and collated them with the *Rule of Benedict* in his *Harmony of Rules* (*Concordia regularum*).[4] Although disparate in size, format, and purpose, these documents reflect a coherent tradition.

3 On this vision, see the commentary by Adalbert de Vogüé in Gregory the Great, *The Life of Saint Benedict*, trans. Hilary Costello and Eoin de Bhaldraithe (Petersham, MA: St. Bede's Publications, 1993), 164–73; and Hugh Feiss, "Dilation: God and the World in the Visions of Benedict and Julian of Norwich," *American Benedictine Review* 55 (2004): 55–73.

4 *Benedicti Anianensis Concordia regularum*, ed. Pierre Bonnerue, CCM 168 and 168A. For a similar procedure in the fourth-century *Comparison of Mosaic and Roman Law*, see Chapter 2 in this volume, by Jill Harries.

They were all written with the same goal of guiding or regulating cenobitic (communal) monastic life, they embrace the same principles, and they have the same ultimate source, namely, the Bible. They are lawlike documents at least to the extent that they prescribe the shape of a life lived in community. Copies of several rules were often collected together in early-medieval manuscripts. This was probably because until Carolingian times most monasteries picked eclectically from various rules for precedents by which to pattern their particular monastic observance. But from the early ninth century until the mid-eleventh, the *Rule of Benedict* was virtually the only rule followed in the monasteries of Western Europe.

There are several ways in which we might study these rules as legal documents. For example, we might consider how their prescriptions (e.g., regarding the donation of property) were related to secular law, or how they envisaged the relationship of the monastery to the authority of the bishops and to the decrees of church councils. Because monasticism was an influential institution in early-medieval times, we might also inquire how the internal workings of monastic communities, their understanding of written and personal authority, and the relations of their superiors to their subjects, influenced ideas of law, authority, and governance in the wider society. For example, it has been suggested that emperor Henry II (d. 1024), who had close ties with several monasteries, modeled his own way of ruling on Benedict's prescriptions for the abbot. Here, however, our chief concern is to study the sources, content, and reception of the *Rule of Benedict* itself, but we shall also look at some sample interpretations of the *Rule*: that of the abbey of Fulda in the eighth century, and that of the abbey of La Chaise-Dieu in the eleventh.

The most important of the early documents that functioned as monastic rules in the West cluster into three groups.[5] To the first group (c. 400–425) belong the Latin translations of the *Rule of Pachomius*, Rufinus's translation of the *Rule of Basil* (*RegBas*), and Augustine's *Praeceptum* and the *Ordo monasterii* attributed to him. To this same era belong the *Conferences* and *Institutes* of Cassian, which were not rules but influenced the writers of rules. The second group resulted from a flourishing of monastic rules during the first half of the sixth century. To this group belong the *Rule of the Master* (*Regula magistri* [RM], before 530), the *Rule of Benedict* (RB), written about two decades after the *Rule of the Master*,[6] Caesarius's rules for monks and nuns, and the rule of Eugippus. To the third group belong the rules of Columban and Donatus (both of which drew on Benedict's *Rule*) and the *Rule of Isidore*. These were composed in the first decades of the seventh century.

5 Adalbert de Vogüé, *Les règles monastiques anciennes (400–700)*, Typologie des sources du moyen âge occidental 46 (Turnhout: Brepols, 1985).

6 Adalbert de Vogüé, *Études sur la Règle de Saint Benoît: Nouveau recueil*, Vie monastique 34 (Bégrolles-en-Mauges: Abbaye de Bellefontaine, 1996), 387–415.

Benedict's Sources

Scripture is fundamental. Over half of the *Rule of Basil* consists of quotations from the Bible, and the Scriptures are the foundation of Benedict's *Rule* as well, although he does not quote them as extensively as Basil does.

After the Scriptures, Benedict's chief source, especially for the prologue and the first seven chapters of his *Rule*, but also for chapters 8–66 to a lesser degree, is the anonymous *Rule of the Master*.

Two other monastic sources influenced Benedict's thinking and sometimes his very words, both directly and via the *Rule of the Master*. In the final chapter of his rule, Benedict recommends that his monks read "the rule of our Holy Father Basil" (RB 73.5), as Benedict himself had done. Although the *Rule of Basil* is twice as long as Benedict's *Rule*, it is less detailed in its practical guidelines. Both it and the *Admonition to a Spiritual Son* (*Admon.*), which was ascribed to Basil, influenced the thought and wording of Benedict's *Rule*: for example, on the awareness of God's presence and his knowledge of hearts and actions (RB 7.10–14, 26–30; 19.1; cf. *RegBas* 2, 34, 46, 60, 66, 79, 108); on how a monk should respond if commanded to do impossible things (RB 68; cf. *RegBas* 69; *Admon.* 6); on the mutual obedience of monks (RB 71; cf. *RegBas* 64); on the interactions between the sick and those who care for them (RB 36.T-4; cf. *RegBas* 36–37); on not eating to the point of satiety (RB 40.6; cf. *RegBas* 9.7); and on the obligation of superiors to provide each monk with what he needs (RB 55.20; cf. *RegBas* 94.3). The most important contribution of the Basilian texts to RB, however, was to place strong emphasis on fraternal bonds. This emphasis counterbalanced the largely vertical approach of the *Rule of the Master*, which emphasizes the relationship of each monk individually to the abbot.[7]

This same fraternal emphasis is found in the short guide for monks (*Praeceptum*) of Augustine of Hippo, which Benedict probably knew in conjunction with the *Ordo monasterii*, another text that was ascribed to the bishop of Hippo. Augustine's writings left their mark on Benedict's chapter 31 on the cellarer, on his prohibition of private property, letters, and gifts, and on his principle that distribution of goods should be made to each according to his needs. Like the *Rule of the Master*, Benedict places a chapter on the abbot as master of the Lord's *schola* at the beginning of his rule (RB 2; RM 2), but later, following Augustine, Benedict adds a chapter on the abbot's role as guardian of the rule (RB 64.20; *Praeceptum* 7.2). The abbot should always remember that he must render an account to God, must love the person but hate his vices, and must seek to be loved rather than feared (RB 64.7, 11, 15; *Praeceptum* 4.10; 7.3). RB 67–73, a section that has no parallel in the *Rule of the Master*, includes a chapter on mutual obedience (RB 71).

Nevertheless, it is to the *Rule of the Master* above all that Benedict owes much of his text – including most of his prologue, which greatly condenses the preliminary matter of the *Rule of the Master*. There are several other places where Benedict

7 De Vogüé, *Études sur la Règle*, 17–32, 47–72, 427–35.

omitted a lengthy section of the *Rule of the Master* entirely. These sections must have seemed to him (as also, in most cases, they do to modern commentators) to be extraneous. For example, he omits RM 1.15–44: a long diatribe against wandering monks. In any case, whatever one thinks of the *Rule of the Master*,[8] it was certainly the chief non-biblical source for the *Rule of Benedict*.

THE *RULE OF THE MASTER* AND THE *RULE OF BENEDICT*

Rather than rehearse this dependency on the *Rule of the Master* in detail, I shall focus on the two rules' respective understandings of their regulations in relation to law (*lex*); on their view of the relation of the abbot and of other superiors to the written rule and to the community; and on how the two documents arrange for hierarchy, officials, and the reception of guests.

Law in The Rule of the Master and The Rule of Benedict

The *Rule of the Master* uses the term *lex* on nine occasions:

- RM Theme 19, 23: The Master speaks to the weight of sins arising from our ignorance of holy **law**. The Christian **law** calls us to a heavenly purpose.
- RM 1.8: Sarabaites (monks living in small groups without the benefit of an abbot or a rule) live without a pastor and their **law** is only the urging of their desires (cf. Rom 7:23)
- RM 7.36: The Master's diatribe against gyrovagues (vagrants who wander from monastery to monastery, taking advantage of the communities) and sarabaites repeats the thought of RM 1.8: that these pseudo-monks live without the guidance of a superior but think they are perfectly observant of every **law** and of all the justice of God.
- RM 10.72–74: A disciple ascends to the eighth step of the heavenly ladder "if he does nothing what but what is required by the common rule of the monastery or the example of the seniors." Apart from the insertion "of the monastery," this is a citation from Cassian, *Conf.* 4.39.2. But RM adds that the disciple says with Scripture, "my meditation is on your **law**" (Ps 118:73), for when he asks his father he will declare this law to him, and if he asks the seniors, they will speak of it to him (Deut 32:7), "that is, the abbot by his teaching." RB 7.55 cites only the first phrase (from Cassian), omitting the rest. This passage is somewhat ambiguous. Cassian did not envisage a written rule. For him, the common rule and the example of the seniors were virtually synonymous, and both pertained to the monastic tradition generally. For their part, RM and RB may be thinking of

[8] De Vogüé, *Études sur la Règle*, 487–505.

their respective written rules, but RM may be equating both the **law** and the example of the seniors with the teaching of the abbot.

- RM 11.9–10: Deans (ministers of the abbot in larger communities, with each assigned to overseeing a group or subset of monks) have a subordinate place in the monastery, analogous to that of officials in a family estate and to that of priests and deacons in a diocese, who represent God to the people and teach them salvific **laws**. Thus, God says to those in positions of authority (*praepositi*) in a monastery, "who hears you hears me."
- RM 13.2: Disobedient monks should be treated not as brothers but as "heretics of the **law**" (*haeretici legis*). The phrase is puzzling. De Vogüé suggests that it may refer to someone who is a heretic in regard to the law.
- RM 15.35: When a brother is tempted by evil thoughts, the abbot should present him with apposite passages of the Bible. Therefore, the abbot himself must be learned in the **law**. If the evil thoughts persist, the whole community should fast so that by bearing one another's burdens they will fulfill the **law** of Christ (cf. Gal 6:2).
- RM 50.25: During their daily labor, the brothers should refrain from speaking, from repeating tales that are not **lawful** (*sine lege*), and from speech about secular matters. Here, *sine lege* seems to mean "illicit."
- RM 93.15: When a new abbot is being installed in his office, the retiring abbot hands him "this rule" and tells him: "Receive this rule, brother, as the **law** of God" (*legem Dei hanc regulam*).

Benedict took only one of RM's references to law (*lex*) into his rule: RM 1.8, on the Sarabaites (=RB 1.8). But Benedict uses the term law (*lex*) in five *other* places, where he is not borrowing from RM:

- RB 43:10: When brothers come late to the day hours, they should stand in the last place according to the "**law** of which we have spoken earlier" (*lege qua supra diximus*). The regulation parallels RM 73.10, but that does not use the term *lex* or refer to an earlier law.
- RB 53.9: Borrowing several sentences taken from RM 71.9, where the Master says that when guests arrive, prayer should be offered before the sign of peace, Benedict adds that the divine **law** should be read to them for their edification.
- RB 58.10, 15: When a new member makes profession, he knows the **law** under which he wishes to serve, the **law** of the rule.
- RB 64.9: The abbot is required to be learned in the divine **law** so that he may know whence to bring forth things new and old (Matt 13:52).

From all this, it appears that the RM has an expansive conception of Christian law as the moral content of revelation (RM Theme 19, 23). Thus, in a monastic context, this law is the framework that defines life in a cenobitic community. Without such a law, a monk is left to follow the urgings of desire (RM 1.8; 7.36). Like the sarabaites, monks who tell stories during work time are also "without law" (*sine lege*, RM 50.25).

Human nature runs amok when it does not have guidelines and boundaries. The law that monks need is found in a shared monastic tradition exemplified in the lives of a community's elders, and with the guidance of the abbot's teaching (RM 10.72–74). This is what the Master has expressed in a written rule. The Master attributes to his rule a quasi-inspired status, and the many details that he lays down are to be followed rigidly. Those with authority in the monastery represent God (RM 11.9–10). Nevertheless, to be able to teach and guide in the community, the abbot must be learned in the law as it is expressed in the Scriptures (RM 15.35). The written rule is the law that guides the abbot in the fulfillment of his office (RM 93.15).

The *Rule of Benedict* agrees with Cassian and the Master that in the absence of any law, the sarabaites follow the urgings of their desires (RB 18). The divine law that all Christians should follow is expressed in written form in the Bible (RB 53.9). To be a teacher, the abbot must know this divine law (RB 64.9). In addition to the divine law, there is the law inscribed in Benedict's *Rule* (RB 43.10; 58.10, 15), which he describes as a little rule for beginners (RB 73).

The authors of both rules are not only abbots but also lawgivers. (This may be the reason why RM equates both the common rule of monastic tradition and the examples of the elders with the abbot's teaching.) The abbot is deserving of obedience both because his office (to which he is appointed in RM but elected in RB) places him in a position of authority, and because he has achieved deep knowledge of divine law and monastic tradition.

In summary, according to both rules, God is the legislator of a divine law that is expressed in the Bible ("law" is sometimes synonymous with "Scripture") and directed to all believers. The Scriptures are the source for the monastic tradition, therefore, which each rule applies to a specific community or communities. Thus, the plurality of written rules does not interfere with the unity of the tradition. Even when a written rule is no longer observed in its original setting, it remains a monument to the monastic tradition.[9]

A Community Under a Rule and an Abbot

Both the *Rule of the Master* and the *Rule of Benedict* are primarily designed for cenobites, that is, for monks living in a community under obedience both to their rule and to their abbot (RM 1.2; RB 1.2). The interrelationships among abbot, rule, and community determine the polity of the monastery.[10]

9 The sequence of divine law > the Scriptures > monastic tradition > written rule parallels the teaching of Hincmar of Reims described in Chapter 21 of this volume. Hincmar thought that human beings need law; that God's eternal law is expressed in the Scriptures; and that church law and human (i.e., secular) law, both of which have varying degrees of authority, are binding but not eternal. Human lawgivers are subject to the laws that they have enacted.

10 Adalbert de Vogüé, *Saint Benoît, sa vie et son Règle: études choisies*, Vie Monastique 12 (Bégrolles-en-Mauges: Abbey de Bellefontaine, 1981), 209–41.

In the minds of both authors, a written rule was extremely important. The Master required that the rule be read every day (RM 24.5), and he begins each section with the words, "The Lord answers through the Master." Benedict wanted his rule to be read often in community (RB 66.8), and he prescribed that the entire rule be read to novices three times during their novitiate so that they would know what the law of the rule required (RB 58.9, 12, 13).

Nevertheless, Benedict regarded his rule as a minimal program for beginners. After fulfilling the rule, trained in the cenobitic life, the monk could proceed to the loftier heights of the eremitic life (RB 1.3–4, 73.5, 8). The Master, on the contrary, does not envisage that his monks will outgrow the rule.

Benedict says that the one chosen to be abbot should be distinguished by the merit of his life and his wise teaching (RB 64.2, 9). He should be discerning (RB 64.17–19), not fanatical or overly suspicious (RB 67.18). "Above all, he should keep the present rule in all things" (RB 64.20; 3.11). Whereas Benedict leaves many things unspecified or to the discretion of the abbot, RM regulates countless things minutely, as if in an effort to cover everything (e.g., see RM 61 regarding monks taking meals outside the monastery). Again, in contrast to the inflexibility of the *Rule of the Master*, Benedict allows the abbot to modify the rule's minute arrangement of the divine office (RB 18.22), although he should make sure the whole Psalter is said each week. Benedict describes a typical wardrobe that he judges adequate for moderate climates, but he leaves the abbot to decide what clothing to provide in hot or cold climates (RB 55.3). More generally, Benedict's abbot should give to each monk what he needs, paying more attention to the needs of the individuals than to the possible ill will of those who need and receive less (RB 56.20–21).

According to Benedict, in the interplay of rule, abbot, and community, the written rule keeps the abbot from arbitrariness and tyranny, but the abbot interprets and adapts the rule, preventing it from becoming a dead weight rather than a source of life. Whereas Benedict warns the abbot that he must render an account to God (RB 2.6–9, 34; 64.7), the *Rule of the Master* does not envisage the abbot's making mistakes or violating the rule. According to Benedict, the abbot should consult all the community before making important decisions (RB 3). His position is sustained by the community's belief that he holds the place of Christ (RB 2.2; 63.13). The abbot and all the community are to prefer nothing to Christ (RB 4.21; 72.11). Christ, their Lord and God, is the source, center, and goal of the Scriptures, which the monastic tradition applies to the life of the communities. Christ is always present in the midst of the community.

Hierarchy, Officials, and Guests

The Rule of Benedict in chapter 63 enumerates a principle of precedence and order: monks follow one another according to the time they entered the community, although the abbot can for good reason advance or put back someone. Age is not to be the deciding factor, nor should the dignity or status that someone had in the world before entering the community. Within the community, there are offices to which the abbot appoints monks who have the requisite qualities: cellarer (RB 31), infirmarian (RB 26), novice master (RB 58), porter (RB 66), prior (RB 65), and deans (RB 21). These carry out their duties according to the directives of the rule and of the abbot, but the abbot should not micromanage their work (RB 64.16–19).

All of this is in sharp contrast to the *Rule of the Master,* which is reluctant to delegate authority. There, two deans of equal rank keep close watch over each group of ten monks, reporting any misbehavior to the abbot (RM 11). Only the cellarer (RM 16) and the keeper of the tools and wardrobe (RM 17) are under the direct supervision of the abbot. The Master prohibits all rank or differentiation of honor below the abbot because he does not want the monks to know whom the abbot favors to succeed him in order to prompt them to compete for his favor (RM 92).

Nowhere is the difference between the Master and Benedict greater than in legislation regarding guests. The Master devotes four chapters to the topic (RM 71–72, 78–79), of which the two most general ones (RM 78–79) express strong suspicions toward guests. Benedict draws on the *Rule of the Master* in some parts of his chapter on guests (RB 53), but he derives his spirit of hospitality from the example of the Desert Fathers, as described in the anonymous *Historia monachorum in Aegypto,* translated into Latin by Rufinus.[11] Benedict reiterates his basic principle: that all who come to the abbey are to be received lovingly and humanely as Christ, although in such a way that the peace and order of the monastery are not upset. The *Rule of the Master* is suspicious of guests and requires that precautions be taken so they will not steal anything. Two brothers from one of the deaneries are to be assigned to assist the guests, but most of all to exercise discrete surveillance at every moment of the day and night. Guests who stay more than two days must work with the brothers or leave, and for that work they will receive only room and board, not clothing.

The two parts of Benedict's chapter on receiving guests reflect the ambiguity in which his monks find themselves. They are followers of Christ, who was open to the world, ate with all kinds of people, and said that whoever receives a needy person receives Christ himself. Benedict is convinced that God is encountered especially in the poor, the sick, and the vulnerable (including the abbot). Because monks are privileged to dwell in God's house, they must share it with others. Yet monks have fled the world to devote themselves single-mindedly to Christ. The tensions between openness and withdrawal, between welcoming all and maintaining monastic peace, between preferential care for the poor and pilgrims and obligations to the powerful, between rule and custom, will recur throughout Benedictine history. The following examples of the reception and life of the *Rule* will illustrate the ways in which these

[11] *The Lives of the Desert Fathers = The Historia Monachorum in Aegypto,* trans. Norman Russell, Cistercian Studies Series 34 (Kalamazoo: Cistercian Publications, 1981).

tensions played out in Benedictine monasteries during the first millennium, particularly regarding the relationships among rule, abbot, the broader monastic tradition, and local custom.[12]

THE ABBEY OF FULDA, 744–822 AD

Fulda was one of several monasteries founded by Boniface, an Anglo-Saxon monk who went to Germany as a missionary early in the eighth century. These monasteries served as places both of prayer and of missionary outreach. In 751, Boniface wrote to the pope asking him to grant Fulda exemption from episcopal control and protection of the monastery's property. (Boniface does not name the monastery that the monks are building, but he says that it is in a deserted place.) The monks are living there according to the *Rule of Benedict*, supporting themselves by the work of their hands, and abstaining from wine, spirits, and meat. Boniface says that he received the land from Carloman, the former prince of the Franks.[13]

Boniface's letter highlights four factors that remained central to the identity of the monks of Fulda: Boniface himself, the Carolingian royal house, the papacy, and the *Rule of Benedict*. Within less than a century, Fulda had become an abbey of six hundred monks, a center of pilgrimage and education, and a great landlord. Boniface's experience of monasticism in England was probably in communities that followed mixed rules, combining selections from several sources. Thus, when he refers to his monasteries in Germany, he usually refers not to a specific rule but rather to a monastic rule or way of life, without further specification. Nevertheless, when he writes about Fulda he mentions the *Rule of Benedict* by name. This may be because it was founded toward the end of his life, when he was presiding over reform councils that required all monasteries to adopt the *Rule of Benedict*.

Boniface installed Sturm as the abbot of Fulda, though he still supervised the community. After robbers killed Boniface in 754, he was buried at Fulda as he had requested. Thereafter, he was regarded as a martyr, and his tomb became a place of pilgrimage. According to the Life of Sturm, written by his relative Eigil, the fourth abbot of Fulda, Sturm had originally wanted to found a hermitage but Boniface gradually led him to embrace cenobitic life. After the monastery was constructed, according to Eigil, the community decided to follow the *Rule of Benedict*. Sturm and two of his fellow monks went to Italy to learn first-hand how those in Benedict's homeland observed his rule. Eigil emphasizes that when they returned to Fulda, they carefully implemented the practices of the *Rule of Benedict*.

Sturm served as abbot of Fulda until 779, when Baugulf (779–802), who seems to have been raised in the abbey, succeeded him. In 791, Baugulf and the community

[12] Terrence Kardong, *Benedict's Rule: A Translation and Commentary* (Collegeville, MN: Liturgical Press, 1996), 419–36.

[13] This section of the chapter is dependent on Janneke Raaijmakers, *The Making of the Monastic Community of Fulda, c.744-c.900* (Cambridge: Cambridge University Press, 2012), 1–174.

began construction of a new church. The church that had been built by Sturm was too small to accommodate the growing number of monks, pilgrims, and donors; a larger church would symbolize the importance of the abbey; and it would provide a better setting for liturgy. Like several other large churches built around this time, it was modeled on St. Peter's in Rome, with an altar at each end. The church could then accommodate the papal form of liturgy, in which mass was celebrated from behind the western altar (of the double-apsed church), facing east. Baugulf employed Ratger as architect of this new church. Near the end of Baugulf's abbacy, Alcuin wrote to say that monks should be kind to Baugulf, who was too ill to observe all the provisions of the *Rule of Benedict*. Alcuin's letter is an indication of unrest at Fulda.

When Baugulf retired to a hermit's cell in 802, the monks elected Ratger as his successor. Ratger was an energetic man. He promoted education and learning. Ratger strengthened the abbey's ties with the aristocracy and increased the community's property. The community grew in size. Yet, there was dissatisfaction, perhaps exacerbated by outbreaks of pestilence in 807 and 810. In 809, the archbishop of Mainz visited the abbey, perhaps to restore harmony. While he was there, he consecrated another new church, which Ratger built on the Frauenberg close to the abbey.

In 812, a group of monks traveled with Ratger to the imperial court to present a document of supplication (*Supplex libellus* [SL]) to Charlemagne. This listed their complaints against Ratger's leadership in twenty paragraphs.[14]

The first paragraph of the *Supplex libellus* objects to changes that Ratger had introduced in prayerful commemorations that "our fathers held" for the living and the dead, particularly for the emperor and his family, for deceased confreres, and in memory of Sturm and other founders of the monastery. That this complaint comes first may indicate the petitioners' priorities, or it may have been an attempt to win the emperor's goodwill. SL 2 asks that, "as it was among our forefathers," worthy priests may have permission and places to celebrate mass more often. SL petitions that important saints' days be celebrated properly, and that on these days the brothers be given time free from work, "just as it was among our forefathers." SL 4 states, "according to the examples of our father who came before us, we should not deny the common practice of sharing in the breaking of bread before eating the daily meal." SL 19 asks that the procession of the cross on Sunday before mass be maintained, "as our forefathers practiced it."

The next paragraphs (SL 5–9) ask for more humane treatment for the sick and elderly and greater readiness to accept sick, elderly, and weak people who come to enter the monastery out of love for the monastic life. Nevertheless, no one should be

14 *Supplex libellus monachorum Fuldensium Carolo imperatori porrectus*, ed. Joseph Semmler, Corpus Consuetudinum Monasticarum 1 (Siegburg, 1963), 319–27. I wish to thank Professor Michael Martin for allowing to me to use his translation of SL that is to appear in H. Feiss, M. O'Brien, and R. Pepin (eds.), *A Benedictine Reader 530–1530* (in press).

forced to embrace the monastic life, and no one should be allowed to join for the wrong reasons.

SL 10 declares: "[O]ur forefathers determined how much food and clothing we were allowed, since our first abbot, Sturm, transformed after spending a year in St. Benedict's monastery, returning afterward to this place, determined their habit and food as approved by St. Boniface. He decided this very ideal for us, for which several witnesses of this event still survive."

The petitioners object in SL 12 to big building projects and other unnecessary works, which tire the brothers beyond their abilities. There should be time for reading and other work. Things should be done with reason and discretion, according to the rule (see RB 48).

Under Ratger, "the longstanding custom of hospitality" is being neglected. Guests' feet are not washed when they arrive, contrary to "the rule, and … the customs of our forefathers" (SL 13). Help should be provided when large numbers of guests arrive, such as during the mass of St. Boniface (SL 14).

SL 18, which may be a later interpolation, reports that Ratger claimed that "he did not disparage the statutes of St. Boniface" (*instituta sancti Bonifatii*) because the synod had already condemned Boniface's decrees, and that other great monasteries were not censured.

The petitioners conclude by naming the things that are necessary above all else: "unity and agreement with our abbot, just as we had with our former abbots, as well as to feel mercy and protection." The abbot should be kind to those in need, forgiving, approachable, supportive, and not vindictive. "We have practiced these privileges and other such actions, lord emperor, as did our former abbots, and we have asked repeatedly for all the above items of this abbot, but we have continued to be unable to obtain them from him even up to the present day" (SL 20).

There are many noteworthy things in this document that illustrate what obedience to Benedict's *Rule* could mean in practice during the first millennium, for it could never be a community's *exclusive* guide to living. None of the liturgical commemorations and other rites that Ratger is accused of changing (SL 1–4, 19) is prescribed in Benedict's *Rule*. Ratger may have trimmed these prayers because they were burdensome additions. In fact, the petitioners do not claim the authority of the *Rule of Benedict*. Instead, they claim that these are things that their forefathers did and that they want to keep doing. The petitioners are appealing to the emperor to intervene and to judge on their behalf, against their abbot, in favor of tradition.

The prescriptions regarding the loving reception of guests, the washing of their feet, and the provision of help for monks who are overwhelmed with work, on the contrary, are in Benedict's *Rule*. On these matters, the petitioners appeal to the *Rule* as well as to the customs of their ancestors against the abbot.

In regard to food and clothing, the petitioners appeal to the two founders of the monastery, Boniface and Sturm. It seems likely that abbot Ratger had called for more austerity in these matters. The *Rule of Benedict* itself is not invoked, probably because the customs that the petitioners wished to retain were not supported there, or perhaps because Benedict left it to the abbot to make adjustments in these matters. In these and other matters, the *Supplex libellus* makes almost no reference to the Bible, the supreme law for all monks.

The petitioners allege that building projects were putting undue stress on the community, and that Ratger was not showing kindly concern for the physical and spiritual well-being of the monks. It is noteworthy that Ratger was not the one who initiated the building of the new church, and that his successor finished it. Hence, the objection to unnecessary building projects may refer to more than the new abbey church. It seems that Ratger was a very good manager of temporalities and a skilled architect, but that he was lacking in pastoral sensitivity. He seems to have been unable or unwilling to win over monks who were reluctant to depart from familiar ways of doing things. He also seems to have had little empathy with the weak and sick. Fulda had changed a great deal from the tiny community that carved out a home in the forest seventy-five years ago. It had become an important royal abbey. It was very difficult for one person to be both the manager of vast temporal estates and projects and a player in secular and religious politics, on the one hand, and at the same time a loving, patient, discerning pastor for the monks, on the other. It is in these last three qualities that Ratger is said to be wanting.

The situation was complicated by the monastic reforms initiated by Charlemagne, which would be continued under Louis the Pious and Benedict of Aniane. (See SL 18, which can be interpreted as meaning that Ratger claimed that his abrogation of long-standing customs at Fulda was in line with the monastic reforms being promoted by the emperor.) Like the reform synods convened at Aachen by Louis the Pious from 816 to 819, Ratger's program was not fully supportive either of a literal interpretation of the *Rule of Benedict* or of the "statutes of St. Boniface" (*instituta Sancti Bonifatii*).

Charlemagne did not side with the petitioners, but Louis the Pious deposed and exiled Ratger in 817, and Eigil was elected to succeed him a year later. Eigil was then seventy years old, widely experienced and deeply immersed in the customs of the abbey. He added two crypts to the new church and a chapel in the cemetery, and he started a new cloister. He made some changes to the liturgy, and he wrote a Life of Sturm, who was now elevated to co-patron of Fulda. During his brief abbacy, Eigil's goal was to restore unity and peace. In this, he seems to have been successful, paving the way for the abbacy of Raban Maur (822–842).

ROBERT OF TURLANDE (1001–1067) AND LA CHAISE-DIEU

A different perspective on the interpretation of the *Rule of Benedict* appears in the founding and early history of the abbey and federation of La Chaise-Dieu.[15]

15 What follows is based primarily on Pierre-Roger Gaussin, *Saint Robert de Turlande et la fondation de la Chaise-Dieu* (Paris: Desfossés, 1964); and H. Feiss, M. M. O'Brien, and R. Pepin (eds.), *The Lives of*

Robert of Turlande was born around 1001 into a family of minor nobility in the Auvergne: a rugged, poor, and not fully evangelized territory in which there were few monasteries. He was educated by the canons of the church of St. Julian at Brioude, whose interests seem to have been as much temporal as spiritual. Robert joined their community, was ordained, and appointed its treasurer. From his own financial resources, Robert opened a hospice for the poor and pilgrims, and he ministered to them personally. Odilo of Mercoeur, who may have been his uncle, had been a canon at Brioude. Odilo left Brioude and went to Cluny where he became abbot in 994. Robert set out to follow Odilo's path, but his confreres and those to whom he ministered prevented him from leaving them. He still wanted to enter the monastic life. There were Benedictine abbeys that he might have joined, but they had drawbacks. Some were wealthy. Some did not observe Benedict's dietary rules. Some were urban. Most had a very heavy schedule of liturgical prayer. Robert wanted to minister to the people. As Pierre-Roger Gaussin put it, these monasteries were both too near the world and too far from it for Robert, whose strong sense of humility and charity prompted him to pursue an austere life devoted to the service of others.

Robert decided to travel to Rome. Like other monastic founders before him, such as Sturm, John of Gorze (d. 974), Romuald (d. c. 1025), and William of Volpiano (d. 1031), Robert went to Monte Cassino to study the *Rule of Benedict* as embodied in the monastic traditions there. He joined up with two repentant knights. One of them, Stephen, found an abandoned chapel on a 3,550-foot butte in the forest of Livradoise, near the sources of the Dore and the Senouire. Robert obtained the land from two clerical members of the Beaumont family, who also sent some supplies to the three hermits. The three worked and prayed together, sharing their faith and their meager supplies with their neighbors.

Because others joined the three companions, they needed to decide on a rule of life for the community. Robert of Chaise-Dieu's dilemma was analogous to that of the later hermit-preachers, such as Robert of Arbrissel (d. 1116), Bernard of Tiron (d. 1117), Vitalis of Savigny (d. 1122), and Stephen of Obazine (d. 1159), who sought solitude but drew large numbers of followers and had to provide institutional settings for them. Gaussin thinks that Robert's uncle, Rencon, bishop of Clermont (1030–1053), counseled him to adopt the *Rule of Benedict.* But some of his community preferred to remain hermits, and some wanted to be canons (clerics living a community that served a collegiate church).

The issue was settled when an angel appeared at the door holding a copy of Benedict's *Rule* (*Tripartite Life*, 1.1), but the way of life that the brothers would follow was not what Benedict had envisaged for his own community. In 1052, the monastery received charters of protection both from Pope Leo IX[16] and from King Henry I of

the Monastic Reformers, 1: Robert of La Chaise-Dieu, Stephen of Obazine, Cistercian Studies Series 222 (Collegeville, MN: Liturgical Press, 2010), 1–101.

16 On the similar aims and contacts between La Chaise-Dieu and the reforming papacy, see Herbert Cowdrey, "Pope Gregory VII and La Chaise-Dieu," in *Maisons de Dieu et hommes*

France. Donations and new members came in abundance. By the time of Robert's death in 1067, La Chaise-Dieu served some fifty churches. Small cells or priories of between three and ten monks, devoted to prayer and ministry, were established to minister to the people who came to these churches. For the next two centuries, La Chaise-Dieu continued to expand beyond the Auvergne and beyond the Alps and Pyrenees. At its apogee around 1260, hundreds of monastic houses were bound directly or indirectly to the motherhouse of La Chaise-Dieu.

When he was near death, Robert is reported to have said to his brothers: "[You know] that the love of Christ led you here, how he taught through us that you should have charity, and how he commanded us to give charitably what is ours to all, whether known or strangers, rich or poor, whether they ask or not . . . Charity is to have first place in this community and its members, so that the evil of possessiveness and greed finds no corner in it."[17] This was his primary law and the tradition he established. He adopted the *Rule of Benedict* and was familiar with how it was lived at Monte Cassino and in the Cluniac monasteries, but there is no evidence that he was particularly concerned with following any particular monastic tradition, even that of Monte Cassino. Although the dispersal of the monks of La Chaise-Dieu with its centralized authority was not new – the majority of the monks of Fulda were not resident in the abbey, and Cluny had introduced a system of centralized authority and dependent priories – the way of life at La Chaise-Dieu was clearly not that envisaged in Benedict's *Rule*. Nor was Robert's emphasis on charity performed for persons outside the monastery. At La Chaise-Dieu, it was the Bible, specifically the law of charity, that was the primary rule of the monastery, and this emphasis was abbot Robert's legacy. The wider monastic tradition and even the letter of the *Rule of Benedict* were secondary.

Robert's combination of monastic life with ministry and practical charity to others beyond the monastery was not without its problems. Marbod of Rennes devoted the first part of the second installment of his life of Robert (*Vita* 2.2–6) to a spirited defense against critics who condemned Robert for embracing the contemplative life of a hermit and then abandoning it for the active life. It is not clear who these critics were, but they could have been other monks (e.g., Cluniacs) or canons (such as those of Brioude or Clermont), who somehow felt challenged by Robert's particular combination of prayer and action.

When Robert died in 1067, Durand succeeded him. Durand, who became bishop of Clermont in 1078, was in turn succeeded by Adelelm. But Adelelm resigned within a year because he had no interest in administration and lacked the education and skills to represent the monastery to the outside world. He was succeeded by Seguin

d'Église. Florilège en honneur de Pierre-Roger Gaussin (Saint-Etienne: Publications de l'Université de Saint-Etienne, 1992), 25–35.

17 Bernard of La Chaise-Dieu, *Tripartite Life of Robert of La Chaise-Dieu* 1.14, in H. Feiss, R. E. Pepin, and M. M. O'Brien, *The Lives of the Monastic Reformers*, vol. 1: *Robert of La Chaise-Dieu and Stephen of Obazine*, Cistercian Studies series 222 (Collegeville, MN: Cistercian Publications, 2010), 79–80.

(1078–94), who did have such skills. Adelelm was invited to the Kingdom of Castile-Leon in 1082/83, presumably at the suggestion of Queen Constance, who would have known of him in France. He stayed on as a chaplain at the royal court, but then he was given a church on the edge of Burgos that served the needs of pilgrims. There, in the vicinity of a monastery that the king entrusted to La Chaise-Dieu, Adelelm lived a very austere life, distributed food to the poor every day, and prayed.[18]

CONCLUSION

This study has taken us from the *Rule of Benedict* and its sources, through the period of mixed rules, and into the Benedictine centuries. It has shown how Benedict's *Rule* was related to the monastic tradition before it, and it has illustrated several ways in which the *Rule* was interpreted.

For Benedict, as for his sources, God's law was the source of all law, and the Scriptures were the fundamental written law. The monastic tradition applied this law to cenobites, for whom many rules were written. Abbots applied these rules as instruments, but they were also in obedience to them. If the abbots were unworthy, they were answerable to God but also to such human authorities as bishops and secular rulers. This was a very dynamic mix of authorities. Creative monastic founders such as Boniface and Robert of La Chaise-Dieu drew on Scripture, monastic tradition, and Benedict's *Rule* to develop new ways of living a monastic life in community – ways that respected the *Rule of Benedict* but departed in radical ways from the life that it portrayed. Robert of La Chaise-Dieu lived on the cusp of a new age, when earlier interpretations of Benedict's *Rule* would be challenged by the Cistercians, and new religious orders would devise and follow new forms of life.

It is impossible to measure the influence that the *Rule of Benedict* has had on the larger society. Surely, its provision of a strong executive, elected by those who were to be governed but subject to the same rule as they, its conviction that human law is not arbitrary but is subordinate to divine law, and its principle that rulers are answerable before God for their actions and for the welfare of their subjects, have influenced law beyond the cloister.

SOURCES

The Oldest MSS of RB

For Bodleian, Hatton 48 (the oldest surviving MS of RB), see http://bodley30.bodley.ox.ac.uk:8180/luna/servlet/view/all/what/MS.+Hatton+48 (accessed April 18,

[18] See *Vita Adelelmi, Vida de San Lesmes*, ed. Rafael Sánchez Domingo (Burgos: Universidad de Burgos, 2004); and the chapter on Adelelm to appear in the forthcoming *Benedictine Reader: 530–1530*.

2018). For Cod. Sang. 914 – the copy made for Charlemagne, now in the monastic library of St. Gallen, Switzerland – see www.e-codices.unifr.ch/en/list/one/csg/0914 (accessed April 18, 2018).

Modern Editions and Translations of RB

RB 1980. The Rule of Benedict in Latin and English with Notes. Timothy Fry et al. Collegeville, MN: Liturgical Press, 1981.

Benedict's Rule: A Translation and Commentary. Terence G. Kardong. Collegeville, MN: Liturgical Press, 1996.

The Rule of Saint Benedict. Ed. and trans. Bruce L. Venarde. Dunbarton Oaks Medieval Library. Cambridge (Mass.) and London: Harvard University Press, 2011. [This is a transcription of Cod. Sang. 914 with Venarde's English translation on facing pages, designed to capture the spirit of Benedict's style.]

La Règle de saint Benoit. Ed. Adalbert de Vogüé. 7 vols. SC 181–86bis (1971–77). [Latin edition with French translation on facing pages.]

Other Sources

Admonitio ad filium spiritualem. Ed. Paul J. G. Lehmann, *Die Admonitio S. Basili ad filium spiritualem.* Sitzungsberichte der bayerischen Akademie der Wissenschaft. Munich: Beck, 1955. Reprinted in Lehmann, *Erforschung des Mittelalters: Ausgewählte Abhandlungen und Aufsätze,* 5 vols. (Stuttgart: Hiersemann, 1959–62), 5:200–45. [There is an old edition in PL 103:683–700. Online English translation: James F. LePree, "Pseudo-Basil's *De admonitio ad filium spiritualem*: A New English Translation," *The Heroic Age* 13 (2010), www.heroicage.org/issues/13/lepree2.php (accessed March 14, 2018).]

Bernard of La Chaise-Dieu. *Liber tripartitus de miraculis sancti Roberti.* In *Acta sanctorum ordinis sancti Benedicti.* Ed. L. d'Achéry and J. Mabillon, 9 vols. (Venice, 1733), 9:213–31.

Cassian, *Conférences.* Ed. E. Pichery, 3 vols. SC 42, 54, 64.

Gregory the Great. *Dialogues.* Ed. Adalbert de Vogüé, trans. Paul Antin. 3 vols. SC 251, 260, 265. [There is an English translation of Book II by Terrence G. Kardong, *The Life of St. Benedict by Gregory the Great: Translation and Commentary* (Collegeville, MN: Liturgical Press, 2009).]

Marbod of Rennes. *Vita beati Roberti.* Ed. Antonella degli'Innocenti. Florence: Giunti, 1995.

Rule of St. Augustine. Ed. Luc Verheijen, *La règle de saint Augustin.* 2 vols. Paris: Études Augustiniennes, 1967.

Rule of the Master. Ed. Adalbert de Vogüé, *La règle du Maître.* 3 vols. SC 105–07. [English translation: *The Rule of the Master,* trans. Luke Eberle, Cistercian Studies Series 6 (Kalamazoo: Cistercian Publications, 1977).]

Supplex libellus monachorum Fuldensium Carolo imperatori porrectus. Ed. Joseph Semmler. Corpus Consuetudinum Monasticarum 1 (Siegburg, 1963), 319–27.

The Rule of St. Basil in Latin and English. Ed. and trans. Anna M. Silvas. Collegeville, MN: Liturgical Press, 2013.

Vita Adelelmi, Vida de San Lesmes. Ed. Rafael Sánchez Domingo. Burgos: Universidad de Burgos, 2004.

FURTHER READING

Adalbert de Vogüé's contribution to the Brepols series *Typologie des sources du moyen âge occidental*, entitled *Les règles monastiques anciennes (400–700)* (Turnhout: Brepols, 1985), is a good introduction to the ancient monastic rules. His list of editions is updated somewhat by Mary Forman and Thomas Sullivan, "The Latin Cenobitic Rules: AD 400–700: Editions and Translations," *American Benedictine Review* 48.1 (1997): 52–68.

For the *Rule of the Master*, the most important source is the edition of de Vogüé. He has written about RM in other places, even suggesting that it might be an earlier edition of the RB, written by Benedict himself, although this interpretation has not been widely accepted. A very useful tool for comparing the Latin texts of RM and RB and their sources is Benedict Guevin, *Synopsis fontesque: Regula Magistri, Regula Benedicti*, Regulae Benedicti Studia, Supplementa 10 (St. Ottilien: EOS Verlag, 1999).

The interpretation of the RB has changed considerably now that it is generally agreed that it depends on RM. De Vogüé's seven-volume edition and commentary is foundational. Parts of it are appearing in English: see Adalbert de Vogüé, *A Critical Study of the Rule of Benedict*, 2 vols., trans. Colleen M. McGrane (Hyde Park, NY: New City Press, 2013, 2015). (A third volume is in press.) Although De Vogüé's work dominates the study of the *Rule of Benedict*, his conviction that Cassian's writings prompted Benedict to put more emphasis on the abbot's relation to each individual monk as his spiritual father than on fraternal relations has been widely questioned. De Vogüé collected some of his more important articles in two collections: *Saint Benoît, sa vie et son Règle: études choisies*, Vie monastique 12 (Bégrolles-en-Mauges, France: Abbey de Bellefontaine, 1981); and *Études sur la Règle de Saint Benoît: Nouveau recueil*, Vie monastique 34 (Bégrolles-en-Mauges, France: Abbaye de Bellefontaine, 1996). Because de Vogüé was always ready to engage with his critics, his articles put the reader in touch with other opinions.

RB 1980: The Rule of Benedict in Latin and English, ed. Timothy Fry et al. (Collegeville, MN: Liturgical Press, 1981), contains a wealth of information. Although by now somewhat dated, it has an excellent concordance of Latin words and a helpful topical index.

Terrence Kardong, the foremost scholar of Benedict's *Rule* working in English today, sums up much of his work in *Benedict's Rule: A Translation and Commentary*

(Collegeville, MN: Liturgical Press, 1996). Aquinata Böckmann has written meticulous studies of the *Rule* in German, and some of these are also available in English: *Perspectives on the Rule of Saint Benedict: Expanding our Hearts in Christ*, trans. M. Handl and M. Burkhard (Collegeville, MN: Liturgical Press, 2005); *A Listening Community: A Commentary on the Prologue and Chapters 1–3 of Benedict's Rule*, trans. M. Handl and M. Burkhard (Collegeville, MN: Liturgical Press, 2015). Georg Holzherr, a scholar who was abbot of the Swiss monastery of Einsiedeln, wrote a fine commentary on the entire RB: *The Rule of Benedict: An Invitation to the Christian Life*, trans. Mark Thamert, Cistercian Studies 256 (Collegeville, MN: Liturgical Press, 2016).

Janneke Raaijmakers, *The Making of the Monastic Community of Fulda, c.744 – c.900*, Cambridge Studies in Medieval Life and Thought, Fourth Series (Cambridge: Cambridge University Press, 2012), is an excellent study that refers to an abundance of relevant literature.

For Robert of Chaise-Dieu, the studies of Pierre-Roger Gaussin are the starting point: *Saint Robert de Turlande et la fondation de la Chaise-Dieu* (Paris: Desfossés, 1964); *Huit siècles d'histoire. L'abbaye de La Chaise-Dieu 1043–1790* (Brioude: Almanach de Brioude, 1967); *Le Rayonnement de La Chaise-Dieu* (Brioude: Watel, 1981). For more recent bibliography and translations of the two early Latin lives of Robert, see Hugh Feiss, Maureen M. O'Brien, and Ronald Pepin (eds.), *The Lives of Monastic Reformers 1: Robert of La Chaise-Dieu, Stephen of Obazine*, Cistercian Studies Series 222 (Collegeville, MN: Liturgical Press, 2010).

17

Gregory the Great

Carole Straw

Pope Gregory I (r. 590–604), also known as Gregory the Great, is celebrated as the fourth doctor of the Latin church and the founder of the medieval papacy. His cultural centrality rested on temporal as well as spiritual power. His writings conveyed the classical heritage of Stoicism as well as the teachings of earlier church fathers, especially Augustine, to the central Middle Ages. His ideal society was one of concord formed from diversity, and his political theology reflected a Byzantine world in which the emperor overshadowed the church. Gregory had his greatest impact in Western Europe. Not only opinions and interpretations from his exegetical works but also legal decisions from his letters entered the tradition of canon law and passed from there to secular law, where his teachings on judicial restraint matter to this day.

LIFE AND WORK

Gregory was born c. 540 to an aristocratic Roman family whose members had served the church for generations. He was educated in law and entered public service. Having risen to the highest office of urban prefect, he resigned suddenly in 574, fearing that the power and fame of the office would cost him his salvation. Retiring to a monastery on his family's estate, he lived in common with the brothers under a rule of ascetic discipline. There he enjoyed the happiest years of his life. But Pope Pelagius II ordered him back into the world, first making him a deacon and then sending him to Constantinople as papal legate (*apocrisiarius*) to the imperial court in 579. Gregory befriended the emperor Maurice's wife and made other important connections at court, although the emperor himself would later become his nemesis. Even after his return to Rome, this Byzantine world continued to be Gregory's frame of reference as pope. Around 585, he returned to Rome and worked again with Pope Pelagius II as his deacon. In 590, Gregory succeeded him as pope, an office carrying worldly responsibilities so great that he likened it to the life of an "earthly nobleman" (*Ep.* 1.24). A recurring theme of his exegesis, which he bequeathed to medieval religious and contemplatives, was autobiographical: the struggle to reconcile an active life of service with the contemplative asceticism of a monk.

Gregory ruled in an era of such turmoil that he thought the world was ending, and this apocalyptic mentality frames his writing. Justinian's wars of reconquest had ravaged Italy. The Lombard invasions soon followed, and cycles of drought, famine, and plague depopulated a wasted land. As the Lombards expanded their domain in northern Italy, the Byzantine forces abandoned Rome and focused on defending Ravenna, the capital of their exarchate. The empire had its own troubles in the Balkans and Persia, and Rome was not a priority. Without tangible support from Byzantium, secular institutions in Rome withered. Although a new military aristocracy arose in Italy, the church remained the most viable complex organization, inheriting the functions of the waning secular government along with its ruling elite. As pope, Gregory saw himself as the guardian, overseer, or watchman (*speculator*) of his people, responsible for their welfare and safety in this life into the next (*HEz.* 1.11.6).[1] He secured the financial future of the Roman church through his careful administration of the papal patrimony and his reform of the papal bureaucracy. Facing challenges from Constantinople and other churches in the empire, he asserted the authority of Peter's successors to judge matters of discipline, settle disputes, and determine doctrine. He worked to expand the church, sending missionaries to convert the English to Roman Christianity. It was among the English that the cult of Saint Gregory first flourished. He also forged connections with other queens and kings of the barbarian successor kingdoms, aiming to evangelize their kingdoms in Gaul, Germany, northern Italy, and Spain. He made minor changes in the liturgy along Greek lines, and he inaugurated the sevenfold penitential procession, or *litania maior*. This litany was repeated in times of distress at Rome, and eventually it became customary throughout Europe.

Gregory is the first major exponent of what would become a truly medieval spirituality in the West, emphasizing the sacramental connections between this world and the next in relics, eucharistic miracles, prayers for the dead, penitential processions, and the intercession of holy men in worldly events. This world and the next are intermingled; indeed, the spiritual world is immanent and immediate here and now. The events (wars, famines, floods) and agents (rulers, soldiers, bandits) of this world are charged with conveying God's grace or wrath: "The invisible judge moves the breath of the gentlest breeze" (*HEv.* 1.1.6). God's communication is constant, although the outcome remains a mystery.

In his preaching, Gregory exhorts Christians to be athletes in the contest and soldiers in the final battle with evil. What makes the struggle bearable is the availability of sacrifices. Various offerings of prayer, penitence, good deeds, and especially the eucharist afford Christians hope of salvation. In encouraging activity and emphasizing the church as a community of charity, Gregory may be considered optimistic. Yet beneath this hopeful edifice lies a dark foundation of fear: grim views

[1] For abbreviations to Gregory's works used in parentheses, see under Sources at the end of this chapter.

about the inevitability of sin, the severity of God's judgment, and the stubborn malevolence of demons.

Gregory's literary works were very popular throughout the Middle Ages, and his impact on the Latin tradition was second only to that of Augustine, whose influence he mediated. His extant works include the *Regula pastoralis*, or *Pastoral Rule* [*Rpast.*]. This manual on leadership, authority, and the exercise of power also illuminates his views of law and social order. His *Dialogues* [*Dial.*], a popular book on the miracles of contemporaneous saints, was soon translated into Greek, and came to define him among Greek Christians, who knew him as "Gregory of the *Dialogues*." Despite these popular works, biblical exegesis was Gregory's forte. His emphasis on the allegorical and moral interpretation of Scripture was followed by later exegetes. In monasteries and cathedral schools, his influence was unrivaled.[2] Among his exegetical works, *Morals on Job* [*Mor.*], *Homilies on the Prophet Ezechiel* [*HEz.*], *On the Song of Songs* [*Cant.*] and *Homilies on the Gospels* [*HEv.*] survive. Among his lost works were commentaries on Proverbs, the Prophets, the Heptateuch, and the First Book of Kings. In an attempt to heal the Istrian schism, Gregory addressed their complaints in a book (*liber*) defending the condemnation of the Three Chapters at the Fifth Ecumenical Council (553).[3] At that time, Gregory was an aide to the bishop of Rome, Pelagius II, and the book was published under Pelagius's name. Here, Gregory tacitly validates the emperor Justinian's role in making church doctrine while emphasizing *concordia* as the defining feature of the church. Of doctrinal importance is a booklet (*libellus*) on the reform Synod of 595 held in Rome, the only one of his papacy.[4] Finally, although Gregory left a registry of over 850 letters, it documents his papacy unevenly and is apparently incomplete. The longest is Book 9 with 240 letters; the shortest, Book 12 with only 16. Many of these letters along with teachings from Gregory's exegetical works were cited frequently in later collections of canons (e.g., Gratian's *Decretum*), in theological treatises and discourses on the law (e.g., Peter Lombard's *Sentences* and Thomas Aquinas's *Summa theologiae*), and in manuals of penance.

Gregory's legacy includes some landmarks in the Western tradition, of which five are worth noting here. First, he made a key contribution to moral theology and literary tradition in his doctrine of principle vices, which was monastic in origin. John Cassian

[2] Henri de Lubac, *Exégèse médiévale: les quatre sens de l'écriture* (Paris: Aubier,1959), 1/2: 538, writes of "le moyen âge Grégorien" when, "Pour la plupart de nos exégètes, en effect, Grégoire est le premier des maîtres."

[3] Under Justinian, the Fifth Ecumenical Council (Constantinople II, in 553) condemned as heretical "The Three Chapters" (i.e., certain writings by Theodore of Mopsuestia, Theodoret of Cyrrhus, and Ibas of Edessa deemed Nestorian). While the papacy supported the emperor and the Fifth Council, the bishops of Istria, Venetia, and Liguria rejected the council, arguing that the condemnation of the Three Chapters violated the Council of Chalcedon (451). The Istrian schism with Rome lasted until 698. See C. Straw, "Much Ado About Nothing: Gregory the Great's Apology to the Istrians," in C. M. Chazelle and C. Cubitt (eds.), *The Crisis of the Oikoumene: The Three Chapters and the Failed Quest for Unity in the Sixth-Century Mediterranean* (Turnhout: Brepols, 2007), 121–60.

[4] *Ep.* 5.57a, MGH Epist. 1 (1887–1891), 362–67.

(d. 435) had proposed a Latin list based on the Greek list of Evagrius Ponticus (d. 399), a monk of the Egyptian desert. Modifying Cassian's list and changing its order, Gregory formulated a degenerative succession of vices – pride, vainglory, envy, anger, melancholy, avarice, gluttony, and lust – that became enshrined in Western tradition as "the seven deadly sins," inspiring writers and artists from Dante and Bosch to modern novelists such as William S. Burroughs. Second, some of his contributions to Western legal tradition had a major impact on its future development, including his affirmation of the various protections that Roman law granted the Jews (*Ep.* 8.25), which entered canon law as the famous "Constitution Concerning the Jews." This became the foundation of papal policy toward the Jews through the fifteenth century. Third, he was important for the ethical tradition of the moral dilemma: If sin cannot be avoided, the choice of the lesser of two evils is recommended.[5] Fourth, several passages from his work counseling judicial restraint entered canon law and Western secular law in cases of uncertainty and reasonable doubt. Fifth, he emphasized the constant need for judicial discretion in determining the seriousness of the crime, evaluating motives, considering extenuating circumstances, matching punishment to crime, and so forth. These humane counsels of restraint and discretion anticipated our modern interest in the social and economic causes of crime, as well as the concern for the rights of the accused, including such reform movements as the Innocence Project, whose lawyers vindicate those wrongly convicted of crimes.[6]

Gregory's legal decisions and opinions follow Justinian's *Corpus Iuris Civilis* and *Novellae*. Indeed, the papacy exercises the role of secular lord and judge in governing the church's massive estates according to prevailing law. And just as Justinian's laws record ecclesiastical as well as secular legislation, so Gregory's decisions deal with secular as well as ecclesiastical disputes. He settles both with the same moderation and discretion. In matters of ecclesiastical discipline, he affirms the first four ecumenical councils – Nicaea (325), Constantinople (381), Ephesus (431), and Chalcedon (451) – but he largely ignores the fifth (Constantinople II in 553), a strategy that the popes hoped would placate the schismatic Istrians (*Ep.* 1.24).

More personally revealing are his justifications for decisions. While he rarely cites Scripture in these judgments, he does claim as moral imperatives several classical virtues, the meaning of which Christians had softened through their emphasis on love and compassion. This chapter illustrates such nuances and changes. Gregory is not Cicero, for whom *iustitia* was generally "righteousness." For Gregory, *iustitia* is "justice" and is associated with discipline, punishment, strictness, authority, and anger, although it is also "doing the right thing." *Rectitudo* is being "upright" or "righteousness." For Virgil, *pietas* connoted duty and obedience to divine law: *pius* Aeneas did what he was supposed to do. In contrast, Gregory understands *pietas* more as "piety," which includes a general religiosity, obligation, and devotion to

[5] Gratian, *Decretum*, dist. 13, c.2, §§1, 3 (*CICan.*, 1:32). See M. V. Dougherty, *Moral Dilemmas in Medieval Thought: From Gratian to Aquinas* (Cambridge: Cambridge University Press, 2011), 27.

[6] See www.innocenceproject.org (accessed May 13, 2018).

divine law but refers more specifically to the love of neighbor. Duty meant responding to the love of God. One must respond sympathetically to others, be it with pity, compassion, clemency, mercy, or kindness.[7] Gregory characterizes these virtues as soft, mild, flexible, and warm, associating them with love (*caritas*) and with *misericordia*. Now, classically, *misericordia* was negative, a wretchedness or pitifulness that made one feel unclean: feelings of disgust, contempt and revulsion evoked especially by the sight of suffering, whether another's or one's own. For Christians, on the contrary, *misericordia* becomes the positive ability to feel pity and compassion for others, to be merciful, forgiving, and humble. Christians embrace the very suffering that pagans despised. This contrast between harsh and soft virtues and emotions is a fixture of Gregory's thought. It defines the ruler's proper behavior, his exercise of power over subjects, and his judgment of cases.

HIERARCHY AS PROVIDENTIAL ORDER: *NATURA* AND THE *IUS GENTIUM*

Gregory's conceptions of the law and justice are continuous with his understanding of how God ordered the divine dispensation according to certain laws. He relies on classical ideas as they had been adapted by Christian writers, beginning with Clement of Alexandria. Following the Stoics, Gregory uses a circular argument to stress that divine providence has ordered the world justly, lawfully, rightly, and fairly (*iuste, iure, recte, aeque*), equating this orderliness with hierarchy and rationality itself. (Compare how we think and organize data by subordinating lesser to greater. The taxonomy of species, genus, family, order, class, phylum, kingdom, domain in biology makes this explicit.) Hierarchy, for Gregory, is order and necessity – how things are and always will be – as well as a self-evident fact of nature. Hierarchy reflects intrinsic worth, meaning that things are in their proper place as God and nature intended. Being an arrangement that is fitting and appropriate, hierarchy is just and providential: a matter of divine law. Just as high is above low, and heaven above earth, so nature has placed angels above humanity, human beings above animals, animals above plants, and plants above rocks. Hierarchy ensures the human community's survival, for if we were all equal, anarchy would prevail. The fact that subjects obey their rulers, in Gregory's view is the *sine qua non* of government (cf. *Ep.* 5.59). Barbarians are subject to Romans, slaves to free men, women to men, and so forth because this is the natural order that God ordained (*Ep.* 11.4). The story of the very creation of Adam and Eve as well as of their fall explains how this order came to exist.

Following Augustine, Gregory recognizes a primordial state of nature (*natura*). In the beginning, God created humanity free and equal (*Ep.* 6.12; *Rpast.* 3.5), below the

7 See *Ep.* 1.24, cited below, where *pietas* (classically, "what is right") is implicitly a "soft" Christian virtue: a clemency that is a mean between laxity and severity.

angels and above animals, in accordance with hierarchical order. Then, God ruled Adam directly, without intermediaries such as kings or emperors. As long as Adam obeyed God, he participated in God's virtue, so that his rational soul dominated the irrational body. This was the rightful submission that an inferior creature owed to his Creator and was justice itself (*Mor.* 34.21.40–41, 29.8.18). A "management of heavenly government" (*superni moderaminis dispositio*) guaranteed that all things would be at peace with themselves when obedience to God's authority was maintained:

> For he who marvelously created all things ordered all creation so that it would harmonize with itself. Where the Creator is resisted, the peace of harmony is dissipated, since things cannot be ordered which lose the management of heavenly government. For the things that are subject to God remain in tranquility, and those that have been abandoned to themselves bring disorder and confusion upon themselves since they cannot find in themselves that peace from above which they reject in the Creator. (*Mor.* 9.5.5)

Humanity's subordination to God was divinely ordained. Conversely, the desire for freedom and autonomy was pride and insolence: *lèse majesté*, defiance of God. Having rejected his proper place, Adam suffered "legitimate" and "lawful" punishment in the rebellion of his own servant, the body:

> For if the spirit is dutifully pressed down under God, the flesh is not illegitimately raised above the spirit. Indeed, the spirit has dominion over the flesh committed to it, as long as it recognizes the law of legitimate servitude to the Lord. For if it despises its Creator in pride, it lawfully undergoes battle from the subject flesh. Whence that first disobedient man, as soon as he sinned in pride, covered his shameful parts. Since the spirit attacked God insolently, soon it was attacked by the flesh insolently. Since it was unwilling to be subject to its Creator, it lost its right to dominate the flesh that it used to rule. (*Mor.* 26.17.28; cf. *Mor.* 34.21.40, 29.8.18, 8.10.19)

Divine justice followed a law of retribution (*lex talionis*), whereby the punishment fit the crime. Human beings were doomed to be dominated by the body's passions unless they subjected themselves to an authority fearsome enough to subdue the body as well as the mind.

Adam's fall ushered in the need for human representatives of God's authority to enforce obedience to God's law. A human law of nations (*ius gentium*) replaced the transcendent order of nature and brought inequality and subjection, whether through slavery or government. Remarkably, this subordination reflected merit: "It is clear that nature brought forth all men as equal, but through the variation of merit sin subordinates some to others" (*Rpast.* 2.6; *Mor.* 21.15.22). Subjugation to superiors was divine punishment, and yet, providentially, it is also redemptive. Individually, obedience to authority is obedience to God and is meritorious (*Rpast.* 1.1, 3.4). This is best seen in the second book of the *Dialogues*, on the life of St. Benedict. The reader learns that the monk must sacrifice self-will in absolute obedience to the superior's command, even as Christ surrendered himself to God in his Passion, confessing, "If it be thy will" (Matt 26:39, Luke 22:42; *Dial.* 4, 60.3–61.1).

CONCORD

Just as submission to authority changed from punishment to cure for individuals in God's paradoxical dispensation, so for society hierarchy is transformed to become concord. In a letter to the bishops of Gaul under the Merovingian king Childebert, Gregory explains a marvelous paradox of the divine dispensation, justifying hierarchy, with its inequality, as the basis of concord, the ideal of a harmonious social order:

> The foresight of the divine dispensation established that there be different stations and separate ranks, so that while inferiors show reverence to the more powerful, and the more powerful extend love to inferiors, one harmonious concord may be created from diversity, and the administration of each office may be rightly managed. For the whole [*uniuersitas*] could not survive with another arrangement [*ratio*], unless it preserved the grand order of these kinds of differences. But since creatures cannot be governed or live in one and the same equality, the example of the heavenly host has taught us that there are angels and archangels. It is clear that they are not equal but differ from one another in power and rank, like us. If, therefore, this distinction continues to exist among those who are without sin, what man would refuse to submit himself willingly to this dispensation, which he knows even the angels obey? For here peace and love embrace each other in turn, and the integrity of concord remains firm in the love for each other that pleases God. (*Ep.* 5.59)

Society, then, is not homogeneous. Trying to achieve equality would invite anarchy. Like the order of heaven, social order depends on differences among the stations (*gradus*) and ranks (*ordines*) of those with less (*minores*) or more power (*potiores*). Each individual fulfills his or her specific role; all know their places in the greater concord or harmony from diversity that brings peace. Through Christian love, diversity generates concord. Love has the capacity to reform society through an entirely peaceful transformation.

The archetypal image of concord comes from Paul – from 1 Corinthians 12:26 ("And if one member suffer any thing, all the members suffer with it; or if one member glories, all the members rejoice with him"), and from Romans 8:17 ("And if sons, heirs also; heirs indeed of God, and joint heirs with Christ: yet so, if we suffer with him, that we may be also glorified with him"). Gregory's ideas about the corporate body of Christ are central to his political theology, which may be characterized as "eastern," "imperial," and "Byzantine." He never speaks dualistically of two realms or "two swords" (cf. Luke 22:38),[8] but instead focuses on the body and its

[8] Although exegesis of the "two swords" is ancient, debates about the political theology of two swords belong to the central Middle Ages in the West. See Bronwen Neil's Chapter on Gelasius I in this volume.

harmonious interconnections. A ruler, whether lay or ecclesiastical, is the head of a corporate body of individuals, be it the priest of his parish, an emperor of the commonwealth. This body and these individuals are then part of the greater transcendent body of Christ. On earth, individual members are arranged hierarchically according to their talents and deficits; just as in heaven, rewards are to be apportioned according to merits.

Gregory envisions the members of the body hierarchically. The spiritual members of the church are the "eyes," while the more carnal members are the "feet."[9] Their strengths and weaknesses are complementary, so that a reciprocal give-and-take unifies the body. The carnal feet are strong, but blind. The spiritual eyes have sight and knowledge, but they are frail and apt to pride themselves on their otherworldly vision. Lest the feet be snared by temptation and trapped in sin, the eyes humble themselves to guide the feet, and this checks their own tendency to pride. And by laboring in this world, the feet are meritorious in protecting the eyes from the "dust" of worldly temptation and sin; and by bearing earthly burdens on their behalf, the feet free the eyes to concentrate on God. This mutual dependence of sharing virtues ensures humility and cooperation in charity (*Mor.* 31.13.25). Acting on behalf of each other, the members form a mystical "unity from diversity"; and sharing a "oneness of mind," they create a harmony or concord. Love binds the members to each other in compassion and to Christ, their head, establishing the interconnectedness of Christ's body (*compago corporis Christi*), or a network of love (*compago caritatis*).[10]

The mystical body is Gregory's favorite image of concord, but other images shed light on the nature of the interconnection of the body's members and are significant for validating the contributions of secular people. In a homily on Ezekiel (*HEz.* 1.7.21), Gregory treats the reciprocity of virtues. Members of the church are like the creatures in Ezekiel's vision (Ezek 1.24). Extending the "wings" of their virtue to touch the "wings" of the others, they both "give" and "receive" virtues in charity. Here, Gregory expands the complementary virtues of the eyes' contemplative understanding and the feet's active service to include the spiritual gifts of preaching, prophecy, and healing, and the earthly virtues of power, influence, and wealth. Signaling his humility, Gregory aligns himself with the earthly group, reasoning that if someone else's preaching "enlightens the darkness of my ignorance with truth," if that man is "oppressed by a power of this world," and if Gregory can give him the

9 *Mor.* 19.25.42 (CCL 143A:990), *Mor.* 3.13.25 (CCL 143:130), *Mor.* 19.25.43 (CCL 143A:991), *Mor.* 28.10.23 (CCL 143B:1414), *Ep.* 2.40 (CCL 140:127), *Ep.* 2.44 (CCL 140:134), *Ep.* 3.65 (CCL 140:215–16), *Ep.* 11.28 (CCL 140A:914), *Ep.* 13.41 (CCL 140A:1045), *Ep.* 13.44 (CCL 140A:1050); *HEz.* 1.7.21 (CCL 142:96); *HEz.* 2.1.6 (CCL 142:211), *Mor.* 30.6.23 (CCL 143B:1506), *Mor.* 31.13.25 (CCL 143B:1568).

10 On the notion of *compago* (referring to something bound together or made fast), see *Mor.* 33.8.15 (CCL 143B:1686), *Rpast.* 3.34.10 (SC 382:310–12), *Mor.* 28.10.22 (CCL 143B:1413), *Mor.* 34.23.48 (CCL 143B:1768), and *Mor.* 30.6.23 (CCL 143B:1506).

"solace of my defense and pluck him from the hand of his oppressor," this illustrates wing touching wing to "share the gift they have received."

In the same homily (*HEz.* 1.7.21), Gregory invokes the long tradition of almsgiving as a form of penitence. The rich feed and clothe the poor, who in turn pray for the rich. The virtue of the poor can compensate for the debts of the rich. But the rich are not the only ones responsible; the laity in general need to give alms. In another passage (*HEz.* 1.8.10), Gregory distinguishes different ranks (*distincti ordines*) of preachers, ascetics, and "good spouses who, [are] living in concord in the love of Almighty God." And of these spouses, "if in some way they offend men, they make amends for it with constant pious activities [*piis actibus*]." Pious activities are meritorious, but how powerful are they? In a gospel homily (*HEv.* 1.20.11), Gregory quotes Luke 11:41 – "Give alms, and behold, everything is clean for you" – and Sirach 3:30 – "Alms atone for sin." These alms are particularly powerful as "works of mercy [*misericordia*] . . . and fruits worthy of penitence." Rather than the prayers of the poor, the laity's own works of mercy have the power to cleanse sins.

Later in the homilies on Ezekiel (*HEv.* 1.20.13), Gregory again acknowledges the contributions of secular persons. The orchards in the desert symbolize the church (Isa 42:18–20). Cedar, thorn, myrtle, olive, fir, and box: Each tree designates a specific spiritual gift. Gregory notes the text's singular treatment of the elm and decides that this tree symbolizes secular men. Just as the elm has no fruit of its own but supports the vines that bear clusters of grapes, so worldly persons, even though they have no spiritual gifts, are able to share in the reward of virtuous men when they use their bounty to support them. Their almsgiving is the "fruit of worthy repentance," which cleanses sin (cf. Luke 11:41) so that through repentance "the kingdom of heaven suffers violence, and the violent take it by force" (Matt 11:12). Although the spiritual achievements of worldly men scarcely merit heaven, nevertheless, their alms allow them to "take heaven by force." Such are the ironies and paradoxes of divine providence.

In fact, the members of God's people are obliged to share the gifts they have received from their head. God is the source of the virtues in which members participate, and they must be good "stewards" of his manifold graces (*HEz.* 1.7.21). Gregory quotes from 1 Peter 4:10, interpreting the words "[a]s every man has received grace, ministering the same to another" to mean that our virtues are "not from ourselves for private use but from God for the common good." Virtues are held in common yet are "owned" by each member's sharing the gifts and participating in the reward. Charity is so powerful that it renders the works of another's labor our own, without any labor on our part (*Rpast.* 3.34). The Redeemer guarantees that one can share in the rewards of another, saying in Matthew 10:41: "He who receives a prophet because he hears the name of prophet will have a prophet's reward, and one who receives a righteous man because he is righteous will have a righteous man's reward" (*HEv.* 1.20.13). Deeds and merits are transferable in the network of love (*compago caritatis*) that is the mystical body of Christ. This imagery and sense of connection have great potential to transform social relationships, the definition of social welfare, and thus politics.

This interconnection explains why the merits and deserts of subjects and rulers are shared. By divine providence, subjects get the rulers they deserve, and vice versa (*Rpast.* 1.1; *HEz.* 1.11.9; *Ep.* 7.7). Gregory sees in the emperor Maurice a punishment for his own sins and for those of the emperor's subjects: "Sometimes, when the sins of man are to be punished, one man is raised up, by whose severity the necks of the people are bowed beneath the yoke of tribulation" (*Ep.* 13.32). Having offended God, Gregory loses the peace that the commonwealth had secured with the Lombards. Agilulf attacks, and grain runs short in Rome (*Epp.* 5.36, 2.38). The sins of the clergy have obstructed their intercession with God, and their flock suffers. Because priests are wicked, the whole empire suffers the cruelties of the barbarians; their sins have sharpened the enemy's swords (*Epp.* 5.37, 7.6). The interconnection of members in the mystical body means that the whole society share the fate of their leaders.

VIRTUE AND JUSTICE

Following classical and early Christian teachings, Gregory believes that virtue, like health, consists in moderation: a "golden mean" between opposite extremes of vice. This moderation is also what was fitting, just, natural, rational, harmonious, and ordained by God. Virtue depends on *discretio* (discernment). It is first the ability to perceive – to scrutinize, sift through data, and make fine distinctions so one can separate the truth from appearances, and focus on the goal. It is all kinds of judgment, including self-judgment and conscience. Discretion is also self-control: the ability to relax or intensify behavior so that one follows the virtuous middle way. Even as the strings of the lute are tightened or loosened to achieve the proper tension, so virtues must be moderated to attain the appropriate harmony (*Mor.* 20.51.78, 28.11.26–29). This applies to governing and justice itself.

Good rulers balance authority with humility and severity with laxity. "The great art of discretion" holds discipline (*disciplina*) and mercy (*misericordia*) together in compassionate severity (*pie saeviens, Ep.* 1.24; *Rpast.* 2.3). Good leaders distinguish vice from virtue lest cruelty appear to be a zeal for justice, or laxity be mistaken for piety (*crudelitas zelus iustitiae, remissio pietas, Ep.* 1.24). Paradoxically (and dialectically) discretion can mean suspending a virtue to keep it. "For virtue is often lost when it is maintained indiscreetly, but when it is discreetly intermitted, it is held more firmly" (*Mor.* 28.11.29). This paradox includes the suspension and enforcement of the law. In Jerusalem, Paul forbids that Gentiles be circumcised (Gal 5:2), but at Lystra, he circumcises the Gentile Timothy (Acts 16:3), lest Jewish Christians be offended. Paul did what he had forbidden from love of the faith, and by this seeming unfaithfulness, he restored to the faith those who might have been lost. Such teachings give leaders enormous power, but Gregory never identified that as a problem.

Gregory's understanding of political and social justice can be traced back to Plato (*Rep.* 4, 427C–45D) and Aristotle (*Nicomachean Ethics* 5, 1129a–1130b; *Politics* 1, 1252a–1253b). This justice is again what is fitting, rational, and proper to an individual: a truth that is considered self-evident, which is to say, validated by social consensus. But because social consensus reflects the status quo, laws, privileges, and punishments depend on social status. By definition, citizens are free and have legal standing, although they are unequal in honor. Their traditional ranks in Roman society – such as *magnifici, gloriossissimi, clarissimi*, or *illustrissimi* – entitle them to various levels of privilege and of deference from others. Slaves have neither freedom nor honor. Unlike slaves, citizens may marry, own property, sign contracts, move about freely, and are not routinely subjected to judicial torture. Gregory shares the elite's view of the lower classes as ontologically inferior – irrational, even bestial – when compared to their superiors. It is permissible to coerce peasants: to use corporal discipline and to inflict fear in other ways to break them (*Epp.* 9.205, 4.26, 3.37). Jews are similarly "carnal" and may also receive harsh treatment. Correspondingly, those of higher status must be given their just deserts. In his charitable donations, Gregory grants "pigments" and "more delicate articles of commerce" to impoverished ladies of high birth, in recognition of their status.[11] But these are all matters subject to discretion.

Recognizing the need for variable treatments, Gregory systematizes social differences and personality types in the *Regula Pastoralis*, book III. Here, he identifies seventy categories of Christians, arranged as thirty-five binary oppositions, such as male or female, young or old. The categories range from the obvious ones of sex and age to considerations of health, marital status, wealth, or class, to distinctions of education and occupation, good fortune, or misfortune. He profiles different temperaments and personality types, with their predispositions to specific virtues or vices. Rulers (*rectores*) are to exercise discretion and calibrate their correction carefully to the needs of different individuals. An excess of severity will break a meek soul with fear and send it to the depths of despair, while too mild a punishment of a confident soul will not eradicate the vice but rather embolden it. This ability to care for souls – to discern what an individual needs and to possess the skill to administer it – makes the ruler a physician of the soul, a practitioner of the "art of arts" (*Rpast.* 1.1).

Whether settling lay or ecclesiastical cases, Gregory sees the purpose of discipline to be as correction and rehabilitation of the guilty party. A pastor wants his sheep cured, not destroyed, and this justifies the liberal exercise of discretion. Certainly, Gregory's distinction of seventy types of Christians in *Pastoral Rule* presumes that the ruler enjoys a wide margin of discretion if he was to treat each subject fittingly. Yet there were other reasons for flexibility and clemency. Not all error sin (*peccatum, crimen*) has the same measure of wickedness. One sin is lesser (*minor*), another more serious (*grauior*), as is

11 Jeffrey Richards, *Consul of God: The Life and Times of Gregory the Great* (London: Routledge & Kegan Paul, 1980), 96–97.

the burden of guilt (*culpa*, cf. *RP* 3.33). Whether unlawful sexual intercourse is the lesser sin of fornication or the greater of sin adultery is "differentiated according to the situation [*locum*] or status [*ordo*] of the person lusting," Gregory writes in *Mor.* 21.11.18. He adds that one should take the previous good deeds of the sinner into account when judging him. Moreover, the motives of the criminal must be taken into consideration as possible mitigating factors. It is one thing to sin from weakness (*infirmitas*) and another from wickedness (*malitia: Mor.* 31.13 24). Those motivated to steal by poverty must be treated differently from those motivated by greed (*Ep.* 8.37). Indeed, charity dictated that "some are to be submitted to while they steal from us." Servants of God should not have property in the first place. "But others are to be prevented, without violation of charity, not from anxiety lest they take away our goods, but lest they ruin themselves by stealing what is not their own" (*Mor.* 31.13.22). Of the several mitigating circumstances Gregory recognizes (situation, status, previous record, motives), he is most sensitive to the role played by economic factors in criminal behavior. Even though human nature is fundamentally flawed, it can be changed for the better with charitable attention to human needs.

In several passages, Gregory deals with doubt as a mitigating factor mandating judicial restraint. Through Gratian's *Decretum* (1140s), the textbook that launched the systematic study of canon law, Gregory's opinion that "doubtful matters should not be dismissed with certain judgment; it is more than grievous and unfitting that a certain judgment should be given in a doubtful matter" entered Western legal tradition as foundational to the theory of "reasonable doubt," one of the most important ideas in jurisprudence in both the East and the West.[12] Even today, guilt must be proved "beyond a reasonable doubt." Gregory's willingness to suspend judgment when there is uncertainty stems from his compassion and his understanding (following Augustine) that human beings are mysteries, even to themselves. Like Augustine, he fears that secret sins, unknown to himself, could be his ruin (cf. *Mor.* 9.25.39; 9.55.84; 24.18.44). Surely to know with certainty all the factors not only of the crime itself, but also the various circumstances shaping someone's nature and character – is godlike omniscience. It would be "grievous" and "unfitting" (the sin of pride) for fallible men to presume to judge in such cases. Humility and self-restraint benefit not only the accused, but also the judges who are accountable to God. This may help explain the wide acceptance of the standard.

A passage from Gregory's early book on the Three Chapters to the Istrians also states the principles of giving the benefit of the doubt in uncertain situations. He went even further here by emphasizing the obligation to presume the best of someone if one does not know otherwise.[13] Whether this be Aristotelian magnanimity, Roman *noblesse*, or supererogatory Christian charity (or all three), its generosity is characteristically Gregorian. A final example is similarly revealing. In *Ep.* 9.48, he

[12] Gratian, C. 11 q. 3 c. 74 (*CICan.* 1:664). James Q. Whitman, *The Origins of Reasonable Doubt: Theological Roots of the Criminal Trial* (New Haven: Yale University Press, 2008), 116, 118.

[13] MGH Epist. 2, *Appendix* III, 467: "in parte semper est interpretanda meliore."

intervenes on behalf of Stephania, a poor widow with a son, who requests return of a house her mother-in-law donated to the church after the death of her son. The issue is less legal (Who owned the house before its donation, the grandmother or the son?), than moral (Who should own the house, and for what reasons?). Gregory orders the house returned to Stephania for her support and that of her son, even though this violated canon law. He advised the defender Romanus, "It is preferable in uncertainties not to pursue strictness but rather bow to kindness [*benigna pars*]."[14] Uncertainty calls for charity.

JOB'S RHINOCEROS: THE CHURCH, THE PRINCE, AND CONCORD

For Gregory, opposition between church and state belonged to a past era of "adversity," when the church had suffered persecution from secular princes, and when martyrs proved the truth of Christianity in heroic deaths while their relics showed the power of God in dazzling miracles. Through the conversion of Constantine, the church had become reconciled with the world, entering an era of "prosperity" in which the church enjoyed the support of princes as well as of secular wealth and power (*Mor.* 28.16.36, 26.40–42, 73–77, 31.2.2; *Ep.* 1.24).

In accordance with this reconciliation, Gregory speaks of the Christian empire (*christianum imperium, Epp.* 5.37, 7.5, 6.64, 7.7), the Christian commonwealth (*christiana respublica, Epp.* 6.64, 9.68), and the holy or pious commonwealth (*sancta/pia respublica, Epp.* 1.73, 2.47, 5.38). Secular and ecclesiastical authorities are not in opposition but rather complementary and mutually reinforcing. They share the same goal of expanding the Christian empire so that the church reaches even "the extremities of the earth" (*Mor.* 27.11.21). Both emperor and priest are God's anointed and rule in his stead to bless or punish his people. This alignment (or synthesis) of contrasts is characteristic of a dialectical thinking that also creates concord from diversity.

In his exegesis of Job 39:9–12, where God inquires if Job has the power to bind the rhinoceros and tame it so that it serves him, Gregory addresses the conversion of secular rulers and the changes that it brings about (*Mor.* 31.1.1–7.10). Only God can tame the savage rhinoceros (the ruler) on Job's behalf. Job (the church) is humbled by his own weakness. Gregory depicts the ruler (the rhinoceros) as carnal. The prince of this world, the devil, is his ancestor. Violent, tyrannical, and cruel, he persecutes the church with his horn of pride, crushing the weak under his massive hooves. Shameless, he is overrun by sins, for pride unleashes a legion of vices: envy, anger, avarice, gluttony, lust, and so forth. On his own, Job (the church) is no match for the rhinoceros, who can only be subdued by divine miracles, which vanquish his

14 *Ep.* 9.48 (CCL 140A:607) shows how the meanings of terms such as *pietas* and *misericordia* were changing.

pride and quell his violence (*Mor.* 28.16.16). But once humbled, the rhinoceros is yoked and given his own office (*ministerium*) of serving the church – to defeat both external and internal enemies, and to advance the church's causes. This has always been God's plan, for the Lord "inclines the powers that he had conferred on an earthly prince temporally for veneration of his worship" (*Mor.* 31.6.8). The rhino's terrible power is now harnessed to good ends of serving the church, conferring on the prince a spiritual aspect as the Lord's anointed, even as the church has its worldly, "carnal" aspect in wealth and temporal power, including command of soldiers. Celebrating the Christian empire, Gregory vindicates the church's prosperity (*Ep.* 1.24). Only hypocrites reject this success, nostalgic for a church militant hardened by persecution and humbled by adversity.

In this Christian empire, the church and the world are reconciled to such an extent that the powers of secular and ecclesiastical rulers are analogous. The princely rhinoceros is said to "preach" by defending the church and promoting its interests. Gregory even goes as far as imagining that rulers have roles akin to that of priests when they make offerings to God. But Gregory sends such patronizing flattery only to barbarian leaders, framing service to the church as a privilege and an honor. In contrast, he lectures the emperor Maurice and can be shrill in his complaints. While barbarian rulers needed to be humored into serving the church, the emperor already knew his duty but had spurned it. Barbarian rulers, too, have their sacred offices. Brunhilda offers a sacrifice of expiation by purging her clergy of immoral behavior (*Ep.* 11.46), and another by repressing simony (*Ep.* 11.49). Ethelbert offers a sacrifice in the conversion of his people (*Ep.* 11.35). Gregory is so pleased by the Visigothic king Reccared's conversion of his subjects from Arian to catholic Christianity that he wonders if he has been outmatched. At the Last Judgment, Reccared will bring with him many flocks of faithful ones. Will Gregory be found wanting? (*Ep.* 9.229). Nor are mass conversions problematic. Even if the first generation of Christian Visigoths is lukewarm, succeeding generations will be true believers (*Ep.* 5.7).

The Christian empire, or holy commonwealth, *is* this harmonious interdependence of ecclesiastical and secular powers: a *concordia*. Writing to Libertinus, the *praetor* of Sicily, Gregory stresses the sacred mission of secular rulers: "From the very beginning of your administration, God has wanted you to proceed in the defense of his cause and has graciously reserved this reward for you with his praise" (*Ep.* 3.37). The emperor's *raison d'être* is sacred and ordained by God: "For power over all men has been given by heaven to my lord's piety [cf. Rom 13:1–7] for this reason, that those who seek good things are given help, that the path to heaven is open more widely, and that an earthly kingdom is in service to the heavenly kingdom" (*Ep.* 3.61). God gave to emperor and empress "the right of such great power" and "established them as rulers of the entire world." Through the "favor of justice," they should reciprocate and "render him service" (*Ep.* 5.39). Several times Gregory reminds the emperor of his obligations to the church that has been entrusted to his protection (*Epp.* 5.39,

5.36, 7.6, 9.154). The ruler's duty is to protect the church with whatever powers he (or she) possesses, to extend its boundaries as he extends his own, to defeat its enemies as he defeats his own (*Epp.* 1.72, 1.73, 2.20, 6.7). Above all, the secular ruler should acknowledge that he owes servile obedience to God, the author of his power, recognizing that he depends on the church's prayers for his own safety and that of his family, as well as for that of the commonwealth (*Epp.* 3.6, 5.30, 7.5, 7.7). At the same time, the church's duty is to pray and obey. All Christians are commanded to obey the ruler as God's anointed (cf. *Rpast.* 3.4). The church has a self-interest in praying for the welfare of secular rulers (*Epp.* 3.61, 5.30, 7.5, 7.7). Gregory can even be chauvinistic on the emperor's behalf. All must pray that heavenly grace will protect the emperor and "subject the necks of all nations beneath the Christian empire" (*Ep.* 7.7).

Gregory goes as far as asserting that the peace of the commonwealth depends on the peace of the church (*Ep.* 5.37). But while prioritizing the church, he places the emperor over it in some respects, assigning to the emperor the task of "managing" the church's unity. He invites the kind of secular interference in internal church affairs that Pope Gregory VII will later condemn and against which Thomas à Becket will die protesting. Gregory advises emperor Maurice to "consider piously and truthfully that no one can rule earthly affairs righteously unless he knows how to manage divine affairs" (*Ep.* 5.37). The emperor must be able to manage the church before he can rule the commonwealth. Prioritizing the church will be to the emperor's benefit because their interests are aligned and interdependent. When the emperor subjects himself to the yoke of heavenly piety, he treads down his own enemies (*Ep.* 7.6). When the emperor presses down the church's enemies, he raises up the commonwealth. And when he cuts away the church's foes, he casts his own enemies out of his kingdom (*Ep.* 5.37). To underscore their common goals, Gregory can even put the secular ruler ahead of the church: "For the more powerful [the prince] is toward the world, the more does he prevail for the Creator of the world" (*Ep.* 5.37). Going further, he makes the relationship reciprocal. Writing to Brunhilda, Gregory points out mutual advantages: "Do what is God's and he will do yours" (*Ep.* 11.49). When he writes to the emperor and empress of their obligation to render God service, he promises in return that they will "receive eternal goodness, for in the causes of his church you have put in debt him who has the power of binding and loosing" (*Ep.* 5.38) – a humble and surprising admission of Saint Peter's vulnerability and need of imperial support.

Gregory was keen to remind secular leaders of their duty to promote the church, asserting his moral authority forcefully in letters, but the needs of the empire and church were not always in tandem. In 593, Maurice issued an edict prohibiting those under obligations to the state (e.g., soldiers, *curiales*, officials) from becoming monks or clerics (*Epp.* 3.61, 8.10). Gregory could accept the ban on their becoming clergy, for often such types were only exchanging one secular career for another. But to forbid conversion to the monastic life threatened the salvation of those too weak to face temptation, for whom salvation depended on seclusion. Gregory used discretion to finesse the situation by protesting to the emperor in a private letter while publicly promulgating the emperor's edict. His explanation to the emperor is noteworthy: "I have thus done my duty on both sides. I have obeyed the emperor, and yet I have not kept back what I felt ought to be said on behalf of God" (*Ep.* 3.61). Rhetorically (but revealingly), both duties were equally compelling.

Even if it is silent and only implied, rebuke fulfills the pastor's duty to God, freeing him from culpability should wickedness persist. As Gregory explains, the Ethiopian enters the bath black and emerges black, but the keeper still receives his pay (*Ep.* 3.62). The loyal subject must be like David, obedient to Saul as the Lord's anointed and honoring him in public. But like David, he could protest silently, though still in God's sight. Just as David cut the hem of Saul's cloak when no one was looking (1 Kgs 24:6), so the subject could disagree discreetly, allowing the ruler to save face (*Rpast.* 3.4). God would take care of the rest. This is how Gregory dealt with Maurice's banning of imperial functionaries from church offices, and he employed similar discretion on other occasions. He will forgive the insults that Maximus of Salona has leveled against him, but he cannot overlook Maximus's sins against God, which render him excommunicate (*Ep.* 6.25). When the emperor moved to replace the archbishop of Prima Justiniana in Illyricum, Gregory protests: "If what he [i.e., the emperor] does is in accordance with the canons, we conform to it; if it is not, we submit to it, as far as we can do so without sin" (*Epp.* 11.29, 13.6). While he considers an imperial decree of Maurice regarding the jurisdiction of the bishop of Corfu to be illegal, Gregory nevertheless refrains from publishing his own decision "lest I should appear to be acting contrary to the commands of my Gracious Lord the Emperor, or in contempt of him – God forbid!" (*Ep.* 14.8). Gregory knew how to make a strategic retreat when necessary.

Yet some principles were worth the battle. Gregory repeatedly calls for the emperor to support him in his dispute with John, patriarch of Constantinople, over his claim to the title "Ecumenical Patriarch" (i.e., patriarch of the entire church). John's presumption is not just an insult to other bishops; it is literally the end of the world. John's pride is diabolical, a sign that the Antichrist is at hand (*Ep.* 5.39). By seeking to subjugate other priests, John threatens the unity and concord of the church: a church that was left in St. Peter's care! Gregory rehearses all the arguments for Peter's primacy, but the emperor is unmoved. Gregory plays his trump card: The empire needs the prayers of priests to survive. But their intercession depends on their virtue, which disunity has compromised (*Ep.* 5.37). Events have proved Gregory right. Barbarians have invaded, and the empire is in ruins as God's punishment for the sins of priests. Priests who should be weeping in dust and ashes instead seek "names of vanity and glory in new and profane titles." Divine vengeance awaits: "Every one that exalts himself shall be humbled" (Luke 14:22, 18:14). Those who will not obey the canons must be coerced by the commands of the emperor, and John must be restrained from injuring the church. Gregory also writes to the patriarchs of Alexandria and Antioch for their support. When John dies, the emperor Maurice orders Gregory to accept John's successor Cyriacus with charity and to cease quibbling over a frivolous issue of titles. Obeying the emperor's orders, Gregory does receive Cyriacus charitably; and although he still protests that what he owes to the "unity of the faith" is one thing and to "the restraint of pride" another (*Ep.* 7.30), he does eventually drop the matter.

Gregory's correspondence suggests that on a practical political level, the balance of power between the emperor and the papacy was overwhelmingly in the emperor's favor.

CONCORD IN PRACTICE: INTERWOVEN AUTHORITIES

Insofar as Gregory's ideal of concord obtained in reality, it did so in the ad hoc cooperation of ecclesiastical and secular authorities in the problems of daily life. Often Gregory acted by default, assuming responsibilities as Roman leader that the imperial authorities had abandoned, such as securing the grain supply (*Ep.* 9.107), paying soldiers (*Ep.* 5.39), ransoming captives (*Ep.* 4.17), and functioning as a secular court. For instance, in *Ep.* 9.46, Gregory wrote to the defender Romanus about an imperial lapse in protecting the elderly in Naples. Many had been robbed, allegedly by agents of an ex-consul. Formerly, the elderly had been "fully protected by the orders of the emperors, but for us, during the time in which we are in power, their rights are strictly protected by my support for their cause and by the command of the emperor" (*Ep.* 9.46). Gregory had the emperor's authority to protect the poor in his stead. Now it was up to Rome to seek justice and to take on the local strongman in a distant province. In addition to such responsibilities, Gregory's involvement with the military and problems of defense is remarkable (e.g., *Epp.* 2.4, 2.10, 2.27, 2.28). In a letter to the military troops in Naples, Gregory commended them for accepting his appointment of the tribune Constantius to command the city's garrison. The letter is remarkable for revealing, once again, how deeply Gregory valued submission to authority:

> The highest military glory among other good rewards is this, to show obedience to the holy commonwealth through services to it, and to submit to whatever has been commanded for its advantage. Just as we have learned even now that you have pledged allegiance to the letter in which we appointed *vir magnificus* Tribune Constantius to command the city's garrison, it is evident that you also show obedience conforming to military oaths of allegiance. For that reason, in our present writing, we take care to warn you to show total obedience to him as you have done so far for the interests of our most serene Lordship, the Emperor Maurice, and for preserving the city; thus, whatever is recognized as being well done you may continue to do through the present emergency. (*Ep.* 2.47)

Here, Gregory acted with all the authority of an imperial official commanding the troops. Although surprising to us, his actions seemed completely routine. He addressed the clergy and people of Nepi similarly: "We have entrusted the care and concern of your city to the *uir clarissimus* Leontius, the bearer of this letter, to show vigilance in all matters and so arrange by himself what he recognizes as pertinent to your advantage and to that of the commonwealth" (*Ep.* 2.10). Gregory was even able to send a tribune and imperial soldiers against the Istrians, in opposition to imperial policy (*Ep.* 1.16). Just as Gregory commanded the troops, so he was their paymaster (*Ep.* 5.39). His independent negotiations with the Lombards provoked a nasty response from the emperor, who ridiculed Gregory as a fool for negotiating a peace with Ariulf, Duke of Spoleto, who had extorted "protection money" for Rome's safety (*Ep.* 5.36). Since the empire failed to defend Rome and southern Italy, Gregory's actions were justified, even if the ransom brought less than two years' peace.

If the church assumed secular power by default, Gregory conversely expected the secular authority sometimes to take up roles that the church had not fulfilled. Writing to Scholasticus, the governor of Campania, Gregory directed that because Naples had no priest, Scholasticus should publish a decree and convoke leaders and citizens of the city to elect a new bishop (*Ep.* 3.15). On other occasions, the secular authority was more of a partner. Gregory informed the subdeacon Antonius that Marcellus, the proconsul of Dalmatia, would help him to oversee the election of a new bishop for Salona (*Ep.* 3.22). In some cases, the entanglement bordered on the risible. Theodore, the notorious Duke of Sardinia, was protecting Donatus, one of his officials, who had taken legal possession of an abbess's convent. Gregory commanded the Duke to make Donatus submit to a judgment of arbitration with the abbess so that "whatever is decided by the verdict of the judges may be put into effect and ascribed to the justice of the law and not to a work of power" (*Ep.* 1.46).

Gregory routinely asked secular officials to support the church in one way or another. He asked the *praetor* of Sicily to make certain that Citonatus supplied the church with the grain he had promised (*Ep.* 1.2), and later to cooperate with the bishop of Tyndari in bringing idol-worshippers, heretics, and lapsed Christians back to the church, some of whom had the protection of local strongmen (*Ep.* 3.59). What really mattered here were ties of friendship and patronage, which throughout Italy cut across the distinction between clergy and laity. Gregory asked Romanus the exarch to support his candidate Constantius, bishop-elect of Milan: "[W]hether or not he has been consecrated ... provide him with your support where it is necessary, with the favor of justice" (*Ep.* 3.31). In another act of patronage, here glossed as Christian charity, Gregory called upon the Pretorian prefect George to "employ piety with compassion" and to earn eternal reward by helping Armenius, an impoverished *uir magnificus* (*Ep.* 3.28).

Gregory's understanding of the church's aims did not match the emperor Maurice's view of the empire's needs. His rhetoric of concord was more wishful thinking than practical reality, for their priorities of defense differed. Ravenna was the seat of the Byzantine exarch, and the capital that had to be defended was Constantinople, whose church was led by the Ecumenical Patriarch – not Rome, not the pope. Maurice did not want an alliance between Rome and the Lombards, much less with the Franks. Gregory's idea of concord meant compelling unity. He sought Maurice's help against the Donatists, complaining that officials did not enforce the laws already in the books (*Epp.* 4.32, 1.72, 1.75, 1.82, 2.39, 4.35, 6.36, 6.62). The Istrians were also targets.[15] But Maurice did not want to disturb the peace by repressing the Donatists or the Istrians. Emperor and pope took the opposing sides on candidates for the see of Salona. Imperial power also overshadowed papal authority in the affairs of the Illyrian church. Whatever concord existed between emperor and pope had to be renegotiated continuously.

GOVERNING THE PATRIMONY AND JUDGMENTS FROM THE EPISCOPAL COURT OF ROME

A majority of the letters in Gregory's register are connected to the papal patrimony in some way. Two basic types are relevant for the study of law: (1) correspondence with rectors who (along with their staffs) administered the papal patrimony, and (2) archival copies of legal decisions given to "the bearer of this letter" – that is, appellants who had sought Gregory's intervention in various kinds of disputes or causes.

The first group dealing with administration of the patrimony illustrates Gregory's fundamental commitment to good government – to honesty and accountability – and highlights the consistency of his beliefs and actions, even in the face of obstacles. Rectors swore an oath on St. Peter's tomb, vowing to defend the interests of the church and protect the poor. Gregory honored these solemn vows when stating that the purpose of governing the patrimony was "not so much to promote the worldly interest of the church as to relieve the poor in their distress and especially to protect them from oppression by anyone" (*Ep.* 1.53). In fact, Gregory ordered rectors to take positive actions: "Before everything we want you to attend to this with care, lest an unjust burden be placed on them in exacting taxes. But if you discover such burdens anywhere, cancel them and establish new and fair ones" (*Ep.* 1.42). In hard times, this could mean that inhabitants "should pay only what they could afford to pay" (*Ep.* 9.205).

When rectors undertook the sacred vow at Peter's tomb, pledging to defend the church and care for the needy, they contracted to suffer Peter's vengeance should

[15] R. A. Markus, *Gregory the Great and His World* (Cambridge: Cambridge University Press, 1997), 138–39.

they fail to keep their promises. While such fear of divine punishment (presumably) guaranteed good behavior, Gregory prudently augmented divine oversight with human vigilance. In nagging letters, he worries about the rectors and their staffs being vulnerable to bribery and intimidation. Worse, avarice often drives them to despoil inhabitants of land and possessions, betraying their vows. Not only does he monitor the rectors closely – demanding reports, sending directives, and enforcing discipline – most important, rectors had to submit accounts annually to the papacy. This assured that human eyes checked for losses and signs of mismanagement or corruption and kept a written record of changes (*Ep.* 13.37). This centralization inhibited the centripetal tendency toward autonomy and anarchy typical of estate managers dominating peripheral areas. This record-keeping – the hallmark of a bureaucracy – laid the foundation for the papacy's future prosperity. It could benefit individuals as well. Lest farmers be overtaxed, Gregory orders Peter the subdeacon to "keep secure accounts of their payments and so stamp them" with the amount each owed in taxes, without any additional charges (*Ep.* 1.42). Henceforward farmers would pay only what they owed.

A blueprint for governing the patrimony can be found in Gregory's long letter of May 591 addressed to Peter the subdeacon, rector of the Sicilian patrimony (*Ep.* 1.42). In it, Gregory outlines policies having the force of law. (Rectors had police and judicial powers, e.g., *Ep.* 9.30.) Fairness in taxation is Gregory's chief concern; taxes are numerous and proliferate freely. Gregory seeks to eliminate, combine, simplify, or lessen the burden (as in the case of the marriage tax). Although Gregory's concern for the overtaxed is genuine, the church as an institution benefited from relieving taxes. Gregory feared that if farmers were crushed by taxes, they would leave the land.

Gregory has other policies for Peter to implement. Farmers are battered by fluctuations in the grain market, becoming vulnerable to moneylenders. Gregory attempts to curb the abuses of moneylenders indirectly by stabilizing the market, chiefly through the storage or release of grain, but also by deferring taxes and dues in kind. To protect families, Gregory forbids rectors from seizing property as punishment for crimes, or reclaiming church land cultivated by farmers, as they lay dying. Hence forward, either the parents or sons could inherit the land. One directive is noteworthy for its revelation of systemic abuse. If a steward is deprived of a possession he has unjustly taken from a farmer, those (clergy) judging the steward cannot keep the property, but must return it to the farmer. Toward the end of *Ep.* 1.42, a testy Gregory refers to Peter "not as your Experience, but as your Negligence." If Peter did not deserve the sarcasm, other rectors doubtlessly did.

In governing the patrimony (as in other matters), Gregory recognized the limits of the church's power and the need to cultivate support from the community to carry out the church's programs. Because nobles and the *praetor* mistreated the poor in Sicily, Gregory charges Peter with rectifying the situation; but he also counsels Peter to act with discretion, using a formula of moderation characteristic of his way of thinking: "Be submissive to them when they act rightly, but stand up in opposition when they act wrongly. But act so that neither your humility is lax, nor your authority unbending, but let justice season your humility and humility soften your justice" (*Ep. Appendix* 1). With such restraint, change can only be incremental.

The second group of letters records Gregory's judgments on a range of complaints appellants brought before the papal court from near and far. Typical complaints involve the usurpation of property or privileges by a relative, neighbor, local strongman, or agent of the church. Other cases deal with marriage and family: adultery, desertion, problems of wills and inheritance. Gregory hears the appellants' complaints and sends them home with official letters recommending a judgment, pending investigation of the case by the local authority (lay or ecclesiastical) whom Gregory selects. To settle a case, Gregory sometimes requests that the local authority simply undertake a thorough investigation of the appellant's complaints. If the appellant is vindicated, he or she is to be indemnified as Gregory recommends, according to "law" and "justice." Alternatively, especially for major cases, Gregory calls on the local authority to select men to establish a court to hear the case and to arbitrate, as he wrote in *Ep.* 8.17: "Disputes should be settled by God-fearing men chosen by both parties." Generally, the case ended there, though in especially important cases, Gregory asked to review the decision of the court. But this is rare. His letters end more frequently with the hope never to hear complaints about the matter again (*Epp.* 3.45, 9.90).

A substantial number of complaints involved the church. Gregory issued a decree forbidding the church from affixing titles on any property in the city or countryside, anathematizing those who attempted to do so (*Ep. Appendix* 1). He reprimands Januarius, bishop of Sardinia, for his avarice in charging for burials and "making profit from grief" (*Ep.* 8.35): a clear case of simony (the purchase or bartering of spiritual things for personal gain). He chastises him also for plowing the fields of Natalis and removing the boundary stones, on a Sunday, no less: "Realize that you have undertaken the care not of things, but of men's souls" (*Ep.* 9.11).The deacon Cyprian cheated a farmer out of three years' wages (*Ep.* 9.43). Pending an investigation, the church will recompense the farmer. Indeed, Gregory's response to property usurpation by the church is consistent: His agents must investigate and return any usurped property. Gregory stated the principle at stake in a letter to bishop Boniface of Reggio: "Just as the church ought not lose its own property, so it should not usurp, with a burning rapacity, the property of others ... For it is very wrong to keep the property of others contrary to church policy" (*Ep.* 3.43).

That the church should not lose property was ordered in the *Codex Justinianus* 1.2.21 and Justinian's *Novellae* 7.46.65.120. The alienation of church property except for the redemption of captives was forbidden. Gregory not only did this (*Epp.* 3.7, 7.13), he made other exceptions for the use (and alienation) of church property for the sake of charity. Secular law is trumped by divine mandates. In the above case of Stephania (*Ep.* 9.48), charity prevails over secular law. Not only did the uncertainty of the title dictate kindness instead of strictness, Gregory was "moved by a widow's tears," and argued that "a strict judgment should at times be moderated when respect for mercy [*misericordia*] calls for it." We should not seem to "follow the path of severity more than embrace the cause of *pietas*." To do the right thing by divine law meant compassion, kindness, mercy – even suspending written law, rather than enforcing it inflexibly, without the exercise of discretion. Recall that in *Ep.* 1.42 above Gregory allowed church land to be inherited by the sons or parents of the men who farmed it. He also forgave debts owed to the church. The sons of Urbicus, the defender from Tivoli, are liable for their father's debt, but they are unable to pay it. Gregory explains that it is his duty to advise orphans and to help them. The church is responsible for alleviating their miseries. He forgives their debts "out of consideration for *pietas*" (*Ep.* 3.21). Gregory often gives grants of property, money, and occasionally goods (e.g., blankets, linens, silver dishes) liberally at the church's expense. After all, charity is the sharing of goods among the members of Christ's body; and to feed the hungry and shelter the stranger is to do the same to Christ, as he quoted Mt 25:40: "Whatsoever you have done to one of the least of my brothers, you have done to me" (*Ep.* 12.2, *Mor.* 16.2.2, *HEv.* 2.20.12).

Gregory was especially solicitous of those who had served the church or taken religious vows. A sense of reciprocity (justice and fairness) obliges him. He gives a slave to Theodore, his eloquent and impoverished counselor, explaining that those "exerting themselves in ecclesiastical services deserve the pleasure of ecclesiastical remuneration, so that those who of their own volition subject themselves to voluntary hardships of obedience, deserve to be repaid in our dispensations" (*Ep.* 3.18). Remuneration is also pragmatic. He advises Gratiosus the subdeacon, "We should take care that hardship does not make those who have chosen religious vocations inactive or undermine their strength," ordering him to give the patrician abbess Flora considerable property for a convent (*Ep.* 3.17). He told his subdeacon Anthelm to help the poor nuns of Nola: "[F]rom the precept of God, it is fitting that we help them and relieve their want as far as we can, with the Lord's giving" (*Ep.* 1.23). Indeed, St. Peter supported the "three thousand nuns in Rome found listed in the census" (*Ep.* 7.23). Finally, he sought to secure the independence of religious foundations, defending nuns from the interference of clergy as well as of laymen (*Epp.* 1.46, 3.58, 9.54), and defending monasteries from the same threats (*Ep.* 8.17).

For Gregory, care for the poor and relief of the oppressed far transcends any need to defend the church's property, even though that was sanctioned by law. Charity is the church's identity (that *compago corporis Christi* and *campago caritatis*) such that to spend the church's money is to take from funds set aside for the poor (cf. *Ep.* 3.55). Everything is rightly theirs. Bishops should not involve themselves in secular cases *except* to defend the poor (*Ep. Appendix* 1). Gregory's charity became legendary. In John the Deacon's time, records existed listing recipients with details of their subvention (*Vita Greg.* 2.30). His generosity was such that critics claimed he had bankrupted the papacy (cf. Io. Diac. *Vita Greg.* 4.5; Paul Diac. *Vita Greg.* 29).

THE CONDITION OF SLAVES AND THE STATUS OF JEWS

In Gregory's day, slaves were chattel, wealth, even a kind of currency. Gregory gave several slaves owned by the church as gifts to friends, and as charity to the needy (*Epp.* 3.18, 3.35, 7.27, 9.99). But the church could buffer the lives of slaves. Gregory ransomed captive slaves, just as he did citizens (*Epp.* 6.32, 7.21). He defended them from abusive owners, sometimes granting them limited asylum in churches, or interceding with their masters (*Epp.* 9.210, 1.53). Gregory treats their unions (*contubernia*) with the same solicitude for stability as he does the marriages of citizens.[16] The church could also be the agent of change. Gregory twice ordered the purchase of slaves, whom he would have converted as their *dominus.* (Indeed, he sanctioned the punishment of slaves who refused conversion: see *Ep.* 9.205.) In Gaul, "Anglish boys" were sent to monasteries to be educated, perhaps to return to England as missionaries (*Ep.* 6.10). The church also bought pagan slaves in Sardinia to help serve the poor and the church (*Ep.* 9.124). For slaves, conversion to monastic life meant freedom from their Christian owners after two or three years as a postulant, though not citizenship. Slaves needed their owner's permission to enter the monastic life, which church-slaves obtained readily. But they could be returned to their masters if their conversions were deemed insincere. Interestingly, on the one occasion when Gregory manumitted two slaves, this was so that one could take monastic vows, while the other was to serve as a notary. He celebrated their citizenship, as if rewarding them (*Ep.* 6.10). The church could compensate Christian owners for their losses. Gregory paid Felix to free a slave who wanted to become a nun (*Ep.* 3.39). He also repaid the debt of the deacon Evangelus, a former slave who had borrowed to buy his own freedom to serve the church (*Ep.* 3.40).

The law forbade ownership of Christian slaves by non-Christians, who might sell them to Christian owners. This prohibition affected Jews greatly, since they could not expect the church to recompense their losses, although sometimes the church did (*Epp.* 4.9, 7.21, cf. 6.30). Gregory's policies were mixed in general. As noted earlier, he affirmed that Jews were permitted to live under Roman law without interference (*Epp.* 2.45, 8.25). That said, his attitude toward the Jews was ambivalent, as was Augustine's. On one hand, unconverted Jews were the enemies of Christ. On the other hand, they were the "forerunners," essential to the divine dispensation. As God's elect in the Old Testament, the Jews' history and prophecies are types foreshadowing those of the Christian elect of the New Testament. Because their prophecies of the Messiah had been fulfilled in Christ, Jews bore witness to the truth of Christianity. Indeed, the conversion of the Jews would finalize God's plan for humanity. Being a part of God's plan, Jews were to be protected. Gregory ordered the subdeacon Anthemius to assist them "with reasonable moderation," lest they suffer from want of food (*Ep.* 4.31). Gregory sought to protect Jewish property. Jewish creditors were not to be defrauded of debts (*Ep.* 1.42). When the defensor Candidus

16 Adam Serfass, "Slavery and Pope Gregory the Great," JECS 14 (2006): 77–103, at 89–92.

seized the ship of Nostamnus, a Sicilian Jew, and imprisoned him to pay a debt, Gregory ordered an investigation. Nostamnus recovered his freedom thanks to Gregory's intervention (*Ep.* 9.40). Gregory rebuked the Bishop of Naples for interfering with the Jews' cult. Christians ought to treat Jews with kind words, not with harsh actions, if they hoped to convert them: "Do not, in future, therefore, allow the Jews to be molested in the performance of their services. Let them have full liberty to observe and keep all their festivals and holy days, as both they and their fathers have done for so long" (*Ep.* 15.13). Gregory ordered the bishop of Palermo to cease consecrating for Christian worship places claimed by Jews, to hold a court with judges from both sides, and to send him any disputed cases (*Ep.* 8.25). Because the bishop had already consecrated buildings, Gregory ordered him to recompense the Jews for their property, including books and ornaments (*Ep.* 9.38). Gregory's reasoning would prove historic: "Just as the Jews ought not have the freedom to dare to do in their synagogues more than the law permits them, so they should not sustain any prejudice in what has been permitted them" (*Ep.* 8.25). This sentence would later become the opening of the papal bull, *Sicut Judaeis*, of Gregory IX (1235), which entered canon law as a *constitution* (a general statement of policy).[17] The bull was reiterated by popes from the twelfth to the fifteenth centuries.

Still, it is curious that in one letter (*Ep.* 1.42), Gregory forbade Jews from being oppressed or persecuted "contrary to the order of reason," implying that an oppression "within the order of reason" was possible. Several restrictions suggest this. "But just as they are permitted to live under Roman laws, with justice assenting, so that they may carry out their own activities as they wish, without hindrance, nevertheless, they are not permitted to own Christian slaves" (*Ep.* 2.45). In another letter (*Ep.* 3.37), Gregory asked Libertinus, *praetor* of Sicily, to free Christians enslaved to the Jew Nasas, who had made them worship at the altar of St. Helias, and to punish him severely. Libertinus must act, "lest the Christian religion be polluted by subjection to Jews." This liberation of Christian slaves entailed economic losses for Jews. Nor was this the only limit imposed. Under civil law, Jews were taxed heavily and excluded from military and civilian offices, and they were punished more strictly than Christians, especially for "insults" against Christians. Nor was the practice of their religion "unhindered." Jews who had converted Christians to Judaism were to be punished (*Ep.* 3.37). Gregory ordered that a Jewish synagogue within hearing distance of a church should be compelled to move, although the bishop was to bear the cost of a new synagogue (*Ep.* 2.45).

The judgments in Gregory's letters are those of an active pope serving the church in the world. They show him to be careful, balanced, and thorough in his attempt to find justice for appellants to the Holy See. Following Roman procedure, he called for an inquiry and the establishment of a court of judges chosen by both sides. In this,

[17] See Solomon Grayzel, "The Papal Bull *Sicut Judaeis*," in M. Ben-Horin et al. (eds.), *Studies and Essays in Honor of Abraham A. Neuman* (Leiden: Brill, 1962), 243–80.

he was efficient and pragmatic. Despite his absolute allegiance to the church – his very participation in it – Gregory was scrupulous in investigating charges of abuse by the church's representatives, and firm in redressing any wrongdoing. Just as he admits St. Peter's weakness in denying Christ (*HEv.* 2.21.4), so he was willing to investigate the failures of his see. More often than not, Gregory acted on the advice that he gave to Anthelm, the subdeacon: that the purpose of governing the patrimony is less the church's worldly interest than relief of the poor and protection of the oppressed.

CONCLUSION

Gregory's contributions to Western legal tradition are significant for his emphasis on judicial restraint, moderation, and the exercise of discretion, all of which allowed him to advance Christian values of mercy, charity, and kindness over strict enforcement of existing law. Discretion gave judges the option of leniency and flexibility in sentencing an accused, instead of mandating severity and rigor in interpreting the law. It encouraged innovation, acceptance, and adaptation to change and so looked toward the future. Debates about judicial discretion continue to this day in controversies over mandatory legal sentencing and the "three strikes and you're out" policies that disproportionately affect minorities and the poor. He believed that if a case were doubtful, judges would be wrong to pass a judgment that was certain and definitive. Going further, Gregory counseled judges to give the accused the benefit of the doubt in uncertainty, even to think the best of the accused, and to act with kindness and mercy. Discretion encouraged relativism as well as restraint. By making judgments fitting and appropriate to individual circumstances, Gregory allowed judges to improvise. All crimes were not equal; some were minor, others serious. The social status of the accused mattered, too, for all the accused were not of the same rank. Those in positions of authority were all the more culpable for having abused that privilege, setting a bad example for their subjects. Gregory insisted that judges consider the motives of the accused, as well as the social and economic disadvantages that shaped their behavior. Poverty and abandonment are mitigating circumstances. It was one thing to steal from greed and another to steal from poverty and want. So, too, the previous virtue of an accused's life had to be counted in his favor when weighing judgment against him. Finally, Gregory was important for affirming, within limits, Roman laws of noninterference with the Jewish community, which became papal policy for the next thousand years. In urging the exercise of discretion, Gregory showed his sympathy for the poor and the weak: for those whose social status prejudiced their access to legal protection. Whether orphans, minors, widows, the elderly, nuns and monks in seclusion, or "the little guy" facing a greater power – even, or perhaps especially the church – all could expect a fair hearing from Gregory.

RECEPTION

Gregory's reception in the canonical tradition is second only to Augustine's. Along with other fathers of the early church, Gregory first appears in an Irish collection of canons, the *Collectio Hibernensis* (c. 700). Pope Hadrian I (r. 772–795) collected Gregory's letters. He also sent a sacramentary to Charlemagne, identified as Gregorian (*a sancto Gregorio papa Romano editum*). This was known as the *Gregorianum* for centuries, but it is now called the *Hadrianum*, or *Gregorianum-Hadrianum*. It contains eighty-two prayers based on Gregory's writings. A canon law collection known as the *Collectio Anselmo dedicata*, dating from the last quarter of the ninth century, used Gregory's letters from Hadrian's collection.[18] Between 912 and 930 in southern Italy appeared the *Sententiae ex codice qui appellatur Regestrum* [sic.] *Epistolarum S. Gregorii papae* and the *Sententiae ex libris moralibus S. Gregorii*, which contains the Roman Council of 595. Abbo of Fleury's *Collectio canonum* (988/96) includes extensive material from Gregory's letters, including the *Responsiones ad Augustinum*. Although Burchard of Worms (d. 1025) took some of his Gregorian material from Regino of Prüm's *Libri duo de synodalibus causis* (c. 906), he also mined Gregory independently, and he had great influence on later canonists. Book 19 of Burchard's *Decretum*, on penance, and book 20, on doctrine and eschatology, use Gregory extensively. Much of Burchard's *Decretum* found its way into the *Decretum* of Ivo of Chartres (d. 1115), who has thirty-eight passages from Gregory, most of them taken from Burchard, although the *Panormia*, compiled from Ivo's *Decretum*, reduces Gregory to a single text (*Ep.* 1.10). The reforms of Pope Gregory VII (1073–1084) during the investiture controversy witnessed further use of Gregory I. Very important in this context is a work by Alger of Liège, the *Liber de misericordia et iustitia* (composed between 1095 and 1121), on which Gratian drew.

The vulgate (augmented) version of Gratian's *Decretum* includes 350 excerpts from Gregory, of which 263 are from his letters. (In comparison, there are 497 excerpts from Augustine in the *Decretum*.) Gaudemet divides the citations of Gregory in the *Decretum* into three classes, respectively on the sources of law, on monastic law, and on matrimonial law.[19] The *Decretum* cites Gregory on doubt and the lesser of two evils (as noted above); on the exercise of power (discipline vs. mercy, gentleness vs. severity, pride and arrogance, obedience owed superiors, etc.); on lying, usury, heresy, sin, penitence, and damnation; on the sacrament of baptism; and on fasting.

[18] Jean-Claude Besse, *Histoire des textes du droit de l'Église au Moyen-Âge, de Denys à Gratien. Collectio Anselmo Dedicata. Étude et textes* (Paris: Librairies techniques, 1960). See pp. 52–56 for a list of manuscripts of collected canons citing Gregory.

[19] Jean Gaudemet, "L'héritage de Grégoire le Grand chez les canonistes médiévaux," in *Gregorio Magno e il suo tempo* (Rome: Institutum Patristicum Augustinianum, 1991), 2:199–21, at 211.

EDITIONS OF GREGORY'S WORKS, WITH ABBREVIATIONS

Letters (Epistulae) [*Epp.*]: Editions: (A) Dag Norberg, *S. Gregorii Magni Registrum Epistularum*, CCL 140–140A. (B) Paul Ewald and Ludwig Hartmann, *Gregorii I papae Registrum epistularum* I–II, MGH Epist. 1–2 (1887–91, 1892–1899). English translations: (A) James Barmby, *Selected Epistles of Gregory the Great*, NPNF, 2nd series, vols. 12–13 (1894, 1898; repr. 1979, 1983). (B) John R. C. Martyn, *The Letters of Gregory the Great*, Mediaeval Sources in Translation 40, 3 vols. (Toronto: PIMS, 2004).

The Book of Pastoral Rule (Regula pastoralis) [*Rpast.*]: Edition with French translation: Floribert Rommel (ed.) and Charles Morel (trans.), Grégoire le Grand, *Règle Pastorale*, 2 vols., SC 381, 382. English translations: (A) Henry Davis, Gregory the Great, *Pastoral Care*, ACW 12. (B) George E. Demacopoulos, *The Book of Pastoral Rule: St. Gregory the Great*, Popular Patristics Series 34 (Crestwood, NY: St. Vladimir's Seminary Press, 2007).

Dialogues (Dialogorum libri IV de miraculis patrum italicorum) [*Dial.*]: Edition with French translation: Adalbert de Vogüé and Paul Antin, Grégoire le Grand, *Dialogues*, 3 vols., SC 251, 260, 265. English translation: Odo Zimmerman, St. Gregory the Great, *Dialogues*, Fathers of the Church 39 (New York, 1959).

Moral Reflections on the Book of Job (Moralia in Iob) [*Mor.*]: Edition: Marcus Adriaen, S. Gregorii Magni *Moralia in Iob*, CCL 143, 143A, 143B. Edition with French translation: *Morales sur Job*, SC 32 bis, 212, 221, 476, 525, 538 (several editors and translators). English translations: (A) *Morals on the Book of Job by Saint Gregory the Great*, Library of the Fathers, 4 vols. (Oxford, 1844; reprinted 2012). (B) Brian Kerns, Gregory the Great, *Moral Reflections on the Book of Job*, Books 1–22, Cistercian Studies 249, 257–259 (Collegeville, MN, 2014-). Series still in progress.

Homilies on the Prophet Ezekiel (Homiliae in Hiezechihelem prophetam) [*HEz.*]: Edition: Marcus Adriaen, Sancti Gregorii Magni *Homiliae in Hiezechielem prophetam*, CCL 142. English translation: Theodosia Grey, *The Homilies of Saint Gregory the Great on the Book of the Prophet Ezekiel* (Etna, CA: Center for Traditionalist Orthodox Studies, 1990).

Gospel Homilies (Homiliae in evangelia) [*HEv.*]: Edition: Raymond Étaix, Gregorius Magnus, *Homiliae in Evangelia*, CCL 141.

FURTHER READING

Blumenthal, Uta-Renate. "The Papacy and Canon Law in the Eleventh-Century Reform." *Catholic Historical Review* 84.2 (1998): 201–18.

Brown, T. S. *Gentlemen and Officers: Imperial Administration and Aristocratic Power in Byzantine Italy A.D. 554–800*. London: British School at Rome, 1984.

Cabassut, André. "Discrétion." *Dictionnaire de spiritualité ascetique et mystique, Doctrine et Histoire*. 1957, 3:1311–30.

Cohen, Jeremy. *Living Letters of the Law: Ideas of the Jew in Medieval Christianity*. Berkeley: University of California Press, 1999.

Dal Santo, Matthew. "Gregory the Great, the Empire and the Emperor." In Neil and Dal Santo (eds.). *A Companion to Gregory the Great. Brill's Companions to the Christian Tradition*. Leiden: Brill, 2013, 57–81.

Damizia, Giuseppe. "Il *Registrum Epistolarum* di S. Gregorio Magno ed il *Corpus Juris Civilis*." *Benedictina* 2 (1948): 195–226.

Gaudemet, Jean. "L'héritage de Grégoire le Grand chez les canonistes médiévaux." In *Gregorio Magno e il suo tempo*. Rome: Institutum Patristicum Augustinianum, 1991, 2:199–221.

Giordano, Lisania. "*Lex fori* e *lex Dei* nel *Registrum Epistolarum* di Gregorio Magno." In Claudio Leonardi (ed.). *Gregorio Magno e le origini dell'Europa*. Firenze: SISMEL, 2014, 259–68.

Grayzel, Solomon. "The Papal Bull *Sicut Judaeis*." In Meir Ben-Horin et al. (eds.). *Studies and Essays in Honor of Abraham A. Neuman*. Leiden: Brill, 1962, 243–80.

Gregorio Magno e il suo tempo. 2 vols. Rome: Institutum Patristicum Augustinianum, 1991.

Hipshon, David. "Gregory the Great's 'Political Thought.'" JEH 53.3 (2002): 439–53.

Neil, Bronwen. "The Papacy in the Age of Gregory the Great." In Bronwen Neil and Matthew Dal Santo (eds.). *A Companion to Gregory the Great*. Leiden: Brill, 2013, 3–27.

Neil, Bronwen, and Matthew Dal Santo (eds.). *A Companion to Gregory the Great*. Brill's Companions to the Christian Tradition. Leiden: Brill, 2013.

Pietri, Charles, and Luce Pietri. "Église universelle et *Respublica christiana* selon Grégoire Le Grand." In *Memoriam sanctorum venerantes: Miscellanea in onore di Monsignor Victor Saxer*. Città del Vaticano: Pontificio Istituto di archeologia cristiana, 1992, 721–39.

Serfass, Adam. "Slavery and Pope Gregory the Great." *Journal of Early Christian Studies* 14.1 (2006): 77–103.

Straw, Carole. "Gregory's Politics: Theory and Practice." In *Gregorio Magno e il suo Tempo*. Rome: Institutum Patristicum Augustinianum, 1991, 1:47–63.

Straw, Carole. *Gregory the Great: Perfection in Imperfection*. Berkeley: University of California Press, 1988.

Wasselynck, René. "La présence des *Moralia* de s. Grégoire le Grand dans les ouvrages de morale du XIIe siècle." *Recherches de théologie ancienne et médiévale* 35 (1968): 197–240, and 36 (1969): 31–45.

Wasselynck, René. "Présence de saint Grégoire le Grand dans les recueils canoniques (X^{e}-XIIe s.)." *Mélanges de science religieuse* 22 (1965): 205–19.

18

Isidore of Seville

Luca Loschiavo

AN IMPORTANT FAMILY, A DUTY TO FULFILL

Archbishop of Seville from 602 until his death in 636, Isidore was a dominant figure in the Visigothic kingdom of Toledo as well as one of the most representative and influential intellectuals of the early Middle Ages. Last of four siblings (all canonized as saints), he was born into an important Hispano-Roman and Catholic family between 556 and 571.[1] His place of birth could have been Cartagena or, more likely, Seville, where his family moved either around 560 or perhaps around 554, when his father Severianus might have left Cartagena under suspicion of collusion with the Byzantine army, which was at that time seeking to capture southern Spain.

Soon orphaned, Isidore grew up under the care of his much older brother Leander (born c. 534) and his sister Florentina. Between the end of the sixth and the beginning of the seventh century, the Visigothic kingdom was in ferment as King Liuvigild recaptured a large part of the territory lost to the Byzantines and strengthened the kingdom. Leander was destined to become a very prominent figure in political and ecclesiastical life. Metropolitan bishop of Seville after 579, he worked together with the Merovingian wife of Hermenegild, son and heir of the king, to convert the latter from Arianism to Catholicism. Exiled by Liuvigild, who aspired to unify Spain under Arianism, Leander spent some years in Constantinople, where he formed a close friendship with the future Pope Gregory the Great. After the death of Liuvigild, Leander returned to Seville and worked to convert the new king, Reccared, and the entire Gothic people from Arian to catholic (i.e., pro-Nicene) Christianity. Leander's efforts were rewarded in 589, when he presided over the Third Council of Toledo, during which the realm became officially catholic.

Throughout his life, Isidore never ceased to consider his brother as exemplary.[2] Leander not only played a key role in the ecclesiastical education and cultural formation of the young Isidore but also instilled in him the consciousness that he

[1] This date depends on the fact that when Isidore became bishop (602), canon law required bishops to be between thirty and forty-five years of age at the time of their election.

[2] Isidore sketches a portrait of Leander in ch. 41 of his *De viris illustribus*.

had a duty to fulfill. It was now time for the Hispano-Roman population to abandon any nostalgia for the Roman Empire and to begin to cooperate with the Visigothic monarchy in the construction of a strong, unitary state. Visigothic Spain had to become a concrete example of *respublica Christiana*: a realm in which monarchy and church supported each other, and where the king would heed the advice of his bishops. To realize this ideal and to win for itself such an influential role, however, the church needed to create the appropriate conditions. First, the church itself had to be reformed, and the cultural level of the clergy improved. Second, the secular elites of the kingdom had to be won over to the new project: Ethnic barriers had to be overcome, and the ruling classes had to be persuaded to come together under that common ideal and to become aware of their role.

Isidore devoted his life to this goal. Like his brother Leander, whom he succeeded as metropolitan bishop of Seville in 602, he played an important role in the kingdom's politics. Isidore was very close to King Sisebut (r. 612–620) and promoted lively conciliar activity. He presided over the provincial Councils of Seville II and III (in 619 and 624, respectively) and over the national Council of Toledo IV (in 633), which affirmed the elective character of the Spanish monarchy and promoted the liturgical unity of the national church. The bishops deemed it essential to standardize Christian rituals and bring them under the control of a central ecclesiastical authority: not only to avoid strife between local communities but also, and more importantly, to ensure the very survival of the kingdom.

AN IMPRESSIVE OUTPUT

Isidore's enduring fame – in medieval Europe as well as today – depends chiefly on his tireless work as a writer. Thanks to contemporaneous testimonies,[3] we know that almost seventeen titles are authentic works of Isidore. He also wrote numerous letters. Some other works should probably be attributed to him as well, although his role in the composition of the first recension of the important canon law compilation known as *Collectio Hispana* or *Isidoriana* is still disputed. The bishop touches on a wide variety of subjects in his writings, from theology to history, from liturgy to the secular sciences, from ascetic theology to both divine and secular law. We can easily suppose that he had at his disposal a vast library, rich in secular and religious texts, for the most part the legacy of his brother and predecessor, Leander. Unfortunately, because Isidore followed the custom of Late Antiquity in only rarely mentioning the authors he used, we can only speculate about the number and kind

[3] The first is that of his disciple Braulio of Saragossa (d. 651), and the second comes from Ildefons of Toledo (d. 667). See the editorial introduction to Andrew Fear and Jamie Wood (eds.), *Isidore of Seville and his Reception in the Early Middle Ages: Transmitting and Transforming Knowledge* (Amsterdam: Amsterdam University Press, 2016), 13–17, for the complete list of works mentioned by Braulio, with indication of accessible editions and translations in modern languages.

of books in his library. The question of Isidore's sources is indeed among the favorite topics in modern Isidorean scholarship.[4]

Isidore never forgot for whom he was writing. His priorities were usually (a) religious unity under the catholic faith, (b) collaboration with the secular authority, and (c) the cultural rebirth of Spain. If we consider that his temperament was not particularly speculative, it is not surprising that he was especially attracted by moral theology, for this easily translates into practically oriented rules of conduct. Typically, Isidore would present a dogma with clarity and certitude while avoiding further discussion and investigation. Less interested in debates about orthodoxy,[5] he was much more committed to indicating to the ecclesiastical and secular societies of his time how to observe the truth of God (*Lex Dei*) in practice. Isidore was first and foremost a theologian of individual and social duties. From this point of view, the most significant work and probably his masterpiece is the *Sentences* (*Sententiarum libri III*), in which it is possible to recognize a program for a Christian life dedicated to the community of all baptized people.[6]

Yet it is only when we consider his writings on secular aspects of society that we can fully appreciate the importance of Isidore's contribution to the Visigothic kingdom. In view of the profound cultural renaissance that he intended to promote, the first of his primary tasks was the retrieval and transmission of ancient knowledge. Aiming to show how useful secular knowledge could be, Isidore was nevertheless keenly aware that the concepts and information to be passed to his contemporaries should not be too vast. He therefore made huge and constant efforts at summarizing classical materials. This conciseness (Isidore speaks of *brevitas*) was useful in maintaining the interest of the reader, but Isidore intended to do more than to avoid overburdening his readers with the subtleties of the ancients. The second primary task consisted in selecting the contents of the exposition. For the bishop of Seville, to offer the best of secular (i.e., classical) culture also meant adapting the knowledge received from the past to serve a well-ordered Christian education, unblemished by sin. Thus, his effort at simplification also served to eradicate any seeds of doubt from the reader's mind: Whatever might tempt or disturb the Christian conscience was best avoided.

Sometimes our Spanish metropolitan bishop wrote in open support of the crown. With his *Historia Gothorum* (after 624), for example, Isidore made the first attempt to

4 The following are fundamental: J. Fontaine, *Isidore de Séville et la culture classique de l'Espagne wisigothique*, 3 vols. (Paris: Études Augustiniennes, 1959 and 1983); and F. Gasti, "Fonti letterarie et fonti 'tecniche' nelle Etimologiae di Isidoro di Siviglia," *Sileno* 42.1 (2016): 21–39.

5 Nevertheless, Isidore wrote a catalogue of heresies (*De haeresibus*; AD 612–15) and attacked the Jewish religion (*De fide catholica ex veteri et novo Testamento contra Judaeos libri II*; 614–15). He also dealt with biblical exegesis, e.g., in the *Liber numerorum qui in Sanctis Scripturis occurrunt* and in the *Allegoriae quaedam Sacrae Scripturae*, both written in the period 612–15.

6 The date of this work is disputed. Isidore probably continued to work on it into the last years of his life. Other Isidorean works of similar character are the *Regula monachorum* (615–18; Isidore was certainly very interested in cenobitic monasticism); the *De ecclesiasticis officiis libri II* (610–15; influenced by Isidore's reading of Ambrose of Milan and Gregory the Great); and the *De viris illustribus* (615–18).

trace a history of the Visigothic kingdom, the aim being to demonstrate that the Goths, and not the Byzantines, were the ideal heirs of the Romans. Here, ethnic difference was forgotten in favor of fusion in a Hispano-Latin-Catholic unity. More often, however, Isidore conceived his works from a much wider perspective, with the purpose of providing precise historical and spatial coordinates. Thus, in the *Chronicon* (after 615) he wrote – under the clear influence of Augustine – a history of the world beginning with the Creation. Similarly, in *De natura rerum*, which he wrote at the request of the literate King Sisebut (612–620), Isidore gave an exposition of physical geography – the seasons, the weather, the course of the stars, the wind, and so on – on the basis of a reading (possibly direct) of Lucretius.

On completion of almost all his other literary works, favored by propitious circumstances and armed, above all, with uncommon courage, Isidore conceived an even greater work, to which he would devote the last twenty years of his life (615–636). Under the title of *Origins*, or *Etymologies*, he compiled a sort of encyclopedia, divided into twenty books and organized according to the system of the *artes liberales*, with some additions that he deemed necessary,[7] and consisting of an interminable series of definitions, beginning in each case with an etymological explanation of the relevant word.[8]

In preparing and editing his material, Isidore followed the methods he had learned from the ancient sages. Vast erudition lay behind his selection and transcription of the most significant passages. The fragments selected were then gathered, classified, and finally summarized to obtain Isidore's precious "brevity." The last step consisted in redacting the content to produce a coherent and clear synthesis. Here, as throughout his literary production, the bishop paid special attention to two particular aims. The first concerned style, which was to be simple and controlled, never prolix or redundant, while reviving and restoring correct Latin against the increasing use of dialects. The second aim was the correct understanding and proper use of words.[9] Isidore also attached enormous importance to the work of transcription, which seems to have bordered on an obsession: The correctness of the text represented the best bulwark against errors in understanding and fruitless debate. Accuracy, clarity, synthesis, and organization thus constitute the frame of an impressive effort, the purpose of which was to present all human knowledge in an exposition that was at once coherent and accessible.

7 The work remained unfinished: Isidore died without having time to correct, polish, and put the finishing touches to the text. It was instead his student Braulio who posthumously edited the *Etymologies* and divided the work into twenty books.

8 As Isidore himself explains (*Etym.* I.29.1–2; trans. Throop): "[1] Etymology is the origin of words, when the meaning of the verb or noun is inferred by interpretation. . . . [2] This knowledge is often necessary for the meaning. When you see where the name came from, you will more readily understand its meaning. Examining anything is clearer when the etymology is understood."

9 The focus on linguistic matters is already present in the early works of Isidore. Even before becoming a bishop, for example, he wrote a synthesis of the differences in meaning in relation to words and things (*Differentiarum libri II*; 598–600). A treatise on oratory also belongs to this group (*Synonymorum libri II*; 610–15).

Visigothic Spain certainly benefited from Isidore's activity, but his work had an even greater influence on the rest of Europe – especially during the Carolingian era, when his writings began to circulate across the Continent. The *Etymologies*, in particular, enjoyed extraordinary success as a schoolbook. For centuries to come, Western Europeans would consider Isidore as an undisputed authority: a trusted guide in approaching every subject.

ISIDORE AND THE CONSTRUCTION OF A COMMON LEGAL CULTURE IN THE EARLY MIDDLE AGES

Even those who were interested in studying law found Isidore's encyclopedia indispensable reading. The space reserved for the law in the *Etymologies* is actually considerable.[10] Almost the entire fifth book (*On Laws and Time Periods*) is devoted to legal matters, as well as many other passages scattered throughout the whole work, particularly in the second, ninth, and eighteenth books. It is immediately clear that Isidore's orientation in all matters of law was the Roman legal tradition. He certainly knew the works of some of the classical Roman jurists, such as Gaius, Paul, and Ulpian, and it is likely that he also benefited from their existing writings (i.e., entire treatises or commentaries) when providing his legal definitions. More than one scholar thinks that Isidore worked only from second-hand materials, compiling excerpts from various works of ancient jurisprudence in which classical ideas had already undergone a process of selection and re-elaboration, but it is impossible to know precisely what texts he had at hand.

What is beyond all doubt is the really extraordinary success of Isidore's legal definitions during the entire Middle Ages. Generations of students had to learn by heart the definitions of sale, loan, property, wills, marriage, rape, theft, and so on found in the *Etymologies*. References to Isidore's work, however, are not limited to basic teaching. During the Carolingian era, any approach to legal texts seems to start with Isidore, and very often quotations from the *Etymologies* may be found in the words of contemporary lawmakers or in those of other "intellectuals" interested in legal matters.[11] As one surveys the legal manuscripts of the early Middle Ages, it is easy to find insertions containing selections from those same Isidorean definitions.

This universal tendency to rely on Isidore in legal matters persisted in the ensuing centuries. Between the eleventh and the early twelfth centuries, for example, even those commentators (i.e., the glossators) who began to study the "rediscovered" legal texts of Justinian seem to have kept "old" Isidore on their desks. What is new in comparison with the Carolingian past is that Isidore's *Etymologies* were now used to

10 Isidore also deals with legal topics in other works, but especially in the two books of *Differentiae* (598–600) and in the three books of *Sententiae* (612–15).

11 A very good example is Jonas of Orléans in his *De institutione regia* (831). See Jean Reviron, *Les idées politico-religieuses d'un évêque du IXe siècle: Jonas d'Orléans et son "De institutione regia." Étude et texte critique* (Paris: J. Vrin, 1930).

explain words or expressions of Justinian's law.[12] It is important to stress that such a tendency to read and interpret Justinian through Isidore would last for a long time and would accompany the diffusion of the Byzantine legal texts throughout Europe – in England, for example, in the teaching of the glossator Johannes Bassianus or, later, through the writings of "Bracton."

Moreover, in the same period, references to Isidore's *Etymologies* began to emerge in contexts far removed from contemporary classrooms and especially in the world of legal practice. This is particularly the case in northern Italy and southern France, where a considerable number of surviving medieval documents allow us to form a less fragmentary idea of that reality: Legal definitions taken from Isidore appear frequently in the records of judicial proceedings and in notarial documents.

Nor was Isidore's importance limited to the civil law. To gain an idea of Isidore's influence on the canon law, it suffices to look at the *Concordia discordantium canonum* (the *Decretum*) of Gratian (c. 1130–1140). Here, we find at the beginning an almost literal copy of most of the legal chapters of the fifth book of Isidore's *Etymologies*. And, naturally, the "decretists" (scholars of Gratian's work) examined these passages with great attention. A good example is the Isidorean passage "On privileges" in *Etymologies* V.18, which became canon 3 of Gratian's Distinction III as well as the occasion for an important *dictum* (*post* C. 25 q. 1 *pars* II.2 *in fi.*). In turn, this last *dictum* became the obligatory starting point for any canon law argument about specific laws and privileges. In the same way, Isidorean definitions were reused in the title *De verborum significatione* of Gregory IX's *Liber Extra* (c. 23 X, 5.40) (1234). Nor did the canonists ignore other Isidorean works, especially the *Sententiae*.

In all, we can say that the works and teachings of Isidore made a decisive contribution to the creation of a common legal grammar across medieval Europe. They functioned as a technical lexicon throughout the early Middle Ages and provided the foundation on which, from the middle of the eleventh century, the great edifice of the *ius commune* was raised. In assessing the impact of Isidore on European legal culture we should not, however, confine our attention to the preservation of legal concepts and definitions from antiquity and their transmission to the post-Roman world. While Isidore cannot properly be considered a jurist, his legal education was nonetheless undeniable. His approach to legal issues was far from naïve or simplistic, as the following examples will show.[13]

12 This use is particularly evident in some manuscripts of Italian origin dating from the eleventh century, such as MS Leipzig; UB, Hänel 5, in which the whole fifth book of the Etymologies is copied in the guise of an introduction; or the MS Vercelli, BC, 122. Both manuscripts reproduce the *Novellae constitutiones* of Justinian in the summarized version of the *Epitome Iuliani*; see L. Loschiavo, "Isidore of Seville and the Construction of a Common Legal Culture in Early Medieval Europe," *Clio@Themis* 10 (2016): 1–21, at 4–5.

13 Cf. Alfonso García-Gallo, "San Isidoro Jurista," in M. C. Diaz y Diaz (ed.), *Isidoriana. Collección de estudios sobre Isidoro de Sevilla en el XIV centenario de su nacimiento* (Leon: Centro de Estudios. 1961), 133–42. García-Gallo may overstate his case, but the criticism of J. de Churruca, "Presupuestos

THE TWO LAWS (*UTRAQUE LEX*): THE ETHICAL FOUNDATION OF THE POWER AND THE CREATION OF A NATIONAL LAW

The fifth book of the *Etymologies* begins with a long series of lawmakers of the past: pagan, Hebrew, and Christian. It begins with Moses, the first who "set forth divine laws" (*Etym.* V.1.1). Surprisingly, the last legislator to be mentioned is not the great Justinian but Theodosius II, author of the code, Isidore explains, that was "called 'Theodosian' after his own name" (*Etym.* V.1.7). This is surely no accident. Isidore never mentions Justinian's law books, but it would be hard to believe that a bishop of Seville was completely ignorant of the existence of the Justinian legislation. Moreover, a little farther on (*Etym.* V.39.40), Isidore recalls the twenty-nine-year reign of Justinian. Rather, in view of the tense relationships at that time between the Visigothic kingdom and the imperial court at Constantinople, as well as the teaching at the hands of his brother Leander, Isidore's intention here is clearly to consider only the secular law that was in force at that time in Spain: above all, the *Lex Romana Visigothorum* (also known as the *Breviarium Alaricianum*, a somewhat abbreviated version of the *Theodosian Code*[14]) and the *Lex Visigothorum*.

We can recognize here an original and important contribution of the Spanish bishop to the evolution of the ideal that modern scholars refer to as *utraque lex* ("both laws"). Typical of Late Antiquity and the early Middle Ages, this concept rested on the double assumption that the catholic Church had in the Roman Empire a necessary counterpart, and that Christian society needed to be ruled by two laws at the same time, both potentially universal: the law of God (*Lex Dei*) and the Roman law.

Isidore believed profoundly in that ideal, but he went further than his models and guides, such as Ambrose, Augustine, and Gregory the Great, in seeking to adapt such an ideal vision to the world of his own day. He not only embraced the cultural change already outlined by Augustine, according to whom the future of Christianity no longer coincided with the fortunes of the Roman Empire; he was also the first to apply to the history of law the theory of the "linear history" elaborated by Augustine.[15] In this way, Isidore replaced the concrete image of the contemporary (and now Byzantine) empire with that of the secular power considered in abstract terms, which therefore became applicable to the different political realities of contemporary Europe. Christian kings – and no longer the Roman-Byzantine

para el estudio de las fuentes juridicas de Isidoro de Sevilla," *Anuario de Historia del Derecho Español* 43 (1973): 429–43, at 430–31, seems excessive.

[14] Including, in the form of an appendix, the *Pauli Sententiae* (the so-called Visigothic Paul). Isidore probably also knew and used the *Institutiones* of the jurist Gaius.

[15] According to Augustine's concept of "linear history," formulated in his *The City of God*, time is not cyclical but rather has a beginning (the Creation) and progresses in a straight line according to God's will toward an end-fulfillment (the second Advent of Christ), so that history has a direction and a meaning.

emperors – were now the best interlocutors of the catholic Church. By the same token, Roman law could still be applied, but only because it was received within the complex legal system of the *respublica Christiana*.

Within this ideal framework, we can better understand why Isidore insists so doggedly on underlining the necessary ethical foundation of any power that claims to be legitimate. Starting from the (Augustinian) premise whereby "kings are said to be *reges* from *regendo*, ruling, and *recte agendo*, acting rightly," Isidore comes to the conclusion that "kings can retain their power only if they govern with rectitude, otherwise they are doomed to lose it."[16] And to reign with rectitude means to follow the advice of the bishops, to cooperate with the church, to become its instrument. When necessary, however, the "good" sovereign may even use his jurisdiction with respect to the church itself. When, in other words, the priest cannot maintain ecclesiastical order by prayers alone, it falls to the prince to impose order using his coercive power (*Sent.*, III.51.6). It is not clear whether such ideas were formulated specifically with the Visigothic kingdom in mind, or whether they should be interpreted from a general and "ecumenical" perspective. In either case, they emerged in all their actuality with the new Carolingian empire and continued to be relevant even after the crisis of this new political structure.[17]

It was not sufficient to address the monarchy alone in order to convert the Visigothic kingdom into a Christian national state. Just like the provincial churches, the inhabitants of the kingdom had to be unified. Isidore knew that in this perspective the legal system played a fundamental role, and it is not surprising, therefore, that quite against the literal tenor of the Visigothic legislation, he interpreted criminal rules as applying to Gothic and Roman subjects alike. In embryonic manner, Isidore here anticipated the thinking of bishop Agobard of Lyon, who some two centuries later would protest to Louis the Pious against the multiplicity of laws in force in the empire: If there was to be one empire, there had better be but one law.

On more than one occasion, however, Isidore had no compunction in deviating from (and also renewing) the Roman law tradition. It is remarkable, for example, how Isidore – particularly in the titles V.24 and V.25 of the *Etymologies* – stresses the importance of the individual will in the legal acts and, more generally, in legal relations between private individuals. The beginning of *Etymologies* V.24 (*On legal instruments*) is already an explicit indication – (§1): "the general name of all legal instruments is 'will' [*voluntas*]. It takes such a name because it comes forth not by force, but by inclination" (trans. Throop). The importance of the individual will is also highlighted in his description of the codicil (V.24.14), of the *cretio* (V.24.16), and of the *fideicommissum* (V.24.17), and especially when he deals with the pact

16 Briefly mentioned at *Etym.* I.29.3, the thought is then developed in *Sent.* III.48.7.

17 Jonas of Orléans, for example, in his *De institutione regia* (831; see especially ch. 5: ed. Reviron, *Les idées*) repeats Isidore's *Sententiae* 3.52.1–3. Similarly, Hincmar of Reims in his *De regis persona et regio ministerio* (873), PL 125:833–56.

(V.24.18–19): "Pact is called a *pactum* because it is a document between parts [*partes*], coming together in peace [*pax*]." In a similar way, the bishop continues, "*placitum* [decree or petition] is so called because it is pleasing [*placet*]." Nevertheless, as other people say (*alii dicunt*), "pact is when someone does what he intends to do." As such, concludes Isidore, "*pactum* is different from *placitum* because the latter forces us to do even what we wish not to do." For Isidore, then, the human will transforms the pact into something more than a simple exception, as it was considered at the time of the ancient jurist Gaius (e.g., *Institutes*, I.84; II.31 and 64; III.179).[18]

Other examples could be given, especially from the section on the criminal law, but to appreciate better the independently minded bishop of Seville vis-à-vis the Roman law tradition, we must now turn to the central topic of the administration of justice.

BUILDING A MODEL OF PROCEDURE FOR THE SETTLEMENT OF DISPUTES

It is useful to remember that the Theodosian tradition, as well as the *Corpus Iuris Civilis* of Justinian, provided no methodical, consolidated, or even coherent framework of judicial procedure. It took a long time – until the twelfth and thirteenth centuries – for jurists to conceive the model that today we call Roman canonical procedure, in reality a medieval creation. Obviously, the interest of the church in settling and resolving disputes long antedated that project. In the long and not always straightforward journey toward the creation of a proper and original law of procedure, the teaching of Isidore of Seville was an important step along the way. He produced an original synthesis by combining different elements from the various normative and legal traditions. While this synthesis did not provide a complete and detailed model of judicial process, it did at least offer a broadly coherent legal framework that would be useful for the entire Christian world.

Isidore's first interesting passage on this issue is to be found in his *Synonyma* (II.86). Here, he admonishes anyone who has the duty to judge to abstain from judgment in the absence of absolute and certain evidence; alternatively, it will be better to rely on God's supreme judgment. In other words, judges have to remember that all human justice is imperfect and that every human court must always be mindful of its limits. Immediately thereafter, Isidore underlines how the path to the truth cannot be improvised but must follow some necessary steps: Judgment has to be based on certain evidence that is verified in an indisputable way, through a verifiable process. Isidore uses here for the first time the expression *ordo iudiciarius*: an expression destined to have a wide and lasting success. The phrase places Isidore

[18] The same peculiar focus on the element of will is also present in Isidore's treatment of sale (*Etym.* V.24.23), where he emphasizes, surprisingly, the "agreement" (*convenientia*) and not, e.g., the exchange of goods.

in an ecclesiastical tradition. Some years previously, Gregory the Great had referred to the orderly achievement of a judgment (*iudicium ordinabiliter habitum*).[19] In describing the *ordo* to be followed in legal tribunals, therefore, Isidore seems to be following Gregory. But whereas the pope was referring to an ecclesiastical judgment (regarding a controversy among the bishops in Spain), Isidore applies the concept to secular tribunals.

Isidore outlines a procedural framework for the law courts in the *Etymologies* XVIII.15. He does not make any distinction here between criminal and civil trials. Such a distinction, which is quite clear in the Roman legal sources, had been lost in the transition to the post-Roman world. Any judgment, then, has to be the outcome of a formalized procedure, not simply of the logical and heuristic mental processes of the judge. The procedure must be controllable and, therefore, public: The public dimension of the trial is a prerequisite of a correct judgment. It is no surprise, then, that Isidore begins his description of the fundamental components of a legal process with the definition of "forum," that is, the court of law. The court, Isidore explains, is the public place devoted to the resolution of disputes. This resolution must come at the end of a proper treatment of the case, conducted in compliance with the law and by the court that, at the end, pronounces its judgment with authority. In this way, the matter under dispute is brought back to justice and regains an ethical-legal equilibrium (*iuris status*).

After this swift but central introduction, Isidore comes to the main issue of the trial: the inquiry about facts and responsibilities (*inquisitio*). The investigation concerning the case at the origin of the dispute is twofold, for it concerns both the law (to establish the scope of the dispute) and the subject matter at the same time. To these two tasks correspond two distinct tools: For the first kind of inquiry, the judge can use logical argumentation (*argumentum*); for the second, he has to avail himself of more technical types of evidence: witnesses and documents.

Isidore continues by indicating the "necessary persons" (*necessariae personae*): those in whose absence no process may be considered regular. Isidore here evokes the four elements of judge, the two parties, and the witnesses, as if in the form of a square.

The judge is the cornerstone of the whole structure, and we can identify in this view an implicit hostility to the procedures generally used among barbarian peoples, where the judge's role was much less relevant than it was both in Roman and in canonical traditions, all the more since Isidore and the church knew very well that the barbarians were the new lords of the Christian West.

In other passages scattered throughout his works, Isidore emphasizes the ethical responsibilities incumbent on the powerful, especially those delegated with the administration of justice. In the *Sententiae* (III.52–54) we read first of all that judges

[19] Gregorii I, *Registrum Epist.*, in P. Ewald and L. M. Hartmann (eds.), MGH Epist. 1.2, p. 411. This is the famous letter of 603 in which Gregory instructs his *defensor* Johannes regarding settlement of the case in Spain of bishop Januarius of Malaca and a certain bishop Stephen.

have to be aware of the importance of the office to which they are called. They have to administer jurisdictional power "solely for the sake of eternal salvation," demanding no gifts in return. They have to escape corruption and avoid using their power to benefit themselves or to achieve goals incompatible with the pursuit of justice. But the judge may fall into error even without malice. This happens, for example, when the judge relies on greedy and rapacious collaborators or falls victim to anger or the temptation to indulge unduly in technical and otherwise redundant argumentation. He must pay no attention to the social status of people whom he has to judge and in general should not let his abilities be dulled for any reason (*Sent.* III.54.7).

To the modern reader, such warnings may seem purely moral, and a lawyer might easily be tempted to dismiss them out of hand. It would, however, be a grave mistake to underestimate the importance of the ethical dimension. The entire judicial framework set out by Isidore is based on it.

In any case, in an encyclopedic work such as the *Etymologies*, Isidore did not need to linger on the point. He limited himself to observing that a judge has to judge in accordance with justice, because "he is no judge, if there is no justice in him" (*Etym.* XVIII.15.6). It is noteworthy, however, that Isidore stresses the necessary presence of both parties if the process is to qualify as correctly ordered. In other words, according to Isidore, the trial cannot take place in the absence of one of the parties. Here, once again, he deviated from Roman law, which admitted and carefully regulated judicial contumacy. Without doubt, Isidore was following here the Judeo-Christian tradition, which treated the presence of both parties as a necessary premise for its fundamental goal of reconciliation between litigants and the recovery of the sinner.[20]

THE EVIDENTIARY PHASE AND THE CENTRAL ROLE OF WITNESSES

After considering the judge and the parties, Isidore arrives at the core of the entire structure: the witnesses and the trial. In his geometric image, the triangle formed by putting the judge and the two parties at the vertices is completed by adding a fourth side, represented by the necessary presence of witnesses. (Three unanimous witnesses are considered as a single person.) Such a schema, it should be emphasized, became typical in the entire ensuing medieval legal tradition.

Isidore had already dealt with the witnesses in two previous passages of the *Etymologies* (V.23 and 24.5–6). In both cases, he speaks only of contractual witnesses, and it is absolutely clear that in doing so he is following the Roman legal tradition. It is not so evident, by contrast, what kind of legal system he has in mind in affirming that no fewer than three witnesses are necessary. With his precise insistence on the

[20] See, e.g., *Didascalia Apostolorum* (Syria, c. 230) II.47.2, 49.1, and 51.1 (trans. R. Hugh Connolly, Oxford, 1929).

point, Isidore was deviating from two venerable traditions, for both Roman law and the Bible require two, not three, witnesses in agreement with each other, on the basis of whose unanimity the judge could pronounce judgment.[21] We do not know why Isidore decided to stray from this twofold, ancient, and quintessentially authoritative tradition, but whatever his reasons, his teaching enjoyed lasting success. It was first confirmed by Pope Nicholas I in his famous letter to the kings of the Bulgars (866),[22] and the rule of the three unanimous witnesses is then repeated by several canonical collections (in particular, the so-called Collections in IX[23] or V[24] Books). It also emerges in some legal instruments of the ninth and tenth centuries.[25]

As well as the question of the number, Isidore deals carefully with the character of the witness (§XVIII.15.9). Witnesses play a crucial role in the economy of the Isidorean pattern: They are "those of whom we ask the truth in court." In agreement with both Roman law and some earlier ecclesiastical authors (it is sufficient to recall Ambrose of Milan, *Epist.* 56), Isidore insists that the judge must carefully verify the trustworthiness of the witnesses. Even in this case, however, Isidore does not follow his models slavishly. What for the Roman jurists was simply a sign of credibility, and so was left to the individual assessment of the judge, now becomes a binding prerequisite. Moreover, once again contravening the Roman law and the canonical tradition, Isidore bars women from giving testimony. The reason behind such a general and a priori exclusion can perhaps be inferred by assuming that there was a vein of misogyny in Isidore.

After dividing the witnesses according to the source of their knowledge (those who report what they have seen are distinguished from those who repeat what they have heard), he continues by dealing with the thorny problem of false testimony. The witness, in fact, can "break the law in two different ways: either by giving false testimony, or in hiding the truth by keeping silent." Here, too, what in the *Etymologies* is only mentioned in passing is discussed in the *Sententiae* in greater detail (III.55.1–7). To begin with, the reticent witness is substantially equated to the false one. Then Isidore specifies that the false witness injures at the same time God, the judge, and one of the parties. Isidore then suggests some useful ways of discovering false testimony before it is too late. The principal method consists in interrogating the witnesses separately and then comparing their testimonies. Already known in ancient times – in Rome as well as in the Jewish courts – this practical solution was

21 See *Digest* 22.5.14 (Ulpian) for the Roman law and Deut 19:15 and Matt 18:16 for Old and New Testament, respectively. The originality of Isidore's position has not escaped scholars from Theodor Mommsen onward.

22 Nicholas I, *Ep.* 99, in E. Perels (ed.), MGH Epist. 6 (1925), 595.

23 Ms. Città del Vaticano, BAV, vat. lat. 1349, f. 125rb (=6.62) (c.920).

24 Ms. Città del Vaticano, BAV, vat. lat. 1339, *sub* 1.214 (eleventh century); ed. M. Fornasari, *Collectio canonum in V libris*, CCM 6, 132.

25 See, e.g., the *placitum* held in Rome in April 998, on which see C. Wickham, "Justice in the Kingdom of Italy in the Eleventh Century," in *La giustizia nell'alto medioevo (secoli IX–XI), Settimane CISAM*, XLIV.1 (Spoleto, 1997), 228–29.

also adopted by the Visigoths, perhaps thanks to Isidore. Later, and again thanks to churchmen, cross-examination was adopted by Charlemagne's judges and those of post-Carolingian Italy.

With the same objective, albeit surely only with regard to secular disputes, Isidore goes so far as to admit the use of torture against dubious witnesses (*Etym.* II.30.16). There was already a tendency to extend the use of torture in the late Roman Empire (e. g., originally only the witnesses of a servile condition could be interrogated under torture; in Late Antiquity, torture was often used also against free witnesses, if of low status). The source of inspiration for Isidore, however, could well have been Augustine (*De civ. Dei* XIX.6). In condemning only the *abuse* of torture, Pope Nicholas I, perhaps because he had read Isidore, does not seem entirely opposed to its proper judicial use[26].

It is tempting to posit a connection between Isidore's concerns over false testimony as a possible cause of error of judgment and the case heard in the council over which he presided in 624 at Seville (Seville III). During that council, Martianus, bishop of Ecija, accused of a series of crimes, had been condemned and stripped of his rank. Finally, his see had been given to his accuser, Aventius. It is very likely that Isidore was among those who voted against Martianus. Very soon, however, it became clear that Martianus had been innocent. Nevertheless, it took fourteen years (by which time Isidore had been dead for two years) and a second appeal by Martianus for the Sixth Council of Toledo (638) to recognize that the charges against him were groundless and part of a vile conspiracy conceived by Aventius. The slandered bishop was then restored to his see, but the "fathers" in Toledo exonerated the authors of the previous judgment. In their view, the bishops gathered in Seville in 624 had acted "neither by craft, nor corrupted judgment," for they had merely been duped by false witnesses. It is difficult, however, to deny the responsibility of the bishops and Isidore himself. Some grievous abuses in the procedure adopted in 624 were evident, and Martianus was clearly the victim of a miscarriage of ecclesiastical justice.

Rachel Stocking is probably right in stressing Isidore's difficulties in managing the scandal that broke out in 624.[27] We know that the first appeal of Martianus was discussed in some haste by the Fourth Council of Toledo in 633 under Isidore's presidency, and that the records of the Third Council of Seville were never inserted into the canon law collection known as *Collectio Hispana*. It does not seem too hazardous to suppose, then, that in the relevant passages of the *Etymologies* and the *Sententiae* – both works on which he was working at the time – Isidore was animated by his preoccupation with that scandal and, most of all, by his concern for the credibility of conciliar justice.

[26] See M. Schmöckel, "Nicolaus I. und das Beweisrecht im 9. Jahrhundert," in R. H. Helmholz et al. (eds.), *Grundlagen des Rechts. Festschrift für Peter Landau* (Paderborn: Schöningh, 2000), 53–76, at 62–63.

[27] See R. L. Stocking, *Bishops, Councils and Consensus in the Visigothic Kingdom*, 589–633 (Ann Arbor: University of Michigan Press, 2001), 139–42, on the trial of bishop Martianus.

SOURCES

Editions of Isidore's works used in this chapter: Isidore's *opera omnia* are edited by Faustino Arévalo in *Patrologiae cursus completus*, I, Roma, typis Antonii Fulgonii, 1797–1803 (reproduced in PL 81–84), but some of his most important works (*Etymologies, Sentences, Synonyms*) are available today in modern editions: *Isidori hispaliensis episcopi Etymologiarum sive Originum libri XX*, ed. W. M. Lindsay, 2 vols. (Oxford: Oxford University Press, 1911; 1989); *Isidorus Hispalensis Sententiae*, ed. Pierre Cazier, CCL 111 (1998); *Isidori Hispalensis Episcopi Synonyma*, ed. Jacques Elfassi, CCL 111B (2009); *Diferencias. Isidoro de Sevilla*, vol. 1, ed. and transl. Carmen Codoñer Merino (Paris: Belles Lettres, 1992).

English translations: *Isidore of Seville's Etymologies*, transl. Priscilla Throop, 2 vols. (Charlotte, VT: MedievalMS, 2005; revised 2013); The Etymologies of Isidore of Seville, trans. S. E. Barney, W. J. Lewis, J. A. Beach, and O. Berghof (Cambridge: Cambridge University Press, 2006); The Letters of St. Isidore of Seville, transl. G. B. Ford Jr. (Amsterdam: Hakkert, 1970).

FURTHER READING

The classic work on Isidore remains J. Fontaine, *Isidore de Séville et la culture classique de l'Espagne wisigothique*, 3 vols. (Paris: Études Augustiniennes, 1959 and 1983). One should also mention P. Cazier, *Isidore de Séville et la naissance de l'Espagne catholique* (Paris: Beauchesne, 1994). Among recent publications, mention should be made of the following: R. L. Stocking, *Bishops, Councils and Consensus in the Visigothic Kingdom, 589–633* (Ann Arbor: University of Michigan Press, 2001), in which see pp. 139–42 for the highly significant story of the trial of Martianus bishop of Ecija; J. Henderson, *The Medieval World of Isidore of Seville: Truth from Words* (Cambridge: Cambridge University Press, 2007); and A. Fear and J. Wood (eds.), *Isidore of Seville and His Reception in the Early Middle Ages: Transmitting and Transforming Knowledge* (Amsterdam: Amsterdam University Press, 2016). These books also provide references to further literature, especially in English. Extensive bibliographies on Isidore of Seville and his work can be found in the introduction of A. Valastro-Canale to his Italian translation of the *Etymologies* (*Isidoro di Siviglia Etimologie o Origini*, 2 vols. [Turin: UTET, 2004] 27–52, which goes up to 2004; and on the website opac.regesta-imperii.de (search for *Isidorus*), up to 2015) (last access: Jan 31, 2018).

In general, on the Visigothic realm, on the ecclesiastical policy, and on the cultural environment in early Spain, see P. D. King, *Law and Society in the Visigothic Kingdom* (Cambridge: Cambridge University Press, 1972); P. Heather, *The Goths* (Oxford: Blackwell, 1998); R. Collins, *Visigothic Spain 409–711* (Malden, MA: Blackwell; Ann Arbor: University of Michigan Press, 2006); and H. Wolfram, *Die Goten und ihre Geschichte* (München: C. H. Beck, 2010).

On the importance of the library of Seville in Visigothic Spain, see J. Orlandis, *Historia del reino visigodo español* (Madrid: Rialp, 1988), 351–54. On the sources and the use of the sources in Isidore, see F. Gasti, "Fonti letterarie e fonti 'tecniche' nelle Etimologiae di Isidoro di Siviglia," *Sileno* 42.1 (2016): 21–39.

On Isidore's position regarding Judaism, see J. Cohen, *Living Letters of the Law: Ideas of the Jew in Medieval Christianity* (Berkley: University of California Press, 1999), which contains a chapter specifically devoted to "Isidore of Seville: Anti-Judaism and the Hermeneutics of Integration"; and W. Drews, *The Unknown Neighbour: The Jew in the Thought of Isidore of Seville* (Leiden: Brill, 2006).

On Isidore's episcopal activity, see R. Kottje, "Isidor von Sevilla und der Chorepiskopat," *Deusches Archiv für Erforschung des Mittealters*, 28 (1972): 533–37.

On the *Collectio canonum Hispana* and the disputed attribution of its first recension to Isidore, see J. Gaudemet, *Les sources du droit de l'Église en Occident du II* ᵉ *au VII*ᵉ *siècle* (Paris: Cerf, 1985), 155–59.

For the diffusion of Isidore's work in the early Middle Ages, see A. Fear and J. Wood (eds.), *Isidore of Seville and his Reception in the Early Middle Ages: Transmitting and Transforming Knowledge* (Amsterdam: Amsterdam University Press, 2016). On the use of Isidore's writings in the work of Jonas of Orléans in particular, see J. Reviron, *Les idées politico-religieuses d'un évêque du IXe siècle: Jonas d'Orléans et son "De institutione regia." Etude et texte critique* (Paris: Vrin, 1930). For the late Middle Ages, see J. Elfassi and B. Ribémont (eds.), *La reception d'Isidore de Séville durant le Moyen âge tardif (XII*ᵉ*–XV*ᵉ *s.)* (Ouzouer-le-Marche, France:Cahiers de recherches médiévales, 2008).

On the legal sources used by Isidore, see the following: Ph. Stella Maranca, *Jurisprudentiae romanae reliquias quae Isidori Hispaliensis episcopi Etymologiarum libris continentur* (Lanciano, 1927) – the work is unfinished and it is very difficult to find, but the thirty-two pages published are now accessible at www.ravenna-capitale.it (search under *materiali per la ricerca / studi*) (last access: Jan 31, 2018); A. García Gallo, "San Isidoro Jurista," *Isidoreana. Collección de estudios sobre Isidoro de Sevilla en el XIV centenario de su nacimiento* (Leon, 1961), 133–42; and J. de Churruca, "Presupuestos para el estudio de las fuentes juridicas de Isidoro de Sevilla," *Anuario de Historia del Derecho Español* 43 (1973): 429–43.

On Isidore and the law, see A. Tabera, "La definición de furtum en las 'Etimologias' de S. Isidoro," *Studia et Documenta Historiae et Iuris* 8 (1942): 23–47; R. R. Gibert Sanchez de la Vega, "San Isidoro de Sevilla y el derecho civil," *Revista de la Facultad de Derecho de la Universitad Complutense de Madrid* 18 (1974): 33–58; M. Lemosse, "Technique juridique et culture romaine selon Isidore de Séville," *Revue historique de droit française et étranger* 79 (2001): 139–52; and P. L. Reynolds, "Isidore of Seville," in R. Domingo and J. Martinéz-Torrón (eds.), *Great Christian Jurists in Spanish History* (Cambridge: Cambridge University Press, 1918), 31–49.

On the influence of Isidore's work on European legal culture, especially regarding procedure, see L. Loschiavo, "Isidore of Seville and the Construction of a Common

Legal Culture in Early Medieval Europe," *Clio@Themis* 10 (2016): 1–21 [www.cliothemis.com]. A complete survey of the medieval tradition of the procedural forms is available in L. Fowler-Magerl, *'Ordines iudiciarii' and 'Libelli de ordine iudiciorum': From the Middle of the Twelfth to the End of the Fifteenth Century* (Turnhout: Brepols, 1994). On the use of torture in the criminal procedure of the Visigothic kingdom, see E. Peters, *Torture* (Philadelphia: University of Pennsylvania Press, 1985), 231–35.

19

Pseudo-Isidorus Mercator

Clara Harder

The author to whom this chapter is devoted was not a real person, although his name is widely known among medievalists and scholars of canon law. Isidore the Merchant (Isidorus Mercator) is the pseudonym used by the compiler (or compilers) of a supposedly late-antique canonical collection. Besides some canons from church councils, the corpus consists of decretals ascribed to the earliest bishops of Rome, from the first century onward. In fact, however, the collection originated in ninth-century Francia. Because roughly one hundred of the decretals are largely falsified, we refer to the compiler today as Pseudo-Isidore, and to the entire collection as the "Pseudo-Isidorian decretals" (or simply "false decretals"). The fact that it was a forgery remained undetected for hundreds of years. It was a resource for ecclesiastical regulation and canon law throughout the Middle Ages and long afterward. It was exposed as a fraud only in the seventeenth century.

One should be careful not to confuse the terms "Pseudo-Isidorian *decretals*" and "Pseudo-Isidorian *forgeries*." The reason for the latter term is that the name of Pseudo-Isidore is associated today with a larger body of related, mainly canonical collections from the same period. Some of these collections seem to have been preliminary studies for the Pseudo-Isidorian decretals (e.g., the *Hispana Gallica Augustodunensis*, also known as *Pseudo-Isidorian Hispana*); some were mainly transmitted along with forgeries of that sort (e.g., the *Capitula Angilramni*); and some are still more loosely connected with Pseudo-Isidore, such as the capitularies ascribed to a certain Benedictus Levita (i.e., Benedict the Deacon), another alleged collector of mainly forged canonical texts. Since the Pseudo-Isidorian decretals are the most complex and successful of these forgeries, the larger body of literature is sometimes referred to collectively (if confusingly) as the "Pseudo-Isidorian forgeries."

THE ORIGINS OF THE PSEUDO-ISIDORIAN FORGERIES

For nearly four hundred years, historians have tried to identify who were responsible for these collections and to discover the intentions that led them to produce what became one of the most successful and formative forgeries in history. For a long time, historians accepted that the forgeries were created by a group of scholars in northern France in the late 840s, probably in the diocese of Reims. Then, at the beginning of the twenty-first century, Klaus Zechiel-Eckes identified the most probable source by detecting traces of the forgers' work in manuscripts derived from the scriptorium of the monastery at Corbie. He argued that Paschasius Radbertus, a monk of Corbie (and abbot 843–850), was the author behind the Pseudo-Isidorian decretals. Radbert is known to historians as one of the most learned men of the ninth century. Zechiel-Eckes showed that he was the only author of the period who used some rare source material otherwise found only in Pseudo-Isidore, such as the works of bishop Ennodius of Pavia. The thesis was consistent with what we know about Radbert: He was the author of a forged letter ascribed to St. Jerome;[1] he was an inventive author, and inventiveness, a rare quality among ninth-century authors, was surely a necessary precondition for assembling a forgery such as the Pseudo-Isidorian decretals;[2] and Radbert shared with Pseudo-Isidore certain political views and thoughts about the church and its organization.

According to Zechiel-Eckes's theory, the main reason for the forgery was the quarrel in the Carolingian realm in the 830s that led to the temporary deposition of Louis the Pious (r. 814–840) in 833. After the emperor returned to the throne in 834, he prosecuted and deposed bishops and other churchmen who had been involved in his downfall. Zechiel-Eckes proposed, therefore, that the forgery was composed in the mid-830s as a direct response to these events, and not in the later 840s as had previously been thought. While many historians celebrated Zechiel-Eckes's findings as a breakthrough, some found his assumptions and reasoning questionable. For example, some pointed out that whereas Paschasius Radbertus was a monk, monastic topics are absent from the collection.[3]

There has also been controversy as to when the work of forgery began and what were the forgers' intentions. Some argue that there had been general dissatisfaction with the rule of Louis the Pious among the Carolingian clergy since the late 820s. The unjust dismissal of bishops, in particular, was already a topic of discussion. Work on the forgery, therefore, could have begun in the early 830s. The decisive moment might even have been in 830, when, after a brief uprising against him, Louis the Pious seems to have deposed bishop Jesse of Amiens and exiled abbot Wala of Corbie.[4] Others have suggested recently that the nineteenth-century scholars Hinschius and Seckel were correct in assuming that the forgery was not carried

1 Klaus Zechiel-Eckes, *Fälschung als Mittel politischer Auseinandersetzung* (Paderborn: Schönigh, 2011), 18–22.

2 David Ganz, *Corbie in the Carolingian Renaissance* (Sigmaringen: Jan Thorbecke Verlag, 1990), 81–83. Clara Harder, *Pseudoisidor und das Papsttum* (Cologne: Böhlau, 2014), 90–91.

3 For example, Mayke de Jong, "Paschasius Radbertus and Pseudo-Isidore: The Evidence of the *Epitaphium Arsenii*," in V. L. Garver and O. M. Phelan (eds.), *Rome and Religion in the Medieval World: Studies in Honor of Thomas F. X. Noble, Church, Faith and Culture in the Medieval West* (Farnham: Ashgate, 2014), 149–78.

4 Steffen Patzold, "Überlegungen zum Anlass für die Fälschung früher Papstbriefe im Kloster Corbie," in K. Ubl and D. Ziemann (eds.), *Fälschung als Mittel der Politik*? (Wiesbaden: Harrasowitz, 2015), 153–72.

out before the late 840s. According to this view, archbishop Ebo of Reims was a central figure in work on the forgery.[5]

The crucial consideration pertains to the forger's intentions. One can find textual support for several different theories by selectively analyzing the vast amount of material contained in Pseudo-Isidore's collection. But any theory about the forger's identity has to take account not only of the content of the collection, but also of additional evidence acquired through detailed textual and comparative analysis. Zechiel-Eckes showed how one could do this by compiling all the points of correspondence between the forgery and Paschasius's known writings. Although Zechiel-Eckes could not definitively demonstrate that Radbert of Corbie was the guiding spirit of the forgery, therefore, he makes a very strong case. The involvement of this monk in the Pseudo-Isidorian project seems at least to be very likely, and to date no one has convincingly refuted the thesis or proposed a more convincing one.

The current consensus among historians concerning the identity of Pseudo-Isidore might best be summarized as follows. All agree that the Pseudo-Isidorian decretals were composed in northern France in the diocese of Reims, most likely in the monastery of Corbie, near Amiens. The date of origin must lie between 830 and the middle of the century, and most historians agree that work on the forgery probably began in the first of those two decades. And it is very likely that Radbert, then a monk of Corbie, was involved in the composition of the forgery. Further particulars regarding the initiators of the forgery and their intentions remain open for discussion.

TEXTUAL VARIATION IN THE PSEUDO-ISIDORIAN DECRETALS

One of the main problems regarding the collection of Pseudo-Isidorus Mercator is the fact that there are several different versions of the collection. We may distinguish to begin with between a shorter version and a longer version, but several ninth-century manuscripts of the longer version vary considerably from one another. This variety is probably the main reason not only for the lack of consensus among historians regarding the forgery's origin, but also for the lack of an adequate, fully critical edition of the collection. As yet, it has not been possible to decide which of the manuscript versions best represents the original source. Indeed, the more historians have examined the various manuscript traditions and their transmission, the more it has become clear that there is really no single "original version" of the Pseudo-Isidorian decretals. Rather, as Horst Fuhrmann put it, these are "versions of equal value and of the same origin," which "stand side by side. They all have the status of an 'original.'"[6]

[5] Eric Knibbs, "Ebo of Reims, Pseudo-Isidore, and the Date of the False Decretals," *Speculum* 92.1 (2017): 144–83.

[6] Horst Fuhrmann, "Reflections on the Principles of Editing Texts: The Pseudo-Isidorian Decretals as an Example," BMCL 11 (1981): 1–7, at 5.

It is possible that the forgers deliberately produced different versions of the texts to make the collection look more authentic. In the ninth century, witnesses to the same canonical text were not always identical. Rather, texts were sometimes abbreviated in various ways, either because of a shortage of writing materials or because of special interest in a particular passage of the original from which they were copied. Sometimes words, sentences, and even whole texts were corrupted and falsely corrected by inept scribes, whose Latin was not good enough to understand what they were copying. And it was common practice to add new texts to a collection whenever this seemed useful or convenient. The variations among the earliest manuscripts of the Pseudo-Isidorian decretals, therefore, might have been deliberately fabricated to make the collection look more authentic.

The Pseudo-Isidorian collection may be divided into three parts. As in most early-medieval canonical collections, each part is arranged internally in chronological order. The contents of the collection as described below are those of the longer version of the collection.

Part one begins with some preliminary texts, including the important foreword by the supposed author, Isidorus Mercator. There follows a collection of sixty decretals by bishops of Rome, from Anacletus (r. c. 79–88) to Miltiades (r. 310–314). All of these papal decretals are false. Indeed, there are no surviving authentic letters from any of these bishops of Rome. This was a bold and unparalleled project: the forging of documents by no less than twenty-nine successive popes.

Pseudo-Isidore did not usually fabricate entirely fresh material, as if making it from whole cloth. Instead, he pieced together his forgeries from authentic material. Among his sources are the Bible, the *Liber Pontificalis* (a collection of papal biographies), authentic papal decretals, ecclesiastical histories such as Cassiodorus's *Historia Tripartita*, and Roman law. Historians have identified about ten thousand pieces of authentic material, which Pseudo-Isidore assembled as if he was making a mosaic. The authenticity of much of the source material is probably one of the main reasons why the forgery remained undetected for so long, for the texts *look* authentic, at least in style. Some of the sources were very rare and hardly known in the ninth century, which suggests that the forgers were well educated and had access to a large and well-stocked library. Pseudo-Isidore sometimes altered the extracted passages, and he sometimes set them a new context. He always gave them a new meaning, if only by attributing the words to a different author. The papal letters in the collection differ considerably from each other in terms of composition. Some are complex items made up from small pieces of original material. In contrast, some are not much more than verbatim rehearsals of biblical texts.[7]

The second part of the corpus is a collection of conciliar texts, ranging from the First Council of Nicaea (325) to the Second Council of Seville (619). Unlike the forged decretals of the first part, these texts are mainly authentic. They were derived

7 See, e.g., the letters of Pseudo-Eusebius in Hinschius, *Decretales*, 230–42.

from the *Hispana Gallica*, an early-medieval canonical collection. The sources are altered only slightly, apparently to make the corrupted text from the *Hispana Gallica* more intelligible. This second part of the collection would have been unremarkable had it not included the first known transmission of the *Constitutum Constantini*, also known as the *Donation of Constantine*. This seminal forged document purports to be an imperial decree by which the emperor Constantine the Great transferred command over the Western empire and the city of Rome to its bishop, Sylvester, and to his successors. As with the Pseudo-Isidorian decretals, historians disagree about the origin of the *Donation*, but there is general agreement that Pseudo-Isidore probably did not fabricate it but rather found it in some source and included it in the collection for reasons unknown.

The third part of the Pseudo-Isidorian decretals is the most complicated. It contains a mixture of papal decretals, both false and authentic, and conciliar texts from the reign of Pope Sylvester (314–335) to that of Pope Gregory II (715–731). The genuine items in this third part were extracted from standard canonical collections, especially from the *Hispana Gallica* but also from others such as the *Dionysio-Hadriana* and the *Quesnelliana*.

The complete compilation of Pseudo-Isidore was not only the most comprehensive canonical collection of its time but also the largest collection of (supposed) papal decretals. It purports to offer access to crucial documents of the early church. It even forged a new history for this church: a history in which the bishops of Rome had a decisive role.

PSEUDO-ISIDORUS MERCATOR ON BISHOPS AND POPES

Why did someone see fit to undertake such a large endeavor, which must have consumed much time and resources? This is among the greatest puzzles regarding the Pseudo-Isidorian decretals. Most historians have tried to find the answer by analyzing the contents of the forgery, but a collection of such scope inevitably covers more than just one topic, and one can find opinions in it on a wide variety of religious and ecclesiastical matters. The bishops of Rome cited in the collection address such important religious matters, for example, as baptism, liturgy, and marriage.

Nevertheless, Pseudo-Isidorus Mercator provides us with decisive clues regarding his intentions in his foreword to the compilation. Here, he complains that many priests have been not only wrongly accused of crimes but also deprived of their authority even before they were tried and convicted. Canonical rules, he claims, explicitly forbid the prosecution of priests who have already been deposed and exiled for crimes. He insists that a deposed bishop can be tried for a crime only after he has been reinstated and his office, authority, and property have been returned to him.[8]

[8] Hinschius, *Decretales*, Praefatio, 18.

This principle, known as *exceptio spolii*, is a key argument in several of the forged decretals dealing with the accusation and prosecution of bishops. Pseudo-Isidore stresses that conflicts involving members of the church hierarchy always have to be settled by an ecclesiastical convocation (i.e., a conciliar assembly of the bishops of the province, usually with some of their clergy).

Another conspicuous topic is the authority of the bishop of Rome over the universal church: the topic of several decretals. Pseudo-Isidore explains the essential point at issue in his foreword, where he states that only the bishop of Rome can summon a church council, and that a council held without the approval of the Apostolic See is invalid.[9] This argument is employed and enlarged in some of the forged decretals. The authority of the council, in the forger's view, depends on papal consent. Not only must the council be summoned by the bishop of Rome, but his legates also have the right to preside over it, and the council's decisions require the pope's approval. Moreover, the Apostolic See is responsible for all important matters of the church (*causae maiores*), which include everything that concerns the higher clergy. Bishops who are being prosecuted locally may appeal to the pope, who has the power not only to protect them but also to revoke any conviction determined by a council and to reinstate bishops who have been convicted. The pope can terminate the proceedings against an accused bishop if he so pleases. Most important, no authority within or outside the church can prevail over the verdict of the Apostolic See in Rome.

The implications of this doctrine for episcopal power are mixed. On the one hand, Pseudo-Isidore enhances the power of the bishops. They have a strong protector in the pope, who stands above all other ecclesiastical institutions and office-holders. Again, the authority of a metropolitan bishop (archbishop) over the suffragan bishops in his archdiocese is diminished, while each suffragan's power over his own subordinates is strengthened. The prosecution and dismissal of bishops by laymen is forbidden. Most important, Pseudo-Isidore introduces a variety of procedural provisions that would have made it extremely hard to press charges against a bishop in a way that was legitimate. On the other hand, Pseudo-Isidore reduces the bishop's authority within the church by making councils subordinate to the pope. Originally, the church council had been the most important ecclesiastical institution for regulation and judgment, and councils were governed by the bishops who attended. But Pseudo-Isidore limits the power and independence of councils by subordinating them to the pope, substantially reducing the bishops' scope for action. Bishops have to have the pope's approval for assembling at all; the pope is entitled to send legates to preside over the council; and the council's decisions are not legally binding without the pope's approval. It is no coincidence that Pseudo-Isidore used the letters of Leo I (see Chapter 13) extensively in the passages concerning Rome's authority over the assembled bishops. But he gave Leo's demands that his bishops

9 Hinschius, *Decretales*, Praefatio, 19.

should obey him new significance by putting them into the mouths of popes who lived long before Leo. Moreover, he generalized them by taking them out of the specific context to which Leo was referring and making them express a universal principle of ecclesiastical procedure.

PSEUDO-ISIDORE AND POWER RELATIONS IN THE CAROLINGIAN REALM

Some have argued that Pseudo-Isidore aimed above all to protect bishops, especially against the power of both archbishops and laymen. Although it is certainly true that he defended bishops in that way, however, he also diminished the authority of church councils in relation to the pope. But there was no fundamental conflict here if one takes into account the realities of the church up to and including the ninth century. The early councils were never as independent as the ecclesiastical documents of the time seem to suggest. Moreover, while papal influence on local councils, with some notable exceptions, was usually very limited, secular powers had dominated assemblies of bishops since Late Antiquity. The Carolingian rulers restored and enhanced this policy, which was well established by the time of Pseudo-Isidore. The Frankish episcopate often met in association with secular assemblies convened by the emperor. By giving the pope authority over councils, therefore, the forgers may have intended not to diminish the power of bishops but rather to reduce or, indeed, to prevent, royal interference and control over the church and its representatives.

In 829, the Carolingian bishops had assembled in four councils to discuss the policies of Louis the Pious, Charlemagne's successor, with which the episcopate was predominantly dissatisfied. They demanded that Louis should respect the bishops' authority over the Frankish church, and they argued for greater independence of the church from secular power, referring to Gelasius's theory of the Two Powers (see Chapter 14).[10] But the emperor did not accede to the bishops' demands, and the conflict soon escalated, partly because of dissatisfaction among the emperors' older sons regarding a plan of succession for the realm. In the *Epitaphium Arsenii*, a biography of his abbot Wala (a highly problematic and widely discussed text), the monk Paschasius Radbertus looked back on the deposition of Louis the Pious. His aim was to demonstrate that episcopal opposition to Louis the Pious had been justified, and that the emperor had been misled by bad advisors. Radbert defended the involvement of Pope Gregory IV (r. 827–844) in this conflict, arguing that it was appropriate because the pope was responsible for the church as a whole. Radbert reports that he and abbot Wala provided Pope Gregory with a dossier of documents from his predecessors confirming the pope's authority and the principle that the bishop of Rome was entitled to judge everyone and could not be judged by others.[11]

[10] *Concilium Parisiense*, 3, ed. Werminghoff, MGH Conc. 2.2, 610–11.

[11] Paschasius Radbertus, *Epitaphium Arsenii*, 2/16, ed. Dümmler, 84.

Did this dossier consist of the Pseudo-Isidorian decretals or selections thereof? Perhaps, but we shall never know. What matters is Radbert's argument: a rare statement during the first half of the ninth century regarding the supreme authority of the Apostolic See from a member of the Frankish clergy. Pseudo-Isidore's view of the church and of papal power over it, therefore, is consistent with the opinions that Radbert articulated under his own name.

Recently, historians have focused on questions regarding which year, which moment, or which person should be seen as decisive in the creation of the Pseudo-Isidorian decretals. But perhaps that is not the crucial issue. Instead, one needs to understand how the false decretals depicted both the organization and the history of the church. The crux was the freedom of the ecclesiastical hierarchy in relation to royal power. The Pseudo-Isidorian forgeries are proof that this was a matter of great concern for at least some of the ninth-century Carolingian clergy.

OTHER FORGERIES ASSOCIATED WITH PSEUDO-ISIDORE

The forgers responsible for the Pseudo-Isidorian decretals seem to have created at least four other canonical collections. The degree to which these collections are connected with the false decretals, however, differs greatly, and the content of the various forgeries is somewhat inconsistent and contradictory, not only among the several works but even within the same work.

Most manuscripts of the false decretals include also a short collection of capitularies (prescriptive legal documents, issued usually in the name of a ruler) called the *Capitula Angilramni* (CA). The short introduction states that Pope Hadrian gave these capitularies to Bishop Angilram of Metz in 786. The text is divided into seventy-one short chapters, which deal mainly with the prosecution of bishops. The CA proposes a legal process that would make such prosecutions virtually impossible. Although the CA and the Pseudo-Isidorian decretals share some of the same source material and were the result of similar methods of composition, they do not cite each other directly. Nevertheless, the CA expresses the gist of Pseudo-Isidore's position regarding prosecution of the episcopate. It does not attribute quite as much power to the papacy as the Pseudo-Isidorian decretals, but it still regards the papacy as responsible for authorizing a council and, therefore, as the most appropriate court for the trial of a bishop.

Another canonical collection that can be traced back to the Pseudo-Isidorian forgers is the so-called *Hispana Gallica Augustodunensis* (HGA), also known as the *Pseudo-Isidorian Hispana*. Its precise relation to the Pseudo-Isidorian decretals is difficult to ascertain. It is clear that Pseudo-Isidore based his collection partly on the *Hispana Gallica*: the Frankish version of a canonical collection, known as the *Hispana* because it originated from Spain. Now, the *Hispana Gallica* consists of two books. The first book contains exactly the same chronologically ordered collection of synodal texts as one finds in the second book of Pseudo-Isidore's compilation; and the second book of the *Hispana Gallica*, consisting of papal decretals, was a source for the third part of Pseudo-Isidore's collection. There is manuscript evidence that a corrected, slightly modified version of the *Hispana Gallica* existed, and it is clear from philological research that this corrected version was the textual basis for many of the authentic passages included in Pseudo-Isidore's collection. Where did the HGA belong in this process? It seems likely that in order to use the *Hispana Gallica* as the basis for his forgery, Pseudo-Isidore would have had to improve the text, for it was apparently heavily corrupted. That said, the known changes made to the text in the *Hispana Gallica* should not necessarily be construed as forgery, for they seem to have resulted largely from an attempt to improve the text. The HGA seems to have been a preparatory work, therefore, rather than a work intended for circulation in its own right, but whether it was prepared deliberately to provide material for the Pseudo-Isidorian decretals remains an open question.

In addition to the *Capitula Angilramni* and the *Hispana Gallica Augustodunensis*, the forgers produced an interpolated (altered) version of the Acts of the Council of Chalcedon (451), known as the *Excerptiones de gestis Chalcedonensis cocilii* (abbreviated to *Excerptiones*). Manuscript evidence shows how the author worked on his version of the Chalcedonian Acts, heavily altering their content.[12] This work differs markedly from the false decretals and the CA inasmuch as it draws on a single authentic source rather than using Pseudo-Isidore's mosaic technique, whereby he combined material from different sources. The text is included in several manuscripts containing the Pseudo-Isidorian decretals, and some of these belong among the earliest surviving copies of the forgery. The alterations made in the *Excerptiones* are substantive and have to do mainly with the relative positions of pope and emperor. Thus, in place of the original statement making it clear that the council depended on the consent of the Byzantine emperor Marcian (r. 450–457), who had summoned the assembly to Chalcedon, we find a statement attributing direct responsibility for the proceedings and decisions to Pope Leo I (r. 440–461) and his legates. This text, too, seems not to have circulated independently, perhaps because of its daring approach, and its purpose is not entirely clear. Since its origin in the Pseudo-Isidorian workshop has been detected only recently,[13] the *Excerptiones* and their relationship with the other forgeries have not yet been studied extensively.

Another, minor forgery can be connected directly to Pseudo-Isidore. It purports to be a decretal of Pope Gregory IV, and it is sometimes known as *Divinis praeceptis*. It was already recognized as a forgery in the nineteenth century, although a few modern scholars have made a case for its authenticity.[14] The decretal's importance

[12] Codex Paris, BnF lat. 11611.

[13] Klaus Zechiel-Eckes, "Verecundus oder Pseudoisidor? Zur Genese der Excerptiones de gestis Chalcedonensis concilii," *Deutsches Archiv für Erforschung des Mittelalters* 56 (2000): 413–46.

[14] See, e.g., Walter Goffart, "Gregory IV for Aldric of Le Mans (833): A Genuine or Spurious Decretal?" *Mediaeval Studies* 28 (1966): 22–38; and Eric Knibbs, "Pseudo-Isidore at the Field of Lies: *Divinis*

lies mainly in the fact that here Leo's concept of the bishop of Rome's "fullness of power" (*plenitudo potestatis*) is revived in the medieval West for the first time.[15] The letter is constructed in a similar fashion to that of the Pseudo-Isidorian decretals, whereby material taken from several authentic sources has been combined. The result is an extensive treatment of papal supremacy over the church: a topic prominent in the false decretals. Besides its content and construction, the surviving manuscript evidence reveals that it is connected to Pseudo-Isidore's work in some way. Whether Gregory IV himself had a role in its composition is still a matter of discussion.

The collection of (false) capitularies ascribed to Benedictus Levita, an extensive and influential ninth-century forgery, has evident affinities with Pseudo-Isidore's work. This purports to be a collection of Carolingian legislation compiled by Benedict, a deacon of Mayence, for his archbishop, Otgar of Mayence. Benedict pretends to continue the work of Ansegisus of Fontenelle, who was responsible for compiling an influential collection of (authentic) early Carolingian capitularies. The collection comprises over seventeen hundred chapters, arranged in three books with four appendices. Like Pseudo-Isidore, Benedict uses authentic source material to construct his forgeries, but his technique is simpler, and the alterations seem to have been less radical than in many of the Pseudo-Isidorian decretals. Some of Pseudo-Isidore's false decretals occur also in Benedict's collection, mostly in the last appendix. It is generally assumed that Benedict took them from Pseudo-Isidore, but the converse might be true. Most of the similarities and points of correspondence apparently stem from shared source material.[16] Although the two forgeries have many common features, therefore, they seem not to be the work of the same person. It has been suggested that the forgers shared their resources at some point in the process and collaborated in making their respective collections. Whether they shared a common goal, however, remains unclear, for there is no general consensus as what exactly the forgers' intentions were. This is especially true of Benedictus Levita. To complicate the issue even further, the CA is closely related with Benedictus Levita as regards shared source material and textual parallels, although its transmission is inseparably connected with Pseudo-Isidore. It is still not clear which of the two collections, the capitularies of Benedictus Levita or the Pseudo-Isidorian decretals, was created first. It seems not only possible but most likely that they were developed simultaneously.

Another collection associated with the Pseudo-Isidorian workshop is the so-called *Collectio Danieliana*. Since the relationship has been acknowledged only fairly

praeceptis (JE †2579) as an Authentic Decretal," *Bulletin of Medieval Canon Law* n.s. 29 (2011–2012): 1–34.

15 Robert L. Benson, "*Plenitudo Potestatis*: Evolution of a Formula from Gregory IV to Gratian," *Studia Gratiana* 14 (1967): 193–217.

16 Gerhard Schmitz, "Verfilzungen. Isidor und Benedict," in Ubl and Ziemann, *Fälschung als Mittel der Politik?* 127–51, at 151.

recently and the collection itself had little historical impact, there has not been much investigation into its relationship to the Pseudo-Isidorian forgeries. But it seems likely that the compilers did not belong to the Pseudo-Isidorian circle, and that the points of correspondence between the *Collectio Danieliana* and the Pseudo-Isidorian decretals result from shared methods and sources.

One should keep in mind that although each of these works has some relation to the Pseudo-Isidorian decretals, they are related in diverse ways. Because their origins remain unclear, therefore, each has to be treated individually. One should not regard the Pseudo-Isidorian forgeries as a single, coherent body of literature, unlike the Pseudo-Isidorian decretals. The observations about reception made in the following paragraphs pertain only to the Pseudo-Isidorian decretals, and not the other forgeries associated with this collection.

THE AGE OF PSEUDO-ISIDORE?

The historian Walter Ullmann referred to the second half of the ninth century as the "Age of Pseudo-Isidore."[17] It is generally accepted today that Ullmann's characterization was exaggerated, but there is some truth to it.

The false decretals were cited for the first time in the middle of the ninth century, probably a few years after they were created. Traces of Pseudo-Isidorian thought can be found in the early 850s, but the first explicit use of the forgery seems not to have occurred before 857. Then, the collection was used extensively both by bishop Hincmar of Laon and by his uncle, superior, and prosecutor, archbishop Hincmar of Reims (Chapter 21). Although Hincmar of Reims explicitly questioned the authenticity of the decretals on which his nephew, in an effort to shield himself from the archbishop's jurisdiction, was drawing heavily, he, too, used Pseudo-Isidorian material when it suited him.[18] Beyond this conflict, however, there is little textual evidence of extensive use of the Pseudo-Isidorian collection during the ninth century, albeit with some noticeable exceptions. Leodoin, bishop of Modena, for example, used the false decretals in the 880s in a letter to abbot Theodoric of Nonantola, whom the bishop had found disobedient. It is interesting that the bishop avoided clear references to his sources when using Pseudo-Isidore, whereas he explicitly cited conciliar canons. Again, he modified the material from the false decretals to suit his purpose, whereas he was careful to record the conciliar canons accurately. It is possible that this difference in Leodoin's use of canonical material was due to the unequal authority he attached to decretals on the one hand and to

[17] Walter Ullmann, *The Growth of Papal Government in the Middle Ages: A Study in the Ideological Relation of Clerical to Lay Power* (London: Methuen, 1955).

[18] Horst Fuhrmann and Detlev Jasper, *Papal Letters in the Early Middle Ages* (Washington, DC: Catholic University of America Press, 2001), 173–81. Horst Fuhrmann, *Einfluß und Verbreitung der pseudoisidorischen Fälschungen*, 3 vols. (Stuttgart: Anton Hiersemann, 1972–1974), 1:195–224.

conciliar canons on the other.[19] Perhaps, in the late ninth century, the doubtful origin of the Pseudo-Isidorian collection was an open secret among clerics, and the false decretals were handled more creatively and with more discretion when used directly in conflicts.

Although citation of Pseudo-Isidorian decretals during the ninth century is rare, at least in the extant literature, the collection must have circulated widely in the Carolingian realm, as can be seen from the many surviving manuscripts. Despite the absence of textual evidence in the form of direct quotations, therefore, one has to assume that Pseudo-Isidore was being not only copied but also read during the second half of the ninth century, and that his thoughts on the church's legal situation did make a difference. There were several cases during this period in which accused or deposed bishops appealed to the pope, with or without success, and this had not been common practice hitherto. On the contrary, such a claim had been denied by the Frankish clergy at the beginning of the ninth century. Moreover, the relationship between the Franks and the Apostolic See changed during the ninth century inasmuch as the Carolingians now not only accepted but even actively sought the pope's authority to confirm privileges and to adjudicate delicate legal matters, such as the divorce of King Lothar II (r. 855–869).[20] It is impossible to determine to what extent this development was a result of the dissemination of the Pseudo-Isidorian decretals, but it seems unlikely that such a drastic change in behavior would have occurred entirely without Pseudo-Isidore's influence. While it would be an exaggeration to characterize the second half of the ninth century as the "Age of Pseudo-Isidore," therefore, it does seem reasonable to give Pseudo-Isidore at least some credit for this shift in Franco-papal relations.[21]

Surprisingly, the papacy during this period, which probably first came into contact with the Pseudo-Isidorian decretals during the 860s, did not make extensive use of them. In 863, the deposed bishop Rothad of Soissons traveled to Rome to seek the help of Pope Nicholas I (r. 858–867). Rothad's deposition seems to have been mainly a result of a conflict with his archbishop, Hincmar of Reims. When the pope reinstated Rothad and declared him to be innocent, he accused the Frankish episcopate of acting in defiance of papal authority, observing that the bishops were ignorant of many decretals. This remark has generally been construed as a reference to the Pseudo-Isidorian decretals,[22] although Nicholas promoted papal supremacy over the church forcefully throughout his pontificate, and it seems that he did not make any direct use of the forged decretals. Nevertheless, it is generally assumed that Rothad brought the collection with him to Rome. Nicholas's successor Adrian II

19 Michael W. Heil, "Bishop Leodoin of Modena and the Legal Culture of Late Ninth-Century Italy," ZRG Kan. Abt. 103 (2017): 1–69, esp. 15–24.

20 Karl Heidecker, *The Divorce of Lothar II: Christian Marriage and Political Power in the Carolingian World*, trans. T. M. Guest (Ithaca: Cornell University Press, 2010).

21 Harder, *Pseudoisidor*, 167–89.

22 Nicholas I, *ep.* 107 (JE 2708), in MGH Epist. 6, 620–21. Fuhrmann, *Einfluß und Verbreitung*, 2:254–63.

(r. 867–872) is generally regarded as the first bishop of Rome explicitly to cite the decretals of Pseudo-Isidore. Nevertheless, the papacy used the Pseudo-Isidorian decretals during the late ninth century only occasionally and randomly, although the claims of the popes during this period regarding their own authority were generally congruent with Pseudo-Isidorian thinking.[23] With the decline of papal power and influence around the end of the ninth century and the beginning of the tenth, Pseudo-Isidore's suggestions about the ecclesiastical order and the papacy's role therein were put aside. They were revived over a hundred years later.

FURTHER RECEPTION, EXPOSURE, AND AFTERMATH

The Pseudo-Isidorian collection was preserved and copied during the ninth and tenth centuries. After Hincmar of Reims, no medieval author seems to have explicitly questioned the collection's authenticity. Compilers of canonical material during the tenth and eleventh centuries, such as Burchard of Worms (see Chapter 23), Anselm of Lucca, and Ivo of Chartres, incorporated Pseudo-Isidorian passages into their collections. The decretals came into full effect, however, only during the central Middle Ages. When Pseudo-Isidore described the supreme position of the pope within the church, he foreshadowed a development that occurred during the eleventh and twelfth centuries, when the papacy's power increased greatly during and after what is now known as the Investiture Conflict. Here, the Pseudo-Isidorian decretals served as an important source of inspiration and as evidence on the papal side. Moreover, the collection included the Donation of Constantine, which provided a rationale for empowering the papacy during controversy with the Byzantine church, as well as in conflicts with European lords regarding investiture. The pro-papal literature that was disseminated during the Investiture Conflict, which was often polemical, drew heavily on the false decretals. Finally, Pseudo-Isidore became inseparable from canon law when Gratian included Pseudo-Isidorian material into his *Concordia discordantium canonum*, also known as the *Decretum*, in the 1140s. Citations from the false decretals account for some 10 percent of the *Decretum*. As Horst Fuhrmann has shown, Gratian probably did not consult Pseudo-Isidore's collection directly, but rather acquired the material from older canonical collections and sources, such as Burchard and Ivo. In general, the Pseudo-Isidorian passages in Gratian pertain mainly to the right organization of the church and support the exclusion of lay influence from the church.[24]

The authenticity of the collection and of its alleged author, Isidorus Mercator, was already beginning to be challenged by the end of the Middle Ages, and the Calvinist preacher David Blondel exposed the work as a fraud in 1628.[25] Blondel noticed that

[23] Fuhrmann, *Einfluß und Verbreitung*, 2:254–88.

[24] Fuhrmann, *Einluß und Verbreitung*, 2:408–585 and 3:769–1005.

[25] David Blondel, *Pseudo-Isidorus et Turrianus vapulantes. Seu editio et censura nova Epistolarum omnium, quae piisimis Urbis Romae Praesulibus a B. Clemente ad Siricium, etc., nefando ausu, infelici eventu, Isidorus cognomento Mercator, Supposuit, Franciscus Turrianus Iesuita [etc.]* (Geneva, 1628).

the alleged early popes in the collection always quoted the Bible from the Vulgate version, which originated in the late fourth century and would not have been quoted before the papacy of Damasus I (r. 366–384). Although the Catholic Church tried to defend the collection's authenticity and authority for a while, Catholic authorities eventually accepted that a substantial part of the church's body of canon law (*Corpus iuris Canonici*) was derived from this forgery. Henceforth, Pseudo-Isidorian material was eliminated from the official law of the church. Nevertheless, Pseudo-Isidore's treatment of some subjects, especially the power and authority of the papacy, had become inseparable from Catholic history and endorsed by tradition. When the First Vatican Council decided in 1870 that the pope not only had "full and supreme power over the whole Church" (Ch. 3.9) but was also infallible, it confirmed and even went beyond Pseudo-Isidorus Mercator. Whether the Pseudo-Isidorian forgeries were causally related to the doctrine is disputable, but any historically informed account of the doctrines of papal supremacy and infallibility has to take into account the contribution of the ninth-century forgers.

SOURCES

The latest printed and only critical edition of the Pseudo-Isidorian decretals dates from the mid-nineteenth century: Paul Hinschius (ed.), *Decretales Pseudo-Isidorianae et Capitula Angilramni* (Leipzig: B. Tauchnitz, 1863; repr. Aalen: Scientia, 1963). While this was arguably an impressive achievement for its time, the edition is problematic and outdated by current standards. Nevertheless, scholars must still rely on it in the absence of anything better, and its extensive introduction, which includes a detailed account of the sources used, is still helpful. A version of the false decretals based on a single manuscript, edited by Jacques Merlin in 1524, is reproduced in PL 130:7–1177. There is a modern edition of one false decretal in Klaus Zechiel-Eckes, "Ein Blick in Pseudoisidors Werkstatt. Studien zum Entstehungsprozeß der falschen Dekretalen. Mit einem exemplarischen editorischen Anhang (Pseudo-Julius an die orientalischen Bischöfe, JK †196)," *Francia* 28.1 (2001): 37–90, at 62–90. Improved versions of many of the false decretals, edited by Karl-Georg Schon, are available online in the "Projekt Pseudoisidor": www.pseudoisidor.mgh.de (accessed June 12, 2017). Unfortunately, work on this project has ceased. One should keep in mind the preliminary state of the versions found there, which are no substitute for a critical edition. Eric Knibbs is now working on a new, fully critical edition: see www.pseudo-isidore.com (accessed June 12, 2017).

There is no complete English translation of the Pseudo-Isidorian decretals. An English translation of Isidorus Mercator's preface can be found in Somerville and Brasington's *Prefaces*, 82–91. There is an English translation of the *Collection in Seventy-Four Titles* (c. 1050), of which the main source was the Pseudo-Isidorian decretals, and that was in turn a major vehicle of their transmission: see John

Gilchrist (trans.), The Collection in Seventy-Four Titles: A Canon Law Manual of the Gregorian Reform (Toronto: PIMS, 1980).

Gerhard Schmitz is currently re-editing the false capitularies of Benedictus Levita. Information on the present state of the edition and some other useful materials and sources are available here: www.benedictus.mgh.de (accessed June 12, 2017). The best printed edition of these capitularies until the new edition is completed is in *Capitularia Regnum Francorum* I, ed. by Étienne Baluze, first published in Paris, 1677, and later reproduced in *Mansis Konziliensammlung*, vol. 17B (Paris, 1780; Paris and Leipzig, 1902). This text can be found online in Gerhard Schmitz's source collection. The edition by G. H. Pertz in MGH LL (in Folio) 2.2 (1837), reproduced in PL 97:699–912, is inferior to Baluze's. For an English translation of the preface, see *Prefaces*, 78–82.

Other Sources and Translations

Die Capitula Angilramni. Eine prozessrechtliche Fälschung Pseudoisidor. Ed. Karl-Georg Schon in MGH Studien und Texte 39 (2006). [Includes a German translation of the Latin text.]

Concilium Parisiense. Ed. Albert Werminghoff in MGH Conc. 2.2 (1908), 606–80.

Constitutum Constantini [*Donation of Constantine*]. Ed. by Horst Fuhrmann in MGH *Fontes Iuris* 10 (Hannover, 1968). [For an English translation, see Johannes Fried, *Donation of Constantine and Constitutum Constantini*, Millennium-Studien (Berlin and New York: De Gruyter, 2007), 138–45.]

"Excerptiones de gestis Chalcedonensis concilii." Edited in Johannes B. Pitra, *Spicilegium Solesmense complectens sanctorum patrum scriptorumque ecclesiasticorum anecdota hactenus opera, selecta e Graecis Orientalibusque et Latinis codicibus*, tom. 4: *In quo monumenta tam Africanae quam Byzantinae ecclesiae proferuntur et illustrantur* (Paris: F. Didot, 1858; repr. Graz: Akademische Druck-U. Verlagsanstalt, 1963), 166–91.

Gregory IV, *Epistola spuria*. Ed. Karl Hampe in MGH Epist. 5 (1899), 72–81.

Nicholas I, Epistolae. Ed. by Ernst Perels in MGH Epist. 6 (1925), 257–690.

Paschasius Radbertus, *Epitaphium Arsenii*. Ed. by Ernst Dümmler. Abhandlungen der königlichen Akadamie der Wissenschaften zu Berlin, Philosophisch-Historische Classe no. 2. Berlin, 1900. [Older edition in PL 120:1557–1650. English Translation in A. J. Cabaniss, *Charlemagne's Cousins: Contemporary Lives of Adalard and Wala* (Syracuse, NY: Syracuse University Press, 1967).]

Unbekannte Texte aus der Werkstatt Pseudoisidors. Die Collectio Danieliana. Ed. by Karl-Georg Schon. MGH Studien und Texte 38 (2006). [Includes a German translation.]

FURTHER READING

One of the most significant and reliable introductions to Pseudo-Isidore, although it is outdated in places, remains Emil Seckel's article in the third edition of the *Theologische Realenzyklopädie* 19 (1905), 265–307. Seckel also published a series of influential articles on Benedictus Levita ("Studien zu Benedictus Levita" I–VIII) in *Neues Archiv* between 1901 and 1917.

For an overview of the manuscript tradition of Pseudo-Isidore, see Schafer Williams, *Codices Pseudo-Isidoriani: A Palaeographico-Historical Study*, with a foreword by Horst Fuhrmann (New York: Fordham University Press, 1971).

Horst Fuhrmann, acknowledged as the leading twentieth-century expert on Pseudo-Isidore, provides an English-language introduction to the topic in Horst Fuhrmann and Detlev Jasper, *Papal Letters in the Early Middle Ages* (Washington, DC: Catholic University of America Press, 2001), 135–95. The following extensive study of the reception of Pseudo-Isidore in medieval canonical collections remains very important: Horst Fuhrmann, *Einfluß und Verbreitung der pseudoisidorischen Fälschungen. Von ihrem Auftauchen bis in die neuere Zeit*, 3 vols., MGH Schriften I–III (Stuttgart: Anton Hiersemann, 1972–1974).

Klaus Zechiel-Eckes published several articles regarding the manuscripts produced in Pseudo-Isidore's "workshop" and the conclusions that may be drawn from them. He summarized his central findings in a lecture that was published in 2010, after his death: *Fälschung als Mittel politischer Auseinandersetzung. Ludwig der Fromme (814–840) und die Genese der pseudoisidorischen Dekretalen* (Paderborn: Schönigh, 2011).

Wilfried Hartmann and Gerhard Schmitz (eds.), *Fortschritt durch Fälschungen? Ursprung, Gestalt und Wirkungen der pseudoisidorischen Fälschungen. Beiträge zum gleichnamigen Symposium an der Universität Tübingen vom 27. und 28. Juli 2001* (Hannover: Hahn, 2002) is an anthology of conference papers on Pseudo-Isidore, including the first article that Zechiel-Eckes published on the topic. The proceedings of another international conference on Pseudo-Isidore, which took place in Cologne in 2013, were published in Karl Ubl and Daniel Ziemann (eds.), *Fälschung als Mittel der Politik? Pseudoisidor im Licht der neuen Forschung. Gedenkschrift für Klaus Zechiel-Eckes* (Wiesbaden: Harrasowitz, 2015).

On the papacy in the Pseudo-Isidorian forgeries, see Clara Harder, *Pseudoisidor und das Papsttum. Funktion und Bedeutung des apostolischen Stuhls in den pseudoisidorischen Fälschungen* (Köln: Böhlau, 2014).

On the reception history of the *Donation of Constantine*, see Johannes Fried, *"Donation of Constantine" and "Constitutum Constantini": The Misinterpretation of a Fiction and its Original Meaning*, Millennium Studies 3 (Berlin: De Gruyter, 2007).

Finally, Eric Knibbs has recently proposed some new theories regarding the genesis of the false decretals. See, e.g., Knibbs, "The interpolated *Hispana* and the Origins of Pseudo-Isidore," ZRG Kan. Abt. 99 (2013): 1–71; and "Ebo of Reims, Pseudo-Isidore, and the Date of the False Decretals," *Speculum* 92.1 (2017): 144–83.

20

Jonas of Orléans

Francesco Veronese

PRELUDE

In a Roman *scriptorium* during the second half of the eleventh century, someone compiled a manuscript, now Codex 122 of the Episcopal Library of Vercelli, that includes a collection of legal and canonical texts.[1] Among these texts (fol. 160 r–162 r) is a little dossier about marriage and incest that includes an image of the *Arbor cognationum*, or kinship tree, the design of which is based on a passage from Isidore of Seville's *Etymologies*. The purpose of such diagrams was chiefly to clarify which relationships were impediments to marriage. A certain Ambrosius Iudex has added below the diagram, perhaps toward the end of the eleventh century, chapter 153 of the *Edictum Rothari*, a seventh-century compilation of Lombard law. Before the diagram of the *Arbor*, however, written by one of the two hands that compiled the manuscript, is a chapter on incestuous relationships (*De incestis*) from the *De institutione laicali* (DIL) by Jonas, bishop of Orléans (d. 840/3), generally regarded as a moral treatise. Thus, we find a chapter from Jonas's moral work included in a collection of legal and canonical texts. The scribe who included this chapter considered DIL to be not only a moral treatise, or *speculum*, therefore, but also a normative, legal text about a highly technical topic.

The Vercelli codex was very probably linked to the needs and debates of eleventh-century church reform. It collects texts that reflect the idea of a comparison, even competition, between secular or imperial law and ecclesiastical regulation. Nonetheless, the use of Jonas's moral treatise here was not inconsistent with the meaning that the author himself attributed to it. In the opening letter of DIL, Jonas wrote that the work was meant to fill a legislative void.[2] At reform councils held in Aachen in 816 and 817, specific *institutiones*, or Rules, had been imposed on

[1] On this manuscript, see Antonio Ciaralli, "Produzione manoscritta e trasmissione dei testi di natura giuridica tra XI e XII secolo: due esempi," in V. Colli (ed.), *Juristische Buchproduktion im Mittelalter*, Studien zur Europäishcer Rechtsgeschichte 155 (Frankfurt am Main: Vittorio Klostermann, 2002), 71–103, at 83–90.

[2] Jonas d'Orléans, *Instruction des laïcs* [DIL], ed. Odile Dubreucq, vol. 1, SC 549, dedicatory letter (120–27), at 122–24.

communities of monks and canons. Jonas, who wrote in the early 820s, felt an equal need to provide the laypeople of the Carolingian empire with their own *institutio*. They were the only *ordo* (social class or group) that still lacked one. Monastic rules and norms were not exactly laws, for they were not issued by secular or ecclesiastical legislators, although as a result of the Aachen councils they *became* laws in effect, since both secular and ecclesiastical authorities imposed them on religious communities by means of capitularies and conciliar acts, respectively, making them legally binding. Jonas associated his work with this Aachen legislation, and he aimed to produce something more than a set of moral guidelines. Presenting his treatise on secular morality as an *institutio*, following the model of those issued for monks and canons at Aachen, he assigned to it a legal meaning, as the compilers of the book of Vercelli clearly recognized. The DIL was just one episode in the constant conversation that characterized Jonas's episcopal and political activity, which embraced morality, law, and Christianity.

Jonas was a "moralist," then, but in his mind there was no sharp division between morality and law or regulation. Moreover, some of his moral teachings effectively *became* statutes through his conciliar activities.

JONAS'S LIFE

Jonas seems always to have enjoyed a special relationship with Louis the Pious.[3] He was from Aquitaine, and he was ordained as a priest and trained in the liberal arts in that region, perhaps at Louis's court. After Louis the Pious succeeded his father Charlemagne as emperor in 814, Jonas remained in Aquitaine for a short period under Louis's son Pippin, but he soon had to flee because of the attacks of "evil men" (*pravi homines*), who had cast a bad light on him in Pippin's eyes.[4] Nevertheless, he maintained links with the court of Aquitaine, as the dedication of his later *De institutione regia* to Pippin shows.

One of the few episodes known to us from this early period of Jonas's career is his journey to the north Iberian peninsula between 780 and 790.[5] There, he met Elipandus of Toledo, who was teaching that Jesus Christ was the adopted son of God. This teaching, a form of what is known today as Adoptionism, was a source of heated controversy in the Frankish world, and it was condemned as heresy at Frankfurt in 794. Jonas's journey to Iberia must have given him a chance to develop his training in religious debates.

3 For detailed biographical portraits of Jonas of Orléans, see Jean Reviron, *Les idées politico-religieuses d'un évêque du IXe siècle. Jonas d'Orléans et son De institutione regia: étude et texte critique*, L'Église et l'État au Moyen âge 1 (Paris: Vrin, 1930), 23–36; Alain Dubreucq, Introduction, in Jonas d'Orléans, *Le métier de roi* [DIR], ed. A. Dubreucq, SC 407, 9–26; and Odile Dubreucq, Introduction, in Jonas d'Orléans, *Instruction des Laïcs* [DIL], ed. O. Dubreucq, SC 549, 33–43.

4 DIR, SC 407, 148–50.

5 Ionae Aurelianensis *De cultu imaginum*, PL 106:305–88, at 307–09.

Immediately after his departure from Aquitaine, Jonas was assigned to the bishopric of Orléans. His predecessor, Theodulf, was one of the most important intellectuals at Charlemagne's court, but he was involved – we do not know exactly how – in the rebellion of King Bernard of Italy in 817–18. In the *In honorem Hludowici* by Ermold, written between 826 and 828, Jonas appears for the first time in the role of bishop, welcoming Louis to Orléans in 818.[6]

In his first years as bishop, Jonas worked to strengthen his position in this new field of action, developing close connections with some of the leading political figures in the region and in the empire. Jonas dedicated the first version of DIL to Matfrid, count of Orléans. Matfrid was one of the emperor's closest advisers until February 828, when he was deposed on grounds of military misconduct.[7] The same fate befell Hugh, Count of Tours and father-in-law of co-emperor Lothar. Jonas had equally close relations with Hugh, as attested by a royal diploma of 835 (referring to events in 827), in which both Hugh and Jonas appear as royal *missi* (envoys), one spiritual and one secular, who worked together as a team.[8] He also showed a strong interest in the monastic communities of his diocese. The ninth-century *Vita Maximini* by Berthold of Micy and the tenth-century *Miracula sancti Maximini* by Lethald both report that the transfer of the bodies of Saints Maximinus and Theodemir to the abbey of Micy (825) took place during Jonas's bishopric and with his consent.[9] We find Jonas operating as an imperial envoy (*missus*) or as a judge in settling disputes involving monasteries in several documents of the 820s and 830s.

It is not easy to follow Jonas's life and career during the years 830–34, when the sons of Louis the Pious led revolts against their father.[10] Scholars have wondered whether Jonas remained loyal to Louis or supported his sons. Ideas that he expressed both in his written works and in conciliar activity may seem to justify the possibility that bishops had the right to exercise authority over their emperor, but Jonas never supported the idea that bishops could *depose* an emperor, as happened in Soissons in 834. Between 832, when he attended a synod in Saint-Denis, and 835, when he participated in the synod of Thionville that reinstated Louis, Jonas is mentioned only once, in a diploma issued by Aldric, archbishop of Sens. (The document was issued in 833 or 834 for the monastery of Saint-Remi in Sens.)[11] Jonas apparently proceeded

6 Ermold le Noir, *Poème sur Louis le Pieux et Épitres au roi Pépin*, ed. Edmond Faral, 2nd edition (Paris: Société d'édition les Belles lettres, 1964), 118.

7 Philippe Depreux, "Le comte Matfrid d'Orléans (av. 815–836)," *Bibliothèque de l'École des Chartes* 152.2 (1994): 331–74.

8 *Die Urkunden Ludwigs des Frommen*, ed. Theo Kölzer, MGH Diplomata Karolinorum 2/2 (Wiesbaden, 2016), no. 357, pp. 888–90.

9 Bertholdi *Vita Maximini*, ed. Luc d'Achery, in Jean Mabillon, *Acta Sancotum ordinis Sancti Benedicti* 1 (Paris, 1668), 591–97, at 597. Lethald, *Liber miraculorum sancti Maximini*, ibid., 598–613, at 602.

10 On this era, see Mayke de Jong, *The Penitential State: Authority and Atonement in the Age of Louis the Pious* (Cambridge: Cambridge University Press, 2009).

11 Alain Dubreucq, Introduction, SC 407, 21–22.

cautiously during the interregnum, therefore, waiting for circumstances to become clearer. When they did, he played a leading role in the process of reinstating Louis the Pious. Hincmar, archbishop of Reims (see Chapter 21 in this volume), says in his treatise on predestination (*De praedestinatione*) that Jonas drafted the sentence deposing Ebbo of Rheims, scapegoat for the revolt of 833–34, at the council of Thionville ("*dictatum est a Iona Aurelianense episcopo*").[12] Jonas was apparently the official who sanctioned Ebbo's punishment.

One other clue sheds light on Jonas's political and social positions. In the aftermath of count Matfrid's deposition in 828, Jonas composed a new version of DIL in which every reference to Matfrid was eliminated. Jonas clearly wished to undo the textual links connecting him to Matfrid. Similarly, in an early manuscript of the version of DIL that had been dedicated to Matfrid, the names of Matfrid and Jonas, mentioned in the introduction, have been erased.[13] Jonas did what he could to distance himself from the disgraced count and to express his full support for Louis.

After 834, Louis the Pious resumed his imperial dignity and his role in convening episcopal assemblies (councils, or synods), and Jonas attended the council in the imperial city of Aachen in 836. His presence is attested by a text ascribed to him: a letter sent from the fathers of the council to King Pippin of Aquitaine (*De rebus ecclesiasticis non invadendis*).[14] Between 834 and 838, Orléans and its diocese were officially part of the kingdom of Aquitaine, so Pippin was the obvious addressee of Jonas's complaints. But Jonas already enjoyed privileged channels of communication with the Aquitanian court, which he had developed when he was a young man and maintained despite his departure. What is more, by that time Jonas already had some experience in giving kings moral instruction (see below). It is not surprising, therefore, that the bishops gathered in Aachen chose Jonas as their spokesman to rebuke Pippin.

Jonas died between 840 and 843. The last sources depicting him as alive are three letters to him from the abbots of Ferrières in the early 840s.[15] By 843, there was a new bishop of Orléans, named Agius, who was probably Jonas's immediate successor. The letters from Ferrières to Jonas reveal that the relationship between the bishop and the monastic communities in his diocese were not always easy. In one of these letters, abbot Lupus of Ferrières accused Agius, Jonas's relative or colleague (*propinquus*), of unjustly seizing the products of the lands dependent on Ferrières, adding that Agius had done so in accordance with Jonas's wishes ("*vestra id fecisse voluntate*"). Jonas was once again dealing with the monasteries of his diocese, therefore, and this activity could generate conflicts and opposition, as the

12 Hincmari Rhemensis *De praedestinatione Dei et libero arbitrio dissertatio posterior*, PL 125:65–474, at 390.
13 The codex is Köln, Erzbischöfliche Diözesan- und Dombibliothek 184, dating from the 820s.
14 The text is edited in MGH Conc. 2.2, ed. Albert Werminghoff (1908), 724–67.
15 *Lupi abbatis Ferrariensis epistolae*, ed. Ernst Dümmler, MGH Epist. 6 (1925), pp. 1–126: no. 21, pp. 29–30; no. 27, p. 33; no. 28, pp. 33–34.

application of secular as well as monastic reforms during the Carolingian period frequently did. Yet Jonas not only applied reforms dictated by his superiors but also cooperated in their elaboration and diffusion, both in his writings and in his conciliar activity.

MORALITY SHAPES CHRISTIANITY: JONAS'S MORAL WRITINGS

Recent scholarship on the life of Jonas has depicted him as an exemplary Carolingian bishop who took care of the monasteries of his diocese, settled disputes as an imperial envoy (*missus*), and defended ecclesiastical property.[16] But what made a bishop exemplary from a Carolingian point of view? This question is crucial to understanding Carolingian debates during the 810s and 820s. A clear distinction between clergy and laity was at stake following the last years of Charlemagne's rule.[17] As well as being prohibited from marrying and bearing arms, clerics were supposed to meet appropriately high standards of moral behavior. Clerics and monks were expected to pray for the safety of the entire empire, and they had to please God morally if their prayers were to be effective. Moreover, the church was experiencing profound changes in the social composition and identity of the episcopacy.[18] In the Merovingian and early Carolingian eras, episcopal authority was almost exclusively assigned to members of the aristocracy. During the reign of Louis the Pious, however, new figures, whose origins were unknown or at least not presented as aristocratic, were elevated to key bishoprics. They succeeded in reaching powerful positions because of their highly specialized religious culture. These changes deeply affected the identity of bishops as a group. Literary and conciliar sources show that noble origins gradually ceased to be emphasized as a salient feature of a bishop's identity. At the same time, social expectations pushed bishops to improve their moral behavior. *Moral* nobility was taking the place of *social* nobility.

Jonas played a key role in these developments. His character and self-image matched what was currently expected of bishops. Thus, he never talked about his social origins in his writings. Clearly, he did not consider such matters to be an important feature of his identity. And he became a bishop not only because he was close to the emperor, but also because he was learned and studious. What is more, he

16 Geneviève Bührer-Thierry, "Épiscopat et royauté dans le monde carolingien," in W. Fałkowski and Y. Sassier (eds.), *Le monde carolingien: Bilan, perspectives, champs de recherches* (Turnhout: Brepols, 2009), 143–55.

17 Rachel Stone, "'In what way can those who have left the world be distinguished?' Masculinity and the Difference Between Carolingian Men," in C. Beattie and K. A. Fenton (eds.), *Intersections of Gender, Religion and Ethnicity in the Middle Ages* (Basingstoke: Palgrave Macmillan, 2010), 12–33.

18 Steffen Patzold, "Redéfinir l'office épiscopal. Les évêques francs face à la crise des années 820–830," in F. Bougard, L. Feller, R. Le Jan (eds.), *Les élites au Haut Moyen Âge. Crises et renouvellements*, Haut Moyen Âge 1 (Turnhout: Brepols, 2006), 337–59.

was the principal voice expressing the bishops' new identity and their efforts to improve their morality.

In 825, Walcaud, bishop of Liège, asked Jonas to compose a new version of the eighth-century Life of St. Hubert (*Vita Hucberti*), which was to be enriched with an account of the removal of Hubert's relics from Liège to Andage in that year. The result was the *Vita secunda Hucberti*, a version revised and improved in language and grammar.[19] Jonas fulfilled his commissioner's requests, but he also pursued goals of his own. Scholars have perceived in the *Vita secunda* something akin to a *speculum episcopale*: a moral guide for Carolingian bishops.[20] Jonas was developing an episcopal morality by the means of a hagiographical text, in order to display a model of behavior to his colleagues. Like Jonas's other moral treatises, the *Vita secunda* begins with a dedicatory letter and a table of contents (both absent from the *Vita prima*), and the main text is now divided into chapters. In updating the *Vita prima*, Jonas uses the vocabulary currently being developed to describe episcopal authority during Louis the Pious's reign. Bishops are called *praepositi* and *praelati* – those who are "set above" their subjects (their *subditi*), whom they have the authority to judge and correct. As a social class, the episcopal "order" (*ordo episcopalis*) must guide and watch over the other principal orders: the monastics and the lay folk. Several of Jonas's contemporaries expounded similar divisions of the community into three orders. Jonas filled his new version of Hubert's hagiographical memory with politically meaningful vocabulary. He was conveying his teachings about the bishops' duties and behavior in a way that the bishops could easily understand. At the same time, he was contributing to the development of a new image of bishops and of their responsibilities: one that was later expressed even more clearly in conciliar enactments.

In Jonas's eyes, however, bishops were not the only ones in need of moral reform. During Louis the Pious's reign, morality was regarded as the driving principle and the standard by which everyone's actions, not only those of the bishops, were to be judged. One of Louis's biographers, known as the Astronomer (writing in the early 840s), emphasizes his wish to reform morality in the empire beginning at its head, the imperial court.[21] Charlemagne's daughters had never married – ostensibly because their father loved them too much, but also, no doubt, because he did not wish there to be a proliferation of little Carolingians who could lay claim to the imperial dignity.[22] Rumors about these courtly women's sexual life began to spread. The first action Louis took as emperor, the Astronomer says, was to send his sisters to monasteries, thus cleaning up the court's moral reputation. The court of Aachen was meant to become an example of morality. The Christian emperor placed himself at

19 Edited by Charles de Smedt in *Acta Sanctorum Novembris*, 1 (Bruxelles, 1887), 806–16.

20 Alain Dubreucq, *Introduction*, 27–28.

21 On the texts of the 830s and what follows De Jong, *The Penitential State*.

22 Janet L. Nelson, "Women at the Court of Charlemagne: A Case of Monstrous Regiment?" in John C. Parsons (ed.), *Medieval Queenship* (New York: St. Martins Press, 1993), 43–61.

the core of the Carolingian society's moral functioning. Morality and penance were conceived as new and powerful tools of legitimation for the emperor. In 822, Louis willingly underwent a public penance. The ceremony gave back to the empire a renewed ruler, restored to the condition of moral perfection expected from him. This role entailed a huge responsibility. Every action of the emperor and his court was scrutinized closely. Purportedly immoral actions became powerful arguments for attacking Louis during the revolts of his sons. In 830, Louis's wife, Judith, was accused of adultery with Bernard of Septimania, and her misbehavior implied that Louis had failed to preserve his household's moral integrity. Morality, and especially conjugal morality, had been so successfully emphasized in the construction of Louis's legitimacy that it could also be used to criticize the emperor and his rule.

It was during the period when morality and conjugality were becoming central to Carolingian political discourse that Matfrid of Orléans asked Jonas to explain from a Christian perspective how to live a righteous conjugal life. Yet what originally inspired Jonas to write this moral reflection for the laity, the *De institutione laicali*, did not come from Matfrid, for Odile Dubreucq has shown that the work was a revised version of an earlier treatise.[23] Jonas had already conceived, perhaps immediately after the reform councils of Aachen of 816–17, the project of compiling an *institutio* for the laity: one comparable to Benedict's rule for monks, to the *Institutiones canonicorum* for communities of clerics, and to the *Institutiones sanctimonialium* for religious women. Matfrid's request gave Jonas the opportunity to give his essay a test drive, but from the beginning Jonas identified the real audience of DIL as all the laypersons of the empire, and especially the nobility. He wished to bring his own bricks to the structure of the morally reformed Christianity that Louis the Pious was building.

Even though Matfrid's request pertained to conjugal life, Jonas produced an all-encompassing treatise on lay morality. Book I contains teachings about baptism, which was the moment in which a person became a rightful member of Christian society. Baptism is presented as an oath that creates a twofold compact, whereby the faithful person (*fidelis*) both renounces Satan and confesses belief in the Trinity.[24] To break this oath is to display *infidelitas*: a lack of faith, or of fidelity. Jonas uses the vocabulary of the oaths of fidelity that subjects made to their emperor. Loyalty to God is expressed in the same way as loyalty to the emperor. Book I goes on to explain the correct way to approach the liturgy, the sacraments, and sacred spaces. Penance, the topic of two chapters in Book I (9–10), was crucial in the contemporary representations of imperial power, and it must have suggested further scenarios for the contemporaneous readers. Jonas regrets that public penance, as enacted in early-Christian times, is no longer practiced. When Louis the Pious undertook his own very public penance in 822, he may have been guided by DIL. If so, DIL must have

23 Odile Dubreucq, Introduction, SC 549, 97–102.

24 DIL I.3, SC 549, 156: "Duarum pactionum nexibus unusquisque fidelis Deo in baptismate se obligauit . . . "

been composed before 822. Jonas was not the only Carolingian cleric to recall the ancient practice of public penance. At the council of Tours of 813, for example, the bishops had stated that this practice ought to be reintroduced.[25] That said, the correspondence between Jonas's endorsement of public penance in DIL and Louis's public acts of penance is striking. Until 828, after all, Matfrid was frequently at court, and by staying in touch with Matfrid, Jonas would have had a privileged channel of communication with the moral and political head of the empire. Jonas perfectly captured the topics at the core of Louis's strategies of moral self-improvement.

Jonas's discourse on marriage in DIL shows correspondences with contemporary debates about conjugality. He addresses men exclusively, but he maintains that men should not suppose they have more rights than women, even if secular laws and social practices might indicate the contrary. Marriage is a partnership between two people who share responsibilities, such as respecting and being loyal to each other and educating their children. The model is that of a husband and wife managing a household that includes their children and others subject to their authority (*subiecti*), over whom the couple were expected to exercise a pastoral ministry (*pastorale ministerium*). In Jonas's view, married couples shared duties that were more commonly associated with priests and bishops.[26] Married couples were like shepherds, expected to keep watch over the little flocks that were their households. Married laypersons, too, were involved in the general effort to bring Christian people to salvation. In Jonas's view, they were an integral part of an all-encompassing moral structure, which placed them alongside all those exercising public and private authority in the empire. Jonas was proposing a highly inclusive model.

The *institutio* that Jonas expounded in DIL was meant to embrace the whole life of the aristocratic laity. Book III expounds the author's theory of vices and virtues. The choice between exercising one or the other determines how one's life will conclude: either with eternal damnation or with eternal salvation. In Jonas's eyes, DIL was meant to become a rule of life for the lay aristocracy of the empire. With that, every class of persons (*ordo*) of the Carolingian *ecclesia* – a term encompassing not only ecclesiastical institutions but the whole of Christendom – was provided with a rule.[27] Jonas was contributing more than a building block to the "moralization" of Christianity. He was providing a wall necessary for the Carolingian moral structure.

Another wall was necessary for that structure to be completed. As Louis the Pious's public penance at Attigny had shown, sometimes rulers were aware that they needed

25 *Concilium Turonense*, ed. Albert Werminghoff, MGH Conc. 2.1 (1906), c. 41, 286–93, at 292.

26 DIL II.16, SC 549, 452.

27 Mayke de Jong, "Ecclesia and the Early Medieval Polity," in S. Airlie, W. Pohl, and H. Reimitz (eds.), *Staat im frühen Mittelalter*. Forschungen zur Geschichte des Mittelalters 11 (Vienna: Österreichischen Akademie der Wissenschaften, 2006), 113–32.

moral reform and were willing to engage in it. In 831, Jonas published another moral text, *De institutione regia* (DIR), sending it to King Pippin of Aquitaine. Here, Jonas described the roles and duties of Christian rulers, their correct relationship to the ecclesiastical authority (which was one of subordination), and other matters of proper conduct. He borrowed his material from the acts of the council of Paris 829 (see below) and, to a lesser extent, from DIL.[28] On this occasion, Jonas was not responding to a request. As he says in his introductory letter, he was concerned about Pippin's eternal salvation, which might be endangered by the ruler's disrespectful behavior toward his father, Louis, since Pippin had been the protagonist of the first revolt by the emperor's sons in 830–31.[29] The respect due to parents is one of the main topics of Jonas's introduction, which he calls an *admonitio*, a warning. While couching his warning in the respectful words of a humble subject addressing his lord, the bishop was advising the king that he was a son before being a ruler – and, what is more, the son of an emperor. Thus, he had to show respect to his father not only as to his emperor but also, precisely, as to his father. The new moral structure was centered on the imperial court that Jonas was helping to shape, which had been undermined in the previous year. Louis's royal sons, no longer young, needed to be led back to a correct hierarchy of power. They had shown that they, too, were in need of moral guidance, which Jonas, as he had done in DIL, expressed by means of a quasi-legal text. His use of the term *admonitio* clearly recalled the *Admonitio generalis* issued by Charlemagne in 789.[30] The term *admonitio*, like *institutio*, recurs frequently in Louis's capitularies and practical instructions to counts, bishops, and envoys (*missi*), indicating an official rebuke.

Jonas's work of moral reform moved in harmony with the guidelines and vocabulary established by the Carolingian rulers. Because the manuscript tradition of his moral guides (*specula*) seems to have been limited, one may wonder how successful were his efforts in supporting the new role of morality. But some points need to be kept in mind here. First, we cannot measure the extent of the works' diffusion by the number of extant copies, for there is evidence that manuscripts containing Jonas's texts were lost. Second, Jonas says that DIL should be read aloud to an audience. The diffusion of his works was oral as well as written. Third, there are hints of the impact of the texts on contemporary political discourses and practices, such as Louis's penance in 822. Finally, these reflections were not the only tool that Jonas used to express his moral ideas. Another medium was available in the enactments and decrees of the councils in which he played a leading part, and here the quasi-legal nature of his moral teaching became fully legal.

28 There is a table of comparison between these texts (albeit one requiring some minor corrections) in Dubreucq, SC 407, 35.

29 DIR, ed. Dubreucq, 160–64.

30 For this text, see H. Mordek, K. Zechiel-Eckes, and M. Glatthaar (eds.), *Die Admonitio generalis Karls des Grossen*, MGH Fontes 16 (2012).

MORALITY BECOMES LAW: JONAS'S CONCILIAR ACTIVITY

The Carolingian era witnessed a strong revival of conciliar activity.[31] Councils became powerful political and legal tools for the pursuit of diverse goals. In the 740s, the Pippinids used councils as means to promote the moral reform of Frankish ecclesiastical institutions, including removal of bishops considered to be unworthy – that is, unwilling to support the Pippinids. After Pippin's royal coronation and anointing, he and his successors continued to convene church councils as features representing their power, and increasingly to demonstrate their religious commitments. Summoning and presiding over councils, such as the council of Frankfurt of 794, to deal with religious controversies was also part of the representation of increasingly imperial Carolingian power. The councils deliberated over the programs of moral reform, and they brought rulers and aristocracies together to debate matters concerning the kingdom. Thus, church councils became part of the routine negotiation between kings and aristocratic groups: a way to involve the aristocracy in the administration of power. Church councils and royal assemblies were often held in the same places at the same times. Conciliar acts were also laws of the kingdom, and they frequently served as grounds for capitulary legislation.

Bishops belonged to the political elite of the empire, but they were not a monolithic group. They experienced deep changes in their identity and duties in the 820s and 830s. The definition of the emperor's power as a "ministry" (*ministerium*) – that is, as a duty to keep all his subjects on the path to eternal salvation by overseeing their moral conduct – led to a redefinition of bishops' own ministry. The conciliar acts of the 820s clearly show that bishops increasingly claimed a place at the ruler's side in the moral supervision of the empire.[32] Correct moral behavior and the bishops' responsibilities to instill it were central issues of debate at the councils of this period, as they had frequently been in Charlemagne's day. Under Louis the Pious, however, the role of moral guidance slowly shifted from the emperor to bishops. All the acts of the five regional councils that Charlemagne convened in 813 stated that their decisions had to be submitted to the emperor for approval or amendment. But in the acts of the Council of Paris of 829, which was convened along with three other regional councils – a procedure very similar to the one followed in 813 – the bishops proclaimed that their own decisions were "by no means to be considered verbose or superfluous."[33] In other words, their decisions should not be amended or modified by anyone else.

Jonas played a very important role in developing, articulating, and spreading this new understanding of the bishops' moral responsibilities. His conciliar activity may

[31] Wilfried Hartmann, *Konziliengeschichte. Reihe A, Darstellungen. Die Synoden der Karolingerzeit im Frankenreich und in Italien* (Paderborn: Schöningh, 1989).

[32] Cristina La Rocca and Francesco Veronese, "Cultures of Unanimity in Carolingian Councils," in S. Ferente, L. Kunčević, and M. Pattenden (eds.), *Cultures of Voting in Pre-Modern Europe* (London: Routledge, 2018), 39–57.

[33] *Concilium Parisiense*, ed. Albert Werminghoff, MGH Conc. 2.2, 605–80, at 609.

be roughly traced through four stages, corresponding to four councils and four different moments in the reign of Louis the Pious: Paris 825, Paris 829, Thionville 835, and Aachen 836. Jonas participated in all four councils, and scholars have argued that he had a leading role in drafting their acts. Here, I shall focus mainly on the first two of the four, for these are crucial for understanding the relations among morality, Christianity, and law in Jonas's thinking and political activity, as well as his contribution to the definition of morality as inherently political during Louis's reign.

The council of Paris of November 825 was part of a public campaign, directed by public power, against Claudius, bishop of Turin. Claudius had criticized the cult of images, relics, and the Cross, as well as pilgrimages to Rome.[34] Some of these issues, especially the cult of images, had already been debated at Frankfurt in 794 under Charlemagne's supervision. Louis the Pious, stimulated in part by a letter from the Byzantine emperor Michael, now intervened to settle the question of the veneration of images, acting to demonstrate his ability to resolve religious controversy in the manner of his father Charlemagne. The acts of Frankfurt were the starting point for debate in Paris, as the summary of the proceedings (*Libellus synodalis*) makes clear. The bishops harshly attacked Charlemagne's statements about the cult of images, accusing him of having "answered with what he wanted to say, not with what was fitting."[35] The change in perspective from the councils of 813, which acknowledged the ruler's role in correcting their enactments, is clear. True, Charlemagne was dead, and Louis the Pious's self-legitimation relied to some extent on moral criticism of his father. But for the first time imperially approved decisions were officially condemned by the bishops assembling at a council. The bishops claimed for themselves the freedom, even the duty, to criticize not only the positions of preceding bishops but also those of a former emperor. Jonas attended the council and was probably tasked with writing down its acts, as suggested by a letter of Louis the Pious addressed to him and his metropolitan, Jeremiah of Sens.[36] Jonas and Jeremiah were also asked to produce a summary of the acts, to be sent to the pope for approval. Because the original acts criticized papal positions on the cult of images, Jonas and Jeremiah had somehow to produce a censored version. Louis the Pious also charged Jonas (as well as the Irish monk Dungal) with composing a theological treatise responding to the iconoclasm of Claudius, bishop of Turin. Jonas started writing his treatise on the cult of images (*De cultu imaginum*) at this time, but he did not complete it until around 840. The reason was that Claudius had died in 827, so that the need was no longer urgent. Jonas participated in Louis's challenge to Claudius both with the treatise *De cultu imaginum* and with the communication of the

34 Jean-Marie Sansterre, "Les justifications du culte des reliques dans le haut Moyen Âge," in Édina Bozóky and Anne-Marie Helvétius (eds.), *Les reliques. Objets, cultes, symboles*, Hagiologia 1 (Turnhout: Brepols, 1999), 81–93.

35 *Libellus synodalis Parisiensis* a. 825 m. Novembri, ed. Albert Werminghoff, MGH Conc. 2.2, 480–532, at 481.

36 Ibid., 533.

conciliar acts to the pope. He was in the front line when bishops were beginning to claim their right to criticize emperors.

During these same years, Jonas composed his *Vita secunda Hucberti*, which, as already noted, was a *speculum* (a moral guide) for bishops. Bishops, too, were in need of moral reform. This idea was openly stated at the council of Paris in 829: one of the four councils that Louis the Pious and Lothar convened in that year to address the increasing moral anxieties spreading throughout the empire. The deposition of Hugh and Matfrid in 827–28 unleashed moral panic. Christian armies had been defeated by hordes of infidels and pagans: specifically, Muslims, Bulgarians, and Danes. It seemed that God was displeased with his people's behavior and had unleashed their enemies as punishment. A moral reform of the whole population would be required to regain God's approval and his protection of the people and, above all, of the emperor. In the *Constitutio* with which Louis summoned the four councils, he asked bishops to "investigate, search and, with the help of God, find [solutions] to the matters concerning the Christian religion and its care."[37] In the acts of the assembly at Paris, which are the only ones that survive, bishops stated their own interpretation of the emperor's requests: They were "daring to take decisions according to the *ministerium* attributed to us."[38] Moral reforms were presented as part of the bishops' ministry: the functions and mission entailed by their charge. After all, the bishops said, rulers had "humbly realized that [such duty] did not pertain to their own office, thinking it should be attributed to the decisions of those of their priests, the *optimates* [senior clerics] and other churchmen [*fideles*] . . . by whom people are set free from the darkness of unfaithfulness."[39] Rulers themselves had charged bishops to show the path of moral reform to the Christian people. Responding to an explicit imperial request, bishops were fulfilling their ministry, which was now enriched with huge moral responsibilities. This work of moral improvement touched all of Carolingian society. The first part of the acts of Paris was entirely taken up with the bishops' own moral self-improvement, for they needed to reform their own behavior in order to prove themselves as authoritative moral examples. But next came the moral reform of the rulers. Bishops claimed a central role in the moral building of the empire. They set themselves up as the ones charged with the duty of correcting and admonishing every other social class. Even self-correction was part of these claims: It was a way to prove that they were able to reform themselves autonomously, thus preventing anyone else from intervening in their work.

Jonas attended the council of Paris, as a contemporary diploma issued by bishop Inchaud of Paris attests.[40] Moreover, he was most probably the author of its written

37 *Constitutio de synodis anno 829. in regno franco habendis*, ed. Albert Werminghoff, MGH Conc. 2.2, 596–97, at 597.

38 *Concilium Parisiense*, ed. Werminghoff, MGH Conc. 2.2, 608.

39 Ibid., 607.

40 Ibid., 605–06.

acts. Twenty-one of their ninety-four chapters and parts of another two correspond almost verbatim to chapters from Jonas's moral works. Ten chapters of Book I of DIL, in the version revised after Matfrid's deposition, were inserted into the acts. And Jonas's later DIR, sent to Pippin in 831, was in turn largely drawn from the teachings for rulers included in the acts of Paris. In this case, therefore, he proceeded in the opposite direction: from conciliar acts to a moral treatise. Jonas had already experimented with something similar in 825, when some contents of his treatise on images (*De cultu imaginum*) were inserted into the official summary (*Libellus synodalis*) of the proceedings at Paris. He regarded his conciliar activity and his moral treatises as two sides of the same coin, in an effort to spread morality and to fight heresy with all the tools available to him. In 829, at least part of Jonas's moral considerations found legal expression in conciliar acts. Beginning as simple guidelines, these became imperial laws, intended to lead the empire out of ideological, spiritual, and moral crisis.

Morality shaped law. Indeed, it became law. This process greatly affected subsequent political events of the empire. Jonas was not the only one who imposed moral standards on the rulers' behavior. Other texts transmitting models of behavior for kings circulated in the Carolingian empire, such as the *De duodecim abusivis saeculi* ("On the Twelve Abuses of the Age").[41] But the councils of 825 and, even more, of 829 officially stated that even emperors would have to be subordinated to the bishops' moral guidance if proper moral and social order were to be restored. These ideas were taken to their extreme in 833, when an emperor, Louis the Pious, judged as unworthy by a number of the Frankish bishops, was deposed. Jonas had apparently not envisaged this outcome when he elaborated the conciliar acts of Paris 829. In the dedicatory letter of DIR, he is eager to remind Pippin of Aquitaine of his duty to respect his father. But no doubt the councils of 825 and 829 opened the way to the capability, even the duty, of bishops to criticize their emperor. Willing or not, Jonas and the other bishops who gathered in Paris in 829 were developing a redefinition of the Carolingian moral structure: one that could even justify an emperor's deposition.

CONCLUSIONS

Jonas of Orléans might be described as a professional moralizer. In his writings and conciliar activity, the relationship between Christianity and law was mediated by morality, the tool by which he tried to shape the society of his time. He participated in the elaboration of new identities for Carolingian bishops, during a period when aristocratic origins were no longer the unifying feature of this group and were being replaced by other measures of worthiness. The proper gauge of fitness became high

[41] Rob Meens, "Politics, Mirrors of princes and the Bible: Sins, Kings and the Well-Being of the Realm," *Early Medieval Europe* 7.3 (1998): 345–57.

moral behavior, which was meant to distinguish the bishops from the other social classes (*ordines*) of the empire. Jonas of Orléans put all his activity and culture at the service of this appropriation of morality by bishops. He wrote texts that were intended, as he explains in the letters introducing them, to have an impact on the everyday behavior of their readers and listeners, such as his two *Institutiones* and his *Vita secunda Hucberti*. He participated in and surely dictated the acts of episcopal councils, claiming for bishops the exclusive right to watch over the empire's morality. Part of his moral teaching, therefore, was issued as conciliar decrees, in this way becoming the law of the Christian empire. His moral texts were meant to convey moral teachings to those social classes – laypeople, bishops, and rulers – still lacking officially recognized codes of behavior. He aimed to fill legal voids and to contribute to the completion of the Carolingian moral structure, so that it would encompass every social category. The whole Carolingian *ecclesia* had to be reached by moral suasions. Morality was the main tool that Louis the Pious wielded to control society, and Jonas tried to show how useful he could be in this regard. Morality was for him what exegesis was for some other authors of the period, such as Hraban Maur, namely, a tool to prove that he was able to contribute to Carolingian power and to define a space of political action for himself and his fellow bishops. In this, he was spectacularly successful, perhaps even beyond his worst nightmares. The bishops' claim to be guardians of morality was turned against the one who originally had used morality for his own legitimation, Louis the Pious.

Christianity in its Carolingian form, where all was subject to the Christian emperor's authority, was deeply affected by Jonas's moral teaching. At the same time, his morality was affected by Christianity, as his moral considerations were inserted into the context of a Christian empire and responded to needs of political legitimation. In a similar way, his morality affected Christian laws and to some extent became law. Conversely, Jonas quoted existing Christian canonical texts, such as papal decretals, making them the basis of some of his own moral teachings. That was one of the aspects characterizing his texts' quasi-legal nature in the wake of the rules issued at Aachen in 816. More than two hundred years later, as we noted at the outset, this nature was still acknowledged by an anonymous Roman scribe.

SOURCES

Jonas's works have recently attracted considerable scholarly attention, and there are new editions of a few of them. *De institutione laicali* [DIL] has been recently re-edited with facing French translation by Odile Dubreucq, *Instruction des laïcs*, 2 vols., SC 549 and 550 (2012–13). For an edition of *De institutione regia* [DIR], also with facing French translation, see Alain Dubreucq (ed.), *Le métier de roi*, SC 407 (1995). An English translation of DIR is available: Robert W. Dyson, *A Ninth-Century Political Tract: The De institutione regia of Jonas of Orléans* (Smithtown: Exposition Press, 1983).

Most of Jonas's work, however, can still be found only in older editions included in standard series, such as PL 106:305–88 for the *De cultu imaginum*, and *Acta Sanctorum Novembris*, vol. 1, 806–18, for the *Vita secunda Hucberti*. For the letters of Odo and Lupus of Ferrières to Jonas, see Ernst Dümmler (ed.), *Lupi abbatis Ferrariensis epistolae*, MGH Epist. 6 (Epp. Karolini Aevi 4), pp. 1–126 (no. 21: pp. 29–30; no. 27: p. 33; no. 28: pp. 33–34). The *Ionae Aurelianensis episcopi epistolae*, edited by Ernst Dümmler in MGH Epist. 5 (Epp. Karolini Aevi 3), 346–57, are the dedicatory letters of DIL, DIR, *Vita Hucberti*, and *De cultu*, which can also be found in the editions of these works. The acts of the councils of Paris of 825 and 829 are edited by Albert Werminghoff in MGH Conc. 2.2 (=*Concilia Aevi Karolini* 1.2) – at pp. 473–551 for Paris 825 (the *Libellus synodalis* is at 480–532, while Jonas and Jeremiah's *Epitome* is at 535–51); and pp. 605–80 for Paris 829.

The codex Köln, Erzbischöfliche Diözesan- und Dombibliothek 184, is available on line via www.monumenta.ch/latein/codex_content.php?c=14 (accessed March 24, 2018).

FURTHER READING

For a first and general approach to Jonas's works, the introductions by Alain and Odile Dubreucq to their editions of DIR and DIL respectively (see Sources, above) are useful. Jonas is also the object of a profound ecclesiological study: Raffaele Savigni, *Giona di Orléans: una ecclesiologia carolingia* (Bologna: Pàtron, 1989).

On Carolingian *specula* for laypeople as a genre, see Alain Dubreucq, "La Littérature des *specula*. Délimitation du genre, contenu, destinataires et réception," in Michel Lauwers (ed.), *Guerriers et moines. Conversion et sainteté aristocratiques dans l'Occident médiéval* (Antibes: Éditions APDCA, 2002), 17–39; and Franz Sedlmeier, *Die laienparänetischen Schriften der Karolingerzeit. Untersuchungen zu ausgewählten Texten des Paulinus von Aquileia, Alkuins, Jonas' von Orléans, Dhuodas und Hinkmars von Reims* (Neuried: Ars Una, 2000).

The redefinition of episcopal identity under Louis the Pious has been brilliantly examined by Steffen Patzold, "Redéfinir l'office épiscopal. Les évêques francs face à la crise des années 820–830," in François Bougard, Laurent Feller, and Régine Le Jan (eds.), *Les élites au Haut Moyen Age. Crises et renouvellements*, Haut Moyen Âge 1 (Turnhout: Brepols, 2006), 337–59. For a more general account of Carolingian bishops, see Steffen Patzold, *Episcopus. Wissen über Bischöfe im Frankreich des späten 8. bis frühen 10. Jahrhunderts* (Ostfildern: Jan Thorbecke, 2008).

The study of lay morality in Carolingian times has been enriched recently by new approaches emphasizing gender. See Thomas F. X. Noble, "Secular Sanctity: Forging an Ethos for the Carolingian Nobility," in P. Wormald and J. L. Nelson (eds.), *Lay Intellectuals in the Carolingian World* (Cambridge: Cambridge University Press, 2007), 8–36; and Rachel Stone, *Morality and Masculinity in the*

Carolingian Empire (Cambridge: Cambridge University Press, 2012). On the role of conjugal morality in Carolingian political discourses, see Stuart Airlie, "Private Bodies and the Body Politic in the Divorce Case of Lothar II," *Past and Present* 161 (1998): 3–38 (albeit focusing on a later and very special case); and Rachel Stone, "Carolingian Domesticities," in J. M. Bennett and R. M. Karras (eds.), *The Oxford Handbook of Women and Gender in Medieval Europe* (Oxford: Oxford University Press, 2013), 229–45.

On Jonas's views about marriage, the classic study by Pierre Toubert is still useful: "La théorie du mariage chez les moralistes carolingiens," in *Il matrimonio nella società altomedievale*, vol. 1, settimane di studio del Centro italiano di studi sull'alto Medioevo 24 (Spoleto: Presso la sede del Centro 1977), 233–85. This should be read alongside Christian Lauranson-Rosaz, "Quod coniugium a Deo sit institutum. Le mariage d'après Jonas d'Orléans (760–841)," in P. Ganivet (ed.), *Identités, marginalités ou solidarités. Droits et histoire des personnes* (Clermont-Ferrand: Presses Univ. de la Fac. de Droit, 2005), 23–37; and Francesco Veronese, "Contextualizing Marriage: Conjugality and Christian Life in Jonas of Orléans' *De institutione laicali*," EME 23.4 (2015): 436–56.

Elisabeth Magnou-Nortier has made stimulating observations (albeit not always supported by manuscript evidence) on Jonas's writings and their role in the revolts of 830–34: see Magnou-nortier, "La tentative de subversion de l'État sous Louis le Pieux et l'oeuvre des falsificateurs," *Le Moyen Âge* 105 (1999): 331–65, 615–41. On the religious, moral, and political dimensions of Carolingian culture during this period, see Mayke De Jong, *The Penitential State: Authority and Atonement in the Age of Louis the Pious, 814–840* (Cambridge: Cambridge University Press, 2009); and Courtney M. Booker, *Past Convictions: The Penance of Louis the Pious and the Decline of the Carolingians* (Philadelphia: University of Pennsylvania Press, 2009).

21

Hincmar of Reims

Charles West

In 845, Hincmar was appointed archbishop of the important see of Reims, a city now in eastern France but then in the kingdom of West Francia. Previously a monk at the prestigious monastery of Saint-Denis near Paris, he threw himself into his new role with remarkable energy, which he sustained until he died almost forty years later in the winter of 882, in flight from the Vikings. Hincmar was a dominating figure in the church and politics of his day. He is perhaps most widely known today as the author of a large portion of the Annals of Saint-Bertin, the mainstay of our knowledge of West Frankish history in the period. But he wrote a great deal besides. As well as dozens of letters, over forty of his works survive, some short, many long, written on a variety of topics.[1]

PRELUDE: AN UNPREPOSSESSING BUT INFORMATIVE MANUSCRIPT

Many of these texts touched on law, and this chapter will concentrate on three of the most important, written at different points in the archbishop's long career (in 860, 870, and 881, respectively). Yet perhaps the best way to approach Hincmar's ideas about law and about its relation to Christianity is offered not by any single text but by a manuscript on parchment stored in the National Library of France in Paris, and known by its shelf mark as Paris, Bibliothèque Nationale, MS lat. 12445. Large but unprepossessing, with few decorative elements to please the eye, what makes this manuscript especially interesting is that it was a legal compilation written in Reims under Hincmar's watch. Its contents, and how Hincmar used

[1] For a convenient summary of Hincmar's career, see Rachel Stone, "Introduction," in R. Stone and C. West (eds.), *Hincmar of Rheims: Life and Work* (Manchester: Manchester University Press, 2015), 1–43. I am grateful to Thomas Faulkner, Emma Hunter, Rachel Stone, and the editorial team for advice on a draft of this chapter, and to the Humboldt Foundation for supporting a period of study in which it was largely written. For publication data for the primary texts cited briefly in parentheses in the main text, see under Sources at the end of the chapter.

them, have much to tell us about the place of law in the archbishop's life, work, and theology.[2]

First of all, the Paris manuscript reminds us that law for archbishop Hincmar was primarily something written. Following Roman-law tradition, Hincmar did not reject unwritten custom (*consuetudo*) as a guide to action, but in his view this was subordinate to the written word (*De divortio*, 167). Consequently, knowledge of the law depended on being able to read it. Hincmar was in a fortunate position in this respect, for when he was appointed as archbishop of Reims, he arrived at an institution that already had an impressive library. Hincmar kept up the momentum over his episcopate, continuing to add more books to the collection. As a result, Paris Lat. 12445 is one of over a dozen ninth-century Reims manuscripts containing law in various forms, now scattered in libraries across Europe and beyond. This steady accumulation of legal knowledge enabled the archbishop of Reims to draw on a wide set of texts, including several that were already rare in the ninth century. Nevertheless, Reims's library was not comprehensive, and there were many surviving legal works from Late Antiquity that not even Hincmar knew at first hand.

The relatively unprepossessing appearance of Paris Lat. 12445 is also significant. As archbishop of a wealthy see, Hincmar could afford to sponsor expensive illuminated manuscripts. And although the most famous decorated manuscript from Reims – the Utrecht Psalter – was probably completed under Hincmar's predecessor, Ebbo, lavishly decorated manuscripts associated with Hincmar do survive, such as the Hincmar Gospels (Reims Mediathèque, MS 57). The legal manuscripts from Reims, however, are more workaday. They were often carefully written by teams of trained scribes, but they are seldom illuminated. These were not presentation pieces or prestige items. Rather, they were practical tools: collections of material intended for use. That suggests that law for Hincmar was not a question solely of grand gestures or ideology. It was also a field of practical expertise, in which he developed an increasing reputation over the late ninth century.

It is above all, however, the contents of MS Paris Lat. 12445 that have much to tell us about Hincmar's understanding and use of law in a Christian framework. The bulk of the manuscript, which was completed around 870, is made up of a canonical collection known as the Dionysio-Hadriana, which Pope Hadrian I had sent to Charlemagne himself decades previously (see Chapter 7 in this volume). This collection was composed of canons (formal decisions) of church councils and selected papal decretals. But the manuscript also has a version of Book XVI of the *Theodosian Code*, an official collection of Roman law that was first issued in the fifth century (see Chapter 2), supplemented here with other Roman legal excerpts. In addition, Hincmar's manuscript preserves some decisions of a church council held in Rome in 853, a decree issued by the Frankish king Charles the Bald, some

[2] For a detailed study of this manuscript, see Letha Böhringer, "Der eherechtliche Traktat im Paris. Lat.12445, einer Arbeitshandschrift Hinkmars von Reims," *Deutsches Archiv für Erforschung des Mittelalters* 46 (1990): 18–47.

material associated with the Pseudo-Isidorian forgeries (see Chapter 19 in this volume), several extracts from patristic writers, such as Augustine of Hippo and Pope Gregory the Great (see Chapters 12 and 17), and some penitential texts (see Chapter 8).

What this variety shows is how wide-angled Hincmar's view of law was. For him, law's overarching purpose was to create order and peace in this world, following God's plan. He borrowed a phrase from a writer whom he thought was Cyprian of Carthage, but whom we know today as Pseudo-Cyprian (he was probably an eighth-century Irishman). This writer identified "people without law" as one of the scourges of the world. According to Hincmar, "the people without law is a people without Christ."[3] Hincmar identified texts that helped to remedy that situation not so much by their form as by their origin and intention. Prescriptive texts that had been produced by authoritative figures were themselves authoritative. Although Hincmar tended to reserve the term *lex* ("law") for imperial and occasionally (and unusually for his time) conciliar legislation, he considered that papal letters and extracts from late-antique exegesis also had a lawlike character, and could all therefore be copied into a single manuscript for later citation. The unbounded nature of law and the absence of any discrete and settled canon of sources posed significant practical problems, since one could never be sure that one had read and digested all the relevant material. But this situation also allowed for a surprising flexibility and creativity in legal thinking, creating an opportunity Hincmar exploited as best he could.

HINCMAR'S CATEGORIZATION OF LAWS

The inherent diversity of the Paris manuscript, in which very different kinds of text rubbed shoulders, does not mean that Hincmar's idea of law was vague and undifferentiated. Far from it. He distinguished carefully between different kinds of regulation, and he did so in different ways.

To begin with, Hincmar frequently drew on kinds of law to express a chronology of world history, which ran from the origins of the world, through the law of Moses, to the Incarnation of Jesus Christ and the New Testament. As Hincmar put it, "After the law of nature, the law of letters was given, appropriate to the hardness of the people, and established on account of transgressions; it was followed by the law of the gospels, later in time but prior in grace" (*Opusculum LV*, 213).

Alongside this chronological approach, Hincmar also drew upon a typology that distinguished laws according to who had issued them. First of all, there was God's law, as expressed in the Scriptures, which was binding and eternal. This provided the

[3] Council of Douzy 871, *Die Konzilien der karolingischen Teilreiche 860–874*, ed. Hartmann, MGH Conc. 4, 501: "Igitur populus sine lege populus sine Christo est" (Hincmar almost certainly wrote this conciliar report). Hincmar also cited this passage in *De divortio*, 261, and in his treatise on royal authority, *De regis persona*, PL 125:833–56.

normative foundation for all earthly action. Like his contemporaries, Hincmar drew extensively on the Bible, and especially the New Testament, in almost all his writings, including those in which he mounted legal arguments. But Hincmar usually referred to the New Testament's commands as "evangelical truth" and not as *lex* ("law"), reserving this Latin word instead for human-made laws. These were binding, too, but they were not necessarily eternal. Some of them were provisional and could be changed to fit changing circumstances. As Hincmar put it, "In truth, just as some of the public laws have been abrogated, changed, and updated, so too some decrees of the catholics that were issued according to time, reason, and necessity have been abrogated or changed" (*Opusculum LV*, 214).

As this quotation shows, the distinction between church decrees ("the decrees of the catholics") and secular edicts was important for Hincmar, though he considered both to be forms of law. Hincmar insisted that clerics had to know the canons and the church's legal traditions, and he cited a decree of Pope Celestine to this effect on half a dozen occasions. He helped put this principle into practice by distributing manuscripts of canons to the newly ordained bishops in his province. For Hincmar, church law meant above all the collective decisions of the six great ecumenical councils, beginning with the Council of Nicaea in 325, which he described as sacred and even "mystical." Although this was in one sense human-made law, Hincmar followed Pope Leo I in considering that the Council of Nicaea had been "divinely consecrated" (*divinitus … consecrata*) with a special authority, and he cited Ambrose to the effect that Jesus himself had to all intents and purposes been present at what was "his" council (*Opusculum LV*, 257). Nicaea and the other ecumenical councils, therefore, occupied a special place within church tradition (see Chapter 4). Inspired by the Holy Spirit, and to that extent almost on a par with Scripture, these councils, in Hincmar's view, had "established laws [*leges*] that will remain until the end of the world" (*Opusculum LV*, 249).

Other forms of church tradition were also important, though less binding and more provisional. Some of these were texts even older than the great councils, but that alone did not make them more authoritative. For example, Hincmar respected the *Apostolic Canons*: apocryphal decisions traditionally attributed to the Apostles themselves. He argued, however, that these canons were not universally binding "because they were not constituted by the authority of episcopal councils," and because they had been transmitted orally before being written down (*Opusculum LV*, 238). Some of their rules were still valid, but others were no longer observed. New problems might require new canonical solutions, ideally issued by councils led by archbishops such as Hincmar. The decisions of such councils were authoritative – for example, the decisions of the council of Worms in 829 were "greatly to be followed" (*Collectio de Ecclesiis*, 83–85) – but not to the same extent as those of the great ecumenical councils. Hincmar also issued his own "legal" guidance in the form of episcopal capitularies directed to the clergy in his diocese. But, in keeping with his preference for collective processes of lawmaking, he seems to have regarded these single-author texts as binding only insofar as they transmitted earlier canonical tradition, and not in their own right.

The other main division of law was worldly, or secular law. This meant above all, for Hincmar, the laws of the Roman emperors, which he cited more often than any early-medieval author had done before him. Although only available in disjointed fragments in the ninth-century West, Roman law remained prestigious and authoritative, which explains why Hincmar had long passages of it copied into the Paris manuscript. He was interested in other kinds of worldly law too, and he freely acknowledged its diversity: "For as there are diverse peoples, so are there diverse laws, which the holy Church does not reject, if they are Christian in their commands, and these are just" (*De divortio*, 183). Hincmar had access to many of the so-called barbarian (or "Germanic") law codes (see Chapter 3), such as the Frankish *Lex Salica*, which were copied in Reims manuscripts. It is striking, however, that he never cited these sources directly and only seldom alluded to them. Perhaps uncertainties about their authorship diminished their authority in his eyes.

What he did cite, sometimes extensively, were the edicts of the Frankish kings, known as capitularies – especially those preserved in the important collection made by Ansegis of Fontenelle around 827, to which Hincmar had access through several manuscripts. He seems to have been unusual in bringing this kind of legislation into focus alongside the Roman legacy.[4] The emphasis that he placed on the collective consensus underpinning the capitulary legislation suggests that he may have seen its relationship to Roman law as equivalent to that between recent conciliar legislation and the foundational ecumenical councils. Kings were morally bound by their own legislation, though Hincmar did not envisage any practical mechanism for enforcing this obligation other than persistent exhortation.

In principle, worldly law did not need to have been issued by Christian rulers for it to be valid. After all, "the kings of the Medes and the Persians, and of the Romans, and the judges of the world, when they were still pagans and idol worshippers, naturally taught what the laws were" (*De divortio*, 225). Law issued by pagan Roman rulers could be authoritative even in a Christian kingdom provided that it could be interpreted as Christian, "that is, as fitting and harmonizing and consonant with Christianity" (*De divortio*, 145). But this last point was crucial for Hincmar. As he observed, rulings "can be called opinions [*arbitria*], but they are not laws [*leges*] unless they are of God, through whom 'kings reign and the establishers of the law decree justice' (Prov 8:15)" (*De divortio*, 248). "The laws of the world ... are sanctified by the justice of God through which everyone is made just" (*De divortio*, 139).

Hincmar considered worldly and ecclesiastical law to be complementary. In his view, many rules developed in one area could be readily applied to the other. Priests did not have to be experts in worldly law, but they too had to obey this law insofar as it

4 Here I draw on Thomas Faulkner, *Law and Authority in the Early Middle Ages: The Frankish* leges *in the Carolingian Period* (Cambridge: Cambridge University Press, 2016).

legitimately touched upon them, "for the church is often accustomed to demand that these [worldly laws] should be promulgated by emperors and kings even for matters of the church, and episcopal authority frequently uses and accepts their decisions in their judgments, together with the sentences of the canons" (*De divortio*, 137). Indeed, Hincmar drew on Pope Gelasius (see Chapter 14) to declare to one Carolingian king that "the bishops of religion themselves obey your laws inasmuch as it pertains to the order of public discipline" (*Collectio de Ecclesiis*, 64 – a citation that Hincmar also used elsewhere). Hincmar even described the constitutions of Christian Roman emperors as "sacred laws" (*sacrae leges*).

Nevertheless, church law and worldly, or secular (*forensis*) law remained distinguishable. Hincmar could conceive of ecclesiastical and secular procedures taking place in parallel, as they did, for example, in cases pertaining to marriage. He also noted that penalties for infraction differed between the two: only the secular ruler, for instance, could impose the death penalty. As he grew older, Hincmar emphasized this distinction more and more, even hinting that the "canons and rules of the fathers" (*canones et patrum regulae*) amounted to a kind of ethnic law for the clergy, equivalent to the Law of Moses for the Jews (*Opusculum LV*, 280). What is more, although it was the ruler's task to ensure peace and order on earth, in eschatological terms worldly law was ultimately and unambiguously subordinated to ecclesiastical law. As Hincmar declared about Christians who tried to defend their crimes by using worldly law (one of his few references to so-called barbarian law), "let them know that on the Day of Judgment, they will be judged not by Roman or Salian or Burgundian laws, but by divine and apostolic laws" (*De divortio*, 145). Precisely what Hincmar meant by "divine laws" in this context is not clear, but since he tended not to use the word *leges* for biblical injunctions, we may suppose he was thinking of conciliar tradition. Certainly, in speaking of "apostolic laws," Hincmar had in mind not the "evangelical precepts" of the New Testament but the rules established by papal decrees (*decreta apostolicorum*, as he usually termed them). The greatest legal authority was wielded by the holy canons and the decrees of the Roman pontiffs; the "laws of the world" (*leges saeculi*) might enjoy a similar status, but only those that were approved by the church (*Opusculum LV*, 153).

LAW IN THE *DE DIVORTIO* (860)

As already emphasized, law for Hincmar was above all written law: texts that existed in manuscripts. Those texts had to be applied if they were to have any effect. And Hincmar sought to apply them to the issues of the day with great vigor. To see how this worked in practice, let us now examine how he used law in three texts written at different points in his career, beginning with the treatise *De divortio* ("On the Divorce of King Lothar and Queen Theutberga"), which he wrote in 860.

Written on commission – an early sign of the Frankish bishops' respect for Hincmar's legal expertise – this treatise dealt with the controversial attempt of a Frankish king, Lothar II, to rid himself of his wife, Queen Theutberga. To establish whether this was permissible, Hincmar drew on the full range of legal and canonical material already mentioned: Roman and Frankish legislation, the pronouncements of popes, late-antique writers and church councils, and Scripture. He applied this material in ingenious ways, some of which might not seem entirely rigorous to modern readers. For example, Hincmar quoted a Roman legal maxim that "the sons are born for the father" to argue that kings should honor their predecessors' legislation. He was not concerned that this maxim had originally applied to liability to private debt, and not to legislative continuity.[5]

The challenge that Hincmar, like everyone else involved, faced at this time in commenting on Lothar and Theutberga's case was that there was no coherent law on ending marriages. Different Christian traditions suggested different and somewhat contradictory answers. Hincmar did attempt to untangle some of the legal knots, but his underlying solution was to focus on the procedure that had been employed by King Lothar II, and here he lent heavily on the distinction between secular and ecclesiastical law. The problem as he presented it was that Lothar II had confused matters procedurally. He had first accused his wife in a secular court, but then he had arranged an ecclesiastical confession in which the king himself, however, had played a role. Hincmar directed his legal firepower on this inconsistency, drawing on a wide range of sources, including the account of the trial of Susanna in the biblical Book of Daniel, to make up for the lack of a clear set of procedural rules.

It is important to emphasize that it was the confusion among different judicial authorities and processes to which Hincmar objected, and not the secular court itself. This is particularly clear in his discussion of the trial by ordeal, a distinctively post-Roman judicial procedure that blossomed in ninth-century Carolingian Francia. Because Queen Theutberga – or, more accurately, her champion – had successfully passed a trial by boiling water in 858, her opponents at King Lothar II's court cast doubt on the validity of that procedure. There was certainly a strand of opposition to the ordeal in the ninth century, articulated most powerfully by archbishop Agobard of Lyon, but Hincmar did not share this skepticism. In the *De divortio*, Hincmar provided the most extended and robust defense of the practice from the early Middle Ages. Hincmar saw no difficulty in justifying the ordeal as a judicial procedure on a scriptural basis, suggesting, for example, that trial by water was prefigured by the Great Flood and the drowning of Pharaoh's army, in both of which the guilty sank and the innocent floated. In other words, Hincmar was perfectly comfortable with the general notion that God intervened directly in legal cases, even though he admitted that diabolical trickery could not be ruled out in specific instances. It is not a coincidence that there are liturgies for the ordeal

[5] See Simon Corcoran, "Hincmar and His Roman Legal Sources," in Stone and West, *Hincmar of Rheims*, 129–55.

associated with Reims in the period. Hincmar's defense of the ordeal illustrates just how closely linked Christian belief and law were in his mind.

LAW IN THE *LITTLE WORK IN FIFTY-FIVE CHAPTERS* (870)

Although archbishop Hincmar chose to emphasize legal procedure in the instance of Lothar II's marriage, on other occasions his arguments were more substantive. A good illustration is his *Little Work in Fifty-Five Chapters* (*Opusculum LV Capitulorum*), written almost exactly ten years after his contribution to the royal marriage case of Lothar and Theutberga. Despite its diminutive title, this is a lengthy text with much to say on law. It was written in response to the efforts of one of Hincmar's suffragans, the bishop of Laon, to cast off his dependence on his archbishop. This Laon bishop happened to be Hincmar's own nephew, and confusingly he was also named Hincmar. Hincmar of Laon used the education that his uncle had lavished upon him to challenge his authority. In response, archbishop Hincmar again drew on the full panoply of his legal knowledge, using manuscript resources such as Paris Lat. 12445. (He may have had this manuscript compiled while he was composing the treatise.)

The issues discussed in the *Little Work* ranged from excommunication to parish churches, but archbishop Hincmar's arguments centered on the question of how to balance contradictory texts, for the bishop of Laon had invoked in his defense a number of apparently very early papal decretals that considerably enhanced the autonomy of bishops in relation to almost everyone else, even including archbishops. In reality, these texts were ninth-century forgeries produced in Frankish ecclesiastical workshops (see Chapter 19). Hincmar did not dispute their authenticity, which he seems not to have doubted. Indeed, he was amongst the earliest writers to cite (from as early as 852) both Pseudo-Isidore and the related collection ascribed to Benedictus Levita (on which, see Chapter 19). But the archbishop attacked the standing of these letters "which you call canons," making the most significant critique of Pseudo-Isidore at any time in the Middle Ages. For the bishop of Laon, the supposed age of these texts made them venerable. For the archbishop of Reims, on the contrary, their antiquity simply meant that they were out of date, for they had been superseded by the great church councils.

Making that argument required some close textual work. For instance, the bishop of Laon had cited a genuine letter by the fifth-century Pope Leo I (see Chapter 13), which appeared to confirm the binding authority of whatever the earlier papal decrees had promulgated. The bishop of Laon took this statement as bolstering the standing of the decretals as a whole. Hincmar of Reims responded with an extensive discussion of the meaning of the Latin word *promulgare*, concluding thus:

> [T]he first thing for us to understand is that it is one thing to promulgate holy orders and canonical discipline, and another to promulgate *about* holy orders and

> canonical discipline, just as it is one thing to promulgate laws and another to promulgate *about* the laws. For to promulgate laws is to establish laws, but to promulgate *about* laws is to take the judgments of these laws and to judge according to them, and to inform everyone about these judgements and observing them. (*Opusculum LV*, 174, my italics)

What Pope Leo had really confirmed, declared Hincmar, was whatever the earlier popes had said *about* pre-existing laws, such as decisions taken by church councils, and not what they had issued on their own legislative account. One might debate whether Leo I's letter could really bear the weight of Hincmar's precise grammatical analysis, but the point to note here is that for Hincmar, focusing as always on the law *as text*, the analysis proved that even popes had to operate within the framework set out by the ecumenical councils.

The bishop of Laon, however, following Pseudo-Isidore, had another tactic available to fend off his uncle's authority. This was to cast doubt on the content of those church councils that Hincmar of Reims prized so highly. Drawing on Pseudo-Isidore, the bishop of Laon claimed that the great Council of Nicaea in 325 had issued many more canons than those that now survived (see Chapter 15). The point was not merely that some of these mysterious extra canons might conveniently confirm Pseudo-Isidorian ideas. Rather, it was that by casting doubt on the textual transmission of ancient councils such as Nicaea, one threw into doubt the whole legislative inheritance of the church. Hincmar of Reims was alert to the possibility that the manuscripts containing canonical regulations could be tampered with, and he even carried out some codicological research to detect interpolations.[6] It is not surprising, therefore, that he was rattled by this attack on the canons of Council of Nicaea. He took great pains to demonstrate in his reply that the council had indeed only issued the twenty canons that had survived to his day.

LAW AT THE COUNCIL OF SAINT-MACRE (881)

Though Hincmar put greatest emphasis on the ecumenical councils of Late Antiquity, he considered that a provincial council, headed by one or more archbishops, was the best means of dealing with contemporaneous problems affecting Frankish society and the church. He described such a council as *perfectum*, meaning "complete" or perhaps "self-standing": a quality that gave extra weight to its decisions. A good example is provided by the council held at the church of Saint-Macre in the diocese of Reims in 881, during King Louis III's brief reign over West Francia. This was a moment of perceived political and spiritual crisis for the region. Hincmar not only presided over this council; he also wrote the synodal report on its behalf. So

6 Hincmar, *Collectio de una et non trina deitate*, PL 125:512, concerning the Council of Constantinople in 680 (as well as a treatise by Saint Augustine), which Hincmar suspected had been interpolated by the heretic Gottschalk.

much does this report bear the stamp of Hincmar's thinking that it has been called his "final testament," for by now he was elderly, and he died not long afterward.

A central issue at this council was the relation between the king and the church, which the council, under Hincmar's leadership, explored with a rare clarity. The report drew on a famous letter of Pope Gelasius I (see Chapter 14) to show "how royal power and bishops' authority should be distinct." Bishops and kings should work together, but only Christ, the synodal report stated, was able to be *both* king *and* priest. The report cited the Old Testament to clarify what was meant: "And we read in the sacred histories that when priests anointed kings to rule the kingdom and placed the diadems upon their heads, they also put the law into their hands, so they might learn and know how they should rule themselves and those subject to them, and how they should honor the priests of the Lord" (*Saint-Macre*, 179). It is noteworthy that the council of Saint-Macre had been summoned by bishops, and not at the king's command. Yet that did not mean that royal legislation had no role to play. Indeed, the synodal report went on to quote no fewer than twenty-three Carolingian capitularies "decreed by previous emperors and kings" as a guide for the young king and his agents.

The council of Saint-Macre's ostentatious reliance on authoritative tradition was entirely in keeping with Hincmar's thinking about the law, as also was the programmatic declaration at the beginning of the conciliar report that "we are not establishing novelties, but rather recalling what was decreed by our elders according to the path of the Holy Scriptures and promulgated by Christian emperors and kings" (*Saint-Macre*, 178). But tradition, however authoritative, still needed to be interpreted before it could be applied to contemporaneous situations, and this allowed plenty of room for both expertise and creativity. Another text issued by the council of Saint-Macre, which was again almost certainly personally written by Hincmar, illustrates this well. A letter addressed to King Louis III, in the name of Hincmar and the other bishops present at the council, asserted that the people and clergy of the city of Beauvais had forfeited their right to choose their new bishop "according to the sacred canons" because they had selected an unsuitable candidate (*Saint-Macre*, 199). This was a bold and unprecedented statement, and in truth it is not clear exactly which sacred canons Hincmar had in mind that could justify a city's losing the right to elect its own bishop through negligence. But by 881, Hincmar had had many years of experience in developing new norms from old texts. Indeed, as the great historian of Pseudo-Isidore Horst Fuhrmann observed, Hincmar had no need of forged decretals, for it seemed that he could make the law that already existed say whatever he wanted.[7]

7 H. Fuhrmann, *Einfluß und Verbreitung der pseudoisidorischen Fälschungen. Von ihrem Auftauchen bis in die neuere Zeit*, 3 vols., MGH 24 (Stuttgart: Hiersemann, 1972–74), 1:121.

SUMMARY

Hincmar was not blind to the problems of working with early-medieval norms. He observed that "there are many things that seem to be contradictory among themselves not only in the canons and in the decrees of the Roman pontiffs, but also in the holy Scriptures of the Old and New Testament inspired by the same Holy Spirit by which the holy canons were established." He went on in an optimistic vein, however: "[B]ut they are not contradictory, but simply arranged or to be arranged according to the nature of the time and matter of the issue" (*Opusculum LV*, 212). Hincmar's legal expertise lay in that process of arrangement, which in turn depended on novel, semi-exegetical, and always erudite interpretation of all kinds of normative text. His method involved the virtuosic combination of norms taken from different traditions – Roman law, ecclesiastical canons, Frankish capitularies, patristic writers, and Scripture – to provide answers to specific questions, in the hope of establishing peaceful and just solutions. His interpretations were flexible in order to bring out what he assumed was an underlying coherence running through all this material. This was his largely implicit theology of law.

Quite how representative of his time his views are is debatable. As we have seen, archbishop Agobard of Lyon (d. 840) certainly had a different perspective on the trial by ordeal. And Agobard also had much less patience with secular legal tradition than Hincmar. Where Hincmar accepted that there was bound to be legal diversity among different peoples, Agobard denounced such diversity and called for it to be replaced with a single Christian law throughout the whole of the Frankish empire. It may be merely by chance that we have so much material regarding Hincmar's views on law, but it may also be that this abundance reflects the unusual efforts that he devoted to the topic and his unusual approach to it. Not all Frankish bishops were as interested in legal traditions as Hincmar was; and not all kings were as receptive to legal ideas as King Charles the Bald, with whom Hincmar worked, mostly in amicable partnership, for over thirty years.

SIGNIFICANCE AND RECEPTION

Hincmar's emphasis on the practical application of laws and canons impeded his direct influence on subsequent writers. Most of his enormous oeuvre was focused on specific issues and cases of his day, and this diminished its interest for later readers. As a consequence, many of Hincmar's most important works survive only in single manuscripts, or even in early-modern editions based on manuscripts that are no longer extant. Only a few extracts from Hincmar's legal work were picked up during the Middle Ages. The *Little Work in Fifty-Five Chapters*, for instance, was cited by later archbishops of Reims and by bishop Ivo of Chartres (d. 1115), through whom a fragment of it, albeit under a misleading title, passed into Gratian's *Decretum*, compiled in the twelfth century (*Opusclum LV*, p. 127).[8] Hincmar's ideas about marriage represent a partial exception, since these exercised considerable influence, albeit partly through misquotation, on the central-medieval coital theory of marriage and in the accumulation of relevant canonical material.[9] Among the few authentic excerpts from Hincmar's work that circulated independently as "canons" during the central Middle Ages, perhaps the most influential and frequently occurring was *Si per sortiarias*, on the course of action to be taken when a couple's failure to consummate their marriage sexually was the result of a hex: a formative and much discussed topic in canon law of the central Middle Ages.[10] Not until the sixteenth century, however, was there a general revival of interest in Hincmar's writings, as they were pressed into the service of polemics about predestination, and, with more interest in his legal ideas, about the "Gallican church."[11]

Yet this does not necessarily mean that Hincmar had little impact on later legal developments, for his weightiest influence may have been exercised indirectly. Whatever the circumstances of Pseudo-Isidore's production, the circulation of this canonical collection in the later ninth century was energized by its value for Hincmar's many rivals, victims, and opponents, such as the already-mentioned Hincmar of Laon, our archbishop's own nephew. Another suffragan bishop who fell out with Hincmar, Rothad of Soissons, may have been instrumental in bringing Pseudo-Isidorian texts to the attention of Pope Nicholas I (d. 867), whose own letters, mediated through various canonical collections, were to be an important source for Gratian's *Decretum*. Hincmar's most profound and enduring legal influence, therefore, may have been less in his own legal ideas than in how his expertise raised the bar for contemporaneous debates about law, compelling his opponents to rise to the challenge.

8 Gratian, C. 24 q. 3 c. 6 (*CICan.* 1:990–92). Cf. Ivo of Chartres, *Decretum* XIV 21, and likewise *Panormia* V 124; *Tripartita* III 27 (28), 13.

9 The source was an epistolary treatise in which Hincmar clarified and explored the legal and theological issues pertaining to the contested marriage of Stephen, an Aquitanian nobleman. The case originated during a council at Tusey (Tusiciacum) in 860. See Philip L. Reynolds, *How Marriage Became One of the Sacraments* (Cambridge: Cambridge University Press, 2016), 222–30. The canon *Si per sortiarias* (see the next note) is from the same source.

10 Gratian, C. 33 q. 1 c. 4 (*CICan.* 1:1150). For discussion of this canon and its reception, see Catherine Rider, *Magic and Impotence in the Middle Ages* (Oxford: Oxford University Press, 2006), esp. 31–42 (with an English translation of the text on p. 40); and John C. Wei, *Gratian the Theologian* (Washington, DC: Catholic University of America Press, 2016), 197–206, who provides further references to canonical collections (see esp. p. 203 n. 41). The canon is an excerpt from Hincmar, *De nuptiis Stephani et filiae Regimundi comitis*, MGH Epist. 8.1 (ed. E. Perels, 1939), no. 136, p. 105.

11 Devisse, *Hincmar*, 1:9–28. M. Stratmann, "Zur Wirkungsgeschichte Hinkmars von Reims," *Francia* 22 (1995): 1–44.

SOURCES

The Paris lat. 12445 manuscript can conveniently be viewed online through the *Gallica* website (http://gallica.bnf.fr/),[12] and the online *Leges* project in Cologne provides a bibliography (www.leges.uni-koeln.de/).[13] Another canon law manuscript to which Hincmar probably had access, Bern, Burgerbibliothek 425, has been transcribed at the Carolingian Canon Law project (http://ccl.rch.uky.edu/).[14] This manuscript mostly contains the Dacheriana canon law collection, but also has some ordeal texts.

Most of Hincmar's works are edited in PL 125–126, but these editions are of very varying quality. This essay has accordingly focused on three of Hincmar's works that have benefited from recent critical editions: the Council of Saint-Macre, in *Die Konzilien der karolingischen Teilreiche 875–911*, ed. W. Hartmann, I. Schröder, and G. Schmitz, MGH Conc. 5 (2012), 166–200; the Opusculum LV Capitulorum, in *Die Streitschriften Hinkmars von Reims und Hinkmars von Laon*, ed. Rudolf Schieffer, MGH Conc. 4, suppl. 2 (2003); and *De divortio Lotharii regis et Theutbergae reginae*, ed. Letha Böhringer, MGH Conc. 4, suppl. 1 (1992). The latter is now available in full English translation with an introduction and annotations: Rachel Stone and Charles West, *The Divorce of King Lothar and Queen Theutberga* (Manchester: Manchester University Press, 2016). An edition and translation into French of Hincmar's innovative treatise on the law of abduction, *De raptu*, by Sylvie Joye is in preparation. Also cited above is Hincmar's *Collectio de Ecclesiis et Capellis*, ed. M. Stratmann, MGH Fontes iuris Germanici antiqui 14 (1990). A list of Hincmar's works available in English translation is available at the "Collaborative Hincmar Project blog," http://hincmar.blogspot.co.uk,[15] administered by Rachel Stone and Charles West.

FURTHER READING

Still fundamental on Hincmar's ideas about law is the book by Jean Devisse, *Hincmar et la loi* (Dakar: Faculté des Lettres et des sciences humaines, 1962), which summarizes Hincmar's conception of law and its divisions but devotes more space to his sources. See also the important updates on the topic that Devisse provided in his much longer *Hincmar, archêveque de Reims 845–882* (Geneva: Droz, 1975–76), vol. 1, 549 ff. For a more recent evaluation in English, see Rachel Stone and Charles West (eds.), *Hincmar of Rheims: Life and Work* (Manchester: Manchester University Press, 2015). The chapter in this collection

[12] The "permalink" to this MS at the time of writing is http://gallica.bnf.fr/ark:/12148/btv1b90726779 (accessed April 21, 2018).

[13] The "permalink" to this MS at the time of writing is www.leges.uni-koeln.de/mss/handschrift/paris-bn-lat-12445/ (accessed April 21, 2018).

[14] Accessed March 15, 2018.

[15] Ibid.

most relevant to Hincmar on law is Simon Corcoran, "Hincmar and His Roman Legal Sources," 129–55, but most of the chapters touch on law to some extent, reflecting its importance to the archbishop.

On the Paris manuscript discussed in the prelude to this chapter, see Letha Böhringer, "Der eherechtliche Traktat im Paris. Lat.12445, einer Arbeitshandschrift Hinkmars von Reims," *Deutsches Archiv für Erforschung des Mittelalters* 46 (1990): 18–47.

Riccardo Bof and Conrad Leyser, "Divorce and Remarriage between Late Antiquity and the Early Middle Ages: Canon Law and Conflict Resolution," in Kate Cooper and Conrad Leyser (eds.), *Making Early Medieval Societies: Conflict and Belonging in the Latin West, 300–1200* (Cambridge: Cambridge University Press, 2016), is useful in emphasizing the difficulties that Hincmar faced in extracting consistent norms from the material available to him. On Carolingian ideas about law, the extent to which Hincmar represented an exception, and how his use of secular law (the *leges*) can be considered "interpretative," or "exegetical," see Thomas Faulkner, *Law and authority in the Early Middle Ages: The Frankish Leges in the Carolingian Period* (Cambridge: Cambridge University Press, 2016), esp. 79–81 and 84–96 for Hincmar.

The rationale for judicial ordeal is best approached through Robert Bartlett, *Trial by Fire: The Medieval Judicial Ordeal* (Oxford: Clarendon Press, 1986). Hincmar's most elaborated arguments about it were presented in his *De divortio* (*On the Divorce of King Lothar and Queen Theutberga*), of which see the translation by Rachel Stone and Charles West, *The Divorce of King Lothar and Queen Theutberga* (Manchester: Manchester University Press, 2016).

For a survey of the wider dispute of which the *De divortio* was a part (with emphasis on "power politics"), see Karl Heidecker, *The Divorce of Lothar II: Christian Marriage and Political Power in the Carolingian World*, translated from the Dutch by T. M. Guest (Ithaca: Cornell, 2010). For a different approach (more sympathetically disposed toward Hincmar, with his quest for peace), see Letha Böhringer, "Gewaltverzicht, Gesichtswahrung und Befriedung durch Öffentlichkeit. Beobachtungen zur Entstehung des kirchlichen Eherechts im 9. Jahrhundert am Beispiel Hinkmars von Reims," in S. Esders (ed.), *Rechtsverständnis und Konfliktbewältigung. Gerichtliche und außergerichtliche Strategien im Mittelalter* (Cologne: Böhlau, 2007), 255–89; and S. Esders, "Das Recht im Dienst der Machtpolitik? Anmerkungen zu einer Neuerscheinung über die Scheidungsaffäre König Lothars II," *Mitteilungen des Instituts für Österreichische Geschichtsforschung* 119 (2011): 146–54.

On Hincmar's attitude to kingship, see the seminal study by Janet L. Nelson, "Kingship, Law and Liturgy in the Political Thought of Hincmar of Rheims," *English Historical Review* 92 (1977): 241–79. For an example of how Hincmar tried to institutionalize one aspect of the distinction and cooperation between the church and worldly law, see Charles West, "The Significance of the Carolingian Advocate," EME 17.2 (2009): 186–206.

For Hincmar's encounter with Pseudo-Isidore and his approach to accusations of forgery, the best guide is still Horst Fuhrmann, *Einfluß und Verbreitung der pseudoisidorischen Fälschungen. Von ihrem Auftauchen bis in die neuere Zeit*, 3 vols., MGH 24 (Stuttgart: Hiersemann, 1972–74), 200–224, 625–726. On Pseudo-Isidore generally, see Chapter 19, by Clara Harder, in this volume.

22

Regino of Prüm

Greta Austin

INTRODUCTION

Regino is included in this volume because of his *Libri duo de synodalibus causis et disciplinis ecclesiasticis* (*Two Books concerning Synodal Investigations and Ecclesiastical Instructions*), a handbook for bishops to consult when making visitations of their dioceses.[1] But Regino was a polymath, and he composed two other, very different treatises: one is on music; the other, his *Chronicle*, is a comprehensive history of the world as it was known to him. Although Regino benefited from the flourishing of learning and study during the Carolingian period, he fell prey to the late Carolingian era's political instabilities when he lost his influential position as abbot of the powerful monastery of Prüm, near Aachen, and fled to Trier. It was during this final period of exile, probably in part in an effort to regain his administrative and political influence, that Regino compiled his *Libri duo*.

The institution of the episcopal visitation, as best we can tell today, was fairly new and still developing during Regino's time. His *Libri duo* is an important historical resource for our understanding of it. It stands out from other Carolingian and late-Carolingian canonical collections in that he states explicitly how he intended it to be used. Regino dedicated the collection to the archbishop of Mainz, explaining that the latter could consult this portable collection "as a guide" when he was traveling and so did not have access to "many volumes of councils."[2] The *Libri duo* was clearly designed as a reference book or manual for bishops, archbishops, and cathedral clergy as they carried out their ministerial duties.

In any modern discussion of Regino's *Libri duo*, some terms familiar in the scholarly literature today, such as "penance" and "canon law," can be difficult to apply consistently, partly because the meanings of these terms had not yet taken on the firm boundaries that they would later have. One way of thinking about the *Libri duo* is to adopt Rob Meens's description: that it positioned itself "on the borderline of canon

[1] The edition of *Libri duo* cited in what follows is Hartmann's. For details, see under Source, below.

[2] *Prefaces*, 93.

law and penitential discipline."[3] In the absence of clear boundaries, Meens's description captures the ways in which the *Libri duo* did not belong definitively to one or the other of these two fields. Although categories such as "canon law" and "penance" can provide a helpful framework for modern scholars thinking about collections such as Regino's *Libri duo* and Burchard's *Decretum*, they can be misleading when they import modern expectations, such as the early-modern preoccupation with the privacy of the confessional and the understanding of canon law as a distinct discipline that was taught in schools, as it became later in the Middle Ages. Obviously, there were no "schools of penance" or "schools of canon law" in Regino's period. Nor would Regino have necessarily seen a clear distinction between canon law and penance, as modern scholars have often noted. John Burden comments regarding Burchard that the "integration of canon law sources and penitentials throughout the *Decretum* suggests that he did not recognize a functional distinction between the two genres."[4] Much the same may be said about Regino's *Libri duo*. Regino assumed that bishops would be using a variety of sources to help them follow proper procedures, correct ignorant priests, assign appropriate penances, maintain moral order, and settle ecclesiastical controversies in their dioceses.[5]

The *Libri duo* can be seen as belonging to the Carolingian tradition of episcopal handbooks. Rosamond McKitterick describes handbooks of this sort as "miscellaneous collections of legal and disciplinary canons, that is, of texts suited for the exercise of the pastoral functions of the priesthood." McKitterick notes, however, that these are not "mere miscellanies. They are deliberately designed handbooks for the bishop and priest to aid him in the running of the diocese and parish."[6] Recent scholarship has also called attention to Carolingian and late-Carolingian manuscripts designed specifically as sources of reference for priests. Thus, Susan Keefe has proposed a typology for manuscript miscellanies of the period, distinguishing between reference books for priests (which she calls "instruction-readers"), school books (with marginal notations and other visible signs of instruction), episcopal reference books, and episcopal pastoral manuals.[7] Unlike the pastoral manuals, the

3 Rob Meens, *Penance in Medieval Europe, 600–1200* (Cambridge: Cambridge University Press, 2014), 141.

4 John Burden, *Between Sin and Crime: Penitential Justice in Medieval Germany, 900–1200* (doctoral diss., Yale University, 2018), 69–70.

5 In this chapter and in the next chapter, on Burchard, I use the terms "canon" and "canonical" cautiously. Some early-medieval collections do describe themselves as "canonical handbooks" or refer to "the canons." Others consist exclusively of penances and describe themselves as "penitentials" (see *Prefaces*, 99). But Burchard and other compilers combined "the laws of the canons" and "the judgments for those doing penances" (ibid.), and it is unclear whether these thinkers saw a clear distinction between the two kinds of texts.

6 Rosamond McKitterick, *The Frankish Church and the Carolingian Reforms, 789–895* (London: Royal Historical Society, 1977), esp. 41–42, and more generally 36–43, on the tradition of episcopal handbooks. For my characterization of Regino's collection, I am indebted to Sarah Hamilton, *The Practice of Penance, 900–1050* (Woodbridge: Boydell Press, 2001), 28 n. 21.

7 Susan Keefe, *Water and the Word: Baptism and the Education of the Clergy* (Notre Dame: University of Notre Dame Press, 2002), 2 vols., 1: 22–38. See also Carine van Rhijin, "Manuscripts for Local Priests

reference books preferred longer texts, often quoted in their entirety, rather than short excerpts. Episcopal handbooks often included multiple texts on the same topic.[8] As has become clear in recent work on liturgical manuscripts of the period, however, modern typologies or categories can be misleading and should be used with caution.[9] Keefe's typology provides a useful way for us to think today about the *Libri duo*, namely, as an episcopal reference book, but other uses were certainly possible as well. Regino's *Libri duo* is best regarded as an episcopal reference book, given his comments in the preface about providing a guide to carry while traveling, but it may also have served pastoral or didactic purposes. There is no need to assign it to categories such as canon law or penitential literature, which were not clearly drawn until a later period.

Regardless of the labels that modern scholars apply to it, the *Libri duo* was so useful that Burchard of Worms, only a century later, modeled his own widely copied *Decretum* on it. Both of these collections stand in the tradition, originally Carolingian, of episcopal handbooks. Unlike the miscellanies described by McKitterick, however, Regino's topical organization and broad range of issues must have made his book especially valuable as a source of reference for bishops, who, as Timothy Reuter points out, played central roles in European life during the tenth and eleventh centuries.[10]

LIFE AND WORK

Regino's episcopal handbook may well reflect his desire to establish or reinforce political and social stability in tumultuous times. Under his eyes, the Carolingian empire was slowly disintegrating. Simon MacLean observes that "the career, mental world and writings of Regino, abbot of Prüm (d. 915) were all defined by the Carolingian empire and, more particularly, by its end."[11] Regino lived in the middle sector of the Carolingian empire, known as Lotharingia. MacLean locates Regino,

and the Carolingian Reforms," in C. van Rhijn and S. Patzold (eds.), *Men in the Middle: Local Priests in Early Medieval Europe* (Berlin: De Gruyter, 2016), 177–98.

8 Keefe, *Water and the Word*, 1:26–28.

9 See the following essays in H. Gittos and S. Hamilton (eds.), *Understanding Medieval Liturgy: Essays in Interpretation* (Routledge: London, 2016): Henry Parkes, "Questioning the Authority of Vogel and Elze's *Pontical romano-germanique*," 75–102, at 99 (on the distinction between "pontifical" and "liturgical book"); Carol Symes, "Liturgical Texts and Performance Practices," 239–67; and Sarah Hamilton, "Interpreting Diversity: Excommunication Rites in the Tenth and Eleventh Centuries," 125–58, at 129.

10 Timothy Reuter, "Ein Europa der Bischöfe: Das Zeitalter Burchards von Worms," in Wilfried Hartmann (ed.), *Bischof Burchard von Worms, 1000–1025*, Quellen und Abhandlungen zur mittelrheinischen Kirchengeschichte 100 (Mainz, 2000), 1–28; English translation in Ludger Körntgen and Dominik Waßenhoven (eds.), *Patterns of Episcopal Power: Bishops in Tenth and Eleventh Century Western Europe / Strukturen bischöflicher Herrschaftsgewalt im westlichen Europa des 10. und 11. Jahrhunderts* (Berlin: De Gruyter, 2011), 17–38.

11 Simon MacLean, *History and Politics in Late Carolingian and Ottonian Europe: The Chronicle of Regino of Prüm and Adalbert of Magdeburg* (Manchester: Manchester University Press, 2009), 1.

therefore, within the political climate of his time, "a world pounded from without by the raids of Scandinavians and Hungarians, and torn apart from within by violent feuds and the disruption of political process."[12]

Regino's origins are unknown. He may have appeared in the list of monks at Prüm when Ansbald was abbot of the monastery,[13] but he first appears in the extant written records of the monastery when the other monks elected him abbot in 892.[14] To be abbot of Prüm was to hold a position of considerable power and influence, for this was a wealthy community. When the monastery surveyed its holdings, probably under Regino in 892, it had about 1,700 estates with some 16,000–20,000 inhabitants.[15] The monastery enjoyed the patronage not only of Carolingian rulers but also of local aristocrats, some of whose relatives were monks there.[16] In addition to overseeing the abbey's property and the many inhabitants, Regino became responsible for the care of King Lothar II's illegitimate son, Hugh. After Hugh revolted unsuccessfully against the Carolingian emperor Charles the Fat, Charles ordered him to be blinded and sent to a monastery. Hugh went first to Saint-Gall but ended up in Prüm, under Regino's care.[17]

Regino's high-profile position as abbot of Prüm exposed him to political maneuvering, which resulted in his loss of office in 889. Regino mentions his own deposition in his *Chronicle*, but this account lacks a narrative that must originally have belonged to it. The reader can tell that a section is missing because Regino apologizes for going "back to the beginnings of the matter" and explaining "in plain language how this affair was brought through to its conclusion."[18] No such explanation exists. In the next section, Regino says he had been "more verbose than is proper." It seems, then, that he had written at length about the circumstances of his deposition, but that this passage was later removed.[19] MacLean argues convincingly that Regino himself probably excised the passage, having had second thoughts about his detailed confession in light of more recent political concerns.[20]

After his exile from Prüm, Regino spent the remainder of his life – some fifteen years – in Trier. It was during this period he composed his three major works, respectively on canonical regulation and penitential discipline (c. 906 CE),[21] history (908), and music (900–915). Archbishop Rathod of Trier had appointed Regino as abbot of a local Trier monastery, but he had clearly come down considerably in the

12 Simon MacLean, "Insinuation, Censorship and the Struggle for Late Carolingian Lotharingia in Regino of Prüm's *Chronicle*," *English Historical Review* 124 (2009): 1–28, at 3.

13 MacLean, *History and Politics*, 4.

14 Ibid.

15 Ibid.

16 MacLean, *History and Politics*, 5.

17 Regino, *Chronicle*, Book II, for the year 885; trans. MacLean, *History and Politics*, 191–94.

18 Ibid.

19 Regino, *Chronicle*, Book II, for the year 892 (p. 213).

20 MacLean, "Insinuation," 10.

21 The two most recent texts in the *Libri duo* (i.e., I.450–51) are dated 906. See *Libri duo*, ed. Hartmann, Introduction, 5.

world.[22] As MacLean suggests, Regino probably "remained preoccupied with regaining high office in the kingdom," given that "he dedicated each of these works to one of the king's three leading advisers, Hatto [archbishop of Mainz], Adalbero [bishop of Augsburg] and Ratbod, respectively."[23] Regino compiled the *Libri duo* at the request of archbishop Rathod. Since the latter had just helped him out of a tight place, the collection may have been a way of thanking him. Moreover, as its modern translators note, the preface "brims with deferential rhetoric praising the virtues of Archbishop Hatto of Mainz,"[24] who was another influential royal advisor. Regino's work as a compiler of canons, therefore, should be seen as his response to tumultuous contemporary events. Perhaps he sought to reinforce the rule of law (broadly understood, in the sense that anthropologists of law use it) rather than rule by force. At a time when nobles were sometimes murdered in church, Regino's interest in contributing to social and ethical order makes sense, for the rule of law must have provided stability and predictability.

Because Regino often worked with existing materials, his innovation and creativity can sometimes be overlooked, especially in the *Libri duo*, but recent scholars have demonstrated his originality in the way that he shaped existing materials. This method belonged to the Carolingian tradition of textual bricolage, whereby existing materials were recombined and often reworked to produce new forms.[25] Regino's creativity expressed itself not only in his *Libri duo* but also in his historical and musical works. As MacLean points out about the *Chronicle*, Regino was "the first major author to begin a history with the birth of Christ, and the first to attempt a comprehensive AD chronology for the entire period since."[26] So also in the *Libri duo*, Regino worked within an existing tradition (that of episcopal handbooks) but used intelligent albeit well-established methods of organizing the information by topics, presenting it on the page with rubrics and subsections, in order to make his collection useful and easy to navigate.

THE PURPOSES OF REGINO'S EPISCOPAL HANDBOOK

As already noted, Regino's *Two Books Concerning Synodal Investigations and Ecclesiastical Instructions* (*Libri duo de synodalibus causis et disciplinis ecclesiasticis*) was above all an episcopal handbook: more precisely, a reference book that bishops could consult as they visited their dioceses, held local synods, and investigated the state of affairs in each parish. The collection developed and popularized a particular genre of such handbooks: ones that were systematically organized and could be used to identify

22 MacLean, *History and Politics*, 6.

23 MacLean, "Insinuation," 9.

24 *Prefaces*, 69.

25 On this method, see, e.g., Celia Chazelle, "Exegesis in the Ninth-Century Eucharist Controversy," in C. Chazelle and B. van Name Edwards (eds.), *The Study of the Bible in the Carolingian Era*, Medieval Church Studies 3 (Turnhout: Brepols, 2003), 167–87.

26 MacLean, *History and Politics*, 6.

proper procedures and rituals, to assign penance or to excommunicate, to hold local episcopal synods, to ensure the correct process for ordination, and to carry out episcopal duties. Book I of the *Libri duo* ends with a text describing how to examine a bishop for his knowledge of church doctrine, noting that a priest or deacon should be examined too.[27] Although chiefly designed for episcopal visitations, therefore, such handbooks could have been used in other ways, such as for consultation as reference books at home and as resources for teaching—an important responsibility for bishops, as we know from various *Lives* of bishops from this period. Burchard's *Decretum* stands in the same tradition, and he clearly modeled his own collection on the *Libri duo*. Burchard mentioned in his preface that he intended his collection to be used for priestly consultation, as well as for teaching and study, and his *Decretum* was clearly useful to bishops in synods and during their annual visitation of their dioceses.[28] Gratian's *Decretum*, too, might be seen as an episcopal handbook, albeit one designed explicitly for teaching and organized on a higher level.

The *Libri duo* is an important source for historians today who seek to understand the developing church practice of episcopal visitations, although it may represent only the local customs during Regino's period and in his part of the world, or possibly even Regino's idealized vision of episcopal duties. Canons 5 and 7 of Book I describe the bishop's duty to inspect his diocese. He should check up on the clergy and instruct the ignorant among them if they are not performing their duties correctly. According to the *Libri duo*, the bishop would investigate first the state of the church and the clergy, and then the laity. The division in two books reflects this two-part process, for whereas Book I focuses on church administration and the clergy, Book II focuses on the laity and their behavior. Each book begins with a long list of questions that the bishop or his ministers or officials (*eius ministri*) should ask at his local synod (*in sua synodo*).[29]

According to Book II, an archdeacon or archpriest should go ahead of the bishop, one or two days before the visit, and gather the people together.[30] This cleric and other priests in the bishop's service should handle minor and lighter cases during this period, in order not to burden the bishop unnecessarily.[31] Seven upstanding representatives of the community should take an oath (which Regino provides)[32] on sacred relics.[33] In due course, the bishop puts a list of questions, which Regino also provides, to the seven oath-takers (II.5).

27 *Libri duo* I.455.

28 See the following chapter, on Burchard's *Decretum*.

29 The note at the beginning of Book I explains that a bishop or his "ministers" (*ministri*) should ask these synodal questions in *vici publici*, estates (*villae*), or parishes. The term *vici publici* seems to refer to settlements with parish churches: see J. F. Niermeyer, *Mediae Latinitatis lexicon minus*, 1st edition (Leiden: Brill, 1997), 1097–1100.

30 *Libri duo* II.1.

31 Ibid.

32 *Libri duo* II.3.

33 *Libri duo* II.2

What was the relationship between the proceedings of the bishop's local synodal court and the practice of penance? The bishop's synod does not seem to be exactly the same as confession and the administration of penance, a practice that is described in Book I (from c. 1. 292 onward). Moreover, whereas the *Libri duo* gives bishops exclusive power over serious offenders and especially over excommunication, it enables priests and even deacons to hear confessions.[34] The *Libri duo* describes what became known in the Carolingian period as "public" penance,[35] but it also mandates that everyone confess their sins on Ash Wednesday. Perhaps all the faithful, as Hamilton has suggested, were supposed to go through the same initial stage of confession, after which those found to have committed serious or public sins were required to do public penance.[36] John Burden has recently argued that Burchard's *Decretum* was designed for public, synodal use rather than penitential use.[37]

One difficulty in determining the relationship between synodal inquiry and penance in Regino's work is that the church's penalties for offenses were primarily derived from penitential practices, sometimes with penance as the alternative to excommunication. People at the time may not have perceived any clear distinction between the visiting bishop's effort to expose and punish crimes and the pastoral prescription of penance after confession to a bishop or a priest. The text itself may contain indications. For example, some canons use the phrase "in this synod" rather than "in penance," and one refers to a miscreant's being in the presence of the bishop "in this synod."[38] Perhaps this refers to a legal inquiry. But to distinguish between "legal" and "penitential" procedures during this period may be going too far.[39] We do not even know, as Wilfried Hartmann reminds us, how the *Libri duo* was actually consulted.[40] Unfortunately, there is little independent attestation for the actual practice of episcopal visitation during the ninth and tenth centuries.[41] Burchard's *Life* does not describe it, for instance. The only tenth-century source that

34 *Libri duo* I.299 says that only a bishop or a priest can assign a penance or hear confession. *Libri duo* I.300 asserts that a deacon can receive a penitent if a priest is not available.

35 *Libri duo* I.295 describes the *ordo* (liturgical script or process) for those undertaking "public" penance.

36 Hamilton, *Practice of Penance*, 43.

37 John Burden, Between Sin and Crime: Penitential Justice in Medieval Germany, 900–1200 (doctoral diss., Yale University, 2018), esp. chapter 2.

38 See, e.g., *Libri duo* II.235. *Libri duo* II.239 and 240 also mention the bishop's presence.

39 Hamilton, *Practice of Penance*, 34–44.

40 Wilfried Hartmann, "Zu Effektivität und Aktualität von Reginos Sendhandbuch," in W. P. Müller and M. E. Sommar (eds.), *Medieval Church Law and the Origins the Western Legal Tradition* (Washington, DC: Catholic University of America Press, 2006), 33–49, at 33.

41 On the texts describing the need for such visitation, see Hartmann, "Zu Effektivität," 37–38. Rudolf Schieffer, "Ludwig 'der Fromme'. Zur Entstehung eines karolingischen Herrscherbeinamens," *Frühmittelalterliche Studien* 16 (1982): 58–73, at 56, concludes that what became known as the synodal court (*Sendgericht*) took shape in the last decades of the ninth century. See also Andrew L. Slafkosky, *The Canonical Episcopal Visitation of the Diocese: An Historical Synopsis and Commentary*, Catholic University of America Canon Law Studies 142 (Washington, DC: Catholic University of America, 1941), 8–24.

describes a bishop carrying out episcopal visitation is the *Life* of Ulrich, bishop of Augsburg.[42]

We might pose the question another way by asking: Was the *Libri duo* a "penitential"? If by "penitential" we mean a book that described offenses and prescribed penances, then the answer would be "partially, but not entirely." The texts on penance seem designed to regulate and explain how priests should hear confession, and how public penance should be performed. After the list of questions in Book I and Book II, a rubric explains that the items or chapters above (*capitulatim*) are "supported by canonical authority" (*auctoritate canonica roborari*).[43] The term "canonical authority" seems to describe authoritative texts in general. In each book, about 455 texts follow the lists of questions. The very first canon of Book I asserts in its rubric that "canonical statutes should be observed by everyone,"[44] and the text itself explains that clerics should not rely on their own judgment in ecclesiastical actions or judgments but rather be led by canonical authority.[45] The *Libri duo* does not, however, address matters of penance alone. It includes multiple texts on church administration, for instance, and Regino does a thorough job of discussing procedure and rituals, such as the blessing of water (e.g., I. 213). A section of Book II provides various oaths, such as that for clearing the name of someone accused of adultery.[46] As a wide-ranging resource, the *Libri duo* provided authoritative proof texts that a bishop and his cathedral clergy, and perhaps even parish priests, could consult in order to check their knowledge of the tradition or to confirm procedures, including not only the administration of penance but also other rituals and practices.

REGINO'S METHODS AS A COMPILER

Regino's collection assumes an episcopal audience of clerics who already possessed the interpretative tools to address potential conflicts or disagreements among the texts that he included. Regino wrote in his preface that he left it up "to the judgment of the reader what he prefers to select and approve as most important."[47] Similarly, in his treatise on music, Regino explained that he worked to dispel confusion, but that he "left it to the judgement of an accomplished singer to assess the value of the additional *differentiae* he

42 See Rob Meens, *Penance in Medieval Europe*, 143–46, for an excellent summary and discussion of episcopal visitation as described in the *Life* of Ulrich of Augsburg, which also refers to the use of canonical rules in debated cases.

43 See *Libri duo*, ed. Hartmann, 38 and 252. The sentence occurs twice: first after the list of questions in Book I, before canon I.1; and later right after the list of questions about lay behavior in Book II (II.5, before II.6).

44 *Libri duo*, ed. Hartmann, 38.

45 The canon is attributed accurately to the council of Meaux-Paris (845/46), c. 34, first part: see *Libri duo*, ed. Hartmann, 38.

46 See *Libri duo* II.232–36, here at 235.

47 *Prefaces*, 94.

considered superfluous."[48] In the *Libri duo*, Regino included texts providing different penances for the same offense and some that might be confusing.[49] Regino apparently expected his readers to be sufficiently skilled at handling such texts. Rather than eliminating ambiguities or apparent contradictions, he provided more texts rather than fewer, leaving the reader to sort out which norms to apply. The only exception to this approach is the list of questions to be asked in confession by priests in Book I, which prescribes specific penances for particular offenses rather than leaving such decisions to the individual priest.[50] For instance, the text says persons who have committed homicide willfully, rather than by accident, should do seven years of penance; if they did so without knowing, they should do five years; if they did it to avenge a relative, one year followed by penances at particular times; and if in war, forty days. Here, Regino did not entrust individual priests with the task of determining the penance to be applied through confession, although presumably the assignment of penance to major crimes, such as homicide, would be supervised by the bishop.[51] But the penitential section in Book I is the exception rather than the rule. The *Libri duo* has texts that could be interpreted differently or that even provide different penances. Book II of the *Libri duo* concludes with Regino's own editorial comment, which again stresses the role of (probably episcopal) interpretation: "[W]e have provided in order various opinions of various Fathers concerning the remedy of sins and regarding the imposition of penance," leaving such decisions to the "judgment of a prudent priest," who must determine "what is more beneficial and useful for the soul of the penitent."[52] These features, again, suggest that Regino's book was intended chiefly for bishops and senior clergy. By contrast, Burchard edited his material in order to eliminate conflicts rather than leaving decisions to the reader's judgment.

A number of texts in the *Libri duo* are of unknown or uncertain origin, since they have no apparent formal sources (that is, there is no known earlier collection or text in which they appear, and on which Regino might have drawn). Did Regino compose these himself? The most famous text in the *Libri duo*, for instance, concerns women who claim to ride on beasts with Diana at

48 Susan Boynton, "The Sources and Significance of the Orpheus Myth in 'Musica Enchiriadis' and Regino of Prüm's 'Epistola de harmonica institutione'," *Early Music History* 18 (1999): 47–74, at 65–66.

49 See, e.g., *Libri duo* II.255, on a person who has fornicated in the manner of a sodomite, where Regino notes that "some require ten years, some 7, others 1. *Item.* Others judge, if they are in the custom of doing so, laity should do penance 5 years, clerics 7, subdeacons or monks 8, deacons ten, priest 12, bishop 14 years."

50 *Libri duo* I.305.

51 *Libri duo* I.304.

52 End of *Libri duo* Book II, after II.454, ed. Hartmann, 468: "Ecce diversorum patrum diversas opinions de remediis peccatorum, vel de leviganda poenitentia in ordine posuimus, in arbitrio prudentis sacerdotis relinquentes, quid salubrius et utilius animae poentienti esse decernat."

night.[53] This text does not have a known precedent, and it is tempting to conclude that Regino wrote it himself. Less dramatically, another text without a precedent prohibits selling wine in a church,[54] and another bans the singing of "diabolical songs" at funerals.[55]

To make matters more complicated, Regino seems to have identified the original sources of some texts incorrectly.[56] Inscriptions ascribing canons to a so-called council of Nantes are often actually excerpts from the capitularies of Hincmar of Reims or Theodulf of Orléans.[57] Perhaps Regino did not consider these episcopal capitularies to have sufficient weight of authority. In addition, there are no precedents in the tradition for *Libri duo*'s excerpts from the so-called councils of Reims, Rouen, and Tours. Hartmann suggests that the Nantes canons that were not from capitularies might have come from an unknown episcopal capitulary or from a council of the second half of the ninth century,[58] or that Regino might even have had access to episcopal or conciliar texts from Rouen and Nantes that do not survive in another source.[59] Hartmann identifies multiple parallels between ninth-century episcopal capitularies and the texts that Regino ascribes to these so-called councils.[60] Thus, it seems that Regino may have taken texts from an episcopal capitulary that no longer existed but altered the inscriptions that identified the sources.

Should we consider Regino to have been a forger? Compilers were supposed to work with the sources in front of them, rather than inventing texts, and Regino says in the preface that he "collected and brought together with great zeal from diverse councils and decrees of the Fathers."[61] Burchard not only edited existing texts but even wove them together to make new ones, especially when the tradition did not supply material relevant to his purpose. Regino, it seems, did not go that far. Instead, he altered the inscriptions of texts that were actually from episcopal capitularies, identifying them as conciliar canons, probably because he did not think that the original sources carried sufficient authority. Among these are several texts describing procedures, oaths, and rituals, including excommunication. These may reflect local practice in Trier, where Regino was residing when he

53 *Libri duo* II.371. See the commentary and translation in Alan C. Kors and Edward Peters, *Witchcraft in Europe, 400–1700: A Documentary History*, 2nd edition (Philadelphia: University of Pennsylvania Press, 2001), 60–63.

54 *Libri duo* I.58, which Regino attributes to a council of Tours, but its source is unknown.

55 *Libri duo* I.398.

56 See Examples of Altered Inscriptions at the end of this chapter.

57 See the chart of texts attributed to Nantes in Wilfried Hartmann, "Die capita incerta im Sendhandbuch Reginos von Prüm," in O. Münsch and T. Zotz (eds.), *Scientia Veritatis: Festschrift für Hubert Mordek zum 65. Geburtstag* (Oxfildern: Thorbecke, 2004), 210–11. Most of these texts come from the capitularies of Theodulf or Hincmar. See also the discussion on 211–16.

58 Hartmann, "Die capita incerta," 216.

59 Ibid., 218.

60 Ibid., 224.

61 *Prefaces*, 93.

composed the *Libri duo*.[62] Two examples of models for letters come from Trier and are dated 906. Yet Hamilton points out that Regino's excommunication rite does not wholly reflect the local practice in Trier but rather fits "what is known of practice elsewhere within the ninth-century Frankish Church from surviving snippets."[63] In 900, the murderers of archbishop Fulk of Reims were excommunicated, and their excommunication was recorded precisely.[64] This procedure matches closely the one that Regino described for excommunication.[65] It is possible that Regino did not invent liturgical rites, but rather recorded contemporary practices, especially but not exclusively those of Trier.[66]

In summary, while Regino's *Libri duo* belongs to the Carolingian tradition of episcopal handbooks, its focus on episcopal visitation, administration, and penance is unique. Among books of the first millennium often described today as "canon law collections," Regino's compilation provides evidence for the use of such books as authoritative texts in contexts that might be described as legal and juridical as well as penitential.[67] In this regard, his accomplishment should not be underestimated. Taking existing canons, often from collections that were organized chronologically, he rearranged them to provide a topical set of texts that a bishop could take as a handbook when conducting a visitation.

RECEPTION AND SIGNIFICANCE

The manuscript life of the *Libri duo* was limited. The compilation existed in two different versions: one known as the "genuine" version (presumed to be the original), and the other as the "interpolated" version. The order of the latter is different, and it contains additional texts. Four manuscripts contain the genuine version, and seven the interpolated version. Most of these manuscripts came from the region around Trier and were made during the tenth and eleventh centuries. For whatever reason, in his *Chronicle*, aside from a discussion of the council of Tribur in 895, Regino did not draw upon his *Libri duo* or use the texts contained in it.[68]

Although circulation of Regino's *Libri duo* itself was limited, Burchard of Worms would later use it both as a model and a source of material for his *Decretum*, which

62 Hartmann, "Die capita incerta," 208.

63 (*Libri duo* I. 450–51). Hamilton, "Interpreting Diversity," 132.

64 Ibid., 129.

65 *Libri duo* II.412–18, 438–46. See Hamilton, "Interpreting Diversity," 130 n. 19. As Hamilton points out, "Hartmann's edition is slightly abridged and omits the second address and one of the alternative formulae, canons II.414–15; these are available in Wasserschleben's original 1840 edition or in the more problematic, but easily available edition in PL 132:361–62 where they are numbered cc. 411–12."

66 Hartmann, "Die capita incerta," 207–26. See Hamilton, "Interpreting Diversity," 132–33, on excommunication.

67 See *Libri duo*, ed. Hartmann, Introduction, 7. See also Kéry, *Canonical Collections*, 128–33.

68 Charles West, "Knowledge of the Past and the Judgement of History in Tenth-Century Trier: Regino of Prüm and the Lost Manuscript of Bishop Adventius of Metz," EME 24 (2016), 137–59, at 149.

enjoyed wide circulation. By this indirect means, the influence of the *Libri duo* was extensive, and many of its texts passed through Burchard's to Gratian's *Decretum*.[69]

SOURCE

The most recent printed edition (with introduction and translation) is Wilfried Hartmann (ed.), *Die Sendhandbuch des Regino von Prüm*, Ausgewählte Quellen zur deutschen Geschichte des Mittelalters 42 (WBG: Darmstadt, 2004). This is based on the edition by F. G. A. Wasserschleben (Leipzig, 1840; reprinted Graz: Akadem. Druck- u. Verlagsanstalt, 1964), but with additions from Luxembourg, Bibliothèque Nationale, MS 29, of which Wasserschleben was unaware.[70]

EXAMPLES OF ALTERED INSCRIPTIONS

The following are examples of places where Regino apparently altered the identification of the original source of a canon. Drawn from Hartmann's work, they are listed here because the details are not available in any English-language literature.

Canons attributed to a Council of Nantes: *Libri duo* I.105 (ed. Hartmann, 82) is in fact from the second capitulary of Theodulf of Orléans; *Libri duo* I.127 (ed. Hartmann, 90): from the second capitulary of Theodulf of Orléans; *Libri duo* I.192 (ed. Hartmann, 112): source not known; *Libri duo* I.210 (ed. Hartmann, 116): source not known; *Libri duo* I.211 (ed. Hartmann, 116): from the first capitulary of Hincmar of Reims; *Libri duo* I.214–19 (ed. Hartmann, 118–22): from the first capitulary of Hincmar of Reims; *Libri duo* I.257 (ed. Hartmann, 138): source not known; *Libri duo* I.342 (ed. Hartmann, 182): from the first capitulary Hincmar of Reims; *Libri duo* I.353 (ed. Hartmann, 184): from the second capitulary of Theodulf of Orléans; *Libri duo* I.405 (ed. Hartmann, 204): source not known; *Libri duo* I.453 (ed. Hartmann, 228): source not known.

Canons attributed to a Council of Reims: *Libri duo* I.60, 68–69 (ed. Hartmann, 66–68) is from an unknown source; *Libri duo* I.121 (ed. Hartmann, 86): source not known; *Libri duo* I.222–23 (ed. Hartmann, 124): Hincmar of Reims, second capitulary; *Libri duo* I.247 (ed. Hartmann, 124): source not known; *Libri duo* I.275 (ed. Hartmann, 144): source not known.

Canons attributed to a Council of Rouen: *Libri duo* I.202 (ed. Hartmann, 114) is from an unknown source; *Libri duo* I.23 (ed. Hartmann, 114) is from Hincmar of Reims, first capitulary.

Canons attributed to a Council of Tours: *Libri duo* I.58 (ed. Hartmann, 64) is from an unknown source; *Libri duo* I.71–73 (ed. Hartmann, 70): source not known; *Libri duo* I. 117 (ed. Hartmann, 86): source not known.

[69] *Libri duo*, ed. Hartmann, Introduction, 7.
[70] Ibid., Introduction, 8.

FURTHER READING

Regino's *Chronicle* has attracted more writing in English than the *Libri duo*. For a recent translation of the *Chronicle*, along with a very helpful introduction to Regino's life and works, see Simon MacLean, *History and Politics in Late Carolingian and Ottonian Europe: The Chronicle of Regino of Prüm and Adalbert of Magdeburg* (Manchester: Manchester University Press, 2009). See also Simon MacLean, "Insinuation, Censorship and the Struggle for Late Carolingian Lotharingia in Regino of Prüm's *Chronicle*," *English Historical Review* 124 (2009): 1–28. Other recent studies of the *Chronicle* in English include the following: Simon Airlie, "'Sad stories of the death of kings': Narrative Patterns and Structures of Authority in Regino of Prüm's Chronicle," in E. Tyler and R. Balzaretti (eds.), *Narrative and History in the Early Medieval West*, Studies in the Early Medieval West 16 (Turnhout: Brepols, 2006), 105–31; Erik Goosmann and Rob Meens, "A Mirror of Princes Who Opted Out: Regino of Prüm and Royal Monastic Conversion," in R. Meens et al. (eds.), *Religious Franks: Religion and Power in the Frankish Kingdoms: Studies in Honour of Mayke de Jong* (Manchester: Manchester University Press, 2016), 296–313; and Charles West, "Knowledge of the Past and the Judgement of History in Tenth-Century Trier: Regino of Prüm and the Lost Manuscript of Bishop Adventius of Metz," EME 24 (2016): 137–59.

Wilfried Hartmann is the leading expert on Regino's *Libri duo*. In addition to his articles cited above, see his *Kirche und Kirchenrecht um 900. Die Bedeutung der spätkarolingischen Zeit für Tradition und Innovation im kirchlichen Recht*, MGH Schriften 58 (Hannover: Hahn, 2008). All of these sources are in German. For discussions of the *Libri duo* in English, see the excellent introductions (focused on penance, but not exclusively) in Sarah Hamilton, *The Practice of Penance, 900–1050* (Woodbridge: Boydell, 2001), 25–44; and Rob Meens, *Penance in Medieval Europe, 600–1200* (Cambridge: Cambridge University Press, 2014), 141–48. On the penitential context, see also Sarah Hamilton, "Interpreting Diversity: Excommunication Rites in the Tenth and Eleventh Centuries," in H. Gittos and S. Hamilton (eds.), *Understanding Medieval Liturgy: Essays in Interpretation* (Farnham: Ashgate, 2016), 125–58; and Pierre Payer, *Sex and the Penitentials: The Development of a Sexual Code, 550–1150* (Toronto: University of Toronto Press, 1984). The Canon Episcopi, on women who believe that they can fly on animals at night, appears in several translations of medieval sources, e.g., Alan C. Kors and Edward Peters (eds.), *Witchcraft in Europe, 400–1700: A Documentary History*, 2nd edition (Philadelphia: University of Pennsylvania Press, 2001), 60–63.

Not much has been written in English on diocesan visitations and synodal courts in Carolingian and post-Carolingian Europe, but see John Burden, *Between Sin and Crime: Penitential Justice in Medieval Germany*, 900–1200 (doctoral diss., Yale University, 2018), passim; and Andrew L. Slafkosky, *The Canonical Episcopal Visitation of the Diocese: A Historical Synopsis and Commentary*, Catholic University of America Canon Law Studies 142 (Washington, DC: Catholic University of America, 1941). Most of the literature in this field is in German: see, e.g., Stephan Dusil, "Zur Entstehung und Funktion von Sendgerichten: Beobachtungen bei Regino von Prüm und in seinem Umfeld," in M. Schmoeckel et al. (eds.), *Der Einfluss der Kanonistik auf die europäische Rechtskultur*, vol. 3: *Straf- und Strafprozessrecht* (Cologne: Böhlau, 2012), 369–409; Wilfried Hartmann, "Der Bischof als Richter. Zum geistlichen Gericht über kriminelle Vergehen von Laien im früheren Mittelalter (6.-11. Jahrhundert)," *Römische Historische Mitteilungen* 28 (1986): 103–24; Wilfried Hartmann, "Probleme des geistlichen Gerichts im 10. und 11. Jahrhundert: Bischöfe und Synoden als Richter im ostfränkisch-deutschen Reich," in *La giustizia nell'alto medioevo (secoli IX-XI)* (Spoleto: CISAM, 1997), 631–72; Wilfried Hartmann, "Zu Effektivität und Aktualität von Reginos Sendhandbuch," in W. P. Müller and M. E. Sommar (eds.),

Medieval Church Law and the Origins of the Western Legal Tradition: A Tribute to Kenneth Pennington (Washington, DC: Catholic University of America Press, 2006), 33–49; Rudolf Schieffer, "Zur Entstehund des Sendgerichts im 9. Jahrhundert," in Müller and Sommar, *Medieval Church Law*, 50–56; and Walter Hellinger, "Die Pfarrvisitation nach Regino von Prüm," ZRG KA 48 (1962): 1–116.

23

Burchard of Worms

Greta Austin

INTRODUCTION

Only recently has Burchard, bishop of Worms, been recognized as a significant contributor to Western intellectual history. In studying the history of marriage, for instance, both Patrick Corbet and Karl Ubl identify Burchard as having played a seminal role.[1] Burchard popularized a very strict method of calculating degrees of consanguinity: a method that the church and the emperor could use to control noble alliances through marriage. Burchard's central contribution to church discipline, however, was his collection of authoritative ecclesiastical rulings and penances, known as the *Decretum*.[2] Burchard designed it as a handbook for the clergy to use at councils and to administer church norms. His main model was the episcopal handbook called the *Two Books* (*Libri duo*), compiled by Regino of Prüm about a hundred years earlier (see Chapter 22). Regino wrote in his preface that he wanted to make a handbook for bishops touring their dioceses and carrying out church law: one that could be easily carried around and consulted – thus, not too large or with too many extraneous laws. Regino seems to have assumed that his users could reason out legal solutions for themselves, even when the texts in his collection gave conflicting penances or rules, but Burchard evidently worked to eliminate such conflicts. He may have assumed a less educated reader, or he may have wanted to make the reader's job as easy as possible. Burchard used a variety of methods to eliminate conflicts: He drew upon the Carolingian heritage of the creative reassemblage of materials; he worked hard to find texts in a wide range of sources; and he altered texts to make them consistent and at least to *appear* authoritative. By these means, Burchard presented an apparently unified body of church law to his readers.

[1] Karl Ubl, *Inzestverbot und Gesetzgebung: Die Konstruktion eines Verbrechens (300–1100)* (Berlin: De Gruyter, 2008). Patrick Corbet, *Autour de Burchard de Worms: L'Église allemande et les interdits de parenté (IXe-XIIe siècle)*, Ius Commune, Sonderhefte, Studien zur Europäischen Rechtsgeschichte 142 (Frankfurt: Klosterman, 2001).

[2] See Kéry, *Collections*, 133–55. The word *decretum* may be translated as "decree," but as Robert Somerville and Bruce Brasington point out in *Prefaces*, 72 n. 21: "no one English word can properly render the Latin *Decretum* when used as a title of a collection."

His *Decretum* was extremely popular and widely copied over the next two centuries, even after Gratian's pioneering work in the mid-twelfth century.

The popularity of Burchard's collection and its chronological proximity to Gratian have sometimes caused modern scholars to underestimate the importance of Burchard's own legal thinking. In working to unify and present a cogent body of law, Burchard's work marked an important accomplishment in its intellectual coherence and its insistence on usefulness.

Church law was not "law" in the secular sense as we think of it today. To live in accordance with church law meant to align oneself with God's wishes. Such law was the practical application of theology, and its ultimate goal was salvific and eschatological, presupposing that humans had an important obligation to understand correctly and to apply God's commands for them. Thus, Burchard's episcopal handbook addresses all aspects of church life and discipline, from speculative theology to administration to ritual to penance.

LIFE AND WORK

Burchard was born into the nobility, rose in the clergy under Willigis, archbishop of Mainz, was appointed bishop of Worms in 1000, and served in that office until his death in 1025. Burchard served as an influential member of the court of emperor Henry II, and he participated in the important local synods of his time, including the councils of Mainz (1007), Frankfurt (1016), and Seligenstadt (1023). Burchard secured control of the city of Worms, in large part because he was an important member of the imperial court, and he governed it both as its secular leader and as its bishop. He expressed a consistent interest in standardizing and writing down law, apparently to provide social stability and consistent legal norms. To this end, Burchard compiled, with assistance, two important legal collections. One was his collection of penances and church regulations, known as the *Decretum*, compiled between 1012 and 1023.[3] The other was a secular legal code that he compiled for his *familia* in Worms (i.e., his dependents): the *Lex familiae* of 1024–1025.[4] Shortly after Burchard's death, a Worms cleric, who is often identified as "Ebbo" in the sources, composed the *Vita Burchardi*, an account of Burchard's life that modern scholars have mined for most of their information about Burchard. According to the *Vita*, Burchard engaged in multiple building and restoration projects, including the cathedral of Worms and the city walls, and he also made Worms a center of learning.

3 Greta Austin, *Shaping Church Law Around the Year 1000: The Decretum of Burchard of Worms*, Church, Faith and Culture in the Medieval West 20 (Farnham, UK: Ashgate, 2009). Hartmut Hoffmann and Rudolf Pokorny, *Das Dekret des Bischofs Burchard von Worms: Textstufen, frühe Verbreitung, Vorlagen*, MGH Hilfsmittel 12 (1991), 32, suggest a date of 1015–1020.

4 Austin, *Shaping Church Law*, 69. Knut Schulz, "Das Wormser Hofrecht Bischof Burchards," in W. Hartmann (ed.), *Bischof Burchard von Worms 1000–1025, Quellen und Abhandlungen zur mittelrheinischen Kirchengeschichte* 100 (Mainz: Selbsverlag der Gesellschaft für Mittelrheinische Kirchengeschichte, 2000), 251–78.

Both the *Vita* and the preface to his *Decretum* attest to his passion for improving the current state of knowledge. The "Worms letter collection," produced in the early eleventh century, consists of texts written by students at Worms, and they displayed considerable familiarity with classical texts.[5]

Burchard's work grew out of his immediate needs and concerns as an influential bishop in the Rhineland, but the *Decretum*'s long-standing success attests to his broad abilities as a thinker whose work had real-life implications for providing order and pastoral care. In going beyond the immediate demands and questions of his day, his handbook supplied a wide range of answers to bishops, priests, monks, and councils, but especially to bishops.

Burchard's pedigree resembled that of many imperial bishops of the Ottonian period. Born to a noble family, he had been a canon of the cathedral of Koblenz, and he studied in several places, probably including Koblenz and Mainz. Willigis, the archbishop of Mainz, appointed him to be a deacon and then head of the archdiocesan treasury. Burchard was also provost of the monastery of Saint-Victor there.[6] Burchard's studies certainly included the Psalter and the Bible.[7] Like Walter of Speyer, he probably also read a wide range of classical authors.[8] Burchard's biographer Ebbo of Worms describes him as "dedicated to study, learned in the pages of Holy Scripture, and full of the wisdom of God."[9] As bishop of Worms from 1000 to 1025, he took an active role in instructing the canons of the cathedral. He also laid out a course of study for his sister, who was an abbess, and he is said to have instructed the future Conrad II.[10]

Burchard devoted himself to building and rebuilding: both literally, in rebuilding the city walls and the cathedral of Worms, and metaphorically, in working to regularize the education and way of life of the canons of the cathedral.[11] Like many bishops in this period, he was both the secular lord and the religious leader of the city. Thus, he was in charge of the *familia* of Worms: not only the clergy but also Burchard's own household members and those who had belonged to the Salian dukes from whom Burchard had taken over Worms. It was for this *familia* that Burchard ordered the customary secular laws to be written down.[12] This text, the *Lex familiae*, represents an important landmark as one of the first written secular law codes of the Middle Ages. Burchard's work in both church and secular law reflects

5 Austin, *Shaping Church Law*, 60.

6 Ibid., 54–55.

7 Ibid., 56.

8 Ibid., 57–58.

9 *Vita Burchardi* 18. For editions see G. Waitz (ed.), MGH SS (in Folio) 4 (1841; repr. Stuttgart, 1981), 829–46; or Heinrich Boos (ed.), *Urkundenbuch der Stadt Worms: Monumenta wormatiensia: Annalen und Chroniken*, Quellen zur Geschichte der Stadt Worms 3 (Berlin: Weidmann, 1893), 97–126.

10 Austin, *Shaping Church Law*, 63–64.

11 Ibid., 65.

12 Ibid., 69.

his broader passion for systematizing and creating greater order, from building to education to regulation of the laity and clergy.

Burchard's relationship to secular authority was complicated. As an imperial bishop, appointed by Otto III, Burchard owed duties to the emperor, and these included frequent travel. In return, he secured gifts for Worms.[13] As already noted, Burchard was both lord and bishop of Worms. This dual role casts light on his treatment of secular law in the *Decretum*, where he regularly separated out church regulations from secular punishments. Burchard not only regularly altered inscriptions to secular law in his *Decretum*, but he also changed references to secular punishments such as the death penalty, so that ecclesiastical penance was applied instead. Burchard worked to distinguish church law from secular law, and in this respect he resembled to some extent the later papal reformers, inasmuch as they sought to assert the autonomy of the church.

BURCHARD'S CHURCH LAW COLLECTION, THE *DECRETUM*

The overarching concern of the *Decretum* is unity. In his preface to the collection, where he signaled his goals for it, Burchard emphasizes that he was concerned above all that in the existing tradition "the laws [*iura*] of the canons and the judgments for those doing penance were confused, inconsistent, and disordered." Only experts could make sense of these legal and penitential rulings, and even then they had difficulty doing so.[14] As a legal thinker, Burchard worked to counter the tradition's tendencies toward confusion, inconsistency, and lack of order. His legal work across the board – from his church law collection to his secular law code, and even to his conciliar work – reflects his concern with shaping and maintaining a consistent body of norms. In his secular law code, the *Lex familiae*, Burchard wrote that he wanted to create "one law for rich and poor," so that nobles could not use law unfairly to oppress his *familia*.[15] Similarly, Burchard played an important role at the council of Seligenstadt in 1023, and the council's preface explained that the gathering would deal with discrepancies among various customs and attempt to reconcile them.[16] Thus, in his compiling, in his directing of

13 Ibid., 72.

14 Burchard, Preface, *Decretorum Libri XX: ex consiliis et orthodoxorum patrum decretis, tum etiam diversarum nationum synodis seu loci communes congesti*, ed. Gérard Fransen and Theo Kölzer (Aalen: Scientia Verlag, 1992), 45. Translated in *Prefaces*, 99.

15 " ... una et eademque lex diviti et pauperi ... communis." See the Preface to the *Lex Familiae Wormatiensis ecclesiae*, MGH Const., *Constitutiones et acta publica imperatorum et regum*, 1, ed. L. Weiland (1893; repr. Hanover, 1963), 640. There is an online translation at https://sourcebooks.fordham.edu/source/lexworms.asp (accessed March 22, 2018).

16 Seligenstadt Preface: "... disparilitas nostrarum singularium consuetudinum honesta consensione redigeretur in unum." For the council of Seligenstadt, see Detlev Jasper (ed.), *Die Konzilien Deutschlands und Reichsitaliens, 1023–1059*, MGH Conc. 8 (Hannover: Hahnsche Buchhandlung,

a secular law code, and in his conciliar activity, Burchard worked to unify customs and practices, making them consistent with each other.

Burchard designed his collection as a comprehensive episcopal handbook. John Burden has recently argued that the *Decretum* was primarily meant to be used at synods during episcopal visitations.[17] In addition, the *Decretum* was clearly designed for teaching, as Burchard also states in his preface.[18] The *Decretum* presents a coherent body of texts, rather than multiple and sometimes conflicting texts from which the experienced reader could choose, as in Regino's collection. Another difference from Regino's collection is that Burchard greatly expanded the range of topics, which also suggests a potentially broader audience than bishops. The *Decretum* surveyed a wide range of topics: clerical hierarchy, synods, church finances, Eucharist and baptism, reconciliation of the sick, and monks and nuns. It also regulated a wide range of lay issues, such as homicide, consanguinity, marriage, illicit sex, gluttony and drunkenness, proper religious practices and beliefs that were not "superstitious," and the behavior of lay rulers. Book 19, *The Corrector*, addresses penance, and Book 20 speculative theology. As George House points out, Book 20 "both justifies the practices and belief systems of the Church (Books I–XIX), whilst offering individuals the answers to fundamental existential questions (Where did I come from? Why am I here? Where am I going once I die?)."[19] The *Decretum* was explicitly designed for the use of bishops and probably for instruction at the cathedral schools. It could have been useful to priests of lower rank as well, including parish priests, although, as Hamilton and Meens have each pointed out, the focus of the collection is episcopal, and the large size of the collection (more than twice the size of Regino's) might have made it too expensive and time-consuming to copy for use in local parishes.[20] In addition, as Kathleen Cushing points out, monasteries, too, owned copies of Burchard's collection: "Monks and abbots, after all, needed canon law quite as much as bishops and other clergy."[21] The *Decretum* provided a soup to nuts guide for the clergy and for monks and nuns in a wide range of

2010), 34–42, at 34. John Ott is publishing a translation of the Seligenstadt preface and canons in an edited volume with Anna Trumbore Jones (forthcoming, PIMS, Toronto). I am grateful to Dr. Ott for sharing a copy of this translation prior to its publication. See also Greta Austin, "How the Local Council of Seligenstadt in 1023 Drew upon Books of Church Law," in *The Use of Canon Law in Ecclesiastical Administration, 1000–1234*, ed. Melodie H. Eichbauer and Danica Summerlin (Leiden: Brill, 2018), 108–20.

17 John Burden, *Between Sin and Crime: Penitential Justice in Medieval Germany, 900–1200* (doctoral diss., Yale University, 2018), especially chapter 2.

18 *Prefaces*, 100.

19 George House, *Pastoral Eschatological Exegesis in Burchard of Worms'* Decretum (doctoral diss., University of Exeter, 2014), 362.

20 Sarah Hamilton, *The Practice of Penance, 900–1050* (Woodbridge, Suffolk, UK: Royal Historical Society: Boydell and Brewer, 2001), 44; Rob Meens, *Penance in Medieval Europe, 600–1200* (Cambridge: Cambridge University Press, 2014), 149.

21 Kathleen G. Cushing, "Law and Reform: The Transmission of Burchard of Worms' *Liber decretorum*," in A. Thier and C. Rolker (eds.), *New Discourses in Medieval Canon Law Research:*

matters: the administering of penances, the regulation of both laity and clergy, the procedures for ecclesiastical business, and the holding of synods.[22] The twenty books were organized topically and covered the following subjects:

Book 1: Clergy (the bishop of Rome and bishops generally) and synods
Book 2: Clergy (priests, deacons, and the rest of the ecclesiastical orders)
Book 3: Church administration, including the administration of church buildings, tithes, oblations, and the canon of Scripture
Book 4: Baptism
Book 5: Eucharist
Book 6: Homicide
Book 7: Consanguinity
Book 8: Monks and nuns
Book 9: Virgins and widows; marriage; concubines
Book 10: Practices and beliefs defined as non-Christian; conspiracy and contentiousness
Book 11: Excommunication; theft
Book 12: Oaths and perjury
Book 13: Fasts
Book 14: Gluttony; drunkenness
Book 15: Secular rulers, the laity, and their relationship to the church
Book 16: Courts: accusations, witnesses, judges
Book 17: Fornication
Book 18: Reconciliation of the sick
Book 19: Penance
Book 20: Speculative theology

In compiling his *Decretum*, Burchard took steps to eliminate conflicts among existing texts. Regino's collection, which was Burchard's main source, sometimes provided different penances for the same offenses. Regino assumed (and said explicitly) that his reader could identify the correct answer from these alternatives,[23] but Burchard seems to have worked out a consistent scale of penances for various offenses. This scale was probably based on Matthew 15:19, where Jesus describes particular offenses that come from the heart, such as "murder, adultery, sexual immorality, theft, false witness, slander."[24] Burchard included texts that assigned seven years of penance to such "criminal" offenses, with modifications as needed. In addition to making texts consistent with each other, and with a general

Challenging the Master Narrative (Zurich, forthcoming). I am grateful to Dr. Cushing for sharing a copy of the paper prior to its publication.

22 Burchard's preface lists each book and its major contents; see the Preface, ed. G. Fransen, *Decretorum libri* XX, 46a–48, and the translation in *Prefaces*, 101–03.

23 See Chapter 22 on Regino; see also Austin, *Shaping Church Law*, 163–65.

24 Burchard, *Decretum* [hereafter DB: *Decretum Burchardi*] 12.14, 16.4, and 19.5.

scale of penances, Burchard often sought to include canons that explained the scriptural underpinnings of rulings. For instance, in *Decretum* 12.17, on oaths, Burchard provides a particular penance for a certain type of offender, but he also quotes the Bible in order to explain the ultimate goal of punishment and reconciliation:

> [Inscription:] From the council of Lleida [Lérida], capitula 6
> [Rubric:] Regarding those who take an oath of eternal hatred among themselves
> [Text:] A person who has disputed with someone and takes an oath that he will never make peace with that person should be separated for a year, on account of his perjury, from the body and blood of the Lord,[25] and should absolve himself of guilt by fasting and giving alms. Indeed, he should return quickly to love, which covers a multitude of sins [cf. Proverbs 10: 12].

Burchard's *Decretum* could be said to have a theological bent (if we use the word "theology" loosely). Scripture was the touchstone for many canons. For example, why should penances for criminal offenses last *seven* years? Burchard included texts that provide a scriptural precedent for this, comparing seven years of penance to Miriam's seven days of punishment (Numbers 13:1–15).[26] Burchard then worked to ensure that all these criminal offenses received seven years of penance. He not only selected canons that already required seven years[27] but also consistently changed the texts of canons so that they required seven years of penance for these offenses.[28] Burchard used editorial intervention – which I do not describe as "forgery," because that term implies malicious intention, as well as a sense of the immutability of written texts – in order to present a coherent, unified body of authoritative church rulings, grounded in Scripture.

Burchard's effort to create a cohesive, intellectually consistent set of rules and ideas based on Scripture enabled his readers to use his collection more easily. The *Decretum* reflects in many ways his concern that the collection should be user-friendly. In particular, the collection includes many helpful organizational features, so that it is easy to find the relevant texts.[29] Scholars who work on reference books readily appreciate the importance of such organizational markers. Thus, chapter summaries, tables of contents, summaries of each text (known as "rubrics"), or numbers for texts enable users to locate the texts that they seek, much like the contemporary index. Burchard's collection has all of these features, and more. For instance, the Preface describes the contents of each book, and each book has a short name and the number at the top of the page, so that one can flip through quite easily. The careful attention to page layout represents yet another aspect of Burchard's thoughtfulness about enabling users to identify legal answers.

[25] In other words, prevented from receiving eucharist, or excommunicated.
[26] See DB 10.67 and 19.82.
[27] Austin, *Shaping Church Law*, 152.
[28] Ibid., 141–42.
[29] On this and what follows, see Austin, *Shaping Church Law*, 91–101.

Burchard put considerable effort into making his texts appear as if they came from only a limited number of sources, which were considered to be authoritative. Texts almost always have a short description of their source (known as the "inscription"). Most strikingly, Burchard did not include any attributions to secular law, such as Roman law or even Carolingian capitularies. He generally avoided such texts if others on the same topic were available. Otherwise, he used them but altered the attributions.[30] More generally, Burchard edited his collection so that the texts would seem authoritative. In his Preface, Burchard listed the types of sources that he viewed as having "authority." All the canons in his collection have inscriptions to these sources – sometimes because he selected them, but occasionally because he altered the inscriptions so that they looked plausible or were vested with considerable authority, such as attributions to Augustine.[31]

Burchard's use of textual alteration is a consistent pattern throughout the *Decretum*. He could be said to have edited according to the motto, "If you can't find the text that fits all your parameters exactly, alter it." But forgers (as we think of them today) often intend to deceive in order to advance their own individual purposes, whereas Burchard's concerns appear more about creating coherence while using limited resources. He was working with a few topically organized collections, as well as with collections that were hard to sort through, especially the decrees of various councils. Burchard sometimes altered texts in order to shape a unified, authoritative set of rulings, but he seems to have done so as a last resort, when his reservoir of texts did not supply anything that fit his high standards exactly. As already suggested, the term "forgery" is too pejorative to apply to Burchard's textual alterations, and in some ways it is anachronistic. His textual alterations function as implicit commentary. Gratian and Abbo of Fleury would use explicit commentary to reconcile conflicts, clarify questions, and assert the authority of the text. But to ask why Burchard did not use explicit commentary is to hold him to later standards. Most other similar collections of his day did not interpolate commentary between the texts, and Burchard was working within the conventions that he knew.

In fact, Burchard's *Decretum* looks like an effort to update and expand Regino's *Libri duo*. The *Decretum* differs from this model in some important regards: it is organized into twenty books, not two; it is much longer than Regino's collection; and Burchard eliminated conflicts, whereas Regino preserved them. That said, both collections were clearly designed as handbooks for bishops in carrying out their pastoral duties.

Fittingly, as a book designed for pastoral care, the *Decretum* has a strong penitential orientation, and it could clearly have been very useful in episcopal synods. The penalties prescribed in the canons are penances, rather than secular punishments of any kind. Book 19 of the *Decretum* focuses exclusively on penance.[32] Book 19, canon

30 Austin, *Shaping Church Law*, 122–26.

31 Ibid., 103.

32 See, e.g., Burden, *Between Sin and Crime*; Ludger Körntgen, "Canon Law and the Practice of Penance: Burchard of Worms' Penitential," EME 14.1 (2006): 103–17; Meens, *Penance in Medieval Europe*, 149; Hamilton, *The Practice of Penance*, 31–44.

5, which is clearly modeled on Regino's interrogations in the *Libri duo*, provides lists of questions that priests and bishops could, at least hypothetically, ask – although it is hard to imagine anyone asking all of these questions, if only because there are so many! Canon 5 catches the eye of readers today because it asks many detailed questions about practices and beliefs that some might call "magical" – practices that the church defined as outside the parameters of proper Catholic devotion. At several points this section seems to provide a window onto folk practices or beliefs, especially concerning women and what today we might call "magic" – that is, beliefs and practices concerning human attempts to manipulate the supernatural.[33] The most famous example is the *Canon Episcopi*, a canon that first appeared in Regino's collection, and that Burchard repeated in his. This canon makes a very early reference to women who today might be called witches. The text condemns beliefs that women fly around the world at night with "Diana, goddess of the pagans."[34] In the Vatican manuscript, the earliest text of the *Decretum*, Burchard made a marginal comment explaining that people called this goddess "Herodiade."[35] This text made its first appearance in Regino's collection.[36] Perhaps the text responded to contemporary concerns, or perhaps it represented an intersection among clerical anxieties, popular beliefs, and textual innovation. The difficulty in reading such legal texts as providing insight into "popular religion" is that legal texts may simply reiterate much earlier texts (some texts are repeated from Martin of Braga, for instance), or they could result from their authors' anxieties or imaginations. But some of Burchard's canons – especially in Book 10 and in the long canon for episcopal visitation and pastoral care in Book 19, the *Corrector* – do seem also to result from an engagement with everyday practice and belief, as mediated, exaggerated, or diminished through Burchard's desire to define the parameters of "true" religion.

THE SOURCES OF THE *DECRETUM*

Burchard's main model and most important source was the *Libri duo de synodalibus causis et disciplinis ecclesiasticis*, or *The Two Books concerning Synodal Investigations and Ecclesiastical Instructions*, compiled by Regino, abbot of Prüm, around 906.[37] Burchard designed his *Decretum*, like Regino's *Two Books*, to be

33 See the excerpts from the *Corrector* translated in John Shinners (ed.), *Medieval Popular Religion, 1000–1500: A Reader*, 2nd ed. (North York, ON: University of Toronto Press, 2009), 459–70; see also the longer translation in John McNeill and Helena Gamer, *Medieval Handbooks of Penance: A translation of the principal 'Libri poenitentiales' and selections from related documents* (New York: Columbia University Press, 1938; repr. 1990), 321–45.

34 Regino, *Libri duo*, II. 371, as repeated in DB 10.1. This idea recurs in the series of questions at DB 19.5.

35 Austin, *Shaping Church Law*, 22.

36 Bernadette Filotas, *Pagan Survivals, Superstitions and Popular Cultures in Early Medieval Pastoral Literature*, Studies and Texts 151 (Toronto: PIMS,2005), 52.

37 See Chapter 22 in this volume, on Regino, as well as Kéry, *Collections*, 128–33.

a handbook for the clergy. About a third of Burchard's canons came from Regino's collection.[38]

At the same time, Burchard updated and expanded the range of topics, especially by working with the Italian collection called the *Anselmo dedicata*, or *The Collection Dedicated to Anselm*, who was bishop of Milan. Like the *Two Books*, this collection had been made about a hundred years before (specifically, between 882 and 896).[39] *Anselmo dedicata* addressed a much wider range of topics than Regino's *Libri duo*, however, and it was divided into twelve books, not two. The organization of this collection may have inspired Burchard to divide his *Decretum* into twenty books.[40] Burchard also took texts from a variety of penitentials and other canon law collections, including ones that were not arranged by topic.[41]

The research of Hartmut Hoffmann and Rudolf Pokorny has unpacked, in careful detail, the various stages by which the *Decretum* came into being.[42] Burchard borrowed manuscripts from the monastic scriptorium at Freising, and he seems to have utilized some of these twice: once in the original making of the collection, and again in making late additions.[43] The "first version" of the *Decretum* has the most topical coherence and order, because later additions do not always fit perfectly at the end of the books. Individual books were organized topically, and within these books it is possible to see unlabeled subsections where Burchard grouped together canons on similar topics, such as homicide committed accidentally. The *Decretum*'s clear organization and topical structure suggest considerable forethought and planning on Burchard's part.

RECEPTION AND SIGNIFICANCE OF THE *DECRETUM*

Burchard's *Decretum* stands as one of the most influential canon law collections of its time. The manuscript numbers alone attest to its popularity. In the eleventh century, only the *Panormia* formerly attributed to Ivo of Chartres has more manuscripts. About a hundred partial or complete manuscripts of Burchard's *Decretum* survive.[44] As Kathleen Cushing points out, Burchard's collection was "especially valued in Italy," where half of the extant manuscripts were copied.[45] In Italy, one version of the collection that was widely copied is called the Italian order of Worms,

38 Austin, *Shaping Church Law*, 39.
39 Kéry, *Collections*, 124–28.
40 Austin, *Shaping Church Law*, 42.
41 Ibid., 43–50.
42 Hoffmann and Pokorny, *Das Dekret*.
43 See Hoffmann and Pokorny, *Das Dekret*, 40–58. Austin, *Shaping Church Law*, 20–24, has a summary in English.
44 Kéry, *Collections*, 133–55; see especially 134–38.
45 Cushing, "Law and Reform: The Transmission of Burchard of Worms' *Liber decretorum*" [unpublished; no page numbers].

Type B.[46] The collection was less well known in France than in Germany and Italy.[47]

Burchard influenced many canon law collections, both minor or local ones and popular ones such as Anselm of Lucca's *Collectio canonum*, Ivo of Chartres' *Decretum*, and the *Panormia*. Sometimes copyists used it as a base and then integrated it with material from other sources, such as the *Collection in 74 Titles*[48] – a process not unlike that which Ivo pursued in his *Decretum*, where he preserved Burchard's texts in blocks within each topical book.

As Martin Brett has pointed out, Burchard's collection continued to be copied and used even after the advent of Gratian's work.[49] The Decretists (scholars who expounded Gratian's *Decretum*) drew upon it as well. The old story told by Paul Fournier was that Burchard's collection was characteristic of those made before the Gregorian Reform, and that it was superseded by Reform thinkers and then by Gratian.[50] But the facts have always shown otherwise. Burchard's *Decretum* influenced other compilers, scholars, clergy, and monks for at least two hundred years after its making. Its ability to do so attests to the collection's design, comprehensiveness, and brilliance.

SOURCES

The *Life* of Burchard of Worms has been edited a few times; see, e.g., the edition by G. Waitz, in MGH SS (in Folio) 4 (1841; repr. Stuttgart, 1981), 829–46. William North has translated the *Vita Burchardi* into English, and his translation is currently available online at https://sourcebooks.fordham.edu/Halsall/source/1025burchard-vita.asp (accessed March 14, 2018). See also the text and commentary in David Bachrach, *The Histories of a Medieval German City, Worms c. 1000–1300: Translation and Commentary* (Farnham: Ashgate, 2014; repr. Abingdon, 2016).

The early modern edition of Burchard's *Decretum* (DB), recently reproduced in Aalen, is very close to the Vatican manuscript, which is the earliest manuscript of the collection: *Decretorum Libri XX: ex consiliis et orthodoxorum patrum decretis, tum etiam diversarum nationum synodis seu loci communes congesti* (Cologne, 1548); ed. Gérard Fransen and Theo Kölzer (Aalen: Scientia Verlag, 1992).

46 Cushing, "Law and Reform: The Transmission of Burchard of Worms' *Liber decretorum*," [unpublished; no page numbers]. Kéry, *Collections*, 137–42.

47 Cushing, "Law and Reform: The Transmission of Burchard of Worms' *Liber decretorum*" [unpublished; no page numbers].

48 Roger Reynolds, "Penitentials in south and central Italian canon law manuscripts of the tenth and eleventh centuries," EME 14 (2006): 65–84, at 76–84.

49 Martin Brett, "Canon Law and Litigation: The Century Before Gratian," in M. J. Franklin and C. Harper-Bill (eds.), *Medieval Ecclesiastical Studies in Honour of Dorothy M. Owen*, Studies in the History of Medieval Religion 7 (Woodbridge, Suffolk, UK: Boydell Press, 1995), 21–40, at 23.

50 Paul Fournier, "Un tournant de l'histoire du droit 1060–1140," *Nouvelle revue historique de droit français et étranger* 41 (1917): 129–80; reprinted in *Mélanges de droit canonique*, ed. Theo Kölzer, 2 vols. (Aalen: Scientia, 1983), 2:373–424.

There are multiple editions of the *Lex familiae*. The most readily accessible is MGH Const. 1, ed. L. Weiland (1893; repr. Hanover, 1963), 639–44; the most recent is *Lex Familiae Wormatiensis ecclesiae*, in Lorenz Weinrich (ed.), *Quellen zur deutschen Verfassungs-, Wirtschafts- und Sozialgeschichte bis 1250* (Darmstadt: Wissenschaftliche Buchgesellschaft, 1977), 88–105; there is an online translation at https://sourcebooks.fordham.edu/source/lexworms.asp (accessed March 14, 2018).

Burchard's *Decretum* has not been translated into English in its entirety. The Preface has been translated into English in Somerville and Brassington's *Prefaces*, 99–104 with a very useful commentary (72–75). There are also translations from Book 19, the *Corrector*, published in John Shinners (ed.), *Medieval Popular Religion, 1000–1500: A Reader*, 2nd edition (North York, ON: University of Toronto Press, 2009), 459–70. George House, Pastoral Eschatological Exegesis in Burchard of Worms' *Decretum* (doctoral diss., University of Exeter, 2014), includes working translations of Book 20 at 376–413.

FURTHER READING

Wilfried Hartmann (ed.), *Bischof Burchard von Worms, 1000–1025, Quellen und Abhandlungen zur mittelrheinischen Kirchengeschichte* 100 (Mainz: Selbsverlag der Gesellschaft für Mittelrheinische Kirchengschichte, 2000), includes articles in German by leading scholars in the field. Otherwise, the bibliography in Kéry, *Collections*, is the best starting point, although many sources listed there, too, are not in English.

The current scholarly attention to bishops in this period has been extremely helpful for understanding Burchard as a bishop: see Greta Austin, "Vengeance and Law in Eleventh-Century Worms: Burchard and the Canon Law of Feuds," in W. Müller and M. Sommar (eds.), *Medieval Church Law and the Origins of the Western Legal Tradition: A Tribute to Kenneth Pennington* (Washington, DC: Catholic University of America Press, 2006), 66–76; Sean Gilsdorf (ed.), *The Bishop: Power and Piety at the First Millennium* (Münster: Lit, 2004); John Ott and Anna Trumbore-Jones (eds.), *The Bishop Reformed: Studies of Episcopal Power and Culture in the Central Middle Ages* (Aldershot, UK: Ashgate, 2007); Timothy Reuter, "A Europe of Bishops: The Age of Wulfstan of York and Burchard of Worms," in Ludger Körntgen and Dominik Waßenhoven (eds.), *Patterns of Episcopal Power: Bishops in 10th and 11th Century Western Europe* (Berlin: De Gruyter, 2011), 17–38; Charles West, "Group Formation in the Long Tenth Century: A View from Trier and its Region," in S. Albrecht and C. Kleinjung (eds.), *Das lange 10. Jahrhundert – Struktureller Wandel zwischen Zentralisierung und Fragmentierung, äußerem Druck und innerer Krise* (Mainz: Römisch-Germanischen Zentralmuseums, 2014), 49–59. The only monograph in English that focuses on Burchard is Greta Austin, *Shaping Church Law Around the Year 1000: The Decretum of Burchard of Worms* (Farnham, UK: Ashgate,

2009). See also Greta Austin, "Jurisprudence in the Service of Pastoral Care: The Decretum of Burchard of Worms," Speculum 79 (2004): 929–59. On the relationship between the *Collection in Twelve Parts* and Burchard's *Decretum*, see Greta Austin's somewhat unwieldy study "Freising and Worms in the Early Eleventh Century: Revisiting the relationship between the *Collectio duodecim partium* and Burchard's *Decretum*," ZRG Kan. Abt. 93 (2007): 45–108.

On the reception and adaptation of the collection – Austin's research focuses rather on Burchard's own editing – see the articles by Kathleen Cushing and Danica Summerlin in the forthcoming *New Discourses in Medieval Canon Law Research* – an edited volume that will represent important contributions in understanding the various ways in which the *Decretum* was adapted and used. The following articles or books on penance discuss Burchard's *Decretum* explicitly: Sarah Hamilton, *The Practice of Penance, 900–1050* (Woodbridge, Suffolk, UK: Royal Historical Society: Boydell and Brewer, 2001); Ludger Körntgen, "Canon Law and the Practice of Penance: Burchard of Worms' Penitential," EME 14.1 (2006): 103–17; and Rob Meens, *Penance in Medieval Europe, 600–1200* (Cambridge: Cambridge University Press, 2014). Recent scholarly interest in *superstitio* and other "magical" practices and beliefs during the Middle Ages has resulted in some writings on this subject in English, including the following: Bernadette Filotas, *Pagan Survivals, Superstitions and Popular Cultures in Early Medieval Pastoral Literature*, Studies and Texts 151 (Toronto: PIMS, 2005); and Martha Rampton, "Burchard of Worms and Female Magical Ritual," in J. Rollo-Koster (ed.), *Medieval and Early Modern Ritual: Formalized Behavior in Europe, China, and Japan* (Leiden: Brill, 2002), 7–34. On Burchard's speculative theology in Book 20, see George House, *Pastoral Eschatological Exegesis in Burchard of Worms' Decretum* (doctoral diss., University of Exeter, 2014); on Book 19 and the reception of Burchard's *Decretum* in abbreviations, see John Burden *Between Sin and Crime: Penitential Justice in Medieval Germany*, 900–1200 (doctoral diss., Yale University, 2018). For some excerpts from Book 19, the *Corrector*, translated into English, see, e.g., John Shinners (ed.), *Medieval Popular Religion, 1000–1500: A Reader*, 2nd ed. (North York, Ont.: University of Toronto Press, 2009), 459–70; see also the longer translation in John McNeill and Helena Gamer, *Medieval Handbooks of Penance: A translation of the principal 'Libri poenitentiales' and selections from related documents* (New York: Columbia University Press, 1938; repr. 1990), 321–45.

24

New Horizons in Church Law

Robert Somerville

A century is an arbitrary measure of history, but the period between Burchard of Worms's death and the First Lateran Council offers a good vantage point from which to see the emergence of new trends in the institutions of the Western church and in church law. Burchard died on August 20, 1025, and Pope Calixtus II (1119–1124) assembled his great Roman council at the church of St. John Lateran in Lent, 1123. That synod or council – sources during this period used the terms interchangeably – promulgated a long slate of influential ecclesiastical legislation.

Lateran I also endorsed the Concordat of Worms (September, 1122). After fifty years of struggle between spiritual and temporal rulers, this compromise between the pope and the emperor Henry V (d. 1125) involved multiple questions about property, customs, and what was emerging clearly as a body of canon law, existing in parallel with Roman civil law and secular customs and statutes. All of these issues get lumped together by modern scholars as "The Investiture Conflict," so named from the ceremony by which bishops and abbots were "invested" with the symbols of their office. When, as often happened, the ceremony of investing was performed by a king or other lay lord, this implied that the latter appointed the former, or at least endowed him with rights and property. From the time of Pope Gregory VII (1073–1085) to Calixtus II, popes decried lay investiture, and after decades of turmoil the Concordat replaced it by an agreement that was ratified by both sides. Historians debate the extent to which this deal was effective, but, however important the Concordat was in the 1120s, the decrees of Lateran I, which were diffused widely and absorbed into the church's expanding legal tradition, had a lasting effect.

Since the scope of the preceding chapters in this millennial volume has extended to Burchard, the aim of this concluding chapter is to preview some of the "new horizons" that would appear in the world of law, especially in the emergence of full-fledged canon law, during the ninety-eight-year "century" between Burchard and Lateran I.[1]

[1] Uta-Renate Blumenthal, *The Investiture Controversy: Church and Monarchy from the Ninth to the Twelfth Century* (Philadelphia: University of Pennsylvania Press, 1988), 106–73. For text of the

Burchard's *Decretum* would become a landmark of canon law. It survives today – wholly or in part, sometimes on its own and sometimes in combination with other works – in dozens of manuscripts written from the early eleventh century to the end of the Middle Ages. Neither Gratian's *Decretum*, the standard textbook for studying church law from the mid-twelfth century into modern times, nor the intellectual energy unleashed by Gratian's work, pushed Burchard into oblivion, as the *Summa* by the late twelfth-century canonist Rufinus readily shows.[2] But notwithstanding the importance of the *Decretum Burchardi*, coming to grips with the many resources for church law available in the Latin world around the year 1050 is a daunting challenge. Lotte Kéry's research demonstrates in a very clear manner just how big this task is, and how pervasive canonical collections were.

Earlier chapters of this volume have mentioned many of these canonical compilations, consisting of conciliar canons, papal decretals, and ancillary material, which date from Late Antiquity down to the time of Burchard. Simply put, Latin Christendom was awash with canonical resources. Professor Kéry provides us with a comprehensive tabulation of what survives of this activity in her survey of canonical collections from around 400 to 1140. In three opening sections, she offers the following divisions: "Part I," collections from Late Antiquity up to the end of the eighth century; "Part II," from the beginning of the ninth to the middle of the eleventh centuries; and "Part III," from the middle of the eleventh century to Gratian. Parts II–III include 130 individual items, of which some, such as the ninth-century Pseudo-Isidorian *Decretals*, exist in multiple recensions and many copies.[3] The surviving exemplars of the books put together between the ninth and the mid-twelfth centuries, therefore, number in the hundreds. Who can know how many more are now lost or have been destroyed?

Even aside from the sheer multitude of canonical codices that must have been available in the mid-eleventh century, trying to understand how the law found in this mélange was appropriated and used in practice in local churches is another matter. The question is of fundamental importance for historians, but it is one that is not easy to answer. Charles Donahue has aptly written, "Bishops had been hearing cases since the late Roman Empire: disputes were resolved and ecclesiastical discipline enforced in local councils and synods . . . "[4] But the records that document these

Concordat of Worms, see Brian Tierney, *The Crisis of Church & State 1050–1300* (Englewood Cliffs, NJ: Prentice Hall, 1964 [and often reprinted]), 91–92. For the canons of Lateran I, see G. Gresser (ed.), "Concilium Lateranense I, 1123," in *Conciliorum oecumenicorum generaliumque decreta: editio critica*, vol. II.1: *The General Councils of Latin Christendom from Constantinople IV to Pavia-Siena (869–1424)* (Turnhout: Brepols, 2013), 73–94; but see also Louis I. Hamilton and Martin Brett, "New Evidence for the Canons of the First Lateran Council," BMCL 30 (2013): 1–20.

2 Rufinus von Bologna, *Die Summa Decretorum des Magister Rufinus*, ed. H. Singer (Paderborn: Schöningh, 1902; repr. Aalen: Scientia, 1963), ciii. For Burchard, see Greta Austin, *Shaping Church Law Around the Year 1000:* The Decretum of Burchard of Worms (Farnham, UK: Ashgate, 2009).

3 Kéry, *Collections*, vi–ix.

4 Charles Donahue Jr., "The Ecclesiastical Courts: Introduction," in W. Hartmann and K. Pennington (eds.), *The History of Courts and Procedure in Medieval Canon Law* (Washington, DC: Catholic University of America Press, 2016), 244–99, at 250–51.

activities are, as Donahue has succinctly summarized, "thin, diverse, and quite intractable. It is obviously difficult to generalize about them."[5]

Such imponderables, nevertheless, did not deter the production of canonical literature, and those books came in various forms. Some were large, chronologically arranged volumes of papal and conciliar decisions, which were gathered together in Late Antiquity and during the early Middle Ages. These included versions of Dionysius Exiguus (the *Dionysiana* and *Dionysiana-Hadriana*), of the Spanish Collection (*Collectio Hispana*), and of its offshoot, the Pseudo-Isidorian *Decretals*. Others, such as the *Two Books* of abbot Regino of Prüm from the early tenth century and the *Decretum* of Burchard from the early eleventh, were put together for specific administrative and educational purposes, as their prefaces indicate.[6] As well as cataloging the wide dissemination of these large collections, Lotte Kéry lists forty-nine works designated "Collections of Local Importance," dating from the end of the eighth to the middle of the eleventh centuries.[7] Canonical literature was to be found everywhere, therefore, but the intellectual tools for handling it remained rudimentary and unsystematic.

How and why that had begun to change by the time of Lateran I is a story that unfolded across "new horizons." First and foremost in that panorama, we must consider the rise to prominence of the revitalized eleventh-century papacy. From the time of Pope Leo IX (d. 1054) onward, the Roman pontiffs strove to move the claims inherent in their office from theory into practice.[8] This entailed promulgation of new law through decretals and other papal letters, and especially through the enactments of synods. Churchmen also transcribed older canonical collections during this period, mining them for texts that in turn, along with recent papal legislation, furnished material for new compilations. At the same time, patristic excerpts were being incorporated in an effort to accentuate the venerability of the church's traditions. Furthermore, the Roman church searched older archives in a hunt for texts that could delineate Rome's special privileges. The second half of the eleventh century, perhaps as a result of these efforts, saw the appearance of previously neglected material from older papal registers.

It was perhaps as a result of these archival excavations that the *Digest* was rediscovered, having virtually disappeared from the West. Commissioned by the Roman emperor Justinian in the sixth century, the *Digest* comprises fifty books of excerpts taken from the writings of the classical jurists. During the late-eleventh and early-twelfth centuries, the *Digest* revived the study of Roman law in the medieval West.[9] No one in the West around the end of the eleventh century was subject to

5 Charles Donahue Jr., "Procedure in the Courts of the *Ius Commune*," ibid., 74–124, at 80.

6 See *Prefaces*, 69–70, 92–94 (for Regino), and 72–75, 99–104 (for Burchard).

7 Kéry, *Collections*, vii–viii.

8 Blumenthal, *Investiture Controversy*, 64 ff.

9 Paul Fournier, "Un tournant de l'histoire du droit 1060–1140," *Nouvelle revue historique de droit français et étranger* 41 (1917): 129–80; repr. in P. Fournier, *Mélanges de droit canonique*, ed.

Roman law, but study of this "grandiose work," as Adolf Berger called it, prompted definitions, comparisons, and reflections that were indispensable for the study of both secular and ecclesiastical law during the central Middle Ages.[10]

By the beginning of the twelfth century, therefore, investigators were surrounded by an ever-increasing corpus of resources for canon law. Not only were older collections such as Pseudo-Isidore and Burchard still very much in play, but fifty years of church reform had also spawned new works presenting reforming agendas, which were found in multiple copies throughout the church. The following new works are worthy of special mention. Three of them are attributed to important Italian reformers, namely, Bishop Anselm of Lucca (d. 1086); Deusdedit, cardinal presbyter of SS. Apostolorum in Eudoxia (d. c. 1100), who was in point of fact a native of France; and Cardinal Gregory of San Grisogono (d. c. 1113).[11] Moreover, a very influential group of compilations was attributed to bishop Ivo of Chartres (d. 1115). Ivo was close to Pope Urban II, who consecrated him as bishop of Chartres in 1090.[12] A few collections of the period had exotic names derived from Greek, such as the *Panormia* ("Collection of all laws") ascribed to Ivo, or cardinal Gregory's *Polycarpus* ("Collection plucked from many things"). But many compilations bore no title, and others were given merely generic titles such as *Decreta, Collectio canonum*, or *Sententiae* ("statements," "opinions"). A well-known example employing this last term is the collection termed *Diversorum patrum sententiae* ("Statements of various fathers"), a work that is better known today as *The Collection in 74 Titles*.[13]

Yet there was more at work in the intellectual life of the Latin church around the year 1100 than the copying of collections, the accumulating of more texts, and the

Theo Kölzer (Aalen: Scientia, 1983), 2:373–424. See also Stephan Kuttner, "The Revival of Jurisprudence," in R. L. Benson and G. Constable (eds.), *Renaissance and Renewal in the Twelfth Century* (Cambridge, MA: Harvard University Press, 1982), 299–322; repr. in Kuttner, *Studies in the History of Medieval Canon Law* (Aldershot, UK, and Brookfield, VT: Variorum, 1990), no. III, with *Retractationes*; and T. F. X. Noble and J. Van Engen (eds.), *European Transformations: The Long Twelfth Century* (Notre Dame: University of Notre Dame Press, 2012).

10 Adolf Berger, *Encyclopedic Dictionary of Roman Law*, Transactions of the American Philosophical Society, New Series 43.2 (Philadelphia: The American Philosophical Society, 1953), 436.

11 For Anselm, see Katherine G. Cushing, *Papacy and Law in the Gregorian Revolution: The Canonistic Work of Anselm of Lucca* (Oxford: Clarendon Press, 1998). For Deusdedit, see Robert Somerville, "Cardinal Deusdedit's *Collectio canonum* at Benevento," in R. F. Gyug (ed.), *Ritual, Text and Law: Studies in Medieval Canon Law and Liturgy Presented to Roger E. Reynolds* (Aldershot, UK: Ashgate, 2004), 281–92. For Cardinal Gregory and his collection, see Uwe Horst, *Die Kanonessamlung Polycarpus des Gregor von S. Grisogono*, MGH Hilfsmittel 5 (Munich: Monumenta Germaniae Historica, 1980).

12 On Ivo's collections, see Christof Rolker, *Canon Law and the Letters of Ivo of Chartres*, Cambridge Studies in Medieval Life and Thought, 4th Series 76 (Cambridge: Cambridge University Press, 2010), 89–126. On Ivo's consecration, see ibid., 14.

13 Ed. John T. Gilchrist, *Diversorum patrum sententie: sive, Collectio in LXXIV titulos digesta*, Monumenta iuris canonici, Corpus collectionum 1 (Città del Vaticano: Biblioteca apostolica vaticana, 1973). English translation: John T. Gilchrist, *The Collection in Seventy-Four Titles: A Canon Law Manual of the Gregorian Reform*, Mediaeval Sources in Translation 22 (Toronto: PIMS, 1980). This and the collection of Cardinal Deusdedit (see Somerville, "Cardinal Deusdedit's *Collectio canonum*," cited earlier) are the only late-eleventh-century collections available in critical editions.

making of new compilations. New intellectual horizons were everywhere in the Latin world at the beginning of the twelfth century. In the canonical tradition, this is vividly exemplified by the innovative treatise produced by a canon in the church at Liège named Alger (d. c. 1131).[14] Alger of Liège's work, entitled *Concerning Mercy and Justice* (*De misericordia et iustitia*), was written at some time between c. 1105 and c. 1121 and survives in a handful of medieval manuscripts. The book is a canonical-theological *florilegium* (literally, "bouquet of flowers"), providing excerpts from the Bible, the church fathers, popes, and councils, arranged under a long series of headings in three large books designated as "parts" (*partes*). What distinguished Alger's work was not his selection of texts but the fact that texts were interspersed with the author's own commentary. Alger wrote with a specific purpose. He arranged the sources and their commentary with the goal of balancing the demands of justice and mercy in dealing with people who received sacraments from schismatics during the prolonged papal schism. From the pontificate of Gregory VII to that of Calixtus II, the church was divided broadly into two ecclesiastical obediences: those loyal to the popes in the Gregorian line, and those supporting the pontiffs in communion with the German rulers Henry IV (d. 1106) and Henry V (d. 1125).[15] Alger wished to solve what was fundamentally a pastoral problem, and in striving to do that he was moving in both canonical and theological territory, asking the question: Who can administer sacraments and under what circumstances? The urgency of the question is obvious, for the church had been fractured into factions for several decades.

Alger's work deserves to be singled out not only as an attempt to deal with a serious current problem but also because the *De misericordia* was one of the sources that Gratian used for the *Decretum*. The desire to resolve conflicts among legal sources, which was central to Gratian's work, was shared by others who were antecedent to him, including Alger. Moreover, the methodology of combining sources and commentary within one treatise, which Gratian will deploy extensively, appeared a generation earlier in the writings of Bernold of Constance (d. 1100): a south-German chronicler, polemicist, canonist, and supporter of the church of Gregory VII. In an untitled *libellus* (tract), Bernold dealt extensively with questions produced by the schism: on avoiding contact with schismatics and with their sacraments, on how schismatics should be received back into the "Gregorian" church, and so forth.[16] He blended citations from the sources with his own statements to produce a narrative that wrestled with both practical and theoretical issues of the time, as Alger's *De Misericordia* had done. In the last section of his *libellus*, which comprises more than half of the entire work, Bernold's discussion turns to the sources of canon

[14] On the intellectual climate of the time, see the opening pages of R. W. Southern, *Scholastic Humanism and the Unification of Europe*, vol. 1 (Oxford: Blackwell, 1995). For Alger of Liège, see Robert Kretzschmar, *Alger von Lüttichs Traktat De misericordia et iustitia*, Quellen und Forschungen zum Recht im Mittelalter 2 (Sigmaringen: Jan Thorbeke, 1985).

[15] Blumenthal, *Investiture Conflict*, 106–34, 167–73.

[16] Bernold von Konstanz, *De excommunicatis vitandis, de reconciliatione lapsorum et de fontibus iuris ecclesiastici* (*Libellus* X), ed. Doris Stöckly, MGH Fontes (2000).

law.[17] Here, Bernold cites long excerpts from popes and councils and looks for ways to handle discrepancies in these selections. He urges readers to take account of differences in time, place, and personal circumstances in treating the canons. An intelligent reader, he wrote, investigates with care the original purposes underlying laws.[18] Reflection on notions such as this gave rise to medieval jurisprudence at the turn of the eleventh into the twelfth century. As Stephan Kuttner wrote: "Bernold of Constance, Alger of Liège, and Ivo of Chartres … began a new and imaginative search for rational principles of hermeneutics … "[19]

Bishop Ivo was one of the churchmen who helped frame the secular-ecclesiastical compromise on investiture that pointed the way to the Concordat of Worms in 1122.[20] His analytical acuity coupled with humane sagacity made his letters and the canonical "Prologue" (*Prologus*) memorable documents, which circulated widely. Ivo's precise relationship to the three well-known canonical collections that have traditionally been ascribed to him – the *Tripartite Collection* (*Collectio Tripartita*), the *Decretum*, and the *Panormia* – is now less certain than it once was, but his authorship of the famous "Prologue" seems secure.[21] This treatise is available in complete translations from Latin into both English and French, and excerpts in English have been at hand for decades.[22] Ivo's work also was copied from the beginning of the twelfth century in canon law collections, and not only in the traditional "Ivonian" compilations, whence it was transmitted wholly or in part. It was known to Bernold, Alger, and Gratian. With its sensitivity to the human circumstances in which law plays out, Ivo's "Prologue" was a work whose time had come. For an age sifting many centuries of church regulations, Ivo explained the need for thoughtful assessment and, when required, for dispensation in order to balance rigor with mercy in applying the law. Furthermore, he suggested ways to think about topics where the canonical tradition was inconsistent or contradictory. The learned bishop was inevitably a politician, but he also was a pastor, and he believed that charity (*caritas*) was the overriding concept that ought to determine

17 "On the sources of ecclesiastical law" (*De fontibus ecclesiastici iuris*), ibid., 120–87.

18 Ibid., 176–77.

19 Kuttner, *Revival of Jurisprudence*, 304.

20 On Ivo, see the following selections from a vast literature: Tierney, *Crisis of Church & State*, 75–78, 82–83; Blumenthal, *Investiture Conflict*, 163–64; Somerville and Brasington, *Prefaces*, 111–18, 131–56; Bruce C. Brasington, *Ways of Mercy: The Prologue of Ivo of Chartres* (Münster: LIT, 2004); and Rolker, Letters of Ivo, passim.

21 As well as the references in the previous notes, see Martin Brett, "Urban II and the Collections Attributed to Ivo of Chartres," in Stanley Chodorow (ed.), *Proceedings of the Eighth International Congress of Medieval Canon Law*, Monumenta iuris canonici, Subsidia, 9 (Vatican City, 1992), 27–46; and Kéry, *Collections*, 244–60.

22 The complete Latin text is available in Jean Werckmeister (ed. and trans.), Yves de Chartres, *Le Prologue*, Sources Canoniques 1 (Paris: Cerf, 1997), 63–129; and in Brasington, *Ways of Mercy*, 115–42. Werckmeister also gives a French translation. For an English translation, see *Prefaces*, 132–58. There are partial English translations in Eugene R. Fairweather, *A Scholastic Miscellany: Anselm to Ockham*, Library of Christian Classics (Philadelphia: Westminster Press, 1956), 238–42, and in Southern, *Scholastic Humanism*, 1:258–59.

how the canons were applied.[23] The appeal of such an idea would have been clear at a time when the loyalties of churchmen were easily divided between secular and ecclesiastical jurisdictions. Sage and compassionate, the "Prologue" circulated widely, and it offered a thoughtful and innovative hermeneutic for handling texts. The fact that the "Prologue" had been composed by a bishop, which was not the case for the treatises of Alger and Bernold, may also have helped to boost its circulation.

Bishop Ivo, as noted above, was closely associated with Pope Urban II, and the pontiff's use of the "Prologue" in one of his letters has been a matter of some debate.[24] Did Urban crib from his friend Ivo, or were Ivo and the pope drawing on a common source? Whatever the truth regarding that question, the "Prologue" was consistently ascribed to Ivo, and it was a methodological landmark. Along with Alger and Bernold but in a more far-reaching way, Ivo's "Prologue" opened the door to a process of evaluating legal and theological texts that became the hallmark of the schools in the central Middle Ages.[25] What Joseph Goering wrote about the history of penitential thought during this period may be applied to medieval thought generally: "The most important development … was the creation throughout Europe of schools and universities where students were introduced to a common tradition through a common curriculum of study and where they developed common methods of thinking about and of teaching … "[26]

That theme would take us to Gratian in the 1140s, who moves the story far beyond the year 1123 and Lateran I. This book has focused on prescriptive normative texts from the first millennium, including canonical texts, which recorded the decisions of councils and popes; and many of these canonical texts were known to Burchard. Gratian's method for treating such texts would prove innovative, systematic, and firmly fixed on the scholastic frontier. When we come to Gratian, we have indeed reached a new horizon in the emergence of church law.

23 See Brasington, *Ways of Mercy*, 7, for Ivo's involvement in political matters.

24 See Robert Somerville with Stephan Kuttner, *Pope Urban II, the 'Collectio Britannica', and the Council of Melfi (1089)* (Oxford: Clarendon Press, 1996), 109–15.

25 See Brasington, *Ways of Mercy*, 8, for attribution to Ivo.

26 Joseph Goering, "The Scholastic Turn (1100–1500): Penitential Theology and Law in the Schools," in A. Firey (ed.), *A New History of Penance*, Brill's Companions to the Christian Tradition 14 (Leiden: Brill, 2008), 219–37, at 219.

Index